STUDIES IN
CONTEMPORARY
JEWRY

The publication of
Studies in Contemporary Jewry
has been made possible through the generous assistance
of the Samuel and Althea Stroum Philanthropic Fund,
Seattle, Washington

THE AVRAHAM HARMAN INSTITUTE
OF CONTEMPORARY JEWRY
THE HEBREW UNIVERSITY
OF JERUSALEM

SEPHARDIC JEWRY
AND MIZRAHI JEWS

STUDIES IN
CONTEMPORARY
JEWRY
AN ANNUAL
XXII

2007

Edited by Peter Y. Medding

Published for the Institute by
OXFORD
UNIVERSITY PRESS

OXFORD
UNIVERSITY PRESS

Oxford University Press, Inc., publishes works that further
Oxford University's objective of excellence
in research, scholarship, and education.

Oxford   New York
Auckland   Cape Town   Dar es Salaam   Hong Kong   Karachi
Kuala Lumpur   Madrid   Melbourne   Mexico City   Nairobi
New Delhi   Shanghai   Taipei   Toronto

With offices in
Argentina   Austria   Brazil   Chile   Czech Republic   France   Greece
Guatemala   Hungary   Italy   Japan   Poland   Portugal   Singapore
South Korea   Switzerland   Thailand   Turkey   Ukraine   Vietnam

Copyright © 2007 by Oxford University Press, Inc.

Published by Oxford University Press, Inc.
198 Madison Avenue, New York, New York 10016
www.oup.com

Oxford is a registered trademark of Oxford University Press

Library of Congress Cataloging-in-Publication Data

Sephardic Jewry and Mizrahi Jews / edited by Peter Medding.
p. cm.—(Studies in contemporary Jewry, ISSN 0740-8625 ; 22)
ISBN 978-0-19-534097-6
1. Sephardim—Congresses.   2. Sephardim—Israel—Congresses.
3. Sephardim—Israel—Political activity—Congresses.   4. Jewish women in literature—Congresses.
5. Women immigrants in literature—Congresses.   6. Sephardim—Religious life—Congresses.
I. Medding, Peter.
DS113.8.S4S455 2007
305.892'4—dc22   2007025549

2 4 6 8 9 7 5 3 1

Printed in the United States of America
on acid-free paper

STUDIES IN CONTEMPORARY JEWRY

Preface

The major and rapid changes undergone by Sephardic Jewry over the last 50 years loom large in the symposium that heads this volume, which features essays from the fields of demography, history, political science, literature, sociology, gender studies, and anthropology. Here I would like to highlight the nature and extent of those changes by placing them in a broader historical and analytic perspective.

The Sephardic/Ashkenazic distinction within Jewry was based initially on halakhic differences. Communities in which halakhah was determined authoritatively in accordance with the principles, rulings, and traditions of the great Spanish sages were characterized as Sephardic (derived from the Hebrew word for Spain), whereas communities that followed French, German, and Polish sages were characterized as Ashkenazic (derived from the Hebrew word for Germany). These differences were crystallized when the great Ashkenazic scholar Moses Isserles published his detailed commentary on Yosef Karo's monumental Shulhan Arukh. Henceforth, Sephardic Jewry's self-identity and sense of distinctiveness were shaped by the differences between its traditions and customs and those of Ashkenazic Jewry as set out in Isserles' dissenting and critical rulings. In other words, the appearance of the Ashkenazic code alongside the Sephardic original could not but help to define Sephardic Jewry by highlighting how its members did *not* behave, what it was they did *not* do and who it was they were *not* like. Significantly, Sephardic Jews' awareness of difference was not contingent on personal contact or social interaction with Ashkenazim. Even when Sephardic and Ashkenazic Jewries lived far apart, the Ashkenazic "other" appeared on every page of Sephardic Jewry's authoritative halakhic code. (The opposite, of course, applied to Ashkenazim.)

However, this Sephardic/Ashkenazic distinction never became a basis for division into separate denominations, much less a split into two Jewries. Rather, the existence of a single authoritative halakhic code made up of both canons attested to an underlying agreement on fundamentals. Indeed, whatever their differences, the other's traditions, customs, and practices were considered a legitimate and authoritative expression of halakhic Judaism. Both Sephardic and Ashkenazic Jews agreed that each were bound by halakhah to practice normative Judaism in accordance with their own distinctive customs and traditions. For there was only one Torah, even if it was interpreted somewhat differently by Sephardic and Ashkenazic sages.

This underlying fundamental halakhic unity had practical consequences. Sephardic and Ashkenazic Jews were often to be found in the "other's" congregation in places in which no congregation conformed to an individual's particular tradition. So, too, Sephardic and Ashkenazic Jewish populations frequently maintained separate congregation-communities side by side, or else joined in establishing an overall

communal framework. Above and beyond these immediate implications, the underlying fundamental halakhic unity made Sephardic and Ashkenazic Jews members of
a single people—Israel—eternally bound to each other by an overarching, divinely-
ordained covenant of mutual responsibility.

By and large, Ashkenazic and Sephardic Jewries were separated by geography and
differentiated by culture. Well into the 20th century, almost all Ashkenazic communities were located in Christian Europe or the New World, and they or their
forebears spoke Yiddish or German. In contrast, the vast majority of communities
adhering to the Sephardic halakhic tradition were situated in Arab or Muslim
countries in North Africa and the Middle East, and their members spoke some
version of Judeo-Arabic. Hence, these communities are generally known as _'edot
hamizrah_, namely, eastern or Oriental communities. (Usually included among them
are Yemenite and Ethiopian Jewries, even though their traditions and practices
predate and differ significantly from those specified by Karo.) In addition, some
Sephardic Jews in Europe, the New World, and Palestine, who traced their origins
directly to Spain and Portugal and who spoke Ladino, are known as Sephardim or as
"pure" Sephardim.

While Jewish communities in the various Middle Eastern, Asian, and African
countries practiced Judaism in accordance with the Sephardic halakhic canon, they
also developed distinctive emphases and particular customs of their own, whether
country-wide, regional, or local. Yet all these communities had two fundamental
elements in common: cultural homogeneity and isolation. Virtually everywhere in
Asia, Africa, and the Middle East, Sephardic Jews did not constitute a mere majority of the community but were the _entire_ community. Moreover, for centuries,
Sephardic communities were relatively isolated. As a result, they were uninfluenced by Ashkenazic Judaism and, until the middle of the 19th century, were
largely unfamiliar with cultural and religious movements within it.

To be sure, European and American Jewish organizations and leaders were involved both in educational and philanthropic activities in some Middle Eastern and
North African Jewish communities and in sporadic international political activity on
their behalf (such as occurred in the 1840s in connection with the Damascus affair).
Such activity brought Sephardic Jewry into the ken of western Jewry's communal,
rabbinic, political, and economic elites. However, the situation of Sephardic Jewish
communities did not take priority on the political, social, or cultural agendas of
Ashkenazic Jewish communities or on those of world Jewry as it became organized
internationally. By the same token, Sephardic Jewish communities and leaders were
not highly involved in the activities and affairs of international Jewish organizations.

In 1948, Sephardic Jewry numbered slightly more than 1.3 million persons of a
total world Jewish population of some 11,500,000. As noted, the overwhelming
majority resided in Arab or Muslim countries including Morocco, Tunisia, Algeria,
Libya, Egypt, Syria, Lebanon, Iraq, Iran, Yemen, and Turkey, with others in
Ethiopia, India, parts of the U.S.S.R., and Israel. Most Sephardic communities were
relatively small (apart from Morocco and Iraq, whose Jewish populations numbered
240,000 and 130,000, respectively). Moreover, in some of these countries, the Jewish
population was both concentrated and dispersed, with the majority concentrated in a

few major (though often geographically distant) cities, with the others residing in a string of very small communities located on the periphery. Thus, for example, in Morocco there were 330 separate points of Jewish settlement, with the number of Jews residing in them varying greatly. While 70 percent of Moroccan Jewry was concentrated in 15 cities (60 percent in five cities with Jewish populations numbering between 12,350–65,570), 25 percent was spread across more than 200 settlements with 150–1,000 Jews, and 5 percent were to be found in more than a hundred settlements with fewer than 150 Jews.

Fifty years later, the geographic, demographic, and cultural situation of Sephardic Jewry had been transformed radically. To begin with, it had undergone significant demographic growth. In absolute terms, the total number of Jews of Sephardic origin (3,403,000) was more than two and a half times greater than it had been in 1950. Although Sephardic Jewry's proportion of the world Jewish population was still much smaller than that of Ashkenazic Jewry, it had more than doubled to 26 percent. Furthermore, geographically, Sephardic Jewry had been almost totally displaced. At the end of the 20th century, only a small number of Sephardic Jews remained in the former areas of concentration; conversely, the vast majority resided in localities in which hitherto only few had resided.

However, the total geographical displacement of Sephardic Jewry did not result in demographic dispersion and communal dissolution, as is common in the wake of mass immigration. Rather, geographic displacement was accompanied by communal transplantation—that is, the large-scale movement to new environments, not only of individuals and families, but of entire local and country-wide communities.

The geographic and demographic data strikingly illustrate these changes. By the year 2000, about two-thirds of all Jews of Sephardic origin (2,295,000) resided in Israel, 18 percent in the Americas (604,000), and 13 percent in Europe (449,000), whereas less than two percent (50,000) were in Asia-Africa. Furthermore, in Israel, Jews of Sephardic origin now constituted 47 percent of the total Jewish population; in France, 70 percent (and in Europe as a whole, 28 percent); in both Mexico and Venezuela, about 40 percent, and in North America, 9 percent. Put somewhat differently, at the beginning of the 21st century, there were almost twice as many Sephardic Jews in Israel as there were in the entire world in 1948; as many Sephardic Jews in France as there were in all the Middle Eastern countries in 1948; and about as many in North America as there were in North Africa in 1948.[1]

Geographic displacement and communal transplantation fundamentally transformed the basic conditions of Sephardic Jewry's collective existence. Today, there are only a few countries—most significantly, France—in which Sephardim constitute a clear majority of the Jewish population. Whereas previously the overwhelming majority of Sephardic Jews were located in homogeneous Sephardic communal environments, they now frequently find themselves alongside Ashkenazic Jews in communities that are predominantly Ashkenazic in character, composition, and outlook. Moreover, whereas in the past Sephardic Jews had rarely encountered Ashkenazic Jewry and its traditions, institutions, and movements, such encounters are now unavoidable. Furthermore, a multiplicity of Sephardic groups of diverse origin with varying halakhic traditions, differing cultural values, and social norms live alongside each other.

In Israel, for instance, Sephardic Jews' self-identity and sense of distinctiveness is now largely defined by their interactions with Ashkenazic Jewry in all its many and varied manifestations. As a result, their self-identity has not only been affected by the need to take account of the Ashkenazic "other" but has also developed and has been promoted in direct opposition to it.

Furthermore, the social, economic, cultural, political, and educational values, achievements, standards, and conditions in the societies in which the vast majority of Sephardic Jews now live are fundamentally different from those of their former countries. For example, most Sephardic Jews moved from Muslim and Arab societies into Jewish and Christian societies; from agrarian to industrialized and technologically advanced economies; from less modernized to more modernized countries; and from authoritarian and autocratic regimes to liberal democracies—all of which add to the complexities and difficulties of the processes of migrant adaptation, adjustment, and acculturation. As shown to varying degrees by Sergio DellaPergola, Michel Abitbol, Yaron Tsur, and Doli Benhabib, the processes of modernization and westernization that Sephardic Jews from Asian and African countries underwent in Israel contrasted greatly with those which some of them had previously experienced in their countries of origin as well as with those undergone by their brethren who migrated to France, Canada, or the United States.

A fundamental difference affecting (not always positively) the process in Israel as compared with that in other countries relates to the changed status of Sephardic Jews from Muslim/Arab countries in the Jewish state and in the western democracies, as compared with their status in their countries of origin. Thus, in Israel, those engaged in the economic, social, and cultural processes associated with modernization compete primarily, even if not solely, with other Jews. (They must also compete with Israeli Arabs, Palestinians, and foreign workers, as well as contending with the forces of globalization). Moreover, they must do so within the framework of ideological values and societal preferences set in place by a predominantly Ashkenazic elite, which inevitably raises questions about the fairness of the competition and gives rise to claims of prejudice and discrimination. This, in turn, has generated profound resentments and has led to the rise of social movements and political parties.

The "Israeli encounter" of Sephardic and Ashkenazic Jews, in the context of a unifying and equalizing national ideology, has highlighted the issue of the former's cultural identity and integration, both before and after immigration to Israel. Over the past half century, this issue has given rise to a number of related questions. For example, prior to their immigration, were Sephardic Jews in the Asian-African countries religiously and culturally Jewish? Or were they religiously Jewish and culturally something else, be it Moroccan and/or French and/or western, as the case may be? Or indeed, were they, as some would argue, religiously Jewish and culturally Arab? And subsequent to their settlement in Israel, were they religiously and culturally Jewish? Or were they religiously Jewish and culturally something else, be it Israeli and/or Moroccan and/or Arab? Or indeed, were they religiously and culturally, something else, say, humanistic, secular, and democratic? Such questions, of course, are as much about the nature of Israeli society and identity as they are about how Sephardic Jews (albeit from different geographic and cultural backgrounds) relate to their past, their present, and themselves.

Three recurring themes in this symposium stand out as particularly worthy of note:

1. The salience of the debate regarding identity, as manifested in the emergence and increasingly wide usage of the terms *Mizrahi* and *Mizrahim* (in place of, or in opposition to) Sephardic and Sephardim,when referring to those sections of Jewry that originated in Asia-Africa. The essays authored by Sergio DellaPergola and by Harvey Goldberg and Chen Bram, in particular, demonstrate that a wide range of general issues is involved in this terminological shift. One relates to whether Mizrahi is a descriptive term—a category, designation, or name—used to distinguish between classes of persons or groups, or whether it connotes identity, relating to a sense of self, to self-image, to how individuals and groups define themselves and their place in their world, to what is distinctive to them and at the same time separates themselves from others. Another relates to who uses the term and how. Is it internally generated and does it reflect how members of the group see themselves; or is it imposed on the group by outsiders such as politicians, government officials, and scholars? Is the term subjective or objective, neutral or value-laden—does it imply praise or convey prejudice? Further, does the term Mizrahi homogenize—that is, does it ignore internal differentiation? Or does it do just the opposite, recognizing internal diversity, variation, particularism and plurality?

2. The invigoration and renewal of Sephardic Judaism, as manifested at both the scholarly and popular levels, in the emergence and growing strength of a haredi form or version of Sephardic Judaism, in the movement of religious return, and in the stated goal of "restoring the crown to its former glory." As shown in the essays by Zvi Zohar, Nissim Leon, and Kimmy Caplan, several factors seem to be significant, among them the concentration of such a large proportion of Sephardic Jewry in Israel; competition between various Sephardic Jewries; the encounter with Ashkenazic Jewry, particularly its rabbinical leaders and halakhic institutions; and the emergence of an entrepreneurial religious leadership seeking to unify all of Sephardic Jewry via a single authoritative halakhic canon. The interaction with Ashkenazic Judaism is particularly complex, including significant elements of Sephardic independence and autonomy along with considerable dependence upon elite haredi Ashkenazic educational institutions and leaders, with cooperation and support in some areas and intense competition and opposition in others. In all, this encounter has proved to be a major stimulant in the invigoration of Sephardic Judaism and, despite the conflicts and differences with Ashkenazic Jewry, has resulted both in cross-fertilization and in the incorporation into Sephardic Judaism of parts of the lifestyle and worldview of Ashkenazic Jewry's haredi sector.

3. The emergence of Sephardic politics, as manifested in Israel by the organization, growth, staying power, electoral success, and political achievements of the Shas party. For a quarter of a century, this party has served as the organized voice of Sephardic Jewry in Israeli society. As such, it competes directly against other parties in the political arena, vying for influence in the making of public policy for the whole of Israeli society and for control over institutions

implementing it. It acts in the name of Sephardic Judaism and Mizrahi Jews, providing them with representation and pursuing their interests. In mobilizing its natural constituency (conceived of and referred to interchangeably as both Sephardic and Mizrahi Jews) it both appeals to and promotes their distinctive group identity in the public arena, using a combination of religious and ethnic motifs and themes to enhance group pride, both as an end in itself and in opposition to Israel's dominant Ashkenazic identities. While the emergence of Sephardic political entrepreneurs has also played a key role in the organization and achievements of the Shas party, even more significant is the close relationship between the Sephardic religious and political leaderships cemented by the former's manifest and firm control of the latter. Put differently, Sephardic Jewry in Israel has developed a single, unified, and effective authority structure, headed and controlled by the religious leadership.

Common to these three themes are the tensions between Sephardim and Ashkenazim, not as separate and distinct ethnic groups, but rather as members of a single people—who can perhaps be viewed as quarreling siblings, with all their perceived slights and feelings of superiority or inferiority. At the same time, there is also a quest for unity, though strikingly, not so much unity between Sephardim and Ashkenazim as among the Sephardim themselves. The oft-stated desire is to transform a multiplicity of diverse communities into a single community, whether by creating an overarching cultural and personal identity; or by restoring the crown of Sephardic halakhah to its former glory; or by mobilizing all Sephardim to act in unison for common goals and purposes. Paradoxically, this quest for unity (in whatever form) seems to require opposition to, distancing from, or conflict with Ashkenazim.

As always, it is difficult to find the words to adequately convey my appreciation for my fellow editors, Jonathan Frankel, Eli Lederhendler, and Ezra Mendelsohn, or for *Studies'* peerless managing editors, Laurie Fialkoff and Hannah Levinsky-Koevary. Thank you, all. On behalf of the entire editorial staff, I would also like to express gratitude to the Samuel and Althea Stroum Foundation and to the Lucius N. Littauer Foundation, whose continuing support is a mainstay of our operation.

P.Y.M.

Note

1. Statistical and demographic data based on material supplied by Sergio DellaPergola, much of which can be found in his symposium essay (see esp. Tables 2 and 4); see also Yaron Tsur's *Kehilah keru'ah: yehudei maroko vehaleumiyut 1943–1954* (Tel Aviv: 2001), 27–30, 411–424.

Contents

Symposium
Sephardic Jewry and Mizrahi Jews

Review Essays

Book Reviews
(*arranged by subject*)
Antisemitism, Holocaust, and Genocide

Biography, History, and the Social Sciences

Symposium
Sephardic Jewry and Mizrahi Jews

"Sephardic and Oriental" Jews in Israel and Western Countries: Migration, Social Change, and Identification

Sergio DellaPergola
(THE HEBREW UNIVERSITY)

In the course of the 20th century, the longstanding presence of Jews in North Africa and the Middle East came virtually to an end.[1] In an extraordinary exodus, sometimes under very stressful circumstances, more than one million Jews left countries in which they had resided for hundreds (if not thousands) of years and emigrated to countries whose Jewish community was often of much more recent origin, and whose members came from very different ethnic backgrounds. This essay assesses the changing profile of "Sephardic and Oriental" Jews since the Second World War, outlining the overall volume and major directions of Jewish international migrations, and examining patterns of demographic, socioeconomic, and cultural change in the context of absorption and integration processes both in Israel and in several western countries. Of particular interest are changes in the composition of immigrants to Israel from Asia and Africa, and their integration into and role in the shaping of Israeli society, as compared with parallel processes among Jewish migrants from those regions in France, the United States, and Latin America.

Analytic Issues and Definitional Problems

Large-scale international migration has long been a key feature of Jewish social and demographic history. It was responsible for major shifts in the global and regional geographical distribution of Jewish populations and for the varied contexts in which Jews conducted their social and cultural life and interacted with the surrounding society. Central to the Jewish historical experience was the degree of social justice, political equality, freedom of expression, and socioeconomic opportunities enjoyed by Jews, both collectively and individually. Once a sizable Jewish community developed in Palestine, and especially after the establishment of the state of Israel, the question of relationships and interactions of different groups within the Jewish majority became increasingly salient.

3

Issues relating to population and social change are worthy of analysis not only in their own right, but also for their impact on politics and public policy. In the case of Sephardic migration, we are dealing not only with quantifiable demographic and sociological data, but also with questions of personal identity that sometimes lie outside the rational realm and are difficult to measure and assess—yet are critical elements in academic and public discourse. With this in mind, there are several key issues that must be addressed in constructing a socio-demographic profile of Sephardic and Oriental Jewish migrants:

1. How do we define Sephardic and Oriental Jewish communities?
2. How do we assess their changing size, geographical distribution, and other socio-demographic characteristics and trends?
3. What were (and are) the distinctive socio-demographic characteristics and trends among Sephardic and Oriental Jewry as compared with those of other Jewish communities and the surrounding non-Jewish populations?
4. In assessing socio-demographic change among immigrants and their descendants in Israel and elsewhere, how should characteristics acquired variously at birth, in country of origin, and country of absorption be weighted?
5. What, if anything, was distinctive about migration to Israel as compared with Jewish migration to other countries, and what, beyond human capital, did Sephardic and Oriental migrants contribute to the new Jewish state?
6. Which model—convergence or divergence, homogenization or pluralism, harmony or conflict—best describes the demographic, socioeconomic, cultural, and identificational changes affecting immigrant groups in Israel and elsewhere?
7. How do we explain differences revealed by such comparative analysis of Sephardic/Oriental Jews versus other migrant Jews in Israel and elsewhere, and what are their broader international implications?
8. When does continuity in group identity give way to identificational change? More specifically, under which conditions and for how long does a "Sephardic and Oriental Jew" remain Sephardic and Oriental?[2]

The terminology of "Sephardic and Oriental" Jews, which derives from the Hebrew "sepharadim ve'edot hamizraḥ" (lit. [Jews] from Spanish and Oriental or eastern communities), is used to define a segment of world Jewry with supposed historical and sociocultural commonalities and distinct socioeconomic and demographic characteristics. It is problematic, however, for a variety of reasons. First, and most obviously, it combines two groups of different geographic origin. Second, even if the "Sephardic" component is removed, the "Oriental" component remains difficult to define objectively. In both scientific literature and public discourse, "eastern Jewish communities" does not reflect a straightforward geographical concept or other objective criterion. Instead, this term is used increasingly in a subjective manner to refer to issues of individual and group identity and collective memory. Moreover, there is no agreement about geographical boundaries between "East" and "West." Whereas scholars of European modernization often cite an imaginary boundary running from Leningrad in the north to Trieste in the south,[3] Jewish communities in the Maghreb (lit., the Occident)—which is geographically located at the west-

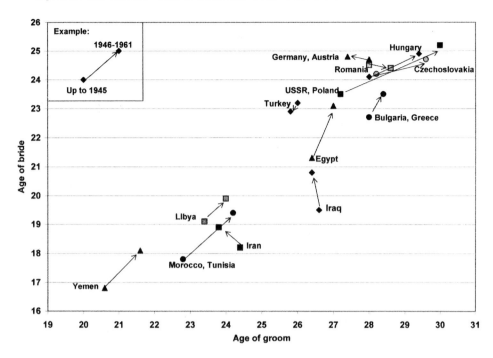

Figure 1. Age at marriage of Jewish brides and grooms in countries of origin among migrants to Israel—marriages until 1945 and from 1946–1961

Each point represents the combined average ages of Jewish brides and grooms in a given country at a given period of time. For each country, arrows go from the earlier to the later period of time.
Source: Created from Israel Central Bureau of Statistics, *Census of Population and Housing* (Jerusalem: 1961).

ernmost end of the Mediterranean area—are typically associated with the "East," whereas those of Eastern Europe are usually located in the "West." Another approach views "Oriental" versus "western" in terms of differing rates and patterns of modernization, the assumption being that eastern cultures experienced modernization at a much later and slower pace. While this may be the case, historical-demographic data indicate that, whereas the *timing* and speed may have differed, the *nature* of socio-demographic change was essentially the same in both the East and the West.

Consider, for example, marriage patterns before 1961 among diaspora Jews who subsequently migrated to Israel.[4] The data in figure 1 depict ages of brides and grooms in marriages performed up to 1945, versus those performed between 1946 and 1961. Each point in figure 1 combines the age at marriage of Jewish brides and grooms in a given country (for instance, in Yemen up to 1945, the average age for brides was a bit younger than 17 and for grooms about 20.5; by 1961, the average age had risen to a bit more than 18 and 21.5, respectively). The data indicate that, during the first half of the 20th century, Jewish brides and grooms in Asian and African countries generally married younger than those in Central and Eastern Europe. At the same time, a widespread trend toward later marriage is apparent among both groups. Indeed, Jewish communities in Egypt, Turkey, and even Iraq do not appear to be distinctly different in this regard from those in Bulgaria and Greece, or even the U.S.S.R. (in the earlier period). All in all, Jewish marriage patterns reveal a sharp modernization gradient across countries of residence, with no clear dividing line between communities "of the East" and "of the West."

Similarly, intriguing evidence based on DNA samples and an analysis of the human genome substantiates a long-held assumption of conventional Jewish historiography—namely, that most Jewish communities have substantially similar origins. Research on male-transmitted genetic characteristics tends to confirm a Middle Eastern origin for most contemporary Jews.[5] It appears that prolonged seg-regation and homogamy reinforced the coherence of Jewish genotypes, notwith-standing the Jews' substantial geographical mobility and their exposure over the centuries to different environments. Keeping in mind the focus on patrilineal origins in these population genetic studies, there appears to be no clear distinction be-tween "eastern" and "western" communities. Jews are more "Oriental" compared with non-Jewish European populations and more "Occidental" compared with non-Jewish North African populations.

A more recent problem relating to the definitional boundaries of Oriental Jews has arisen due to the consequences of intensive international migration during the 20th century. In the wake of large-scale intercontinental mobility, especially since the Second World War, contemporary Oriental Jewish identity no longer reflects the actual *residential location* of Jewish communities but rather *global diffusion*—in Israel, France, and other western countries. With the passage of time and the birth of new generations geographically removed from the group's place of origin, Oriental Jewish identity has tended increasingly to become the product of cultural trans-mission in a physically, religiously, and institutionally different context from that of the original culture. Thus, the question of "who is an Oriental Jew?" becomes ever more removed from its actual environmental roots.

The growing frequency of marriage between persons of different geographic origins has also complicated the meaning of "Sephardic and Oriental." For a rapidly increasing proportion of the Jewish population both in Israel and elsewhere, ancestry and sub-ethnic identity are linked to more than one origin.[6] Consequently, the determination and role of ancestry among Jews has tended to become similar ana-lytically to the familiar and value-laden process of ancestry attribution in the United States and other major countries of immigration.[7]

All in all, somewhat echoing more general contentions about the concept of "Orientalism,"[8] it appears that "eastern," in the Jewish sense, is most commonly defined not in *objective*, but rather in *symbolic* terms. "Eastern" often appears in the context of value-laden assumptions about *difference*—or more precisely, *hierarchic inequality*. In such statements, the paradigm of *'edot hamizrah*, or "Oriental com-munities," while expressed in the plural, is not posited against any similar paradigm of *'edot hama'arav*, or "western communities." Instead, Oriental Jews are consis-tently contrasted with an aggregate of "Ashkenazim" who are assumed to form a coherent alternative paradigm. So, too, "eastern" and "Sephardim" commonly go together even though the history of Jews from Spain has little in common with that of Jews from Oriental communities. What this means is that all those who are not "western" (actually Ashkenazic) constitute a single group. Put somewhat differently, "eastern-ness" is defined not by the *existence* of a given property, but rather by the *absence* of another property: "western-ness." Furthermore, "West" and "western" are commonly (whether explicitly or implicitly) associated with modernization, progressiveness, and rationality—all of which are endowed with positive connotations and deemed desirable both for individuals and groups. In contrast, "East" and "eastern" represent the alternative—perhaps more expressive and colorful, probably less orderly and efficient, maybe good for *them*, but surely less desirable for *ourselves* or for *us all*.

To be sure, the East/West dichotomy may and has been employed by scholars of Jewish life without negative intent and pejorative assumptions, although the latter are also to be found, both above and below the surface, and implicit value judgments are difficult to avoid. A more neutral definitional criterion is the one long followed by Israel's Central Bureau of Statistics, which classifies Jews, for analytic purposes, by continents of origin (Africa, Asia, Europe, America) while explicitly avoiding the popular Ashkenazic-Sephardic dichotomy.[9] From a cultural-historical perspective, it is useful to distinguish between Jewish communities (past or present) by location in a Christian versus a Muslim environment.[10] There has also been a recent attempt to characterize the cultural background of Jewish cuisine by means of a dichotomy between the use of olive oil—predominant around Mediterranean shores—and goose fat, which was the norm in continental Europe as well as along Italy's eastern coast.[11] Jewish culinary preferences appear to be intriguingly intertwined with the diffusion of Sephardic and Ashkenazic communities, but also illustrate the dependency of sub-group Jewish identities on environmental factors such as climate and food supply.

Finally, it is worth mentioning that the "North-South" typology frequently used in contemporary studies of global development and modernization might more correctly capture both the straightforward geographical and cultural derivates of the Jewish sociohistorical experience. This, of course, assumes the validity of using dichotomous typologies to describe world Jewry. In fact, the Jewish historical experience exhibits far greater variation, nuance, and identificational fluidity. Nevertheless, as do others, we adopt such a typology here as an operational device for handling a vast mass of detail and reducing complex phenomena to their essentials, albeit at the price of oversimplification.

Defining and Characterizing Jewish Ethnic and Sub-ethnic Identities

In attempting an evaluation of the thicker and more binding identificational components of Jews of Sephardic and Asian-African ancestry today, one must first consider how group identity shaped itself (or became reshaped) in the course of migration and absorption in new societies. In the process, certain aspects of ethnic identity were presumably eroded, whereas others were either created or reinforced. In the specific cases examined here, "Sephardic," "Oriental," or "Asian-African" are all used to define sub-ethnic identities within the broader framework of Jewish ethnic identity (see fig. 2).

Sub-ethnic identity among Sephardic and Oriental Jews, both in Israel and else-where, reflects a number of factors, including the pre-migration background of migrants, the modalities of the migration and absorption processes, and the nature of the receiving society. A further question is to what extent preexisting ethnocultural characteristics affected the socio-demographic patterns of immigrant absorption, and to what extent the consequences of immigrant absorption affected the patterns of group identity. On the one hand, the possibility existed that narrower particularistic identities could become integrated into broader, more encompassing, and possibly less specific identities. On the other hand, the cultural residue of the absorption process could have the opposite effect—of reviving or even generating new forms of more specific, communal sub-identities. The speed of these processes varied. In France, for instance, a strong assimilationist ethos promoted the immigrants' acquisition of French national identity, whereas in Mexico, which was characterized by deep socioeconomic cleavages and where an exclusive approach to national identity prevailed, the formation of ethnic enclaves was legitimated.[12]

Sub-ethnic identities may be portrayed, as in figure 2, as rungs on an imaginary ladder, with its bottom rungs representing very narrowly defined particular identities, and those at the top, broad and encompassing pan-ethnic identities. The following discussion reflects identificational changes that may occur in the context of international migration. Referring to the examples in figure 2, the initial situation is one in which a Jew in a given place experiences his or her Jewish identity vis-à-vis the non-Jewish environment, regardless of the existence of other Jews. The awareness of being of a particular geographic origin usually emerges only after such a Jew, following migration, comes into contact with other Jews of different geographical origins.

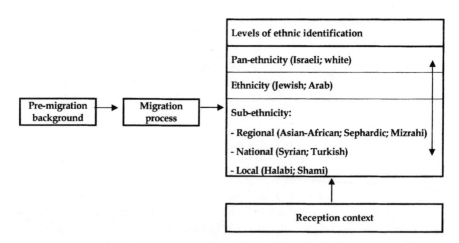

Figure 2. Hierarchic levels of ethnic and sub-ethnic identification

Source: Adapted from Sergio DellaPergola, Georges Sabagh, Mehdi Bozorgmehr, Claudia Der-Martirosian, and Susana Lerner, "Hierarchic Levels of Subethnicity: Near Eastern Jews in the U.S., France and Mexico," *Sociological Papers* 5, no. 2 (1996), 1–42.

Thus, during the process of absorption, integration, and acculturation of the immigrants, sub-ethnic identities may evolve and broaden geographically—for instance, from "Halabi" (Aleppan), to "Syrian," to "Sephardic" or "Mizrahi," before giving way to a generically inclusive ethnic category. (In Israel or in the United States, for instance, "Jewish" is the product of a merger of different Jewish sub-ethnic identities, and yet remains distinguished from other ethnic identities. Similarly, pan-ethnic identities tend to develop in both countries. The term "Israeli" encompasses Jews, Arabs, Druze, and other subgroups, whereas in the United States, the term "white" still leaves room for meaningful distinctions prior to a hypothetical grand merger into "American.")[13] Moreover, awareness of association with a given subgroup often increases when members of a given group meet those of other groups similarly located on the ethnic hierarchy. Among Jewish migrants from Syria, for example, the feeling of being "Halabi" may increase when those belonging to that community meet others of Shami (Damascene) origin. In a similar fashion, the feeling of being "Syrian" may increase when Syrian Jews come into proximity with Turkish Jews. In a broader sense, "Sephardic" identity (which contains many particularistic sub-ethnic identities such as "Iraqi" or "Moroccan") is highlighted by contrast with the "Ashkenazic" community, which is also the product of many distinct sub-ethnicities. "White"—itself the merger of many ladders of distinct and even conflicting sub-ethnic identities such as "Italian," "Polish," "British," and "Irish"—retains its distinctive identity as against "black" or "Asian," which encompass their own powerful and often competing subgroups.

In other words, identifying as a "Sephardic," "Oriental," or "Mizrahi" Jew may represent a shorter or longer transitional stage between, say, a limited and local Halabi identity and a more encompassing national Israeli identity. Or else it may be part of a simultaneous identification with different levels of the sub-ethnic/ethnic ladder—the same person sometimes feeling more "Sephardic," sometimes more "Halabi," sometimes more "Israeli," depending on context. This "Sephardic," "Oriental," or "Mizrahi" property, in spite of its transitional or shared character, can nonetheless represent a very important component in one's identity and outlook, as well as in public perceptions regarding the fundamental sociocultural structure of society.

Another feature of immigrant absorption (particularly of Jews) is a phenomenon we may define as "identity translation" by members of the absorbing society. Thus, for example, the popular perception of all recent immigrants from the former Soviet Union (FSU) to Israel as "Russians," even though many of them came from Ukraine, Belarus, or even Moldova or Kazakhstan. By the same token, North American, British, South African, and Australian immigrants in Israel are all called "Anglo-Saxons," Mexicans are "Argentinians," and the significantly different groups of immigrants from Gondar, Tigris, Addis Abeba, and Quara all become "Ethiopians." In Latin America and in some West European countries, Jewish immigrants from the Middle East became known as "Arabs." Significantly, although artificially and externally imposed—and lacking in depth or even plausibility—these societal perceptions have tended over time to have an impact on the bearers of these sub-ethnic identities, whether in rejecting or internalizing them.

As shown in table 1, the same identity (Sephardic/Asian/African) can encompass smaller or larger groups of people in a given country at a given time, depending on

Table 1. Jews of Sephardic/Asian-African Origin in Selected Countries, by Various Definitions, 1960–2002 (percent of total Jewish population)

Definition	Argentina 1960	Italy 1965	France 1970s	Israel 1983–1984	USSR 1989	Brazil 1990	U.S. 1990	Canada 1991	Mexico 1991	South Africa 1991	Venezuela 1998–1999	Israel 1998–1999	France 2002
Birthplace Asia-Africa	3	10	49	19		5	2	5	4	2	10	12	44
Same as above, plus Balkans	3	14		20					5			12	
Father's birthplace Asia-Africa			61	44								33	
Same as above, plus Balkans				46								34	
Asian-African origin after allocating Israeli-born with Israeli-born father				52								45	
Same as above, plus Balkans				54								47	
Self-identified Sephardic Jew							8		32	2	39	70	
Member of Sephardic organization							9		39		42		
Birthplace Asia-Africa and/or self-identified Sephardic Jew													
Self-identified "special" ethnic Jew					7								
Resident of Asian republic					14								
Knows Judeo-Arabic or Judeo-Español			15										
Voted for Shas party				3								13	

Sources: U.O. Schmelz and Sergio DellaPergola, *Hademografiyah shel hayehudim beargentinah wearaẓot aḥerot shel amerikah halatinit* (Tel Aviv: 1972); Sergio DellaPergola, *Anatomia dell'ebraismo italiano* (Rome/Assisi: 1976); Doris Bensimon and Sergio DellaPergola, *La population juive de France: sociodémographie et identité* (Jerusalem-Paris: 1984); Israel Central Bureau of Statistics, *Statistical Abstract of Israel* (Jerusalem: 1984); Mark Tolts, "Trends in Soviet Jewish Demography since the Second World War," in *Jews and Jewish Life in Russia and the Soviet Union*, ed. Ya'acov Ro'i (London: 1995), 365–382; René Decol, "Judeus no Brasil: explorando os dados censitários," *Revista Brasileira de Ciências Sociais* 16, no. 46 (2001), 147–160; Sergio DellaPergola and Uzi Rebhun, "Hebeitim sozio-demografiyim udfusei hizdahut shel yehudim sefaradim veashkenazim bearẓot habrit bishnat 1990," in *Hevrah vetarbut—yehudei sefarad leahar hagerush*, ed. Michel Abitbol, Galit Hazan-Rokem, and Yom-Tov Assis (Jerusalem: 1997), 105–135; Leo Davids, "The Jewish Population of Canada, 1991," in *Papers in Jewish Demography 1993 in Memory of U.O. Schmelz*, ed. Sergio DellaPergola and Judith Even (Jerusalem: 1997), 311–323; Sergio DellaPergola and Susana Lerner, *La comunidad judía de México: perfil demográfico, social y cultural* (Jerusalem: 1995); Sergio DellaPergola and Alie A. Dubb, "South African Jewry: A Sociodemographic Profile," *American Jewish Year Book*, vol. 88 (New York: 1988), 59–140; Sergio DellaPergola, Salomon Benzaquen, and Tony Beker de Weintraub, *Perfil sociodemográfico y cultural de la comunidad judía de Caracas* (Caracas: 2000); Israel Central Bureau of Statistics, *Statistical Abstract of Israel* (1999); Erik H. Cohen with Maurice Ifergan, *Les Juifs de France: valeurs et identité* (Paris: 2002).

its previous definition. In Israel of the late 1990s, for example, the percentage of Jews of Sephardic/Asian/African origin ranged from 12 to 47 percent, depending in large part on whether it included only first-generation immigrants or members of the second and third generation as well (or was further extended to Jews of Balkan origin). In France of the 1970s, 49 percent of the Jewish population was born in Asia or Africa (mostly in Algeria, Morocco, or Tunisia) but their proportion rose to 61 percent when the second generation was included. Both in Mexico (in 1991) and in Venezuela (1998–1999), the proportion of Sephardim was larger when defined in terms of membership in a Sephardic or Middle Eastern organization than when based on self-identification. In France, where Jewish organizational reach is quite limited, self-identification along sub-ethnic lines is particularly high: in 2002, 70 percent of the total Jewish population identified as Sephardic.

A further distinction emerges from Soviet and post-Soviet censuses that, based on criteria of ethnicity, distinguish between "mainstream" and relatively small numbers of "special" ethnic Jews such as Georgian Jews, Bukharan Jews, and Tats. Knowledge of a native language offers another criterion for sub-ethnic distinctions. In this regard, there is clear erosion over time. For instance, in France of the 1970s, only 14 percent of French Jewry still knew Judeo-Arabic or Judeo-Español.

Yet another definitional option is based on political party preferences. In Israel, there are a number of political parties aimed explicitly at sub-ethnic constituencies. Although such parties had hitherto been short-lived, Shas, a religious Sephardic political party, has been represented in the Knesset since 1984. In the elections of 1999, Shas gained more than one fourth of its theoretical total vote—that is, of those with an Asian-African background extending back three generations.

Changes in the Geographic Dispersion of World Jewry

Having come to terms with the complexities, uncertainties, and contradictions of identificational definitions, we may now turn to some descriptive data on Jewish population change.[14] Table 2 outlines the changes in the regional distribution of world Jewry between 1948 and 2005, showing in particular the implications for the size and distribution of Jewish communities in Asia and Africa. The main determinant of change was mass emigration of Jewish communities from Asia, Africa, and the Balkans (as well as Eastern Europe) and their relocation to Israel and to several countries in Western Europe, North America, and Latin America. The continuing shift of the major centers of world Jewry brought about a greater Jewish population concentration in the more developed areas of the globe. Of the estimated 1.2 million Jews living in 1948 in Asia (including parts of the former Soviet Union) and North Africa, only about 44,000 remained in 2005—a decline of some 97 percent. During this same period, the immigration of more than one million Jews from Asia and Africa was a major determinant of rapid Jewish population growth in Israel.[15]

As shown in table 3, the world Jewish migration system over the last 50 years consisted of two main supply areas (Eastern Europe, and the region comprising North Africa and the Middle East) and two major reception areas (the western countries, and Israel).[16] Although annual migration numbers varied greatly, between

Table 2. Jewish Population by Major Regions, 1948–2005

Region	Number (thousands)[a]			Percent[a]			Percent change		
	1948[b]	1970[c]	2005[d]	1948[b]	1970[c]	2005[d]	1948[b]–1970	1970–2005	1948–2005
World total	**11,500**	**12,662**	**13,034**	**100.0**	**100.0**	**100.0**	**+10**	**+3**	**+13**
Israel	**650**	**2,582**	**5,238**	**5.7**	**20.4**	**40.2**	**+297**	**+103**	**+706**
Asia-Africa	**1,325**	**569**	**118**	**11.5**	**5.5**	**0.9**	**−57**	**−79**	**−91**
Former USSR in Asia	350	262	20	3.0	3.1	0.2	−25	−92	−94
Other Asia[e]	275	100	19	2.4	0.8	0.1	−64	−81	−93
North Africa[f]	595	83	5	5.2	0.6	0.0	−86	−94	−99
South Africa[g]	105	124	74	0.9	1.0	0.6	+18	−40	−30
Europe-America-Oceania	**9,525**	**9,511**	**7,678**	**82.8**	**74.1**	**58.9**	**−0**	**−19**	**−19**
Europe, West[h]	1,035	1,119	1,066	9.0	8.9	8.2	+8	−5	+3
Europe, East and Balkan[h]	765	216	94	6.7	1.7	0.7	−72	−56	−88
Former USSR in Europe[i]	1,950	1,906	360	17.0	13.9	2.8	−2	−81	−82
North America[j]	5,215	5,686	5,652	45.3	45.0	43.4	+9	−1	+8
Latin America	520	514	397	4.5	4.1	3.0	−1	−23	−24
Oceania[k]	40	70	109	0.3	0.5	0.8	+75	+56	+173

[a] Minor discrepancies due to rounding.

[b] May 15 (Israel independence day).

[c] December 31.

[d] January 1.

[e] Asian parts of Turkey included in Europe.

[f] Including Ethiopia.

[g] South Africa, Zimbabwe, and other sub-Saharan countries.

[h] East European countries that joined the European Union included in Eastern Europe.

[i] Including Asian parts of Russian Republic.

[j] U.S., Canada.

[k] Australia, New Zealand.

Sources: Adapted from Sergio DellaPergola, "World Jewish Population 2005," in *American Jewish Year Book*, vol. 105 (New York: 2005), 103–146; Sergio DellaPergola, Uzi Rebhun, and Mark Tolts, "Prospecting the Jewish Future: Population Projections 2000–2080," in *American Jewish Year Book*, vol. 100 (New York: 2000), 103–146.

1948 and 2002, an average of nearly 90,000 Jews moved each year. Overall, nearly two thirds of total Jewish migration after 1948 was to Israel, with the propensity to choose it over a western destination higher in Asia-Africa than in Eastern Europe. The rate of emigration per 1,000 Jews at origin (which reflects the weight of the push factors) was also much higher in Asia-Africa than in Eastern Europe. Emigration propensities were extremely low in the western countries and also quite low in Israel. In the exchange between Israel and the western countries, the net balance tended to be in favor of the latter.

World Jewish migration needs to be assessed in a comprehensive rational framework. While the idealistic aliyah motives should not be underestimated, global

Table 3. Estimated Jewish International Migration, by Major Areas of Origin and Destination, 1948–2002

Areas of origin and destination	1948[a]–1968	1969–2002	Total
Total (thousands)	**1,880**	**2,815**	**4695**
Yearly average (thousands)	91	83	86
Percent, total	**100**	**100**	**100**
From Eastern Europe[b]	*33*	*55*	*46*
To Western countries	6	22	16
To Israel	27	33	30
From Asia-Africa[b]	*52*	*16*	*30*
To Western countries	15	3	8
To Israel	37	13	22
From Israel to Western countries[c]	*10*	*16*	*14*
From Western countries to Israel	*5*	*13*	*10*
% to Israel			
Of world total[d]	69	59	63
Of total from Eastern Europe	82	60	65
Of total from Asia-Africa	71	81	73
Rate per 1000 Jews, total	**8**	**6**	**7**
From Eastern Europe[b]	*12*	*51*	*37*
To Western countries	3	20	14
To Israel	10	31	23
From Asia-Africa[b]	*83*	*97*	*92*
To Western countries	28	27	27
To Israel	55	70	65
From Israel to Western countries[c]	*5*	*4*	*4*
From Western countries to Israel	*1*	*1*	*1*

[a] May 15 (Israel independence day).

[b] Since 1990, Asian regions of FSU included in Asia-Africa.

[c] All emigration attributed to Western countries.

[d] Including emigration from Israel.

Source: Sergio DellaPergola, "Israel: Demographic and Economic Dimension of International Migration," in Euro-Mediterranean Consortium for Applied Research on International Migration—CARIM, *Annual Report 2005* (Fiesole: 2005), 123–130, 137–140.

Jewish migration flows generally reflected levels of socioeconomic development and political stability. Thus, whenever possible, Jews tended to move upward, from places that ranked lower on these scales to those that ranked higher. Consequently, the geography of world Jewry came to mirror that of the leading industrialized, developed—and also democratic—countries.[17] In the process, the vast majority of Jews of Sephardic and Oriental origin left their historical areas of settlement and created a new type of diaspora.

Table 4 provides an estimate of the total number and geographical distribution of Jews of Sephardic and Asian-African origin around the year 2000.[18] The estimates are based on rough evaluations of objective indicators such as countries of origin in Asia, Africa, and the Balkans, as well as on subjective indicators such as self-identification or membership in Jewish community organizations that are linked in some way with Sephardic culture. Within these limits, we suggest a world Sephardic/

Oriental population estimate of 3.4 million, out of a total world Jewish population of slightly more than 13 million (amounting to 26 percent of the total). In Israel, Jews of Asian-African origin, including both foreign- and Israeli-born, constituted about 47 percent of the total Jewish population in 2000, in contrast with a total of about 25 percent some fifty years earlier, growing to about half by 1990, before again declining somewhat due to the massive influx of immigrants (mainly Ashkenazim) from the FSU.[19] In the diaspora, Sephardic and Asian-African Jews were estimated to constitute less than 15 percent of total Jewish population, with shares varying according to region. While small communities remained in the historical areas of

Table 4. Total Jewish Population and Estimated Jews of Sephardic/Asian-African Origin, 2000

Region	Total Jewish population (thousands)	Sephardic/Asian-African origin[a]		
		Number (thousands)	Percent of total Jews in region	Percent of worldwide Jews of Sephardic/ Asian-African origin
World total	**13,192**	**3,403**	**26**	**100.0**
Israel	**4,882**	**2,295**	**47**	**67.4**
Diaspora total	**8,310**	**1,108**	**13[b]**	**32.6**
Asia	**51**	**37**	**73**	**1.1**
FSU	30	18	60	0.5
Other[b]	21	19	90	0.6
Africa	**90**	**13**	**14**	**0.4**
North[c]	8	8	100	0.2
South[d]	82	5	4	0.2
Europe	**1,583**	**449**	**28**	**13.2**
European Union	1,027	411	40	12.1
Other West	20	4	20	0.1
FSU[e]	438	5	1	0.1
Other East and Balkans[f]	98	29	30	0.9
America	**6,484**	**604**	**9**	**17.7**
North[g]	6,062	546	9	16.0
Central	53	21	40	0.6
South	369	37	10	1.1
Oceania[h]	**102**	**5**	**5**	**0.2**

[a] Highest estimate based on various available criteria.

[b] Asian parts of Turkey included in Europe.

[c] Including Ethiopia.

[d] South Africa, Zimbabwe, and other sub-Saharan countries.

[e] Including Asian parts of Russian Republic.

[f] Including Turkey.

[g] U.S., Canada.

[h] Australia, New Zealand.

Source: Sergio DellaPergola, "He'arot 'al hameḥkar hasoẓio-demografi shel 'kehilot yisrael bamizraḥ'," *Pe'amim* 93 (2002), 149–156.

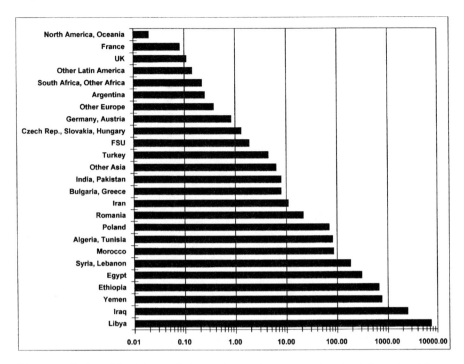

Figure 3. Ratios of Jewish population in Israel of given country of origin, to Jewish population in same country, 2000

The horizontal bars are presented in logarithmic scale.
Source: Computed from Israel Central Bureau of Statistics, *Statistical Abstract of Israel* (2001), Sergio DellaPergola, "World Jewish Population 2000," *American Jewish Year Book*, vol. 101 (New York: 2001), 484–495.

origin, those in Western Europe and Central and South America were much larger. In fact, in some countries, especially France, Mexico, and Venezuela, higher rates of natural increase or lower levels of loss due to assimilation or aging has resulted in Sephardic and Asian-African Jews—once a tiny minority—attaining parity or forming the majority among the younger age groups. These trends are also manifest within the emerging cadre of younger Jewish communal leaders.

Of the estimated global total, about two thirds of Sephardic and Asian-African Jews live nowadays in Israel, with two other significant concentrations located in North America and Western Europe. Jews of Sephardic or Asian-African origin actually living "in the East" (Asia, apart from Israel, and Africa), today account for no more than 1–2 percent of the total, and this figure continues to decline.

What are the overall results of such migration for Israeli society and for world Jewry more generally? In order to answer this question, it is useful first to compute a ratio between the number of Israeli Jews originating from a given country and the Jewish population currently living in the country of origin (see fig. 3, displaying a logarithm scale). The results provide a measure of the cumulated historical odds of staying in the country of origin versus permanently moving to Israel—an indication of relative attractiveness within each pair of countries. The shorter the bars in the diagram, the greater the propensity of Jews from a given country to remain in that country. The longer bars indicate that more of them live in Israel than in the country of origin. The pattern is highly differentiated, reflecting mass movement mostly from countries in North Africa, the Middle East and, to some extent, the Balkans and Eastern Europe to Israel, as against resilience and sometimes attraction of new migrants in countries in North America and Western Europe. The "crossover point" between a larger number living in the original country versus living in Israel (appearing on the diagram as 1.00) passes between Germany-Austria and the Czech Republic-Slovakia-Hungary.

In examining the ranking of aliyah propensities by country and comparing it with indicators of a given country's quality of life such as the UN Human Development Index (HDI),[20] there is a clear reverse correlation between propensity to move to Israel and quality of life in the respective countries. In other words, aliyah is a selective form of immigration that strongly reflects the negative quality of life in the countries where Jews previously lived. One may try to draw a rough balance of the overall impact of immigration on the nature of Israeli society, and vice versa, by first keeping in mind Israel's population composition by countries of origin, and then attributing to each subpopulation the appropriately weighted HDI of its respective country. The resulting average HDI might be considered a predictor of Israel's expected ranking worldwide. In making such a calculation, Israel's predicted HDI ranking comes out between the 60th and 70th place, out of a total ranking of 170 countries. In reality, however, Israel was ranked 23rd in 2005—substantially better than would have been predicted.

What accounts for this striking inconsistency? Two explanations may be offered. First, one should take into account the *sociocultural and socioeconomic selectivity* of migrants, who in general might not reflect the typical human capabilities of their societies of origin. More specifically, and significantly, those making aliyah were overwhelmingly Jewish,[21] and evidently the social structure of Jewish diaspora populations, and of the migrants among them, was not representative of the general society in each country of origin—for instance, they tended to be overrepresented at the higher levels of educational attainment and professional capabilities.

There is also, however, a further explanation that is specific to Israel, one that has to do with the societal "added value " produced by social trends connected with the longer-term process of immigrant absorption. Israeli society succeeded in enabling its immigrants to attain upward social and economic mobility, and in consequence, most of the immigrants to Israel improved their socioeconomic standing relative to that which they might have been expected to achieve in their countries of origin. Put somewhat differently, Israel's significant socioeconomic achievements and institutional growth cannot be attributed solely to the import of human resources via immigration, but reflect as well the success of a collective project that involved the participation of many sectors of the society.

Immigrant Absorption: Failures and Achievements

I now turn to a more problematic aspect of immigrant absorption, examining in greater detail the occupational characteristics of migrants and the modalities of their economic absorption. As noted, Jewish international migration was quite selective in terms of both the countries of origin and the demographic and socioeconomic characteristics of the migrants. What follows is an analysis of immigrant absorption patterns in Israel as compared with those in other countries.[22]

Table 5 shows the basic occupational patterns of Jews of Asian and African origin in different countries, as compared with the general Jewish population in each country. In general, Jewish communities display a relatively high proportion of better-educated professionals and managers and a visible concentration in commerce and sales, alongside a relatively low presence among lower-status service and manual

Table 5. Occupational Distributions among Total Jewish Adults and Those of Sephardic/Asian-African Origin in Selected Places, 1970s–1990s (percent)

Place and population	Professional	Managerial	Clerical	Sales	Blue-collar
Greater Paris, 1970s					
Total Jewish population	25[a]	43[b]		21[c]	10
Born Morocco-Tunisia (gap)	−3	+6		−10	+7
Born Algeria (gap)	−11	+12		−2	+1
U.S., 1990					
Total Jewish population	37	16	20	15	12
Sephardim (gap)	+4	+2	−5	−3	+2
Mexico City, 1991					
Total Jewish population	27	53	11	5	4
Aleppo Jews (gap)	−11	+5	+4	0	+2
Damascus Jews (gap)	−20	+14	+2	+3	+1
Turkish-Balkan Jews (gap)	−1	+4	−4	+1	0
Istanbul, 1988					
Total Jewish population[d]	11	15	7	61	6
Caracas, 1998–1999					
Total Jewish population	17	28	31	21	3
Sephardim (gap)	−6	0	+3	+2	+1
Israel, 1998					
Total Jewish population	29	6	19	18	28
Born Asia-Africa (gap)	−12	−1	−2	+5	+10
Israeli-born, father b. Asia-Africa (gap)	−9	−1	+5	+2	+3
Intergenerational difference	+3	0	+7	−3	−7
France, 2002					
Total Jewish population	13	30	42	9	6
Born North Africa (gap)	+6	−4	−3	+1	+1

[a] Including higher-ranking managers.

[b] Including lower-ranking managers.

[c] Including artisans.

[d] Overwhelmingly of Sephardic origin.

Sources: Bensimon and DellaPergola, *La population juive de France*; DellaPergola and Rebhun, "Hebeitim soziodemografiyim udfusei hizdahut"; DellaPergola and Lerner, *La comunidad judía de Mexico*; Shaul Tuval, *The Jewish Community in Istanbul 1948–1992* (Jerusalem: 2004); DellaPergola, Benzaquen, and Beker de Weintraub, *Perfil sociodemográfico y cultural de la comunidad judía de Caracas*; Israel Central Bureau of Statistics, *Statistical Abstract of Israel* (1999); Cohen with Ifergan, *Les Juifs de France*.

workers. The proportion of Jews in academic and liberal professions is significantly and positively correlated with the general level of economic development of a given country; in the United States, it is significantly higher than in any other country. In countries with a comparatively lower level of economic development, such as Mexico or Turkey,[23] Jews are overrepresented in the sales sector (often in management roles) and in manufacturing (as owners and managers). Often they have benefited from protectionist trade policies, but recently they have been hurt significantly by liberalization and globalization of international trade.

These occupational characteristics often reflect the dynamics of a relatively small minority within the general economic context.[24] The situation is somewhat different in Israel, where in the context of a Jewish majority, the share of Jews employed in services, manufacturing, and agriculture is significantly larger than in the diaspora. Public employment is much more predominant in Israel, whereas the proportion of self-employed is higher in diaspora communities. At the same time, Israel has undergone significant economic modernization and industrialization and hence the proportion in professional, academic, and technical occupations is similar to that in other western countries.

While conforming generally to the occupational pattern of Jews as a whole, the data pertaining to Sephardic and Asian-African Jews points to certain differences between them and Jews of European and American origin. Among Sephardic and Asian-African Jews, the share of professionals and academicians—which is tied directly to higher levels of educational attainment—is somewhat lower. This was particularly true of the Algerian-born in France in the 1970s, who were highly visible among lower-rank administrative and clerical positions, and of the Damascus-origin group in Mexico in the 1990s. However, the generally lower share of professionals and academicians was often balanced by a comparatively higher proportion of managers—frequently an indication of self-employment. Overall, Jews from Asia and Africa were slightly more concentrated in sales and blue-collar positions than Jews from other origins. In France in 2002, following a prolonged and successful process of upward social mobility, Jews of North African origin had a higher proportion of professionals than Jews from other origins, alongside a slightly lower than average proportion in managerial and clerical positions, while differentials in sales and blue-collar employment were virtually non-existent.[25]

This contrasts starkly with the situation in Israel, where immigrants from Asia and Africa have not closed the negative occupational gaps, remaining underrepresented in high-status positions and overrepresented in low-status positions. This finding calls for an in-depth examination of the process of economic absorption of the masses of Jewish immigrants to Israel in the early years after independence. One way of doing so is to compare Jewish immigration to Israel with that to other countries during the same period.

The two columns in bold characters in table 6 provide a simplified representation of the occupational characteristics of Jewish migrants to Israel (until 1961) and France (until the early 1970s). These two time frames cover the major migration waves following Israel's independence and the process of French decolonization in North Africa. While France drew primarily from North Africa and from Central and Eastern Europe, Israel's migrants came from a wider range of countries in Asia and

Africa (particularly North Africa) and Eastern Europe, with smaller numbers from Western and Central Europe.

Occupational differences in these countries of origin before emigration are striking. Among those who went to Israel, the differences might not at first seem significant. A somewhat higher proportion of professionals and administrators (managers and other white-collar workers) were to be found among Jewish immigrants from Europe (23 percent) than among those from the Asian and African countries (15 percent). While initially not remarkable, the difference later had a significant impact. At the same time, there was a significant difference between Jews from Muslim countries who immigrated to France and those who went to Israel. The bulk of North African Jewry's social, cultural, and political elites chose to move to France rather than to Israel. As a result, in France there were four times as many professionals and administrators among them (61 percent) as in Israel (15 percent). The initial selectiveness of these migrants' choice of overseas destination may be dubbed, the original "sin."

But there was a second and worse "sin" relating to the early absorption of immigrants in the new countries. Table 6 shows the percentages in the same occupational category after immigration. Of particular note is occupational retention for those in the professional and administrative categories, for whom presumably the post-migration adaptation was less traumatic. The differences in retention rates between migrants born in Asia or Africa and those born in Europe or America are striking: the latter were much more likely to retain their positions, both in Israel (61 percent versus 49 percent) and in France (59 percent versus 43 percent). The same pattern appears for migrants previously employed in sales. Of the European-American migrants to Israel, 25 percent retained a position in sales, compared with 15 percent of the Asian-Africans; in France, the figures were 41 and 29 percent, respectively. The lower retention figures in Israel of those engaged in sales (among both Asian-Africans and European-Americans) clearly reflect the greater difficulties of migrant absorption into a normal national economy, as compared with the economic advantages and opportunities enjoyed by specialized economic minorities.

The pattern of occupational retention within the administrative (managerial and clerical) sector is mixed: in Israel, 48 percent of the migrants of European origin versus 42 percent of those from Asia-Africa retained their positions compared with 35 percent and 49 percent, respectively, in France. There the higher rate of retention for Asian-Africans—in this case, mainly North Africans—may be explained both by the significant number of Jews in the French colonial administration in North Africa and the reintegration into their posts after their repatriation to France (this applied in particular to Algerian Jews, who had been granted French citizenship in 1870).

Clearly, immigrants from Asia and Africa paid a much higher price in the post-migration process of occupational absorption than immigrants from Europe or North America. The large majority of Asian-African immigrants underwent downward socioeconomic mobility. For instance, of the immigrants who had been professionals in Asia-Africa and moved to a different occupation in Israel, 69 percent went to blue-collar, or to "no or unknown" occupations, compared with 44 percent of professional immigrants from Europe-America. In France, in contrast, 72 percent of North African professionals moved to administrative jobs and 28 percent to blue-collar or to "no or unknown" occupations, while some two thirds of European immigrant professionals

Table 6. Patterns of Occupational Mobility among Jewish Immigrants to Israel and to France, Asian-African vs. European-American Origin, 1960s and 1970s

| | Born Asia-Africa | | | | | Born Europe-America | | | | |
| | | | Of all occupationally mobile, % moved to: | | | | | Of all occupationally mobile, % moved to: | | |
Occupational status	% distribution abroad	% retention after migration	Professional, administrative	Trade and sales	Blue-collar, none, unkn.	% distribution abroad	% retention after migration	Professional, administrative	Trade and sales	Blue-collar, none, unkn.
Israel, 1961[a]	**100**					**100**				
Professional	**5**	49	23	8	69	**10**	61	50	6	44
Administrative	**10**	42	9	11	80	**13**	48	8	16	76
Sales	**30**	15	9	[e]	91	**23**	25	25	[e]	75
Blue-collar	**44**	79	16	17	67	**36**	75	41	25	34
None, unknown	**11**	40	15	8	77	**18**	19	39	10	51
Greater Paris, 1970s[b]	**100**					**100**				
Professional[c]	**29**	43	72	0	28	**32**	59	35	65	0
Administrative	**32**	49	31	64	5	**17**	35	16	49	35
Sales[d]	**24**	29	86	[e]	14	**24**	41	88	[e]	12
Blue-collar	**15**	38	75	25	[e]	**27**	18	87	13	[e]

[a] Occupational mobility of immigrants.

[b] Occupation abroad of immigrants to France before 1961. The data on occupational mobility were computed from occupation abroad of fathers of heads of households, and occupation in France of heads of households.

[c] Including higher-ranking managers.

[d] Including artisans.

[e] Same occupational status before and after migration.

Source: Computed from Israel Central Bureau of Statistics, *Census of Population and Housing* (1961), vol. 9 (1963); vol. 27 (1965); Bensimon and DellaPergola, *La population juive de France,* Table 9.7 (p. 214); Table 17.4 (p. 370).

took up employment in trade rather than in blue-collar jobs. Similar patterns are apparent for migrants who had held administrative positions in their countries of origin. With regard to those in sales, 91 percent of the Asian-African immigrants to Israel moved down to blue-collar or "none or unknown" jobs, as did 75 percent of those from Europe-America. But in France, the experience was totally different—the vast majority of sales personnel moved up into professional and administrative positions (86 percent of those born in Asia/Africa and 88 percent of those born in Europe-America).

Most likely, the individual characteristics of immigrants turned out to be somewhat subordinate to perceptions (whether positive or negative) regarding the overall global prestige ranking of their countries of origin. Further country-by country evidence of the process of occupational change soon after the large immigration before 1961 shows that many immigrants from English-speaking and other West European countries with relatively little education rapidly moved from blue-collar occupations abroad to white-collar in Israel, while the opposite occurred to relatively better-educated immigrants from North Africa and the Middle East.[26]

In sum, there were both commonalities and sharp contrasts in the immigrant absorption processes affecting Jews born in Asia-Africa and those born in Europe-America. Both population subgroups experienced a general downward mobility in their new countries, though those coming from Europe-America usually fared better than those from Muslim countries. Among the former, much of the post-migration mobility was lateral (that is, to a different occupation with similar socioeconomic status). In contrast, many of the Asian-African immigrants to Israel—particularly those with a background in the professions and sales—were forced to move to blue-collar jobs. Thus, they paid a much higher socioeconomic price than did European-American immigrants. On the whole, the mostly North African Jewish immigrants to France benefited from a smoother absorption process.

Sub-ethnic Convergence, Divergence, and "Catch-up"

As a consequence of the mass waves of immigration in the late 1940s and early 1950s, Israel became a highly heterogeneous society. As has been seen, there was an initial gap between immigrants from Muslim countries versus those from Europe or North America, with the former group experiencing a greater drop in socioeconomic status. The question is whether this gap persisted over time, or whether sociodemographic trends that developed in the wake of mass immigration worked in the direction of promoting greater equality among the different Jewish subgroups. The following data focus on variables pointing to increasing convergence/integration versus increasing divergence/segregation among the Israeli Jewish population.[27]

Residential Distributions

A primary concern of multiethnic and multicultural societies is the allocation of residential space to different groups, whether more clustered or diffused. Previous analyses have shown a clear trend toward greater residential diffusion and declining segregation among different origin groups in Israel.[28] This is true with regard to both regions and cities, and to the more specific level of urban neighborhoods and smaller territorial units. A model of the countrywide and regional geographical location of different origin groups in Israel is shown in figure 4. This Smallest Space Analysis of the 1995 Israeli census data synthesizes a matrix of 26 groups of countries of birth,

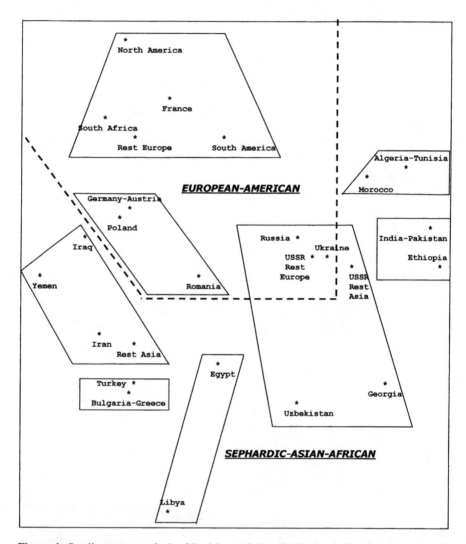

Figure 4. Smallest space analysis of Jewish population distribution in Israel, by countries of birth and sub-districts, 1995

Each point on the Smallest Space Analysis (SSA) synthesizes the distribution of a given origin group across Israel's 16 sub-district divisions. Closeness or distance between points indicates more or less similar distributions of two populations across sub-districts. The Israeli-born group was not included. The polygons were drawn to stress the proximity between groups with some geographical similarity, such as Western countries, the FSU, Northwest Africa, and Northeast Africa.

Source: Created from Israel Central Bureau of Statistics, *Census of Population and Housing 1995*, Public Use Sample.

subdivided by 16 sub-district territorial divisions. The closer the points representing two given origin groups, the more similar their respective regional distributions. A more central position on the map means greater diffusion over Israel's territory; less central positions indicate peculiar patterns of regional clustering. Eight regional residential clusters of immigrants from geographically proximate countries—presumably sharing similar cultural backgrounds—appear for Western Europe and North America, Central and Eastern Europe (predominant among veteran immigrants), the different republics of the FSU (predominant among more recent immigrants), and the Balkans, Asia, and different areas in North Africa. The significant distances between the clusters formed by the last three groups of countries further underlines the previously noted analytic deficiencies of the single overall Asia-Africa aggregate category for the study of ethnicity and identity.

The salience of countries of origin as a factor in creating proximate communities and social networks, and in reinforcing particularistic identities, is confirmed by these data. Four major factors explain the varying residential distribution of different groups of origin: the timing of immigration to Israel and the availability of housing in each period; Israel's policies concerning national population dispersion; the socioeconomic status of members of each group and their ability to negotiate housing in convenient locations; and the ideological orientation of different groups toward living in the territories occupied by Israel after the Six-Day War of June 1967. At the same time, no clearly hierarchical residential patterns based on the geography of origin are apparent, as would be the case if all countries-of-origin groups in Asia-Africa appeared on one part of the diagram, with all those in Europe-America located elsewhere. Differences in the geographical distribution of immigrant groups in Israel are not necessarily related only to inequality but also to residential preferences that reflect a voluntary search for proximity with persons of similar background in a culturally diverse society. One significant exception seems to be the peculiar clustering of Jews from India and Ethiopia. The only rationale for the residential closeness of two groups from different continents that immigrated at very different times would seem to be their nearly total dependence on the settling authorities—which would explain their being directed to similar peripheral and semi-rural areas in accordance with a rigid interpretation of national population dispersal goals.

In the case of Jewish communities outside Israel, residential differences are apparent at the neighborhood level. In France, for instance, North African Jews who had immigrated more recently than the veteran (mostly Ashkenazic) population and who, as in the case of the Algerians, could rely partly on public assistance in relocating, were initially more dispersed residentially. Over time, however, the residential spread of the two groups became narrower as the North African immigrants and their descendants came increasingly to reside in more central locations—the Paris metropolitan area rather than provincial towns—or else, like the more veteran Jewish population, gradually moved to the suburbs of the capital city. Similarly, in Mexico City and Caracas, Sephardic Jews initially displayed distinctive patterns of residential concentration that differed markedly from those found among the European-origin Jews. However, over time, heightened socioeconomic status and mobility within the Jewish population gradually led to greater residential proximity and similarity as all moved to newer urban and suburban locations.

Health and Marriage

From the early stages of Israel's statehood, active public intervention brought about improvements in public health and increased life expectancy. Over time, Asian-African immigrants succeeded in erasing their initial disadvantages in these regards.

As more similar lifestyles developed, the frequency of interethnic marriages between Jews from Asia-Africa and from Europe-America increased. Figure 5 illustrates the historical decline in the propensity of Jewish brides and grooms in Israel to marry within their own geographic origin group. During Israel's early years, very high—indeed nearly exclusive—sub-ethnic homogamy prevailed, since the cultural patterns of each immigrant group were reinforced by the great similarity in length of time in the country, socioeconomic status, and residential proximity. Over time, however, sub-ethnic homogamy declined, such that by the end of the 1990s, the frequency of heterogamic marriages (that is, those occurring between members of different sub-ethnic groups) was more than half as likely as it would have been had marriages occurred randomly across the main origin groups.[29] Sub-ethnic intermarriage tends to dilute or even to alter partly the cultural bases of group-of-origin identities, thereby accelerating the process of cultural integration. A further study based on data from the 1983 and 1995 censuses confirms that, when social class is controlled, the statistical overrepresentation of marriages among Jews sharing the same continental origin tends to diminish.[30]

At the same time, figure 5 indicates a cessation or even a reversal of these converging trends, beginning in the year 2000. Part of the explanation may be related to the inherent limitations of the data: the continental origin of a growing proportion of Jewish brides and grooms is not specified, as they and their parents were born in Israel. Thus, although marriage across sub-ethnic boundaries is presumably quite widespread within this group, it does not register in the data. One must also consider the large number of immigrants during the 1990s from the FSU and Ethiopia, many of whose children married in the following decade. As immigrants from the FSU constitute a very large group, in-marriage will in all likelihood be enhanced temporarily, as was clearly the case during the years 1948–1953. The Ethiopians, while a much smaller group, are still frequently homogamous—and this, too, contributes to a heightening of overall rates of in-marriage. While the possibility cannot be ruled out that the data in figure 5 reflect the beginning of a reversal of the historic trend toward sub-ethnic convergence in marriage, longer-term evidence is required before it can be substantiated or disproven.

In France, too, intermarriage between North African and European Jews became increasingly frequent, indeed even more so than in Israel. At the same time, marriage with non-Jewish partners (outmarriage) also tended to increase over time. In contrast, Jewish marriage patterns in Mexico were singularly homogamic. Until the 1970s, for instance, more than 90 percent of Ashkenazic spouses in Mexico married within the same sub-ethnic group; among Sephardim, sub-ethnic endogamy was well over 80 percent even in the 1990s. In addition, among the Halabi (Aleppo) and Shami (Damascus) communities in Mexico, 65–70 percent of marriages involved partners from the same community group within the sub-ethnicity.[31] Similar marriage patterns obtain for the Iranian immigrant community in Los Angeles.[32] It is only since the 1990s that some of these trends have begun to weaken.

Fertility

Fertility patterns in Israel indicate a growing convergence between Asian-African and European-American origin groups. Jewish total fertility rates (TFR)[33] were comparatively stable in Israel, diminishing from 3.6 children in the 1950s to 2.6–2.7 in the 1980s, and remaining steady thereafter into the early 2000s. However, the initial gap between different origin groups was quite large. As figure 6 shows, by the mid-1950s an immigrant woman from Asia-Africa had, on average, over three more children than her immigrant peer from Europe-America. This marked gap in family-size decreased steadily throughout the 1960s and 1970s, and by the early 1980s, it had been reduced to a minimum. The subsequent reappearance of a fertility gap between these two groups reflects recent immigration of Jewish women from the low-fertility FSU and from high-fertility Ethiopia. Thus, by 1992, the TFR gap again reached 1.5 children, but within a few years, immigrant women once again began to conform to the established norm of Israeli society. A decline of fertility among the

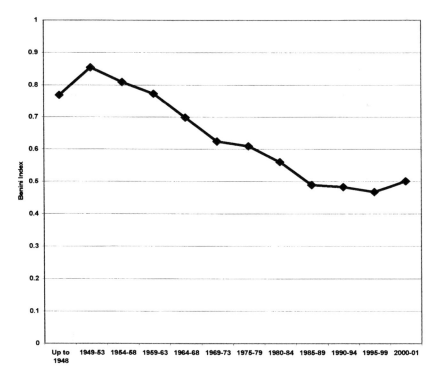

Figure 5. Indexes of marriage attraction within main origin groups in Israel, Asian-African vs. European-American Origin, 1948–2001

For explanations, see note 29 to the text.

Source: Computed from Israel Central Bureau of Statistics, *Statistical Abstract of Israel* (Jerusalem: various issues).

higher-fertility group of immigrants concurred with some increase of fertility among
the lower-fertility group. The stability attained in Israeli fertility patterns is manifest
in the data for the second, Israeli-born generation of women, where the initial differences between immigrant groups have long since disappeared.

In other countries—for instance, France and Mexico—similar processes of Jewish
sub-ethnic fertility convergence have also occurred. Generally, their levels of fertility were significantly lower than that in Israel, and at no time did fertility increase
among Jews of European origin. In the 1970s, the fertility level of French Jewry fell
below replacement level and subsequently remained fairly stable. In Mexico, it was
somewhat higher—possibly because of the community's comparatively high level
of income and the ready availability of household help, but still somewhat lower
than in Israel.[34]

Educational Attainment

Especially during the initial period of mass immigration to Israel, the educational
levels of immigrants were far from uniform. Many immigrants from the Middle East
and North Africa had little or no education and relatively few had any university
training, as compared with immigrants from Europe and America. One of the priorities of the newly established state was to reduce gaps in educational attainment; to
that end, it invested considerable resources.[35] By the 1950s, nearly universal literacy
had been attained, and by the 1980s, a vast majority of Israeli schoolchildren were
completing at least 12 years of schooling.

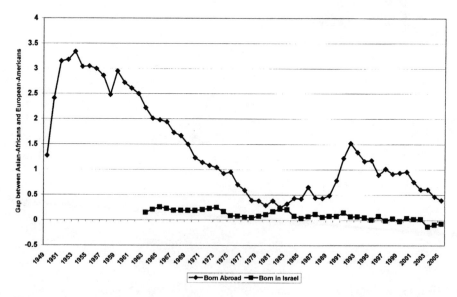

Figure 6. Total fertility rate gaps in Israel between Jewish women of Asian-African vs.
European-American origin, 1949–2005

Source: Computed from Israel Central Bureau of Statistics, *Statistical Abstract of Israel* (Jerusalem: various issues).

The extent of the educational gaps between the two main origin groups can be assessed over time at various levels, from entrance into the system at age 6 to completion of a college or university degree. Figure 7 examines the gap by means of three measures: median years of study completed; successful completion of high-school matriculation examinations; and enrollment in an institution of post-secondary education among individuals aged 20–29. By positing the respective percentages achieved by the European-American origin group at a level of 100, a measure of relative disadvantage may be obtained for the Asian-African origin group. Thus, by the early 2000s, the gap in years of schooling between Israeli-born children of Asian-African origin and those of European-American origin stood at 13 percent, as against about 30 percent in the 1960s.

Convergence of levels of educational attainment was incomplete in at least two other respects. More youngsters of Asian-African origin were enrolled in vocational high schools, where the chances of attaining a matriculation certificate *(te'udat bagrut)*—a prerequisite for admission to an Israeli university—were considerably lower than at academic high schools. Nevertheless, the gap between youngsters of Asian-African origin and those of European-American origin in reaching that level was reduced significantly over the years—from 70 percent in the 1960s to 12 percent by the early 2000s.[36] However, further analysis of these data indicates that the closing of this educational gap is proceeding more slowly than earlier anticipated, and has emphasized the need for affirmative action so as to provide equal educational opportunities for all, irrespective of group origins.[37]

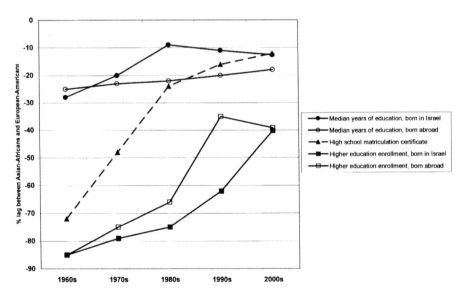

Figure 7. Educational gaps in Israel between Jews of Asian-African vs. European-American origin, 1960s–2000s

Source: Computed from Israel Central Bureau of Statistics, *Statistical Abstract of Israel* (Jerusalem: various issues).

Closely related to the latter is the underrepresentation of Israelis of Asian-African origin among university and college students. In the early 2000s, among both Israeli-born and immigrants, enrollment in higher education among those of Asian-African origin was 40 percentage points lower than among those of European-American origin. While this gap had diminished over time—from 85 percent for both immigrant- and Israeli-born Asian-African and European-American origin in the 1960s, to 60 percent for Israeli-born Asian-Africans and European-Americans in the 1990s—the remaining 40 percent gap is highly significant, given the rapidly increasing educational attainments among all sections of Israel's population. The rate of exposure of the whole Israeli population (including Arabs) to at least some post-secondary education rose from 9 percent in 1961 to 39 percent in 2001. Among Jews aged 25–34, the figure was 58 percent, compared with 29 percent among those aged 65 and over. Moreover, access to post-secondary education was eased considerably by the establishment, in the 1990s, of colleges with lower admission standards and academic requirements than the research universities. This, in turn, led to greatly increased college enrollment among the younger generation, a situation that augurs well for the further narrowing of the gap between those of Asian-African and European-American origin, with regard to higher educational achievements.

Occupation

The pattern of occupational stratification within Israel's Jewish population—a direct outcome of educational attainment—has changed considerably since the 1960s, as is clearly evident from the data reported in table 7. Between 1966 and 2004, the combined proportions of professionals, managers, and clerical personnel among Jews of Asian-African origin were consistently lower than among those of European-American origin, although within both groups those proportions rose during that period. Thus, among Jews of Asian-African origin (including Israeli-born), the total of those in academic, technical, managerial, or clerical positions increased from 16 percent in 1966 to 49 percent in 2004, whereas among persons of European-American origin, the figures were 38 percent and 58 percent, respectively. This rise was counterbalanced by higher (albeit steadily declining) proportions of workers in industry, construction, transport, and agriculture among those of Asian-African origin: 60 percent in 1966 and 28 percent in 2004, as compared with 40 percent and 24 percent, respectively, among those of European-American origin.

The general direction of change in Israel's social stratification involved a growing predominance of white-collar over blue-collar occupations. On the one hand, the state as the primary employer facilitated the large-scale access of those of Asian-African origin to lower level white-collar jobs. On the other hand, following the Six-Day War, Jewish employees in lower-level occupations became upwardly mobile as Palestinian laborers from the West Bank and Gaza replaced them.

An assessment of the relative occupational disadvantage of those of Asian-African origin as compared with those of European-American origin can be attained through an index of dissimilarity that measures the hypothetical percentage of individuals in a given group who should change their occupation in order to match the occupational distribution of some other group. The (+) or (−) sign reflects the

Table 7. Occupational Gaps in Israel between Jews of Asian-African vs. European-American Origin, 1966–2004

	1966		1992		2004	
Occupation	Asian-African Origin[a]	European-American Origin[a]	Asian-African Origin[a]	European-American Origin[a]	Asian-African Origin[a]	European-American Origin[a]
Total (thousands)	291.9	371.1	627.3	681.2	749.6	916.3
Total %	100	100	100	100	100	100
Academic and technical	6	17	17	36	21.5	36
Managerial, clerical	10	21	24	22	27.5	22
Trade, services	24	22	26	19	23	18
Workers	47	33	31	20	26	23
Agriculture	13	7	3	3	2	1
Asia-Africa relative disadvantage index:[b]						
vs. European-American same year	−22%		−18.5%		−14.5%	
vs. European-American 1966	−22%		+7%		+12%	

[a] Country of birth (foreign-born) or father's country of birth (Israeli-born).

[b] Indexes of dissimilarity of percent distributions. The positive or negative sign of the index reflects the direction of the different incidence of academic, technical, managerial, and clerical positions among the Asian-African group in a given year versus the matching group.

Source: Computed from Israel Central Bureau of Statistics, *Statistical Abstract of Israel* (Jerusalem: various issues).

greater or lesser frequency of academic, technical, managerial, and clerical occupations among Jews of Asian-African origin relative to those of European-American origin. The index of dissimilarity shown in table 7 indicates that the occupational gap diminished, from −22 percent in 1966 to −18.5 percent in 1992 and −14.5 percent in 2004. To put this admittedly slow improvement in relative stratification into perspective, it should be noted that it occurred within a general Israeli context of significant upward mobility. Thus, in 1992, the occupational profile of the Asian-African origin group was only slightly better than that of the European-American origin group in 1966 (26 years earlier), with an index of dissimilarity/relative gap of +7 percent, and by 2004 that gap (versus the Europeans-Americans in 1966) was +12 percent. In other words, while both groups have undergone significant upward social mobility, the manifest differences in socioeconomic achievements between Jews of Asian-African origin (including both first- and second-generation Israelis) and those of European-American origin currently amount to a 20–25 year lag, although this time lag is diminishing.

Income

A final indicator of socioeconomic inequality is income distribution. Figure 8 shows the relative income gap between urban employees of Asian-African and European-American origin at four different points of time, between 1975 and 2003. Income

gaps are measured for each decile of income among Jewish households of urban
employees, that is, not including the self-employed. Group 10 represents the highest
level of income, and group 1 represents the lowest. For each point, the graph
indicates the overrepresentation or underrepresentation of Asian-African households
as compared with their share of total Jewish households in Israel. Under a theoretical
situation of equal income distribution, the share of Asian-African households would
be identical for each income decile.

The comparisons for 1975–1976 and 1986 show that Asian-African origin households were strikingly overrepresented at the lowest level, and underrepresented at
the highest levels of income distribution. In 1975–1976, the gap amounted to 35
percent—more at the bottom level, less at the top level—versus what might have been
expected, had income been equally distributed across the different origin groups. The
more recent data indicate virtually equal distribution by origin in the middle-income
deciles, with the continued presence of inequality (albeit considerably reduced) at the
top and bottom income levels. However, the pace of change in income distribution
equalization has considerably slowed down during the 2000s as compared to the
1990s.

Several caveats should be noted: the data do not include the urban self-employed,
the rural sector, or the Israeli-born. The last are significantly more concentrated at
higher income levels, even allowing for the fact that income inequality tends to be
transmitted from generation to generation across all origin groups. Neither do the data
take into account the even greater income inequality between Jews and non-Jews.
Significantly, the recent immigration from the FSU created a large group of European-origin individuals at the bottom of the income scale that served to dilute somewhat the concentration of Asian-African households at those lower levels. But overall

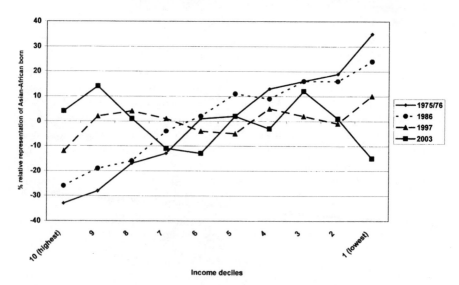

Figure 8. Income distribution in Israel of Jewish urban employees born in Asia-Africa:
actual vs. expected representation by income deciles, 1975–2003

Source: Computed from Israel Central Bureau of Statistics, *Statistical Abstract of Israel,* various issues.

it seems that persisting sub-ethnic educational and occupational differences do not preclude the attainment of greater income equality among the various sub-ethnic groups within the Jewish population. In spite of the continuing impact of education and occupation on income, the Israeli socioeconomic system evidently allows for alternative paths to comparatively similar income attainment.

Patterns of Jewish Identification

Social, demographic, and economic change are bound to leave their mark on identity and culture. Frequencies of adherence to selected indicators of Jewish identification among Jews of Sephardic and Asian-African origins in France, the United States, Mexico, Venezuela, and Israel between the 1970s and the early 2000s are presented in table 8. The data show the levels of Jewish identification of the selected origin groups and the total Jewish population in each place. The indicators cover a wide variety of elements relating to individual and family religious practice, choice of marital partner, activity in Jewish organizations, Jewish educational background, and attitudes toward Jewishness.[38]

It should be recalled that, in each country, Jewish migrants came from a number of different places of origin. In France, for instance, the "Asian and African" Jews were predominantly from the Maghreb (Morocco, Algeria, and Tunisia). The United States countrywide data on "Asian and African" Jews refer to a heterogeneous group, including a veteran component that arrived in the United States during the 19th century alongside more recent arrivals from Israel and other Middle Eastern countries—not to mention the tiny remnants of the original Sephardim who were the earliest Jews who settled in North America during the 17th century. The more visible recent addition included several thousand Iranian immigrants living in the Los Angeles area. In Mexico, the predominant "Asian and African" groups came from Syria (Aleppo and Damascus) and Turkey. In Venezuela, the single largest group was from Morocco, with a strong representation from the former Spanish territories in Morocco. The heterogeneity of the Sephardic and Asian-Africans was at its highest in Israel, whose immigrants came from all of the above-mentioned countries as well as from Iraq, Yemen, Ethiopia, Libya, and Egypt.

Remarkably, in spite of the varying levels of Jewish identification of the different Jewish populations surveyed here, the popularity and frequency of performance rankings of different Jewish rituals and traditions are quite similar among all Jews regardless of origin. This would suggest that Jews nearly everywhere display a similar understanding of the relevance of Jewish practices and values—whether or not they are personally involved with them. Apart from the high frequency of in-marriage in the observed period, the highest frequencies pertain to Passover observance and synagogue attendance at least once a year. The frequencies of choice of a sub-ethnic spouse, membership in Jewish organizations, and attaching importance to being Jewish are generally somewhat lower, with consistent observance of Jewish rituals such as kashruth and weekly synagogue attendance much lower.

In most cases, Jews of Asian-African origin display higher levels of Jewish commitment and community cohesiveness on a range of attitudinal and behavioral

Table 8. Jewish Identification Gaps, Total Jewish Adults and Selected Sephardic/Asian-African Origin Jews, Various Places (percent), 1970s–2000s

Place and population	Attend synagogue — At least once a year	Attend synagogue — At least once a week	Observe Pesach	Jewish spouse	Sub-ethnic spouse[a]	Member of Jewish organization	Ever received Jewish education	Important to be Jewish
Greater Paris, 1970s								
Total Jewish population	60	9	82	80	57	42	35	86[b]
Born Morocco-Tunisia (gap)	+30	+2	+12	+15	+22	-4	+23	+7
Born Algeria (gap)	+25	+5	+11	+6	+25	+4	+24	+4
Los Angeles, 1987–1988								
Total Jewish population	61	7	n.a.	74	n.a.	24	n.a.	n.a.
Iranian Jews (gap)	+33	+16	n.a.	+22	c	+17	n.a.	n.a.
U.S., 1990								
Total Jewish population	83	11	70	71	n.a.	39	76	53[d]
Sephardim (gap)[e]	-3	-4	n.a.	-5	n.a.	=	=	+11
Mexico City, 1991								
Total Jewish population	89	17	93	97	88	97	69	76[f]
Allepan Jews (gap)[g]	+10	+7	+6	+3	+8	+3	-8	+8
Damascene Jews (gap)[h]	+9	+9	+6	+3	+8	+2	+7	+4
Turkish-Balkan Jews (gap)[i]	+1	-10	-4	+1	-19	+1	-5	-7
Caracas, 1998–1999								
Total Jewish population	97	38	91	98	88	97	74	66[f]
Sephardim (gap)[j]	+2	+11	+5	+1	-2	+2	+5	+8
Israel, 1991								
Total Jewish population	81	24	89	X	68[k]	X	92[l]	65[m]
Born Asia-Africa (gap)	+8	+13	+4	X	+7[k]	X	+4[l]	+17
Israeli-born, father Asian-African (gap)	+6	+4	+5	X	+12[k]	X	+4[l]	=
Intergenerational difference	-2	-9	+1	X	+5[k]	X	=[l]	-17

Israel, 1999						
Total Jewish population	58	23	77	X	n.a.	63[n]
Born Asia-Africa (gap)	+23	+15	+16	X	n.a.	+16
Israeli-born, father Asian-African (gap)	+11	+3	+16	X	n.a.	+12
Intergenerational difference	−12	−12	=	X	n.a.	−4
France, 2002						
Total Jewish population	22		70	48[o]	28[p]	
Born North Africa (gap)			+5			

[a] Married to Jew of same origin.

[b] Interested in Judaism.

[c] 96 percent of cases.

[d] Very important to be Jewish.

[e] Self-defined Sephardic Jew and/or born in Asia-Africa.

[f] Very important to be part of Jewish people.

[g] Maguen David community.

[h] Monte Sinai community.

[i] Sephardic community.

[j] Asociación Israelita Caracas (AIC) community.

[k] As reported for "close family."

[l] "Important to have Bar Mitzvah."

[m] "Definitely" proud to be Jewish.

[n] "Feel part of a world Jewish people."

[o] Donates to Jewish organizations several times a year.

[p] Day school only. If part-time Jewish education is included, the figure would be higher than in the 1970s.

Source: Bensimon and DellaPergola, *La population juive de France*; DellaPergola, Sabagh, Bozorgmehr, Der-Martirosian, and Lerner, "Hierarchic Levels of Subethnicity," 1–42; DellaPergola and Rebhun, "Hebeitim sozio-demografiyim udfusei hizdahut"; DellaPergola and Lerner, *La comunidad judía de Mexico*; DellaPergola, Benzaquen, and Beker de Weintraub, *Perfil socio-demográfico y cultural de la comunidad judía de Caracas*; Shlomit Levy, Hanna Levinsohn, and Elihu Katz, *Beliefs, Observances and Social Interactions among Israeli Jews* (Jerusalem: 1993); Shlomit Levy, Hanna Levinsohn, and Elihu Katz, *A Portrait of Israeli Jewry: Beliefs, Observances and Values among Israeli Jews 2000* (Jerusalem: 2002); Cohen with Ifergan, *Les Juifs de France.*

indicators. For instance, the data on France for 2002 indicate that the percentage of
Jews of Asian-African origin married to non-Jews is somewhat lower than that of the
total Jewish population.[39] The exception to the general pattern of higher observance
and affiliation is the Sephardic and Asian-African born community in the United
States, whose measures of Jewish identification are marginally lower than those
among the overall Jewish community (except for the importance attached to Jewishness, where it is significantly higher).[40]

In Israel, significant weakening in Jewish attitudes and practices is apparent in the
second generation of Asian-African immigrants.[41] This accords with a common
pattern among migrants, whereby traditional attitudes, patterns of behavior, and
communal structures maintained in the first generation after migration become attenuated as the migrants—and especially their children—adapt to the host society.

A further issue relating to identificational patterns and immigrant absorption
concerns the mutual perceptions of different sub-ethnic groups. One long-term
follow-up study indicates that Israeli Jews of European-American origin tended to
have more positive perceptions of Asian-African Jews during periods of economic
or security crisis, whereas periods of normalcy were marked by more critical attitudes on the part of both groups.[42] Between the 1970s and the late 1990s, Jews from
Asia-Africa (including the second, Israeli-born generation) had relatively more favorable perceptions of Jews from Europe or America, than the latter had of them.
Interestingly, they also appear to have internalized some of the negative stereotyping
of their group by persons of European-American origin, for example concerning
mutual perceptions of consistency and reliability.[43]

Changing Perceptions of Sub-ethnic Identities

What weight should be given to ethnic and sub-ethnic identity in evaluating the
consequences of large-scale international migration of "Sephardic and Oriental"
Jews to Israel and to the main western countries? Among Israeli scholars, there
are several schools of thought on the matter. Historically, the emphasis on nation-
building meant that ethnicity was perceived mainly along cultural lines. As part of
the process of immigrant integration, the salience of cultural diversity—hence sub-
ethnic identity—would decline and the structural assimilation into society would
occur over time.[44] An opposite view holds that sub-ethnic cleavages in Israeli society
overlap fundamentally and permanently with divisions and conflicts of class.[45] In an
extreme formulation of this view, it is argued that ongoing ethnocultural inequalities
in Israel are the outcome of the conscious exploitation of the immigrants from Asia
and Africa by the earlier European Jewish immigrants.[46] A third school of thought
recognizes the existence of various forms of sub-ethnic stratification but regards
these not as the result of exploitation, but rather as a constituent (if not inevitable)
feature of Israeli society.[47]

In fact, the data pertaining to educational attainment, occupational status, and
income suggest that persisting gaps between the two major origin groups might better
be described as time-related evolutionary lags rather than as insurmountable obstacles inherent in Israel's social structure. If this is the case, the main cause for

concern should not be the absence of a trend toward closing these gaps, but rather its relatively slow pace. As has been shown, social gaps between the two main origin groups continue to be significant at the higher levels of the Israeli educational ladder, which implies that the acquisition of higher levels of training required for upward mobility continues to be affected by imbalances of the past. At the same time, the gradual closure of sub-ethnic demographic gaps provides a more egalitarian starting point for the younger, Israeli-born generation. Thus, the frequency of interethnic marriages, the gradual disappearance of family-size differentials, and growing residential integration of members of different origin groups are all indicators of continuing reduction in the extant socioeconomic gaps. Such gaps, however, will not be eliminated in the foreseeable future without preferential policies and incentives aimed at improving the educational achievements of the weaker social groups, which are still disproportionately of Asian and African origin.

Among Jewish communities in the diaspora, the observed patterns of Jewish immigrant integration from Asia and Africa share many commonalities with those in Israel. However, since their initial social resources and skills tended to be higher than those of their peers who went to Israel, the period of recovery after the initial shock of absorption was much shorter. Their successful socioeconomic mobility is manifested, for example, in the growing involvement of immigrants and their children in the highest levels of Jewish communal leadership. In France, since the 1980s the chief rabbis have been of North African origin, as are many influential lay leaders, professionals, academics, intellectuals, and politicians prominent in French society and culture. Similarly, in a number of Latin American communities—in Mexico, Argentina, Venezuela, and Brazil, for instance—a growing number of individuals of Middle Eastern ancestry (in particular, from Aleppo) serve as Jewish communal leaders. Such growing involvement reflects a commitment to Jewish communal life that is characteristic of many Asian-African Jews. On the whole, these migrants remain more strongly attached to Jewish community life in comparison both with members of the veteran Jewish communities that absorbed them and with other Jewish migrants who arrived at the same time. Finally, in countries as different as France, Mexico, and Venezuela, there is an emerging demographic predominance of Jews of Asian and African origin in place of Jews of Central-Eastern European background. A true *Sephardization* of the community is thus underway, starting from the younger age groups and moving up to encompass the entire community.

All in all, the basic trend is one of a gradual convergence among Jewish immigrants from different continents, and especially among their children, in terms of residential dispersion, family size, and socioeconomic status. In Israel, however, there is a possible major obstacle to continued convergence, namely, the growing influence of ethnic political parties – in particular, Shas. The question is whether sub-ethnic political entrepreneurs enhance or hinder the long-term process of assimilation into the Jewish mainstream. On the one hand, vested political interests tend to stress ethnic and sub-ethnic cleavages and in this way actually reinforce them. On the other hand, in Israel (not unlike certain Jewish communities in Latin America), Jewish sub-ethnic separatism has worked to mobilize Jews of Sephardic and Asian-African origins to greater political involvement and has resulted in a more equal distribution of power and resources. Thus, by promoting sub-ethnic separatism and particularistic interests—in part, by stressing sub-ethnic tensions—attaining the ultimate goal of more equitable representation actually may be accelerated.

When assessing social inequality and its relationship to sociocultural origins, it is not enough simply to read the story conveyed by measurable data. It is also essential to evaluate the actors' subjective perceptions and expectations. What counts is not only what actually happened but also what people wanted to happen and what they thought actually did happen. Thus, the overall evaluation of sub-ethnic convergence versus divergence must consider more subjective changes in identity as well as quantitative data regarding sociodemographic change. In light of the convergent trends described above—albeit occurring more slowly in Israel than in other Jewish communities—I would suggest that, in the long run, sub-ethnic identities are likely to be largely subsumed within a more broadly defined ethnic identity. In the past, to be sure, varying intensities of sub-ethnic identity coexisted with a broader Jewish identity, and these may continue to coexist, both in Israel and in western societies that have absorbed significant numbers of Jewish migrants. For a relatively small minority, homogeneity or even segregated cultural and socioeconomic environments may continue to reinforce strong and nearly all-encompassing sub-ethnic bonds. For many more individuals, the consciousness of ethnic origin may persist as an enriching frame of reference within broader societal orientations toward universal socioeconomic goals and cultural expressions. For others, any cultural residue of sub-ethnic (or, for that matter, Jewish) identity may eventually be lost. These approaches correspond, respectively, to a cohesive self-contained community, a distinctive social group, and a segment of the population whose ethnic origin can no longer be traced.

While the effects of time and generational changes in Israel and abroad have operated in the direction of strengthening the second and third approaches, sub-ethnic identities are not likely to vanish completely, in part because of the activities of various political and communal sub-ethnic entrepreneurs. Shas, for instance, has created a network of religious educational institutions that attempt, among other things, to strengthen Mizrahi identity among the younger generation. Moreover, past accomplishments in the realm of closing socioeconomic gaps have led to legitimate demands for even greater parity. As noted, ethnic origin stereotypes are often associated with social status. The socially mobile Israeli-born of Asian-African origin (or, more significantly, the upwardly mobile children of sub-ethnic intermarriages) can both identify with and be identified by a broader Israeli Jewish ethnic identity or even a neutral Israeli pan-ethnic identity; they may no longer feel the need for the protective shell of a strong sub-ethnic frame of reference. In contrast, those located on the lower socioeconomic rungs are more likely to identify, or be identified by others, with a Mizrahi sub-ethnic identity and to become the focus of sub-ethnic political lobbying.

Such pockets of social marginality and disadvantage, existing at the margins of successful absorption and integration, can become fertile ground for the preservation or even revival of sub-ethnic identities that militate against convergence between the two main origin groups. Yet as already noted, even at the peak of its success, Shas never garnered more than a fourth of the potential Mizrahi vote. The party's fluctuating degrees of electoral success can be explained by the periodic widening or narrowing of that part of the constituency which feels excluded from the mainstream of Israeli development and personal achievement.

As against the interplay between socioeconomic and cultural identificational trends among the two main origin groups in Israel, the maintenance of sub-ethnic identities in the diaspora has been manifested mainly by certain cultural traits, such as familiarity with specific languages and customs, that are gradually disappearing. Of greater significance is the generally stronger adherence to various patterns of Jewish identification among diaspora sub-ethnic groups originating in Asia and Africa. In a context in which Jews constitute a small minority of the general population and are primarily struggling for their own role as a collective vis-à-vis the majority, Jews from Asian and African countries have become the principal element in ensuring the overall continuity of the community. In other words, the sub-ethnic identity of Jews of Asian-African origin tends to become a proxy for Jewish identity at large, whereas Jews of European origin, who are more likely to assimilate, exhibit declining interest in Judaism. From the point of view of socioeconomic stratification, unlike in Israel, where another Jew is the typical "competitor" in terms of economic resources (and all the more so if he or she belongs to a different sub-ethnic group) the "competitor" in diaspora communities is typically a member of the majority group. Therefore, among diaspora communities, any feelings of frustration or sense of personal discrimination tend to relate to the society at large vis-à-vis Jews, whereas in Israel the same feelings may be channeled toward Jews of a relatively more upwardly mobile sub-ethnic group.

In some countries, sub-ethnic identification is strengthened by organizations that can encompass—as is the case in Mexico—the entire gamut of Jewish community services, including primary and secondary schools. Given the virtual disappearance of Jewish communities in most Asian and African countries of origin and the wide diasporization of the original communities across many countries of destination, it was not possible to maintain or reconstitute an inspiring cultural center in a single place. If any, such a central place of resonance for communities located elsewhere tended to be represented by Israel, its phenomenology, and its religious and political leadership. It thus appeared that Jewish communities of Middle Eastern and North African origin in Western Europe and in Latin America were increasingly importing religious services, ideas, identificational traits (including some of Shas patterns) and also ideological cleavages from their Middle Eastern and North African peers in Israel. The long-term effects of this export of Israeli cultural patterns to Jewish diaspora communities remain to be seen.

France, the country of destination for nearly a quarter of a million North African Jews in the late 1950s and early 1960s, represents a success story with regard to immigrant absorption. As has been seen, the initial stages of absorption were less traumatic than in Israel, and the immigrants' long-term socioeconomic integration has been quite impressive. The immigrants and their French-born children have created a vibrant and intensely identified community that has changed the face of French Jewry by replacing the classic *Israélite* pattern of accommodation with a more self-confident Jewish communal orientation. The problem with this momentous transformation is that it appears to be on a collision course with the notion of Republican unity, which opposes the concept of *communautarisme* (particularistic communalism)[48]—all the more so, at a time of increasing tension sparked by the assertive (and growing) Muslim population. In spite of French Jewry's personal attainments over the years, the concerns of Jewish identity are shifting from cultural continuity and social equality to the sphere of political survival. The comfort attained as a result of years of skillful cultural and socioeconomic integration is now at risk, and there is uncertainty regarding the future of the Jews in general (let alone North African Jews), in a context in which increasing Muslim ethnic unrest has led the government to initiate measures restricting religious freedom of expression.

Conclusion

Perhaps the main conclusion of this study concerns the importance of a comparative approach in investigating processes occurring in a given context, whether Israeli society or diaspora Jewish communities. In seeking to interpret the transformations of Jewish populations and communities over the course of the 20th century, it is a mistake to focus exclusively on the internal dynamics of Jewish society at the local level. As has been repeatedly demonstrated in the past few decades, external determinants have been of critical importance in the fate of Jewish communities worldwide. Israel, for example, would not be what it is—or might not exist at all— were it not for geopolitical developments in Europe, North Africa, and Asia. This obvious point is often overlooked by those who limit their analysis to internal Israeli politics and social trends.

This leads us to a more ideologically laden comment. In the process of immigrant absorption, Israel did not act in the manner of a utopian society, as some would have liked to believe.[49] Such an ideal society, dedicated to perfect equality, would either have ignored variations in human capital in its allocation of power and resources or else would have intervened more vigorously in order to achieve total equality. In the latter instance, given the significant gaps among Jewish groups originating in vastly different places and cultures, it would have been necessary to implement an extreme policy of affirmative action—the government in effect acting as Robin Hood, taking away resources from "stronger" groups so that others might "catch up." Rather than following this path (which, for a democracy, would have entailed clear risks), the government by and large allowed free-market competition to prevail. Although government agencies and the Jewish Agency did implement corrective policies to ease social gaps, their primary focus was on overall national strategic goals such as security, infrastructure, and land development.

On further consideration, a country in which free-market mechanisms were in place and where competition between individuals was based on personal initiative and free association (as is the norm in most western societies) really *was* utopia for a people who historically had been dispersed, often discriminated against, alienated, and significantly dependent on philanthropy or other public support. Jews who went to Israel were seeking a return to "normalcy," yet normalization exacted a much heavier price on some individuals than on others. The more veteran immigrants of the pre- and early post-1948 years, who were mainly of European origin, tended to be centrally located in Israel's physical and social space and as such were closer to better market and educational opportunities. Immigrants of the subsequent period, from 1948 through the 1960s, many of whom came from Asian and African countries, were both more dispersed and more apt to reside in peripheral towns and settlements. As a result, they paid a higher price to enter Israeli society, even though they, too, reaped the benefits of rapidly improving standards of living. Significantly, the more decisive socioeconomic and technological take-off of Israeli society took place during the 1990s under the impact of the most recent immigration waves from the FSU. The latter—many of them armed with advanced technological training—arrived during a window of opportunity created by the temporary breakthrough in the Middle East security impasse and substantial economic investment in Israel.

The pace of development of each of the different demographic and sociological processes that I have examined has been quite unequal over time, encompassing phases of slow-down or even temporary reversal. Notwithstanding, the removal or downgrading of sub-ethnic identity (and of the more inclusive "Sephardic and Oriental" identity, for that matter) from its formerly central role as a social determinant has largely been accomplished.

In the diaspora, the absorption of Jewish immigrants relied somewhat less on normative-utopian expectations and considerably more on self-reliance and private networks. Yet some of the mechanisms of immigrant absorption were very similar to those seen in Israel. As noted, immigrant absorption outside of Israel also entailed a temporary loss of socioeconomic status. In France, as in Israel, the veteran European-born members of the Jewish community had acquired a more central location on the national and urban territory, whereas the mass of immigrants from North Africa who arrived in the 1950s and the 1960s were initially much more geographically dispersed in locations with lesser access to economic and educational opportunities. Although French Jewish organizations provided assistance, individual initiatives played a much more significant role. The crucial differences between the French and Israeli contexts were the French Jews' status as a minority (as, of course, was true of Jewish immigrants in other countries of the diaspora), their freedom from responsibility in the realm of security and development, and the abundant availability of other, lower-status population groups to fulfill the less desirable functions in society. In consequence, Jewish upward mobility in France was faster and more visible than in Israel, albeit accompanied by periodic frustration reflecting periods of antisemitism and fear from the surrounding society. A certain compensation for the painful mobility experiences among immigrants to Israel may have been the pride and the privilege associated with citizenship in a Jewish state.[50]

It is very difficult to predict whether the political and socioeconomic discontinuities that produced mass Jewish emigration in the past will recur in the future. Jewish history has had many such moments, and might have more in the future—some of which might generate new massive dislocations. No matter what the country of destination, migration brings with it the challenges of immigrant absorption. The goal of having different group identities coalesce—but not disappear—into a coherent national social structure is one facet of that challenge. The experience of "Sephardic and Oriental" Jewish migrants in Israel and in other environments highlights the challenges related to the maintenance of Jewish heritage versus the pursuit of social mobility; sub-ethnic clustering versus global geographical diffusion;

equality versus relative deprivation; and adherence to ideal norms versus pragmatic realism. The lessons of this experience need to be learned for the future.

Notes

Research for this essay was undertaken at the Division of Jewish Demography and Statistics, The Avraham Harman Institute of Contemporary Jewry, The Hebrew University of Jerusalem. I thank Uzi Rebhun and Benjamin Anderman for processing of the Israeli 1995 population census. Earlier versions of this essay were presented at the Ben-Zvi Institute in Jerusalem, at the American University in Washington, D.C., and at the Oxford Centre for Hebrew and Jewish Studies where I was a Skirball Visiting Fellow in 2002/3.

1. For general reference works, see Michel Abitbol, Shlomo Bar Asher, Ya'akov Barnai, Yoseph Toubi, and Shmuel Ettinger (eds.), *Toledot hayehudim bearzot haislam (History of the Jews in Muslim Countries)* (Jerusalem: 1986); Bernard Lewis, *Semites and Anti-Semites: An Inquiry into Conflict and Prejudice* (New York: 1986); Norman A. Stillman, *The Jews of Arab Lands in Modern Times* (Philadelphia: 1991); Jane S. Gerber, *The Jews of Spain: A History of the Sephardic Experience* (New York: 1994); Esther Benbassa and Aron Rodrigue, *Histoire des Juifs sépharades. De Tolède à Salonique* (Paris: 2002).

2. For an earlier, systematic evaluation of the issues discussed here, see Uziel O. Schmelz, "Be'ayot musagiyot bamehkar shel 'edot yisrael," *Pe'amim* 56 (1993), 125–139; for a short outline, see Sergio DellaPergola, "He'arot 'al hamehkar hasozio-demografi shel 'kehilot yisrael bamizrah,' " *Pe'amim* 93 (2002), 149–156.

3. See, for instance, Ansley J. Coale and Susan Cotts Watkins (eds.), *The Decline of Fertility in Europe* (Princeton: 1986).

4. Uziel O. Schmelz, "'Aliyah hamonit measiyah uzefon afrikah: hebeitim demografiyim," *Pe'amim* 39 (1989), 15–63.

5. M.F. Hammer, A.J. Redd, E.T. Wood, M.R. Bonner, H. Jarjanazi, T. Karafet, S. Santachiara-Benerecetti, A. Oppenheim, M.A. Jobling, T. Jenkins, and B. Bonné-Tamir, "Jewish and Middle Eastern NJ Populations Share a Common Pool of Y-Chromosome Biallelic Haplotypes," *Proceedings of the National Academy of Sciences of the USA* 97 (2000), 6769–6774. The analysis also indicates genetic similarities between Jews and Arabs.

6. In Israel, the Central Bureau of Statistics indicates the origin of Israeli-born children according to the father's birthplace. After two generations, the notion of ancestry is thus lost in official data. However, although less readily available, data on the mother's birthplace can also be obtained, thus making possible the attribution of origin by either parent. See Israel Central Bureau of Statistics, *Census of Population and Housing 1961* (Jerusalem: 1961); idem, *Census of Population and Housing 1995* (Jerusalem: 1995); idem, *Statistical Abstract of Israel* (Jerusalem: yearly publication).

7. Mary Waters, *Ethnic Options: Choosing Identities in America* (Berkeley: 1990).

8. Edward W. Said, *Orientalism: Western Conceptions of the Orient* (London: 1978).

9. On the problematics of this policy, see Chen Bram and Harvey E. Goldberg, "Sephardic/Mizrahi/Arab-Jews: Reflections on Critical Sociology and the Study of Middle Eastern Jewries within the Context of Israeli Society," in this volume, esp. 230–231.

10. Unlike other Jewish communities, Spanish Jewry was exposed to both the Muslim and Christian cultures, albeit during different historical periods.

11. Ariel Toaff, "Culture ebraiche nel mondo," in *Atlante dell'alimentazione e della gastronomia*, vol. 1, ed. Massimo Montanari and Françoise Saban (Turin: 2004), 229–241.

12. Pierre Chaunu, *La France: histoire de la sensibilité des français à la France* (Paris: 1982); Judit Bokser de Liwerant, "Imagines de un encuentro," in *La presencia judia en México durante la primera mitad del siglo XX* (Mexico: 1992).

13. Waters, *Ethnic Options*; Sergio DellaPergola, Georges Sabagh, Mehdi Bozorgmehr, Claudia Der-Martirosian, and Susana Lerner, "Hierarchic Levels of Subethnicity: Near Eastern Jews in the U.S., France and Mexico," in *Sociological Papers* 5, no. 2, ed. Ernest Krausz and Gitta Tulea (1996), 1–42; Richard Alba and Victor Nee, *Remaking the American Mainstream* (Cambridge, Mass.: 2003).

14. The analysis in this essay relies in the main on primary data available from the Israel Central Bureau of Statistics and on a systematic monitoring of diaspora Jewish communities as documented in Sergio DellaPergola, "World Jewish Population, 2005," in *American Jewish Year Book*, vol. 105 (New York: 2005), 87–122; see also Sergio DellaPergola, Uzi Rebhun, and Mark Tolts, "Prospecting the Jewish Future: Population Projections 2000–2080," in *American Jewish Year Book*, vol. 100 (New York: 2000), 103–146.

15. Roberto Bachi, *The Population of Israel* (Jerusalem: 1977).

16. Sergio DellaPergola, "The Global Context of Migration to Israel," in *Immigration to Israel: Sociological Perspectives*, ed. Elazar Leshem and Judith T. Shuval (New Brunswick: 1998), 51–92; idem, "Jewish Diaspora," in *International Encyclopaedia of the Social and Behavioral Sciences: Demography*, ed. Neil J. Smelser and Paul B. Bates (Oxford: 2001), 7963–7969.

17. Sergio DellaPergola, Uzi Rebhun, and Mark Tolts, "Contemporary Jewish Diaspora in Global Context: Human Development Correlates of Population Trends," *Israel Studies* 10, no. 1 (2005), 61–95.

18. Minor inconsistencies in total population estimates reflect the provisional character of some of the data.

19. Central Bureau of Statistics, *Statistical Abstract of Israel* 57 (Jerusalem: 2006).

20. The Human Development Index is a composite measure of socioeconomic development based on country performances in the areas of health, educational attainment, and real income. See United Nations Development Programme, *Human Development Report 2005* (New York: 2005).

21. The main exception was the major wave of immigration from the FSU that began in December 1989, which included numerous non-Jewish spouses and children of mixed marriages.

22. The following discussion relates to a large data sample in the greater Paris area. However, a control sample collected in French provincial cities provides a similar picture, thus justifying the use of "France" rather than "greater Paris." See Doris Bensimon and Sergio DellaPergola, *La population juive de France: sociodémographie et identité* (Jerusalem and Paris: 1984).

23. Shaul Tuval, *The Jewish Community in Istanbul 1948–1992* (Jerusalem: 2004).

24. Simon Kuznets, *Economic Structure of U.S. Jewry: Recent Trends* (Jerusalem: 1972); Gabriel Sheffer, *Diaspora Politics: At Home Abroad* (Cambridge: 2003).

25. Erik H. Cohen with Maurice Ifergan, *Le Juifs de France: valeurs et identité* (Paris: 2002).

26. Sergio DellaPergola, "Some Occupational Characteristics of Western Jews in Israel," in *Papers in Jewish Demography 1977*, ed. Uziel O. Schmelz, Paul Glikson, and Sergio DellaPergola (Jerusalem: 1980), 255–281.

27. Given the limited scope of this essay, the comparable position of Israeli Arabs is not discussed, even though Jewish-Arab interactions undoubtedly influenced the nature of internal interactions among the various Jewish subgroups.

28. Uziel O. Schmelz, Sergio DellaPergola, and Uri Avner, *Ethnic Differences among Israeli Jews: A New Look* (Jerusalem: 1991).

29. One way of measuring the frequency of homogamy (that is, marital attraction between brides and grooms belonging to the same group) is provided by the Benini index, which measures actual versus theoretically expected frequencies of given combinations of marriage partners whose group of origin is known. An index value of 1 indicates exclusively in-group marriages; an index of −1 indicates exclusively out-group marriages; an index of 0 indicates random distribution of marriages reflecting the respective sizes of different population groups.

The Benini index results from (a-e)/(m-e), where: a = the actual number of homogamous marriages in a given group; e = their expected number if marriages were proportionally distributed according to the size of groups; m = whichever of the total number of brides or grooms is the smaller or the upper limit of homogamous unions possible among the spouses of the given group. If there are only two categories, as in the present case, the index value is the same for both. For additional materials, see Schmelz, DellaPergola, and Avner, *Ethnic Differences among Israeli Jews*. The material here is computed on the basis of census data and vital statistics on marriages in which the origin of both the bride and the groom was specified.

30. Barbara Okon, "Insight into Ethnic Flux: Marriage Patterns among Jews of Mixed Ancestry in Israel," *Demography* 41, no. 1 (2004), 173–187.

31. Sergio DellaPergola and Susana Lerner, *La comunidad judía de Mexico: perfil demografico, social y cultural* (Jerusalem: 1995); Sergio DellaPergola, Salomon Benzaquen, and Tony Beker de Weintraub, *Perfil sociodemográfico y cultural de la comunidad judía de Caracas* (Caracas: 2000); Sergio DellaPergola, "Jewish Out-marriage: Mexico and Venezuela," paper presented at International Roundtable on Intermarriage, Brandeis University, 2003, online at http://www.brandeis.edu/hbi/pubs/FinalPapersIntermarriage/SDPMexicoVenezuelaFinal.doc.

32. Mehdi Bozorgmehr, "Internal Ethnicity: Armenian, Bahai, Jewish, and Muslim Iranians in Los Angeles" (Ph.D. diss., University of California, Los Angeles, 2002).

33. The Total Fertility Rate is a measure of fertility based on the assumption that current age-specific fertility rates will remain constant over time.

34. Cohen with Ifergan, *Les Juifs de France*; DellaPergola and Lerner, *La comunidad judía de Mexico*.

35. Chaim Adler, "Jewish Education in Israel: A Sociological Perspective," in *Jewish Education Worldwide: Cross-Cultural Perspectives*, ed. Harold S. Himmelfarb and Sergio DellaPergola (Lanham: 1989), 485–503.

36. In-depth follow-up conducted by Dov Friedlander, Zvi Eisenbach, Eliahu Ben-Moshe, Dan Ben-Hur, Shlomit Lunievski, Ahmed Hleihel, and Lilach Lion Elmakias, *Religion, Ethnicity, Type of Locality and Educational Attainments among Israel's Population: An Analysis of Change Over Time*, Working Paper Series, Parts 1–2 (Jerusalem: 2000). An article by Dov Friedlander, Barbara S. Okun, Zvi Eisenbach, and Lilach Lion Elmakias, "Immigration, Social Change and Assimilation: Educational Attainment among Birth Cohorts of Jewish Ethnic Groups in Israel, 1925–29 to 1965–69," *Population Studies* 56 (2002), 135–150, confirms the findings broadly outlined here.

37. Dov Friedlander, Eynat Aviv, and Lilach Lion-Elmakias, *Beḥinot habagrut bishnot hatish'im: pe'arim behekefei limud, ẓiyunim, zakaut* (Jerusalem: 2006).

38. The data reported in this respect are not entirely consistent for different Jewish populations. In some cases, the level of identification of "very important" was preferred, given the extremely high (close to 100 percent) and undifferentiated response given at the "important" level.

39. Cohen with Ifergan, *Les Juifs de France*.

40. Sergio DellaPergola and Uzi Rebhun, "Hebetim soẓio-demografiyim udfusei hizdahut shel yehudim sefaradim veashkenazim bearẓot habrit bishnat 1990," in *Ḥevrah vetarbut: yehudei sefarad leaḥar hagerush*, ed. Michel Abitbol, Galit Hazan-Rokem, and Yom-Tov Assis (Jerusalem: 1997), 105–135.

41. Shlomit Levy, Hanna Levinsohn, and Elihu Katz, *Beliefs, Observances and Social Interactions among Israeli Jews* (Jerusalem: 1993); idem, *A Portrait of Israeli Jewry:Beliefs, Observances and Values among Israeli Jews 2000* (Jerusalem: 2002).

42. Shlomit Levy and Elihu Katz, "Dynamics of Inter-Group Relations in Israel: 1967–2002," *Social Indicators Research* 74 (2005), 295–312.

43. Zeev Ben-Sira, *Hizdahut menukeret baḥevrah hayisreelit hayehudit: yaḥasim bein'adatiyim veintegraẓiyah* (Jerusalem: 1987).

44. Shmuel N. Eisenstadt, *The Absorption of Immigrants* (London: 1954); Eliezer Ben-Rafael and Stephen Sharot, *Ethnicity, Religion and Class in Israeli Society* (Cambridge:

1991); Eliezer Ben-Rafael and Yochanan Peres, *Is Israel One? Religion, Nationalism, and Multiculturalism Confounded* (Leyden: 2005).

45. Gershon Shafir and Yoav Peled, *Being Israeli: The Dynamics of Multiple Citizenship* (Cambridge: 2002).

46. Shlomo Swirsky, *The Oriental Majority* (London: 1989); Yehouda Shenhav, *Haye-hudim-ha'aravim: leumiyut, dat, veetniyut* (Tel Aviv: 2003).

47. Sammy Smooha, *Israel: Pluralism and Conflict* (London: 1978); Calvin Goldscheider, *Israel's Changing Society: Population, Ethnicity, and Development* (Boulder: 1996); Noah Lewin-Epstein, Yuval Elimelech, and Moshe Semyonov, "Ethnic Inequality in Home Ownership and the Value of Housing: The Case of Immigrants in Israel," *Social Forces* 74, no. 4 (1997), 1439–1462.

48. [Shmuel Trigano], "French Jewry—The End of an Era," *The Jewish People Policy Planning Institute Annual Assessment 2005* (Jerusalem: 2005), 48–51.

49. See a discussion in Dan Horowitz and Moshe Lissak, *Trouble in Utopia: Overburdened Polity in Israel* (Albany: 1989).

50. See an earlier analysis in Michael Inbar and Chaim Adler, *Ethnic Integration in Israel: A Comparative Case Study of Brothers Who Settled in France and in Israel* (New Brunswick: 1977); and more recently, Cohen with Ifergan, *Les Juifs de France*.

Jews of Muslim Lands in the Modern Period: History and Historiography

Michel Abitbol
(THE HEBREW UNIVERSITY)

Paradoxically, never has the history of the Jews in Muslim lands been as intensely observed, written about, or discussed as it has been in the last 40 years, when the Jewish presence in these lands has all but vanished. As recently as the mid-20th century, there were scores of ancient Jewish communities in the region, their total population numbering approximately one million. Today, however, with the obvious exception of the Jewish community in Israel, there are no more than 65,000 Jews in this part of the world: some 25,000 in Iran; fewer than 20,000 in Turkey; 10,000–13,000 in Azerbaijan; 3,000–4,000 in Morocco; 2,000 in Tunisia; 300 in Yemen; barely 100 in Egypt and in Syria, and a mere handful in Iraq, in Lebanon, and in Afghanistan. Of these, about 6,000 are to be found in Arab countries, which is undoubtedly less than the total Jewish population on the Arabian peninsula alone at the time of the prophet Muhammed.

For centuries, Muslim theologians, philosophers, and polemicists attached little importance to Judaism, choosing instead to direct their attention—and critical barbs—at Christianity. In the last half century, however, this approach has been completely reversed, as indicated by the Arabic-language bibliographical listings and catalogs of the world's major libraries. Until the mid-1950s, the subject of Jews and Judaism in the Middle Eastern and North African countries was considered esoteric. But with the mass departure of Jews from the area beginning with the establishment of the state of Israel and the decolonization process in the 1950s, and far more so following the Six-Day War of June 1967 and with the rise of radical Islam in the 1970s and 1980s, interest in the Jews and in Judaism increased significantly.[1]

Apart from political and military volumes that directly address the Arab-Israeli conflict, contemporary Arabic literary output on the Jews may be divided into two main genres: theological works (more specifically, those examining the place of the Jews and Judaism in the Quran and in Muslim religious tradition) and historiography (with an emphasis on stages in the development of Judaism and the historical development of the Jewish populations of Palestine and the diaspora). In addition to these major themes, a rather special type of "literary genre" has recently come to the fore: antisemitic literature. For instance, Egypt's new Alexandria library, rebuilt through the generosity of UNESCO and a number of European countries, had no hesitation in displaying a copy of the first Arabic translation of the classic antisemitic tract *The Protocols of the Elders of Zion* alongside basic texts of Judaism.

How did this situation come about? The ongoing Israeli-Palestinian conflict is clearly a factor, but its roots actually go much further back in history, to the French "short invasion" of Egypt in 1798 and the expansion of European influence in the Middle East and North Africa. For this reason, I begin this essay with a brief account of the differing Muslim and Jewish "encounters" with the modernizing European powers. Following this is an overview of general historical writing on Jews in the region (authored by European Christians, Muslims, and Jews) in both the colonial and modern eras. Finally, I examine trends in Arab historiography since the Six-Day War.

The Historical Overview

European expansion in the Middle East and North Africa ushered in a new era in the history of Arab lands and their Jewish communities. Both Muslim and Jewish societies were compelled to adapt themselves to the modern world as a wide range of economic, political, and legal reforms were introduced by the local authorities under European control. In some areas—for instance, the Ottoman Empire—de facto abrogation of the old *dhimmi* (protected minority) status of Jews and Christians had occurred long before the colonial conquest. By the turn of the 19th century, however, other parts of the region were forced to open their borders to European trade, culture, and immigration, which seriously affected the economic and social life of the local population. Among many other things, foreign penetration led to the growth of a practice known as consular protection, whereby thousands of local Christian and Jewish agents of foreign companies were transformed into "protégés" of the European powers, thereby enjoying the same legal privileges as the European émigrés. Soon, foreigners and protégés gained many other concessions, such as the right to own land or to enter into commercial partnership with rural peasants. Many native Jews who entered into such partnerships were able to travel to Europe and beyond, to Latin America, India, or even China. In the process, they often acquired naturalized European citizenship. Returning home, they were considered by Muslim governments to be western citizens, with all that this implied in terms of personal security and legal rights.[2] Moreover, from the second half of the 19th century, Jews were able to enroll their children in schools that had been founded by European Jewish organizations such as the Alliance Israélite Universelle and the Anglo-Jewish Association. As a result, thousands of Jewish boys and girls acquired western culture long before the colonial conquest of their countries by France, Italy, Spain, or England.

Understandably, then—and unlike their Muslim compatriots—the Jews generally had a positive reaction to the European presence. Many of them began working for European firms or acquired western manners and languages, and before long, Jews as a group were accused of being in collusion with Europe. As a Moroccan historian, 'Abd al-Wahab ibn Mansur, put it: "Jews left the Muslim dhimma in favor of the European dhimma."[3] This accusation, one must say, was not totally inaccurate: the "minorities question" was in fact exploited by certain representatives of European powers. By compelling local governments to introduce liberal reforms such as the granting of equal rights for Jews and other religious minorities, the European powers were essentially increasing their own influence in the region.

This point is illustrated by an event that became known as the Batto Sfez affair. In 1856, a young Tunisian Jew named Batto Sfez was arrested and later executed for having insulted Islam and the prophet Muhammed. This event triggered a large wave of protest among the European émigrés in Tunisia, which was then still part of the Ottoman Empire. A delegation was sent to the French emperor, Napoleon III, who responded by dispatching his navy to Tunis. In consequence of the affair, the Tunisian Bey had no choice but to publish a "fundamental pact" (*'Ahd al-Aman*) granting civil rights to the Jewish minority. However, in the eyes of the local political and religious establishment, this state of affairs appeared to have come about as a result of a Parisian-based "Jewish plot" led by the Rothschild and Péreire banking families on behalf of their Tunisian Jewish brethren.[4]

Seven years later, Moroccan *'ulama'*, or religious clerics, reacted in similar fashion to a journey made by Sir Moses Montefiore to Marrakech. The Anglo-Jewish leader had set forth in an effort to persuade the sultan of Morocco to issue a decree that would ameliorate the very bad situation of Moroccan Jewry. Not only did Montefiore fail, but his mission was regarded as a plot conceived by western powers (abetted by European Jews) to undermine Moroccan sovereignty and territorial integrity.[5]

Thus in mid-19th-century Morocco, as in most Arab countries, the "Jewish question" was no longer merely a religious problem but also had become a political issue. This marked the most important change in the relations between Jews and Arabs at the beginning of the modern era.

As dhimmi, or "tolerated people," Jews in Muslim societies suffered traditionally from religious discrimination that placed them in a permanent and immutable state of social inferiority, somewhat akin to the status of women and slaves in those societies. At times, the Jews were subjected as well to outbursts of anger on the part of the populace—mostly in the context of incitement by religious leaders, court overthrows and violent seizures of power, epidemics and starvation—during which the Jews were made the scapegoats. Nevertheless, prior to the modern period, the Jews, unlike their Christian neighbors, were not regarded as an alien element or as the agent of a foreign power. With the strong European penetration of these societies, however, the situation changed radically: the Jews were now counted among the enemies of the Islamic peoples both because of their religious distinctiveness (which hitherto had not aroused special problems) and as allies of the Europeans who constantly demanded the amelioration of their situation as well as that of other minorities.

Indeed, following the Damascus affair of 1840, when Montefiore, together with Adolphe Cremieux of France, first visited an eastern Jewish community, a new image of the Jews and a new perception of the Jewish question had begun to emerge.[6] Perceived by their neighbors as more or less conscious agents of European imperialism—an image that was later strengthened with the emergence of Zionism and the first waves of aliyah, or immigration to Palestine, at the end of the 19th century and during the first half of the century that followed—the Jews were depicted in local sources as insolent and aggressive people who had little respect for the laws of Muslim countries, and who were eager to get rich at their neighbors' expense. Furthermore, the Jews were no longer considered to be (if indeed they ever had been) a separate religious and ethnic group that was cut off from global society. In the new Muslim perception, conveyed in particular by the Arab Christian press, the Jews were part of a great and powerful entity—world Jewry—whose nerve centers were located in Europe and which, at the slightest moan emanating from the Jews of the Maghreb or the Middle East, would bring all of its vast influence to bear on the French, English, or American governments.

This new vision gradually came to dominate Arab opinion. In contrast to the traditional Islamic framework that lumped Jews together with other non-Muslim groups, this perception drew upon Christian stereotypes of Jews that originated in the Middle Ages. Thus, for instance, the classic Christian accusation of ritual murder began to gain credence in the Muslim world, and charges of this sort were leveled from time to time against Jews in Syria, Turkey, and Egypt.[7] Since the Sublime Porte's ineffectual denunciations of these libels rarely had any effect, the Jews were forced to rely on intervention by European Jewish institutions and the consular representatives. Such intervention subsequently justified the (mostly Christian-based) charges of connivance with European imperialism, to the extent that Muslims eventually came to believe that Jews indeed were guilty of ritual murder.

From the end of the 19th century, calumnies of European antisemitism were increasingly adopted by the Arab world. Initially, it was the exclusive province of Arab Christians, who were the first in the Levant to publish antisemitic tracts in Arabic. One of these was a pamphlet in French by Najib Azoury that later appeared in Arabic translation as *The Awakening of the Arab Nation or the Universal Jewish Peril* (1905). Another was Georges Corneilhan's *Jews and Opportunists—Jewry in Egypt and Syria*, which was first published in Paris in 1889 and translated four years later by Naji al-Hajj, a Lebanese Christian journalist who specialized in rendering European anti-Jewish texts into Arabic.[8] On the whole, the initial intrusions of European antisemitism had only slight impact on general Muslim opinion. Apart from low literacy levels that kept down the number of readers of incendiary anti-semitic prose, the continued dominance of traditional views about Jews was a major obstacle to the acceptance of antisemitic ideas in the Arab world. Over time, however, significant inroads were made among the Muslim population as well—and in the meantime, champions of Muslim reformism—notably Muhammad ʿAbduh and his follower, Rashid Rida—offered a modern restatement of Islam's traditional criticisms of the Jews and Judaism.

In the first half of the 20th century, ʿAbduh, Rida and their later followers engaged in a form of "dejudaization" of Muslim tradition in their efforts to "purify" the exegetical tradition of the Quran and the *Hadith* (traditions of the Prophet). They applied a fine toothcomb of rationalist critique to the literature of the *Israʾiliyyat*[9]— written in the first four centuries after the rise of Islam, which had for ages been an inexhaustible source of inspiration for exegetes—attributing the often "irrational" and fantastic nature of this literature to the Jewish origins of its main authors and transmitters, in particular the "Jewish trio" of Kaʿb al-Ahbar, Wahb b. Munabbih and ʿAbd Allah b. Sabaʾ, all of whom had converted to Islam.[10] Cautiously challenged by 'Abduh,[11] these authors were more explicitly criticized by Rashid Rida. In his *Tafsir al-Manar,* Rida charged that their legendary tales (authored as well by Persian converts) had distorted Muslim tradition. As proof, Rida cited the fables about the lives of the biblical prophets that were recounted by Ka'b al-Ahbar and those about the exodus from Egypt that were handed down by Wahb ibn Munabbih. Among other things, he compared them to the original Hebrew biblical texts in order to prove their fallaciousness.

One of Rida's most talented disciples, Mahmud Abu Rayya, went even further, publishing an article in 1946 under the resounding title of "Ka'b al-Ahbar Huwwa al-Sahyuni al-Awwal" ("Ka'b al-Ahbar is the first Zionist"), in which he denounced not only the role that Ka'b had played in establishing the *Isra'iliyyat* literature, but also his "Zionism." According to Abu Rayya, Ka'b had contemplated assassinating Caliph 'Umar, who, by taking Palestine and Jerusalem, had destroyed the Jewish dream of the Promised Land once and for all. In reprisal, Ka'b is said to have waited for 'Umar to die before "larding" the Muslim oral tradition of *hadiths* with base-less tales taken from the Bible and other Jewish sources.[12] Citing the medieval Egyptian theologian Ibn Taymiyya, Abu Raya accused Ka'b of having yielded to his Jewish leanings by maliciously placing praises *(fada'il)* to the glory of Jerusalem in the Prophet's mouth—attempting in this way to minimize the central status of Mecca.[13]

In sum, as a result of several factors, including European expansionism, European and Arab Christian antisemitic propaganda, the appearance of Zionism, and Islamism, the Arab perception of Jews was gradually transformed. Although the traditional view of the Jew as a dhimmi, an inferior but tolerated other, did not entirely give way, it was increasingly supplanted by the image of the Jew as a political rival using any and all means to draw closer to Europe and to benefit from its protection.

In contrast with the situation prevailing in Western Europe, where Jewish emancipation coincided with sociocultural transformations—in particular, modernization and secularization—Muslim countries experienced modernization while continuing to adhere to religious tradition. Even the Reformist movement founded in Egypt and Turkey in the second half of the 19th century did not endorse the concept of secularization as understood in western culture. Instead, it formulated a new system of values leading, on the one hand, to the modernization of Islam and, on the other hand, to the islamization of modernity.[14] This left no room for the emergence of a new social order that could allow for integration or assimilation of non-Muslims. Indeed, assimilation was perceived neither by the society at large, nor by the Jews themselves, as either a desirable aim or a logical outcome of their legal emancipation. Since Islam remained the main component of Arab collective identity, the Jews (except for those of Iraq) generally refused to be assimilated into Arab modern culture. They preferred to pursue western culture, which in their eyes was less religiously oriented.

The cultural and political divorce of Jews from their host societies was more pronounced in North Africa (including Egypt) than in the Middle East (in particular, as noted, in Iraq). It became strengthened during the colonial period when, in contrast to the Muslim population, Jews for the most part welcomed the advent of French rule in Algeria (1830), Tunisia (1881), and Morocco (1912); the British rule in Egypt (1882); and the Italian rule in Libya (1911).

Beyond its obvious military and political meaning, colonialism may be defined as the domination of a native population by a foreign minority, on the grounds of a supposed racial and cultural superiority. This sense of superiority found expression in the desire to transform the "backward" native culture. France and, to a lesser extent, Italy were more representative of this state of mind than was England, which was far more moderate in terms of seeking to impose cultural change in its colonial provinces.[15] Colonial society was also strongly hierarchal in nature. At the top were the colonial expatriates and the naturalized locals, who controlled all major administrative and economic functions and who were the only segment of the population to enjoy real political freedom. At the bottom was the native population, which as a group lacked civil and political rights. Moreover, in general, the colonial authorities viewed and dealt with the colonized population as a mixture of ethnic divisions, sects, and denominations rather than as a homogenous entity. In Muslim countries, accordingly, certain ethnic groups that were considered to be more open to western culture—for example, Berbers, Jews, and Copts—were favored by the authorities. This generated tensions between Muslims and non-Muslims in general and between Jews and Muslims, in particular.

More than any other colonial power, France encouraged its colonized peoples to believe that if they renounced their traditional way of life by adopting the French language, pursuing secular education, and embracing traditions such as monogamy, they would be assimilated into the dominant colonial group. Not surprisingly, the Jews showed a greater willingness than their Muslim countrymen to go along with these terms. Thus, Jewish children were sent to secular schools (in the main, those belonging to the Alliance network); women began to work outside the home, as they had begun to do in Europe; and Jews, whenever possible, applied for French (and, in other places, Italian or British) citizenship, whereas the local Muslim population generally maintained a much more reserved attitude toward the colonial powers and European culture. Statistics illustrate the gap between the two groups. For example, by the end of the Second World War, less than 20 percent of Muslim children in Algeria, Tunisia, and Morocco went to modern elementary schools, as compared with 60 percent among Jews in Morocco, 70 percent in Tunisia, 75 percent in Egypt, and 100 percent in Algeria. The gap was even greater in the realm of post-secondary education. In 1914, of the 90 Tunisian students who completed their baccalaureate, 27 were Jews and only 5 were Muslims. A similar situation prevailed in Libya: in 1931, only 5 percent of the Muslim population was fluent in Italian, as opposed to 47 percent among the Jews of Tripoli and 60 percent among the Jews of Benghazi.[16]

To be sure, modernization did not affect all Jewish communities equally, and clearly, one cannot view Yemen and Kurdistan, on the one hand, and Egypt and Algeria, on the other, as similar in this regard. Likewise, the differences within communities were no less deep, as for example, those between the Jews of Tunis and the Jews of Djerba, whose leaders opposed the introduction of European education into their country until the middle of the 20th century. And, indeed, as is attested to by all accepted sociological indicators, a not inconsiderable proportion of Jews in Muslim countries maintained their traditional lifestyle right up until the mass immigration to Israel. Nevertheless, one cannot fail to note that modernization left its mark on their way of life, even in the most outlying regions of North Africa and the

Middle East—whether as a result of the building of roads and new means of trans-
portation; the penetration of the modern economy into daily affairs (the flooding of
local markets by imported European goods, which had disastrous consequences for
itinerant Jewish traders); internal immigration from village to city; increased personal security on roads and within the big cities; improved sanitation (with all that
this implied for reduced mortality rates and larger family size); and, of course, the
opening of new schools with the assistance of international Jewish organizations
such as the Alliance, whose teachers reached even the Jewish cave dwellers of
southern Morocco.

As was India for Great Britain, so was Algeria in many respects a French colonial
laboratory. Immediately after the French conquest in 1830, Algeria's small Jewish
community, numbering no more than 6,000 persons, found itself under the patronage
of French Jewry. Its leaders persuaded the French authorities that their Algerian co-
religionists should be accorded treatment similar to that which it had received in the
wake of the French Revolution. Put somewhat differently, Algerian Jews should be
encouraged to leave the paths of Algerian history and to follow those of their French
Jewish brethren. In order to bring this about, the Algerian Jewish communal organization, with its traditional rabbinical courts and means of taxation, was abolished in
1845 and replaced (as in metropolitan France) by the Napoleonic consistoire system.
French rabbis were sent to Algeria to replace native rabbis and to lead the local Jewry
on the path of modernization and French assimilation.[17] In 1870, the Cremieux
decree, named after the French minister of justice, Adolphe Cremieux (Montefiore's
former companion on his journey to Damascus) granted French citizenship to the
Algerian Jews. Thus they were transformed from dhimmi into French citizens, an
extraordinary promotion within the colonial context.

In other European-ruled parts of North Africa and the Middle East, colonial authorities, while refraining from extending citizenship to the local Jewish population,
abolished the last remnants of the discriminatory Covenant of Umar. Thus, for the
first time in their long history in Muslim lands, the Jews were permitted to dress as
they wished, to move from place to place without restriction, and, above all, to feel
that their origins would not be a bar—theoretically at least—to improving their social
and economic situation. Most Jews, therefore, felt indebted to France and the other
colonial powers, and very few of them joined the Arab nationalist movements that
spread throughout North Africa and the Middle East between the two world wars.[18]
The fact that Islam played a decisive role in the consolidation of local nationalist
movements deterred Jews from joining them. Thus, for example, the political parties
that arose in Morocco and Tunisia prior to the Second World War appeared to be
more like parties for the defense of Islam against the colonial power than as pan-
nationalist parties open to all sections of society, including the Jews.

Relationships between Jews and Muslims deteriorated in most parts of the Arab
world after the First World War as a result of the rise of Arab nationalism, the Balfour
Declaration, and the first clashes in Palestine between Jews and Arabs. Other noteworthy factors were the world economic depression and German propaganda among
the Arab population during the 1930s, which exploited the fact that Nazi Germany
was not a colonial power. Hitler—or "al-Hajj" Hitler, as he was called in some North
African villages during the Second World War—enjoyed huge prestige throughout

the Muslim world, and a number of Arab nationalist leaders, including al-Hajj Amin al-Husseini (Palestine), Rashid ʿAli al-Kaylani (Iraq), Ahmad Hussein (Egypt), Antun Saadeh (Syria), and ʿAbd al-Khaliq Torres and Ahmad Balafredj (Morocco) developed strong ties with Nazi Germany and Fascist Italy. Without exaggerating its impact, it is clear that Arab pro-Nazi and pro-Fascist sympathy did not improve relations between Jews and Arabs on the eve of the Second World War.[19] Antisemitic incidents occurred in Palestine, Iraq (following Rashid ʿAli's ascent to power) and, most seriously, in Algeria, where thousands of Muslims attacked the Jewish quarter of Constantine for two days in August 1934, killing some 20 Jews and injuring dozens of others.[20]

In many respects, the Second World War was a watershed in the history of Jews in Arab lands in general, and in their relationships with their Muslim countrymen, in particular. In Algeria, the Jews were stripped of their French citizenship and fired from the civil service in accordance with the racial "Statut des Juifs" promulgated by the Vichy regime, which were implemented not only in the French "free zone" but also in North Africa.[21] In Tunisia, which was occupied by the Nazis, Jews were subjected to racial laws and sent to forced labor camps. Similarly, in Italian-ruled Libya, racial laws regarding the Jews were put into effect, and Jews throughout the country were sent to forced labor camps.

Deeply disillusioned by their wartime experiences with the French, many young North African Jews began to explore alternative avenues in their quest for political emancipation and cultural identity. Zionism and Communism both made serious inroads among the younger generation in the 1940s and the 1950s (even in Iraq, in the wake of anti-Jewish riots in June 1941). In the meantime, the Middle East began undergoing a process of decolonization. As noted, few Jews joined the local independence movements that spread throughout North Africa after the war. Arab nationalist leaders drew inspiration from anti-Zionist (and later, anti-Israeli) propaganda issued in Egypt and Syria. As a result of militant Arab nationalism, Jews were expelled from Libya in 1951 and from Egypt in 1956, and in Iraq, they left en masse after losing their citizenship in 1950. Elsewhere, for instance, in Petijean and Oujda (Morocco) or in Bizerte (Tunisia), they were the targets of violent demonstrations that marked the beginning of the end of these old communities at the very time their countries were gaining political independence.

The Historiography of Jews of Arab Lands

In comparison with those studying other non-European societies, scholars dealing with the history of Jews in Arab lands do not have the impression that they are sailing in uncharted waters. On the contrary, they have at their disposal a plethora of diverse sources in many languages, including a considerable number of scientific studies dating as far back as the European penetration of Muslim countries in the late 18th century. Over the years, the topic grew in interest, particularly with the French conquest of the Maghreb. Until the 1960s, however, the historiography of Jews in Arab lands was essentially a by-product of the colonial historiography of North Africa and the Middle East, and as such was mainly influenced by western cultural perceptions and ideological formulations. Until recently, the French, for example, viewed the history of the Maghreb, and that of Africa as a whole, as a series of foreign conquests, whereas the "indigenous" society—be it Arab, Berber, or Jewish—was perceived as a passive entity manipulated both by external forces and by obscure, unchanging religious impulses.

This approach is most clearly reflected in the work of a large number of non-Jewish historians and ethnologists. For instance, Paul Monceaux, Jean Mesnage, and Marcel Simon researched the beginning of Jewish settlement in North Africa as part of a broader effort to uncover North Africa's Christian past.[22] Similarly, it was the unabated search for the real (or imaginary) roots of the Berber-Arab conflict on the part of French colonial authorities and the French academic establishment that prompted the inquiry into Ibn Khaldun's epic tale of al-Kahina, the eighth-century "Jewish" Berber princess of the Atlas mountains who fought against the Arab invaders.[23] While it is not at all certain that al-Kahina was actually Jewish, this story plays an important role in shaping the historical experience of the Jews of the Maghreb in modern times. Aside from providing an unlimited source of livelihood for those dealing with Jewish onomastics (who sought to prove the Berber origins of the indigenous Jews), this legend granted legitimacy to the feeling of alienation felt by many Jews of the colonial period toward the Arab population—an attitude that accorded with the anti-Arab orientation of French colonial policy and historiography.[24]

Not everything written about Jews by Europeans was inspired by extraneous or non-professional considerations. H.J.M. Haddey's essay of 1871 on the economic history of the Jews of Algiers in the beginning of the 19th century is based on meticulous archival work and contains a great deal of precise economic data.[25] The history of Algerian Jewry since the French conquest was painstakingly and professionally reconstructed by an avowed antisemite, Claude Martin, whose book, published in 1936, is still considered (despite its shortcomings) the best analysis of the community written during the French period. Many years before Jews of the Moroccan Atlas mountains became the sole province of Israeli anthropologists, Pierre Flamand wrote a doctoral dissertation on the subject; preceding him were Vincent Monteil, an Africanist, who concentrated on southern Morocco; Jean Huguet, who researched the Jews of Mzab in southern Algeria; and Hubert Cornet, who wrote a historical monograph on the Jews of Gafsa, in southern Tunisia.[26] Earlier monographs were also written by Jean Goulven, on the Jews of Rabat, and José Bénech, on the Jews of Marrakech.[27]

In general, it appears that non-Jewish scholars of the Maghreb were most interested in Moroccan Jewry. Both Roger Le Tourneau and Paul Marty devoted themselves to the study of this community. The former, considered to be among the foremost historians of precolonial North Africa, studied gold thread production in the mellah (Jewish quarter) of Fez, whereas the latter (author as well of an authoritative work on the spread of Islam in black Africa) examined the Moroccan Jewish communal organization both before and after the establishment of the French protectorate in 1912.[28] Finally, a special place in the French historiography of Morocco and its Jews is reserved for Jean-Louis Miège, whose painstaking work in European archives resulted in definitive works dealing with the crucial role of the Jews in the economic history of Morocco in the second half of the 19th century. Another non-

Jewish scholar, Renzo de Felice, wrote the best overall history of Libyan Jewry from the middle of the 19th century to the last quarter of the 20th century.[29]

French Jewish scholars form another category of historical researchers in the field of colonial North Africa. Included in the colonial service were a number of individuals who lived in the region, including Abraham Cahen and Isaac Bloch, who served respectively as "commissioned" rabbis (sent by the consistory) in Constantine and Oran in Algeria in the second half of the 19th century, and Maurice Eisenbeth, who served as the chief rabbi of Algeria in the late 1930s and during the Second World War.[30]

Among the teachers employed by the Alliance in its dozens of schools in the Maghreb, Yom-Tov Semach deserves special mention for providing scholars with the French translation of R. Abner Hasarfati's chronicle, *Yaḥas Fas*, five decades before it appeared in the original Hebrew in an edition produced by R. David Ovadyah. Also noteworthy is the contribution of the orientalist Robert Brunschvig, whose book on precolonial Tunisia includes a chapter on the social and economic life of the Jews that is based on data culled from contemporary responsa literature. The *Chronicles of Fas* (1951), a work that was compiled over a period of centuries by rabbis of the Ibn Danan family and others, was translated from Hebrew into French by Georges Vajda and also subsequently published in a Hebrew edition by David Ovadyah.[31] All in all, the history of the Jews in North Africa was written by persons representing a wide spectrum of scholarly interests and published in a variety of professional periodicals focusing on the Maghreb, including *Hesperis, Revue Africaine, Revue du Monde Musulman* and *Archives Marocaines*.[32]

Some Jewish scholars were born in the Maghreb, and until the end of the colonial era, most of their research dealt with two main areas—the intellectual history, and the legal status, of Jews under Muslim and French rule. Outstanding in the former field are David Cazes on Tunisia; Yaacov Toledano on Morocco; and Yosef Ben-Naim, who published the first bio-bibliographical dictionary of the Moroccan rabbis in 1931.[33] Works on the Jews' legal status in Tunisia were written by Rodolphe Arditti, Salomon Tibi, Raoul Darmon, and Jacques Chalom; and in Morocco, by André Chouraqui, Elie Malka, and Abraham Zaguri.[34] Several individuals, including André Chouraqui (1952) and Isaac D. Abbou (1953) sought to cover all North African Jewish communities, but the quality of these works was uneven.[35] Only in 1965, with the publication of Hayim Zeev Hirschberg's two-volume work, did a comprehensive historical study of North African Jewry become available.[36]

The process of decolonization and the mass exodus of Jews from North Africa led to qualitative changes in both the general and the Jewish historiography of the region. Although the two disciplines developed independently and within different contexts, they do share certain characteristics. First, since the end of the 1960s, the French have ceased to be the sole contributors to the general historiography of the region. An increasing number of scholars from English-speaking countries, Israel, and the Maghreb have been attracted to the historical study of North Africa in general, and of its Jewry in particular.[37] Second, Jewish historiography has become specialized professionally, with many of its practitioners trained in departments of Jewish history in Israeli universities, whereas scholars from other disciplines are far less prominent. So, too, the boundaries and conceptions typical of previous periods with regard to the study of North Africa and its Jews have been broken down. For example, the geographic framework no longer coincides with the colonial division of North Africa: Libyan and even Egyptian Jewry are now included as a matter of course in "North African" Jewish studies.[38] Alongside this geographic extension, recent studies on the Jews in the Maghreb are increasingly viewed from the perspective of the history of the Jewish people. The first to move to this direction was Hayim Zeev Hirschberg, whose repudiation of the theories of the conversion of the Berbers to Judaism restored to Jews of the Maghreb their ancient Palestinian or Middle Eastern origins, thus reinstating them in the framework of Jewish history. Hirschberg was also the first to apply to them the research techniques, terminology, and periodization common to students of that field. The Israeli and foreign scholars who followed him have gone further, exploring subjects and areas directly related to the central themes of Jewish history: the life and internal structure of Jewish communities;[39] the relations between Jews and their surroundings;[40] hatred of Israel and antisemitism;[41] Hebrew and Judeo-Arabic poetry;[42] the Haskalah and modern education;[43] the impact of the Second World War, Zionism, and aliyah and resettlement in Israel;[44] gender studies;[45] and integration in Israel and France.[46] This linkage with Jewish history and the raising of issues that hitherto had been studied solely in a European Jewish context did not merely give expression to the assumption that Jews shared a common fate. Primarily, they reflected the desire to prove both that the central processes of Jewish history had not bypassed these "peripheral" communities, and that these communities had not remained static for centuries prior to their encounter with the "West" (whether in the form of European colonialism or of Zionism and the state of Israel).

A further assumption common to both the new general and Jewish historiography of the Maghreb is that earlier scholarship not only neglected certain historical periods but also failed to grasp the cultural uniqueness of local societies. When it did attempt to do so, it generally employed ethnographic concepts and terms external to those societies, borrowed either from the realities of the pre-European period or else from the work with which the researcher, the traveler, or the colonial clerk was familiar. Postcolonial scholars, in contrast, have made extensive use of a variety of sources, including Arab sources, Geniza documents, Hebrew chronicles, communal regulations and responsa literature, and oral traditions, in the belief that via them, they could more authentically reconstruct the life of the various communities and identify what changed over the centuries.[47]

As might be expected, the colonial period is the subject of spirited argument between the new historians and their predecessors. While Jewish historians do not generally take as critical a view of this period as do their Muslim colleagues (for instance, Mohammed Kenbib), no one considers North African Jewry's "march toward the West," as it was called by André Chouraqui in a book of that name, to have been a journey along a rose-strewn path.[48] More recent studies authored by Doris Bensimon-Donath, Michel Abitbol, Yaron Tsur, Rachel Simon, and others focus on issues that colonial historiography either played down or ignored, such as the Algerian Jews' lack of enthusiasm for French citizenship; the long period of decline in their economic status after 1830; and the intense antisemitism to which they were subjected from the proclamation of the Cremieux decree in 1870 until the end of the Second World War.[49]

With regard to one question, however, that of relations between Jews and Muslims, contemporary Israeli scholars and some of their colleagues abroad, both Jews and non-Jews, have differed sharply. While no one today claims that Jewish life in Islamic lands actually reflected the covenant of Omar with its strict segregation between Muslims and non-Muslims (whether for good or for evil), non-Israeli scholars tend to paint Jewish-Muslim relations in terms of "coexistence" or a "symbiosis," some of them going so far as to attribute all of the anti-Jewish outbursts occurring in the Maghreb over the past hundred years to external factors such as imperialism, colonialism, and Zionism.[50] Israeli scholars, for their part (even those not diametrically opposed to that view), emphasize the fact that during the modern period, the Jews, for a variety of political and cultural reasons, ceased to regard themselves as an integral part of the history of the lands in which they had lived for centuries.[51] Thus, in their view, in not participating in their home countries' struggle for independence, the Jews distanced themselves from the fate of the North African peoples and, subsequently, willingly departed from the Maghreb along with the colonial powers that had ruled the region since 1830. For Jews as a religious minority, the question of national membership became an actual issue during and at the end of the colonial period, whether as a result of the appearance of nationalist movements that demanded that the Jews identify themselves politically, or of the appearance of Zionism and the establishment of the state of Israel, which cast a heavy shadow on the continued existence of a Jewish collectivity in Muslim countries, the avowed enemies of the Jewish state.

Trends in Arab Historiography of the Jews since the Six-Day War

What is the basis of Jewish history in the Arab lands? The following is an outline of Jewish history in Palestine according to Ahmad Soussa, an Iraqi-born Jew who later converted to Islam and wrote a best-selling and highly influential book titled *Arabs and Jews in History*.[52] Soussa's views, an elegant blend of religious interpretations and pseudo-scientific theses, summarize the predominant view of the Jews and Judaism in the contemporary Arab world.[53]

As Soussa presented it, Palestine was always, and in all respects, an Arab country. Although it served as a kind of way station for the Patriarchs, the children of Jacob (most of whom were born in Haran, near Mosul in Mesopotamia) soon left Canaan (Palestine) for Egypt. There was thus no direct relation between Abraham, Isaac, and Jacob and "the Hebrews," a group that appeared on the scene, according to Soussa, only during the period of Moses, some 700 years after Abraham—who, during his wanderings, had passed through Mecca, where Muslim tradition attributes to him the founding of the sacred site of the *Ka'ba*.

Basing himself on a number of sources, in particular Sigmund Freud's *Moses and Monotheism*, Soussa also argued that Moses was an Egyptian prince at the court of Akhenaton, a monotheistic ruler who was overthrown by his countrymen. In the resultant turmoil, Moses was forced to flee Egypt, heading a motley band comprising survivors of the ancient Hyksos (whom the Egyptians had ill treated) and an undefined number of "Israelites" who had entered Egypt in the wake of Joseph and Jacob.

Since the latter were Egyptian by language and civilization, there was no justification for the Bible's calling them the "Children of Israel." Be that as it may, during the crossing of Sinai, God revealed the "true" Torah to Moses—a document written in an Egyptian language, whose authenticity is acknowledged by the Quran but which the Israelites would later discard, replacing it with a text that was a forgery and a complete fabrication.

According to Soussa, the "Mosaists" were too few and too weak to impose their will on the native population of Canaan. Forced to adopt the local customs and mores and making their livelihood from agriculture and trade, they ultimately proved inferior to their Canaanite neighbors and to Canaan's other populations of Arab origin. As indicated by the Bible itself, this state of affairs lasted until the period of King David and his son Solomon, who managed to expand their territory, setting up larger and more viable states than the tribal fiefdoms that had come into being in the time of the Judges. But these were still largely polytheist states, linguistically and culturally Arab-Canaanite (Hebrew, Soussa claimed, did not come into being until after the period of the Kings) under the permanent tutelage of the major empires of the time, notably Egypt and Assyria. In any event, the state established by David and Solomon was doomed to end in chaos and division, split between two separate political and religious entities, the kingdoms of Israel and Judea, before being conquered first by the Assyrians and then by the Chaldeans, who drove out the Jewish inhabitants and dispersed them throughout Babylon.

It was during this first period of exile that, in the sixth century BCE, the "Judeans," or Jews, composed in Hebrew—as directed by Ezra—the new version of the Torah. This "perverted" text, according to Soussa (and all other Arab historians), falsified the "authentic" portraits of Abraham, Isaac, and Ishmael, deliberately failed to refer to the future coming of Mohammed, and above all created the apocryphal notions of the "chosen people" and the "promised land." In so doing, Ezra, as it were, established a new Jewish religion based on the preeminence of the priests and rabbis, which no longer had any connection to the monotheism of the Patriarchs and Moses.

Given permission by the Persians to return from exile, the Jews were eventually able to rebuild the Temple that had been destroyed under Nebuchadnezzar. However, as in the earlier periods, they did not put down roots in the country but instead remained eternal intruders and aliens before being expelled once again, this time by the Romans at the beginning of the Christian era.

Incapable of becoming established in Palestine, the Jews nevertheless managed to disseminate their religion among the diverse peoples of the earth with whom they came into contact, either through trade or by dispatching missionaries. Thus Judaism infiltrated the Arabian peninsula during the period of King Solomon. The Jews of the peninsula, who were actually Arabs of Jewish faith, had become so well integrated there by the 6th century that it was only their religion that differentiated them from their polytheist neighbors, whose language they spoke and whose lifestyle they shared. According to Soussa, there is no evidence that the Jews of Arabia came from Palestine and Babylon, as proven by their ignorance of the Talmud, whose redaction in Babylon dated back to the 6th century. The same is true of a goodly proportion of the Jews living in the other Mediterranean countries: these were natives who had converted to Judaism, later bolstered by a few handfuls of people with a Palestinian, Babylonian, or later, Hispanic background.[54] The same phenomenon of religious dissemination, Soussa contended, took place in Europe, where Judaism was spread through the Judaized Khazars in Russia and Eastern Europe, whereas further to the west, "Ashkenazic" Jewry adopted the cultural, ethnic, and linguistic characteristics of the surrounding populations. Altogether, Soussa concluded, religion has always been the sole common denominator of Jewish communities worldwide; it is the Jewish religion, not the existence of a mythical "Jewish people," that has enabled the Jews to survive all the vicissitudes of history.

Against the background of the rise of Zionism and the emergence of the state of Israel, the modern and contemporary era is by far the most thoroughly discussed topic among Arab historians of Judaism. Given the perceived links between these two historical events and some of the most painful episodes in Muslim history—European expansion, the abolition of the Ottoman caliphate, colonization, the loss of Palestine, and the Six Day War, among others—it is understandable that Arab writers are tempted to explain their own decline by the success of Jews. Frequently drawing upon the most hackneyed conspiracy theories of European antisemitic literature, the Jews are depicted as the *deus ex machina* of a vast global plot, a people who, since the end of the 18th century, have sought to destroy Islamic civilization by any and all means, whether on their own or in collusion with the Christians.

As already seen, the appearance of antisemitic themes in Muslim countries is no recent development. Since 1967, however, one topic has been the main focus of attention: Zionism—its historical and cultural origins and inherent racism; its relationship with Judaism and with the "Jewish mindset"; its expansionist and colonial nature; and its close ties with highly influential cosmopolitan and "Jewish" organizations (including the mysterious "Elders of Zion" along with the Communist International, the Freemasons, the Jehovah's Witnesses, B'nai Brith, and even the Rotary Club). All of these provide grist for works published in Cairo and Beirut as well as in Damascus, Riyadh, or Amman and share a basic hypothesis, namely, the intensifying of Jewish influence in the world and, conversely, the weakening of Christianity and Islam in the wake of the expansion of secularism and modernity.[55]

More specifically, the authors of such works attempt to reply to a single, burning question: Why did the Jews manage to achieve their goal by establishing a state in Palestine, whereas the Arabs remain incapable of achieving unity among themselves? The basic reply is that the historical drama in which contemporary Arabs are the main victims begins with the French Revolution, which, on the one hand, led to the erosion of religious sentiment in the West and, on the other, to emancipation and the establishment of a democratic regime, both of which improved the condition of the Jews throughout Western Europe. From this point on, the Jewish thinkers, bankers, and politicians set out to incite political, social, and cultural upheavals along the same lines as those initiated in 1789 by the French revolutionaries. Thus they were responsible for all the ways of thinking that seek to wipe out religious feeling—such ideas and ideologies as the separation of Church and state, Karl Marx's Communism, Freud's psychoanalysis, Emile Durkheim's sociology, and Einstein's theory of relativity. Wishing to control the world, the Jews also set up central organizations and omnipotent lobbies acting on a global level, including, among others, the "Elders of Zion" and the Freemasons.

Moreover, flushed with their success in Western Europe, the Jews took on Orthodox Holy Russia, where they fomented the Bolshevik revolution of 1917. Then they set their sights on the Muslim world, bringing about the abolition of the last Muslim caliphate, the Ottoman Empire. Musatafa Kemal Atatürk is held to have been directly responsible for this last catastrophe, acting as he did because of his alleged Jewish and Freemason roots (shared, it is charged, by many other Young Turks), and it is he who paved the way for the Zionists to march into the Holy Land. This time, the Jews did not work alone. They were in cahoots with the Europeans, with whom they had been eager collaborators in all the Muslim countries that had fallen under the colonial yoke—for instance, in Algeria, Egypt, Tunisia, and Morocco.

The centerpiece of the Jewish scheme to dominate the world—the establishment of the state of Israel—was thus no accident of history, but was rather the result of an anti-Muslim conspiracy hatched by westerners and Jews: a conspiracy that Jewish "fabrications" about the Holocaust could scarcely conceal. As a result, it is also, and above all, one of the most painful and humiliating reminders of the Muslim decline that began with Napoleon Bonaparte's expedition to Egypt and climaxed in the years following the First World War with the Balfour Declaration and the colonial conquest of the entire Arab world.

This view was well summarized in 1968, a few months after the Six-Day War, in a work published in Lahore, Pakistan under the title *Islam versus the People of the Book*. The practically unknown author was one Maryam Jameelah, alias Margaret Marcus—who, like Soussa, had converted from Judaism to Islam. In this book, Jameelah called for a no-holds-barred war against Judaism and the Jews, demonstrating an outspoken and virulent hatred for her former religion. Caring little for spiteful comments regarding her extremist positions (a characteristic of converts and others who have "seen the light"), Jameela took pleasure in the fact that her book received a stamp of approval from no less a figure than Abu al-ʿAla al-Mawdudi (1903–1979), the Pakistani sheikh who had founded Jamaʾat al-Islami, a radical Islamic party. Together with Hassan al-Banna, the founder of the Muslim Brotherhood (who was assassinated by King Farouk in 1949), and Sayyid Qutb, the preeminent ideologist of the ever-changing Islamist scene (whom Nasser put to death in 1966), al-Mawdudi was one of the key figures in 20th-century radical Islam. Like his two counterparts, al-Mawdudi, who acted as Jameela's spiritual adviser following her conversion to Islam and her arrival in Lahore, shared opinions that ran counter to what the "modernists" promoted, namely, a more conciliatory attitude toward "peoples of the Book."

Struck by the religious ardor displayed by this young American who had grown up so distant from any Muslim environment, the Pakistani scholar felt the greatest admiration for her categorical stands against the way that Muslim life had been adversely affected by materialism and nationalism, which he regarded as two manifestations of one and the same illness—western modernism. Like her mentor, Jameelah roundly denounced Muslim statesmen and intellectuals who called for the westernization of their countries. She was particularly scathing about the Turkish Atatürk, who set up the first secular regime in an Islamic country; Habib Bourguiba, the Tunisian president who went on record arguing that the Ramadan fast was responsible for the underdevelopment of Muslim countries; and the Egyptian writer Taha Husayn who, citing 19th-century arguments by Khedive Isma'il, had the audacity to declare that Egypt was an integral part of Europe.

In the years following the publication of her book, Jameelah became a much-admired essayist and lecturer. Most of her writings focus on combating western influence and promoting the struggle against Zionism. Her deeply held conviction is that Islam is in mortal danger from both of these phenomena, whether separately or in collusion. Given her Jewish and American roots, Jameelah views herself as the Muslim figure best equipped to explain and combat the two-pronged threat of western influence and Zionism, both of which had acquired ever greater currency since the June 1967 war between Israel and the Arabs.

Thus, when she addresses the relationship between Islam and Judaism, Maryam Jameelah violently rejects the "deceptive" discourse about the two religions' shared roots and the possibility of reconciliation between Jews and Muslims. On the contrary, she argues, the struggle between the two groups is destined to last until the end of days. In order to provide a basis for her rulings, she cites an obscure *hadith* to the effect that when the Last Judgment comes, those Jewish survivors who have managed to outlive this all-out Jewish-Muslim war will not even be able to seek shelter between trees and rocks in order to escape the vengeance of those pursuing them ("And the rocks and trees will say: O servant of Allah, o Muslim warrior, a Jew is trying to hide behind us, come quickly and kill him!").[56]

Thus, in Jameelah's presentation, the war between Jews and Muslims is not about to come to an end. In response to the question as to why, of all the *Ahl al-Kitab*, the Jews are the most hated, she argues that it is because the Jews are guilty of having rejected the message of the Prophet for "reasons of racial and national pride," being unable to accept the idea that an "illiterate" Arab should become their supreme guide. In their perfidy, the Jews went so far as to alter the content of their own Scriptures in order to remove from them all signs heralding the coming of Muhammed. Despite this, the Muslims did not treat them with excessive harshness. Instead, for centuries, the Jews were allowed to practice their religion freely as dhimmi in all the countries of the Caliphate.

This state of affairs lasted, she argues, until the 19th century, at which point it came to an abrupt end as a result of Jewish initiatives connected with European imperialism and then Zionism. At this point the Jews once again became the implacable enemies of Islam, reverting to the demonic attributes that were characteristic of them during the early period of the Hegira. Back then, Jewish traitors and "prophet-killers" had indirectly caused the death of Muhammed (who, Jameelah claims, was poisoned by a Jewish woman from Khaybar whose husband was killed in fighting against the Muslims). The vindictive hypocrisy of 'Abd Allah ibn Saba', a convert with a Jewish background, was responsible for triggering the unrest that led first to the assassination of Caliph 'Uthman, then to the martyrdom of Caliph 'Ali, and finally to the schism of the *Shi'a*, which divided the lands of Islam once and for all. Five centuries later, in 1258, the Jews helped the Mongols to destroy the final remnants of the Baghdad Caliphate, and at the beginning of the 19th century, it was once again the Jews—or, more precisely the *dunmeh*, descendants of former followers of Sabbetai Zevi who had converted to Islam—led by Atatürk and the Young Turks, who abolished the Ottoman caliphate, the last Muslim bastion against the Zionist invasion of Palestine. These developments paved the way for the Balfour Declaration, the proof par excellence of the Judeo-Christian "plot" hatched against Islam.

The fact is that the Christians, having persecuted the Jews for centuries, had in the meanwhile become their best allies when it came to attacking Islam and the Arab world. This connivance was not just the upshot of a transient partnership of interests between Jews and westerners. Rather, it was the outcome of Jewish domination in Europe and the United States, a domination that spread its tentacles as far as the Holy See, which, following Vatican II in 1964, formally absolved the Jews of any responsibility for the death of Christ.[57]

Jameelah heaps the same opprobrium on the Christians, the Jews, polytheists, irreligious Muslims, the Freemasons, and Orientalists. *Jihad*, or all-out war, is the fate reserved for all of them, and the Jews, even though a "people of the Book," are not to enjoy any special treatment. In a conclusion that is shared by many in the Muslim world today, Jameelah writes:

> We must realize that under the existing circumstances, no friendship is possible. Jewry and Christendom have joined hands to destroy us and all we cherish. Zionism, freemasonry, Christian missionary activity and Orientalism have combined to annihilate us religiously, culturally and even physically. It would be sheer folly to kiss the hands that are beating us!
>
> Peaceful relations and mutual respect among us can only be achieved through strength. We must cease indulging in apologetics and present the Islamic message to the world honestly and forthrightly. Before we can hope to succeed with Tabligh [piety] on a large scale, we must first convert the nominal Muslims into true believers. We must establish a full-blooded Islamic state where the world will witness our precepts translated into action. Finally, we must crush the conspiracies of Zionism, freemasonry, Orientalism and foreign missions both with the pen and with the sword. We cannot afford peace and reconciliation with the Ahl al Kitab until we can humble them and gain the upper hand.[58]

The Hamas covenant of 1987 puts the matter more succinctly: "The day of judgment will not arrive before the destruction of all the Jews."[59]

Notes

1. One indication of this growing interest is the number of books written in Arabic that contain the word *Yahud* (Jew) in their title. A search that I conducted on the WorldCat site yielded the following results: five titles (1890–1929); four (1930–1939); four (1940–1949); five (1950–1959); 38 (1960–1969); 51 (1970–1979); 101 (1980–1989); 151 (1990–1999); and 89 (2000–2003).

2. Mustafa Bouchara, *Al-Istitan wa-l-Himaya bi-l-Maghrib*, vol. 1 (1984), 128–129; Mohammed Kenbib, "Structures traditionnelles et protection étrangère au Maroc au XIX° siècle," *Hespéris-Tamuda* 22 (1984), 79–101.

3. ʿAbd al-Wahab ibn Mansur, *Al-Wataʾiq*, vol. 5 (Casablanca: 1981), 19.

4. Ibn Abi Diyaf, *Athaf Ahl al-Zaman bi-Akhbar Muluk Tuns wa-ʿAhd al-Aman*, vol. 4 (Tunis: 1963), 235.

5. Mohammed Kenbib, *Juifs et musulmans au Maroc, 1859–1948* (Rabat: 1994), 142–172.

6. On the Damascus affair, see Jonathan Frankel, *The Damascus Affair—"Ritual Murder," Politics and the Jews in 1840* (Cambridge: 1997).

7. Jacob M. Landau, " 'Alilot dam uredifot yehudim bemiẓrayim besof hameah ha-19," *Sefunot* 5 (1961), 417–460.

8. Sylvia G. Haim, "Arabic Antisemitic Literature—Some Preliminary Notes," *Jewish Social Studies* 17 (1956), 307–314.

9. On this literature, see in particular Georges Vajda, "Isra'iliyyat," *Encyclopédie de l'Islam*, 2nd ed. (Leiden: 1979), 4:212–213; Roberto Tottoli, "Origin and Use of the Term Isra'iliyyat in Muslim Literature," *Arabica* 46 (1999), 193–209.

10. On this debate, see Gautier H.A. Juynboll, *The Authenticity of the Tradition Literature—Discussions in Modern Egypt* (Leiden: 1969), 121–138; Johannes J.G. Jansen, *The Interpretation of the Koran in Modern Egypt* (Leiden: 1974), 18–34.

11. Jansen, *The Interpretation of the Koran in Modern Egypt*, 27.

12. On this issue, see the introductory article by Ronald L. Nettler, "Early Islam, Modern Islam and Judaism: The Isra'iliyyat in Modern Islamic Thought," in *Muslim-Jewish Encounters, Intellectual Traditions and Modern Politics,* ed. Ronald L. Nettler and Suha Taji-Farouki (Amsterdam: 1998), 1–14; Hugh S. Galford, "Sayyid Qutb and the Qura'nic Story of Joseph," in ibid., 39–64; William M. Brinner, "Soferet miẓrit anti-miẓrit," in *Sofrim muslemim 'al yehudim veyahadut: hayehudim bekerev shekhenehem hamuslemim*, ed. Hava Lazarus-Yafeh (Jerusalem: 1996), 247–266.

13. Juynboll, *The Authenticity of the Tradition Literature*, 131. In fact, the words ascribed to 'Umar by the great 9th-century Muslim chronicler Tabari, supposedly reporting the conversation between the conqueror of Jerusalem and Ka'b Ibn Ahbar, followed similar lines: when asked by 'Umar where the first mosque should be located, Ka'b replied that the Rock (in other words, the Temple Mount), appeared to him to be the most appropriate place for such an initiative:

"By God, Ka'b," said 'Umar, "you are following after Judaism. I saw you take off your sandals [following Jewish practice]."

"I wanted to feel the touch of it with my bare feet," said Ka'b.

"I saw you," said 'Umar. "But no . . . Go along! We were not commanded concerning the Rock, but we were commanded concerning the Ka'ba [in Mecca]"(quoted in Bernard Lewis, *The Jews of Islam* [Princeton: 1987], 70–71).

14. Michel Abitbol, *Le passé d'une discorde Juifs et Arabes depuis le VIIe siècle* (Paris: 1999), 184–210.

15. Albert Memmi, *L'homme dominé* (Paris: 1968), 58–59.

16. Michel Abitbol, "Hayehudim upetiḥat hamagreb,"in *Toledot hayehudim bearẓot haislam*, vol. 2, ed. Shmuel Ettinger (Jerusalem: 1986); Sergio DellaPergola, "Haukhlusiyah hayehudit bameot ha-19–20," in *Toledot yehudei miẓrayim bitkufat ha'otomanit*, ed. Jacob M. Landau (Jerusalem: 1988).

17. Simon Schwarzfuchs, *Les Juifs d'Algérie et la France* (Jerusalem: 1981).

18. Once again, the exception was Iraq, where Jews actively participated in their country's political and cultural life and expressed pride in their Arab heritage and Babylonian origins. Two factors underlying the Jews' allegiance to Iraq are the relatively short term of British colonial rule and the positive role played by King Faisal, who encouraged the Jews (along with Sunnites, Shiites, Kurds, and Assyrians) to feel that they were an integral component of the newly born Iraqi nation. See Nissim Kazaz, *Yehudim be'irak bameah ha'esrim* (Jerusalem: 1991).

19. On this issue, see Bernard Lewis, *Semites and Antisemites: An Inquiry into Conflict and Prejudice* (New York: 1986), ch. 6.

20. Charles-Robert Ageron, "Une émeute antijuive à Constantine (août 1934)," *Revue de l'Occident Musulman et de la Méditerranée* (1973), 23–40; Yves Aouat, "Un pogrome en

Algérie française: les émeutes antijuives d'août 1934 à Constantine" (Master's thesis, Université de Nice, 1980).

21. Michel Abitbol, *The Jews of North Africa during the Second World War*, trans. Catherine Tihanyi Zentelis (Detroit: 1989); Renzo de Felice, *Jews in an Arab Land: Libya, 1835–1970*, trans. Judith Roumani (Austin: 1985); Robert Assaraf, *Yehudei maroko: tekufat hamelekh Muḥamed V* (Tel Aviv: 1997).

22. Paul Monceaux, "Les colonies juives dans l'Afrique romaine," *Revue des Études Juives* 44 (1902), 1–28; Jean Mesnage, *Le christianisme en Afrique* (Algiers: 1904); Marcel Simon, "Le judaïsme berbère dans l'Afrique ancienne," *Revue d'Histoire et de Philosophie religieuses* 36 (1946), 1–31; 105–114.

23. On this episode, see Hayim Z. Hirschberg, "Haberberit Kahina," *Tarbitz* 26 (1957), 370–383.

24. Daniel Schroeter, "La découverte des Juifs berbères" in *Relations judéo-musulmanes au Maroc, perceptions et réalités*, ed. Michel Abitbol (Paris: 1997), 169–187.

25. H.J.M. Haddey, *Le livre d'or des Israélites algériens; recueil de renseignements inédits et authentiques sur les principaux négociants Juifs d'Alger pendant la période turque* (Algiers: 1871).

26. Pierre Flamand, *Diaspora en terre d'Islam* (Casablanca: 1959–1960); Vincent Monteil, "Les Juifs d'Ifrane," *Hespéris* 35 (1948), 151–162; Jean Huguet, "Les Juifs du Mzab," *Bulletins et Mémoires de la Société d'Anthropologie de Paris* 3 (1902), 559–573; Hubert Cornet, "Les Juifs de Gafsa," *Cahiers de Tunisie* 10 (1955), 276–315.

27. Jean Goulven, *Les Mellahs de Rabat-Salé* (Paris: 1927); José Bénech, *Essai d'explication d'un Mellah* (Paris: 1949).

28. Roger Le Tourneau, *Fès avant le Protectorat* (Casablanca: 1949); Paul Marty, "Les institutions israélites du Maroc," *Revue des Études Islamiques* (1930), 297–322.

29. Jean-Louis Miège, *Le Maroc et l'Europe* (Paris: 1959–1960); Renzo de Felice, *Jews in an Arab Land*.

30. Abraham Cahen, "Juifs d'Afrique à la limite du désert,"*Archives Israélites* (1866), 84–89; Isaac Bloch, "Les Israélites d'Oran de 1792 à 1815," *Revue des Études Juives* 13 (1886), 85–104; idem, *Inscriptions tumulaires des anciens cimetières israélites d'Alger* (Paris: 1888); Maurice Eisenbeth, *Le judaïsme nord-africain: étude démographique sur les israélites du département de Constantine* (Paris: 1931); idem, *Les Juifs d'Afrique du Nord: démographie et onomastique* (Algiers: 1936); idem, *Pages vécues, 1940–1943* (Algiers: 1945).

31. Yom Tov Semach, "Une chronique juive de Fès, le 'Yahas Fas' de Rabbi Abner Hassarfaty," *Hespéris* 19 (1934), 79–94; Robert Brunschvig, *LaTunisie sous les Hafsides* (Paris: 1940–1947); Georges Vajda, *Un recueil de texteshistoriques judéo-marocains* (Paris: 1951); David Ovadyah, *Fas veḥakhameiha* (Jerusalem: 1979).

32. Nahum Slouschz, author of *Hebraeo-phéniciens et Judéo-berbères—introduction à l'histoire de des Juifs et du judaïsme en Afrique* (Paris: 1908), *Travels in North Africa* (Philadelphia: 1927), and *The Jews of North Africa* (Philadelphia: 1944), published some of his best work in the *Archives Marocaines*.

33. Yaacov Toledano, *Ner hama'arav* (Jerusalem: 1911); David Cazes, *Essai sur l'histoire des Israélites de Tunis* (Paris: 1888); Yosef Ben-Naim, *Malkhei rabanan* (Jerusalem: 1931).

34. For Tunisia, see Rodolphe Arditti, *Recueil des textes législatifs et juridiques concernant les Juifs de Tunisie de 1857 à 1913, annotés et commentés* (Tunis: 1915); Salomon Tibi, *Le statut personnel des Israélites et spécialement des Israélites tunisiens* (Tunis: 1921–1923); Raoul Darmon, *La situation des cultes en Tunisie* (Paris: 1930); Jacques Chalom, *Les Israélites de Tunisie—leur condition civile et politique* (Paris: 1908). On the Jews' legal status in Morocoo, see André Chouraqui, *La condition juridique de l'Israélite marocain* (Paris: 1950); Elie Malka, *Essai sur la condition juridique de la femme juive au Maroc* (Paris: 1952); Abraham Zaguri, *Le régime successoral des Israélites marocains et les réformes actuelles en la matière* (Casablanca:1959).

35. André Chouraqui, *Marche vers l'Occident—Les Juifs d'Afrique du Nord* (Paris: 1952); Isaac D. Abbou, *Musulmans andalous et Judéo-espagnols* (Casablanca: 1953).

36. Hayim Zeev Hirschberg, *Toledot hayehudim bizfon afrikah*, 2 vols. (Jerusalem: 1965).

37. See Michel Abitbol (ed.), *Relations judéo-musulmanes au Maroc—perceptions et réalités* (Paris: 1997), and Sonia Fellous, *Juifs et Musulmans en Tunisie* (Paris: 2003), which contain contributions by many historians from Morocco and Tunisia, including Larbi Mezzine, Mustapha Bouchara, Khaled Kchir, Ibrahim Jadla, Ridha Ben Rejeb, Mohammed Larguèche, Larbi Chouikha, and Habib Kawadagli. Nonetheless, only a few Moroccan scholars (among them, Ahmad Toufiq, Mostafa Hassani-Idrissi, and Idris Khalil) took part in the International Colloquium on Moroccan Jewry organized in Paris in 1978 by Identité et Dialogue, a Jewish organization.

38. This phenomenon is well illustrated in Shmuel Ettinger (ed.), *Toledot hayehudim bearzot haislam*, 3 vols. (Jerusalem: 1981–1986), which contains contributions on North Africa, the Ottoman Empire and Asia by Michel Abitbol, Shalom Bar-Asher, Yaacov Barnai, and Yossef Tobi.

39. Shalom Bar-Asher, "Hakehilah hayehudit bemaroko—fes, meknes, vesefru bameah hashemonah 'esrei" (Ph.D. diss, The Hebrew University, 1981); Menahem Ben Sasson, *Zemihat hakehilah hayehudit bearzot haislam: kayrawan, 800–1057* (Jerusalem: 1996).

40. Rachel Simon, "Yehudei luv usvivah hanokhrit beshilhei hatekufah ha'otomanit," *Pe'amim*, 3 (1980), 5–36; Yaron Tsur, "Takriyot august 1917 betunisiyah" (Master's thesis, The Hebrew University, 1981).

41. Eliezer Bashan, "Sinat hamuslemim layehudim bameah hatesh'a 'esreh," *Mahanayim* 1 (1992), 216–223; Menahem Ben Sasson, " 'Iyun behishtamdut bitkufat al-Muwwahidun," *Pe'amim* 42 (1990), 16–37; Michel Abitbol, *MiCrémieux lePétain: antishemiyut bealgeriyah hakoloniyalit, 1870–1940* (Jerusalem: 1992).

42. On Hebrew poetry, see Haim Zafrani, *Poesie juive en Occident musulman* (Paris: 1980); Ephraim Hazan, *Shirei Farji Shaouat* (Jerusalem: 1976); and Joseph Chetrit, *Shirah upiyut beyahadut maroko* (Jerusalem: 1999). On Judeo-Arabic poetry, see Yosef Tobi, "The Flowering of Judeo-Arabic Poetry in North Africa, 1850–1950," in *Sephardi and Middle Eastern Jewries: History and Culture in the Modern Era*, ed. Harvey E. Goldberg (Bloomington: 1996).

43. Joseph Chetrit, "Nizaneha shel tenu'at haskalah 'ivrit bemaroko beshilhei hameah hatesh'a 'esreh," *Mikedem umiyam* 2 (1986), 129–168; Michael Laskier, *The Jewish Communities of Morocco and the Alliance Israélite Universelle, 1860–1960* (Albany: 1979).

44. On the impact of the Second World War, see Michel Abitbol, *Les Juifs d'Afrique du Nord sous Vichy* (Paris: 1981); Yaron Tsur, "Yehudei tunis bitkufat hakibush hanazi," *Yahadut Zemaneinu* 2 (1985), 153–175; and Robert Assaraf, *Mohammed V et les Juifs du Maroc à l'époque de Vichy* (Paris: 1997). On Zionism, see Zvi Yehuda, "Hairgun haziyoni bemaroko bashanim 1900–1948" (Ph.D. diss., The Hebrew University, 1981); Michael Laskier, *The Jews of Egypt, 1920–1970 in the Midst of Zionism: Antisemitism and the Middle East Conflict* (New York: 1992); David Cohen, "Lyautey vehaziyonut bemaroko (1912–1925)," *Kivunim* (1983), 105–153; Hayim Saadon, "Haziyonut betunisiyah, 1918–1945" (Ph.D. diss., The Hebrew University, 1993); on aliyah, see Shmuel Segev, *Mivza' yakhin: 'aliyatam hahashait shel yehudei maroko leyisrael* (Tel Aviv: 1984); Michael Laskier, "Jewish Emigration from Morocco to Israel: Government Policies and the Position of Jewish International Organizations, 1949–1956," *Middle Eastern Studies* 25 (1989), 323–362; Yaron Tsur, *Kehilah keru'ah: yehudei maroko vehaleumiyut* (Tel Aviv: 2001).

45. Rachel Simon, *Change within Tradition among Jewish Women in Libya* (Seattle: 1992); Esther Schely-Newman, " 'The Peg of Your Tent': Narratives of North African Israeli Women," in Goldberg (ed.), *Sephardi and Middle Eastern Jewries*, 277–287; Yedida K. Stillman, "Attitudes des femmes musulmanes et juives à l'égard de la féminité et de la modernité," in Abitbol (ed.), *Relations judéo-musulmanes au Maroc*, 237–246.

46. On integration in Israel, see Harvey E. Goldberg, *Cave Dwellers and Citrus Growers: A Jewish Community in Libya and Israel* (Cambridge: 1972), and Shlomo Deshen and Moshe Shokeid, *The Predicament of Homecoming: Cultural and Social Life of North African Immigrants in Israel* (Ithaca: 1974); on integration in France, see Doris Bensimon-Donath, *L'intégration des Juifs nord-africains en France* (Hague: 1971); Claude Tapia, *Les Juifs sépharades en France (1965–1985)* (Paris: 1986).

47. On Arab sources, see David Corcos, *Studies in the History of the Jews of Morocco* (Jerusalem: 1976); Norman A. Stillman, *The Jews of Arab Lands* (Philadelphia: 1979); idem, *The Jews of Arab Lands in Modern Times* (Philadelphia: 1991); Michel Abitbol, *Les Commerçants du Roi: Tujjar al-Sultan: une elite economique judeo-marocaine au XIXe siècle* (Paris: 1998); Kenneth L. Brown, "Mellah and Madina—A Moroccan City and Its Jewish Quarter," in *Studies in Judaism and Islam*, ed. Shelomo Morag, Issachar Ben-Ami, and Norman A. Stillman (Jerusalem: 1981), 253–281; Daniel J. Schroeter, *The Sultan's Jew: Morocco and the Sephardi World* (Stanford: 2002); Kenbib, *Juifs et Musulmans au Maroc*; and Abdelhamid Larguècke, "Nasim Shamama: un caïd face à lui-même et face aux autres," in Fellous (ed.), *Juifs et Musulmans en Tunisie*.

On genizah documents, see Menahem Ben Sasson, *zemiḥat hakehilah hayehudit bearzot haislam*.

On Hebrew chronicles, see Harvey E. Goldberg, *The Book of Mordechai: A Study of the Jews of Libya* (London: 1993); Samuel Romanelli, *Travail in an Arab Land*, trans. Yedida K. Stillman and Norman A. Stillman (Tuscaloosa: 1989); Shlomo Deshen, *The Mellah Society: Jewish Community Life in Sherifian Morocco* (Chicago: 1989).

On communal regulations and responsa literature, see Haim Zafrani, *Les Juifs du Maroc: vie sociale, economique et religieuse: etudes de taqqanot et responsa* (Paris: 1972); Itshaq Abrahami, "Kehilat kodesh portugezim betunis upinkasah," (Ph.D. diss., Bar Ilan University, 1982); Shalom Bar-Asher *Yehudei sefarad uportugal bemaroko (1492–1753): sefer hatakanot* (Jerusalem: 1990); and Moshe Amar, *Sefer takanot ḥakhmei meknes* (Jerusalem: 1996).

On oral traditions, see Issachar Ben Ami, *Moroccan Jewry: A Chapter in the Study of Their Culture* (Jerusalem: 1975); Joseph Chetrit, "Strategies discursives dans la langue des femmes judéo-arabophones du Maroc," *Massorot* (1986), 41–66; and Lucette Valensi and Avram Udovitch, *The Last Arab Jews: The Communities of Jerba, Tunisia* (London: 1984).

48. Cf. André Chouraqui, *Marche vers l'Occident: les Juifs d'Afrique du Nord* (Paris: 1952).

49. Among other works, see Doris Bensimon-Donath, *Evolution du judaïsme marocain sous le Protectorat français* (Paris: 1968); Michel Abitbol, "The Jews of North Africa and Egypt under Colonial Rule," in Ettinger (ed.), *Toledot hayehudim bearzot haislam*, 2: 363–466; Yaron Tsur, "Zarefat vihudei tunisiyah, 1873–1888 (Ph.D. diss., The Hebrew University, 1988); Rachel Simon, "Language Changes and Socio-political Transformations: The Case of Nineteenth and Twentieth Century Libyan Jews," *Jewish History* 4 (1989), 101–121; Simon Schwartzfuchs, *Les Juifs d'Algérie et la France* (Jerusalem: 1981); Geneviève Dermenjan, *Juifs et Européens d'Algérie; l'antisémitisme oranais (1892–1905)* (Jerusalem: 1983); and Aouat, "Un pogrome en Algérie française: les émeutes antijuives d'août 1934 à Constantine."

50. Leland Bowie, "An Aspect of Muslim-Jewish Relations in Late Nineteenth Century Morocco: A European Diplomatic View," *International Journal of Middle East Studies* 7 (1976), 3–19; Lawrence Rosen, "Muslim-Jewish Relations in a Moroccan City," *International Journal of Middle East Studies* 3 (1972), 388–404; Mohammed Kenbib, "Protections, Protectorat et Nationalisme au Maroc, 1904–1938," *Hespéris-Tamuda* 18 (1978–1979), 199–210.

51. Yoram Bilu and André Lévy, "Nostalgia and Ambivalence: The Reconstruction of Jewish-Muslim Relations in Oulad Mansour," in Goldberg (ed.), *Sephardi and Middle Eastern Jewries*, 288–311; Michel Abitbol, *Le Passé d'une discorde*.

52. The original title is *Al-'Arab wa-l-Yahud fi al-Ta'rikh*. First published in Baghdad in 1972, this work quickly became a standard reference work in all Arab capitals and subsequently has been published in numerous editions. Ahmad Soussa briefly relates the circumstances of his conversion in a work titled *Fi Tariqi ila al-Islam* ("My path to Islam"), although the thrust of this autobiography, which was published in Cairo in 1936, is an attempt to demonstrate Islam's theological superiority over Christianity and Judaism. Soussa's conversion was the subject of much discussion among the Iraqi Jewish community, which followed his remarkable progress in the Iraqi world of letters with great attention. His "case" is referred to in a number of Hebrew-language novels published recently by Israeli writers of Iraqi descent, including Eli Amir's *Mafriaḥ hayonim* (*Farewell Baghdad*) (Tel

Aviv: 1994) and Simon Ballas' *Vehu aher* (Tel Aviv: 1991), which recently appeared in English as *Outcast*, trans. Ammiel Alcalay and Oz Shelach (San Francisco: 2007).

53. Among the many other works promoting similar theses are the following: Ahmad 'Uthman, *Ta'rikh al-Yahud* (Cairo: 2002); Mahmud Na'na', *Ta'rikh al-Yahud* (Amman: 2001); Ahmad Dawud, *Al-'Arab wa-i-Samiyyun wa-l-'Ibraniyyun wa Banu Isra'il wa-l-Yahud* (Damascus: 1991); Ahmad Shalabi, *Al-Yahudiyya* (Cairo: 1978); 'Abd al-Jalil Shalabi, *Al-Yahud wa-l-Yahudiyya* (Cairo: 1997); Muhammad al-Shirazi, *Ha'ula' al-Yahud* (Beirut: 1984).

54. This idea is to be found just below the surface in most of the monographs written in recent years about Jewish communities in Muslim countries. See, for example, 'Abd al-Majid Muhammad Nahr, *Al-Yahud fi Andalus* (Cairo: 1970); 'Ali Ibrahim 'Abdu, *Yahud al-Bilad al-'Arabiyya* (Beirut: 1971); Muhammad al-Habib Ibn Khudja, *Yahud al-Maghrib al-'Arabi* (Cairo: 1973); Ma'mun Kiwan, *al-Yahud fi al-Sharq al-Awsa* (Amman: 1992); Muhammad Husni Sa'ida, *Al-Yahud fi Misr* (Cairo: 1993); Abbas Shiblak, *The Lure of Zion: The Case of the Iraqi Jews* (London: 1980).

55. Among the works dealing with the historical origins of Zionism are Sabri Jirayis' *Al-Turath al-Yahudi al-Sahyuni wa-i-Fikr al-Fruyidi* (which posits a link between the "Judeo-Zionist heritage" and Freudian thinking) (Cairo: 1970); and Hasan Tantawi, *Al-Sahyuniyya wa-l-'Unf-al-Falsafa wa-l-Istratijiyya* (Beirut: 1977). Books dealing with Zionism's racism include Muhmmad Kamal Dassouqi, *Al-Sahyuniyya wa-i-Naziyya* (Cairo: 1968); Hamid Rabi', *Al-'Unsuriyya al-Sahyuniyya* (Damascus: 1973); Ahmad Yusuf al-Qar'i, *Al-Sahyuniyya wa-i-'Unsuriyya* (Cairo: 1977); Na'na', *Ta'rikh al-Yahud*; and 'Ahmad al-Wahab al-Miri, *Al-Sahyuniyya wa-l-Naziyya wa Nihayat al-Ta'rikh* (Cairo: 1997). On the link between Zionism and Judaism, see As'ad Razzuq, *Al-Talmud wa-l-Sahyuniyya* (Beirut: 1970); Muhammad Sabri, Al-*Talmud, Shari'at Bani Isra'il-Haqa'iq wa Waqa'i'* Cairo (1978); Ahmad Ibrahim Khalil, *Isra'il wa-l-al-Talmud* (Cairo: 1983). On Zionism and the "Jewish mindset," see Muhammad Nimr al-Khatib, *Haqiqat al-Yahud wa-l-Matami' al-Sahyuniyya* (Beirut: 1969).On the expansionist and colonial nature of Zionism, see Muhammad Hamdan, *Al-Isti'mar wa-l-Sahyuniyya al-'Alamiyya* (Beirut: 1967); As'ad Razzuq, *Isra'il al-Kubra* (Beirut: 1968); Mahmud Diab, *Al-Sahyuniyya al-'Alamiyya* (Cairo: 1976); Muhammad 'Abd al-Rahman Hussayn, *Al-'Arab wa-l-Yahud fi al-Madi, wa-l-Hadir wa-l-Mustaqbil* (Cairo: 1991); Hasin 'Azi, *Isra'il al-Kubra* (Damascus: 1992).On alleged ties between Zionism and cosmopolitan and "Jewish" organizations, see Fuad Muhammad Shibi, *Mushkilat al-Yahud al-'Alami* (Cairo: 1970); Muhammad al-Samak, *Al-Yahud al-'Alami* (Beirut: 1993); Sabir 'Abd al-Rahman Tu'aymah, *Al-Masuniyya wa-i-Sahyuniyya wa-l-Shuyu'iyya* (Beirut: 1978); Muhammad al-Shirazi, *Ha'laa' al-Yahud* (Beirut: 1984); Khalil Ibrahim Hassuna, *Al-Masuniyya Qadiman wa-Hadhithan* (Tripoli: 1994).

56. Maryam Jameelah, *Islam versus Ahl al-Kitab*, 5–6.

57. Ibid., 13.

58. Ibid., 412.

59. Hamas covenant (Gaza: 1987), par. 7.

The Brief Career of Prosper Cohen:
A Sectorial Analysis of the North African Jewish Leadership in the Early Years of Israeli Statehood

Yaron Tsur
(TEL AVIV UNIVERSITY)

In November 1948, about half a year after the establishment of the state of Israel, a 38-year-old attorney landed at Haifa's airport: Prosper Cohen, a former secretary of the Zionist Federation in Morocco. Married and the father of a young girl, he nevertheless arrived alone—the plan being that his wife and daughter would join him within months. In time, he described his arrival as follows:

> It was the Sabbath. I was choked with emotion. Around me, I heard Hebrew, police, porters, women, children, everyone was turning to one another, shouting in a language I did not understand, though I was overwhelmed by merely hearing it. I thought of Renan [the renowned French biblical scholar and philosopher] as he defined the language of the Bible: "A quiver of steel, a hawser made of mighty twine, a trombone of bronze rending the air with two-three sharp notes—that's Hebrew."[1]

No kneeling to kiss the sacred soil; no remembered prayers for the Jewish return. Instead, Cohen recalls his excitement at the sound of Hebrew, a language incomprehensible to him, whose impact he could define only by reference to his French cultural identity. Far different is the account of another Moroccan immigrant, Shmuel Ben-Harosh, who had arrived on the very day that the state of Israel was established, on May 14, 1948. Ben-Harosh had headed the Em Habanim yeshiva in Sefrou, a small town renowned both for its rabbinical Jewish elite and as a moderate-religious local center of the Hebrew Enlightenment (Haskalah).[2] Ben-Harosh and his family, nine people in all, reached the port of Tel Aviv by ship amid Egypt's bombing of the city and were whisked off to an immigrant camp in Netanya before they were able to perform the ceremony of kissing the ground. But when one of the rabbi's sons later reminded him, the omission was quickly rectified.[3]

These two initial encounters with the Jewish state rest on different cultural heritages. What do they signify for the different courses taken by Cohen and Ben-Harosh in Israeli society? This essay focuses in the main on Prosper Cohen (though Ben-

Harosh will make another appearance toward the conclusion), recounting his brief, unsuccessful foray into Israeli politics and his subsequent career during the first years of Israeli statehood. Beyond Cohen's personal saga, this essay examines the characteristics of the new Jewish elites that developed in colonial Morocco and argues for attributing greater importance to their varied nature in describing how their members fared in Israel. As these characteristics were the product of the colonial situation whose influence was manifest not only in Morocco but also in other Jewish communities in Asia and Africa, the present analysis offers a methodology that is applicable to them as well, and also to that in Mandatory Palestine and the state of Israel. A further and important aim of this article is to add another layer to the ongoing research concerning the encounter between the colonial order and the national order in the Zionist society in Israel. Whereas Israel's "old" historiography and sociology tended to blur the influence of the colonial heritage on internal Jewish relations, some critical sociologists and most post-colonial researchers have leaned in the opposite direction and have emphasized mainly the colonial face of Zionism, internally as well. But the critical historiography of the Jews of the Islamic countries, and of their history in Israel, has a voice of its own in this matter—a voice that warns against downplaying the impact of either one of the two global orders: colonialism and nationalism—and this article seeks to strengthen that voice.[4]

From Colonial and Sectorial to a National Society

Prosper Cohen and Shmuel Ben-Harosh represent two Moroccan elites that developed under French colonial rule in Morocco (1912–1956). Cohen's elite included an intellectual circle that transferred the focus of its high culture to the French sphere, the language of the western conquerors. In contrast, Ben-Harosh's elite was firmly grounded in Morocco's indigenous cultures: Arabic for the Muslim majority; Judeo-Arabic and Hebrew for the Jewish minority.[5] For purposes of clarity, the members of this second elite—both Muslim and Jews—will here be referred to as *maskilim*. Many of these maskilim were also able to communicate in French, but their command of the language did not approach the level of westernized individuals, such as Cohen, who had attended a French high school and French institutions of higher learning.

The difference between the two elites had its origins in the colonial condition. Colonial societies are generally characterized by a rigid socio-hierarchical dichotomy separating "Europeans" from "natives," the local inhabitants. This dichotomy stems from a perceived racial, or at least cultural, superiority of the former in the social realm, accompanied both by legal status differentials that privilege Europeans and by a variety of social practices that reinforce the hierarchical ladder and segregation. In the case of Morocco, the French rulers were interested in the country's modernization, primarily to advance their own interests. The resources of western education, industrialization, and economic development were thus managed differentially, being meant primarily for European officials and settlers. The local majority had little access to these resources. Nevertheless, because Morocco was now open to modern Arab and Jewish external influences, there was increased opportunity for modernizing the native cultures. Hence the circle of local maskilim (both Muslim and Jewish) expanded considerably. In addition, the colonial government also allocated some funds to select groups of Muslims and Jews who had acquired a French education at the elementary school level and occasionally beyond. Some of those who were fluent in French were the intermediaries par excellence between the overseas extension of European economy and culture and the local systems. And some adopted French as the higher culture, distancing themselves from that of their "native" brethren, which remained Arabic or Berber of various types. This group will hereafter be denoted as "westernized" (to distinguish them from maskilim who underwent modernization within their own non-European culture, even if they could communicate in a western language).

The differences at the elite level reflected a general division within colonial society into three groups of social networks within which economic mobility was dependent on culture:

a. the *European sector*—networks of European officials and settlers dependent on mastery of western culture;
b. the *native sector*—networks of local inhabitants dependent on mastery of the local culture (in the North African case: Arab or Berber);
c. the *westernized sector*—networks of local inhabitants who had attained mastery of a western-national culture (in Morocco's case: either French or, in the narrow northern strip, Spanish), and made it their high culture.

As opposed to the common class-based analysis, the importance of the sectorial perspective is that it places the emphasis on the influence of the concurrent existence of different *cultural systems* (rather than on the accumulation of wealth and property) within a single territorial society. In fact, each of the sectors outlined above had its own class divisions—within the native sector, for example, were individuals who had great wealth, both in land and in assets. At the same time, insofar as different cultural groups vary in their capacity to accumulate wealth, it is clear that sector and the socioeconomic will become linked. In colonial societies, the European sector of settlers and officials—which succeeded in dominating the local territory and population because of superior technological, military, and political capabilities—seeks to perpetuate its privileged position by means of various restrictions and restraints, some hard and fast, some vague and diffuse; some anchored in law, such as economic and political privileges, and some anchored in belief systems and patterns of conduct. As noted, these privileges included full access to European education, which was accorded to locals sparingly and only to select groups. But even westernized locals such as Cohen, who was fully schooled in European culture, came up against the formal and informal bars to social mobility within the European sector. At the same time, they belonged to the local Arab (or Arab-Jewish in the case of the minority) cultural circle, which meant that the boundaries to their economic and social mobility spilled over into areas that Europeans could not penetrate. Consequently, even though they lacked a delimited economic system, they may be defined as a sector distinguished by the unusual mobility boundaries its members created. The "native" Arab (or more precisely, Arab and Berber) sector, for its part, was distinguished by its complete mastery of the local languages and agrarian economy, despite evident seeds of modernization cultivated by the maskilim and the westernized. Just as Arabic/

Berber speakers lacking modern education were not mobile within the European sector, so too the exclusively French-speakers, products of the modern educational system, were not mobile in the Arab sector, certainly not in its agrarian realms.[6]

Clearly the quasi-autonomy of the economic-cultural systems did not constitute equal opportunity. There was a striking difference in the degree to which members of the different colonial sectors could accumulate wealth under the new conditions. In the case of Morocco (and also elsewhere), this situation led to external Jewish intervention. For complex reasons of Jewish solidarity and French patriotism, Jews of the mother country strove to westernize local Jewry as much as possible, primarily via the educational arm of the Alliance Israélite Universelle. Cohen, a product of Alliance education in Meknes, went on to become a teacher and a principal in the Alliance network before turning to law. The Alliance sought to move children from the local Judeo-Arab sector into the westernized sector as quickly as possible, and it would make impressive progress in this direction on the eve of Israel's establishment.[7]

Most of the Moroccan *'olim* (immigrants) in the first aliyah wave belonged to the native local Arab sector, or were located on the "seam" between the native and the westernized sectors. In his memoirs, Cohen speaks of Zionist fervor sweeping over the whole of Moroccan Jewry. But in discussing the first immigrant wave, he mentions the difficulty of obtaining exit permits and the distinctive social profile of those who chose to emigrate at all costs, illegally crossing the border into Algeria en route to the Jewish state. He pinpoints the two main groups of immigrants: impassioned youth, and large families from the community's lower socioeconomic strata. While he does not relate to the social origins of the former (who enlisted in the Israel Defense Forces immediately upon arrival), most of them came from the "seam" between the native and the westernized sectors. The large poor families stemmed from the native sector, and Cohen emphasizes that aliyah was aimed at rescuing them from the serious housing and educational distress that they suffered in Morocco. In other words, not only were they poverty-stricken but they were deprived of access to modern educational resources. According to Cohen's memoirs, they were encouraged to immigrate by community members who did not join them, but who shared the hope that aliyah would solve both these social problems.[8]

There were noteworthy sectorial and class differences between the large immigrant population that made its way to the Jewish state and the sole Zionist leader who did so. As noted, most of the immigrants stole across the border to Algeria and required the services of passport forgers and smugglers, who were apt to blackmail them and their communal backers. Once across the border, the immigrants were processed by envoys from the Yishuv (and eventually by the Israeli government or the Jewish Agency), upon whom they were utterly dependent. They were held in temporary camps in Oran and Algiers, then transferred to Marseilles for embarkation to Israel, all in accordance with orders from above.[9] In Israel, they were sent off to immigrant camps or else made their way to abandoned Arab neighborhoods in the big cities (Jerusalem, Jaffa, and Haifa), where they struggled to find their place along with other groups of new olim. The Moroccans quickly acquired a reputation as "bad" immigrants, as "troublemakers," and as prone to violence. Those who had been mobilized also came into conflict with their surroundings, but this was ameliorated by their reputation for bravery in combat. During this period, there were only a few large families from the Judeo-Arab native sector whose breadwinners were maskilim, such as Shmuel Ben-Harosh, and they had no impact on the Moroccan image. In short, within months of their arrival, Moroccan immigrants became associated with a turn for the worse in the Yishuv's societal development—adding, as it were, a group with prominent negative characteristics to the Yishuv's poorest strata. In the context of social relations within the evolving national Jewish society, this constituted an additional blow to the non-European section, being largely identified with Arab origin and culture as well as with backwardness and primitiveness. North African immigrants, most of whom were from Morocco, were placed at the bottom of Israel's new social prestige rankings.[10]

The situation of Moroccan immigrants in the young state of Israel may also be analyzed from the sectorial perspective. Notwithstanding the ongoing debate concerning the nature of Zionist settlement in Palestine and its connection with European colonialism, Ashkenazic immigrants may certainly be perceived as forming a European sector with clear cultural and economic boundaries, whereas the country's Arabic-speaking inhabitants—Muslims, Christians, and Jews—constituted a local Arab sector, partially modernized since the twilight of the Ottoman period. However, in contrast with other European colonial settlements, the Yishuv did not share the identity or national culture of any colonial power. It evolved well before the British takeover of Palestine, in the form of a national movement and society—the "national Yishuv," in Zionist terms, in opposition to which local Muslim and Christian inhabitants—but not native Jews—established a Palestinian national movement and society of their own. Thus the two prototypical colonial sectors, the European and the native, assumed a national character.

A westernized sector of local inhabitants who adopted the culture of the European sector (in this instance, Hebrew) as their high culture did not develop during the Mandate period among Muslims or Christians, since neither were interested in integrating into the rival Zionist nationalist sector. Nor could they play a middleman role. Although limited circles of both Muslims and Jews were attracted to English culture and colonial society, there was no substantial Palestinian sector of English officials and settlers in which to integrate. Another notable difference between the local sectorial situation and that of classic colonialism was the presence of a non-Zionist ḥaredi (ultra-Orthodox) Jewish sector that was heir to the pre-Zionist Ashkenazic Yishuv. Its heritage included a particular culture resting on a separate linguistic base (Yiddish) and a defining religious ideology. It was also characterized by a distinctive economic pattern and the financial support of haredi diaspora communities, and not just on integration into one or both of the national economies.

Cultural and economic boundaries may be mutually reinforcing, and commonly the various wings of the sectorial structure are underpinned by mobilizing and organizing ideologies. Ostensibly, Moroccan and Palestinian colonial societies differed in this respect, for while it is easy to discern these ideologies in the Palestinian-Arab/ Zionist/haredi case, this is not true of Morocco's non-European (Arab and westernized) sectors. In fact, however, the Moroccan social order was determined by the hegemonic European sector, and it was its colonial ideology that defined the internal boundaries.[11] The contrast between these two societies in this regard reflected, among other things, the difference between French colonialism and that of the British in Palestine. The latter lacked a settler class made up of members of the ruling power. Instead, natives and Europeans had earlier on developed national sectors. In Morocco, too, with the development of a local national movement at the end of the Second World War, Muslim maskilim and a handful of westernized Muslims (and some Jews) joined together to overturn the colonial order. At this stage, it seemed as if the two local sectors, Arab and westernized, sought to unite in the name of a Moroccan Arab national ideology. In this way, clear identity and cultural boundaries were established between the unified national sector and the European one.

An interesting issue in the Palestine/Eretz Israel arena, and one obviously closely connected with our subject, is what transpired with the Arabic-speaking Jews of the Yishuv, who, as noted, did not join the Palestinian national sector. On the whole, they joined the Zionist sector and its dominant Ashkenazic majority, though without becoming fully assimilated into it. Two contrary concepts of identity left their mark on relations between the European and non-European Jews in the modern era. On the one hand, a common religious identity and an ethnic view of Jewish nationalism fostered unity and rapprochement. On the other hand, the dichotomous conception typical of the colonial era—which perceived "white" Europeans and their cultures as superior, and the inhabitants of other regions and their cultures as inferior—promoted estrangement and discrimination. Against this background, the Zionist Yishuv was plagued from its inception by a unique social problem later to be designated the "ethnic problem": the unequal relations between members of European versus Asian or North African origins. The first to sense this were immigrants from Yemen who had been recruited during the Second Aliyah period as agricultural workers in the moshavot in place of cheap Arab Muslim labor.[12] Meanwhile, the veteran non-Ashkenazic inhabitants of the pre-Yishuv period, who were called "Sephardim" and who were often financially better off than the Ashkenazic halutzim, also sensed the feelings of superiority and patronization on the part of the European olim.[13] Although the Jewish national ethos did not allow for the construction of rigid legal or statutory boundaries separating European and non-European Jews, it could not prevent the establishment of invisible and diffuse boundaries of labeling, social distance, and discrimination.

Another difference between colonial sectorial society and the Zionist Yishuv related to the question of a uniform culture. The colonial situation is based on the perpetuation of the multicultural reality in the conquered territory and on the distancing of the broad native masses. In Morocco, for example, the French did not have an ideology that sought to encourage cultural unification. The situation was different in the Jewish national territory, where the vision and building of a national economy required cultural unification based on reviving and modernizing Hebrew as the normative spoken language. The choice of Hebrew, both a Semitic language and the sacred language common to all Jews, should have made it significantly easier for Asian and North African Jews to adapt culturally and function in the national society. So too should the choice of Sephardic rather than Ashkenazic pronunciation of Hebrew. It must be kept in mind, however, that modern Hebrew culture had been fashioned chiefly in Eastern and Central Europe, and also by Ashkenazic immigrants to Palestine from those regions, who, for the most part, were devotees of Europe's Enlightenment. It was thus saturated with western and European Jewish influences, and the adaptation to it by Asian and African immigrants was a form of westernization, sometimes referred to as *hishtaknezut* (becoming "Ashkenazic"), along the lines of *françisation* (becoming "Frenchified") in French colonial territories.

In any event, there remained the question of the extent to which the Zionist Ashkenazic elite would seek to encourage the complete assimilation of the non-European elements into the new Jewish society. Over a few decades, the Zionist sector had developed virtually ex nihilo out of successive immigration waves and the need both to populate essential societal strata and to fill economic niches. There were fewer than 25,000 Jews in Palestine in 1882. With the bringing in of Yemenite immigrants during the Second Aliyah—as noted, the formative affair of Zionism's "ethnic problem"—came the possibility of attempting to "translate" the (somewhat imagined) agrarian profile of a Judeo-Arab population group into that of a proletariat of hired agricultural laborers within the national society. That phenomenon was apt to recur and turn into a syndrome.[14] The Ashkenazic elites engaged in society-building were thus liable again and again to encounter a conflict between the vision of cultural unification and the interest of exploiting existing cultural differences for the urgent needs of nation-building, or for the legitimation of the entrenchment of European Jews at the upper levels of the emergent society.

Creating a uniform linguistic base for the Zionist sector was one thing; establishing educational mechanisms to facilitate mobility between the different strata was another. One possibility was to translate the initial sectorial situation of the immigrants into social stratification, in other words, to move them from "sector" to "class."

Unlike classic immigrant nations such as the American, Zionism sought to build a society based on members of a single religion and on an ideology that regarded all members of the national group as emanating from a single origin, as having a common history of exile and persecution, and as possessing the right to return to the land from which they had been exiled in the distant past. But this task could not be free of the influences establishing hierarchical relationships between Europeans and non-Europeans that originated in overlapping eras of colonialism and nationalism. Neither could it escape the conflicts between those with power and the powerless, which are endemic in human society. On the contrary, since the Zionist sector in Palestine/Eretz Israel constituted a national society-in-the-making, its leaders possessed an unusual degree of power to steer the members of all the various Jewish diaspora communities into what the former perceived to be suitable societal niches for the latter—as farmers, independent artisans, wage laborers, clerks, and professionals, among others. At the same time, the power of the Ashkenazim often served to blur, both in popular opinion and academic historiography, the reality of the immigrant "others"—the non-Ashkenazim—their identities, and their interests and strategies as they sought to make their way to membership within the Yishuv and the Jewish state. To help shed light on this somewhat obscured aspect of the building of Israeli society, we shall focus on the story of the Moroccan Zionist leader, Prosper Cohen, in the years 1948–1949.[15]

In the Service of the Herut Party and the Jewish Agency

As Cohen began to make his arrangements for aliyah, news of the unsavory reputation his countrymen were acquiring in the young state was reaching Morocco,
along with accounts of the negative treatment the new immigrants were receiving.
Feeling a great sense of responsibility not only for the Jewish state but also for his
fellow Moroccan Jews, Cohen set his sights on a position in Israel's emergent
government, as director of a special Jewish Agency department for the absorption of
North African immigrants. Such a job, of course, was also meant to ensure him an
income and a position in his new society, and thus to continue the process of upward
social mobility he had begun in Morocco. He wrote to an acquaintance of his, a senior
Jewish Agency official named Samuel U. Nahon, telling him of his plans and re-
questing his assistance.[16] However, he left for Israel with no promising news from
Nahon.

Upon his arrival, he traveled from Haifa to Tel Aviv and took a hotel room near
the beach. "That evening," he wrote,

> I beheld the merriest, noisiest, youngest, motliest crowd, clad in the most disparate
> uniforms, graced by the wildest hairdos. The gaiety, the smiles that burst out like fire-
> crackers, the unself-conscious carriage, the total absence of snobbism and formality—
> here was a world, an atmosphere, I had never before encountered.[17]

Yet the festive atmosphere soon gave way to disappointment. The next day, as the
first step toward securing the senior position he coveted, Cohen traveled to Jerusalem
to meet with the director of the Jewish Agency's aliyah department, Giora Yoseftal.
He could not get to see him. Instead, he was ultimately furnished with a note to the
department's regional director in Haifa, Kalman Levine. In Cohen's memoirs, Levine comes across as the embodiment of inflexibility and obtuseness, treating the
newcomer discourteously before finally offering him the post of a functionary in an
immigrant camp, where he would be expected to live as well. Between one meeting
and another, Cohen managed to spend several days at a camp, gaining an idea of the
conditions and type of work he would be doing, as a result of which he angrily
rejected the offer.[18] He, the only member of the Moroccan Jewish leadership to arrive
in the first wave of immigrants, had not expected this sort of "integration." He had
come to lead the immigrants, not to share a hut with them and ply away at a
monotonous bureaucratic job. Levine's suggestion was an attempt to "exile" him, he
wrote. It is interesting, however, that Cohen's account of his contacts with the Jewish
Agency gives no hint that his "ethnic" origins carried any special weight. He was
brushed aside, he believed, because the bureaucracy regarded him as a tiresome
"immigrant."[19]

Following his unpleasant experience with the Jewish Agency and the ruling establishment, Cohen sought a curative experience in the rival political camp, the Herut
party. This was not a sudden development; by Cohen's own testimony, he had had
initial contacts with representatives of the Zionist Revisionist movement while still
in Morocco, though he had not thrown in his lot with them before arriving in Israel.[20]
His path to the establishment blocked, he was welcomed with open arms by the main

opposition party. From his first days at Herut's offices, while still acquainting himself with the various departments, he began to fill a role commensurate with his aspirations, receiving North African immigrants, listening to their problems, and directing them to the relevant party officials. As elections to the First Knesset approached, Herut utilized his French oratory talents, sending him to spread the party word in immigrant camps that had many North Africans. He also accompanied party leader Menachem Begin to rallies in Jaffa and Jerusalem.[21]

Cohen thus entered Israeli public life very swiftly. Within weeks of his arrival, he had landed a relatively senior position in Herut. In addition to dealing directly with North African immigrants and helping out with party propaganda, he soon became secretary of a new Herut-affiliated organization aimed at Jews in Muslim countries, the International League for the Rescue of Arab Jewry.[22] The League's temporary chairman, Yirmiyahu Halperin, earned high praise from Cohen. In his memoirs, Cohen juxtaposes the warmth showered on him by Halperin in particular, and Herut members generally, with the "unconcealed hostility and gruff, brutal cynicism I found among all the Jewish Agency's petty officials."[23] For all the differences between his traumatic Jewish Agency experience and the restorative experience of Herut, in both, Cohen's primary social reference group was the same: the European sector's elite, with its Ashkenazic stamp. In his endeavors to be admitted to the elite, one circle rejected him, while another accepted him.

Soon after joining Herut, Cohen published an article in the party's French-language newsletter, *Liberté*, urging the immigrants not to allow absorption difficulties to cloud their motives for aliyah—mainly, the desire to live freely in their ancestral land—while stigmatizing the surrounding Arab society as the major factor in the oppression of Moroccan Jewry.[24] Elsewhere, however, he was quick to express a more critical view of what was happening in the Jewish state. For instance, among the League documents, there is a memo undoubtedly authored by Cohen titled "The Situation of the New Immigrants from North Africa." It opens by citing a letter from 400 immigrants in the Haifa region who decried their substandard housing and sanitary conditions. Following this, the memo summarizes an investigation undertaken by the League in immigrant camps in Pardes Hannah, Netanya, Binyamina, Atlit and Raanana, as well as in selected city neighborhoods, in particular, Jabeliya (Jaffa). In all, the memo not only corroborated the complaints in the immigrants' letter, it actually took them further.[25]

Clearly, Cohen saw his two positions—at the League, and as a Herut party official dealing with North African immigrants—as complementary. In fact, he came up with an apt formula combining them: along with rescuing Jews from Muslim countries who had not yet immigrated, it was necessary to rescue those who had already done so and were suffering from serious problems such as hunger, appalling housing, and no educational opportunities. Cohen could not, of course, make this internal social slogan the main message of the diaspora-oriented League for the Rescue of Arab Jewry. But he could add it to the League's original mandate.[26]

Results of the League investigation were published in another article written by Cohen for *Liberté*, which elicited an angry reaction in *Davar*, the Histadrut labor federation newspaper (affiliated with the ruling Mapai party). *Davar*'s reporter accused Cohen of comparing the immigrants' living conditions to those in the Nazi

concentration camps of Majdanek and Treblinka.[27] Cohen's response to *Davar* did
not mention the comparison, but rather stood behind the figures cited in the memo; he
also took the opportunity to attack the differential handling by the government censor
of establishment newspapers such as *Davar*, on the one hand, and *Liberté*, an opposition party organ, on the other.[28]

While Cohen was busy crafting his rhetorical explanation of his route to Herut—
and, in the process, blackening Jewish Agency personalities—individuals connected
with the establishment, whose identities he did not reveal, set out to defame him. He
was accused of having "betrayed" his mission of playing his part within the administrative bodies dealing with the North African immigrants in the camps, opting
instead for a cushy city job for reasons of personal convenience, and in the lap of the
opposition, to boot. These charges made their way to Morocco, and in February 1949,
two of Cohen's colleagues from the Moroccan Zionist Federation, Ayouche Cohen
and Maurice Timsit, came to Cohen's office while on a visit to Israel and demanded
that he part company with the opposition and try his luck once again at the Jewish
Agency.[29] Together with them, Cohen returned to the offices of the absorption
department, and what had been denied him as an immigrant—a meeting with its
director Giora Yoseftal—was readily granted to the two honored tourists. According
to Cohen, they even managed to get a promise that he would receive the appointment
he desired—head of a new department for the absorption of North African immigrants.

Thus it was that Cohen entered the ranks of the Jewish Agency in early March
1949. His first project was to prepare a memo with a blueprint for his new department
and proposed measures to improve immigrant conditions.[30] The memo was written
in French; prior to its translation, it was circulated among friends in Morocco and in
Israel for their comments. It began by listing a number of basic facts. First, it charged,
Israeli envoys had mismanaged Moroccan immigration and were thus responsible for
the quality of the arrivals, perhaps having received "instructions to bring immigrants
at any price." The obvious conclusion was that one should not rely on emissaries who
had not proved themselves and had created problems for the state. At the very least,
the management of aliyah from North Africa should not be left solely in their hands.
Turning to the Israeli arena, Cohen suggested that there were 20,000–30,000 North
African immigrants (in fact, the correct figure was about 12,000), most of them from
Morocco. His assessment of them was as follows:

> The human material that came to settle here does not represent the healthy mass of the
> Jewish population in North Africa. This is what earned the immigrants from this area a
> bad name. Further explaining the quality of this material is that, in all countries, people
> with a rather high average standard of living—culture, financial means, etc.—generally
> do not venture or do not want to give up their relative comfort.[31]

This paragraph appears in the French original (found in the personal archive of a veteran Zionist leader in Morocco), where it is crossed out; it is absent from the Hebrew
translation that was circulated in Jewish Agency and government offices.[32] Although
an uncomplimentary assessment of North African immigrants, particularly of Moroccans, was widespread and was shared also by the local Moroccan Zionist leaders,
they were not interested in reinforcing such negative stereotyping of the immigrants.

In fact, North African leaders' sensitivity about the new immigrants' image in Israel rested on solid ground, as was soon shown. A few weeks after Cohen submitted his memo, in late April 1949, the *Haaretz* daily published an article about North Africans written by Arieh Gelblum, a rising star in Israeli journalism. Titled "The Yemenite Aliyah and the African Problem," the article was part of a 17-part series based on Gelblum's visits to immigrant camps and became a milestone in the history of Israel's ethnic problem.[33] In a preceding article, Gelblum had outlined a three-tiered social ranking of new immigrant groups. Occupying the top tier were Ladino-speakers from the Balkans. On the next tier were the Ashkenazim, most of them refugees and former inmates of concentration camps ("inferior goods," Gelblum called them). On the bottom were those who posed a real threat to the fledgling society—immigrants of the "Arab-African bloc."[34]

In this "bloc," as yet outside of Israel, Moroccans constituted the largest community (more than half of some 500,000 North African Jews). Having arrived in the state's early days in relatively large numbers (some 9,000 of about 100,000 immigrants in Israel's first year), they symbolized the transformation of Israeli society and drew most of the journalist's fire. Apart from the basic incompatibility of North African immigrants, as a group, with the Yishuv's accepted, desirable cultural criteria, Gelblum depicted them as destroying social norms and hence posing a serious threat to the public. The slew of stereotypes he listed included "idlers," "boors," "lawbreakers," and "knife-wielders."[35]

In the background to Gelblum's series was to be found a general goal—one of whose main promoters was Dr. Yoseftal, head of the Jewish Agency's aliyah department—to institute aliyah restriction by considering the quality of the olim and not just their number.[36] Moreover, an analysis of the anti-North African article indicates that Gelblum expressed a prevalent anxiety in the veteran Ashkenazic Yishuv concerning the possibility of changes in the demographic, cultural, and political character of the Zionist society in the wake of large-scale immigration of Jews from Muslim countries. It thus laid out concepts and ideas that stood no chance of ever receiving an official public imprimatur, but that nonetheless accurately reflected the world of impressions, images and prejudices, serious absorption problems, and most of all, societal apprehensions and fears that gripped the Zionist Yishuv. Consequently, it was not pushed aside and forgotten but rather aroused an outcry. The ensuing public controversy gave expression to the very real crisis stemming from the fear of demographic transformation: from immigration dominated by Ashkenazim to heterogeneity, and to the steadily increasing significance of Jews from Muslim countries, what Gelblum defined as the "Arab-African bloc." This was the first serious outburst of the ethnic problem in the state of Israel; significantly, it emanated from the Ashkenazic, not the Mizrahi, side of the evolving society.

Though Cohen's memo was composed under the gathering storm and largely forgotten while Gelblum's article sent sparks flying, there seems to have been an unconscious dialogue between the two documents. Himself not overly impressed by the collective profile of North African immigrants, Cohen was nevertheless able to appreciate the fact that misgivings about them did not derive solely from objective traits. In the months since his arrival and his initial Zionist fervor, he had learned a thing or two about prejudice toward Asian and North African immigrants. Personally, he had been received fairly well by the European majority, even if in opposition circles, but his group of origin was both under public attack and socially marginalized. Although, in the context of his attempt to return to the Jewish Agency, Cohen had no interest in voicing radical criticism, his memo did not duck the issue of discrimination, especially with regard to employment. Thus, he noted:

> In the concentrations of North Africans, most are unemployed. One dare not suppose that this is intentional, but even if it is due to mere chance, the distortion must be fully or partially rectified and as quickly as possible. "An empty belly has no ears," an old folk saying rightfully declares. This is true sevenfold and especially dangerous when it is not one hungry belly but many at one and the same time.

Cohen also took aim at the arrogance and hypocrisy of bureaucrats:

> The staff at the employment office does not always take into account how sensitive their job is. To tell someone looking for work, "I have nothing for you" or "come back in 4 or 5 days," is to sentence him to death by starvation.... That person's reaction becomes even more hostile when he sees—[and] unfortunately this happens too often—that behind him, the *very same slot* is given to someone else.[37]

Interestingly, Cohen's accusations of hypocrisy and job discrimination were corroborated by Gelblum, albeit with a different slant:

> When they started coming ... we began with our habitual, typical hypocrisy. On the one hand, we continued to insist on the principle of free and unrestricted immigration of North African Jewry; on the other—we did not, and do not, know what to do with them.... [O]n the one hand, Jewish and worker solidarity, and on the other, private and Histadrut job contractors know that the Moroccan worker is unproductive and unreliable....[38]

In sounding the alarm of those who warned against overly rapid shifts in the Ashkenazic-Mizrahi demographic balance, Gelblum's article gave voice to their serious reservations, even to the point of complete estrangement, concerning the North African immigrants.[39] In contrast, Cohen's memo emanates from the would-be leadership of the immigrants under attack that seeks to protect them via integration into Israeli society. The two authors, each from his own perspective, had to contend with the rhetoric of Jewish equality that followed Zionist ideology. Cohen, entering the arena first, sought the reinstatement of the values and ideals of equality; Gelblum suggested giving them up for the sake of securing the western, European character of Israeli society. But because the negative view of North African immigrants and the conflict between the integrating and estranging attitudes were already manifest, both authors had to contend with the blurring of existing inequality—a blurring that was the product of a hegemonic Zionist ideology that demanded unity.

The gulf between the two documents was also evident in the realm of the immigrant's identity and culture. Gelblum saw North African Jews as symbolizing all the evils of the "Arab-African" Jewish bloc, whereas Cohen does not mention an Arab, much less an African, identity. As far as he was concerned, North African immigrants belonged to the French cultural orbit, and all his proposed absorption reforms are stamped with a French seal. He suggested, for instance, that French-speaking officials meet the immigrants on arrival and that the directors and staff of immigrant camps include people able to communicate in French. Announcements via the camp public address system as well as printed matter should also be in French. To be sure, the immigrants should begin the process of adjustment to the Yishuv's Hebrew culture, but not necessarily by shedding their prior European culture. Thus, Hebrew should be taught by French-speaking teachers; lectures should be given in French; and French newspapers should be circulated. In short, French was to be the primary language in camps and settlements of North African immigrants. Whereas Cohen's memoirs note his proficiency in Moroccan Arabic as one of the qualifications that should have made the Jewish Agency "jump" at the opportunity to hire him,[40] his memo makes no mention of the Arabic dialects used by North African Jewry. Their connection with Arab environments was totally expunged.

Was Cohen's emphasis on French due to purely technical considerations, for instance, the existence of multiple Judeo-Arabic dialects (Moroccan, Algerian, Tunisian) as opposed to French, the colonial language in much of North Africa? It does not seem likely, since his own memoirs acknowledge that many of the immigrants were not fluent in French. Cohen's overemphasis on that language therefore warrants explanation. To some extent, it can be explained by the desire to obtain jobs for North African immigrants, an aim that would have been promoted by stressing the demand for French-speaking agents. Beyond this, however, there can be no doubt that the denial of the immigrants' Judeo-Arab identity derived from the fact that this identity label only further weakened their status in Israeli society. For his part, Gelblum took this likeness to Arabs to the extreme, denigrating the North African Jews as being, in the main, "only a cut above the general level of the Arab black and Berber inhabitants at home; in any case, this is even a lower level than we encountered in the Arabs of former Palestine."[41] Since Israel in early 1949 was at war against Arab states perceived as the ultimate enemy, it is understandable that Cohen, the would-be leader of North African immigrants, was quick to obscure the Arab element in their identity by going to the extreme of highlighting its French element. Doing so, moreover, required no change or innovation in his own personal identity evolution, since he, as with other westernized Moroccan Jews, had long since distanced himself from his original Judeo-Arabic cultural milieu. As previously described, this process had begun and been accelerated in Morocco's colonial society—it merely had to be adapted to new conditions. Cohen acted in accordance with his understanding of Israeli reality without betraying his own identity and cultural heritage, but rather by veiling the differences in this regard between himself and most of his fellow North African immigrants. This is one of the memo's pathetic aspects; no doubt his readers from establishment ranks remained unconvinced by his overemphasis on the immigrants' Frenchness. It could only have elicited their agreement with Gelblum's sarcastic assessment: "None of these immigrants would be happy to acknowledge that he is African. *Je suis français*!—they are all French, all from Paris and almost all were captains in the Maquis."[42]

Another issue emphasized by Cohen was educational opportunities for the immigrant children:

> In this sphere, too, we saw sorry scenes of children being prevented from registering in school for lack of space while other children were being admitted to the same institution.

There is no need to mention that the children represent the potential upon which the future of the nation rests. . . . The author of this memo spent 15 years teaching in various cities in Morocco, and he can confirm that the children of this country are a fertile seed that, if wisely managed, will flourish into wonderful fruit for the nation's future. In contrast, if they are abandoned, they will become, like children everywhere, a dangerous reservoir spawning all sorts of wrongdoers.[43]

Read between the lines, the memo reveals that Cohen and his colleagues sensed a design to discriminate educationally against North African youth, based on a stereotype that attributed to them inferior intellectual qualities. Soon thereafter, Gelblum confirmed their sense of the presence of such stereotypes:

We have before us a people of unparalleled primitiveness. Their level of education borders on utter ignorance and, graver still, intellectual inaptitude. . . . The special tragedy of this [group], in contrast with the worst human material from Europe, is that their children are also without hope. To raise their general level at the depths of their ethnic being will take generations.[44]

Given such prejudice, Cohen felt compelled to invoke his personal experience in Morocco's educational arena to issue a severe warning: discrimination in education, rather than the children's innate qualities, constituted the danger to Israeli society. His memo demanded that the existing situation be corrected by ensuring that the initial education given to North African immigrant children be adapted to their particular economic and cultural circumstances, by providing free schooling for immigrant children, and by hiring teachers proficient in French. Yet immediately following that, it was necessary to see to their being integrated fully into the general educational system: "If once a child who has already attended school in his country of origin has learned sufficient Hebrew, he should be admitted to a class commensurate with his educational level."[45] Aliyah was pointless if in Israel, even more than in Morocco, the process of social integration into the dominant sector was liable to be cut short. Here, too, Cohen's goal is integration. His emphasis is on the acquisition of Hebrew, with even French to be used in schools only as a temporary initial measure (he seems to have been eager to emulate the successful Alliance educational project, but this time in Hebrew).

Throughout the memo, Cohen draws on his French heritage. This is evident in his stress on values such as the sanctity of human and civil rights, the importance of representation, and the priority given to modern education. The French tradition was evident as well in the nature and formulation of his proposals, which reflected centralism, rationalism, and systemization. As a western tradition that itself served as a model for many modernist movements, including Zionism, the French heritage did not necessarily contradict the political tradition that Cohen found in Israel. But his memo adopted a different, somewhat unusual note that was particularly prominent in his proposal for the establishment of a voluntary organization of North African Jews. He addresses this in the memo's closing chapter, setting out an elaborate democratic and centralized organization patterned after the French Jacobin model, which would be linked to the formal immigrant absorption agencies and would serve as the representative body of North African immigrants.

The Association of North African Immigrants

After completing his memo, Cohen spent all of March trying unsuccessfully to
realize his plan. At the end of the month, he was summoned by the absorption
director for the Tel Aviv area, Dr. Haikes, who requested that, since Cohen was
drawing a salary without doing anything, he should at least help out with his knowledge of French. "Within three weeks," he wrote, "my name had made the rounds of
Turkish, Bulgarian, Iraqi, Syrian, Egyptian, English, and Indian immigrants, as a
result of which I inadvertently became a multilingual interpreter [for] Spanish, Arabic, English and sometimes even French. Only for Yiddish did the immigrants rely
on assistance from another quarter."[46]

At about the same time, Cohen was notified that his appointment as countrywide
director of North African immigrants had been downsized to the Tel Aviv area, and
that the senior position was to go to Ephraim Friedman.[47] Friedman, a member of
Ahdut Ha'avodah, had formerly been the chief Zionist emissary in North Africa.[48]
During his stint in Morocco, Friedman and Cohen had occasionally collaborated;
indeed, Cohen writes that when he arrived in Israel, the socialist Friedman had
promised to support his candidacy for department director. Now, however, following
Cohen's association with Herut, the two men found themselves on opposite sides
with regard to politics, ethnic affiliation, and in the contest for administrative appointments and power. As it happened, Friedman's appointment did not materialize.
According to Cohen, Friedman's kibbutz refused to authorize the move, and so the
job went to Dina Werth, another veteran of the Ashkenazic Yishuv. Cohen once
again felt slighted. Just as he was unqualified to head the section responsible for
Hungarian or Polish immigrants, he argued, so, too, neither Friedman nor Werth was
qualified to direct the absorption of North Africans.[49] At this point, frustrated at
every turn, Cohen began a new chapter in his political career as he turned his energies
to the formation of the immigrant organization he had proposed in his memo. Originally envisioned as part of the Jewish Agency framework, the organization was
now conceived as an independent body. Known as the Association of Immigrants
from North African and French-Speaking Countries (Histadrut 'Olei Zefon Afrikah
Vehaarazot Dovrot Hazarfatit), the new body began its work in June 1949, with
Cohen as its president. Contributing to its establishment was the public outcry in the
wake of Gelblum's article. As is evident from Cohen's writings on the subject,
members of the immigrant elite felt a sense of emergency and were determined "to
create a long-needed defense organization."[50]

In Cohen's view, the Association was to play a role in planning immigration,
absorption, and integration. Apart from reorganizing the patterns of reception, it
would advocate special camps for North Africans "to grant them suitable living
conditions and prevent the daily clashes and frictions in existing camps," and it
would serve as a watchdog against discrimination in housing, employment, and
education. In addition, it would organize Hebrew classes, clubs, and activities
marked by "the characteristic warmth and emotion of our social gatherings." One
innovative addition to Cohen's memo was the idea of an organizational newsletter
for "defense and information."[51]

The greatest innovation, however, referred to immigration. Cohen wanted to accord the organization an active role in directing the Zionist federations in North Africa regarding the extent and rate of immigration.[52] While he played this down in a newspaper article on the organization's goals, his report on the situation of North African immigrants presented at one of the first meetings of its central committee at the end of June 1949 concluded by recommending that "responsible organizations" of North African Jewry should consider halting aliyah from their end so long as this situation remained unchanged.[53] The report cited statements by Ben-Gurion and others to the effect that the aliyah from Muslim countries was absolutely vital on demographic grounds. Therefore, to curtail it by the olim themselves might be disturbing enough to force the authorities to act. "The deliberate, desired inertia of the authorities," Cohen wrote, "should be countered clearly: either they stopped the discrimination, in which case North African Jewry would continue to be Israel's population reservoir, or, if they did not stop, the responsible organizations of North African Jewry would have to rethink the issue of aliyah."[54] Meanwhile, until serious steps were taken, the flow of immigrants should be stemmed. In short, Cohen proposed going over the heads of the Jewish Agency and the government—an idea that could be interpreted as a call to revolt against the veteran Zionist and new Israeli establishment, and which was also prone to be viewed as the product of subversive influence of the Revisionist opposition.

Another of the report's anti-establishment aspects was Cohen's interpretation of the problems of North African immigrants in Israel. By this point, he had formed the opinion that a form of racism—not altogether unlike antisemitism—was involved:

What is happening in Israel vis-à-vis North Africans or, more precisely, against Francophones, who are referred to by what has become an ominous word, "Moroccans," is not unlike what is to be seen in a number of antisemitic countries. From the highest official to the lowliest gatekeeper, from the factory foreman to the simplest laborer, you will most likely [not] hear a bad word against North Africans, yet from the first moment, you are asked where you're from. Hanging in the balance is your employment, your life and the lives of your children, your future in Israel. You may mask your true character as a North African under the more complimentary French label, but you will not avoid the lurking disaster: "French" is equivalent to "Moroccan," and the label draws another in its wake: "knife." Thus, should you be walking on the street and speaking Voltaire's language, you are apt to hear around you, often [in a tone of] blatant fear, "Moroccan."[55]

Cohen rejected the claim that the lot of North African immigrants was essentially no different from that of other immigrants at the start of the process, and that Ashkenazic immigrants, too, Poles for example, suffered from discrimination on the part of their Russian predecessors. "The root of the opposition of Russians and Poles did not lodge in racial difference," he argued. "These two groups shared a number of factors that drew them together—language, cuisine, synagogue—and these were sufficient for them soon to resolve their problems and cause them to perceive one another as brothers [belonging] to the same people."

Generally racism accords prime significance to origin—not culture. Cohen, however, attempted to illustrate his claims by means of referring to neutral, non-hierarchical cultural features such as language and cuisine. He may have done so chiefly out of sensitivity for his fellow immigrants who, like him, knew that the misgivings about them rested on an assumed association between "Arab" or "African" origin and its ostensibly inferior culture—an assumption that was the central motif in Gelblum's article, which Cohen cited at length in his report. The colonial conception of European superiority prevailed within the Ashkenazic public but clashed with the unifying egalitarian national conception, which made it necessary to conceal one's reservations about the immigrants from Africa, just as the anti-semite committed to act in accordance with a liberal ethos is not permitted to vent his rejection of the Jews. But while this comparison was, in my view, apt, Cohen himself shared the conception of European superiority. Hence, neither here nor in other public documents did he give expression to the sensitive aspects of Moroccan aliyah—namely, the lowly social origins of most of these immigrants and their Judeo-Arabic culture. When the Association sought to introduce North African Jews to the Israeli public by means of a small pamphlet, it did indeed note that they spoke various dialects of Arabic. In deciding what to name the Association, however, its heads took care to identify the immigrants with French, not Arabic, culture.[56]

Europeans, the Westernized, the Maskilim, and the "Ashkenized"

In the summer of 1949, the Association of Immigrants from North African and French-Speaking Countries came into conflict with a rival North African immigrant body set up by Mapam and its representatives within the Jewish Agency's department for Middle Eastern Jewry. More broadly, this development was part of the ongoing political, ideological, and electoral struggle between Mapam and Mapai over the North African immigrants. Interestingly, this may partly explain why, according to documents of the period, Mapai was initially prepared to back the Association in its conflict with its Mapam-led opponent, and in fact some Mapai members served on its board alongside the "Herut-nik" Cohen.[57]

In contrast with Cohen's memo, which strove to advance his fellow westernized, Zionist-conscious, and French-speaking new immigrants, the Mapam-affiliated officials of the Jewish Agency who created the new organization, named Ahiezer, turned to an entirely different source: youthful members of a hitherto overlooked group, the Mughrabim—descendants of 19th-century immigrants from North Africa (the Maghreb) who had lived in the country for generations. These youngsters, who came from Arabic-speaking families but who had long been integrated into the hegemonic Ashkenazic workers' culture, were, in our terms, "Ashkenized." In a memo titled "Ahiezer Circle for North African Immigrants," they defined themselves as veteran members of the Yishuv society who had demonstrated their commitment to basic Zionist and labor values, and they went on to note the differences between themselves and their potential veteran rivals for leadership of the new aliyah both from within their own group and outside it.[58] Unlike the "inactive" ethnic community elders, the youngsters saw themselves as an avant-garde taking on a national task. And, unlike Ashkenazic officialdom, they were able to mediate between the new immigrants and the Yishuv veterans because of their origins and cultural traits. "All members of the group speak fluent Moroccan," they wrote. Judeo-Arabic—omitted from Cohen's memo because it was liable to be damaging to the westernized immigrant seeking to integrate into the Jewish European sector—was put back into the picture by this Ashkenized avant-garde, as it was the very cultural asset that could help them serve as a bridge between the European sector and the Moroccan immigrants from the Arab sector. At the same time, the Ashkenized, like the "Frenchified," insisted that their European transformation was complete. Arabic was of positive worth provided that it became a secondary instrument and not the fundamental defining element.

Once they had highlighted their credentials and announced their intention of participating in the battle over the North African immigrants' public image, members of Ahiezer turned directly to the immigrants. Discerning that the immigrants "had no voice," they undertook to organize them in the Jerusalem area and represent their interests. Following this, they arranged a meeting in August at Jerusalem's Semadar cinema, but the event was opposed by the Association and was disrupted by Cohen's followers.[59]

Since that meeting constituted the first major event in the battle over the leadership of North African immigrants, it is worth taking a look at the gallery of figures involved, who represented different cultures and ethnic identities. Naturally, members of the Yishuv's dominant European-born Ashkenazic leadership were present. From the elite's East European wing came Yaakov Zerubavel, the head of the Jewish Agency's department for Middle Eastern Jewry, who was the main speaker,[60] and Y. Weinstein, also from the Jewish Agency, but from Hapoel Hamizrachi, a religious Zionist party. From the elite's West European wing came the aforementioned Ephraim Friedman, who was born in Holland. These three individuals were entrenched at various levels of the party and Jewish Agency bureaucracies, whose backing made the meeting possible. Significantly, certain Ashkenazim—Mapai leaders whose influence far outweighed that of those in attendance—were conspicuously absent, but their opposition to Mapam's initiative probably made it easier for Cohen's group to break up the meeting. In any event, Cohen's memoirs mention only the abrupt end, not the meeting's "disruption" or the underlying party struggle within the workers' camp.[61] "Continuing its destructive work," he wrote, "the Jewish Agency, guided by Ephraim Friedman, tried to split the North African camp."[62]

Even so, at this stage the Ashkenazim thought it better to remain behind the scenes with regard to the leadership of the North African immigrants and to advance others to center stage: the Association members, in the case of Mapai, and the Ahiezer group, in the case of Mapam in Jerusalem. Although both were "North African" in identity, they were actually very different. The Association consisted of new immigrants who personified the varied cultural and identity paths traversed by Moroccan Jews in recent generations—some of them westernized, some maskilim, others who were the product of French westernization along with varying degrees of Hebrew or Judeo-Arabic modernization. In contrast, members of the Ahiezer group defined themselves as young sabras of Maghreb extraction. Broadly speaking, however, they had undergone a similar process of westernization by assimilating into the Ashkenazic Zionist sector of Yishuv society. This, however, was but one aspect of the complex history of the Mughrabi group in Palestine in recent generations.[63]

In the pre-Zionist Yishuv, the central element in the Mughrabi community was a veteran core of Moroccan immigrants who had arrived in the 19th century. Forming at first a traditional community characterized by both Arabic and Jewish cultural features, they were subsequently influenced (as was the case throughout the Middle East and North Africa) by the Alliance elementary school system. Thus, as in Morocco, a thin westernized stratum of Francophones was formed. Before long however, the Ashkenazic Zionist presence became dominant in the local Jewish arena, leading most of the westernized Mughrabim to adapt to that majority culture. This complex cultural profile was characteristic of the prominent public figures connected with the Mughrabi community when the state of Israel was proclaimed: Bekhor Shalom Shitrit, Avraham Elmaleh, and Avraham Harcarmeli (Lulu), all of whom were elected to the First Knesset, with Shitrit serving as a minister.[64] His-torically, the three were connected with the Mughrabi community, but within the identity structure that developed in the Zionist Yishuv, they were regarded as part of another social formation as well—"Sephardim"—that is, members of any of the long-established, non-Ashkenazic communities in Eretz Israel.

The Yishuv's Sephardic elite, headed by the descendants of the Ladino-speaking Ottoman Jewish leadership, had lost their hegemonic status in the Jewish Yishuv to the Ashkenazim, first to the haredim and then to the Zionists.[65] In an attempt to preserve their elite status, they formed a new political alliance with descendants of Arabic-speaking Jews from various communities, mainly the Mughrabim. Not in-cluded in this alliance were the leaders of the new Yemenite immigrants, but neither was it based solely on length of residence in the Yishuv. Rather, there was a basis of cultural affinity, since its members had undergone similar processes of moderniza-tion either in Alliance schools (or similar institutions) or under the impact of Ash-kenazic Zionism.

Not surprisingly, the hegemonic Ashkenazic Zionist parties frowned on this al-liance, branding its founders "separatists" and accusing them of being consumed by an inferiority complex. While certainly not separatists, they undoubtedly did suffer from a sense of discrimination and, in some cases, a sense of inferiority, since their contacts with Europeans often injured their self-esteem. In this respect, they re-sembled many of the westernized individuals who found themselves in a similar situation in various non-national societies.

Apparently none of this veteran non-Ashkenazic elite attended the August meeting; certainly nobody from their ranks addressed the audience. The Sephardic population boasted thin middle- and upper-class layers,[66] and neither were overly sympathetic to radical socialism or Mapam. The members of the latter, for their part, had their own reservations about this Sephardic bourgeoisie. Although westernized and even Ash-kenized, they were nevertheless suspected to some degree or another of "Levantin-ism," meaning that their Europeanization was only partial and incomplete. Only a handful who were close to the socialist camp had received endorsement (albeit limited) from Mapam's avant-garde. Thus, for example, Eliahu Hacarmeli, a Mapai func-tionary involved in the Histadrut's department for Mizrahi immigrants, was invited to attend the meeting, though he did not show up.[67] Mapam, as noted, looked more to members of the younger generation whom it had cultivated and whose class and ideological loyalty had passed the test. It found suitable candidates in Jerusalem (in the Ahiezer forum), and among members of Zeirei Zion (Zion Youth) in Tunisia and other westernized youth groups in French North Africa's large cities.[68]

Prosper Cohen did not fit the Tunisian Zeirei Zion's profile. He was older, nearing 40, and his political and cultural socialization reflected the interwar period, whereas members of the generation that had come of age during the Second World War were much more pro-socialist or pro-Communist in their outlook. Cohen's relatively advanced age was also reflected in his cultural profile. Prior to his aliyah, he had not seriously studied modern Hebrew. The young westernized Zionists, in contrast, had taken pains to learn the national language while still on North African soil and had arrived in the Yishuv prepared to integrate smoothly into the European Jewish sector's structures.

It is not known to what extent the cultural and social profile of his colleagues in the Association resembled that of Cohen. But we do know who succeeded him after his retirement. Two of its more prominent officials were Asher (Prosper) Hassin, later a Mapai representative in the Knesset, and Hanania Dahan. Both were younger than him (Hassin by some ten years and Dahan by seven), and neither had attained his social rank in Morocco.[69] Both were located on the seam between the Judeo-Arab and westernized sectors. They, of course, knew French, but unlike Cohen, they had also taken the path of modern Hebrew education. They were far less "French" than he. Cohen had been an Alliance teacher and attorney; Hassin and Dahan had been Hebrew teachers in Morocco and had arrived in Israel knowing the language. Culturally, they were part of the maskilim camp, not the westernized. Their preferred high modern culture looked to the original "native" cultures, Judeo-Arabic and Hebrew. In age and language, they were closer to the westernized youth who had been cultivated by Friedman and drawn into the orbit of the socialist camp. But unlike them, they had not undergone French modernization either in high school or beyond before adopting Hebrew.

Thus, the relocation from colonial territory to the Jewish national state entailed changes in the cultural-linguistic capital required for integration into the hegemonic order. Hebrew, not French, was now the prime linguistic resource, and in it was located the potential for overturning the leadership hierarchy that the immigrants brought from North Africa. Cohen's maskilic colleagues from Morocco emphasized their command of Hebrew, not French. The decline of French is also evident in the Ahiezer memo, whose author—virtually boasting of his lack of mastery in French—stresses his Eretz Israel cultural competencies and suggests Moroccan Arabic as a temporary but necessary language of communication with the immigrants. Indeed, for the bulk of their immigrant target audience, Moroccan Arabic was far more suitable than French. In 1949, Cohen did all he could to preserve the dominant status of French among the leadership of North African immigrants. Yet this was an anachronistic attempt. It was better suited to North African colonial society and to his own sector than to the Jewish national order or the Moroccan Arab sector of most of the immigrants.

From Sector to Class

The break-up of the Mapam-sponsored meeting in Jerusalem took place soon after Cohen's appointment at the Jewish Agency ended officially in August 1949 (effectively, his work had ceased several months earlier).[70] Following his second unsuccessful encounter with the establishment, Cohen took action to put his public activities on the right track: he now concentrated on the Association, which he sought to strengthen by means of ties with his former colleagues in the Moroccan Zionist Federation. Although such an approach had been adumbrated in the Association's founding principles, it had until then not been realized.

In our terms, Cohen now sought to strengthen the bond with his sector of origin. Immigration generally entails an initial sectorial disability, since the individual is cut off from his original cultural and economic network and considerable time is required before he becomes integrated into an alternative network. Cohen, who perceived his personal disabilities as reflecting a general problem of his compatriots, sought to rehabilitate his connection to his original sector, if only partially. Though he was not aware of it, his pattern of behavior was reminiscent of that of the haredi sector, in which the cultural and economic interdependence of diaspora communities within its social orbit is considerable. What applied to the haredi sector, however, did not apply to Zionist immigration, especially after statehood. In Morocco, the autonomous functioning of the local Zionist movement was weakening continually in favor of the direct involvement of departments of the Jewish Agency, representatives of the Israeli government, and emissaries from Israeli political parties and movements. The veteran cadre of activists was now engaged in defending its influence in the burgeoning Zionist activity, whose outcomes were dependent on the goodwill of the centers of power in Jerusalem and Tel Aviv, which in turn cooperated closely with Jewish power centers in Paris and New York.[71] Needless to say, it never occurred to the Federation leaders to worsen their defensive situation by being dragged into a confrontation with the centers of power in Israel, as would be the case if they supported an immigrant association headed by someone identified with the political opposition in Israel and the Zionist movement.

The varying interests of Cohen and the Association of Immigrants from North African and French-Speaking Countries, on the one hand, and the distant Moroccan Zionist Federation, on the other, soon became apparent. The latter sought to make the Association its Israeli collaborator, albeit without assisting it with funds raised in Morocco and without granting it a foothold in the inter-diaspora Zionist arena. The Association, for its part, was reluctant to give its colleagues in Morocco full and free access to the data it had gathered concerning the problems facing their compatriots in Israel, or to accept the right of the Federation alone to represent the olim in national forums abroad. The attitude of the Federation to the question of participation by Cohen and his colleagues in an upcoming Zionist conference, to be held in Paris in October 1949, turned out to be the test case for relations between the two organizations. Cohen and some other members of his board wanted to attend and asked for financial help from the Federation—which they did not get.[72]

Over and above the conflicting interests of the two organizations, the Federation members had serious misgivings about Cohen's leadership of the Association, and these became absolutely clear in October 1949. At the end of that month, prior to receiving a letter from his Moroccan colleagues demanding that he resign from the leadership of the North African community in Israel, Cohen quit of his own accord.[73] He does not mention his Moroccan friends' demand in his memoirs. Rather, he writes in general terms about the Association's financial straits and lack of assistance, and he attributes his resignation solely to Israeli pressures on him and on his colleagues. According to him, they were threatened with dismissal from their jobs (presumably in the Histadrut or in government offices) if he remained president.[74] Nevertheless, Cohen's personal archive does not permit one to downplay the significance in this affair of his relationships with his own social circle in Morocco. Indeed, it makes clear that Cohen regarded his image in the eyes of his Zionist colleagues in Morocco as of ultimate importance; when he realized that they had turned their backs on him, he gave up hope, retiring not only from the Association but from all public activity.[75] Neither did he go back to work for Herut, though he claimed that he could have. Instead he was unemployed and became destitute:

> The Via Dolorosa lasted seven months, seven long months. We, my wife, my daughter and myself, bore our cross with courage, with dignity. When our meager means gave out, we fell on poverty. It is easy to say this. But it was not at all pleasant. The days and hours of unemployment, the vain wandering in search of work, the belly that knew only bread and margarine, the lodging bare as only the room of a jobless pauper can be, the inability to meet the fees for the education of our daughter, who was under constant threat of expulsion—all this was what may be tersely called a life of hardship . . . seven months, as long as the Exile.[76]

At this point, the Cohen family had seemingly fallen near to the bottom of Israel's socioeconomic ladder. Following a process of upward mobility in Morocco, the crisis of immigration had brought the family down—almost to the level of the majority of large, poor Moroccan families now crowded together in appalling living conditions in Israel's new centers of poverty in Haifa, Jaffa, and Jerusalem. Once again, however, the differences between those coming from the various classes and sectors of Morocco were soon manifest. During the early period of his employment, Cohen's income enabled the family to rent a room or two in apartments in Tel Aviv and Holon, and thus avoid moving to a disadvantaged neighborhood. Later, during his second term at the Jewish Agency, Cohen's name was placed on a list of Zionist leaders from abroad who were entitled to housing after their aliyah. In 1949, he received a refurbished two-room apartment, with a small garden, in Tel Giborim (near Holon). In 1952, the family moved from there to Tel Aviv.[77]

If Cohen's privilege or status sufficed in obtaining the Tel Giborim home, his cultural capital was what prevented him from descending to poverty and what enabled him to locate himself relatively quickly within the middle class. After being unemployed for seven months, he found work at an elementary school near his home, where, of all things, he was expected to teach Hebrew.[78] But he rose to the task. While this fact may serve to illustrate his personal abilities and the extent of his progress in learning the language of his new country, it is above all indicative of the implications of his sectorial position. More than anything else, schools in fledgling Israel needed qualified persons with teaching experience in modern educational systems, whereas the degree of mastery of the national language was secondary. Acquiring the rudiments of a new modern language was neither an insurmountable hurdle for the westernized, nor did it require years. From this perspective, Cohen's talents, level of European modernization, and rich experience as a teacher and educator in the Alliance schools in Morocco far exceeded what was generally available in the teaching market of 1949. Little wonder, then, that the first school principal to hire him was quick to do so. Cohen did not remain a minor elementary school teacher for long, but soon moved into curriculum administration in a Tel Aviv vocational school. For this appointment, too, he writes proudly, a brief interview sufficed.[79]

No doubt Cohen regarded his return to teaching as a step backwards in his professional-social career. After all, he had already filled such positions in Morocco, and he had used them as a springboard toward law and public life. In Israel, he had already been hurt by public life, but his future professional plans did include a return to the practice of law. Already during his period of unemployment, he had begun to prepare for the Israeli bar exam, which he passed. He then began to work as a lawyer, but after a short time closed his office. According to his daughter, he did so because of economic difficulties, though she ascribes even greater importance to other causes. She writes in her memoir: "Father is not happy. He does not at all like this legal system which he regards as 'bastard,' for it is made up of Hebrew, Ottoman, British, and Israeli laws. It cannot be compared at all with the Cartesian spirit of French law!"[80]

Cohen's French cultural identity, which had so strong an impact on his public activities in his first year in Israel, thus continued to leave its mark on his life in later years. He returned to teaching, this time to the sphere in which he truly excelled— French. He became a French teacher in a Tel Aviv high school and held this position until his retirement in 1974. His wife, Laurette, also returned to her profession as a French teacher. The couple thus remained devoted in Israel to the high culture that they had brought with them and in which they had been brought up culturally and socially. This was manifest not only in their work but also in other activities, such as giving lectures at the French Cultural Institute as well as in their reading and leisure patterns, overseas studies, vacations, and so forth.[81] Cohen may have indeed withdrawn from public life, but his writing abilities, which found an outlet in newspaper articles in 1949, did not disappear, and neither did his love of writing in French. His spheres of interest were many, and he tried his hand at writing on many and varied topics. His personal archive (housed at the Ben-Zvi Institute) is of interest not only with regard to his short political career but also to his intellectual development and interests in Israel. His professional and socioeconomic trajectory in Israel was thus influenced profoundly not so much by material assets as by the cultural capital he had brought with him.

For comparative purposes, it is worth recalling the other figure mentioned at the beginning of this essay, Shmuel Ben-Harosh of Sefrou. As noted, Ben-Harosh was not a member of the westernized sector in Morocco but was rather a religious Jewish maskil of the native sector. Culturally and socially, he was thus closer than was

Cohen to the broad mass of olim. His own large family reflected this, having grown from nine to 11 in the state of Israel. So, too, the path he traversed in getting to Israel, and the trials and tribulations he encountered on the way, were characteristic of those of the vast majority of immigrants from North Africa. The Ben-Haroshes' journey to Israel included stealing the border to Algeria; enduring hunger and hardship prior to their transfer to Marseilles; attempted illegal immigration via a clandestine sea voyage; and capture and detention in Cyprus.[82] In Israel, they were briefly housed in an immigrant camp before being directed, in June 1948, to housing in the abandoned Arab neighborhood of Salameh (Kfar Shalem), south of Tel Aviv. Formerly a yeshiva teacher, Ben-Harosh found work first as an unskilled laborer and was then assigned to the military industry, where he was injured in an accident and thereafter restricted to light work. At this stage, however, his situation relative to other immigrant members of his sector began to improve. He sat for and passed ordination exams, and was appointed local rabbi of his community. According to the memoirs published by his son Eliyahu, his meager salary could not support his family, and so the Ben-Haroshes sought to increase their income by raising goats, setting up a poultry coop in their backyard, and attempting to trade in vegetables in Jaffa. However, within two years, Ben-Harosh went up another rung both in the rabbinical hierarchy and on the social ladder by passing further exams and being appointed a marriage registrar for the religious council of Tel Aviv-Jaffa.[83] Though it was modest, a public service salary signified the beginning of the Ben-Harosh family's entry into Israel's middle class. While the family continued to live in Kfar Shalem (which became a typical, economically depressed Mizrahi neighborhood), its head fulfilled a leadership role. He ran the local North African synagogue, participated in the political system of the religious Zionist movement, and wrote and published essays on rabbinical topics.[84] His eldest son, author of a book about the family, became a battalion commander in the IDF, helped train the army of Zaire, and in time served in the senior command of the Israeli police force.

The key to the family's quick exit from the crisis of immigration and the cycle of poverty was the connection that was formed between the rabbi and the religious Zionist party, Hapoel Hamizrachi.[85] Culturally, this connection was based on the common links of the Moroccan rabbi and Ashkenazic party functionaries to religious literature and the Hebrew language. The rabbi possessed Torah and Hebrew-maskilic cultural capital at a level that was rare among the immigrants. Without the religious similarities, this specific connection would not have been created, yet it was his mastery of the national language, above all, that advanced Ben-Harosh at this stage. Unlike his peers in the native sector who spoke Judeo-Arabic (and perhaps in addition some broken French), his Hebrew was fluent, and this enabled him to navigate his way within the Zionist sector. In Hapoel Hamizrachi, the rabbi filled the same role as the westernized in Morocco, that of a mediator and a connecting link between the local European sector and immigrants from the Arab sector who were likely to increase the religious party's electoral support.[86] Knowledge of the language and the connection with the Yishuv Zionist party guaranteed the Moroccan rabbi an entry point into the Zionist sector's social networks. Just as, in Morocco, such a mediating role gave the westernized a good starting point for upward social mobility, so in Zionist society it favored the Hebrew-speaking maskil and community leader. Of course, there were also notable differences between a maskilic "Arab Jew" in Morocco and one living in Israel. Ben-Harosh's original "native" high culture— Jewish religious culture—which had been considered inferior in the colonial territory, now enjoyed a higher status, at least in certain European Jewish circles. Another difference was the absence of rigid legal and judicial boundaries between Jews on opposite sides of the colonial fence. What is more, the demands (and sentiments) of the national ethos weakened the diffuse and unclear boundaries. Consequently, Moroccan immigrant maskilim, like the westernized, were ultimately able to move up the political, class, and social ladders and to integrate into the original "European" sector to an extent impossible in French Morocco. "Native" maskilim, like "Frenchified" immigrants of the westernized sector, quickly joined the middle class in their own national society.

It is instructive to consider the different starting points from which Cohen and Ben-Harosh advanced upwards into the Israeli middle class. Cohen's immigration and integration took place from the outset in spheres dominated by the European Jewish majority: the Jewish Agency; Herut; the educational system; the Israeli bar association; and Tel Aviv's Ashkenazic neighborhoods. His route continued a process of social development begun in Morocco, and he tied himself immediately to the European sector. His retirement from public activity on behalf of his North African group of origin signified as well the fact that he was cut off physically from the mass of immigrants who found themselves in the bottom layer of Israeli society and in impoverished neighborhoods that increasingly took on the character of "Mizrahi" enclaves. Ben-Harosh's social rise, in contrast, was accomplished entirely within such an enclave. The different social and geographic spheres within which they moved also indicated the continuation of their original divide, with Cohen remaining loyal to French culture and Ben-Harosh to Moroccan Jews' religious culture.

Ben-Harosh's Israeli biography reflects processes that developed in the new poverty enclave: the exit of European Jewish immigrants and the entry of various groups of Jews from Asia and North Africa who, over time, crystallized into a single Mizrahi "ethnic" unit.[87] For the immigrants from colonial sectorial societies in North Africa, the westernizing option in its French or Italian version had of course disappeared. But what was to replace it? Ashkenization? Or the development of a new version of Israeli culture that was characteristic of the Jews from Muslim countries in the poorer strata? What weight did the old Judeo-Arabic culture carry in these enclaves? Can one speak of the formation of a new sector, a cultural-economic system with quasi-autonomous boundaries, or of a lower class that was integrated into the majority economic system but had its own distinctive cultural characteristics?

The Arabic cultural origin of North African immigrants, their negative labeling as "Arab Jews," and the explicit misgivings about them in Israel's early years begs a comparison with Israel's Arab population. In this regard, it is important first to note that Israel's early statehood was marked by realignment in the sectorial structure inherited from the Ottoman and Mandatory eras. The 1948 war put an end to the Palestinian national sector's existence as a self-sustaining economic entity. The question faced by Arabs remaining in the Jewish state and by Israeli leaders was how to integrate the Arab national minority into the Zionist sector's economic system. The government's policy of cultural unification, the "melting pot," was not applied equally to Jews and Arabs, and consequently the latter's economic mobility was limited. This situation was exacerbated by the institution of a military government for the Arab population (in place until 1966), which variously restricted physical mobility. Despite the declared equality between members of different religious groups, the various policy practices actually preserved the outlines of the national sectorial structure of the Mandate period. Within the Jewish community as well, the "melting pot" policy was not applied equally to haredim and Zionists. Here, too, policy practices developed that preserved the former sectorial outlines.[88] In both cases, the maintenance of sectorial lines was not solely the work of governmental bodies; rather, to one degree or another, those within the sectors themselves sought to preserve the national, religious, cultural-ideological, or social boundaries between them and the majority.[89] Nevertheless, economically, the situation of haredim and Arabs differed. By and large, the haredim managed to retain the infrastructure of their traditional *ḥalukah* (allotment) economy, which ensured their religious elite's control over the public, and rested to a large degree on the links between them and the diaspora haredi communities. In contrast, the transition from the Mandatory regime to a Jewish national state severed the links between Israel's Arabs and other Arab populations, turning the former into a minority unable to sustain an autonomous economic system. Against this background, from the early years of statehood, most Arabs entered the lower ranks of the economy, which was controlled by Jews. The economic boundaries between the national sectors had never been perfectly sealed, but now the breaches in them widened greatly, albeit without blurring the cultural boundaries. The Arab minority's sectorial autonomy weakened considerably, but both the Zionist establishment's interests and the minority's own inclinations militated against further lowering of the barriers between them. Thus, Israeli Arabs underwent a perceptible process of transition from sector to class—in particular, the lower class—but without closing the door on the rehabilitation of their autonomous sectorial status should conditions change.

Unlike the Arabs, who were interested in protecting their special sectorial status on both cultural and national grounds, the North African immigrants arrived in Israel without any ideology that accorded significant value to the Arab aspect of their profile, but rather with one that sanctified its Jewish aspect. Although it was an integral, vital, and intimate part of their culture, their Arabism was not consciously esteemed, cultivated, or admired. In their Judeo-Arabic culture, which rested entirely on their Arabic dialect, it was Judaism in various forms—popular or conservative religion, maskilic, Zionist—that was at the heart of their identity and identification. This "balance" between their Arab and Jewish foundations did not necessarily hold for other Judeo-Arabic communities, even those in North Africa, and neither was it static. But at this historical stage and for these immigrants to Israel from that region, this was the picture. As for the Israeli establishment, the "melting pot" policy of unification was not merely a declared ideological vision and ideal, it was also essential for the harmonious running of the national economy.[90] Linguistic and cultural uniformity was therefore the imperative of the time, and if the perpetuation of cultural diversity could be tolerated in the case of the older Arab and haredi sectors, this was not so when it came to the new immigrants. All the languages brought by the immigrants from their various countries of origin were rejected.[91] Judeo-Arabic was especially disvalued because it was identified both with the non-European side of the world and with the enemies of the nation. Neither the immigrants from the Arab sector in North Africa nor the state authorities left any leeway for maintaining and developing the linguistic boundaries between the new olim and the veteran Yishuv.

The intellectual and cultural level of North African immigrants was quite another matter, however. Already in 1949, Cohen and his colleagues blamed discriminatory policy for what they saw as inordinate neglect in the modern Hebrew education of North African immigrant children. Since most of the immigrants from the Arab sector arrived in any event with no, or only a low, level of modern education, a deficient Hebrew education was destined to perpetuate the economic mobility gaps and consign those immigrants and their offspring to the bottom rungs of Israeli society. Despite the national and cultural differences between these Jewish immigrants and Israel's Arabs, the same transition from sector to social proletariat was liable to occur. The founders of the Association of Immigrants from North African and French-Speaking Countries did not note this likeness, perhaps because they were unaware of it. But they did warn that discrimination in education would place the immigrants in an inferior class situation, with disastrous social consequences. They, the maskilim and the westernized Moroccans, had learned from experience that the roots of social advancement lay in the cultural capital acquired through modern education, which facilitated access to the dominant networks of the local society. Only a clear policy of cultural change in the spirit of the West, such as that offered by the Alliance to Moroccan Jews, could put this population on the path of upward social and economic mobility. Cohen was the first to raise the issue and to attempt to provide leadership committed to this policy. But he was not the first leader to think in these terms; the heads of the Yishuv's Sephardic community had preceded him.[92]

One future development that was not foreseen by the North African immigrants' leadership was the joining up of some of their followers with the minority Jewish sector—the Ashkenazic haredim. As noted, for most immigrants of the Judeo-Arab sector, religion remained at the core of their identity. Thus they viewed their aliyah and the status of the land of Israel in religious, not necessarily modern nationalist, terms. Even when they had been exposed to secular European conceptual and behavior patterns in Moroccan, Algerian, and Tunisian urban centers, such patterns were largely alien to them. Secular nationalism still had a long way to go before it could capture the minds of most North African immigrants, and so long as this had not occurred, the way was open for other Jewish movements. In Morocco, for instance, several haredi networks had by then penetrated large Jewish population centers, and one of them, Chabad, later branched out from there to southern villages and the Atlas Mountains.[93] There is no evidence of vigorous activity by the haredi sector in Israel among Moroccan immigrants in 1948–1949. However, from the end of 1949, haredi emissaries were active among the Yemenite immigrants—all from Yemen's sole Arabic sector, whose wholly traditional-agrarian character beckoned instantly to religious and haredi camps within the veteran Ashkenazic public.[94]

At about the same time, the option of joining up with the haredi camp made its first appearance among North African immigrants. One example is to be found in the person of David Sabah, the former president of the religious court in Rabat.[95] Though he was close to the Sephardic chief rabbi, Ben-Zion Uziel, Sabah leaned toward the haredi camp and even joined in its petitions.[96] While Prosper Cohen appealed unsuccessfully to North African synagogue worshippers in Jerusalem for financial assistance for his organization,[97] Sabah was held in the highest esteem, as evidenced by his inclusion in a list of holy persons and rabbis revered by North African immigrants in Israel.[98]

The target audience of Cohen's leadership, the North African immigrants, was not endowed with his western cultural capital, and their sectorial origins made them prime candidates, alongside Israel's Arabs, for direction to the bottom rungs of the evolving society and/or for joining up with its haredi sector. After Cohen failed in the public sphere and lost the support of his Zionist and westernized Moroccan associates, he could nevertheless pursue his personal social advancement in the Jewish state. This was not true of the average Moroccan immigrant from the Arab sector or from the Arab-westernized "seam." No other public figure of Cohen's social and cultural standing rose to lead Moroccan Jewry in Israel, and he soon faded from public memory. The first Moroccan hero to become etched in national memory was David Ben-Harosh, the hero of the second ethnic outburst in Israel (this time from the Mizrahi side), the Wadi Salib riots of 1959. Like Shmuel Ben-Harosh, he had arrived in Israel in 1948 after first being detained in Cyprus.[99] Yet he did not come as either a senior or minor representative of a Moroccan Jewish elite. Rather, he was one of the youngsters of the lower strata, just embarking on westernization, who had been swept up by Zionism. In Israel, his path to the middle class was blocked, and he became the voice of the poor and the frustrated from his own former sector and new social class. Thus, he, and not Prosper Cohen, was inscribed in memory both as the first hero of the North African immigrant social struggle and as the instigator of "the Mizrahi discourse."[100]

The time frame of this article covers the first year and a half of the developing Moroccan immigration wave, which overlapped the period of mass immigration to the state of Israel (1948–1951) and brought in a total of about 33,000 Moroccans. Westernized and maskilic immigrants represented only a tiny fraction of this total, but in the succeeding waves—consisting of some 70,000 people (1954–1956) and 100,000 people (1961–1964)—their proportion increased. In investigating the influence of Asian and North African Jews' identity on their absorption in Israel, two schools of thought have predominated: functionalism and critical sociology. During Israel's first years of statehood, the functionalist school held sway, arguing that the decisive stratification factor was the immigrants' cultural capital. That is, those who arrived suitably equipped to integrate into the modern Zionist economy found appropriate places without encountering discrimination. Arguing against this notion, Shlomo Swirsky, a pioneer of Israeli critical sociology, claimed that the functionalists essentially compared Israeli society to a bookcase that was passively waiting for immigrants to fill its shelves, which were ordered according to their cultural level. This was not so, according to Swirsky. Instead, he argued, the powerful in society placed the weak where they wanted them; thus the Ashkenazim placed Asian and North African immigrants (or *Mizrahim*, in his terminology) on the bottom shelves, thus actively depriving them and benefiting from the cheap labor they provided.[101]

There are substantial grains of truth in both the functionalist and critical perspectives. Conceptions deriving from the colonial heritage did influence public opinion and thinking and did encourage the channeling of Asian and North African immigrants to less choice niches and areas in the emergent society. Yet the importance of capital, particularly cultural capital, as a factor that molded their fate cannot be dismissed. Not all immigrants from Asia or North Africa lent themselves to manipulation: even if placed "on the bottom shelf," the westernized and maskilim of various types were often able to quickly find a way up. Furthermore, if they had their fill of the treatment they received in Israel, they were able to emigrate from the Jewish state. The absence of rigid legal discriminatory barriers, resulting from the dominance of the national principle and order, made it easier for those suffering from a "stigmatizing label"[102] to advance themselves. Suitable cultural capital had the potential to facilitate the entry of the Jewish immigrant from Asia/North Africa into the middle class and even quite rapidly into leadership positions in Israel, as is evident from Cohen's early days in the country.

Cohen's failure as the first contender for the leadership of North African Jewry was the result primarily of political mistakes on his part—if initially he had joined forces with Mapai rather than Herut, or if he had simply stuck to his choice of the opposition party, he might have made it all the way to a Knesset seat. He certainly did not lack the qualifications, although perhaps his personality may have been wanting. In any event, his path into Israel's middle class was paved. As noted, there were not many like Cohen in the first wave of Moroccan immigration, although among Iraqi immigrants, for example, who arrived in 1950–1951, there were more, including many maskilim in the realm of modern Arabic culture (a type of Jewish maskil that was extremely rare in Morocco). Thus, sticking to stereotypical, overgeneralized conceptions such as the "Arab/African bloc," or, in contrast, the "Mizrahim," distorts the complex and varied character of the immigrants from Muslim countries, and hinders investigation of their histories and paths in the development of Israeli society's class system.

Notes

This article was translated by Evelyn Abel.

1. Prosper Cohen, *La grande aventure: fragments autobiographiques* (Jerusalem: 1993), 59.

2. Eliyahu Ben-Harosh, *Shorashim: toledot mishpahat Ben-Harosh* (n.p.: 1987), 76, 147. Em Habanim was a small school system established in the region of Fez to counter the influence of the secular education provided by the Alliance Israélite Universelle. For its more talented pupils, a higher class was created and this, apparently, was the yeshiva headed by Ben-Harosh.

3. Ibid., 176.

4. On the trends in sociology, see Uri Ram, *The Changing Agenda of Israeli Sociology: Theory, Ideology and Identity* (Albany: 1995); on the development of research into Israel's ethnic problem as a whole and Israeli historiography in particular, see Yaron Tsur, "Hahistoriografyah hayisreelit vehabe'ayah ha'adatit," *Pe'amim* 94 (2003), 1–4, esp. the bibliography;

an English version appears in a collection edited by Benny Morris, *Making Israel: The Historiographic Controversies in Israel* (Ann Arbor: forthcoming).

5. Morocco's indigenous cultures included that of the Berbers, but since it lacked a written language and a center of internal modernization such as the Arabs had in the Middle East, it was not part of this process at this historical stage. Most of Morocco's Jews lived in Arabic-speaking areas, though there were also many communities in Berber neighborhoods.

6. For an extensive discussion of the sectors in Morocco's Jewish society, see Yaron Tsur, *Kehilah kru'ah: yehudei maroko vehaleumiyut 1943–1954* (Tel Aviv: 2001).

7. Ibid., 24–25, 146–148; for a more general discussion of the Alliance, see Michael M. Laskier, *The Alliance Israélite Universelle and the Jewish Communities of Morocco 1862–1962* (Albany: 1983).

8. Prosper Cohen, memoirs (photocopy deposited in the Jews of Islamic Countries Archiving Project, Tel Aviv University), 60.

9. Tsur, *Kehila kru'ah*, 253–260.

10. Yaron Tsur, "Carnival Fears—Moroccan Immigrants and the Ethnic Problem in the Young State of Israel," *The Journal of Israeli History* 18, no. 1 (1997), 73–103; idem, *Kehilah kru'ah*, 253–272. To date, little research has been done on the Yishuv's non-European Jewish population, which accounted for some 20 per cent of the Jewish population at the end of the British Mandate. For an instructive brief treatment, see Yoav Gelber, "Hitgabshut hayishuv hayehudi beerez yisrael, 1936–1947," in *Toledot hayishuv hayehudi beerez yisrael meaz ha'aliyah harishonah*, vol. 2, part 2, *tekufat hamandat habritit*, ed. Moshe Lissak, Anita Shapira, and Gabriel Cohen (Jerusalem: 1995), 343–347.

11. On the development of the colonial thinking of the founder of the Moroccan regime, General Hubert Lyautey, see Daniel Rivet, *Lyautey et l'institution du protectorat français au Maroc 1912–1925*, 3 vols. (Paris: 1996).

12. There is a good deal of research literature on this topic. See especially Nitza Druyan, *Beain marvad kesamim: hahityashvut hateimanit beerez yisrael, tarma"v-tara"d* (Jerusalem: 1981); Gershon Shafir, *Land, Labor and the Origins of the Israeli-Palestinian Conflict 1882–1914* (Cambridge: 1989), 91–122.

13. The veteran Sephardic community is discussed later in this essay; see p. 84.

14. See, for instance, their status in the experts' plan for mass immigration (*tokhnit hamilyon*), prepared at David Ben-Gurion's demand during the Second World War, as discussed in Esther Meir-Glitzenstein, "From Eastern Europe to the Middle East: The Reversal in Zionist Policy vis-à-vis the Jews of Islamic Countries," *The Journal of Israeli History: Politics, Society, Culture* 20–21 (2001), 24–48.

15. The story of Cohen's life rests considerably on his memoirs, which were written in the 1970s (see n. 8). Nevertheless, the part relating to 1948–1949 in the memoirs is based almost completely on documents he wrote during the events themselves, in the summer of 1949. I have also relied on other documents and correspondence from this period, which remained in Cohen's personal archive and which were eventually deposited at the Ben-Zvi Institute in Jerusalem. Apart from certain cuts, the memoirs were published by his daughter, Matilde Tagger, after his death as *La grande aventure*. I would like to thank Ms. Tagger for kindly allowing me to peruse the original manuscript and for placing at my disposal two short biographical texts written by her ("Papa"; "La famille en Israël").

16. Cohen, *La grande aventure*, 56–58; the correspondence in full is cited in Cohen, memoirs (manuscript), 70–71.

17. Cohen, *La grande aventure*, 59.

18. Ibid., 60.

19. Ibid.; also see the memoirs (pp. 77–81), where this episode is given more prominence.

20. Cohen, *La grande aventure*, 49–50, 60.

21. Ibid., 62–64.

22. Ibid., 61; on the League, see the pamphlet authored by Y. Halperin, *Yeziat mizrayim mearzot 'arav* (Tel Aviv: 1949); see also the report on the League's activities up to June 1, 1949 (Jabotinsky Institute Archive, 8/2–15 and the League Bulletins there, 8/6–15).

23. Cohen, memoirs, 83.

24. P[rosper] Cohen, "Aux Nord-Africains," *Liberté* (9 Dec. 1948).

25. "Maẓavam shel ha'olim haḥadashim miẓfon afrikah," 22 Dec. 1948, Jabotinsky Institute Archive, 8/5–15.

26. See, for instance, the protocol of a League meeting, 10–12 Dec. 1948, pars. 11–12, where, following an account of means that should be taken to rescue North African Jews, there is a demand for immediate improvement in the situation of those who have already arrived in Israel (ibid., 8/9–15).

27. H.S., "Ta'amulat zeva'ah shel haḤerut," *Davar* (5 Jan. 1949). I was unable to locate Cohen's original article in *Liberté*, but the accusations in *Davar* may have been based on a misunderstanding of Cohen's rhetoric. The Nazi concentration camps Buchenwald and Majdanek had been cited in par. 12 of the League's decisions of December 1948 (see preceding note), which also dealt with the immigrants' situation in Israel. The language used in this paragraph warned against such camps being created in "the neighborhood of free Israel"—a reference to the *Arab* countries, not Israel. Reflecting Cohen's strategy to combine the external menace with the internal one, the paragraph resorted to the same rhetoric when it warned against creating slums in Israel. It may be that the League's decisions were translated and published, and that this was the source of a misunderstanding. On the "Shoahization" of public discourse surrounding North African immigrants, see Yaron Tsur, "Mekoman shel kehilot ẓefon afrikah bapezurah hayehudit leaḥar hashoah," in *Hashoah bahistoriyah hayehudit: historiografyah, toda'ah ufarshanut*, ed. Dan Michman (Jerusalem: 2005), 275–291.

28. A copy of the response to the *Davar* article, "Non, ce n'est pas de la propogande" (undated), is found at the Ben-Zvi Institute, Archive of Prosper Cohen, Container 2, File titled "Mes premières tribulations en Israël."

29. Cohen, *La grande aventure*, 86.

30. "Le double problème de l'immigration des Juifs nord-africains et de leur absorption dans le pays," Ben-Zvi Institute, J.R. Ben-Azzeraf archive, file 5. The document is dated 1 Mar. 1949.

31. Ibid.

32. See the translation in archive of Prosper Cohen, "Mes premières tribulations en Israël."

33. Arieh Gelblum, "'Aliyat teiman uve'ayat afrikah," *Haaretz* (22 April 1949). For a detailed analysis of this document, see Tsur, "Carnival Fears."

34. Arieh Gelblum, "Haemet 'al haḥomer haenoshi" *Haaretz* (21 April 1949).

35. Gelblum, "'Aliyat teiman uve'ayat afrikah."

36. Ibid.; for a detailed discussion of the trends within the Israeli leadership with respect to aliyah in general, see Devora Hacohen, *'Olim bese'arah: ha'aliyah hagedolah uklitatah beyisrael, 1948–1953* (Jerusalem: 1994), 105–115. On the Moroccan immigration, see Tsur, *Kehilah kru'ah*, 262–272, 281–301.

37. Cohen, "Le double problème de l'immigration des Juifs nord-africains."

38. Gelblum, "'Aliyat teiman uve'ayat afrikah."

39. From this period on, two basic orientations were discernible among state leaders: some believed it both vitally important and possible to quickly integrate a mass immigration of Jews from Asia and Africa, whereas others had reservations. See Tsur, "Carnival Fears"; idem, *Kehilah kru'ah.*

40. Cohen, *La grande aventure*, 57.

41. Gelblum, 'Aliyat teiman uve'ayat afrikah."

42. Ibid.

43. Cohen, "Le double problème de l'immigration des juifs nord-africains."

44. Gelblum, 'Aliyat teiman uve'ayat afrikah."

45. Cohen, "Le double problème de l'immigration des juifs nord-africains."

46. Cohen, *La grande aventure*, 65.

47. Prosper Cohen, "Le problème nord-africaine en Israël," in archive of Prosper Cohen, "Mes premières tribulations en Israël," 13.

48. On Friedman's work in North Africa, see Ephraim [Friedman] Ben-Haim, "Haha'apalah miẓfon afrikah: shalosh haoniyot, 1947," in *Shorashim bamizraḥ: kevaẓim leḥeker hatenu'ah haẓiyonit vehaḥaluẓit bearẓot haislam*, vol. 1, ed. Y. Avrahami (Ramat Efal: 1986), 241–320; idem, "Mivẓa' 'Zebu'—Algeria 1947–1948," ibid., vol. 3 (Ramat Efal: 1991), 213–231; Tsur, *Kehilah kru'ah*, passim (see index).

49. Cohen, "Le problème nord-africaine en Israël," 14; idem, *La grande aventure*, 68–69. In fact, Werth was appointed to the department dealing with all immigrants from all the lands of Islam, not only North Africa, and she worked there briefly before being inducted to the IDF's women's corps, where she went on to become the chief officer (1959–1964). She had studied medicine in France and been an envoy to North Africa on the eve of Israeli statehood. Cohen situates her in Mapam, but she was in fact affiliated with Mapai (interview with Ephraim [Friedman] Ben-Haim, 25 Feb. 2006). Friedman, as will be seen, was later appointed to a senior position in the Jewish Agency's department for Middle Eastern Jews.

50. "Nous avons gagné la première manche" (undated article with no reference to newspaper of publication), archive of Prosper Cohen, "Mes premières tribulations en Israël"; see also "La seule défense des nord-africains" (a copy of a [typewritten] article, one of a series published in *Journal de Jérusalem*, apparently a French-language party organ), ibid.

51. Ibid.

52. Ibid.

53. Cohen, "Le problème nord-africaine en Israël," 15.

54. In drafting the report, apparently for his mission to the Zionist Federation in Morocco, Cohen erased the words "deliberate" and "desired."

55. Ibid.

56. *Ha'aliyah haẓefon afrikait beyisrael*, issued by Histadrut 'olei zefon afrikah Vehaarazot Dovrot Hazarfatit, archive of Prosper Cohen, "Mes premières tribulations en Israël."

57. Yaakov Zerubavel to Berl Locker, 4 Oct. 1949, Central Zionist Archives (CZA), S20/555-I.

58. "Ḥug Aḥiezer le'olei ẓefon afrikah," in file titled "Hitaḥdut 'olei ẓefon afrikah 11/1948–6/1950," CZA S20/620.

59. Ibid.; Y. Belais, "Asefat 'olei ẓefon afrikah birushalayim," *Hed hamizraḥ* (2 Sept. 1949).

60. Yaakov Zerubavel (1886–1967), Ukrainian-born, was one of the fathers of socialist Zionism, a founder of the Poalei Zion-Left faction.

61. Cohen, *La grande aventure*, 69–70. The article in *Hed hamizraḥ* on the Assembly remained among his papers of this period, and it is quite clear that he used it when speaking of the affair.

62. There is of course no reason to identify the Jewish Agency as a whole with Friedman. However, Cohen was not mistaken in assigning Friedman a major role in this affair. In 1949 he joined the staff of Zerubavel's department in the Jewish Agency as Mapam's expert to the North African communities (interview with Ephraim [Friedman] Ben-Haim, 25 Feb. 2006), and he certainly was among the main organizers of the Ahiezer meeting. Apart from being one of the speakers at the meeting, Friedman had arranged for Nadia Cohen—a prominent representative of the young, westernized socialist group from Tunis that he had cultivated, who had since become a kibbutz member—to be invited as well. See Zerubavel to Locker, 4 Oct. 1949.

63. On the development of the Mughrabi community at the end of the Ottoman period, see Michal Ben Yaakov, "'Aliyatam vehityashvutam shel hayehudim hama'araviyim (yehudei ẓefon akrikah) beereẓ yisrael bameah hatesh'a 'esrei" (Ph.D. thesis, The Hebrew University, 2001). According to the census of 1916, the Mughrabi community in Jerusalem numbered 1,029, or 3.9 percent of the Jewish population; comparable figures for the census of 1939 are 2,499, or 3.1 percent of the Jewish population of Jerusalem. See Avraham Hayim, *Yiḥud vehishtalvut: hanhagat hasefaradim birushalayim bitkufat hashilton habriti (1917–1948)* (Jerusalem: 2000), 32.

64. For brief biographical details on Shitrit, see *Encyclopaedia Judaica,* 14:1417; on Elmaleh, see ibid., 6:681–682 and, in greater detail, the article by Isaac R. Molkho, "Le veteran Abraham Elmaleh," in *Minḥah leAvraham: sefer hayovel likhvod Avraham Almaliah* (Jerusalem: 1959), 49–55 (non-Hebrew entries); on Hacarmeli, see his book *'Ad 'alot ha-shaḥar,* ed. Yisrael Yishayahu and Yonah Cohen (Jerusalem: 1978), vii–xix. On their work during the Mandate period, see Hayim, *Yiḥud vehishtalvut* and Yitzhak Levy, "Hape'ilut hapolitit vehairgun shel hakehilah hasefaradit bayishuv uvimdinat yisrael 1945–1955" (Ph.D. diss., The Hebrew University, 1998).

65. On the Sephardim, see Penina Morag-Talmon, "Hishtalvutah shel 'edah vatikah be-ḥevrat mehagrim: ha'edah hasefaradit beyisrael" (Ph.D. diss., The Hebrew University, 1980); Rachel Sharabi, *Hayishuv hasefaradi birushalayim beshilhei hatekufah ha'otomanit* (Tel Aviv: 1989); Hayim, *Yiḥud vehishtalvut;* Yitzhak Levy, "Defusei pe'ilut ẓiborit ufolitit shel ha'elitah hasefaradit beereẓ yisrael 1895–1931" (Master's thesis, The Hebrew University, 1987); idem, "Hape'ilut hapolitit vehairgun shel hakehilah hasefaradit bayishuv uvimdinat yisrael."

66. Hayim, *Yiḥud vehishtalvut,* 35–36; see also the list of Sephardic organization heads (ibid., 343–358); Moshe Lissak, *Ha'elitot shel hayishuv hayehudi beereẓ yisrael bitkufat hamandat* (Tel Aviv: 1981), 108–112; Levy, "Defusei pe'ilut ẓiborit ufolitit shel ha'elitah hasefaradit beereẓ yisrael."

67. Zerubavel to Locker, 4 Oct. 1949.

68. On the development of these Zionist circles in North Africa, see Chana Avrahami, "Reshitah shel tenu'at hano'ar haḥaluẓit biẓfon afrikah (1943–1948)," *Shorashim bamizraḥ—kevaẓim leḥeker hatenu'ah haẓiyonit vehaḥaluẓit bearẓot haislam* 1 (1986), 191–240; Hayim Sa'adon, "Haẓiyonut betunisiyah" (Ph.D. diss., The Hebrew University, 1992), 178–183; Tsur, *Kehilah kru'ah,* 241–243, 247, 252, 273–281.

69. See the personal details supplied by the Association to the Jewish Agency aliyah department in August 1950, A. Hassin to B. Duvdevani, 2 Aug. 1950, CZA S6/6245.

70. Cohen, *La grande aventure,* 92.

71. Tsur, *Kehilah kru'ah,* 104–109, 112–113, 133–137, 142–144, 272–282.

72. See the correspondence on the topic at the Ben-Zvi Institute, Prosper Cohen archive, container 1, file "Hitaḥdut 'Olei Ẓefon Afrikah" and "Mes premières tribulations en Israël."

73. Paul Calamaro (president) and others to Cohen, 25 Oct. 1949, ibid. ("Mes premières tribulations en Israël").

74. Cohen, *La grande aventure,* 70.

75. The work of his successor at the Association in the early 1950s is described in brief in Tsur, *Kehilah kru'ah,* 30, 305–306.

76. Cohen, *La grande aventure,* 71, although I chose to translate from the original, which is somewhat different; see Cohen, memoirs, 96.

77. Tagger, "La famille en Israël."

78. Cohen, *La grande aventure,* 72.

79. Ibid.

80. Tagger, "La famille en Israël."

81. Ibid.

82. Ben-Harosh, *Shorashim,* 141–144; Tsur, *Kehilah kru'ah,* 244, 249–250, 260.

83. Ben-Harosh, *Shorashim,* 181–182.

84. Ibid., 187. The family lived in its original home in Kfar Shalem for 22 years, at which time the parents moved into a nearby apartment building (ibid., 77).

85. Ibid., 77–79, 180.

86. For a broad discussion of the political factor in the ethnic arena, see Hanna Herzog, *'Adatiyut politit: dimui mul meẓiut, nituaḥ soẓiologi-histori shel hareshimot ha'"adatiyot" leasefat hanivḥarim velakneset (1920–1984)* (Tel Aviv: 1986).

87. Something similar happened in the synagogue Ben-Harosh headed, which over the years became less "Moroccan" and more generally "Mizrahi" in its composition and customs. See Ben-Harosh, *Shorashim,* 180, 183; on Kfar Shalem as a pocket of poverty in the 1970s, see Reuven Ogen, "Shekhunat 'oni betel aviv," in *Yisrael: antropologyah mekomit,*

ed. Orit Abuhav, Esther Herzog, Harvey Goldberg, and Emanuel Marcus (Tel Aviv: 1998), 109–139.

88. There is quite extensive literature on the Arab sector and the policy toward it in the first decade; see, for instance, Ian Lustick, *Arabs in the Jewish State: Israel's Control of a National Minority* (Austin: 1980); Dina Greitzer, "Ben-Gurion, Mapai ve'arviyei yisrael," in *Ha'asor harishon: tasha"h-tashya"h*, ed. Zvi Zameret and Hanna Yablonka (Jerusalem: 1997), 151–168; on the haredi sector in Israel's early years, see Menachem Friedman, *Hahevrah haharedit: mekorot, megamot vetahalikhim* (Jerusalem: 1991).

89. For an analysis of the haredi sector's preserving its boundaries, as based on Mary Douglas' "Cultural theory," see Emmanuel Sivan, "Tarbut hamuvla'at," *Alpayim* 4 (1991), 45–98.

90. On the industrial importance of cultural and modern national unity, see Ernest Gelner, *Nations and Nationalism* (Oxford: 1983). See also the attack on Gelner from the perspective of post-colonial Mizrahi research in Israel in Yossi Yonah and Yizhak Saporta's "Hahinukh hakedam mikzo'i viyzirat ma'amad hapo'alim beyisral," in *Mizrahim beyisrael: 'iyun bikorti mehudash*, ed. Hannan Hever, Yehouda Shenhav, and Pnina Motzafi-Haller (Jerusalem: 2002), 68–104.

91. A certain tolerance was extended only to those West European languages—primarily English and German—that were useful in connecting the Israeli national economy to the world economy.

92. Shlomo Alboher, *Hizdahut, histaglut vehistaygut: hayehudim hasefaradim beerez yisrael vehatenu'ah haziyonit bimei hashilton habriti, 1918–1948* (Jerusalem: 2003), 139–154.

93. Tsur, *Kehilah kru'ah*, 185–186, 207–209; Yaakov Lupu, *Shas delita: hahishtaltut halitait 'al benei torah mimaroko* (Tel Aviv: 2004).

94. Zvi Zameret, *Yemei kur hahitukh: va'adat hakirah 'al hinukh yaldei ha'olim (1950)* (Sdeh Boker: 1993).

95. David Sabah left Morocco in 1948 and settled in Jerusalem in 1949. See the biographical review by Moshe Amar, "Letoledot rabi David Zabah, tekufato vizirato (1869–1956)," in the responsa volume authored by Sabah and published by his family, *Shoshanim leDavid* (Jerusalem: 2000).

96. This information is based on a survey of Sabah's writings that was conducted by his great-grandson, Shalom Ratzabi. My thanks to Prof. Ratzabi for this information. However, judging from Sabah's Hebrew and Judeo-Arabic writings in 1949, in which he lauded the process of mass immigration resulting from the creation of the state of Israel as the "beginnings of Redemption" (ibid.) he certainly did not adhere at this stage to the anti-Zionist ideology of haredi Orthodoxy.

97. According to the Ahiezer memo, Prosper Cohen went to the synagogues to request donations to finance the Association's participation in the Paris-based Zionist conference.

98. According to Shalom Ratzabi, this list remains in the possession of the Sabah family.

99. Tsur, *Kehilah kru'ah*, 250–251.

100. Sami Shalom Chetrit, *Hamaavak hamizrahi beyisrael* (Tel Aviv: 2004), 351 (n. 191).

101. Shlomo Swirsky, *Lo nehshalim ela menuhshalim: mizrahim veashkenazim beyisrael: nituah soziologi vesihot 'im pe'ilim ufe'ilot* (Haifa: 1981), 13.

102. This term was coined by Vicki Shiran, a pioneering researcher and activist regarding the ethnic problem. See "Hatiyug hamakhtim: 'edot hamizrah beyisrael" (Master's thesis, Tel Aviv University, 1978).

From Arab Diaspora to Eretz Israel: Literary Portraits of Mizrahi Female Immigrants in the 1940s and 1950s

Doli Benhabib
(THE OPEN UNIVERSITY OF ISRAEL)

In Eli Amir's *Scapegoat* (1987),[1] a girl named Nilly comes to live on a kibbutz as part of an Iraqi group of young immigrants. She quickly obtains for herself a pair of shorts, but she takes care to wear modest attire when she goes home to her parents in the *ma'abarah* (transit camp). Over time, Nilly not only adopts the gender norms of the culture of "the New Hebrew" in the kibbutz but also becomes romantically involved with a sabra, a young kibbutznik. Eventually she becomes pregnant, a situation that causes her father to sit shiva.

What happens to young girls and women who are located on the boundary between life in the Arab diaspora and pre- and post-independence Israel? This essay takes a look at the immigration experiences of Mizrahi girls and women as depicted in five novels written by Israeli writers between 1955 and 1995.[2] In particular, I will examine the following questions: Is Eretz Israel (or later, the state of Israel) represented as a site of liberation from the patriarch or of empowerment for these girls and women? Does the image of the diaspora serve to advance that of Israel as a liberating environment, and if so, how? In other words, is it possible to trace the manifestations of the Zionist conception of "negation of the exile" (*shelilat hagalut*), which calls for the liberation of the Jew from the yoke of exile, in the literary representations of Mizrahi girls and women?[3] What is the relationship between the girls and their fathers (or, in some instances, their mothers), who are perceived as representing exile or as simply not willing to change their exilic ways? Is there a certain duality in the fate of these girls or women: to some extent empowered, are they at the same time subjected to ethnic or class-based oppression? And finally, who functions as an object of desire or, in general, as an "other" of some significance for the Mizrahi girls?

Of the five novels, Naomi Vishnitzer's *Ḥaruz kaḥol shel mazal o, keḥu oti habaitah* (The blue bead of luck or, Take me home) (1975) is the only one with a pre-independence setting (the others take place in the "transit camp" era of the 1950s). Zakia, soon to be renamed Esther, is cut off from her family in Aleppo, Syria by her immigration in 1946 to Eretz Israel. She is placed in the foster care of a veteran Ashkenazic family in the village of Yehonadav, outside Jerusalem. There she undergoes a complex, painful, and emotionally unsatisfying adjustment. From an economic point of view, the move from Aleppo represents an improvement. Although she has memories of rich Jews living in this city, Esther herself comes from an impoverished background: following her father's death, she had spent time in an orphanage where the daily fare consisted of bread, olives, and cheese (only on the Sabbath was there cooked food). In Yehonadav, there is no lack of food and moreover, as an uncle points out, Esther will be able to attend school instead of being sent out to work, as were her cousins.

One may observe here a story of salvation that is reminiscent of the "white men saving brown women" of India, an interpretation of the abolishment of the rite of Hindi widow sacrifice by the British (as discussed by Gayatri Chakravorty Spivak),[4] or the fantasy of saving Mizrahi women that is triggered by various Israeli films.[5] At the same time, Vishnitzer makes it clear that Esther is emotionally unsatisfied and insecure. Her status in the foster family is low, and she is not provided with a supportive or caring environment. The mother of the family expresses no love or tenderness toward her—at a certain point, she even tells Esther that she is a person other families would not want. The attitude of the foster family's younger daughter, Sorke, is even worse: she actively makes Esther's life miserable by mocking her, both at home and at school, often bringing her to the point of tears. For much of the novel, Esther is miserable, self-effacing, and unassertive. Whenever the older daughter, Leah, comes home from her service in the Palmach and speaks about matters of national importance, she takes center stage. Esther, meanwhile, vacates her place for neighbors and becomes someone who "sees but is not seen."[6] When a letter from her brother is read aloud by the foster mother, people around her laugh at its ornate style. Esther, glued to her seat, wants to protest but can do no more than smile feebly. Afterwards she feels that she has been degraded like a dog.

According to the foster mother, there is no reason for Esther to feel homesick. Syria is conceived by her as a place of scarcity, whereas Eretz Israel, in her eyes (as per the Zionist narrative), is the site of redemption. However, until late in the plot, Esther expresses a desire to return home, to Aleppo. For this, she is branded an "ungrateful creature—here she is in the land of Israel, for which so many yearn, and she wishes she weren't here!"[7]

In school, as in the foster home, Eretz Israel does not offer Esther emotional gratification. When the youth group leader suggests that Esther (and other immigrant children) be accepted into the group, the latter, including Sorke and her friend, vote against the idea. Sorke also calls Esther a "Negro" (*kushit*) and suggests that she be given the part of the queen's slave in the annual Purim play, since "all the Negroes are slaves!"[8] Atara, the teacher, reprimands Sorke and gives Esther the role of Queen Esther. But Esther does not manage to hold onto the part, as her guttural accent is mocked by the other children. Here it is interesting to note that, in a diary passage written about this time, Esther expresses dissatisfaction with her looks, in particular her facial features and frizzy hair. She even writes a poem about her longing for straight hair and inserts it in her diary. In line with Frantz Fanon's discussion of the black man in the colonial context,[9] Esther displays some self-alienation. Though it is not entirely clear whether this is the direct outcome of her uneasy interaction with the other children, the juxtaposition of the two issues in the diary makes the linkage between them plausible.

Adults and children from the veteran settlement display insensitivity and intolerance to Esther and her cultural practices, as seen in their reaction to her guttural accent. The "blue bead of luck" of the book's title is yet another example highlighting the distance between Esther and her new surroundings. The blue bead is part of a neck amulet that Esther never removes. Sorke jeers at this practice, in the way that she and her friends often mock Esther at school; the foster mother claims that, in due course, Esther will grow ashamed of the talisman and will throw it away. That is, the custom that Esther brought with her from Syria is considered to be a future source of humiliation. (Interestingly, as will be seen, a Holocaust survivor who becomes Esther's friend reacts more positively to the amulet.) Another source of ridicule is Esther's lack of knowledge of her exact age or date of birth; in Syria at that time, such lack of knowledge was presumably not uncommon. She also continues to cling to traditional religious observance. For much of the novel, she refrains from work on the Sabbath. As she writes in her diary: " . . . on the Sabbath I feel ostracized sevenfold since I exclude myself from society."[10] Vishnitzer highlights the uniqueness of Esther's emotional reaction to her situation by depicting another option for coping with it: her Syrian friend proudly goes for a walk on the Sabbath. However, this young female friend is given very little attention in the text. Surprisingly, the only external critical reaction to Esther's faith comes from Yoel, her European-born friend. Yoel undermines the value of religious conviction by claiming that her religious belief is something temporary that, like her childhood, will be shed. Nevertheless, he also mentions that in the past he himself was religious, thus underlining a link between himself and Esther.

In striking contrast to these varied sources of frustration in her life, school turns out to be a major source of empowerment for Esther. Already in Aleppo, the reader learns, she was a talented student, known there as "the sheikha," a title given to a woman having high position or status. (The novel notes that the word corresponds in Hebrew to *malkah*, or queen—yet another allusion to Queen Esther.) But in Yehonadav, in contrast to Aleppo, Esther is held in regard only by her teachers. Sorke, after all, calls her a "Negro," whereas the teacher chooses her to play the role of Queen Esther. Because she has learned Hebrew in Syria (unlike other immigrants in the school, who have studied at the French-sponsored Alliance schools), Esther is moved up to a much higher grade. Another teacher, Elkana, praises her written compositions in front of the class, at one point telling her that she has the makings of a poet. Elkana, like Atara, also complements her on her looks. Esther warms to his compassion. "When I looked at him, I realized that I love him because he is goodhearted, he listens to my stammering, he enriches me, he is my father and my home. He is a spider, may God forgive me. . . ."[11] (Earlier in the diary passage, Esther notes that in Syria, it was considered lucky to dream of insects.)

Elkana, in this passage, is seen as both home and family for Esther: a compensation for what she is not getting from her foster family. Later on, Esther is able to reciprocate some of the empathy she has received when she comforts her teacher at a time of distress. What is not clear from the text is the extent to which the affinity that develops between Esther and Elkana should be understood as stemming from their similar background. Elkana, like Esther, is an immigrant (from Iraq): he, too, has a guttural accent. In fact, as the plot develops, it becomes increasingly apparent that Esther's meaningful relationships, those in which she is cherished and reinforced, are not with sabras but with "others," immigrants like herself, whether new or more veteran.

Another of these meaningful relationships, as already noted, is with a Holocaust survivor. Esther meets Yoel one night under difficult circumstances. She has left Yehonadav following an incident in which she is unfairly blamed for her foster father's arrest at the hands of the British. An uncle in Jerusalem cannot offer her a home; she next seeks her brother, who, she discovers, has returned to Syria; finally, she travels to Tel Aviv in search of another uncle, who in the meantime has moved without leaving a forwarding address. In the course of her flight from her foster family, Esther's true family seems to be disappearing, leaving her with no refuge. At this stage, she runs into Yoel and, in a scene indicating her sense of trust, goes to sleep on a bench with her head resting on his knees.

Shortly after Esther returns to Yehonadav, Yoel comes there to find work and to spend time in Esther's company. They have a platonic relationship. Yoel, like Elkana, admires Esther's looks. Describing a young woman beloved to him, he adds that "Milenka was a dark-looking girl like you."[12] At another point, he calls her "Ketsele," which means, he explains, a small, black, and pretty cat whose fur is curly like an ewe. He is open in his affection. Esther's blue bead, he claims, brings him luck as well, for it has brought her into his life.

Esther develops no romantic feelings toward Yoel, who is himself still searching for Milenka. Rather, the significance of their connection lies in the fact that Esther now has a friend in Eretz Israel, a person who can make her feel welcome. It also allows her to feel her own strength. Although both of them are outsiders, Yoel is even more on the margins, having left the kibbutz to which he was sent upon his arrival, both because he found it too reminiscent of the camps in Europe and because he had plans of looking for Milenka. He has spent much of his time on the streets and does not even have an identity card. When Esther bumps into him in Yehonadav one Saturday, she plays the gracious hostess, taking him to some rocks she regards as her own special place, her own private "house of prayer." The implication is that Esther now feels less uprooted and more connected to the village, that, following her night in Tel Aviv, she has gone through a process of accepting her life in Yehonadav. In another encounter, seeing that Yoel is feeling desolate about Milenka, she caresses the back of his neck. Later she muses about the incident: "Only yesterday, she was reaching out for a bit of affection, yet tonight she was able to give something of herself, without any thought of recompense."[13] In exercising her capacity to give, Esther behaves in a stronger and more mature manner. In another scene, she serves as a socializing agent for Yoel, introducing him to Hebrew songs—almost as if, while in company with him, she is assuming the place of a veteran resident.[14]

In sum, the Esther who returns to Yehonadav is different from the girl who left. She no longer fears what people will say or whether they will interrogate her about where she has been. Instead, she enters the house as does the elder daughter, Leah, full of confidence. She is less vulnerable, in the sense of being able to close herself off from slights. These changes are not explicated in the text, but it appears that they are the outcome of her having dared to leave the village, to have survived even after failing to find her family.

In other words, Vishnitzer constructs a turning point of return to the village and not to Syria, and leads Esther to adjust to life with her foster family in Yehonadav. This point of adjustment is marked by Esther's growing sense of maturity and accomplishment: she helps a cow give birth, for instance, and aids Yoel in his search for Milenka. In the final diary passage, Esther comments that she has not written in her diary in a long time because she has been busy with life itself—perhaps an indication that she is feeling far less lonely and thus not tending to withdraw into her inner world. In this passage, Esther further notes that she has selected Rosh Hashanah to be her birthday, as if she has invented herself anew and chosen the day of her renaissance. The newfound strength and energy Esther has toward the end of the book, accompanied by a progress into maturity and enhanced self-confidence, are also manifested in a scene in which she scans her reflection in a shop window. She sees how she has developed physically and, contemplating her eyes, she decides that they are pretty. This moment of contentment with her own image in the window contrasts with the way in which she could not come to terms with her own looks in the beginning of the novel. This scene incorporates, in Vishnitzer's design, another source of gratifying mirroring—Yonatan, Esther's foster brother, who has already begun to stir her emotions, appears in the window just then. He, too, is at a critical juncture, having lately enlisted, apparently in the Palmach.

Vishnitzer brings her novel to a happy ending via interethnic matchmaking. While Esther's most satisfying and supportive relationships up to this point have been with "others," the binding eros in the life of a Syrian immigrant is imagined by Vishnitzer as related to the Ashkenazi sabra Yonatan, a true child of the land. In the novel's concluding passage, Esther gives Yonatan her amulet, feeling that she no longer needs it. Does this act imply spiritual growth, or does it indicate that the Ashkenazi acculturizing has been successful enough to lead her to give up her Mizrahi custom? It is difficult to determine which of these interpretations is more correct, although it does seem clear that, had Esther stopped believing in the amulet's power, she would not have chosen to give it to Yonatan. In any event, the book ends at the beginning of the romance between the two, a formula employed by many of the "bourekas" movies produced in Israel during the 1960s and 1970s. As Ella Shohat has noted, this formula reflects a belief in social integration and the ideology of national unity.[15]

In Eli Amir's *Scapegoat*, we observe the experiences of a group of adolescent immigrants being absorbed on a kibbutz. The story is narrated in first-person by one of the group, an Iraqi-born boy named Nuri. The female characters are fairly marginal, with Nilly (known in Iraq as Laila) receiving more attention than the others.[16]

Much of *Scapegoat* focuses on the mechanism of socialization and acculturation that is imposed on the group (for example, exposing them to classical music) and the conflict that consequently ensues in the soul of Nuri, the novel's main protagonist. Youth group counselors serve as acculturizing agents. The newcomers also have contact with the children of the kibbutz. These are referred to as the "regional" (*azori*) youth, and they serve as the model that Nuri and Nilly choose to imitate.

According to Sonia, one of the youth group counselors, the transformation of people in general, and that of the Iraqi youths in particular, is a goal of the kibbutz. As she explains to Nuri: "If you join an existing kibbutz it will be like coming to a half-cooked meal. If you set up a kibbutz of your own, it will prove not only that the kibbutz is capable of changing people, but also that you are capable of changing."[17] If the educational method imposed upon the Iraqi youth group in the kibbutz is laid bare in these words, then Nilly represents a case of success. She adopts various cultural elements—norms of behavior, dress, songs—from the repertoire of the "regional" youth. The fact that the sabra functions as an object of desire in her soul is also manifested in her choice of boyfriend. Indeed, Nilly's behavior is reminiscent of Fanon's discussion of black men who, in the colonial context, adopt the dominant white culture and desire white women.[18]

Nilly is not alone in her acculturating behavior. Nuri is going through similar psychic processes, often articulating a desire to be like the "regional" youth. Thus it is no accident that Nilly chooses him as her confidant. When Nuri asks her why she discloses her secrets only to him, she responds: "You're like me . . . you know that Baghdad is dead and that we have to be like them."[19] She is clearly among the more rapidly acculturating members of her group, adopting with greater enthusiasm the culture of the New Hebrew as represented by the sabra and also, of course, internalizing the gender norms of this culture.[20]

The book enables the reader to get to know some of the Iraqi gender arrangements that undergo change in the context of the kibbutz. In the beginning, Nuri is loyal to the notion of strict segregation between males and females. The kibbutz, however, not only houses boys and girls in relatively close quarters (on opposite sides of the same building) but also has them studying and working together. This naturally leads to friction—for instance, the boys tease the girls by loosening their kerchiefs, which causes shame to them, since they always keep their hair covered. Iraqi gender norms are also expressed in the group's reaction to the clothing worn by the kibbutzniks. At the outset of the novel, one of the characters, Ilana, expresses criticism of the shorts worn by one of the women: how could the woman not be ashamed? Nuri, for his part, thinks that the socks and military-looking shoes worn by another woman are not at all suitable—unsuitable, that is, because they lead to a blurring of sharp gender distinctions. In dealing with the encounter between two cultures, one that may also be conflictual, *Scapegoat* raises a number of questions regarding dress codes and appropriate attire. For instance, the Iraqi boys are initially reluctant to put on the standard-issue work clothes and are repulsed by the idea of removing their undergarments in the communal showers. Clothing, in this novel, is not only a site where cultural identity is inscribed but also a site of intercultural struggle. Laila is not simply transformed into Nilly, but receives as well a nickname: "Nilly-short pants."

Nilly, however, exhibits none of the internal intercultural rupture felt by Nuri. This, of course, may be merely a function of the first-person narration that exposes only Nuri's consciousness. Nonetheless, it is also possible that Nilly does not, in fact, feel any conflict—that at this point, Amir is employing a strategy that tightly links the process of the liberation of an Iraqi girl with Israel; or specifically, connects the existence of liberating gender norms with the culture of the mythological sabra. Thus Nilly encourages the other girls to participate in the group's internal elections, is elected to the group committee, and perseveres in her plan to plant a garden around the group clubhouse, something she had seen near the "regional" clubhouse. Following Nuri, she also attends classical music quiz sessions and asks him to explain this music to her. When one of the Iraqi boys (who was attached to her) sings Arabic music, Nilly disrupts his singing with a rendition of Hebrew songs. Such actions stamp her as a leader, whom many of the girls follow enthusiastically.

In a scene revealing that Nilly has adopted the sexual mores of the "regional" youth, she defends a Romanian girl who is running after one of the Iraqi boys. Ilana attacks the girl, calling her a prostitute, whereupon Nilly silences her and threatens reprisals if the harassment continues. It is unclear whether Nilly's main motivation is to stand up for a stranger or to defend the notion of greater sexual freedom for the girls. In any event, she applies the "regional" sexual mores to herself, whether because she is attempting to adjust to the surrounding culture or else (as one of the youth group counselors believes) because she is acting as a revolutionary. When a relationship begins to develop between Nilly and Zvika, one of the boys of the kibbutz, she not only drops her guttural, Arab accent but also changes her appearance to more closely resemble the "regional" girls, and encourages the other Iraqi girls to do likewise: "His world had become her world. . . . A bronzed body, a Russian belt; an embroidered blouse, the old mania for short pants, and a new dream of long plaits."[21] She starts to develop her own image of what is feminine and sexually appealing, advocating small waists and firm breasts and shamelessly wiggling as she walks. Yet, as noted, she goes home to her religiously observant parents dressed modestly.

Amir chooses not to deal with the implications of Nilly's double life, showing only her enthusiastic adherence to sabra culture and her relationship with Zvika, which eventually leads to her becoming pregnant. Nilly justifies her sexual behavior by saying that this is how the "regional" girls act. This pregnancy and the wedding plans of the young couple are denounced on all sides. Zvika's friends deride his willingness to wed a girl from an Iraqi family and attempt to frighten him with stories about her parents' cultural backwardness and rigid clinging to religious ritual. These warnings bring to mind both an earlier scene in the novel in which the Iraqi youths were labeled "Asiatic" and "primitive" by one of the kibbutz members and the characterization of the Arabic music played at their parties as "wailing" (*osef shel yelalot*).[22] Nilly's friends are no more encouraging. The girls (especially Ilana) demand her expulsion from the group even though many of them had previously looked up to her as a leader. Yet Amir's account of their reaction reveals an ambivalence that is missing in his depiction of Nilly's world. As his narrator, Nuri, notes of the girls:

> They were full of righteous satisfaction, and not a little spite, as well as an unconscious envy of the daring Nilly. In the secret places of their hearts they longed for the revolution that Nilly symbolized, and at the same time they were afraid of the consequences she was suffering now.[23]

Here we see, on the one hand, a mixture of malice and fear, and, on the other, a desire for Nilly's sexual freedom and perhaps for women's liberation in general. Without such desire, the girls would have no cause for jealousy. Yet when Sonia summons the girls to a meeting in which she explains what can happen when two people are in love and gives practical advice as to how to avoid such consequences, the girls give public expression to the traditional mores that they had internalized in Iraq. At the meeting, their internal conflict is not manifested. Rather, they protest that what happened to Nilly could never happen to them because they have their pride, are respectable, and were properly brought up in good families. Such a response reflects Iraqi norms of appropriate female behavior—though one might inquire whether in the Israel of the 1950s, members of other ethnic backgrounds did not similarly view out-of-wedlock pregnancy as a violation of feminine propriety. In any event, Nilly's father, a cantor, reacts gravely to his daughter's pregnancy and her plans to marry. He sits shiva, pardoning her only when the baby is born, when he asks that his grandson be given a name signifying Iraqi generational continuity. However, in the dialogue (or lack of dialogue) with her father before the baby's birth, Nilly realizes the kibbutz imperative of rebelling against the past, as represented by her parents, and chooses the world of the New Hebrew. Her new life constitutes a negation of her father's expectations.

In a number of passages, Amir hints at the youth group counselors' interest in severing the bond between the Iraqi youngsters and their parents. For example, after Nuri, representing the group, writes a letter to the local Aliyat Hanoar office demanding that the youths be given a vacation at home with their families, the counselors summon a meeting in which Sonia declares heatedly that "after every trip to the *ma'abarah*, all our work here is undermined."[24] The parents, then, are perceived as a corrosive element threatening the new educational scheme. And when Nahche, a member of the central committee of the kibbutz movement, talks to Nuri about his educational mission in the transit camp, he emphasizes that it is targeted at the younger generation only: "What are you saddling me with parents for? It's the children we're interested in."[25]

Sonia tries to impose her European path of rebellion on the Iraqi youths (as is known, indigenous Communist and Zionist movements also existed in Iraq prior to the mass emigration of Iraqi Jews to Israel). She appeals to the group to rebel, as she has, against the old world—the *galut* and the fathers. "I too discarded the old world I came from and put it behind me," she tells them, "and you'll discard it too, and in the end it will be for your own good."[26] The sociopolitical and sociocultural line pursued in the European context, involving the "negation of exile," is presented to the Iraqi youth as the model they must adopt. In Nuri's case, the strategy works. He begins to wish that his father—a lawyer in Baghdad who in Israel became a manual laborer in the forests of the Jewish National Fund—would be more like Dolek, who is a self-taught expert in garbage disposal. At the same time, in response to Sonia's urgings to make a complete change and establish a new kibbutz, he explains that he, unlike her and other kibbutz members such as Dolek, did not come to Israel alone but rather with an extended family. That is to say, he adamantly refuses to cut himself off from his family—despite the fact that he is confused about his identity: "I'm always running between the hilltop where the 'regionals' are and the *ma'abarah*."[27]

As seen, Nilly, unlike Nuri, makes an unambiguous choice in favor of the kibbutz and the liberation it is perceived to offer to women. Interestingly, it is the struggle over a woman's freedom that leads, in an earlier episode, to the first instance of collaboration between the youth group and the kibbutz members, a collaboration that, not incidentally, works against the parents. In this earlier scene, a girl named Farida fights for her freedom against her parents, who have come to take her from the kibbutz in order to marry her off to a much older man who is a stranger to her. Her rebellion succeeds because of the intervention of the kibbutz members, supported by the immigrant youths. This event denotes a growing affinity between the youths and the kibbutz members, a point of reconciliation that emerges as a result of the parents being cast aside. It is noteworthy that the representation of kibbutz life as a source of change in the gender norms of Iraqi youth is constructed by Amir in quite deliberate fashion. In his depiction of Iraqi youth, Amir gives great weight to those who are religiously observant while repressing the presence of those Iraqi girls and boys who were exposed to western gender norms back in Iraq—for example, via the Alliance Israèlite Universelle schools.[28]

The tension that emerges between parents and Mizrahi girls subsequent to their immigration, as can be observed in *Scapegoat*, lies at the center of Milo Ohel's *Bridge*, published in 1955. Ohel molds the intergenerational tension as the leading conflict in the novel, so that here we witness the internal drama of a Libyan family, the Inaras from the city of Benghazi. This family is now living in a transit camp in Israel. Esther, the eldest daughter, defies her father's wishes by obtaining work in a cooperative restaurant in the city. The job appears to be a means of empowerment, promising access to economic well-being, friends, and more generally, a new world. Esther imagines the material comforts coming with the job in the form of an acquired ornament, a dress for herself, movies, and significant economic assistance for her family. In addition, the job neither belittles her nor is constructed textually as the source of education forgone. Actually, Ohel totally ignores the question of education. In this, *Bridge* differs from Sami Michael's ma'abarah novels in which Mizrahi girls find themselves in blue-collar jobs that lower their self-esteem and often signal the end of their schooling or, in some instances, become prostitutes who are exposed to male tyranny and violence.[29]

Esther, however, takes to her job enthusiastically, viewing it as a significant opportunity, since she emanates from a background of relative poverty in Libya and also faces severe hardship in the transit camp. Ohel shows how Esther, who is physically underdeveloped for her age, matures both physically and psychologically at work. She gains in self-confidence and subsequently displays courage and determination when she insists on keeping her job rather than engaging in domestic work. Some of this newfound strength, as will be seen, can be attributed to her work friendship with other Mizrahi girls.

Going out to work creates a duality in Esther's life between the restaurant milieu and the world of the city, between veteran residents and those of the ma'abarah where her family lives. Describing her feelings as she returns home after her first day at the restaurant, Ohel's omniscient narrator comments that Esther had not yet realized that she had been cast on that day into the chasm between the two worlds. On the rare occasions when she reflects on the matter, Esther regards this chasm as material in nature. But in general, the cleft between the two worlds in Esther's psyche is not developed at any length, nor is ambivalence toward the city, the world of veteran residents, a major theme in the book.

Similarly, the move of a young girl from a religious home in Benghazi to the ma'abarah, and from there to a work ambiance managed by veteran Israelis, does not engender an internal cultural conflict. Rather, the cultural conflict is externally situated in the relationship between father and daughter. The daughter rebels against her father in going out into the public sphere, whereas the father steadfastly adheres to norms anchored in deep religious belief. Haim Inara is depicted as both patriarchal and oppressive, in keeping with Israeli myths of Mizrahim—in particular, their sexism—that are discussed by Ella Shohat.[30] It should be noted, however, that Ohel does not intend him to be representative of all Jewish men from his community. Both the mother and the narrator reflect on the fact that many men in Benghazi, among them religious figures and highly esteemed people in the Jewish community, had given their own daughters comparatively more freedom.

Unlike some works written by other authors such as Eli Amir and Sami Michael, *Bridge* does not revolve around a once affluent Mizrahi family whose fortunes decline in the Jewish state. The Inaras have always been poor, whether in Libya (where the father was a tailor) or in Israel (where he does road work). Though not the only reason, the family's economic distress is certainly the main factor compelling Esther to look for a job in town. Her father's opposition stems from fear of her falling into errant ways. In explaining her father's position to her friend Lizzy, Esther points out that, being very pious, he fears for her, believing that a girl is easily seduced or manipulated. For her part, going out to work while still living at home, Esther hopes that her father will eventually get used to the idea.

At first, this appears to be the case. One day, however, he storms into the restaurant, sees his daughter in her waitress uniform, spits in her face, angrily shouts "accursed, accursed!" and slaps her with all his might. A moment before this occurs, when her father has just seen her, Esther is described in the following manner: "her gait erect, her head tilted back, her apron shining white." Following his outburst, Esther has "a bowed back and lowered head, her body shrunken, her apron stained and wet."[31] In these two snapshots, we behold Esther flourishing at work and, a moment later, devastated by her father's violent intrusion.

And yet Esther has already begun to feel a certain sense of empowerment vis-à-vis her father. In an earlier scene, she has shown incipient signs of rebellion. She looks at her father, and despite his height and eyes filled with rage, she beholds a weak and sickly creature who only appears to be powerful. In the face of his threat several weeks later to throw her out of the house if she does not give up her job, Esther is temporarily cowed but then determines to assert herself. She no longer views her father as a figure inspiring respect or obedience but rather as someone who is weak and lacking in understanding—even a bit ridiculous. This crisis-struck relationship is shown in its moment of greatest tension in the restaurant incident, subsequent to which Esther deserts the arena of strife and finds sanctuary at a friend's place.

On the margins of the conflict between Esther and her father is another female character: the mother. When Esther is working but still living at home, her mother emerges as a significant source of support for her ambitions. At a certain moment her husband is even convinced that the mother and daughter are conspiring against him, and this may well be the case. For example, the mother readily agrees to shorten Esther's apron when she brings it home after her first day of work, and she listens

with great interest to her daughter's stories about the restaurant. Her thoughts indicate that for years she has been carrying a grudge against the father for his behavior
toward their daughter. In her consciousness, there emerges an image of "a bird in a
cage" to describe Esther's situation even back in Benghazi.[32] Esther's struggle to
work outside the house is thus likened to that of an imprisoned creature seeking
freedom, which her mother not only supports but also identifies with.

Yet far more attention is devoted to Esther's female friends, who accompany her
in her new life outside the home and provide her with an alternative protective space.
Ohel's strategy of representation thus differs from that of Naomi Vishnitzer in *The
Blue Bead of Luck*, whose heroine forms nurturing relationships only with males.
Moreover, in contrast with some of the Iraqi youths in *Scapegoat* who choose to
model themselves in the image of the "regional" kibbutz members, Esther is trying
to mimic two of her closest friends, who are, like her, North African immigrants. As
already noted with regard to *Scapegoat*, Nilly's choice of a sabra youth is more in
line with Fanon's view of the black man's object of desire in the colonial context. In
Bridge, Esther's object of desire may even be said to be the world outside the transit
camp, with her two close North African friends mediating between her and the world
outside the ma'abarah.

Miriam, like Esther, is from the ma'abarah. She becomes a waitress in the cooperative restaurant, and it is she who paves the way for Esther to obtain employment
there as well. At the beginning of the novel, she represents the ideal to which Esther
aspires: free of unpleasant domestic chores such as laundry and taking care of babies.
Instead she gives her father cash, dresses like one of "their" girls, and is destined to
be on an equal footing with others in the restaurant cooperative, expressing her
opinions in the same way as any of the veteran girls. During a conversation between
the two girls and a counselor from the Histadrut's organization for working mothers,
Miriam comes across (in Esther's perception) as purposeful, decisive, and courageous. At this moment, Esther's desire is to be like her; at one point in the conversation, when Miriam gives her advice on how to handle the veteran residents, she
even feels envious, since it is clear to her that Miriam can stand up to them. At this
point in the novel, Ohel's depiction of the two girls underlines the differences between them: "this one [Miriam] upright and that one bent down, this one well-
dressed and that one in what passes for clothing, this one demanding and that one
pleading. . . ."[33] In another scene set against the background of the conflict with her
father, Esther hears Miriam as an inner voice ("don't give a damn about home"),
which suggests that Miriam's assertiveness and independence have been internalized, at least to some extent.

At a later stage, the connection with Miriam is cut, and Esther moves on to an
alternative source of authority, protection, and guidance—Lizzy. But by then, she
begins to wonder whether she herself or Lizzy should be the guide. As with Miriam,
Lizzy arouses in her a desire for imitation, and at a certain point Esther considers
whether she wants to be like Lizzy and live on her own. Lizzy, after all, is more
experienced than Esther. She has seen the world and knows something about going
out with young men; like Miriam before her, she is more familiar than Esther with the
norms of the other world. While living at Lizzy's, Esther starts to think that she is
already becoming like the other young women around her—Lizzy, Miriam, and

Shoshana (another girl working at the restaurant), and even a girl who happened to stand next to her at the movie theatre. This, in part, is wishful thinking. Whenever she considers other girls, the qualities that come to Esther's mind are assertiveness, courage, and knowing how to behave around young men. These are the attributes that she wants to adopt as her own, and in this regard, she feels that she has already made some progress.

As noted, Esther's significant friendships are with girls who, like her, originally came from North Africa. This fact is part of the general representational strategy of the novel: although Ashkenazim and veteran Israelis do make an appearance in the text, they play a marginal role in Esther's world, and the sources of satisfaction or frustration in her life are primarily North African immigrants, including her father. As for the veteran Israelis, there is Rivka Saharuni, for one, the manager of the cooperative's restaurant. She is condescending and judgmental, condemning and accusatory toward immigrants in general, while at the same time giving herself credit for "rescuing" immigrants such as Miriam and Esther. This rescue fantasy is held up to question in the novel both by Esther's thoughts and by Miriam's statement to the effect that if the two girls don't pull themselves up out of the mud, no one else will do it for them. Another Ashkenazic character, Avraham Hoter, is a public figure in the city and a leading member of the restaurant's board of directors. Visiting the ma'abarah in an unsuccessful attempt to mediate between Esther and her father, Hoter chooses not to preach to Haim Inara about Zionism or to compare the hardships of the immigrants of the 1950s with those of the early pioneers. Rather, as someone long settled in the country and perhaps also as an influential public figure, he has guilt feelings toward the residents of the ma'abarah. He has high regard for the sacred value of family unity among Mizrahim, believing it to be no less important than the value of labor (*'erekh ha'avodah*), a key tenet of Zionist thinking. Hoter's thoughts about the crisis of the family among Ashkenazic Jews puts the intensity of the intergenerational conflict in the Inara family, with its traditional Mizrahi background of family cohesion, in a much broader context.

At a certain point in the novel, Ohel moves away from depicting Esther's inner life and emotional development. Once Esther moves from one mentor (Miriam) to another (Lizzy), the question that emerges is whether she will eventually become fully independent. Some progress in this direction is indicated when Esther makes an attempt to leave Lizzy's and find a place of her own. Here, however, Ohel shifts the focus to Esther's father. Thus *Bridge* concludes differently from *The Blue Bead of Luck*—not with a happy match between an established settler and an immigrant, or between an Ashkenazic man and a Mizrahi woman (although Esther does have a romance with an "almost sabra," it ends badly), but rather with a psychological turnabout by Haim Inara that leads him to accept his daughter and her right to work. The novel's center of attention remains the intergenerational family drama.

Toward the end of the novel, Haim Inara's deeply held convictions are shaken up. He looks around him, noticing that both young and older women are contributing to their families' incomes. He himself is physically frail and jobless and, visiting the employment exchange, he witnesses violent displays of despair there—all factors leading him to sober up. Following the visit to the employment exchange at the end of the novel, the sidewalk in front of him takes on the aspect of a bridge in his eyes.

Striding along it, he murmurs a prayer of thanksgiving for the job of road-paving that
was taken from him and the job of "bridge construction" that has been granted to
him. He then approaches his daughter's restaurant, gazing at her through its window.
In this context, the word "bridge" operates on the symbolic level as a linkage, a
mediator between different worlds: that of the ma'abarah and the established settlers;
the father and the daughter; or between the world of Jewish tradition and a new world
of women's liberties.

In conclusion, the function of Israel as a location of women's liberation is evident in
this novel, but not totally dominant. On the one hand, *Bridge* is the tale of a young
woman who rebels against her father, the patriarch, by going out into the world, a step
that leads to her empowerment and blossoming as a woman. All of this happens to
Esther Inara in Israel, and in this sense it is indeed a site of female liberation, as is also
underscored by the heroine's mother when she tells her husband that in Israel, women,
too, are human beings. On the other hand, Ohel makes it clear that Haim Inara's
rigidly patriarchal attitudes and behavior are by no means characteristic of Jewish
men in Benghazi. From this perspective, Arab exile and Israel are not polar opposites.
Nonetheless, a formative transformation does occur in a specific territorial location—
Israel. It is here that the father eventually accepts his daughter's right to go out and
work, if only because of the helplessness imposed on him in the world of the employment exchange, though, as previously pointed out, this is only one of the catalysts
of change. As for the daughter, her story has a certain redemptive dimension.

In Eli Amir's *Mafriah hayonim*, or *Farewell, Baghdad*, written in 1994, we witness a
similar struggle by a woman for the right to work, although here the protagonist of the
struggle is a married woman and the patriarch is her husband. The novel, a saga with
multiple narratives and points of view, focuses mainly on the Imari family of
Baghdad (and later, Israel). In its Baghdad section, set in the late 1940s, the reader
encounters a variety of Jews and Muslims and a panorama of views regarding Zionism, Communism, and where Jews should live. Overall, the Baghdad exile is
represented as hostile toward Jews; we witness events in which Jews, particularly
Zionists, are persecuted, and there are sections dealing with the *farhoud* (pogrom) of
June 1941. With regard to another political "minority" group—women—*Farewell,
Baghdad* offers a very critical perspective. According to the comments of the omniscient narrator, women in Iraqi society are slaves, and one of the novel's main
characters, a Communist teacher named Salim Afandi, says that Baghdadi women
are submissive and self-effacing in the presence of men, and that independence and
assertiveness among them is rare.

Against this background, Kabi's mother is both typical and exceptional. Kabi
Imari, an adolescent who narrates much of the novel, contrasts the cyclical regularity
of his mother's life, which is very much attuned to nature, with his father's moving
along the path of history. This view, of course, reflects the patriarchal representation
of women being located on the nature pole of the nature-culture continuum, and as
existing outside history. Kabi depicts his mother in traditional female spaces, her life
revolving around home and family, engaged in nurturing activities such as serving
food and taking care of the sick alongside other endeavors such as gardening and
embroidery, which she handles like an art. However, she does not entirely accept her

place in the patriarchy. She is openly bitter about the fact that her husband imposes his decisions in crucial matters such as where the family should live in Baghdad and whether they should immigrate to Israel. In the course of frequent marital arguments, she stubbornly maintains her own position.

Toward the conclusion of the novel, the family arrives in Israel and the subjects of domestic disputes change. That is, in Israel, we witness the same personality structure in Kabi's mother but one in contact with a different set of norms and options. In Baghdad, the Imari family was well-to-do. The transit camp, a sea of tents, comes as a shock:

> It is clear that she [Kabi's mother] could barely control the trembling that took hold of her when she first caught sight of the immigrants' place of residence. Time had to pass before she would recover from the sight of thousands of immigrants; the dirt and neglect; the idleness; the living amid constant noise; the atmosphere of hopelessness hanging like a heavy cloud over our heads.[34]

The father, an enthusiastic and active Zionist in Baghdad, has come to Israel with the dream of growing rice, as his family had done. He begins making the rounds of bureaucrats, all of whom tell him that his plan is impossible because the country lacks sufficient water. Sunk in despair yet unable to abandon his dream, he refuses to work with a watchmaker and exploit the expertise he had brought from Baghdad. When he finally agrees to go to work in road construction, he discovers that he does not have the physical stamina required for the job. In these passages on Israel in the novel, we witness the tragic story of a downfall.

At this point, the father's position as patriarch of the family is threatened both by someone who in Baghdad had been subservient to him in the socioeconomic structure and by a woman: that is to say, by a former servant named Abed and by his own wife. The former, who preceded them to Israel, acclimated successfully, in part because of his willingness to accept and to be grateful for any work that came his way. Upon the Imaris' arrival, Abed becomes their mentor and guide in the process of absorption. The mother views Abed as a model for survival and success; the father disagrees, and maybe angrily so. She, for her part, declares her intention to take charge and get the children gainfully employed, since her husband is caught up in his dream of growing rice. She also announces her plan to acquire a trade, go out to work, and earn money of her own.

Such a declaration is naturally seen as a threat to the father's position of power as family head and main breadwinner. He cannot countenance being financially maintained by a woman. His pride is involved. Yet his wife, depicted in this passage as being more realistic and able to adjust than he is, points out that in Israel, as opposed to Baghdad, women commonly work. Moreover, "women's work"—washing floors, housecleaning, fruit-picking—is readily available. Such menial work she views uncritically with the calm of a person who is reconciled with reality. She puts off working only because she is pregnant but informs her husband that one day she will realize her plans. In addition, she will no longer let him impose his will on her, as he used to do in Baghdad. At this point, the argument between the mother and the father mostly revolves around the topic of women's status, a topic that is related to financial issues and derives from it in the specific Israeli context.

Shortly thereafter, Abed finds some customers for Kabi's mother's embroidery. Yet despite this success, and despite her general readiness to adapt (which includes her desire to attend classes in order to learn Hebrew), she does not view Israel as the place of her redemption. "Since the moment I put my foot on Israeli soil, I have not had a single hour of joy," she tells her husband. "I am cursed for having followed you."[35] It is left to her son, looking back years later, to perceive that this unwanted move to Israel "enabled her to become more independent and to remove the yoke of the father who had imposed 'aliyah upon her."[36]

Kabi's mother's story is only one strand in the panoramic *Farewell, Baghdad.* In contrast, Sami Michael's *Victoria* (1995) places a Mizrahi woman at the center of the text, following her from pre-First World War Baghdad to Israel of the 1990s. Both novels portray the change yielded by immigration in the power balance between a married Iraqi woman and the husband, but Michael illuminates the sources of the change in a somewhat different manner. In *Victoria*, although most of the action takes place in Baghdad, Michael inserts a number of flash-forward portrayals of Victoria and other characters in their later years in Israel. As in other novels set (or set in part) in the ma'abarah, Victoria's family suffers severe economic hardship in the new country. Victoria, like Kabi's mother, is determined to pull the family up— "thread by thread," as she describes it decades later to one of her sons, a successful businessman who is nevertheless bitter about his lack of education. Over time, the family does succeed in gaining a firm economic grounding, as is shown in an en-counter from the 1990s, which takes place in a comfortable apartment in Ramat Gan, where the extended family has gathered for a sumptuous family seder.

To some extent, *Victoria* also depicts the manner in which its protagonist and two other women from Victoria's Baghdadi milieu are empowered in the new state. A specific statement even points this out as a general phenomenon among immigrant Iraqi women. This empowerment, however, should not be seen as the "redemption and freedom offered by Zionism to Jewish women who were condemned to be prisoners and servants, first to their parents and later to their husbands," as Batya Gur suggests, and as is implied, to some extent, in Eli Amir's *Scapegoat.*[37] Rather, the power that women accumulate is represented as a survival mechanism, as a direct response to a breakdown of status among the male immigrants from Iraq. Put somewhat differently, the men's loss of economic power and authority is the nec-essary condition for the women's empowerment and, in a way, its cause. Iraqi men, by and large, are broken by the new and difficult circumstances of the ma'abarah and Israel in general. Victoria, who faces this process in her husband Rafael's life, has no choice but to endure and persevere.

As Michael shows, this endurance is the product of a certain continuity in Vic-toria's life. Victoria is no stranger to hardship. Back in Baghdad, already married but with her husband, Rafael, gone to a sanatorium in Lebanon, she has worked in a cigarette factory to help support herself and her little daughter. Her class position in this period and her position as a woman throughout her life in Baghdad prepare her for the ma'abarah. The transit camp is merely another in the series of hardships she faces during the course of her life, and her endurance is more to be traced to her Iraqi past than to any salvation offered by the Jewish state. At the same time, she does undergo certain changes in the new environment. For instance, she fears her husband less and begins to fight back when he beats her. Moreover, as indicated by her "thread by thread" analogy, Victoria views herself as responsible for "pulling the strings" as it were, in order to coordinate her family's rise from poverty.

Viewed together, this novel by Michael and the aforementioned works by Amir, Ohel, and Vishnitzer offer variations on the theme of Israel as a zone of liberation and/or empowerment for immigrant Mizrahi girls and women. Amir's *Scapegoat* constructs the closest linkage between Israel (or, more specifically, the kibbutz) and female liberation and empowerment. His second novel, *Farewell, Baghdad*, also describes an Israel that offers new norms and opportunities to its Mizrahi heroine. Struggling against her husband as she did in Iraq, Kabi's mother draws support from the special character of the new environment and, as a result, is able to liberate herself somewhat from the patriarchal yoke. Indeed, it is precisely Israel, the state that she did not choose, that offers her new life chances. Similarly, Ohel's *Bridge* features a heroine in conflict with the patriarch over the right to work. Esther's refusal to give up working and her father's surrender at the end of the novel, together with her own thoughts and her mother's words about Israel's uniqueness, show it to be a locus of female liberation and empowerment (though this image is blurred somewhat by the fact that the father's rigid patriarchalism is not characteristic of the behavior of Benghazi Jewish men). Michael's *Victoria* also unrolls a narrative of some empowerment and a certain degree of liberation from the patriarch, in this case, the husband. And yet, as opposed to Amir, for example, Michael does not find the sources of change in the new opportunities offered to women by a more enlightened, less sexist Israel. Rather, these are to be found in the breakdown of male authority in the context of the harsh socioeconomic circumstances of the ma'abarah.

In contrast to these four novels, Vishnitzer's *The Blue Bead of Luck, or Take Me Home*, does not construct a story of struggle against or liberation from the patriarch. Esther's story, before the low ebb of her failed quest among her relatives, depicts economic comfort, achievement at school (something known to her also from Syria), and deep emotional dissatisfaction. In fact, she wants to go back to Syria. But toward the end of the plot, she also undergoes emotional and personal "empowerment," the outcome of her growing maturity. In this regard, *The Blue Bead of Luck* could just as easily have been the story of a Syrian Jewish boy—except that Esther's adjustment to her new home is inextricably linked to her growing acceptance of her female appearance. This, in turn, leads to the question of ethnic-racial oppression. At the beginning of the novel, Esther is taunted for her looks, her dark skin; at the end, she is beginning a romance with an Ashkenazic sabra, a product of the dominant New Hebrew culture. This ending may be seen as pointing to interethnic unity, or may instead suggest that Esther has not yet freed herself from her ethnic shackles. In this sense, *The Blue Bead of Luck* offers a complex and elusive variation on the theme of Israel as a zone of liberation or empowerment for Mizrahi women immigrants.

Does each one of the novels, then, represent the complexity of the lot of Mizrahi female characters following immigration? In other words, is liberation from patriarchy shown to be accompanied by ethnic and/or class oppression? In Vishnitzer's work, the ethnic/cultural oppression that was exercised in the beginning of the plot is partially uplifted at the end. Moreover, Eretz Israel does not lead her to financial deprivation since she is actually absorbed by a veteran Ashkenazi family. In *Scapegoat*, too, absorption within a wide, veteran framework solves financial problems for immigrant Iraqi girls whereas the parents in the transit camps face keen economic hardships. This novel exposes the efforts made to change and erase the culture of the immigrant girls and boys from the Arab exile. And yet it should be pointed out that Amir's Nilly cooperates with this mechanism of acculturating and does not experience it as an oppressive mechanism. It is rather the other way around, that is, the change empowers her. In *Farewell, Baghdad* by Amir, we witness material difficulties of different types that the mother faces together with her family, but it is indeed this problem that gives birth to the mother's plans of liberation and empowerment. In *Bridge*, the economic hardship encountered by Esther in the ma'abarah compels her to the path of a struggle for independence against the patriarch, a path that results in a certain degree of empowerment and a certain degree of economic well-being that changes the initial situation. In *Victoria*, immigration brings Victoria's family and the father in this family to economic downfall, but this very fact forces her to grow and accumulate power as a woman.

Notes

This article is dedicated to Shula Keshet, an artist devoted to the Mizrahi women's cause.

1. Eli Amir, *Tarnegol kaparot* (Tel Aviv: 1984) (English version, *Scapegoat*, trans. Dalia Bilu [London: 1987]).
2. Apart from Eli Amir's *Scapegoat*, the other novels discussed, in order of their appearance, are: Naomi Vishnitzer, *Ḥaruz kaḥol shel mazal, o, keḥu oti habaitah* (Tel Aviv: 1975); Milo Ohel, *Gesher* (Tel Aviv: 1955); Eli Amir, *Mafriaḥ hayonim* (Tel Aviv: 1994) (although this novel does not appear in English translation, an English title, *Farewell, Baghdad*, appears opposite the title page; the literal title would be *The Pigeon Runner*); Sami Michael, *Victoria* (Tel Aviv: 1993) (English version, *Victoria*, trans. Dalya Bilu [London: 1995]). The last novel is discussed only briefly; I deal with it at length in "Sami Michael: be'ayot shel beniyat subyektiviyut mizraḥit" (Ph.D. diss., Tel Aviv University, 2002); idem, *Yemei hapaḥonim veaḥareihem be'olamo shel Sami Michael* (forthcoming).
3. "Negation of exile" was a tenet of Zionism at least until the 1970s, and arguably to the present day. According to Amnon Raz-Krakotzkin, mainstream Zionist ideology believed in the concept of the "negation of exile" and viewed the founding of territorial Jewish sovereignty in the land of Israel as a return of the Jewish people to its homeland. According to this view, there is continuity between the ancient past and the present. The negation of exile was conceived as the "normalization" of Jewish existence via the creation of a new national culture. There emerged a belief that the return of the people to its land would give rise to an authentic cultural renaissance. Different images of the "New Jew," the representative of this authentic culture, emerged against this background. The terms "Hebrew," "sabra," and "Israeli" are all connected to the notion that the erasure of the exilic consciousness is the necessary condition for liberation. Each one of them, in its own manner, points to an image of the "redeemed" Jew. According to Raz-Krakotzkin, the construction of the "New Jew" implied the rejection of exilic traits, or sometimes of entire cultural traditions considered to be exilic, and this was "especially conspicuous with respect to the Jews from Arab countries" (Raz-Krakotzkin, "Galut betokh ribonut: lebikoret 'shelilat hagalut' batarbut hayisreelit," part 1, *Theory and Criticism* 4 [Fall 1993], 23–55, quote on 24; part 2, ibid. 5 [Fall 1994], 113–132).

117

In *From Hebrew to Canaanite*, Yaacov Shavit points out that the idea of "Hebrewness" (*'ivriyut*) originated in the ideological conceptual world of the European Jewish society in the 19th century and was also influenced by the Romantic movement. "Hebrewness" was a utopian model for the identity of the Israelite people, and its attributes were perceived as opposing those of Jewishness. For example, it focused upon national-secular instead of religious consciousness; modernism and rationalism instead of tradition; and a powerful sentiment for the land, the landscape, and the soil, instead of landlessness (Shavit, *Mi'ivri 'ad kena'ani* [Jerusalem: 1984]). Anita Shapira differs from Raz-Krakotzkin in her analysis of the connection between this concept and Zionism. Although she, too, points to the salient presence of the "negation of exile" in the first stage of Zionist ideology, she argues that this line of thought was neither the sole nor the dominant strand in Zionism. Her discussion is devoted in the main to the slow but constant retreat from this line of thought in Israeli society from the 1960s, and especially in the 1970s, with the Eichmann trial constituting a turning point (Shapira, "Lean halkhah 'shelilat hagalut'?" *Alpayim* 25 [2003], 9–54).

4. Gayatri Chakravorty Spivak, "Can the Subaltern Speak?" in *Colonial Discourse and Post-Colonial Theory*, ed. Patrick Williams and Laura Chrisman (New York: 1994), 66–111.

5. On this last issue, see Ella Shohat, *Israeli Cinema: East/West and the Politics of Representation* (Austin: 1989); idem, "Making the Silences Speak in Israeli Cinema," in *Calling the Equality Bluff: Women in Israel*, ed. Barbara Swirski and Marilyn P. Safir (New York: 1991), 31–40.

6. Vishnitzer, *Ḥaruz kaḥol shel mazal*, 21. There is also a brother, Yonatan, whose relationship with Esther becomes more significant at a later stage of the plot.

7. Ibid., 73.

8. Ibid., 31.

9. Frantz Fanon, *Peu noire masques blancs* (Paris: 1965).

10. Vishnitzer, *Ḥaruz kaḥol shel mazal*, 19.

11. Ibid., 66.

12. Ibid., 100.

13. Ibid., 124.

14. It is noteworthy that Esther's significant and nurturing relationships are only with men. Atara occupies a more marginal place in Esther's world as compared with Elkana or Yoel. In addition, the foster father is also a man whom Esther feels is good to her. Perhaps this can be attributed to the fact that Esther's father is dead; in any event, it is here a consistent textual strategy employed by the author, who in this way tends to close off the possibility of female bonding or solidarity.

15. See Shohat, *Israeli Cinema*; idem, "Making the Silences Speak in Israeli Cinema."

16. For a very brief (and different) discussion of the representation of the female characters in this novel, see Nancy Berg, *Exile from Exile: Israeli Writers from Iraq* (New York: 1996).

17. Amir, *Scapegoat*, 198 (all quotes are from the English translation).

18. Similarly, a white object of desire is observed in the lives of women of color, to whom Fanon devotes a single chapter; see *Peu noire masques blanc*, ch. 2.

19. Amir, *Scapegoat*, 148.

20. Berg observes that those characters who come from more marginal social circles in Iraq are more willing to adjust to Israel. Nilly comes from a village in the north of Iraq. See Berg, *Exile from Exile*.

21. Amir, *Scapegoat*, 138.

22. See Berg, *Exile from Exile*, where she points out that music in this novel is an arena of social conflict.

23. Amir, *Scapegoat*, 152.

24. Ibid., 93.

25. Ibid., 167.

26. Ibid., 93.

27. Ibid., 200.

28. On this social layer of Iraqi women, see Aziza Khazzoom, "Lahafokh lemi'ut, livḥon et hamigdariyut: nashim 'irakiyot yehudiyot bishnot haḥamishim," in *Mizraḥim beyisreel: 'iyun bikorti meḥudash*, ed. Hannan Hever, Yehouda Shenhav and Pnina Motzafi-Haller (Tel Aviv: 2002), 212–243. On the relatively westernized layer of Iraqi Jewry, see also Benhabib, "Be'ayot shel beniyat subyektiviyut mizraḥit"; idem, *Yemei hapaḥonim veaḥarehem be'olamo shel Sami Michael*.

29. Sami Michael, *Shavim veshavim yoter* (Tel Aviv: 1974); idem, *Paḥonim veḥalomot* (Tel Aviv: 1979). See also Doli Benhabib, "Margalit moladeti: migdar ve'edah besifrei hama'abarah shel Sami Michael," *Theory and Criticism* 20 (Spring 2002), 243–258.

30. Shohat, *Israeli Cinema*. It is noteworthy that both the daughter's attempt at going out into the public sphere and her materialistic desires are associated in the father's mind with impurity and pollution.

31. Ohel, *Gesher*, 140, 141.

32. Ibid., 100.

33. Ibid., 33.

34. Amir, *Mafriaḥ hayonim*, 440.

35. Ibid., 442.

36. Ibid., 444.

37. Batya Gur, "Lo beta'am ḥalav udevash," *Haaretz* (19 Feb. 1993).

The Sephardic Halakhic Tradition in the 20th Century

Zvi Zohar
(BAR ILAN UNIVERSITY)
(THE SHALOM HARTMAN INSTITUTE)

This article consists of two parts. The first section is an overview and discussion of Sephardic halakhah in the 20th century. Following this is a survey, by decade, of works of rabbinic responsa published between 1901 and 1990 that conform to the following criteria: a) the author was of Sephardic ethnicity; and b) he was alive during at least part of the century.

Neo-classical Sephardic Halakhah

Who best embodies Judaism's religious-cultural ideal-type: the individual who totally immerses himself in the study of Jewish texts and traditions, or the one who combines command of Jewish texts and traditions with serious knowledge and a fundamentally positive evaluation of non-Jewish "general" culture? In the high Middle Ages—the 11th and 12th centuries—Ashkenazic Jewry seems to have identified the first type as paramount, whereas Sephardic Jewry espoused the second model.[1] After the expulsion from Spain and the Sephardic cultural renaissance of the 16th century, the actual involvement of Sephardic rabbinic intellectuals in "general" culture became much more limited, especially in Muslim lands. Nevertheless, the classical Sephardic model seems to have retained its viability, at least as a latent cultural option, and sometimes as more than that. Thus, when political, social and cultural changes that occurred during the 19th and 20th centuries enabled realization of aspects of the classical model, Sephardic rabbis advocated it, in a variety of ways.[2]

Some characteristics of this neo-classical Sephardic response were: support for a revised curriculum of Jewish education that included both "Jewish" and "general" topics; respect for non-Jewish society, culture, and religion; support of modern Jewish nationalism; and recognition that modern contingencies may require creative halakhic responses not entailed by mainstream precedent. While there were some who held rejectionist attitudes toward modernity,[3] the neo-classical response was the dominant one among Sephardic rabbis.[4] Let me illustrate aspects of this response by citing several quotations from leading 20th-century Sephardic rabbis, reflecting their views with regard to links and relations between the Jewish and the non-Jewish realms of culture, religion, and human relationships.

In advocating an expanded curriculum for Jewish education in Aleppo to include secular as well as Torah topics, Hakham[5] Yitzhak Dayan (c. 1890–1964), scion of that community's most illustrious rabbinic lineage, contrasted traditional Sephardic cultural horizons with the outlook of the secular European Jewish Haskalah movement, and called for a return to the classical Sephardic ideal:

> The first intellectuals [*maskilim*] in the period of the wise men of Spain realized and knew well the depth of the spirit of Judaism and its glorious power. The Torah and rational knowledge walked among them like twin sisters. And there was a true peace between their spiritual tendencies. And therefore in their wisdom and their intelligence they strengthened and validated the Torah and the tradition, and made them intellectually accessible. . . . But the new intellectuals of the past generation did not realize this. They did not penetrate the great depth of Judaism. They did not know that the spirit and the great ideas of the Bible and the midrash are the homeland of the people's soul, [a homeland] that developed and attained perfection over the course of millenia . . . and therefore they strayed a great distance and changed the order of things.[6]

Another case in point is Hakham Avraham Abikhezir.[7] In 1912, while serving as head of the rabbinical court in Alexandria, he penned an approbation (*haskamah*) to a book in Arabic on Jewish family law composed by the chief *dayan* (rabbinical judge) of Cairo. His positive attitudes toward non-Jewish readers of this work and toward the Arabic language, as well as his explicit invoking of the classical Sephardic cultural ideal (exemplified by Saadyah Gaon and Maimonides), come through clearly in the following quote: "Your opus," he wrote to the author, "the work of a wise man and a thinker, is sui generis." He continued:

> No gold can equal its value, nor any silver pay its worth. You devoted days and nights, and banished sleep from your eyes, in order to retrieve pearls from the depth of the sea of Talmud and rabbinic decisors (*poskim*). And from them you fashioned a necklace, inlaid with precious onyx and jasper, to adorn the members of your nation and to publicly sanctify the Name of Heaven. . . . Moreover, lest it remain a sealed book for those who do not understand our pure and holy tongue, you toiled—and succeeded—in presenting it in the language spoken here in Egypt, the harmonious and pleasant Arabic tongue. In doing so, you followed in the footsteps of our intellectual giants of old, Saadyah Gaon and Maimonides, of blessed memory. Thereby, you fulfilled a keenly felt lack: the people, heretofore treading in darkness, who have never seen the light of Torah, will now see a great light and will happily rejoice. The legislators and the lawyers, of all peoples and tongues, will taste of this honeycomb and say, "Hurrah! we have become warmed and enlightened by just laws and regulations!"—they will thank and praise your name, for you will be to them a father and a teacher of justice. And they will sanctify the God of Jacob and give adoration to the laws of Israel, saying: "What great people has laws so just, as the laws of Torah which Moses set before the people of Israel?!"[8]

Hakham ʿAbdallah Somekh (1813–1889), the chief rabbi of Baghdad, was responsible for reviving rabbinic learning in that community. The following excerpt deals with the question of whether it was permissible to employ a Gentile to extinguish the synagogue lamps on the Sabbath. In the past, tensions and enmity between Jews and Gentiles had been invoked to justify the relaxation of some rabbinic ordinances, thereby permitting the employment of a Gentile to extinguish synagogue illumination after the Sabbath evening prayers were over. It was argued that if the lamps were not extinguished at night, a fire might break out and spread, for which the Jews would be blamed and consequently attacked. Somekh ruled that improved relations between Jews and Gentiles, and the development of municipal services in modern times, called for a change in halakhic ruling:

> In our times—thank God—Jewish life in exile has been sweetened, especially in the cities of Europe and also in Turkey. And they will not cast libel upon us if a fire happens to break out, and no one will raise his voice to say that Jews started the fire in order to harm Gentiles; *for all have become almost as one people.*
>
> In addition, when a fire breaks out, Jews are not required personally to extinguish it, for in such a case the firemen come quickly, with all their equipment, and it is they whose task it is to put out fires.
>
> Therefore, all the reasons [for permitting such employment of Gentiles on the Sabbath] offered by R. Poppers [an 18th-century German halakhist] are irrelevant in our times.[9]

In another instance, R. Yosef Mesas (1892–1974) ruled in 1951 that the halakhah permits Jews to donate organs to non-Jews. Among other justifications, he noted that, "by this [donation], love of man for man—with no differentiation on religious grounds—will become apparent. For all are created by God. . . . All the more so, since all peoples today have faithful knowledge of God, and believe in His Unity and Providence."[10]

Respect for Muslim tradition and Jewish-Muslim cooperation are exemplified in the following description by R. Nisim Ohana (1882–1962)[11] of events during his term as rabbi of the Jewish community of Gaza in the first decade of the 20th century:

> In Gaza, [Christian] missionaries established a clinic in which they accepted all patients, and also conducted prayers and preached to the assembled about Jesus and the New Testament. They also distributed evangelical tracts about the messiah etc., including the book "Speak Truth" in which they proved that the Quran was a book compiled from the Torah, the Prophets and talmudic *agadot* and not—as they [the Muslims] were told— the product of Muhammad's prophecies.
>
> The mufti of Gaza, Sheikh ʿAbdallah alʿAlami, sought to prove to the missionaries that the Quran was in fact true, since indeed its contents were found in the Torah, the Prophets and talmudic *agadot,* whereas the same was not the case with regard to the [biblical] verses cited in the New Testament as proof for Jesus of Nazareth: those verses do not fit him, and do not foretell him at all.
>
> The mufti turned to me, and visited me twice weekly in my home. He brought me questions with regard to all the chapters and verses found in the New Testament and asked me to give him clear answers based on the Bible itself. He sat and wrote out my answers in his own hand, in Arabic. His manuscript remains in my possession to this day.[12]

Above, I cited Yosef Mesas' views on the halakhic significance of human brotherhood; he clarified his view with regard to the basically monotheistic character of

Christianity by arranging (c. 1935) to have himself invited to a church in Algeria, where he discussed Christian beliefs with the priest and also inquired about the significance of Christian religious sculpture.[13] Toward the end of the century, R. Hayim David Halevi (1924–1998), the Sephardic chief rabbi of Tel Aviv, also ruled that Christians should be regarded, halakhically, as monotheists.[14] He generalized this insight, writing:

> It is self-evident that all human beings are created in the divine image, and therefore all persons from all nations of the world can become righteous men and attain high spiritual degrees by virtue of the spirit of life that God instilled in Adam, father of all humanity. This is why Ben-Azai held that the verse "This is the Book of Adam's descendents" (Gen. 5:1) is of greater significance than the verse "Love thy neighbor as thyself" (Lev. 19:18).[15] Clearly, Ben-Azai sought to indicate not the opening words of the verse, which in themselves are meaningless, but rather its conclusion: "... in the image of God was he made."[16]

And, to conclude this section, a quotation from R. Ben-Zion Meir Hai Uziel, the first Sephardic chief rabbi of the state of Israel:

> Each country and each nation that respects itself does not and cannot be satisfied with its narrow boundaries and limited domains; rather, they desire to bring in all that is good and beautiful, that is helpful and glorious, to their national [cultural] treasure. And they wish to give the maximum flow of their own blessings to the [cultural] treasury of humanity as a whole, and to establish a link of love and friendship among all nations, for the enrichment of the human storehouse of intellectual and ethical ideas and for the uncovering of the secrets of nature. Happy is the country and happy is the nation that can give itself an accounting of what it has taken in from others; and more importantly, of what it has given of its own to the repository of all humanity. Woe unto that country and that nation that encloses itself in its own four cubits and limits itself to its own narrow boundaries, lacking anything of its own to contribute [to humanity] and lacking the tools to receive [cultural contributions] from others.[17]

The modern, neo-classical manifestation of the Sephardic worldview is eminently apparent in this series of quotes. However, the rabbis quoted here have another common denominator: all completed their rabbinic studies before 1950. As we shall see in the following section, developments in the realm of rabbinic education during the 20th century led to a situation in which the religious ethos advocated by rabbis born into ethnically Sephardic families is increasingly out of step with neo-classical Sephardic culture and values, to the extent that the continued existence of this culture is in doubt.

Sephardic Rabbinic Education in the 20th Century

The past century witnessed great transformations in Jewish life throughout the world—including, of course, in Sephardic and Oriental communities. Most Sephardic communities became increasingly influenced by West European culture and lifestyle, and also experienced a rise in economic well-being. Secularization was widespread, especially among those of upper and middle socioeconomic status.

Concurrently, the goals of institutionalized education changed. In the past, educational institutions had focused on religio-cultural socialization, seeking to provide the young with the skills and knowledge necessary for participation in the community's religious life. In the 19th and 20th centuries, however, schools aimed to provide tools for future economic success and for participation in *civic* life and culture. Secular secondary and higher education also came to be regarded as keys to upward social mobility. Indeed, options of non-Torah-centered post-elementary institutionalized education were created for the first time in the Middle East and North Africa, mostly by non-Jewish organizations. Rabbinic education became only one of several avenues that a young, intellectually inclined man might follow. Because of secularization, rabbinic status seemed less attractive than before.

Thus it was that talented young men, who in previous generations would naturally have aspired to Torah scholarship, increasingly opted for other occupations. Put otherwise: a young man who in pre-modern times might have become an outstanding halakhist was now far more likely to become a distinguished professor or practitioner of medicine, law, or literature.

The turn from rabbinics to other professions is illustrated, inter alia, by the history of rabbinic dynasties. The Mani family is a case in point. R. Eliyahu Mani (1818–1899), a leading halakhist and kabbalist from Baghdad, came to Eretz Israel in 1856 and settled in Hebron, where he was appointed chief rabbi in 1864. He had five sons. Suleiman (1850–1924) received rabbinic training, served in Hebron as a dayan and as head of a yeshiva, and from 1905 was himself chief rabbi of Hebron. Three other sons received rabbinic training but made little public mark: Yehezkel-Shalom (1854–1940), Avraham-Barukh (1855–1882), and Yaakov (1864–1940). However, his fourth son, Yitzhak-Malkiel (1860–1932), while also versed in rabbinics, chose a different path, studying classical Arabic, Quran, and Islamic law in Hebron, and then training in Turkish jurisprudence in Beirut. He became the first Jewish judge in the Ottoman court system in Eretz Israel; after serving the full number of allowed terms, he became a private lawyer in Jerusalem, where he represented the legal interests of the sultan's private properties in the region. In 1918, he was appointed a judge on the highest court of British-administered Palestine. The children of all five Mani brothers achieved prominence as jurists, physicians, civil servants, and educators. None served as rabbis.[18] The histories of other leading Sephardic families reflect a similar pattern.[19] As R. Makhlouf Fahima[20] noted with regard to Morocco under the French Protectorate:

> All the elite of Morocco—the sons of rabbis and the grandsons of rabbis—went to study in the Alliance.[21] From the day that this [educational] network entered Morocco, there was no dayan whose son became a dayan. After the entry of the Alliance, a dayan's son became a doctor, an engineer, a pharmacist or an architect—but not a dayan. . . . [T]his is very bad, because Torah requires honor and distinguished descent. There is a difference in level [of scholarship] when the father is a dayan and his son after him is also a dayan, as opposed to a dayan who crops up from some householder who does not know Torah. Torah passes as inheritance: the father's nobility passes to the son.[22]

As scions of aristocratic rabbinic dynasties moved on to other occupations, the realm of Sephardic rabbinics opened up opportunities for men from lower socioeconomic backgrounds. Such was the case both with the aforementioned Hayim

David Halevi and with Ovadia Yosef, two great Sephardic halakhists active during the second half of the 20th century, both of whom came from humble background. Following the establishment of the state of Israel, Torah study became an avenue of upward mobility for young men from poor immigrant families, some of whom later became leaders and activists in the Shas movement.

The 20th century was also a time of transition with regard to institutional modes of Torah study for Sephardic rabbis. At the beginning of the century, there were no institutions in Islamic lands that were devoted specifically to rabbinic training, with the exception of Beit Zilkha in Baghdad.[23] The traditional institution of Torah study was the *midrash*—typically, a large room in which accomplished rabbinical scholars ranging widely in age engaged in study and research. Many of them attended the midrash on a part-time basis, spending the rest of their time as communal rabbis, judges, teachers, *shohatim* (slaughterers), or else as merchants and businessmen. Upon completing his elementary religious education, a young teenager aspiring to a scholarly career would typically join a midrash. There he would study together with the older scholars, hear them debate, observe them responding to actual halakhic questions, and participate in lectures given by the most expert among them or by distinguished visitors. Over time, he would progress in talmudic and halakhic methodology and acquire growing knowledge of canonical texts. If recognized as talented, he might be asked by a local rabbi or dayan to field a halakhic query— researching the topic and then writing a draft responsum that was submitted for the senior scholar's approval. At some point, he would be acknowledged as a *hakham* in his own right, but might well continue studying in a midrash, serving in turn as mentor and inspiration to younger students.

Midrashim were usually funded by munificent individuals who received public approbation and, all agreed, heavenly reward for their support of Torah study. However, as secularization spread, philanthropic priorities shifted and financial support for the midrashim decreased. The previous, rather common practice of a wealthy patron setting aside a room in his residence as a place of study for scholars (who were also, either wholly or in part, maintained by him) seems to have ceased almost entirely by the First World War. Moreover, as standards of living rose, the minimum cost of funding a scholar and his family also increased, whereas philanthropic contributions for Torah study, as noted, were now scarcer than in the past.

Thus, by the First World War, there were fewer midrashim, attended by scholars who were generally older and who had a relatively lower standard of living than their predecessors. At the same time, there was a paucity of young halakhic scholars in almost all Sephardic communities of the Middle East and North Africa. In the former, the only significant center of Torah study was in Eretz Israel, whereas in North Africa, such centers were to be found in Djerba, a small island in Tunisia, and in the less modernized Moroccan cities. This crisis in traditional Jewish learning was already a matter of concern to leading rabbis early in the 20th century. Thus, in 1907, R. Eliyahu Hazan initiated the establishment of a Sephardic yeshiva in Jerusalem, though his untimely death in 1908 disrupted the project. Ultimately it evolved (though perhaps not as Hazan had envisioned) into Yeshivat Porat Yosef, which in 1923 officially opened the doors of its handsome Old City premises and was, for more than two decades, the only institution of its kind in Eretz Israel.

In Morocco, controlled by France after 1912, midrashim went on the wane even in cities that had once been bastions of Torah. Twenty-year-old Yosef Mesas, destined to become one of the most brilliant and innovative halakhists of the 20th century, vividly describes the situation in his hometown of Meknes at that time:

> From the day that the French came to our city, there began a new era in the arrangements of life. He who calls it a good era—is not in error; and he who calls it a bad era—is not in error. For peace and quiet did increase in the land; but the calm and relaxation that had been in people's hearts, with everyone feeling happy with his lot, whether good or bad—completely vanished. For in all that men have need of, luxuries increased: in clothing and in livelihood, in housing and in utensils; this was especially so with regard to the women and girls, who smelled the powerful scent of new times. All this led to the increase of trouble, toil, and work, and involvement in all fields of commerce—accompanied by envy and competitiveness, and by the lust to ascend the rungs of wealth and pleasure. In this way, all hearts and all minds were filled with many thoughts, both deep and simple, to devise artifices, to cunningly act, to craftily deceive—so as to fill one's hands with reams of money, by hook or by crook. . . .
>
> And also those engaged in Torah began to leave their mother's bosom [that is, Torah study], and to go out each one to make his profit; for their souls, too, yearned to taste of the new era's delights. And so the pillars of Torah began to weaken—and there was no one to prop them up, to support them, or to admonish at the gate.[24]

At this crucial juncture, writes Mesas, a dramatic intervention took place: an unknown rabbi, Zeev Wolff Halperin, born in Russia and hailing from London, appeared one day in the mellah (Jewish quarter) of Meknes. After sizing up the scene for several days, he asked a young rabbi to convene all the young Torah scholars of the city in one of the synagogues, early on a Sabbath afternoon:

> And I, too, came there with the others who were invited. And he [Halperin] delivered in our ears a beautiful speech about Torah and worship; and his pleasant speech aroused our hearts to love him and to cleave to him and to heed his voice. And he decided to establish a permanent yeshiva in which Talmud and the Codes would be studied every evening, in accordance with the regulations that he set out.[25]

Soon thereafter, Halperin organized all the city's schoolteachers and outlined new modes for teaching the young. Subsequently, he convened a meeting of merchants and artisans, encouraging them to participate in evening Torah-study classes. A month or two later, he began to persuade these laymen to each donate a modest weekly sum for the support of a full-day yeshiva program for young Torah scholars. By mid-summer, the yeshiva was a reality, maintained by funds collected by an enthusiastic public committee.

The establishment of a rabbinical seminary in Rhodes in 1926 represents a third type of response to the crisis in Torah scholarship. Operating under the aegis of the Jewish community of Turin, the seminary's establishment was made possible by the support of the Italian government. The students were talented Jewish youngsters from Mediterranean Sephardic communities; the language of study was Italian and, apart from rabbinics, the students studied Bible, Italian history, and literature.[26]

There are two significant differences between these new institutions and the classic midrash that are worthy of note. First, the former were not places of Torah study catering to scholars of varying ages and scholarly levels who studied texts of their own choice and progressed at their own pace. Rather, they trained young scholars (and future rabbis) in accordance with a structured curriculum. Second, they were dependent neither on the goodwill (nor the wealth) of a few munificent individuals but instead had a broader base of financial support, whether deriving from small donations by many individuals in the local community (as in Meknes), or support from foreign donors (Jerusalem and Rhodes). While the Meknes approach reflects innovative integration of certain European practices with local traditions and priorities, in the other two cases, the vision was completely European. Porat Yosef was modeled on the East European Volozhin higher yeshiva (*yeshivah gedolah*), and the Rhodes seminary was set up by the Turin community along the lines of its rabbinical seminary. Moreover, both in Jerusalem and in Rhodes, the teachers and the student body formed a self-contained unit that was independent of, rather than integrated into, the local community's social or religious structure. This was illustrated in striking manner when the Rishon Leziyon (Sephardic chief rabbi), Ben-Zion Uziel, noticing that Porat Yosef students knew nothing of the writings of the great medieval Sephardic philosopher-theologians, offered to teach a class on the religious thought of Yehudah Halevi but had his proposal rejected by the yeshiva staff. In classical Sephardic institutions of Torah study, where teachers were part of the local rabbinate, such an occurrence would have been unthinkable.

A major change in the rabbinic training of Sephardic young men took place after the Second World War. Several haredi rabbis who had survived the Holocaust took upon themselves the heroic task of reviving talmudic learning in accordance with the prewar East European ("Lithuanian") model. Since there was no hope of doing so in Eastern Europe itself, they turned their attention to Western Europe (France and England), the United States, and Eretz Israel. It quickly became clear to them that few in the younger generation of Holocaust survivors wanted to study Torah. The renaissance of the "yeshiva world" thus required the mobilization of students elsewhere. In 1946, the leaders of this nascent movement noted the existence of a reservoir of potential candidates in North Africa—especially in Morocco, where many Jews, having only recently been exposed to European modernity, were still positively disposed to Torah study. Accordingly, emissaries were dispatched to Morocco, offering young men the opportunity of studying Torah at prestigious institutions abroad.

Tens and then hundreds of Moroccan Jewish teenagers responded to this call and entered East European-style yeshivot such as Shearith Bnei Yosef in Fublaines (France), Sunderland in England, Mir in New York, and Ponevezh in Bnei Brak (Israel).[27] There they internalized the outlook of their teachers, who considered Moroccan sages to be culturally inferior to those of Eastern Europe. The Moroccan students received sound training in the Lithuanian mode of study and were acculturated into the ethos of the haredi *musar* yeshivot, but they learned nothing of the modes of Torah study and halakhic decision-making that were characteristic of the North African Jewish tradition. Rather, they were taught to regard the prewar, East European yeshiva world as the epitome of Jewish religious existence and to revere the great talmudic scholars of that tradition. In 1952, a center of Lithuanian haredi Torah learning was established in the city of Tangiers. A long and laudatory eulogy of its founder and head, R. Zushe Waltner, reveals clearly what haredi Ashkenazic rabbinic leaders think about Moroccan Jewry and its traditions of Torah:

> The tradition of Torah study in Morocco was utterly different from the norm in Europe. They learned a lot of *Zohar, medrashim* and *Tanach.* Those *talmidei chachamim* who took an interest in *gemora,* learned "on the *daf,*" without much sophistication. Their *shiurim* culminated in a precis of the halachic conclusions of the topic studied. They started with the *gemora* and finished with the four volumes of *Shulchan Oruch....* It's true that there were *chadorim* and yeshiva high schools in Morocco even before... but the approach to teaching there was very primitive. The teachers were devoted and were good Jews but they didn't know how to educate.... They learned by rote and by heart, more than in depth.... Before Rav Waltner came, the idea of spending years learning in yeshiva was foreign to them. Gifted *talmidim* learned in a yeshiva framework for a year or two at most and then left to earn a living.... Rav Waltner brought the Eastern European tradition of Torah study in breadth and depth, ambition for Torah greatness and the self-discipline of *mussar* and planted them, for the first time, in Moroccan soil. He thus wrought a real and startling revolution in the minds and characters of many among the local Jewish population.
>
> Hitherto, a mother's greatest ambition might have been to see her son a *chazan,* a *shochet,* or a successful businessman. Now, parents and youth alike began to see a new ideal—the *talmid chochom,* the *ben Torah,* the Jew whose calling in life was his quest for Torah knowledge and for self-improvement. They tasted the sweetness of *lomdus* and of comprehension. They experienced the tranquility that comes with introspection and self-knowledge. They saw the happiness that prevails in Torah homes and they were fired to try and achieve the same in their own lives.[28]

This transformation led to the emergence of a growing cadre of younger scholars who were ethnically Sephardic but culturally converted to the worldview and religious ideals of the haredi, "Lithuanian," musar-type yeshivot. Conversely, there was a dramatic decline in the number of scholars trained in the original Sephardic tradition. Many members of the new cadre became teachers and ultimately headed yeshivot of their own; in time, they became the mainstay of the Sephardic rabbinic world. This generational transition of rabbinic leadership began to crystallize in the 1970s, and within a decade, "Lithuanian" Sephardic rabbis were already clearly in the majority. As of 2005, virtually all young Torah students from Sephardic ethnic backgrounds were studying in yeshivot that did not subscribe to the neo-classical Sephardic ethos.

Returning the Crown to Its Ancient Glory: Ovadia Yosef's Reformation

In the last decades of the 20th century, R. Ovadia Yosef emerged as the towering rabbinic leader within Sephardic Jewry.[29] Born in Baghdad, Yosef came to Eretz Israel as a child and grew up in an ethnically mixed religious neighborhood of Jerusalem where observant Sephardim lived side by side with haredi Ashkenazim. Indeed, his early years of study were spent in Bnei Ziyon, a haredi school established by Ashkenazic teachers for Sephardic boys. Later, he continued his studies in the Porat Yosef yeshiva. Significantly, for a variety of reasons—possibly connected to his early education and the Porat Yosef curriculum—he did not internalize a major core component of neo-classical Sephardic culture, namely, the religious value of openness to general human culture. On this issue, he is quite close to the haredim. However, he does identify with two other elements of the classical Sephardic worldview. First, he gives considerable weight to the real-life halakhic implications of the Talmud, regarding public service as a dayan or as a community rabbi as a far more desirable choice than remaining in the yeshiva throughout one's entire life. Second, he advocates moderation and leniency as guiding considerations in halakhic decision-making.

Beyond this, Yosef has placed the reconstruction of Sephardic halakhah at the top of his agenda. Since his late teens, he has decried the influence of Ashkenazic halakhah on Sephardic religious behavior and norms, calling on Sephardic and Mizrahi Jews to reject it and "to return the crown to its ancient glory" (*lehahazir 'atarah leyoshenah*). It is important to realize that, for Yosef, this phrase has a very specific meaning. Authentic Sephardic norms are those that comply with the Shulhan Arukh of R. Yosef Caro, often referred to as "Maran." What Yosef advocates is for all to return to and follow the halakhic path set forth by Caro. In terms of the history and sociology of religion, this call is reformationist, as it posits an earlier, "pure" form of religion that is to be preferred over later, "corrupt" religious forms. In Yosef's view, not only has pure Sephardic halakhah been corrupted by "external" (Ashkenazic) sources, but quite a few Sephardic halakhic authorities of recent centuries, have, in one way or another, deviated from the "authentic" Sephardic path set down in Caro's Shulhan Arukh.

In addition to Yosef's general position with regard to the primacy of Caro, he also advances a specific argument concerning Jews who reside in Eretz Israel. He writes that, whereas Sephardim everywhere are obliged to follow Maran, those living in Israel have a specific duty to do so, since Caro has the status of supreme local rabbinic authority (*mara deatra*) for the land of Israel. Indeed, according to certain of Yosef's writings, this duty is incumbent upon all Jews in Israel—regardless of ethnic or geographical origins. Thus, it would seem to follow that not only Sephardim but also Ashkenazim living in Israel must follow the rulings of Maran.[30]

In practice, this leaves Yosef himself as the arbitrator of which decisions by Sephardic rabbis are "truly" Sephardic, and which are not. In total command of classical, medieval, and modern halakhic sources, Yosef is a confident and fearless decisor. Yet by inclination and biography, he is basically conservative rather than creative. Symbolically, in the photograph of his graduating class at Porat Yosef, he is the only person wearing a beard. Ultimately, his halakhic fearlessness is at the service of an agenda that is quite narrowly framed, both socially and religiously, as compared with other leading Sephardic rabbis of the 20th century.

Sephardic Rabbinical Responses to Ovadia Yosef

Yosef first called for a "return" to the rulings of Yosef Caro in the late 1930s. However, it was not until 1984, when he became the spiritual head of the Shas party, that his campaign acquired mass influence. At this point, thousands of ethnically Sephardic students who had experienced discrimination and denigration in Ashkenazic-Lithuanian yeshivot responded to Yosef's message of Sephardic dignity and pride. Having been trained to look up to authoritative Ashkenazic rabbis reputedly gifted with *da'as torah*[31] such as R. Eliezer Schach, many of them now transferred their allegiance to Yosef.[32] In so doing, they accepted him as their religious authority and began to follow his halakhic rulings. A significant literature of halakhic handbooks and compendiums has appeared over the past two decades, providing the Sephardic public with a well-ordered and accessible digest of Yosef's halakhic rulings on many topics and in many areas of life. Many of these publications have been compiled by his sons and students, such as the well-known *Yalkut Yosef* by his son Yitzhak. In general, the traditional Sephardic public seems to rely on these works. However, the same cannot be said for all Sephardic rabbis. The latter fall into four main subgroups.

The first and largest subgroup accepts Yosef as the supreme guide and arbitrator of Judaism in general and of the halakhic tradition in particular. The other three groups of Sephardic rabbis, who do not accept Yosef's primacy, are each smaller in scope than the first group, and are not cut of one cloth. One such group consists of rabbis who consider their birth to Sephardic parents to be irrelevant to their current allegiances. Having been educated and socialized in a Lithuanian haredi milieu, they identify as "simply" haredi Jews. Thus, members of an organization based in Bnei Brak, Irgun Marbizei Torah Sepharadim, are ethnically Sephardic rabbis who reject Yosef in favor of Ashkenazic Lithuanian *gedolei torah* ("Torah greats"). In their view, God gave Israel one Torah, and there is no justification for persons of Sephardic descent to take a racist position and reject the great leaders of the authentic milieu of Torah just because those leaders are Ashkenazic. Indeed, at least one version of the (originally) Ashkenazic Lithuanian "musar" movement—that of Novardohk—exists today only because of its ethnically Moroccan followers.[33]

Members of the third group (of the four) reject Rav Ovadia's contention that in Eretz Israel, Maran holds (halakhic) sway, to the exclusion of practices and customs that characterized Jewish communities in the diaspora. They argue that the move to Eretz Israel does not uproot the right (nor the duty) of, say, children of Tunisian parents to follow Tunisian Jewish customs—even if these customs are not supported by Caro. Rabbis of this group acknowledge in principle the obligation to follow Maran, but in their halakhic works argue that Caro himself upheld the maintenance of local community customs even when these went against his rulings.[34] In addition, rabbinic opponents of Yosef's delegitimization of Sephardic sub-ethnic traditions publish prayer books (*sidurim*) according to those traditions. Thus, in the introduction to *Sidur tefilat hahodesh ner Yitzhak* that he published in 1998, R. Shimon Abihatzeirah, scion of a famous Moroccan rabbinic dynasty, writes:

> In recent years, the customs of our fathers and their traditions of prayer have been disappearing, and all pray in the uniform Sephardic rite (*nusah ahid Sepharadi*), even in synagogues that claim to follow the rite of Moroccan Jews. Because of this, they do not retain the legacy of authentic prayer (*nahalat hatefilah haamitit*) for us and our seed after us. By publishing this magnificent prayer book, we have tried to return the crown to its ancient glory.[35]

The phrasing of the final sentence is both striking and pointed. Whereas Abihatzeirah, too, views "returning the crown to its ancient glory" as an important goal, this will not be achieved by discarding sub-ethnic traditions in favor of a single common *nusah*. Rather, the exact opposite is the case: only by renewed commitment to each community's particular heritage will tradition be authentically renewed.

Finally, a fourth group of rabbis more generally contests Yosef's basic contention that loyalty to Sephardic tradition entails the recognition of the primacy of Caro's rulings over all other halakhic and religious considerations. In their view, important as he is, loyalty to Caro's rulings must be balanced against other values and goals. A programmatic exposition of this position appears in R. David Chelouche's *Hemdah genuzah*, in which he disproves the claim that Caro should be regarded as the supreme halakhic authority of Eretz Israel. For one thing, he writes, the position of chief rabbi of the land of Israel did not exist in Caro's lifetime, and Caro himself was not even the *mara deatra* of his own town of residence, Safed. More important, however, the status of *mara deatra* can apply only to an individual in the present, not to a rabbinic personage from the past. Thus, even if Caro had been the supreme authority in Eretz Israel in his own lifetime, this is of no relevance today. While his Shulhan Arukh is in fact accepted as a canonical work, this is a matter of convention: no formal, binding commitment was ever made by rabbis worldwide never to deviate from Caro's rulings as set down in that work. In addition, Caro himself did not necessarily regard his statement of the halakhah as foreclosing the possibility of future rabbinic initiative and innovation. In sum, all rabbis, argues Chelouche, should have deep regard for Caro's views. Nevertheless, if their own thorough analysis of a halakhic question or issue leads them to a different conclusion from that which they would have reached by relying solely on Maran, they may (and should) rule in accordance with the halakhah as they see it.[36]

Similarly, R. Hayim David Halevi held that contemporary halakhists are not obliged to slavishly follow Caro's rulings. Criticized by a certain rabbi who argued that true adherence to halakhah meant absolute adherence to the Shulhan Arukh, Halevi replied that dynamic (albeit organic) change was in fact the very lifeblood of halakhah. Indeed, he wrote, the eternal relevance of Torah over the course of millennia had been possible

> only because permission was given to Israel's sages in each generation to renew halakhah in accordance with the changes of times and events. Only by virtue of this was the continuous existence of Torah in Israel possible, enabling Jews to follow the way of Torah.... There is nothing so flexible as the flexibility of Torah.... it is only by virtue of that flexibility that the people of Israel, through the many novel and useful rulings innovated by Israel's sages over the generations, could follow the path of Torah and its commandments for thousands of years.[37]

To a greater or lesser degree, mainstream Sephardic halakhah in recent centuries followed the ethos explicated by Halevi. Today, however, with halakhists of Sephardic origin divided between the Ashkenazic haredi ethos and that of Ovadia Yosef, voices advocating a neo-classical Sephardic orientation seem to be almost totally submerged. Apart from several places in which the neo-classical Sephardic approach is advocated and taught,[38] it appears to be in serious danger of being lost. Thus, while the future of ethnically Sephardic Jews is not in doubt, the same cannot be said of Sephardic Judaism.[39]

Sephardic Halakhic Writing in the 20th Century: Responsa

Halakhic writing includes several genres such as responsa (*teshuvot*), novellae (*ḥidushim*), handbooks and codes, and commentaries on earlier halakhic works. Little of the halakhic literature published in the 20th century has been the topic of academic study. In this section, I present a decade-by-decade survey of published Sephardic responsa of the 20th century up until 1990, based on the holdings of the National and University Library in Jerusalem and the Bar-Ilan University library (see table 1 on p. 143).[40] Given the interest these libraries have in maintaining a complete collection of Judaica, and given the fact that books from the 20th century are more easily available than older publications, it seems reasonable to assume that these library holdings account for no less than 95 percent of published works of responsa. Readers are encouraged to bring additional works to my attention.

1901–1910

During the first decade of the century, halakhists active in the land of Israel published more works of responsa than did rabbis in any other country in the Middle East and North Africa. Another general fact to be noted is the relative weight of the Middle Eastern Sephardic rabbinate (outside of Israel): Iraq, Syria, and Egypt account for 38 percent of published responsa, compared with 28 percent for North Africa (Morocco, Gibraltar, and Libya).

Two major Sephardic halakhists died during this decade: Yosef Shaul Eliashar of Jerusalem (1906) and Yosef Hayim of Baghdad (1909). Eliashar—the most influential rabbi in Jerusalem during the last decades of the 19th century—was appointed Rishon Leziyon (chief rabbi of Jerusalem) in 1893. His final volume of responsa, *Shaal haish*, appeared posthumously in 1909. Yosef Hayim was both the greatest rabbi of Iraqi Jewry in modern times and an extremely prolific writer. The four volumes of his *Rav pe'alim* were published in 1901, 1903, 1905, and 1912, respectively. In addition to halakhic responsa, each volume also contained responsa devoted to theological and kabbalistic topics, which were gathered under the title *Sod yesharim*.[41] In this respect, Hayim was very different from Eliashar, who seems to have advocated a strict demarcation between the realms of halakhah and kabbalah.

Other works of responsa published during this decade reflect the geographical spread of Sephardic halakhic expertise at the time. These include works by rabbis from the diaspora communities of Syria, Iraq, Egypt, and Morocco. In Damascus, *Sha'arei 'azarah*, by Ezra Tarab (1851–1920), head of its rabbinical court, was published in 1906. Around the same time, the sixth and last volume of *Penei Yiẓhak*, authored by Yitzhak Abulafia (1830–1910), also appeared.[42] These were among the last volumes of responsa written by rabbis living in Syria. This was also the case in Baghdad, with the publication in 1910 of *Akim et Yiẓhak*, by Yitzhak ben Avraham Shlomo (1835–1920). Damascus and Baghdad had been home to leading rabbis in the 19th century and prior to that time, but already by the first decade of the 20th century, halakhic creativity in these cities was but a shadow of its former greatness.

Moving on to Egypt, we find responsa by Eliyahu Hazan (c. 1845–1908), the grandson of Jerusalem's chief rabbi Hayim David Hazan, who had grown up in Jerusalem. After serving as chief rabbi of Tripoli (from 1874), he took up a similar position in Alexandria in 1888. There, the final two volumes of his responsa work, *Ta'alumot lev*, were published in 1903 and 1907.

The three works of Moroccan responsa include two by members of the illustrious Abendanan family of Fez: *LeYizhak reiah* (1902), by Yitzhak Abendanan (1836–1900), and *Asher liShlomo* (1906),[43] by Shlomo Abendanan (1848–1928). The author of the third work, *Karnei reem* (1910), was Raphael Enkaoua (1848–1935), who later became the chief rabbi of Morocco. *Rahamim peshutim* (1910)[44] was authored by Raphael Hayim Ben-Naim. Born in Tetuan in 1845, he was brought to Tiberias as an infant but in 1881 returned to North Africa (Gibraltar), where he served as rabbi until his death in 1920.

Ben-Naim's biography brings to light the significant links between Moroccan Jewry and Tiberian halakhic scholarship during the 19th and early 20th centuries. Thus, three of the Tiberian rabbis whose responsa were published in this decade were born in Morocco: Raphael Ohana (1850–1902), the author of *Nizkar halakhah* (1906); Yaakov Hai Zrihan (1869–1953), the author of *Bikurei Ya'akov* (1907); and Eliyahu Ilouz (1860–1929), the first volume of whose *Yesh me'ayin* appeared in 1909 (and the second in 1932). Only Aharon Bekhor el-Hadef (1835–1909), who published *Mipi Aharon* in 1907, was born in Tiberias.

During this decade, the literary production of Jerusalem's rabbis was negligible as compared with that of Tiberias. The abovementioned *Shaal haish*, by Yaakov Shaul Eliashar, also contained some responsa authored by his son, Hayim Moshe Eliashar (1845–1924), titled *Penei hamah*. The only other "Jerusalemite" volume of responsa published during this decade was *Vayashev Yosef* (1905), by Yosef Nisim Burla (1828–1903). Another work, *Hod Yosef* (1905), included some reponsa by its author, Yosef Arawas, a Moroccan-born rabbi who grew up in Jerusalem as a member of the local Mughrabi community. In 1903 Arawas moved to Jaffa, where he served in various rabbinic capacities until his death in 1925.

1911–1920

The First World War was the major, but not the sole reason for the paucity of published responsa during this decade. The years before it witnessed the appearance of works of responsa by rabbis from Egypt, Djerba,[45] Bulgaria, and Jerusalem. Raphael Aharon Ben-Shimon, the chief rabbi of Cairo and an innovative halakhist, published *Umizur devash* in 1912.[46] *Gan Ya'akov,* a posthumous volume of halakhic writings (including responsa) by Yaakov Cohen-Gadeisha (d. 1909), who had served as chief rabbi of the Hara Kebira neighborhood of Djerba, was published in 1913, as was *Avnei haefod*, by Salonika-born David Pipano, then rabbi of Sofia (and chief rabbi of Bulgaria from 1920 until his death in 1925).

In that same year, two works were published by rabbis living in Jerusalem. Aleppan-born Yosef Mordekhai Yedid (1866–1930) published his first volume of responsa, *Yemei Yosef* (a second volume of this work was published posthumously in the 1970s), and Avraham Alsheikh (formerly of Yemen) published *Maor degel hatorah*. During the next seven years, however, only one other work appeared, *Zidkat Moshe* (1916) by Moshe Zaken Mazouz (1851–1915), formerly head of the rabbinical court of Djerba.

1921–1930

Eretz Israel regained its primacy in published responsa during this decade, but the Middle East, as a whole, registered a decline: no works were produced by rabbis from Iraq or Egypt, and only one by a Syrian rabbi. Neither did the Sephardic communities of the former Ottoman empire in Europe (Bulgaria, Greece, and Romania) make any contribution in this regard. Half of the responsa works published during this period originated in North Africa (Libya, Tunisia, and Morocco), and two in the far-flung Sephardic diasporas of Argentina and China.

Moroccan authors included two aforementioned figures: Chief Rabbi Raphael Enkaoua, whose *To'afot reem* appeared in 1930, and Shlomo Abendanan, who published *Bikesh Shlomo* in the same year. In Tunisia, the list included *Yashiv Moshe* (1924), by Chief Rabbi Moshe Sitruk (1846–1928),[47] *Yizhak yeranen* (1926), by Yitzhak ben Yeshua Cohen; and *Ohev mishpat* (1928), by Fraji Aloush of Gabes (d. 1920). Another scholar, Hananyah Haviv Azulai, was an expatriate of Eretz Israel who had spent much of his life abroad.[48] During this decade, he resided in Casablanca, where his responsa volume, *Moreh zedek,* appeared in 1924. Hayim ben Shlomo Cohen was a native of Djerba who served as rabbi in Tripoli (Libya) until his death in 1905. His work *Devar hamishpat* was published in 1928, and is listed under Libya.

In Damascus, another work by the aforementioned Ezra Tarab, *Milei de'Ezra,* appeared posthumously in 1924, the only collection of responsa by an indigenous Syrian author published during the 1920s. However, rabbis of Syrian ethnic roots had formed a "colony" in Jerusalem toward the end of the 19th century. During this decade, that community's elderly rabbi, Yosef Mordekhai Yedid, published a second volume of his responsa (*Vayehi Yosef,* 1929).

Yet another Syrian rabbi, Shaul David Sutton (1851–1930), had emigrated in 1913 from Aleppo to Buenos Aires and had been instrumental in the establishment of the Sephardic rabbinate there. He is best known for innovating an outright ban on all conversions to Judaism, which has since become canonized among Syrian émigré communities. His *Devar Shaul* appeared in 1928.

The responsa of Eliyahu Yitzhak Hazan, published as *Yedei Eliyahu* in 1930 (two additional volumes appeared in 1936 and 1937), reflect the experiences of an Iraqi-born rabbi in Hong Kong and Shanghai. David Hai Edrei of Safed (1888–1932), who served as a rabbinical emissary and then as a rabbi in several Central Asian communities during the second decade of the century, later returned to Safed, where he published *Bad David* in 1922. The indigenous Sephardic community of Jerusalem was represented by Hayim Moshe Eliashar (1845–1924), whose *Penei Moshe* appeared in 1921.[49] David Papo (1848–1927), born in Istanbul and educated in Jerusalem, served as chief rabbi of Tripoli (Libya), Bursa (Asia Minor), Monastir (Balkan region of the Ottoman empire), and Baghdad before returning to Jerusalem, where he served as president of a rabbinical court. He published a volume of responsa, *Penei David,* in 1924.

1931–1940

This decade is marked by the striking predominance of responsa authored in Eretz Israel: even prior to the mass emigration of North African and Middle Eastern Jews, almost as many works of responsa were composed by rabbis active there as by halakhists of all other Sephardic communities combined. Almost a third of the volumes of Sephardic responsa published in this decade were by North African authors (Morocco, Algeria, Tunisia, and Djerba). The surprising salience of China is due to the publication of an additional two volumes of Eliyahu Yitzhak Hazan's *Yedei Eliyahu*, in 1936 and 1937. Significantly, there are no works by halakhists active in Damascus, Aleppo, or Baghdad, or in the entire area of the Balkans. It is clear that, outside of Israel, responsa were being written mainly in North Africa (Morocco, Algeria, Tunisia, Djerba, and Egypt).

Tiberian rabbis produced a further cluster of responsa works during this decade: *Hilkhot ishut*, by the Moroccan-born Eliyahu Ilouz (b. 1860, came to Tiberias in 1872, d. 1929), in 1934; *Korban Eliẓur*, by Eliezer Mansour Sithon (1860–1937), in 1936; and *Vayomer Meir*, by Meir Ouaknin (1885–1975), in 1939. (After serving abroad from 1910–1930, Ouaknin returned to Tiberias, where he was chief rabbi until his death.) In 1931, another Tiberias-born and educated rabbi, Yaakov Moshe Toledano (1879–1960), then serving as head of the rabbinical court in Alexandria, published a work of responsa, *Hayam hagadol*.[50] Also serving in Egypt (but hailing originally from Damascus) was Yehudah Hayim Maslaton (1872–1945), whose two volumes of responsa, *Vezot liYehudah* and *Sheerit Yehudah* appeared in 1937 and 1938, respectively.

In Algeria, David Hacohen Scali (1861–1948) of Oran published the two-volume *Kiryat Ḥana David* in 1935/1936, while Moroccan-born Yosef Mesas (1892–1974), who was serving as rabbi of Tlemcen, brought out the first volume of his *Mayim ḥayim* in 1934 (the second volume appeared in 1965).[51]

Two works of responsa by Moroccan rabbis were published during this decade: *Shoshanim leDavid* (1935), by David Sabah[52] (1869–1956) and *Lekhah Shlomo* (1937), by Shlomo Yosef Cohen (1882–1909). In addition, Shimon Abicasis of Mogador included five of his responsa in a book titled *Rakh vatov* (1937).

During this period, the only other volume of Sephardic responsa that appeared during the author's lifetime was *Yerekh Ya'akov* (1940), by Yaakov Arguetti (1862–1944) of the Istanbul rabbinical court. (It was also the last such publication by rabbis active in Turkey.) However, a number of posthumous works appeared. In Djerba, the first volume of *Zera' David*, by Sassi Cohen-Yehonatan (d. 1905), was published by his grandson in 1940 (the second volume came out 12 years later), while in 1932, the responsa of Damascus-born Yaakov Tarab (1862–1923), the chief rabbi of Beirut from 1900 until his death, appeared as the second volume of his *Sheerit Ya'akov*. This turned out to be the last published work of responsa authored by a rabbi who resided in 20th-century Syria (Beirut was the seat of the French Mandatory government of Syria-Lebanon until Lebanon became an independent country in 1943).

In Eretz Israel (outside of Tiberias), Hizkiyah Shabetai (1862–1955), who was born in Salonika but educated in Jerusalem, published the first volume of his *Divrei*

Ḥizkiyahu in 1935 (a second volume appeared in 1952). Also appearing during this decade were volumes of responsa by a father and son from Jerusalem's "Syrian" community. *Vediber shalom*, by Shalom Hedaya,[53] was published in 1934. A work by his son Ovadyah (1890–1969), titled *Yaskil 'avdi*, first appeared in 1931, and two further parts of it came out later in the decade. By the time of his death, Ovadyah Hedaya was a leading member of the supreme rabbinic court of Israel, and *Yaskil 'avdi* ultimately consisted of eight volumes.[54] Ovadyah Hedaya was also a leading kabbalist, and like the works of Yosef Hayim before him, most volumes of *Yaskil 'avdi* contain not only hakakhic responsa but also a section devoted to responsa in the field of kabbalah, separately titled *De'ah vehaskel*.

Contrasting halakhic perspectives are clearly represented by two works of responsa published in Eretz Israel during this decade. Shlomo Eliezer Alfandari, who was more than 100 years old at his death in 1930, hailed from Istanbul and arrived in Eretz Israel in 1904. Known from his youth as a radical anti-modernist, his staunchly, fundamentalist positions were not well received by his peers. This may explain why, after briefly serving as rabbi of Damascus and then of Safed until 1918, he held no other public appointment. He published no responsa during his lifetime; the first volume of his halakhic rulings (*Sheelot uteshuvot MaHaRSHa*) appeared posthumously in 1932.[55] Later in the 20th century, Alfandari came to be regarded as a harbinger of Sephardic haredism, and he was accorded great importance by those loyal to its postulates.

Very different was the halakhic worldview of Ben-Zion Meir Hai Uziel, who published the first volume of his responsa work *Mishpetei 'Uziel* in 1935.[56] He was then chief rabbi of Tel Aviv, and later in the decade, he became the Sephardic chief rabbi of Eretz Israel. In the introduction to the first volume of *Mishpetei 'Uziel*, he wrote:

> In every generation, conditions of life, changes in values, and technical and scientific discoveries—create new questions and problems that require solutions. We may not avert our eyes from these issues and say "the Torah prohibits the new," that is, anything not expressly mentioned by earlier sages is ipso facto forbidden. A fortiori, we may not simply declare such matters permissible. Nor may we let them remain vague and unclear, each person acting with regard to them as he wishes. Rather, it is our duty to search halakhic sources and to derive, from what they explicate, responses to currently disputed issues. ... In all my responsa, I never inclined toward leniency or strictness according to my personal opinions; rather, my intention and striving were always to search and discover the truth. To the extent that my understanding enabled me, I walked in the light of earlier halakhic masters, whose waters we drink and whose light enlightens us; with this holy light, which issues from the source of the hidden, concealed Light, I illuminated my eyes.

Fully within the neo-classical Sephardic tradition, Uziel remained its most prominent protagonist until his death in 1953.

1941–1950

This decade saw little new Sephardic halakhic writing. The declining role of Middle Eastern communities is manifest: although they remained intact (at least until 1948), no works of responsa by rabbis active there were published during the 1940s. Until 1947, only two volumes of responsa by "first-time" authors had appeared: *Minḥat heḥag*, by Hananyah Gavriel Yehoshua (1875–1954), a rabbi from Jerusalem's Ladino-speaking Sephardic community, which was published in 1942, and *Shivat ẓiyon*, by Zion Cohen-Yehonatan of Djerba (d. 1935), which came out in 1943, with a second volume published in 1948. The first volume of *Yayin hatov*, by Yitzhak Nisim (1895–1981), who later served as the Sephardic chief rabbi of Israel, was published in 1947 (a second volume appeared in 1979). *Sheerit Yosef*, the work of another prominent rabbi of Jerusalem's Ladino-speaking community, Yosef Mordekhai Halevi (1875–1947), was published in 1948, a year after his death. (It should not be confused with the responsa by Yosef Mordekhai Yedid Halevi that appeared under the same title in the 1970s.)

Two works written by Moroccan-born rabbis were published at the end of the decade: in 1948, *Pirḥei kehunah*, by Masoud Hacohen (d. 1950), born in Tafilalt and at the time rabbi of Ein Temouchent in western Algeria; and *Vaya'an Avraham*, by Avraham Revah (d. 1938), a disciple of Raphael Enkaoua, published posthumously in Djerba two years later.

1951–1960

What is striking about this decade is the total absence of Sephardic rabbinic centers except for Israel and North Africa. Moreover, within North Africa, works of responsa were produced only by rabbis from Djerba and Morocco, with the former's output surpassing that of the latter. During this decade, several major responsa series began to appear. Khalfon Moshe Hacohen (1874–1949), Djerba's greatest scholar of the 20th century, was no longer alive when the first of his (to date) eight volumes of responsa, titled *Shoel venishal*, was published there in 1952 (after volume 3 appeared in 1961, Israel became the publication venue).[57] His successor, Rahamim Hai Houita Hacohen,[58] published the first of his seven volumes of reponsa, *Simḥat kohen*, in Djerba in 1953, before moving to Israel.[59] These two series constitute the most important halakhic contributions of Djerban rabbis in the 20th century. Another Djerban rabbi, Boaz Hadad, published a volume of responsa in 1955; this was the third volume in his collected works, titled *Vayomer Bo'az* (the first two, appearing in 1948 and 1953, did not include responsa).

A third multi-volume responsa work began to appear in Israel in 1954: *Yabi'a omer*, whose author was a young, Iraqi-born and Jerusalem-educated scholar named Ovadia Yosef.[60] Other works of Sephardic responsa published in Israel during this decade were *Naeh meshiv* (1958), by Nisim Benyamin Ohana (1882–1962)[61] and *Halakhah leMoshe* (1959), by Moshe (ben Eliyahu) Maimon (b. 1924), who came to Israel from Tunisia in 1949 and ultimately served as rabbi of Kiryat Ata, near Haifa.

Works by Moroccan rabbis published during this decade include *Yismaḥ levav* (1952), by Yeshua Shimon Ovadyah (1872–1952); *Gevul Benyamin* (1956), by Benyamin el-Khreif of Meknes; *Hagam Shaul* (1959), by Shaul Abendanan (1882–1972), who was chief rabbi of Morocco from 1949–1965 before settling in Jerusalem; and *Vaya'an Shmuel* (1959), by Shmuel Murciano (1881–1962).[62]

1961–1970

The prominence of Djerba as a center of halakhic creativity, already apparent in the previous decade, became even more manifest in this decade. Indeed, during the 1960s, more works of responsa were published by rabbis indigenous to North Africa (Djerba, the rest of Tunisia, and Morocco) than by Israeli-based Sephardic rabbis. Moreover, relatively few "new" halakhic authors emerged. A second volume of the collected works of David Idan (1873–1954) of Djerba, titled *Maskil leDavid* and including some halakhic responsa, appeared in 1961 (the first volume, published in 1954, was devoted entirely to homilies [*derashot*] in Hebrew and Arabic). Similarly, a work by Khmous Mamou (1892–1947) of Djerba, which included some of his responsa, was published in 1963 as *Benei Makhir*. A further volume of responsa, *Veheshiv Moshe*, by Moshe ben-Shimon Hacohen (1906–1966)—an important halakhist of Djerban origin who moved to Israel in 1958[63]—was published in 1968. Finally, some halakhic responsa by Hayim Eliyahu Avraham Shitrit (who had served as a dayan in Sefrou at the turn of the 20th century) were included in the volumes titled *Melel leAvraham* (1963).

An omnibus volume (*Or ḥadash vezemah zadik*) containing several responsa together with other writings by Yitzhak Alfia (1878–1955), a member of Jerusalem's Syrian community, appeared in 1969. A year later, Syrian-born Shaul Matloub Abadi (1889–1970), who had served as a rabbi and an educator in the Syrian community of Brooklyn, published some of his responsa together with other of his rabbinic writings in *Magen ba'adi* (1970). Yaakov Arguetti of Istanbul (mentioned above) died in 1944; his second work of responsa, *Zekher 'asot* appeared in 1963.

It seems that of the halakhists who first published in the 1960s, only four did so during their lifetimes. One was Yitzhak Rahamim Boukhnik (1915–1975) of Gabes and Tunis, whose opus *Vayomer Yizḥak* (1965) included responsa. The second was Zekharyah Yehiel ben Avigad Sharabi, a Yemenite rabbi in Israel, who strongly opposed establishing an *'eruv* anywhere in Eretz Israel and ruled that to do so was invalid halakhically. He published two works containing responsa on this matter: *Ner Yehudah* (1968) and *Kol bamaḥaneh* (1970). Moshe Malka (1911–1997) was born and educated in Morocco, served as a dayan in Casablanca and, after moving to Israel following the Six-day War, was appointed rabbi of Petah Tikvah. The first volume of his responsa, titled *Mikveh hamayim*, appeared in 1968 (followed by others in 1971, 1976, 1980, and 1984). The fourth living rabbi to begin publishing in this decade was Moshe Avidan, a resident of Acre, in Israel, whose volume of responsa, *Or miziyon* was published in 1965.[64]

A number of responsa (some quite courageous) were also to be found in Yosef Mesas' three-volume *Ozar hamikhtavim*, which began publication in 1968 and covered many areas of traditional Jewish scholarly concern.[65]

In sum, then, the 1960s were not a particularly prolific period of Sephardic responsa publication. This situation, however, was soon to change dramatically.

1971–1980

The 1970s were marked by a dramatic increase in the publication of responsa. The ratio between responsa originating in Israel and in the Sephardic diaspora also changed dramatically. Although quite a few works of responsa by rabbis active mainly in North Africa (Djerba, Tunisia, Morocco, and Algeria) appeared, they were significantly fewer in number than responsa published by authors active primarily in Israel. Indeed, the publication of the works by North African rabbis was itself facilitated by the existence of Israel, where most of these volumes were printed.

Responsa appearing during this decade can be divided into several categories. One consists of "new" works (from manuscript) authored by already-published scholars of the first part of the century. Among these new works were three volumes of Shlomo Eliezer Alfandari's *Saba kadisha* (1973–1974); Yosef Hayim's pseudoepigraphic *Torah lishma'* (1976); Yosef Mordekhai Yedid's four-volume *Sheerit Yosef* (1974–1979); the second volume of his *Yemei Yosef* (1974); and yet another volume by him titled *Yemei Yosef Batra* (1972).

The second category consists of posthumous works by previously unpublished, early 20th-century rabbis. Responsa volumes by rabbis of Tunisian origin figure prominently: these include *Beit halahmi* (1975), by Yitzhak Hai Boukhabza (1853–1930); *Mikhtam leDavid* (1976) (included in the eclectic *'Et dodim*), by David ben Berekhiyah Hacohen, a prominent Djerban rabbi (d. 1950); *Hesed veemet* (1977), by Makhlouf Idan (1882–1946); *Zayit ra'anan* (1977) by Nisim Idan (a brother of Makhlouf), and Yisrael Zeitoun's *Mishpat katuv* (1980).[66] In addition to these works, the responsa of David Moshe Sutton, who was born in Aleppo, became a dayan in Buenos Aires, and subsequently served as chief rabbi of Argentina (d. 1950), were published in 1974 under the title *Ya'aleh hadas*.

The third category consists of responsa volumes written by rabbis active in the second half of the century. Nisim Ezra Khdouri, born and educated in Iraq, came to Israel soon after its founding and lived in Jerusalem until his death in 1972. An omnibus volume of his writings, *Ma'aseh Nisim* (1976), includes a section of responsa. A number of other works were authored by Tunisian rabbis. Two volumes by Mazliah Mazouz (1911–1971), titled *Ish Mazliah*, appeared soon after his 1971 murder at the hands of a Muslim assassin in Tunis. A volume of collected works by Eliyahu Demri (1902–1974), the rabbi of the Tunisian town of el-Hama, titled *Kol Eliyahu* (1975), contained a section of responsa under the separate title of *Vaya'an Eliyahu*. In that year, the writings of Nisim ben Rahamim Cohen (b. 1912, Djerba; d. 1974, Moshav Sharsheret) were published as *Ahimelekh Hakohen*, which included responsa. The responsa of Djerban-born Mordekhai Amias (1886–1973), who served as chief rabbi of Tunisia, were published as *Gedulat Mordekhai* (1976). The responsa of Khmous Yehonatan Hacohen of Djerba, who spent his last years in Israel (d. 1973), appeared in the omnibus volume of his writings, *Kamus 'imadi* (1979). The same year saw the publication of *Ohel Moshe*, by the above-mentioned Moshe ben Shimon Hacohen of Djerba and Tiberias. Responsa by Djerban-born Minyani Raphael Hadad (who died in Israel in 1961, after a long illness) appeared posthumously in *Peter rehem* (1973, 1976), a two-volume compendium of writings by several Tunisian scholars.

Born in Ein Temouchent (Algeria), David Ibn Kalifa studied under Yosef Mesas in Tlemcen and David Scali Hacohen in Oran. He was rabbi of his hometown from 1947 until 1962, when he (as did most of the Algerian Jewish community) emigrated to France. There he continued his rabbinical career, and in 1980 published his work of responsa, *Beit David*.

Rabbinical activity in Morocco is reflected in the responsa of Makhlouf Abi-hatzeira (*Yafah sha'ah*, 1971), Shimon Barukh Ohayon (*Halikhot shva*, 1972), Yehoshua Maman ('*Emek Yehoshua*, 1977),[67] Shimon Dayan (*Zehav shva*, 1977), Yitzhak Hazan (*Yehaveh da'at*, 1974),[68] and Yosef Sharvit (*Orhot yosher*, 1978),[69] all of whom were living in Israel when their works appeared.[70] Makhlouf Shitrit had been a rabbi in several Moroccan cities before moving to Israel and taking up a position in Afula. After retiring, he published the first volume of *Minhat Yehudah* in 1980 (the second appeared in 1989). The most prominent Moroccan rabbi to arrive in Israel during this decade was Shalom Mesas (1908–2003). In 1978, he relinquished his post as chief rabbi of Morocco to become chief rabbi of Jerusalem.[71] Within a few years of his arrival in Israel, he published four volumes titled *Tevu'ot shamesh* (1979, 1980, 1981, 1982), which contain responsa originally written in Morocco. Another rabbi born and initially educated in Marrakech (Morocco), who came to Israel as a youngster, was Avraham Hafuta. The son of Yair Hafuta, the rabbi of the town of Beer Yaakov, he headed the Rambam Ubeit Yosef yeshiva (first in Tel Aviv and then in Petah Tikvah). He published the first and second volumes of his responsa, *Ma'aneh lashon*, in 1976 and 1979 (and a third in 1995). In contrast, Aharon Ben-Hasin (1891–1964) remained in Morocco, where, at the time of his death, he was president of the rabbinical court of Mogador. His responsa work, *Mateh Aharon*, was published in 1971.

The responsa of two rabbis who began their careers in Tunisia but spent much of their lives in Israel appeared during the 1970s. These were *Shemo Avraham* (1976), by Avraham Bitan of Djerba (d. 2001), and *Hehayim bayad* (1974), by Sousou Joseph Cohen (d. 1980), who arrived in Israel in 1956 and later became chief rabbi of Beersheba. Scholars of Yemenite origin who published responsa in this decade were Shalom/Salem Halevi (b. 1891, Sana; d. 1973, Tel Aviv), widely regarded as the "head of all Yemenite rabbis in Israel," whose *Divrei hakhamim* appeared in 1972; and Saadiyah Hozeh, of the Sharab region of Yemen, whose responsa collection *Minhah sheluhah* formed part of the omnibus volume *Sefer toledot harav Shalom Shabazi* (1973).

Israeli-educated authors of responsa include Shimon Hirari, who served as a rabbi in the Kiryat Shalem neighborhood of Tel Aviv (*Sha'ar Shim'on ehad*, 1973);[72] Shlomo Tovim, who studied in a haredi yeshiva in Yahud before becoming a ritual slaughterer and, later (in 1980), rabbi of the town—his work, *Dover shalom* (1973), contains approbations written by leading Sephardic and haredi Ashkenazic rabbis; Ezra Batzri (b. 1937), a Jerusalem-based dayan who is both a halakhist and a kabbalist—the first volume of his *Sha'arei 'Ezra* appeared in 1978 (and the second in 1993); Yitzhak (ben-Yosef) Ben-Shoushan, whose *Toledot Yizhak* (1980) included responsa;[73] and Zekharyah Yehiel ben-Avigad Sharabi, an abovementioned rabbi of Yemenite origin, who included a number of responsa in the first volume of his *Yavo Shilo* (1976).

This decade also witnessed the publication of the first parts of multivolume responsa works by two prominent Israeli-educated rabbis: *'Aseh lekha rav*, by Hayim David Halevi (1924–1998),[74] and *Ḥemdah genuzah*, by David Chelouche, the chief rabbi of Netanya (vols. 2 and 3 appeared in 2000). Finally, Ovadia Yosef, while continuing to publish further volumes of his magnum opus *Yabi'a omer*, also began to publish another responsa series, intended for a less specialist audience, titled *Yeḥaveh da'at* (1977).[75]

1981–1990

Israel continued to be the predominant source of Sephardic halakhic responsa literature during this decade (the inclusion of three works by Iraqi rabbis is slightly misleading, as all three were published posthumously). Again, this decade's responsa may be divided by category. One consists of "new" works by already-published scholars who lived in the first part of the century. Thus, a collection of responsa by Yosef Hayim of Baghdad, published in 1983 as *Hod Yosef*, was culled from earlier published sources, that is, periodicals and publications of his contemporaries. Another volume of his writings from manuscript sources was published in 1988 as *Yedei Ḥayim* and included some responsa he authored, as well as others by his son Yaakov (see below).

Posthumous works of responsa by rabbis of the first half of the 20th century, whose opus had hitherto gone unpublished, make up the second category. Thus, *Zikhronei ish*, by Avraham al-Nadaf (1866–1940), who came from Yemen to Eretz Israel in 1891 and later led the Yemenite community's struggle for autonomy from control by the Sephardic community of Jerusalem. This work was published in 1981, alongside some of his other writings, in the second volume of a two-volume work titled *'Anaf ḥayim*. Responsa by Yaakov ben-Yosef Hayim of Baghdad (1854–1921) appeared in 1983 as *Tal orot*; as previously noted, other responsa of his were published in *Yedei Hayim* (1988). Those of Masoud Mehadar (d. 1959) of Djerba, titled *Mayim tehorim*, were published in 1984; a year later, responsa by Eliyahu Taieb of Tunisia[76] were published under the title *Zekher Eliyahu*. Michael Khmous Hadad (d. 1926) had been rabbi of Medenine (Tunisia); a volume of his work, including responsa, was published in 1986 as *Devek tov*. A son of Khalfon Moshe Hacohen, Avraham Cohen of Djerba (1897–1931), left responsa that were collected and published as *Vayashev Avraham* (1989). The leading rabbi of Djerba until his death in 1919 was Yosef Brabi: a collection of his responsa, titled *Ben porat Yosef* (vol. 3), was published in 1989, bound together with vol. 7 of Khalfon Hacohen's *Shoel venishal*. Also included in this category is *Zon Yosef* (1990), by the Moroccan rabbi Yosef Ben-Naim (1882–1961).

The third category covers responsa by rabbis who were active during the second half of the century, who may be further subdivided according to education in the diaspora or in Israel.

Diaspora-educated rabbis included Yitzhak Elmaliah (1906–1974), who was rabbi of Tlemcen (Algeria) until moving to France in 1962; his responsa were published in 1981 under the title of *Siaḥ Yiẓḥak*. Yitzhak Barda, who had been a rabbi in Morocco before serving as rabbi of Sharsheret (Israel), published the first volume of his *Yiẓḥak yeranen* in 1981.[77] Hayim Amsalem, another Moroccan rabbi who later resided in Sharsheret, published two volumes of responsa, titled *Minḥat ḥayim*, in 1985 and 1986. Aharon Saada Boukhris (1919–1982), who served as rabbi of Ferryville (Tunisia) and then of various villages in Israel, authored *Bigdei Aharon* (1985), which was published by his family in Netanya. Yisrael Hadad (1908–1980) served in several Tunisian communities (the last of which was Sousse) prior to moving to Israel in 1953, where he was a rabbi first in a number of agricultural settlements in the Sharon plain and later in Netanya. A book of his scholarly writings, *Koh leḥai* (1983), includes more than 70 responsa.

The Djerban-born Saghir Ashush (1901–1985) published both *'Et sofer* (1983), a work of responsa relating to the work of scribes, and *'Eẓ shatul* (1988), whose responsa focused on issues of festival observance (an expanded version appeared in 1994). Raphael Khdeir Zaban, educated and trained in Djerba and later chief rabbi of Netivot until his death in 1985, authored *Nefesh ḥayah* (1984), which included several responsa. Shlomo Mazouz (1908–1982), who was chief rabbi of Djerba from 1950 until 1956, later moved to Israel but refused rabbinical appointment there. In 1984, a volume of responsa he had written in 1926–1928 as part of his training as a respondent under Khalfon Moshe Hacohen was published as *Shoel umeshiv*, and in 1987, a collection of more recent responsa, *Kiseh Shlomo*, appeared.

Eliyahu Hadad, formerly secretary of the rabbinical court and head of the community committee in Djerba, authored a work titled *Ḥedvat Eliyahu* (1985), which includes some responsa. Shoushan Khalfon Cohen (1906–1976), a son of Khalfon Moshe Hacohen, who served as a rabbi both in Djerba (until 1956) and in Eitan (Israel), was the author of *Sha'ar Shoushan* (1988).

Rounding out this list of diaspora-educated rabbis are Moshe Ouizgan (1905–1995), who served in several rabbinic capacities in Morocco—ultimately, as rabbi of Marrakech from 1963 until 1983—before retiring to Israel, where he published his responsa *Vayaged Moshe* (1988); Djerban-born Alter Mazouz (1932–1987) moved to Israel in 1956 and in 1976 became rabbi of the village of Eitan, succeeding Shoushan Khalfon Cohen—his *Em labina* (1988) appeared after his death in a traffic accident; and Yahya ben Masoud Shneiur, a rabbi in Jerusalem's Morasha neighborhood, who published vol. 3 of his *Yesh me'ayin* in that same year (the first two volumes did not include responsa). Bougid Hanina Saadon (c. 1900–2006), chief rabbi of Djerba until his departure for France in 1985 and highly venerated by the North African Jewish community, published two responsa works, *Meshiv amarim* and *Magid teshuvah*, as a single volume in 1990 (by 2003, another six volumes had appeared). In that same year, he published another volume titled *Meshiv amarim*, which contained halakhic correspondence with Nisim Hayim Madar, as well as *Higid Mordekhai*, containing halakhic correspondence with Nisim Hayim and Mordekhai Amias Hacohen.

Several works of responsa by Israeli-educated rabbis were published shortly after their death in the 1980s. These included *Naḥalat 'Ezra* (1984), by Ezra Hedaya (1910–1980) the younger brother of Ovadyah Hedaya, and *Asher liShlomo* (1985), by Shlomo Ilouz, who (like Hedaya) had served as a dayan in Haifa.

Among the living Israeli-educated rabbis whose responsa works were first published during this decade were Eliyahu Bakshi Doron, then chief rabbi of Haifa and subsequently chief rabbi of Israel, the first volume of whose *Binyan av* appeared in 1982 (with further volumes in 1989, 1995, and 2001); and two Israeli Yemenite rabbis, Hayim Ksar (*Hehayim vehashalom*, 1982–1984), and Yitzhak Ratzabi (*'Olat Yizhak*, 1989).

Shimon Hirari published an additional volume of responsa, titled *Sha'arei zedek,* in 1982, while Yosef Bar Shalom, chief rabbi of Bat Yam (Israel), published the first volume of his responsa *Nezah Yosef* in 1983 (a second volume appeared a decade later). In 1987, Ben Zion Aba Shaul (d. 1998), head of the Porat Yosef yeshiva, published *Or leziyon* (a second volume appeared in 1993 and a third in 2005). Also in 1987, Yosef Pinhasi, later to become rabbi of Kiryat Sefer, published the first volume of *Yefeh mareh*, which included a section called *Yefeh to'ar*—responsa devoted to "issues of essential importance" (*'inyanim mahutiyim*). Some responsa by Moshe Horev (formerly Khori, a well-known Djerban surname) appeared in his *Keren or* (1987). The following year, *Merosh zurim*, by Shmuel David of Yeshivat Har Etzion[78] (later to become chief rabbi of Afula), was published. Its appearance is significant insofar as David is one of the few younger Sephardic rabbis whose halakhic writings reflect a non-haredi and neoclassical Sephardic approach.

Three volumes of responsa that appeared in 1989—*Hemdat Yosef*, by Yosef Palavani, a disciple of Aba Shaul;[79] *Revid haavrekh*, by Yitzhak Dayan, a member of a *kolel* in Safed; and *Hesed Shaul*, by Avraham Cohen—are indicative of a new trend: relatively young (and peripheral) scholars publishing their responsa in order to establish or enhance their status in the world of halakhic scholarship. The publication in 1990 of Shabetai Levi's *UleLevi amar* and of Pinhas Zevihi's *'Ateret paz*[80] are further indications of this trend.[81]

Summary of Sephardic/Oriental Responsa Publication, 1901–1990

Table 1 summarizes the production of responsa volumes authored by Sephardic/ Oriental rabbis who lived for at least one year during the 20th century. Several points are worthy of note. First, the number of works published in any given decade varies significantly. Clearly, decades experiencing major wars (1911–1920 and 1941– 1950) showed a great decrease in the quantity of publication, whereas the decades immediately following witnessed moderate increase. Interestingly, the post-Second World War resurgence was weaker than that after the First World War, perhaps because of the significant dislocations/relocations of Sephardic/Oriental Jewry in the 1950s and 1960s.

Second, the 1970s and 1980s manifest a quantum leap in the quantity of responsa publication. This undoubtedly reflects conditions in Israel, where most of them appeared. Apart from the relative stability of living conditions for Sephardic/Oriental Jews and the relative availability and affordability of Hebrew publishing in Israel during these decades, there was also a growing market for rabbinic books due to the presence of an ever-larger audience of readers who had acquired rabbinic education

Table 1. Number of Sephardic Responsa Volumes Published (by decade and country)

	1901–1910	1911–1920	1921–1930	1931–1940	1941–1950	1951–1960	1961–1970	1971–1980	1981–1990	Total
Algeria	—	—	—	3	1	—	—	1	1	6
Argentina	—	—	1	—	—	—	—	1	—	2
Bulgaria	—	1	—	—	—	—	—	—	—	1
China	—	—	1	2	—	—	—	—	—	3
Djerba	—	2	—	1	1	5	8	11	13	41
Egypt	2	1	—	2	—	—	—	—	—	5
Eretz Israel/Israel	8	2	5	14	7	9	9	44	46	144
Gibraltar	1	—	—	—	—	—	—	—	—	1
Iraq	4	1	—	—	—	—	—	1	3	9
Lebanon	—	—	—	1	—	—	—	—	—	1
Libya	1	—	1	—	—	—	—	—	—	2
Morocco	3	—	3	3	1	4	4	9	7	34
Syria	2	—	1	—	—	—	—	—	—	3
Tunisia	—	—	4	2	1	—	2	9	8	26
Turkey	—	—	—	1	—	—	1	—	—	2
United States	—	—	—	—	—	—	1	—	—	1
Total	21	7	16	29	11	18	25	76	78	281

in yeshivot (and other institutions of Jewish learning) that were the beneficiaries of government funding. These general trends were accelerated in some communities by specific factors: thus, for example, South Tunisian Jewry (and especially the Djerban community) maintained traditions of communal funding for the publication of works by the community's scholars.[82] As can be seen in the table, the salience of responsa publications by Djerban and Tunisian authors increased notably over the course of the century.

Throughout the century, beginning well before the uprooting and mass emigration of most members of the Sephardic diaspora in Muslim lands, Eretz Israel plays a major role (if not *the* major role) in the production of Sephardic responsa literature. During the first half of the 20th century, a million Sephardic Jews were located in the Middle East and North Africa, and only a small fraction of this number in Eretz Israel. Nevertheless, in all decades except for the second (when relatively few works were published because of the First World War), rabbis based mainly in Eretz Israel published more works of responsa than did their counterparts in other Sephardic communities. The centrality of Eretz Israel became even more pronounced after the 1960s.

A related point concerns the geographical diversity of Sephardic responsa authors, which declines after 1940. In the first three decades of the 20th century, responsa were published by rabbis who were active in seven, six, and seven countries, respectively—peaking to a total of nine in the 1930s. That level of geographical diversity was never reached again: over the next five decades, five, three, six, seven, and six countries were represented, respectively. (Preliminary data for the 1990s do not indicate any increase in geographical diversity.) To my mind, these figures indicate that halakhic creativity dwindled drastically in several Sephardic communities from the 1930s onward (and, given the time lag of responsa publication, probably even before that).

The decline in halakhic creativity, however, was not equally spread among the various communities. Specifically, the data reflect the dramatic decline in the halakhic creativity of Sephardic communities in the Middle East (Iraq, Syria, Egypt) and in parts of the former Ottoman empire (the Balkans, Turkey, Libya), but not in Eretz Israel or North Africa. Moreover, this decline was not caused by the massive relocation of these communities after 1948, but should rather be attributed to the decline of rabbinic culture in those communities, which was caused by factors such as secularization and westernization.

A further point, obvious against the backdrop of the above, is the continuation of halakhic creativity in the Maghreb—Tunisia (and Djerba), Morocco, and even Algeria—during the middle decades of the 20th century, despite the significant French presence. The conditions that enabled this continued vibrant halakhic activity seem to have been different for each country, but the contrast between the Maghreb and all other Sephardic communities is stark. Between 1951 and 1990, the halakhic legacy of the Jewish people was enriched by close to 80 volumes of responsa authored by scholars whose main area of activity was the Maghreb, as opposed to less than 10 volumes authored by rabbis from all other countries of the Sephardic diaspora.

Notes

1. Daniel Elazar has characterized these two great Judaic cultures as "Romantic" [Ashkenazic] versus "Classic" [Sephardic]. See Daniel J. Elazar, "Sephardim and Ashkenazim: The Classic and Romantic Traditions in Jewish Civilization," *Judaism* 33, no. 2 (1984), 146–159. I follow this terminology here with regard to Sephardic culture.

2. For the purpose of this article, "Sephardic" is shorthand for "Sephardic and Mizrahi." Included are rabbis who were born and educated in North Africa and the Middle East (including areas that were ruled by the Ottoman Empire in Europe, and including residents of Israel who were/are ethnically Sephardic/Mizrahi).

3. See my response in *Akdamot* 11 (5762), 139–151 ("Orthodoxy is Not the Exclusively Authentic Halakhic Approach to Modernity: A Reply to Benjamin Brown") to Benjamin Brown's article "On Oriental Rabbis and Religious Zealotry: Towards a Re-Examination" (*Akdamot* 10 [5761], 289–324), in which he discussed four rejectionist Sephardic rabbis.

4. For an account of the dominance of the neo-classical approach, see Zvi Zohar, *Masoret utemurah* (Jerusalem: 1993); idem, *Heiru penei hamizrah: halakhah vehagut ezel hakhmei yisrael bamizrah hatikhon* (Tel Aviv: 2001). For articles in English, see, for example, idem, "Sephardic Rabbinic Response to Modernity: Some Central Characteristics," in *Jews Among Muslims: The Anthropology of Communities in the Pre-Colonial Middle East,* ed. Shlomo Deshen and Walter P. Zenner (London: 1996), 64–80; idem, "Sephardic Halakhic Tradition on Galut and Political Zionism," in *From Iberia to Diaspora: Studies in Sephardic History and Culture,* ed. Yedida K. Stillman (Leiden: 1999), 223–234; idem, "Religion: Rabbinic Tra-

dition and the Impact of Modernization," in *The Jews of the Middle East and North Africa in Modern Times,* ed. Reeva S. Simon, Michael M. Laskier, and Sara Reguer (New York: 2003), 65–84; idem, "On European Jewish Orthodoxy, Sephardic Tradition and the Shas Movement," in *Jewry Between Tradition and Secularism,* ed. Eliezer Ben-Rafael (Leiden: 2006), 133–150.

5. "Hakham" literally means "man of wisdom." This is the standard Sephardic apellation for a rabbi.

6. R. Yitzhak Dayan, "Torat yisrael ve'am yisrael," printed as a preface to Yehudah Nisim Atiya's *Minḥat Yehudah* (Aleppo: 1924).

7. Born in Morocco in 1866, his parents immigrated to Palestine in 1872. In 1892, he became personal assistant to Alexandria's chief rabbi and head of the city's rabbinical court. In 1929, he retired to Jerusalem, where he was elected honorary president of the Moroccan community council.

8. Approbation (*haskamah*) to Hakham Masoud Hai Ben-Shimon, *Kitab al-Aḥkam ash-Shar'iyyah fi-l-Akhwal ash-Shakhsiyyah li-l-Isra'iliyyin* (Cairo: 1912). The last sentence is an allusion to Deut. 4:8.

9. R. 'Abdallah Somekh, *Zivḥei ẓedek haḥadashot* (Jerusalem: 1981), no. 134.

10. R. Yosef Mesas, *Mayim ḥayim,* vol. 2 (Jerusalem: 5785 [1985]), no. 109.

11. R. Ohana was born in Algeria, educated in Jerusalem, and served as rabbi in several communities, including Port Said and Cairo. In 1947, he was chosen to be chief rabbi of Haifa, a post he held until his death.

12. From R. Nisim Binyamin Ohana's introduction to his treatise *Ved'a mah shetashiv laepikoros* (Jerusalem 5719 [1959]). For a detailed account of the relationship between Ohana and Sheikh al'Alami, and how the sheikh's manuscript came into the rabbi's possession, see: Aharon Rahamim Ohana-Ronen, *Sefer hamishpaḥah—mishpaḥat harav Nisim Binyamin Ohana: ma'asim, zikhronot, sipurim (*published by the family, 5761 [2001]), 63–67.

13. Mesas, *Mayim ḥayim,* 2:108.

14. R. Hayim David Halevi, *'Aseh lekha rav,* vol. 9 (Tel Aviv: 1989), no. 30.

15. Cf. *Sifra,* Kedoshim, 2:4; JT Nedarim 9:4.

16. Hayim David Halevi, "Adam harishon veAvraham avi hauma," *Hazofeh* (10 Nov. 1989). Ben-Azai was a second-century rabbi; the statement quoted here appears in *Sifra,* Kedoshim, 2:4:12.

17. Ben-Zion Meir Hai Uziel, *Hegyonei 'Uziel* (Jerusalem: 5714 [1954]), 2: 118. This paragraph was translated by Rabbi Dr. Marc Angel and cited in idem, *Loving Truth and Peace: The Grand Religious Worldview of Rabbi Benzion Uziel,* (Northvale: 1999), 50.

18. Avraham Ben-Yaakov, *Yehudei bavel beereẓ yisrael: meha'aliyot harishonot 'ad hayom* (Jerusalem: 1980), 68–105.

19. This can be seen, for example, in the Eliashar, Pardes, Uziel, Malka, Somekh, Toledano, Hazan, Meyuhas, and Berdugo families.

20. Rabbi Fahima was a teacher in the Ashkenazic Etz Hayim yeshiva in Tangier until 1967. Currently, he is spiritual leader of the Sephardic haredi community in Bnei Brak.

21. The Alliance Israèlite Universelle was founded in 1860 by prominent French Jews to benefit Jews in underdeveloped countries. One of its major activities was the establishment and maintenance of elementary schools where most hours of study were devoted to a modern/western curriculum, and the rest to a limited Jewish studies curriculum.

22. Quoted in Yaakov Lupu, *Shas delita: hahishtaltut halitait 'al benei torah mimaroko* (Tel Aviv: 2004), 156.

23. Beit Zilkha was established in Baghdad by R. 'Abdallah Somekh in 1840 with the explicit goal of training young rabbis. Structurally it resembled the midrash model, with scholars of a wide range of ages sitting together and discussing texts and halakhic issues, and with funding coming from one major source.

24. Yosef Mesas, *Oẓar hamikhtavim,* vol. 1 (Jerusalem: 1998), 93.

25. Ibid., 94.

26. Israeli filmmaker Rami Kimchi is working on a documentary about this institution, at which his father studied.

27. On the induction of young men of Moroccan and North African origin into the recreated world of Lithuanian yeshivot, see Yaakov Lupu, "Haẓalat yahadut maroko latorah: hahashpa'ah haashkenazit 'al 'olam hatorah bemaroko" (Master's thesis, The Hebrew University, 1997); idem, *Shas delita*. For a list of the main yeshivot receiving students from Morocco, see ibid., 75. Of special interest are the interviews Lupu conducted with four Moroccan-born rabbis who studied in Lithuanian-style yeshivot, who had very different reactions to that experience (ibid., 143–169).

28. From the testimony of Rabbi Eli Rothschild regarding Rabbi Waltner's influence on Moroccan Jewry, cited in part 2 of Moshe Musman's "Torah for the Taking, Torah for the Giving: HaRav Zushe Waltner Zt'l," *De'ah-veDibbur* (2 July 2003). Part 1 of this article, which appeared on June 25, 2003, can be found online at http://chareidi.shemayisrael.com/archives5763/KRH63features2.htm.

29. For a rather laudatory biography of Rav Ovadia, which appears with a handwritten approbation written by the book's subject, see Benyamin Lau, *Mimaran 'ad maran* (Tel Aviv: 2005). For a more critical assessment, see Ariel Picard, "Pesikato shel harav 'Ovadyah Yosef lenokhah temurot hazeman" (Ph.D. thesis, Bar Ilan University, 2004). And see my own analysis of Ovadia Yosef's work, in the following note.

30. See Zohar, *Heiru penei hamizraḥ*, ch. 16.

31. *Da'as torah* is best translated as "Torah clairvoyance"—the ability to perceive the correct answer on issues of Torah and halakhah in a trans-rational manner.

32. This transfer of allegiance, however, had its price. Aryeh Deri, the brilliant young political strategist of Shas, later regarded his transfer of allegiance from Shach to Yosef as one of the roots of his subsequent entanglement in corruption, which then led to his trial and imprisonment. It was reported that Deri's last words before entering jail in 2000 were a plea that he would be forgiven by R. Shach.

33. Lupu, *Shas delita*, 133–137.

34. See for instance R. Shalom Mesas' three-volume responsa work, *Shemesh umagen* (Jerusalem: 1986–2000), where he devotes much space to the validation of Moroccan customs and norms seemingly contradicted by Caro's rulings as interpreted by Yosef. And see Shlomo ben Haviv David Toledano, *Divrei Shalom veemet* (Jerusalem: 2000), a volume of more than 300 pages that is devoted to "defending halakhic rulings of North African rabbis from Morocco to Libya against attacks that have been mounted upon them in the Holy Land."

35. Shimon Abihatzeirah (ed.), *Sidur tefilat haḥodesh ner Yiẓḥak* (Jerusalem: 5759 [1998]).

36. R. David Chelouche, *Hemdah genuzah* (Jerusalem: 1968), no. 23 (pp. 235–289).

37. R. Hayim David Halevi, *'Aseh lekha rav*, vol. 7 (Tel Aviv: 1986), no. 54.

38. Among the places teaching in accordance with neo-classical Sephardic tradition are Yeshivat Ahavat Yisrael in Netivot and the study program for young rabbis conducted by the Mimizrah Shemesh organization in Jerusalem.

39. Daniel Elazar sounded a warning back in 1992; see his article "Can Sephardic Judaism be Reconstructed?," *Judaism* 41, no. 3 (1992), 217–228.

40. Responsa published after 1990 will be dealt with in a subsequent paper. I take this opportunity to thank my research assistant, Racheli Carmon, for painstakingly going through tens of thousands of catalogue listings, separating out works of Sephardic and Oriental rabbis relevant to this project, and constructing a series of charts enabling the chronological analysis of the data.

41. Many of Yosef Hayim's writings remained in manuscript form and were published over the course of the century, especially after the Iraqi Jewish community relocated to Israel in 1950 and 1951.

42. The previous five volumes appeared between 1871 and 1898. The date of publication of the sixth volume is variously given by university catalogues as 1903, 1906, and 1908, while the correct date seems to be 5669/1909.

43. A few libraries give the publication date as 1901.

44. This date appears on the title page. Other information, however, indicates that the book may have been published in 1914.

45. Although the island of Djerba was politically part of Tunisia, it functioned as a separate cultural entity. To indicate its great importance for rabbinic creativity, I differentiate between rabbis active in Djerba and those active in the rest of Tunisia.

46. Born in Morocco, Ben-Shimon came to Jerusalem as a child with his father, David, a renowned rabbi in his own right. In 1891, he was appointed chief rabbi of Cairo, a post he held for 30 years. In 1921, he retired to Tel Aviv.

47. A second volume of *Yashiv Moshe* appeared in 1928 and again in 1932. A new printing of both volumes, with addenda, was published in 1980.

48. Born in Jerusalem, Azulai left in 1898 on a fund-raising mission, taught in the rabbinical seminary in Paris in the first decade of the 20th century and, in 1908, moved to Liège (Belgium). Subsequently he lived for a time in London before moving to Casablanca.

49. Another work of responsa was published in Jerusalem in 1921—*Simḥat Kohen* by the long-lived Masoud Hacohen el-Hadad (1820–1927), head of Yeshivat Hamekubalim Beit El. However, since the issues discussed in this work are kabbalistic rather than halakhic, it is not included in the present survey.

50. In 1942, Toledano was appointed chief rabbi of Tel Aviv; his final public position was in the Israeli government, where he served as minister for religious affairs.

51. Another "Algerian" work, *Zakhor veshamor,* by Yosef Renassia, was published in 1940. Although it is classified as a responsa volume, it is actually a didactic work that presents the laws of ritual slaughter in question-and-answer form.

52. Born in Rabat, Sabah served as rabbi in Mazagan, Kuneitra, and Rabat, then moved to Jerusalem in 1949, where he resided until his death.

53. Born in Aleppo in 1864, this halakhist and kabbalist came to Jerusalem in 1895. In 1927, he took charge of Yeshivat Hamekubalim Beit El; three years later, he was appointed the head of the Sephardic rabbinical courts of Jerusalem. He died in 1945.

54. Other volumes appeared as follows: vol. 2 (1935); vol. 3 (1939); vol. 4 (1948); vol. 5 (1958); vol. 6 (1959); vol. 7 (1965); and vol. 8 (1980).

55. Three additional volumes of responsa (*Saba kadisha*) were published in 1973–1974.

56. By the time of his death, five additional volumes had appeared: vol. 2 (1938); vol. 3 (1940); vol. 4 (1947); vol. 5 (1950); vol. 6 (1952). Other volumes were published posthumously in 1964 and 2001.

57. Other volumes were published as follows: vol. 2 (1956); vol. 3 (1961); vol. 4 (1970); vol. 5 (1980); vol. 6 (1986); vol. 7 (1989); and vol. 8 (1991). Vol. 9, an index of the preceding eight volumes, came out in 1998.

58. Rahamim Hai Houita (or Hawita) Hacohen was born in 1901, appointed dayan in Djerba in 1930 and, following the death of Khalfon Hacohen, became head of the rabbinical court in Djerba in 1949. He moved to Israel in 1954, where he resided in the village of Berekhia until his death in 1959.

59. Other volumes appeared as follows: vol. 2 (1966); vol. 3 (1967); vol. 4 (1970); vol. 5 (1971); vol. 6 (1974). The seventh and final volume was published in Jerusalem in 1979.

60. In 1924, Yosef came with his parents from Iraq to Jerusalem. He has since resided there, except for brief stints as rabbi in Cairo (1947–1950) and in Tel Aviv (1969–1973). Additional volumes of *Yabi'a omer* appeared as follows: vol. 2 (1956); vol. 3 (1960); vol. 4 (1964); vol. 5 (1969); vol. 6 (1976); vol. 7 (1993); vol. 8 (1995); vol. 9 (2002); and vol. 10 (2004).

61. Born in Algeria in 1882, Ohana came to Eretz Israel at the age of six and was educated in Jerusalem. He served as rabbi in many communities, including Gaza, Malta, the Syrian Jewish community in Brooklyn, Port Said, and Cairo before becoming chief rabbi of Haifa in 1947, a post he held until his death in 1962.

62. Shmuel Murciano served as rabbi in the Moroccan towns of Taorit and Outat before joining the marriage and divorce department of the Casablanca rabbinate. He emigrated to

Israel in 1956. A second volume of *Vaya'an Shmuel* appeared in 1977; a new edition of both volumes was published in 2004.

63. Born in Djerba in 1906, Hacohen served as rabbi of the Diget quarter until 1958; he then moved to Tiberias and served there as a dayan until his early death in 1966.

64. Avidan was a grandson of Maimon Ben-Atar (d. 1957), who had been a rabbi in Alexandria. At the time his work was published, Avidan directed the Agudat Israel school in Acre. Subsequently, he became superintendent of the (haredi) teacher seminars in the Ministry of Education.

65. See, for example, his ruling in vol. 3 (1975) that modern changes in public mores in Europe with regard to women's apparel made it unnecessary, and in fact inappropriate, for the halakhah to require that married women cover their hair (*Ozar hamikhtavim*, 3:212).

66. Yisrael Zeitoun was chief rabbi of Tunis, 1917–1922.

67. Subsequent volumes appeared as follows: vol. 2 (1981); vol. 3 (1988); vol. 4 (1994); vol. 5 (1997).

68. Vol. 2 appeared in 1980; vol. 3 was published in 1991.

69. Vol. 2 appeared in 1989; vol. 3 was published in 2000.

70. Makhlouf Abihatzeira was born in Tafilalt (Morocco) some time before the First World War. He served as a rabbi in various communities, and eventually became head of the rabbinical court (*av bet din*) of Marrakech. At some point around 1969, he moved to Israel, where he resided in Jerusalem. He was a grandson of the famous rabbi and kabbalist Yaakov Abihatzeira (d. 1880). Shimon Barukh Ohayon was born in Essaouira/Mogador in 1906 and taught in the Keter Torah yeshiva in Casablanca from 1931 until that institution was taken over by Ozar Hatorah in 1947. He then taught in the Em Habanim yeshiva, serving at the same time as overseer of all ritual slaughterers in Casablanca. He moved to Israel in 1955, and became rabbi of Jaffa in 1958. Yehoshua Maman was born in Safi in 1918. After serving as a rabbi and dayan in Safi and Rabat, he became chief rabbi and *av beit din* in Marrakech in 1964. He emigrated to Israel in 1968, where he was appointed chief rabbi of Nahariya; later, he served as a dayan in Beersheba. See the biography written by his son, Raphael Maman, *Yad ramah* (1991), 91–94. Shimon Dayan (1918–1975) served as a dayan in Demnat, Marrakech, and Casablanca. He moved to Israel in 1973. Born in 1919 in the town of al-Masuriya in southern Morocco, Yitzhak Hazan served in various rabbinical capacities in the Dera province until 1948, when he moved to Casablanca. In 1954, he was appointed rabbinical judge in the city of Agadir, and in 1955, he became a member of the rabbinical court of Casablanca. In 1968 he emigrated to Israel; the following year, he was appointed a dayan in the rabbinical court of Haifa.

71. Shalom Mesas was the nephew of Yosef Mesas (whose *Mayim hayim* had been published in the 1930s). The elder rabbi had retired from his position in Morocco in 1964 and subsequently emigrated to Israel, where he served as chief rabbi of Haifa until his death in 1974.

72. Three more volumes appeared in 1976, and a fifth in 1980.

73. At the time, Ben-Shoushan was living in the town of Rishon Leziyon. Toward the end of the century, he moved to the newly established haredi town of Kiryat Sefer. A second, expanded edition of *Toledot Yizhak* appeared in 1989.

74. Other volumes appeared as follows: vol. 2 (1978); vol. 3 (1979); vol. 4 (1981); vol. 5 (1983); vol. 6 (1985); vol. 7 (1986); vol. 8 (1988); vol. 9 (1989).

75. Subsequent volumes appeared as follows: vol. 2 (1978); vol. 3 (1980); vol. 4 (1981); vol. 5 (1983); vol. 6 (1984).

76. Eliyahu Taieb was a contemporary of Moshe Sitruk, who died some time in the first half of the 1930s.

77. Subsequent volumes appeared as follows: vol. 2 (1984); vol. 3 (1988); vol. 4 (1991); vol. 5 (1994); vol. 6 (1998).

78. Har Etzion is a "religious Zionist" yeshiva located in the town of Alon Shevut. Its students serve in the Israel Defense Forces.

79. A second volume of *Hemdat Yosef* appeared in 1991.

80. Vol. 2 appeared in 1995; vol. 3 came out in 1998.

81. Indeed, for not fully understandable reasons, Zevihi's work has been included in the database of the Bar-Ilan responsa project; in consequence, he has attained near-celebrity status among users of that ubiquitous research tool.

82. This characteristic has been described and analyzed by Shlomo Deshen, the foremost scholar of the Jews of South Tunisia. See his "Kitveihem shel ḥakhmei tunisiyah," in *Dor hatemurah*, ed. Shlomo Deshen and Moshe Shokeid (Jerusalem: 1977), 122–137.

"Zikui Harabim": Ovadia Yosef's Approach toward Religious Activism and His Place in the Haredi Movement within Mizrahi Jewry

Nissim Leon
(BAR-ILAN UNIVERSITY)

For more than two decades, the religious culture of Mizrahi Jews, both in Israel and abroad, has been marked by ferment.[1] A major source of this ferment is the growing haredi movement within Mizrahi Jewry, the most prominent manifestations of which are organizations promoting religious return (*haḥzarah bitshuvah*)[2] and the appearance of a haredi ethnic political party—Shas.[3] I use the term "haredi movement" in the sense of a historical dynamic, central to which is the growing influence of haredi elements over the infrastructure of Mizrahi religious culture, namely, rabbinical elites, institutions, and symbols.[4]

One of the outstanding rabbinical figures in the haredi movement within Mizrahi Jewry is Ovadia Yosef, the Sephardic chief rabbi of Israel from 1973 to 1983 and the current spiritual leader of Shas. Yosef's halakhic thought—in particular, his emphasis on "restoring the crown to its past glory" (*lehaḥazir 'atarah leyoshenah*)—has been the subject of scholarly discussion and research.[5] Yosef, a renowned scholar and halakhic authority, did not seek to become a political leader but rather was drawn into the political vortex in the early 1980s when he agreed to head a political campaign aimed at combating the institutionalized Ashkenazic discrimination against Mizrahim within haredi society.[6] Much of the research on "Rav Ovadia," as he is popularly known, has focused on the question of what impelled him to enter the political arena. Why would this foremost halakhic authority, immersed in the world of Torah, choose to go out and mobilize mass support for Shas, appearing at political rallies at which many of those present were far from the pious and demanding religious way of life?

In answering this question, scholars commonly point to the ethno-political significance attributed to Yosef's halakhic work by the communities that regard him as their spiritual leader. Yosef's project of restoring the crown of Sephardic halakhah to its past glory fits in well with the identity politics of Shas activists. On the one hand, the organized power of Shas serves to put this project into practice. On the other hand, promoting this project serves as a marker of ethnic identity for Shas activists, functionaries, and voters, whether in opposition to Ashkenazic hegemony in the haredi world or to the dominant culture in Israeli society.[7] As Sami Shalom Chetrit points out: "For the religiously attuned, the term 'crown' connotes rule and monarchy within a Jewish *religious* context. Nevertheless, in a free political translation, this is the myth of the 'Sephardic revolution,' or 'Mizrahi power,' analogous to 'Black Power.' "[8] These claims are problematic, on two counts.

First, the current research on Yosef's thought emphasizes that, rather than being aimed at transforming Central and East European Jews' halakhic identity, the project of restoring the crown of Sephardic halakhah to its past glory principally addresses Jews from Muslim countries who follow patterns of religious *minhag* (custom) referred to in general as "Sephardic and Oriental."[9] Indeed, the precise location of Yosef's struggle is his ethnic "home court," where for years he has sought to establish his approach. In other words, if there is a Sephardic halakhic project aimed at contesting Ashkenazic hegemony, it has been swallowed up by the internal halakhic struggle. Prominent among Yosef's "home court" rabbinic rivals are Meir Mazouz (of the Djerban/Tunisian community) and Mordekhai Eliyahu (Yosef's successor as Sephardic chief rabbi), whose halakhic rulings adhere closely to the approach of the renowned late 19th-century Iraqi halakhist, R. Yosef Hayim, popularly known as the Ben-Ish Hai (1834–1909). Thus, while Mazouz, Eliyahu, and others may regard Yosef as a distinguished religious leader and as an outstanding figure in the realm of halakhah, they continue to maintain the line of ethnic or community minhag and halakhah in their rulings, often in direct conflict with those of Yosef.[10]

Second, my recent research on the haredi movement within Mizrahi Jewry has come to the conclusion that Yosef's project of "restoring the crown to its past glory" has made major inroads into the routine patterns of religious life. My fieldwork observations (conducted in 23 Mizrahi congregations) attest to Yosef's central and prominent status within them: his halakhic approach is routinely given expression in liturgical practices, on the shelves of synagogue libraries, and in halakhah classes. Significantly, however, the observed population may be divided into three subgroups. One group accepts Yosef's halakhic rulings as authoritative and follows them implicitly at all times. Another relates to his approach while studying halakhah, but maintains its own ethnic community *minhagim*—which increasingly have been backed up by new halakhic texts, some of which were produced specifically as a counter to the influence of Yosef's project. The third group consists of persons indifferent to halakhic subtleties and variations who follow the local rabbi's minhag or that practiced in their family. This is the case with the religiously observant, and even more with the "traditionals" (*masoratim*) whose religious practice is inconsistent, and for whom the fine distinctions between Yosef's halakhic approach and that taken by various other rabbis are even less relevant.

In other words, Yosef's halakhic project has not achieved hegemony, though this is certainly its aim as it competes against other leading halakhic systems in the Sephardic world. Be that as it may, differences in halakhic approach are matters for experts (primarily rabbis and scholars), whereas most worshippers, who are concerned less with halakhic theory than with its practice, are guided by their familial, congregational, and ethnic community traditions. This insight provides the key to understanding Binyamin Lau's conclusion regarding Yosef and his halakhic enterprise:

> It remains difficult to evaluate the whole of Rav Ovadia Yosef's halakhic work or its success, although in certain instances the matter has undoubtedly been resolved. For example, with respect to the [ethnic] origin of rabbinical judges (*dayanim*) in the state of Israel: if, in the past, Rav Ovadia had to demand that in each court (*beit din*) there be at least one Sephardic judge, today the situation is entirely reversed.... Clearly, this revolution in the rabbinical courts is connected to the dramatic rise of the Shas movement, but in no way is it possible to separate that revolution from Rav Ovadia Yosef's declared aim of "restoring the crown to its past glory." With regard to the creation of a united Sephardic front, no definitive assessment can be offered. Notwithstanding his unchallenged position in Israeli public life and his firm leadership among all the ethnic communities, there is no way of knowing whether [his] attempt to create a Sephardic "melting pot" will succeed. The power of the tradition that passes from mother to daughter and from father to son is likely to be even stronger than Rav Ovadia's halakhic rulings.[11]

Notwithstanding, it does appear to be the case that Yosef's concepts have become routine elements in Mizrahi Jews' religious culture, following their dissemination since the early 1990s by Shas functionaries. The latter used their institutional positions and access to financial resources to subsidize the printing and distribution of Yosef's writings as well as of prayer books bearing his imprimatur. In similar fashion, Yosef's halakhic lectures were distributed via the network of Shas-affiliated schools. Yet it would be mistaken to assume that Yosef's power and influence in recent years have rested primarily on politics. While there is some truth in this assumption, it overlooks the crucial fact that Yosef was widely known and venerated in the Mizrahi public many years before the establishment of Shas, and even before he became the Sephardic chief rabbi in 1973. Nearly a decade earlier, for instance, Yosef served as a dayan in the rabbinical court of Petah Tikvah. An article appearing at that time in *Kol Sinai*, a journal published by haredi Mizrahim, described him as follows:

> This young genius has a special talent for going out to the people and winning their hearts with his folksy sermons, while also elevating them in the paths of faith and knowledge.... This young rabbi, involved in the affairs of both community and state, is paving a halakhic path to the solution of actual problems...[yet] in spite of his workload, he never stops expounding Torah to the public by day and by night, on both Sabbaths and festivals, unique in his commitment and concern to restore the crown and greatness of Torah to members of the Mizrahi ethnic communities and to Sephardim.[12]

At the end of the 1970s (several years before Shas was founded), a Moroccan-born rabbi, interviewed for a sociological study of Mizrahi Jews conducted by Shlomo Swirsky, called for the establishment of an ethnic political party—one that would be unlike earlier Mizrahi protest movements such as the Black Panthers. As he explained:

> The Panthers called themselves "Panthers," and this sent voters away. Second, their leaders lacked stature. As we now have a Sephardic president [Yitzhak Navon] [and] a Sephardic [chief] rabbi, Rav Ovadia Yosef, who is a great Torah scholar, all Sephardic

Knesset members will make the sacrifice of giving up their seats within their [various] parties, and because they are already well-known, they will [be able] to come together to form an umbrella organization and establish a political party in their own right.[13]

As these two examples indicate, Yosef's renown as a halakhic authority and spiritual guide does not rest necessarily on his political prominence during the past 20 years. If, as we have just noted, he was already a recognized rabbinic leader within Mizrahi Jewry in the 1960s, the question that needs to be asked is what brought about his deviation from the conventional mold of halakhic scholar and decisor immersed in his books; what transformed him into a figure whose stamp has been imprinted on the haredi movement within Mizrahi Jewry.

In my view, the answer to this question is not only to be found in Yosef's halakhic canon, his elite position in the rabbinical hierarchy, or recent ethno-religious political developments. It is also to be found, as this essay will show, in a hitherto neglected aspect of his career—namely, his religious activism. In other words, the key to understanding Yosef's place in the haredi movement within Mizrahi Jewry lies in the public's identification with his religious activism, as embodied both in his halakhic project and in the emphasis he gives to popular-level public lectures and teaching in the fulfillment of his rabbinical role. As yet unresearched, but of cardinal importance in Yosef's attitude and approach to the public, is the concept of *zikui harabim*, understood broadly as the conduct of activities that enable the masses to attain religious merit or virtue. Indeed, that concept constitutes the defining principle of Yosef's project of halakhic study, decision-making, and teaching. According to him, the obligation to engage in zikui harabim is an integral element in the mission of every rabbi, talmudic scholar, yeshiva student, and simple believer within a religious community facing modernization and secularization. In what follows, I shall show how this principle has informed Yosef's rabbinic career and played a central role in the popular and political Torah discourse that has been used to mobilize and expand the haredi movement within Mizrahi Jewry.

Highlights of Ovadia Yosef's Life and Rabbinical Career

Ovadia Yosef was born in Iraq in 1920 and came to Jerusalem with his family in 1926. As a boy and later as a young man, he studied in various haredi educational institutions, including the newly established Sephardic yeshiva, Porat Yosef, which was known for the piety of its students and their withdrawal from the outside world.[14] Yosef, however, made it a habit to teach publicly. It appears that this unmediated contact with the public made him aware of the gap between what was practiced in the Sephardic communities and the halakhah that, in his view, ought to have been the norm in the land of Israel—namely, that set out systematically in the Shulhan Arukh, the monumental 16th-century code of law authored by R. Yosef Karo ("Maran").[15] The attempt to establish Karo's Shulhan Arukh as the sole halakhic authority in the land of Israel later became the centerpiece of Yosef's halakhic project, earning him a reputation for not paying due heed to local ethnic community minhag and traditions in his halakhic rulings.

In 1948, a few years after his marriage, Yosef was chosen by the chief Sephardic rabbi of the Yishuv, Ben-Zion Meir Hai Uziel, to be deputy chief rabbi of Cairo and head of its rabbinical court. During his years in Cairo, Yosef acquired a firsthand knowledge of the impact of secularization and modernization on a once traditional Jewish community, in particular, the weakening of rabbinical authority even in such spheres as kashruth. There, too, his halakhic discourses (given either in the synagogue or in a private home) served both as an instrument for explaining the minutiae of halakhah and minhag and as a base for rebuilding Jewish religious life; such lessons, he felt, were vital elements in the struggle against westernization and assimilation.[16]

Returning to Jerusalem in 1949 in the aftermath of the Arab-Israeli war, Yosef joined an Ashkenazic *kolel* named Midrash Bnei Zion, some of whose members later became prominent "Lithuanian" haredi rabbis. In the *kolel*, Yosef was exposed both to the method of halakhic argumentation and analysis known as *pilpul*, which was dominant in the Lithuanian haredi yeshiva world, and to the strong ideological tendency within it toward separation from the external world—similar to that which he had encountered earlier at Porat Yosef. In the mid-1950s, he was engaged briefly, but unsuccessfully, in efforts to establish a yeshiva named Or Torah. Following this, Yosef took the first step in what turned out to be a three-decade involvement in the state religious court system at both the municipal and national levels. Both Yosef's erudition (which became increasingly known via his voluminous halakhic writings) and his earlier connections paved the way for the first of a series of appointments to official religious offices, as a member of the Petah Tikvah rabbinical court. In this position, he acquired a reputation for consistently following Sephardic halakhic principles in his decisions and rulings. By the early 1960s, although still only in his mid-40s, he was promoted for the post of Sephardic chief rabbi of Israel by a marginal ethnic haredi movement known as Neemanei Hatorah (the Torah faithful), though the initiative did not get far. This movement, which was active throughout the 1960s, accepted Yosef's rabbinical authority and articulated political aims similar to those later advanced by Shas.[17]

In 1968, Yosef was elected Sephardic chief rabbi of Tel Aviv. Five years later, he became the Sephardic chief rabbi of Israel, holding that office until 1983, when he and his Ashkenazic counterpart, R. Shlomo Goren, reached the end of their statutory term.[18] At that time, Yosef might have been expected to return full-time to his scholarly activities at the head of his own distinctive Torah institution. As a prolific and renowned religious authority with a unique halakhic approach, and as a former chief rabbi, Yosef was certainly well placed to mobilize the resources needed to establish and maintain such an institution. Rather than do so, however, he chose to focus on political activity.

Within three months of leaving office, Yosef issued a public message of support for the rabbis, yeshiva heads, and religious functionaries who had founded a new haredi Mizrahi political organization, the Association of Sephardic Torah Guardians, which was aimed at "strengthening Sephardic Jewry . . . through Torah education . . . and bolstering Torah and welfare institutions."[19] Candidates associated with this organization successfully ran in the municipal elections of 1983 in several places, notably in Jerusalem, Tiberias, and Bnei Brak, and these initial successes were followed by the establishment of a political party under that name, which presented a list of candidates for the 1984 Knesset elections and won four seats. Since then, it has been known as the Shas party, the name consisting of the Hebrew letters *shin* and *samekh* that were chosen to identify it on the ballot papers. (Not coincidentally, Shas is also a common acronym for the Talmud.) Yosef became the new movement's spiritual leader from its very inception and effectively imprinted his rabbinical personality upon it. Indeed, over the years, Shas evolved into a powerful institutional base for disseminating Yosef's halakhic approach. This was accomplished by means of its network of bodies variously offering formal and informal education and kashruth certification and supervision, and via the many religious congregations assisted by officials of the Ministry of Religious Affairs who were also Shas loyalists. Yosef's halakhic approach, if not yet the standard for all Mizrahi communities in Israel and outside it, was fast laying claim to that status, especially among second- and third-generation immigrants from Muslim countries.

Restoring the Crown to Its Former Glory

As we have seen, the scholarly literature on Ovadia Yosef focuses on his halakhic project, viewing it as the key to understanding the political and religious relevance of Shas for many Mizrahim in the 1990s. Specifically, scholars identify two distinctive elements in Yosef's halakhic approach. The first is an avowed general preference for adopting the less-strict halakhic position as authoritative.[20] The second, which was previously touched upon, but which I would now like to explore at greater length, is the project of reinstating Karo's Shulhan Arukh as the sole halakhic authority within the boundaries of the land of Israel.

Scholars have suggested that this project has two underlying rationales. The first is that it represents a reaction to the Ashkenazic dominance of the rabbinate in Israel. In Yosef's view, that dominance had given rise to procedural errors in the religious courts in cases involving Jews from eastern countries.[21] According to the second rationale, the project provides a means of coping halakhically with the diversity of minhag arising from increased numbers of immigrants from varied countries of origin. The mass and variegated immigration to Israel from both Europe and Muslim countries in the 1940s and 1950s led not only to a "carnival of identities," as Yaron Tsur has termed it,[22] but also to a mosaic of religious ways of life, halakhic approaches, and minhag. These were given expression in the establishment of ethnic community synagogues and in the printing of prayer books following their particular liturgy and customs—in effect, via the recreation, as far as possible, of the whole fabric of religious life of the place of origin.[23] Already in the 1930s, Yosef drew attention to the necessity of addressing the question of heterogeneity that had become more prominent with the large influx of olim from European countries along with smaller numbers from the Balkan and Muslim countries. In his view as a halakhist, this state of affairs called for a new order in the realm of halakhah and minhag, which could be found by returning to the rulings of the Shulhan Arukh.[24]

But why the Shulhan Arukh? There were three advantages to following the rulings of Maran, all of which were also indirectly related to what might be termed the "halakhic politics of identity." The first advantage was geo-halakhic—that is, the a priori assumption that the rulings of Karo's Shulhan Arukh (and not the Ashkenazic glosses of R. Moshe Isserles) were binding in the land of Israel. At issue here was the principle of priority in Jewish law which held that in locales with diverse communities and ritual practices, precedence was to be given to the initially instituted set of halakhic rulings as reflected in the established minhag. In the case of the land of Israel, Karo's Shulhan Arukh had been accepted by its inhabitants in the 16th and 17th centuries and hence continued to be authoritative.

Second, the Shulhan Arukh enjoyed a historical and sociological advantage. That work, reflecting the halakhic approaches, principles, and instructions that had crystallized by the 16th century, constituted (in the language of post-modern sociologists) the required halakhic "zero-point." Not only was it commonly found in the religious Jewish home and widely studied as a core text, the Shulhan Arukh also marked the halakhic baseline—the point at which it was possible to distinguish the clearly separate halakhic approaches of "East" and "West," Sephardim and Ashkenazim. At the same time, even though the Shulhan Arukh (with all these varying interpretations) was the source of divided halakhic rulings, the fact that it was a commonly studied basic source text enabled it to serve sociologically as an instrument for the (re)integration of Jewish halakhic identity.

A third advantage, mainly an outgrowth of the latter, was political—or what might again be termed the "halakhic identity politics." Despite an approach that sought to unify the many and varied halakhic customs, practices, and rulings stemming from centuries of multi-diasporic Jewish existence, the Shulhan Arukh was nevertheless identified in common halakhic parlance with the "Sephardic halakhic tradition." While the concept of "Sephardism" was not used here in an ethnic sense, in the common parlance of mid-20th century Israeli society, it served as the basis for the politics of identity.

As a canonical text, the Shulhan Arukh played a dual role. On the one hand, it was indeed avowedly blind to ethnic divisions, intended by its author, Yosef Karo, to serve as a means of creating unity among varied Jewish publics. On the other hand, the historical and sociological layers of text were, as noted, identified more with the halakhic world of Jews in Muslim countries, and less with that of the masses of Jews dispersed across Eastern and Central Europe. In other words, the text of Karo's Shulhan Arukh provided a clear delineation of the dividing lines between "Sephardim" and "Ashkenazim," which were institutionalized in 20th-century Israel in official religious institutions and rabbinical offices. Furthermore, in daily speech in Israel, "Sephardic" and "Mizrahi" (which has manifest ethnic connotations) are used interchangeably or are virtually synonymous.

The above reasoning provides the key to understanding the reformative-Orthodox position taken by Yosef, as cited in *Yalkut Yosef*, a compendium written by his son:

> And even if a hundred *aharonim* [later halakhic authorities] disagree with him...he who issues a binding halakhic ruling is not permitted to adopt a more stringent position in opposition to lenient rulings by Maran, even if there are many authorities who disagree with Maran; neither may individuals follow stricter custom in contradiction to a lenient ruling by Maran pertaining to the same matter, because all of the rulings of Maran—the *mara deatra* [lit. "master of the place"], whose authority we accept—are

like the law of Moses at Sinai, with which there can be no disagreement, and he who diverges from his edicts, whether to the right or the left, treats his masters with disrespect.[25]

The revolutionary implications of Yosef's halakhic project were already apparent in his first book, *Hilkhot 'olam*. This work, summarizing public halakhic discourses delivered by Yosef in one of Jerusalem's ethnic community synagogues in the 1930s, has received considerable attention from scholars such as Lau, largely because it is the first book in which Yosef directly takes issue with the halakhic approach of the Ben-Ish Hai by pointing to the discrepancies between it and that of the Shulhan Arukh. Yosef's line of thought did not go unnoticed by the rabbis of the Porat Yosef yeshiva in which he studied. In that yeshiva, which had been built on the basis of the Ben-Ish Hai's vision and whose teachers and students followed his halakhic rulings and minhag, the direction in which Yosef was moving appeared to be close to heretical. In their eyes, for its leading student to oppose the Ben-Ish Hai's approach was without doubt a problematic reformatory tendency, and for years Yosef was roundly criticized for it. What is important here, however, is not so much the fierce halakhic controversy between the two sides as the manner in which Yosef eventually chose to resolve it. Here, for the first time, the political implications of Yosef's heuristic approach—teaching Torah in a local setting, and the unmediated connection with the public—begin to be revealed. That approach establishes him as a rabbinical figure known to all, with some seeing him as a walking halakhic encyclopedia. In order to disseminate his views, Yosef employed a heuristic method of inculcation that, in modern marketing terms, may be described as the door-to-door approach. The neighborhood halakhic class; the mass meeting; the wall posters in synagogues; short articles on the weekly Torah portion in leaflet hand-outs for worshippers—all of these became an integral part of Yosef's struggle to bring his halakhic approach to the people. The concept that he continues to employ to characterize and justify this practical effort is zikui harabim.

Enabling the Many to Acquire Religious Merit

While the evaluation and appreciation of Ovadia Yosef's halakhic project is a matter for scholars, it seems that the high public esteem for his work does not stem only from the impressiveness of his vast erudition in matters of Torah or from his transformative approach toward the halakhah and minhag within Mizrahi ethnic communities. Indeed, something entirely different was much more frequently mentioned in my many fieldwork conversations. Time and again, Rav Ovadia was described as someone who was close to the people, who understood their language and inner thoughts; a rabbinical figure projecting both accessibility and authenticity, as manifest, for example, in his dress and manner of speaking. This is quite surprising because, since the founding of Shas, Yosef has if anything become further removed from the people. Notwithstanding, his public image is that of a rabbi who, with all his knowledge, erudition, and elevated status, is still within reach—one who seeks to be close to members of his flock. This image, I believe, is the outcome of his application of the principle of zikui harabim, which underlies Yosef's rabbinical (or more precisely, pastoral) approach.

The source of the term zikui harabim is a passage found in Pirkei Avot (5:18):

Whosoever enables the people to attain religious merit will not come to any sin, but whosoever leads the people astray will not be permitted to repent. Moses enabled the people to attain religious merit, and hence their merit is ascribed to him, as is written: "He executed the justice of the Lord, and His ordinances for Israel" [Deut. 33:21].

According to most interpretations of this passage, "religious merit" is attained by fulfilling the commandments, and to "enable the people" refers to teaching them Torah and, more generally, leading them on the path of righteousness. Such an approach was manifest both in the struggle to reinforce an existing religious community being eroded by the processes of modernization and secularization, and in the Sisyphean effort to expand that community by means of religious activism. In contrast, Yosef's concept of zikui harabim formed part of his criticism of the self-segregating world of the haredi "society of learners" (hevrat halomdim) of which he regarded himself as a member.[26] Yosef's criticism, it should be emphasized, appears to have been directed not only at Ashkenazic haredism but also at his own alma mater, the Porat Yosef yeshiva—the place where a historically based Mizrahi haredi identity had begun to crystallize.

Yosef dealt with this theme in the introduction to Yabi'a omer, his main responsa work, subsequently revising and publishing it in expanded form under the title "Igeret leven torah" (Letter to the Torah scholar).[27] In both works, Yosef's demands of the contemporary ben torah—the yeshiva student, or even the community rabbi— are made clear. The latter's calling is not just halakhic expertise; even more important is disseminating his knowledge and teaching the public. Thus, at the center of the life of Torah study is not learning per se but rather turning it into an instrument of public guidance—a tool by means of which the rabbi can become rooted in the life of the community to which he turns. Torah study is an instrument for acquiring religious knowledge, on the one hand, and for expanding the influence of the religious life in an era of modernization and secularization, on the other.

As Yosef writes:

By learning well the halakhot that apply today, he can teach the people the way of the Lord, and enable the masses to attain religious merit, as has already been said in the Gemara Baba Batra 8a: "And they follow Your footsteps and are the bearers of Thy word" [Deut. 33:3].... These are the Torah scholars who weary their feet trudging [from town to town and country to country] to learn Torah.... And [the Sages] also said, "those who make the masses righteous are like eternal stars" [Dan. 12:3], for just as the stars look small to us but are infinitely larger than the earth, so too is the value of those who make the masses righteous.[28]

In other words, the neighborhood Torah class as well as the countrywide Torah gathering—every framework from the smallest to the largest whose purpose is to transmit knowledge of the Torah to the public at large—is crucial not only for communal leadership but also, and even more so, for the rehabilitation and strengthening of the religious community. It is incumbent upon the Torah scholar to leave the confines of the study hall to teach Torah and halakhah wherever he can be of influence.

As Yosef comments:

> In truth, every married Torah scholar, and especially one with divinely endowed teach-
> ing gifts, is obliged to give classes in halakhah to the masses and to teach them the
> way of the Lord with regard to frequently encountered halakhot, for instance, laws
> relating to the recitation of the Shem'a and 'Amidah prayers; laws about the Sabbath and
> forbidden foods; laws regarding family purity and the festivals. . . . [T]he most righteous
> person, even one whose soul has attained divine perfection and comes close to the
> angels' moral qualities, behavior, and striving to serve the Lord, does not reach the
> heights of religious merit of whosoever teaches and guides others to the good and right
> path. . . .[29]

Interestingly, Yosef's interpretation of zikui harabim as portrayed in the figure of
the rabbi who accompanies the people in their daily lives and who uses teaching
frameworks to establish an unmediated connection with the public he seeks to lead,
brings to mind the very leader whose halakhic heritage he is variously and frequently
accused of opposing: R. Yosef Hayim. The latter was known not only for his rich
halakhic opus but also for public sermons on halakhah that were spiced with stories
and legends (*agadot*) presented in everyday language. In the introduction to his
eponymous halakhic work, the Ben-Ish Hai writes: "Indeed it is well known that
sermons based solely on halakhah do not attract the masses; rather, the essence and
bulk of the sermon should relate to *agadah* and ethics."[30] From his early days, Yosef
has clearly followed this injunction, giving halakhic discourses to varied publics in
many places, and later extending his contact with the masses via live video transmissions, later widely distributed as CD and DVD recordings.

Yosef's demand to engage in zikui harabim has also made a powerful impression on the rabbinical elite surrounding him. Thus, for example, Meir Mazouz (who,
as noted, is sometimes critical of Yosef's halakhic approach), portrays him as
follows:

> There were great rabbis in the world, from the time of the Patriarch Abraham to the
> present, but they were great men who located themselves in a corner and stood there
> alone. Two hundred years ago there was a famous *gaon* who never saw the light of the
> sun: he would close the window during the day so that he could sit and study, undis-
> turbed by the buzzing of a fly or bee.[31] He studied all the time. However, *Maran shelita*
> [a reference to Yosef] studies all the time and also constantly gives the people Torah.
> And with such love and with such devotion! I remember the first time that I heard his
> sermon, I was studying *Yabia' omer*. I was then a new immigrant. On one occasion I
> prayed in the Great Synagogue of Bnei Brak. An Ashkenazic *kolel* student came over to
> me and said: "You know, Rav Ovadia, may he live long, is giving a Torah discourse
> after the Sabbath is over. He delivers it all without notes—it's worth coming to, it's
> worth hearing." Fine, I said, if an Ashkenazi says so, then it must certainly be
> worthwhile attending. So I went after the Sabbath, arriving at 8:30 p.m.—and gentle-
> men, I will tell you what I felt—this is the absolute truth, to this day I am stunned by the
> power of that feeling. The discourse lasted until 12:30 a.m., and I felt that if the rabbi
> had kept on giving it until the morning, no one would have felt the need for sleep, [no
> one would have felt hunger]. . . .
>   On arriving home, I was asked, "Why were you so late?" I told them: "It's a pity the
> rabbi didn't deliver his discourse in the cemetery."

"Why?" they asked.

I said: "If the rabbi had given it there, I assure you the dead would have arisen to hear it." I felt—my soul had come to life.

Mazouz continues his account:

This discourse was geared to Torah scholars and kolel students. But there was also another class at the Rashbi yeshiva, which the rabbi . . . used to give weekly, and I would see how the people arrived there dressed in all kinds of clothes. Plasterers, building laborers, and house painters would come to listen straight from the construction sites. Once, just before Tisha B'av, the rabbi discussed the custom of extending the prohibition against eating meat on the 9th of Av until midday on the 10th of Av, because the destruction of the Temple had continued during part of that day. After the rabbi explained it for half an hour, and referred to the talmudic tractate Ta'anit and to the views of the halakhic authorities, someone asked him, "Rabbi, is it forbidden to eat [meat] on the 9th and 10th of every month?"

That's what he asked . . . someone else would have mocked him and laughed at him . . . and in such a case, one could guarantee that he would rush off never to return. But the rabbi took him seriously, answering, "I was referring only to the month of Av, to the 9th and 10th of Av," with such fondness, with such love. One does not receive this kind of love everywhere. Someone else would have said that it was a waste of his time to explain the matter to this tiresome fool. . . . But [if] a Jew asks, your must encourage him [lit., "give him life"].[32]

The Rashbi synagogue (named after R. Shimon bar-Yohai) to which Mazouz refers is located in the heart of the Hatikvah neighborhood in south Tel Aviv. During the 1970s, Yosef used to give a weekly discourse there to a diverse audience of yeshiva students, rabbis, laborers, artisans, and businessmen, both neighborhood residents and outsiders. This was only one of many such discourses regularly delivered by Yosef at the time. What was distinctive about this discourse, and indeed, of Yosef's heuristic style as a whole, was, as Mazouz noted above, the smooth transition from the popular manner of speaking when addressing a diverse mass public to the elevated language of the academy when speaking to Torah scholars. While some may detect a hint of an attitude of superiority in such popularization, what is important for our purposes is the dynamic use Yosef made of the language of the Torah discourse as an instrument in the work of zikui harabim.

There can be no doubt that the principle of zikui harabim has had a marked impact on many rabbis and activists. These followers have adopted Yosef's patterns of activity as their model and inspiration for what should be the role of the rabbinate among Mizrahi Jewry; and this, in turn, serves as the basis for a critical view of the past. Thus, Aryeh Deri, the former political head of the Shas party, said the following about Yosef's role among his "dear and beloved brethren," the mass of good people and true believers. According to Deri:

[F]or them and for their sake, our father and shepherd, Maran—the Rishon Leziyon, Ovadia Yosef, may he live long—descended "from the mountain to the people." This most elevated [spiritual] shepherd, the Torah master whose every hour is so precious and whose every moment is spoken for, has directed attention to spreading the network of Torah study, to establishing Torah youth centers around the country. . . . [F]rom his words, we learned the way to return the people to its heritage—to go down to the people and to take them by the hand, one by one! To speak, to converse, to persuade with pleasantness.[33]

This statement gives expression to the place occupied by the principle of zikui harabim in the haredi Mizrahi movement's mythologization of the figure of Ovadia Yosef. But one should also take note of its latent critique: "from his words, we learned the way to return the people to its heritage." What it suggests is that Yosef's appearance signals the dynamic turn that was required of Mizrahi Jewry's rabbinical elite. That claim, in my view, is connected to Shlomo Deshen's important observation that, prior to coming to Israel, many rabbis within Mizrahi Jewry were graced with the aristocratic quality of distance from the public. According to Deshen, this quality may explain in part the Mizrahi rabbinate's moderate reaction to the challenges of modernization and secularization, as compared with that in Central and Eastern Europe. The rabbinate's limited interaction with the masses and relative confinement within the synagogue and study hall sheltered them from full awareness of the meaning of the processes of secularization for the traditional order.[34] The symbolic figure of Rav Ovadia, actively engaged in zikui harabim, highlights the turn required of the Mizrahi rabbis—namely, coming closer to the masses, rubbing shoulders with them, and being involved in their lives. In this sense, the principle of zikui harabim signifies a historic dividing line.

Zikui Harabim in Mizrahi Religious Popular Culture

During the past few decades, as has been seen, Ovadia Yosef has been transformed into the leader of a mass movement. To further clarify his status within haredi Mizrahi Jewry's mass public, I would like to focus on a realm that is relatively far removed from halakhah and the rabbinate, namely, popular Israeli music of the 1990s. By "popular music," I refer not to songs played on mainstream Israeli radio stations or to compact disks or cassettes sold in major music store outlets, but rather to works found on the margins of "Mediterranean" or "Mizrahi" music. Beginning in the 1990s, a number of Mizrahi singers and songwriters, who were either newly religious or becoming more devout (*mithazkim*),[35] increasingly produced religious songs. Popular Mediterranean singers such as Benny Elbaz, Ofer Levi, and Jackie Makaiten made the switch from songs that appealed to the secular public to popular religious songwriting that focused on the revolution in their lives and in those of many Mizrahi Jews in Israel and abroad. In the main, recordings of their songs could be purchased in religious music stores or heard on the pirate radio stations that were the mouthpiece of the movement of religious return. Instead of making women the object of desire, these songs expressed a longing for God; in place of the tribulations of love, they spoke of the difficulties of coming close to the Creator; in lieu of confessions of unfaithfulness, these singers bared the sins of their secular past.

There were also songs of love in which musicians and songwriters dedicated their voice and their arranging skills to extol the name of the person they regarded as the leader of the "spiritual revolution"—Rav Ovadia Yosef. Song collections with titles such as "Haosef hagadol: kulam sharim lemaran" ("The grand collection: everyone

sings to Maran") attest to the cult of Yosef as a "living saint" (*haẓadik heḥai*) that
pervades religious return activities and the haredi movement within Mizrahi Jewry.
Songs from these collections are part of the run-up to the satellite video transmissions
of Yosef's weekly sermons that are beamed to many places in Israel and around the
world, and they are played over the loudspeakers at local and national mass gatherings attended by Yosef. The audience knows the words and often sings along. Here,
for example, is an excerpt from one of the better-known songs on the cassette,
"Hamalakh hatov" [The good angel], which is commonly heard on the haḥzarah
bitshuvah radio stations that broadcast Yosef's weekly Torah discourses:

> The good angel has appeared, and he will give us his discourse—
> Our master Ovadia has arrived, he will shower us with words of Torah.
> Behold, the beloved of us all—[may he live] until one hundred and twenty!
> Until the arrival of our Messiah—the head of the sages!
> Here he [comes] by helicopter—the lion of the rabbis!
> Here he [comes] via satellite—he is the leader of the shepherds!

Rather than highlighting the power of Yosef's halakhic decisions, this song emphasizes the active and dynamic dimension of his public persona. Yosef is portrayed
as a rabbi who accompanies his community/audience wherever it goes—even, if
necessary, by means of helicopters or other sophisticated technology; in fact, by any
means that will enable him to convey his words of Torah to the public as part of zikui
harabim. In a different song, "Histaklu 'alav" (Look at him), the significance of
Yosef's image for the Mizrahi religious renewal movement is made even more
explicit. The following is an excerpt from this song, originally performed by Amir
Eliyahu, a popular singer in the Mizrahi haredi movement:

> Purity of virtues, a vessel full of mitzvot—
> We aspire only to rise to his [level of] righteousness.
> He is a shepherd and leader in our generation,
>   we will follow in his path without stopping.
> His words are spoken calmly
>   for the ears of the entire Jewish people.
> Wisdom and knowledge radiate from his words—
> He teaches the way of the Torah.

> [*chorus*]:

> Look at him, look at him,
> Our master, the splendor of the generation, look in his eyes!
> Look at him, look at him,
> Our master, the splendor of the generation, look in his eyes—Rav Ovadia!

> On the night after the Sabbath and on Tuesdays
> He gives his discourse by way of satellite.
> The rabbi prays for all our brethren
>   that they will not stray from the path of God.
> We will all raise our arms,

We will call out in prayer to the heavens,
That our rabbi should be given long life,
[Spend] his days and also his years in pleasantness.

[*chorus*]:

Look at him, look at him,
Our master, the splendor of the generation, look in his eyes!
Look at him, look at him,
The splendor of the generation, look in his eyes—
Rav Ovadia! Rav Ovadia! Rav Ovadia![36]

Set to the tune of a familiar Israeli melody, this song is the opening number of a cassette bearing the title "Borei olam" (Creator of the universe). What is most striking about this particular song is that Yosef is described not as an ethnic figure, set apart in terms of ethnicity, but rather as precisely the opposite, as belonging to all Israel. His Torah teachings—regular public discourses delivered from a variety of public platforms—are not intended solely for the Mizrahi public in Israel and abroad, but for the entire Jewish public ("His words are spoken calmly/ for the ears of the entire Jewish people"; "The rabbi prays for all our brethren/ that they will not stray from the path of God"). Furthermore, Yosef is presented as a figure transcending the historical moment. He personifies "the splendor of the generation," that is, the purpose of the generation, and he sets the standard for the religious way of life: "We aspire only to rise to his [level of] righteousness." In this song, it seems, Yosef has become both a personal model to be emulated and an inspiration for religious activity.

The activity of the haredi movement within Mizrahi Jewry in recent years has made the concept of zikui harabim part of the idiom as well as the source of widespread efforts to stem the tide of secularization by expanding the mobilizing capacity of religious return organizations. Activists and preachers in the hahzarah bitshuvah movement, alongside community rabbis and the believing public, perceive the task of zikui harabim as integral to their religious way of life. This goal finds practical expression in various forms of religious activism, such as distributing cassettes, teaching daily Torah classes, and organizing prayer quorums—indeed, anything that can bring the nonobservant public closer to a religious way of life. This activism blends in well with the efforts of Torah scholars, as well as with those of the newly religious (*ba'alei teshuvah*) and those engaged in spiritual "strengthening," to live according to the halakhah in religiously mixed social situations. For it is the case that not all Mizrahi newly religious move into religiously homogenous neighborhoods even after they marry; many of them remain in their original religiously mixed environment and come into daily contact, whether in their own extended family or among the members of their synagogue, with what haredim characterize as a secular (*hiloni*) way of life.

In fact, religiously mixed nuclear families are relatively common in Mizrahi society: one spouse may be newly religious or undergoing spiritual strengthening while the other may maintain a lifestyle that, while respectful of tradition, is far from being strictly religious. Such situations are recipes for conflict and family breakup. Rabbis active in the hahzarah bitshuvah movement are well aware of the problem and seek remedies more basic than verbal encouragement and reinforcement. One remedy is found in the principle of zikui harabim. Thus, for example, Amnon Yitzhak, a well-known religious preacher, specifically devotes audio and video cassettes to that end, urging his followers to disseminate them widely as part of the effort to further religion. Many newly religious engage daily in the work of zikui harabim, whether by disseminating religious-return cassettes, organizing local religious activities, or re-invigorating the neighborhood synagogue. Such activity, in turn, creates a sense of religious purpose that assuages the complexities of their situation. The concept of zikui harabim thus translates the constraints of living in a religiously mixed environment into a life mission, one that merges with the path that Ovadia Yosef affirms in his own way of life.[37] "We are all Rav Ovadia," I was told by a man who had returned to religious observance (we were speaking in a synagogue in south Tel Aviv, a mainly secular area). "We are all Rav Ovadia," he repeated, "we are all part of the spiritual revolution. Everyone contributes something of himself to bringing distant people closer, at home, in the synagogue, in the neighborhood, in the family."

Conclusion

Up until this point, I have sought to account for Yosef's prominent position in the haredi Mizrahi movement. In this concluding section, I would like to deal with Rav Ovadia's more symbolic role as a kind of "bridge" between the haredi leadership and the traditional (*masorati*) masses—that is, between the world of a self-segregating contemporary Mizrahi haredi Judaism that tends to close itself off in the study hall and stick closely to the written halakhic text, on the one hand, and the world of the community outside the study hall, whose religious life rests largely on mimetic traditions, on the other. Underpinning this symbolic role is Rav Ovadia's demand to effect zikui harabim, which is also a demand to renew the connection between the "rabbi," the Torah scholar, and the traditional masses. The result of such a connection is a new form of haredi community with far more fluid boundaries, a community based on joint observance of the halakhah as a way of life. In such a community, the balance moves from the responsibility of the religiously observant public for what happens in the world of nonobservant individuals to the responsibility of observant *individuals*—be they rabbis or lay believers—for the nonobservant collectivity that nevertheless maintains some link with religious life. An observant individual is caught between the self-segregating demands of the *ḥevrat lomdim* and the contrary demand to engage in religious activism and seek to influence what happens both in the community and beyond it. Under such circumstances, Yosef warns,

> one who repairs only his own soul attains only small merit, but one who repairs his own soul and many other souls with him attains double merit, as it is taught: "Whosoever enables the people to attain religious merit will not come to any sin, but whosoever leads the people astray will not be permitted to repent." One who teaches his friend's son Torah attains the merit of "sitting" in the yeshiva on high [that is, in the world-to-come].[38]

It is this approach, rather than politics or even his halakhic leadership, that clarifies Yosef's role as *the* prominent symbolic figure in the life of contemporary

Mizrahi Jewry. Mizrahi Judaism, it should be recalled, is not freighted with a historical tradition of confrontation with modernization and secularization, but rather is characterized by its moderate and relaxed reaction to them. However, late 20th-century developments also brought to the fore within Mizrahi Jewry a third option: a haredi existence that stands out by virtue of the link that it maintains with the traditional, nonobservant masses. It seems that, for the purpose of dealing with such a complex situation, the public sees Yosef as a figure who offers it not only the option of halakhic living as the basis of community, but also the option of a new halakhic-tradition community structure that arises out of halakhic study, in particular the interaction between the rabbi, the newly religious, and the religiously mixed environment that characterizes the local Torah study session.

In my fieldwork, I noted the significance of such interaction between these religiously heterogeneous publics. It was epitomized in a dialogue that took place in one of the synagogues, in which the main participants were the young neighborhood rabbi (who belonged to the new and increasingly haredi rabbinical elite within Mizrahi Jewry) and a traditional Mizrahi Jew who had come to say kaddish in memory of his mother. The dialogue arose during a class on halakhah conducted by the rabbi in the short interval between the weekday afternoon and evening prayers. This class dealt with the question of whether a traditional—but not strictly observant—Jew is entitled to receive religious honors such as being called to the Torah during the Sabbath morning prayer service. Significantly, from our present perspective, the discussion turned quickly from a dry legal analysis of the halakhic issues into an emotionally charged, multi-person debate over the nature of Jewish identity and the contemporary Jew's ultimate purpose. Following it, I went over and talked with the rabbi. In the course of the conversation, it emerged that one of the rabbi's underlying aims was to use halakhic study sessions as a springboard for exactly this kind of discussion of questions related to faith, thereby opening up the opportunity to influence the traditional, but not strictly observant, masses who frequent synagogues to return to religion, or at least to consider that possibility. "That is my contribution," he said, "to zikui harabim." It was perhaps here that I first came to appreciate the transformative importance of this practice in Mizrahi religious life.

My analysis would suggest that the significance of the figure of R. Ovadia Yosef extends beyond the realms of the specific history, sociology, and anthropology of Mizrahi Jewry. Indeed, his image and halakhic project to a large degree represent an attempt to resolve the constant tension in which Orthodox Judaism finds itself due to the deep inroads of the turn to modernity. On the one hand is the structural threat to the observant community that leads to self-segregation and isolation; on the other is the acknowledgement of its responsibility for the Jewish collectivity beyond the boundaries of the Orthodox enclave. Tension of this nature seems to be more prevalent within groups in which the observant and the nonobservant are located on the same societal continuum. Prior to the appearance of the Shas party in the mid-1980s, discussions on how to bridge the gap between the religious and secular publics took place primarily within religious Zionist frameworks. The link between the haredi leadership and the traditional publics forged by the Shas party made this question relevant outside those frameworks as well.

There are a number of explanations for Shas' emphasis on this link. One may be found in functionalist models, whereby the pursuit of political power gives rise to strategies of voter mobilization that are based on a pragmatic approach to religious observance and identity-based political marketing. But attention must also be paid to the new religious emphases and patterns of religious life engendered by a link between the haredi leadership and broader, traditional publics. Thus, for example, the concept of zikui harabim accords heightened significance to the figures that forge the link between the conservative religious approach and a religious activism that is given expression in the effort to extend to the utmost the boundaries of the religious community. Herein, perhaps, lies the secret of Yosef's influence as the model and source of inspiration for the haredi movement within Mizrahi Jewry: a movement that combines a dynamic activism directed at changing social reality with the conservative world of religious traditionalism and the haredi society of learners, in order to shape and firmly establish a new religious institutional reality.

Notes

1. In the context of this essay, "Mizrahim" refers broadly to Jews originating in Muslim countries. It should be noted that the terms "Mizrahim" and "Mizrahi Jewry" are not generally employed within the haredi (ultra-Orthodox) and *dati* (religious Zionist) world. The more common term is "Sephardim" or "Sephardic Judaism"—an allusion both to the mythology surrounding the historical origins of Mizrahi Jewish communities and to the pattern of ritual performance and halakhic approach adhered to in most of these communities. For instance, prayer books used in the ethnic community synagogues maintained by Jews from Muslim countries usually bear the subtitle: "In accordance with the custom of the Sephardim and the Eastern Jewish Communities." In this essay, I use the term *Mizrahi* to refer generally to Jews in Israel who originated from Muslim countries. In all matters relating to religious life, however, I use the term *Sephardic*.

2. *Hahzarah bitshuvah* refers to activities designed to bring—or return—people to religious belief and observance, whereas the term *hazarah bitshuvah* refers to those who choose to return to a life of religious observance. The newly religious or "returned" religious are known as *ba'alei teshuvah* or (with more of a stress on the return to religious observance) *hozrim bitshuvah*. On the hahzarah bitshuvah movement among Mizrahi Jewry, see Yehuda Goodman, *Hahzarah bitshuvah vezehuyot datiyot hadashot beyisrael bithilat shenot haalpayim* (Tel Aviv: 2002); Nissim Leon, "Kenes hateshuvah hehamoni baharediyut ha-mizrahit," in *Haredim yisreelim: hishtalvut belo temi'ah?*, ed. Emmanuel Sivan and Kimmy Caplan (Tel Aviv: 2003), 82–98; Benjamin Beit-Hallahmi, *Despair and Deliverance: Private Salvation in Contemporary Israel* (1992); Kimmy Caplan, "Israeli Haredi Society and the Repentance (Hazarah Biteshuvah) Phenomenon," *Jewish Studies Quarterly* 8, no. 4 (2001), 369–398. See also idem, "Studying Haredi Mizrahim in Israel: Trends, Achievements, and Challenges," in this volume, 169–192.

3. On political expressions of this ferment, see Yoav Peled, "Hidah ushmah Shas," in *Shas: etgar hayisreeliyut*, ed. Yoav Peled (2001), 52–74; Neri Horowitz, "Shas vehaziyonut: nituah histori," *Kivunim hadashim* 2 (2000), 30–60; Ricky Tessler, *Shas vehamahapekhah hadatit* (Jerusalem: 1993); Aaron Willis, "Sepharadic Torah Guardians: Rituals and Politics of Piety" (Ph.D. diss., Princeton University, 1993); David Lehmann and Batia Siebzehner, *Remaking Israeli Judaism: The Challenge of Shas* (London: 2006).

4. See Nissim Leon, "Hatenu'ah haharedit ezel mizrahiyim beyisrael barei uvehayei hapraktikah hadatit" (Ph.D. diss., Tel Aviv University, 2005).

5. See, for instance, Zvi Zohar, *Hairu penei hamizrah: halakhah vehagut eẓel ḥakhmei yisrael bemizrah hatikhon* (Tel Aviv: 2001), 312–352; Hayim Shain, *Medinat hayehudim: shelav hasikumim: harav 'Ovadyah Yosef vehanasi Aharon Barak* (Tel Aviv: 2003); Binyamin Lau, *Mimaran 'ad maran: mishnato hahilkhatit shel harav 'Ovadyah Yosef* (Tel Aviv: 2004); Yossi Elituv and Zvi Alush, *Ben porat Yosef: ḥayav, mishnato umahalakhav hapolitiyim shel 'Ovadyah Yosef* (Tel Aviv: 2004); Nizan Chen and Anshil Pepper, *Maran: 'Ovadyah Yosef, habiyografiyah* (Jerusalem: 2004).

6. See, for example, Aryeh Dayan, *Hama'ayan hamitgaber: sipurah shel tenu'at Shas* (Jerusalem: 1999), 85–103; Menahem Rahat, *Shas: haruaḥ vehakoaḥ* (Bnei Brak: 1998), 32–43.

7. Eliezer Ben-Rafael, *Zehuyot yehudiyot: teshuvot ḥakhmei yisrael leBen-Gurion* (Sde Boker: 2001), 70–80; Baruch Kimmerling, *Mehagrim, mityashvim, yelidim: hamedinah vehaḥevrah beyisrael, bein ribui tarbuyot lemilḥamot tarbut* (Tel Aviv: 2004), 282–336; Shlomo Fischer and Zvi Bekerman, "'Kenesiyah' o 'kat'?," in Peled (ed.), *Shas—etgar hayisreeliyut*, 321–342; Lehmann and Siebzehner, *Remaking Israeli Judaism*, 74–119.

8. Sami Shalom Chetrit, "Milkud 17: bein haredivut lemizrahiyut," in Peled (ed.), *Shas—etgar hayisreeliyut*, 46.

9. For a definition of minhag as it relates to Yosef's approach, see Lau, *Mimaran 'ad maran*, 325–366.

10. Ibid., 190–201.

11. Ibid., 373.

12. *Kol Sinai* (Shvat [Jan.-Feb.] 1964), 4.

13. Shlomo Swirsky, *"Lo nehshalim ela menuhshalim": mizrahim veashkenazim beyisrael, nituah soẓiologi vesihot 'im pe'ilim ufe'ilot* (Haifa: 1981), 312. The rabbi's name is not given.

14. This section is based on biographical studies that deal with Yosef, in particular, Neri Horowitz, "Yeshivat Porat Yosef," lecture given at the Forum on the Sociology of Higher Education, Tel Aviv University, 2003; Lau, *Mimaran 'ad maran*, 25–150.

15. Horowitz, "Shas vehaẓiyonut"; Lau, *Mimaran 'ad maran*. The honorific title "Maran" is often appended to the names of respected rabbinical figures, particularly among Mizrahi Jewry. Standing alone, however, it generally refers to R. Yosef Karo.

16. Horowitz, "Shas vehaẓiyonut."

17. This marginal movement would have been forgotten, were it not for the fact that as early as the 1960s it suggested a political program very similar to that of Shas. For instance, in 1962, the year the movement was founded, its activists proposed the establishment of a Council of Torah Sages whose members would come from the ranks of the Mizrahi rabbinical elite. *Kol Sinai*, the movement's publication, was used by Yosef as a platform for disseminating his halakhic approach to the public at large, in particular, new immigrants from Muslim countries.

18. Previously, although the chief rabbis faced periodic reelection, there were no term limits, but in 1979 the law was changed in favor of a single, non-renewable ten-year term.

19. Lau, *Mimaran 'ad maran*, 114.

20. This preference is in accordance with the classic Sephardic approach toward halakhah. For a theoretical discussion, see ibid., 255–268; see also Zvi Zohar's essay in this symposium, "The Sephardic Halakhic Tradition in the 20th Century," esp. 119–130.

21. Lau, *Mimaran 'ad maran*, 86–100.

22. Yaron Tsur, "Aimat hakarnival: 'hamarokayim' vehatemurah beve'ayah ha'adatit beyisrael haze'irah," *Alpayim* (2000), 19.

23. Leon, "Hatenu'ah heharedit eẓel mizrahiyim beyisrael," 113–155; Yoram Bilu, *Lelo meẓarim: ḥayav umoto shel rabi Ya'akov Vazanah* (Jerusalem: 2004) (in English, *Without Bonds: The Life and Death of Rabbi Ya'akov Wazana* [Detroit: 2000]); Moshe Shokeid, *The Dual Heritage: Immigrants from the Atlas Mountains in an Israeli Village* (Manchester: 1971).

24. On the meaning of Yosef's halakhic work with regard to the halakhah practiced by Ashkenazic Jews, see Zohar, *Hairu penei hamizrah*, 312–347; Lau, *Mimaran 'ad maran*, 190–201.

25. R. Yitzhak Yosef, *Sefer yalkut Yosef* (Jerusalem: 1971), 207.

26. Samuel Heilman and Menachem Friedman, "Religious Fundamentalism and Religious Jews: The Case of the Haredim," in *Fundamentalisms Observed*, ed. Martin E. Marty and R. Scott Appleby (Chicago: 1991), 197–267.

27. The fact that this book appeared in Rashi script rather than in conventional Hebrew letters would seem to indicate that it was intended for a scholarly audience.

28. R. Ovadia Yosef, *Igeret leven Torah* (1997), 23.

29. Ibid.

30. R. Hayim Yosef, introduction to *Ben ish-ḥai* (Jerusalem: 1991), 3.

31. The reference is to the Vilna Gaon (R. Eliyahu b. Shlomo, 1720–1797).

32. Quoted in M. Katzir, *Baasher talekh* (Jerusalem: 1997), 264–265.

33. Aryeh Deri, *Shaagat Aryeh* (n.p.: 2001), 9–10.

34. Shlomo Deshen, "Hadatiyut shel hamizraḥim: ẓibur, rabanim, veemunah," *Alpayim* 9 (1994), 44–58.

35. See Caplan, "Studying Haredi Mizrahim in Israel," 181–182.

36. "Histaklu 'alav," lyrics by Leah Eliyahu, melody by Zeev Nehama and Tamir Kaliski. The original song, "Histakli 'alai" (lyrics by Zeev Nehama) was sung by Eyal Golan, a well-known Israeli singer.

37. Goodman, *Haḥzarah bitshuvah vezehuyot datiyot ḥadashot beyisrael.*

38. Yosef, *Igeret leven torah*, 24.

Studying Haredi Mizrahim in Israel: Trends, Achievements, and Challenges

Kimmy Caplan
(BAR-ILAN UNIVERSITY)

In 1984, Rabbi Chaim S. Karelitz, a well-known mitnagdic haredi publicist in Israel, wrote an article that appeared in *Diglenu*, published monthly by Zeirei Agudat Israel. "We must realize," he wrote,

> that haredi Jewry, those who came from Ashkenazic countries, were trained for generations to do battle against the maskilim, against secularism, Zionism, and all kinds of ideologies that appeared primarily in European countries, whereas Sephardic Jews essentially did not know of these wars until they came to Israel.[1]

Since the early 1980s, the religious sector of Israeli society has witnessed the emergence of a new subgroup, haredi Mizrahim. Notwithstanding the fact that various aspects of its development and its social and religious boundaries remain unclear, this subgroup is distinctive both organizationally and politically. However, as we shall see, its members' identification as haredim is a novelty in the Sephardic world.

This essay, which is based primarily on a representative survey of scholarship on the phenomenon of haredi Mizrahim, pinpoints both its achievements and challenges. In order to characterize the extant scholarly works in this field, we must look at two related bodies of research findings, one dealing with traditional Mizrahi Jews in Israel, the other with Israeli haredi society. This approach provides us with clues as to which aspects of research on haredi Mizrahim have been well covered and which have been either neglected or have only recently begun to receive scholarly attention. In the course of this essay, I note several unresolved aspects of those issues that have already been investigated, in addition to raising questions and suggesting a number of further avenues and topics of research.

Terminology, Characteristics, and Demography of Haredi Mizrahim

The terms "Mizrahim" and "haredim," whether separately or in conjunction, are not self-explanatory. As to the first, scholars of Israeli society have increasingly characterized Jews from Middle Eastern and North African communities as Mizrahim rather than "Sephardim." The latter term originally referred to Jews whose forebears were expelled from Spain in 1492 (as distinct from "Ashkenazim," whose origins lay in Germany or Eastern Europe), but during the modern era it was broadened to apply as well to Jewish communities of non-Iberian background whose ritual and liturgical practices followed the Sephardic rather than the Ashkenazic tradition. More broad distinctions were carried over into the Yishuv and the newly established state of Israel, although in the latter it became increasingly common to use the term " 'edot hamizrah" (communities of the East) to refer collectively to the large numbers of recently arrived Jews from Middle Eastern and North African countries.[2] Over time, some of them began to eschew the Sephardic designation and to identify culturally and politically as Mizrahi, which literally means "eastern" or "Oriental." Even though this term is not without problems—it is far from clear where the geographic boundaries of the "East" lie and how these relate to cultural differences—we use it in this essay to refer to Jews from North African and Middle Eastern countries whose families immigrated to Israel either before or shortly after its establishment.

Attaching the term "haredim" to Mizrahi Jews is also somewhat problematic. As illustrated in Karelitz's article, those who use the term are generally referring to the 19th-century European Ashkenazic social, cultural, and religious milieu, which had little in common with the Mizrahi Jewish experience.[3] Identified mostly with R. Moses Sofer (1762–1839; known as the Hatam Sofer), Jewish Orthodoxy regards itself as the only natural, authentic, and therefore legitimate continuation of traditional Judaism. This contrasts with the scholarly approach that defines it as a modern phenomenon with marked dissimilarities from the traditional Judaism that it inherited.[4] The most basic difference between traditional and Orthodox Judaism lies in the contrast between living a traditional life and consciously inventing a tradition, or, in other words, between traditional Jews and "traditionalized" Jews.[5]

Jewish Orthodoxy, then, is seen as a modern response to the decline of traditional Jewish society, to the emergence of rival Jewish movements and ideologies—primarily the Enlightenment (Haskalah) and Reform—and to increasing secularization and nonobservance. During the 20th century, Orthodox leaders continued to grapple with these challenges as well as with those emanating from Zionism and Conservative Judaism, giving rise to such a diversity of response that the term "Orthodoxy" requires further specification along historical, geographical, philosophical, sociological, or other lines.[6]

Above and beyond their intrinsic interest, these terminological complexities compound the difficulties of clearly delineating the boundaries of the contemporary haredi Mizrahi phenomenon in Israel. Thus, current definitions of Israeli haredi society that emphasize historical and ethnic elements are only partially applicable to haredi Mizrahim. In 1985, Menachem Friedman and Yosef Shilhav characterized haredim as wholly committed to the strict interpretation of halakhah exemplified in the East European Jewish tradition, and claimed that this applied as well to haredi Mizrahim.[7] By 1991, however, Friedman had added several additional criteria: neo-traditionalism, the obligation to learn Torah, anti-Zionism, and a collective "fear of erosion" resulting from the choice of many Jews (actually, the majority of them) to abandon traditional life in favor of other Jewish religious or secular options.[8] He identified four Ashkenazic groups—Lithuanians, Polish hasidim, Hungarians, and Jerusalemites—as representing the main haredi types.[9] Elsewhere, he emphasized the centrality within haredi society of the "society of learners" (*ḥevrat halomdim*), pointing to the latter's influence on its ethos, internal authority structure, and standards of religious observance, all of which had come to be dominated increasingly by the halakhic texts rather than, as hitherto, by oral traditions.[10] A similar "Ashkenazocentric" approach is manifest in the extensive and programmatic article on haredi society co-authored by Friedman and Samuel Heilman that appeared in 1991 in the first volume of the Fundamentalisms Project sponsored by the University of Chicago.[11] A year later, Heilman published an ethnographic study of haredi society that ignored haredi Mizrahim.[12]

In contrast to the Ashkenazic haredim described in these works, haredi Mizrahim do not subscribe to East European Jewish traditions but rather have created their own, derived from historic Sephardic Judaism; as we shall see, R. Ovadia Yosef opposes the strict Ashkenazic reading of halakhah. Thus, as compared with Ashkenazic haredim, haredi Mizrahim are neither opposed to Zionism on theological grounds, nor do they view Israeli national institutions negatively. Yosef, who served as the (Sephardic) chief rabbi of Israel from 1973 to 1983, has ruled that the Hallel prayer recited on various Jewish religious festivals may also be recited, albeit without a blessing, on Israel's independence day (contrary to the Ashkenazic haredi position);[13] the very fact that Yosef over the years held several positions in Israel's official rabbinical structures is in itself indicative of a more positive approach toward the Zionist state, notwithstanding the fact that this approach is not presented in theological terms.[14] In addition, the extent to which haredi Mizrahim have adopted the Ashkenazic model of a "society of learners," with all of its concomitant influences, is unclear.

Furthermore, there are certain common behavioral patterns among haredi Mizrahim that are both rare and frowned upon in Ashkenazic haredi circles. For example, although the former's involvement in army service (both compulsory and reserve) has been on the decline in recent years, it is still more prevalent among them than among their Ashkenazic counterparts. By and large, haredi Mizrahim seem more favorably disposed to secular education—even if only for pragmatic reasons—and they are also less segregated in their marriage choices: whereas Ashkenazic haredim from birth rarely marry newly religious haredim, let alone traditionally observant non-haredi Jews, such marriages are both more common and more acceptable in haredi Mizrahi circles. In sum, Mizrahi haredism rests on its own distinctive halakhic values and behavioral foundations and is not some watered-down version of the Ashkenazic model.

To be sure, haredi Mizrahim are influenced by their mitnagdic Ashkenazic haredi counterparts—in their manner of dress, in their unquestioning acceptance of rabbinic authority (*da'at torah*),[15] and in their political organization, as evidenced by the establishment of an authoritative council of rabbinic leaders, Moezet Hakhmei Hatorah, whose decisions, like those of the similarly structured Moezet Gedolei Hatorah of the Agudat Israel party, are binding upon their delegates in the political arena.

Notwithstanding recent advances in the study of the phenomenon of haredi Mizrahim, it still requires clearer definition, not only on its own account but also for the light it sheds on Israeli haredi society and culture as a whole, within which the size and significance of the Mizrahi segment is growing rapidly. According to some estimates, haredim constitute about 10 percent of the Israeli Jewish population— some 500,000 persons—of whom about a third are Mizrahi.[16] As we shall see, this quantitative base has enabled haredi Mizrahim to become a significant force in Israeli society.

The Unnoticed Rise of Mizrahi Haredism

As has been seen, the study of haredi Mizrahim was divided between two fields of research on Israeli society: one focusing on Mizrahim and the other on haredim. For various reasons, the initial appearance of Mizrahi haredism went unnoticed. Only in the early 1980s did this phenomenon begin to attract attention, and almost a decade passed before the first sociological and anthropological studies appeared.

Up until that point, several developments had taken place in the study of Israeli Mizrahim. Research began not long after the establishment of the state and culminated in 1954 with the publication of Shmuel Eisenstadt's sociological study of the trends and characteristics of the absorption of immigrants in Israel.[17] This study, together with later works that were mostly influenced by the "melting pot" ideology, provided sociological guidelines for understanding the process of nation-building in Israel. Special emphasis was laid on the various types of rural settlements in Israel, in particular the moshavim, many of which were populated largely by Mizrahi immigrants.[18]

Other studies that combined sociological and anthropological approaches were published in the 1970s by such scholars as Shlomo Deshen, Harvey Goldberg, and Moshe Shokeid. Their research was concerned primarily with the cultural and symbolic aspects of the immigrants' lives in their countries of origin and in Israel, as well as with social structure and religious beliefs and practices.[19] Several additional works of this type came out during the 1980s and 1990s.[20] The earlier works in particular focused on the more traditional rural immigrants from North Africa and the Middle East who had been sent to settle on Israel's periphery. Few scholars in the 1960s and 1970s, however, explored urban Mizrahi communities such as those of Jerusalem.[21] During these decades, several anthropologists did investigate the role played by saints, rabbis, and traditional healers among Mizrahi Jews.[22] But in focusing on "colorful" and "exotic" groups of Mizrahi immigrants, these scholars, it has been suggested, while presenting their culture as "authentic," on the one hand, essentially excluded them from the Israeli mainstream, on the other.[23]

To the best of my knowledge, none of the research appearing in the 1960s and 1970s reported on developments that might indicate the impending emergence of a self-conscious and vibrant haredi Mizrahi society. On the contrary, some of these studies concluded that the considerable changes experienced by Mizrahi immigrants to Israel in the religious, communal, and personal spheres pointed in the direction of a weakened role for religion and traditional religious authority in their lives.[24] To be sure, such a conclusion had some basis in fact. Many Mizrahi immigrants indeed experienced a weakening of religious observance as they struggled both to survive economically and to become integrated into Israeli society.[25] The spread of this phenomenon did not encourage consideration of the possible development of "strong religion" among Israeli Mizrahim.[26] In addition, as noted, most of the research on them was conducted on Israel's periphery. Yet most of the initial activists and leaders of Shas, the haredi Mizrahi political party, came from the heart of Israel's urban areas, primarily Jerusalem and Bnei Brak, where many of them were learning in mitnagdic Lithuanian yeshivas in which they increasingly felt discriminated against because of their ethnic origin.[27] This phenomenon was overlooked, as were the efforts of Mizrahi rabbis such as Eliezer Ben-David and Eliyahu Schrem in the 1950s and 1960s to elevate knowledge and commitment to religious observance among Mizrahim, in part by encouraging parents to enroll their children in the religious school system.[28] Finally, as noted, at least some of the early scholarly research was designed to assist Israeli policymakers in dealing with the mass immigration of North African and Middle Eastern Jews and their subsequent absorption into Israeli society. These studies were understandably influenced by the sociological paradigms of modernity and secularization current at the time, which were predicated on the assumption, among other things, that religion, and especially its conservative expressions, was in decline.

Not only did scholars of Israeli Mizrahim miss the rise of Mizrahi haredism, so, too, did scholars of Israeli haredi Jewry. As we have seen, Jewish Orthodoxy arose as a response to developments that took place in Ashkenazic Jewish society in Europe beginning in the late 18th century. Thus, the characteristics of haredi society as set forth by Menachem Friedman were based upon a specifically Ashkenazic paradigm. This approach, as well as his reservations regarding the capacity of Mizrahi haredism to maintain itself in the future (both because of a lack of sufficient financial resources to sustain a "society of learners" and the absence of a tradition of learning in traditional Mizrahi society)[29] probably explains why Friedman defined the Shas party as being situated midway between "haredism and traditionalism."[30] In sum, for a long time, the rise and distinctive features of Mizrahi haredism went unnoticed.

The Political Phase of Mizrahi Haredism

The exception to the belated scholarly response to Mizrahi haredism (to which we will return later) is the research conducted by scholars in a different field entirely—political science—in response to the extraordinary success of the Histradrut Hasepharadim Shomrei Torah party (Association of Sephardic Torah Guardians), or Shas, as it is more commonly known.[31] The founding of Shas in 1983 was precipitated primarily by three factors. First, as already noted, was the ongoing frustration among both Mizrahi yeshiva students in Ashkenazic mitnagdic institutions and Mizrahi rabbis within the Ashkenazic haredi establishment, who felt discriminated against and excluded. Second was a concrete example of such exclusion: the fact that meetings of Agudat Israel's Moezet Gedolei Hatorah were conducted in Yiddish. Finally, internal rivalries within Agudat Israel led some of its members to support the establishment of a rival party.[32]

Shas' first foray was on the municipal level, in the elections held in Bnei Brak, Jerusalem, and Tiberias in October 1983. Following its relative success in these cities—most significantly in Jerusalem, where it won three seats on the municipal council—the party's leaders decided to organize at the national level and compete in the next Knesset elections, which were held in July 1984.[33] To their surprise, and that of many others, Shas won four seats. Over the next decade and half, the party grew steadily, winning six seats in the Knesset elections of 1988 and 1992. In 1996, with the introduction of separate direct elections for prime minister, which encouraged split voting, Shas won 10 seats and became the third-largest party in the Knesset. Under the same system in 1999, its electoral strength increased dramatically to 17 seats. Subsequently, however, Israel abolished direct elections for prime minister, and in the 2003 Knesset elections Shas was reduced to 11 seats (and was replaced as the third-largest party by Shinui, which ran a strident anti-haredi and anti-Shas campaign and won 15 seats). In the elections of March 2006, Shas increased its Knesset representation to 12 seats and retained its position as the fourth-largest party (while the Shinui party disappeared from the scene after failing to win any seats).

Shas was not the first Israeli political party with a specifically ethnic agenda. Several others preceded it, but either failed completely or existed for only a few years. These included a Yemenite party (Hitahdut Hateimanim Beyisrael) that won one seat in both the 1949 and 1951 Knesset elections; and Tami (Tenu'at Masoret Yisrael), founded by Aharon Abuhazira, formerly of the National Religious Party (NRP), that won three Knesset seats in 1981 and one in 1984 (when it competed with Shas), before merging with the Likud party.[34] The unprecedented electoral successes and staying power of Shas attest to its capacity to gain support outside haredi circles. Thus, for example, most of its voters in 1984 were Mizrahim located in the lower socioeconomic strata who may be described as observant or traditional but not haredi in their religious orientation and behavior. Most of these voters had previously supported either Tami or the Likud. In addition, a number of Ashkenazic haredim voted for Shas, as did a number of supporters of Meir Kahane.[35]

Over the years, Shas has attracted considerable scholarly interest. Whereas Samuel Heilman's discussion of the Orthodox and haredi camps in the 1988 elections barely mentioned Shas,[36] other scholars at the time began to focus on the Shas phenomenon. Among the first was Eliezer Don-Yehiya, who attributed its success in 1988 to a number of factors: the party's use of strong and attractive symbols of traditional Jewish identity; the inclusion on its list of Mizrahim from different countries of origin (Morocco, Iraq, Yemen, and Afganistan); a highly effective campaign; and its capacity to exploit the governmental and municipal offices it attained (following its initial electoral successes) for purposes of patronage in the form of administrative appointments and funding for its institutions and projects. In addition, Don-Yehiya noted, Shas had benefited from the support of R. Eliezer M. Schach (1898–2001), at the time arguably the most prominent leader of the mit-nagdic Ashkenazic haredi camp and one of the key figures in Agudat Israel's Moezet Gedolei Hatorah.[37] Schach's opposition to developments and personalities within Agudat Israel led him to call on his many followers to support Shas in the 1988 election campaign, and this played no small part in gaining it two additional Knesset seats.

Aaron Willis conducted an anthropological study of Shas' 1992 campaign (tactics, symbols, images), its activists (mainly yeshiva students), and its targeted audiences (in particular, traditional Mizrahim and the newly religious) but did not address the question of its electoral success.[38] One aspect of the latter was taken up by Hillel Frisch, namely, the symbolically significant rise in the Arab vote for Shas, which he attributed both to the influence within the Arab sector of the Ministry of the Interior headed by Aryeh Deri and to Shas' "ideology of reducing inequality."[39]

In a study by Gideon Doron and Rebecca Kook of the 1996 elections, Shas' success in winning 10 seats was explained in terms of the party's political flexibility and ability to exploit institutional changes, and of general sociopolitical trends within Israeli society such as a "growing preoccupation of the Israeli public with issues of identity." In addition, Doron and Kook highlighted two main strategies aimed at broadening Shas' population base beyond that of traditional Mizrahi Jews: the provision of improved social services and a campaign designed to "strengthen the spiritual bond between the voters and their leaders."[40] Similarly, Eliezer Don-Yehiya found that "the growing penetration of SHAS into non-haredi and even non-Orthodox circles" contributed to the party's increased vote in 1996. Don-Yehiya noted in particular the ongoing organizational changes within the religious parties between 1981 and 1992, which led to instability and fragmentation, and the competition between Shas and the NRP for Mizrahi voters.[41]

Shas' striking achievements in 1996 and 1999 (in both instances, well beyond the pollsters' pre-election predictions), led political scientists to look beyond previous explanations. In analyzing those elections, Yoav Peled, for instance, presented a refinement of the theoretical model of cultural division of labor (CDL), in order to "explain the persistence and growth of ethnic identification [with Shas] in a modernizing society," and to conceptualize the relationship between social structure and political culture. In his view, Shas appealed particularly to Mizrahim of low socioeconomic status because of "its ability to direct their resentment . . . not against the *Ashkenazic,* but against the secular, modernizing component of the dominant culture. In counterposing *Jewish,* rather than *Mizrahi* identity to this dominant culture, Shas provided its followers with an *integrative* rather than a *separatist* principle of organizing 'contrary to state aims.'"[42] Agreeing with Peled on the importance of Shas' expanded support among Mizrahi voters, Etta Bick also noted that much of the support for Shas was essentially a protest vote—in particular, against the Shinui party, which espoused a secular and stridently anti-haredi platform, and against Yisrael Ba'aliyah, a Russian immigrant party.[43] Furthermore, she pointed out (as had others) that Shas had picked up votes from religiously observant Mizrahim who had traditionally supported the National Religious Party.[44]

As mentioned, following the Knesset elections of 2003 (after the abolition of direct elections for prime minister), Shas reverted to its pre-1999 parliamentary strength (11 seats). In analyzing the results, Michael Shalev and Gal Levy offered an explanation combining identity and ethnic considerations, social status, and the specific political circumstances (most significantly, the degree of tension and violence in relationships between Jews and Arabs in Israel, and between Israel and the Palestinians at the time of the elections).[45] In seeking to account for Shas' loss of six seats—despite its gains in the Bedouin and Druse sectors—Bick drew attention to shifts in voter allegiance from Shas to (and sometimes back to) the Likud, which was led by the incumbent prime minister, Ariel Sharon; to the internal structural and personnel changes within Shas, occasioned by the departure from the scene of the party leader, Aryeh Deri, to whose political astuteness and ministerial prominence much of Shas' earlier electoral successes were commonly attributed;[46] to disappointment with Shas' parliamentary performance as exemplified, for instance, in its failure to block significant cuts in child allowance payments; and to the party's decision to focus on a religious message, at the center of which stood "belief in God and reverence for Rabbi Yossef."[47]

Some studies (such as Peled's) explained the significant support for Shas among non-haredi voters in terms of ethnic identity, economic status, and protest against the larger parties.[48] Others focused on Shas' organizational networks and grass-roots activities. Thus, Riki Tesler presents a fascinating analysis of how Shas utilized the formal opportunities made available to it via the parliamentary system and the bureaucracy to obtain generous government funding that enabled it to establish and conduct a nationwide network of educational and social service bodies and activities. In many cases, its dependents and beneficiaries reciprocated by voting for the party. One of her main conclusions is that Shas' ultimate aims are not concerned solely with Mizrahi Jewry, but extend to Israeli society as a whole.[49]

Viewing Shas from the perspective of the literature dealing with the forces and factors involved in the establishment of new political parties, Anat Feldman focuses on the processes and developments within Israeli society and politics that gave rise to the establishment of Shas. These include the multiple cleavages within Israeli society (especially between secular and religious and between Sephardim and Ashkenazim), changes within the political system, such as the weakening of the "party-camp" model with its stable loyalties and internal discipline, and the perception that sociocultural groups on the peripheries of society were either not represented or mistreated. According to Feldman, in the early 1980s, haredi Mizrahi rabbis and activists began to take note of these developments. For example, members of the Sephardic religious elite were no longer willing to support Agudat Israel if they did not receive their fair share of the funds allocated to the party by the state. On the broader communal level, the difficult situation of many Mizrahim (the fact, for example, that most Jewish prisoners in Israeli jails were of Mizrahi origin) also contributed to the impetus to establish a new Mizrahi political party.[50]

Another approach has been to attempt to apply broader theoretical categories to the study of Shas. Thus, Shlomo Fischer and Zvi Beckerman sought to determine whether Shas constitutes a sect or a kind of church, similar in certain ways to the Catholic Church, and concluded that it is a kind of "church movement."[51] However, their analysis, which is based on the rhetoric of Israeli haredi preachers as well as on propaganda from the 1999 elections, is flawed both by problematic assumptions and by a reliance on unrepresentative sources. For example, one of the individuals highlighted in Fischer and Bekerman's study is Uri Zohar, formerly a popular Israeli actor and entertainer, who later became associated with the mitnagdic Ashkenazic haredi camp. The authors argue that Zohar's sermons mention only Mizrahi or Sephardic rabbis. In fact, Zohar's sermons to Mizrahi audiences differ considerably from those he delivered to Ashkenazic or Ashkenazic haredi audiences, and even some of the former make reference to Ashkenazic rabbis. Similarly problematic is Fischer and Bekerman's anecdotal use of one or two (out of hundreds) of documented sermons and lectures delivered by Amnon Yitzhak, a leading figure in the haredi Mizrahi "return to religion" (*haḥzarah bitshuvah*) movement—who, for many years, distanced himself from the Shas party, although subsequently he moved closer to it.

A number of researchers have explored Shas' public image, both as perceived by voters and as portrayed in the media. Ephraim Yuchtman-Yaar and Tamar Hermann, for instance, apply a "reality check" to Shas' dovish image by comparing this with its supporters' attitudes, which generally are hawkish. They conclude that "this [dovish] image does not have a solid foundation in reality, and also that the degree of its validity alters according to the point in time that is considered."[52] Another study, by Sara Helman and André Levy, explores Shas' image as reflected in *Haaretz*, a leading Israeli newspaper. Until the late 1980s, they write, Israeli newspapers covered Shas as a marginal phenomenon. Over the course of the following decade, the coverage gradually shifted and Shas and its values came to be portrayed as a challenge to "hegemonic Israeliness" and as a threat to Israeli society; both the party and its supporters were characterized as representing "ignorance" and "fundamentalism."[53] More broadly, Shlomo Fischer has examined the ways in which Shas offers alternative categories for understanding social realities in Israel and the legitimate boundaries of political propaganda. For instance, in the legal controversy surrounding Shas' use of religious amulets during the municipal elections in Jerusalem in November 1998, Aryeh Deri contended that banning the use of amulets contradicted liberal and democratic values of personal autonomy and freedom as well as the right of any group to adopt its own methods of discourse and persuasion.[54]

Interest in Shas is not confined to academic researchers. Three books written by journalists appeared in the late 1990s, two of which dealt with the party and the third with Aryeh Deri.[55] Despite their flaws, which include a dearth of analysis and a failure to differentiate between significant and insignificant data, they are rich in information and anecdotal material, especially with regard to Shas leaders' complex interpersonal relationships.

Cultural Aspects of Mizrahi Haredism

A decade after political scientists "discovered" Shas, historians, sociologists, and (primarily) anthropologists began to deal with the wider haredi Mizrahi phenomenon. Despite the relatively later start, the quantity and variety of research on haredi Mizrahim since the 1990s is impressive. For instance, there are two comprehensive anthropological studies based primarily upon participant observation, interviews, discussions, and analysis of rituals and symbols. Aaron Willis' doctoral thesis, completed in 1993, is the first.[56] Although, as noted, Willis explores the political dimensions of the haredi Mizrahi experience (mainly in Jerusalem) exemplified by Shas, he focuses primarily on the religious and cultural meaning of that experience and not on Shas as a political actor. The second ethnographic study, conducted by Nissim Leon, looks at the impact of Shas on Mizrahi and haredi identities as well as the discourse concerning these identities. Leon tracks communal developments in the greater Tel Aviv area, primarily in the realm of synagogue life and rituals, and shows that the haredi Mizrahi phenomenon cannot be understood if it is viewed solely as a response to being situated on the geographic peripheries and lower economic rungs of Israeli society. According to Leon, it must also be seen as an attempt to reshape the Mizrahi collective religious identity.[57]

Different scholars have given attention to the historical, halakhic, and theological aspects of Mizrahi haredism. Neri Horowitz, for example, probes the relationship between certain Mizrahi rabbis and some mitnagdic Ashkenazic rabbis from the 1940s through the 1960s, showing how the former were influenced by the latter's ideological rejection of Zionism, their alienation from the state of Israel, and their opposition to many of its policies in the educational and religious spheres. Many Mizrahi rabbis during this period were angered by the culturally insensitive manner in which state representatives treated Mizrahi immigrants in general and dealt with their children's educational needs, in particular. In consequence, they founded an organization, Hever Hape'ilim Hatorati, which was aimed at ensuring that Mizrahi immigrant children not be deprived of a traditional religious education, as was the case at that time in many immigrant camps and *ma'abarot*.[58] Another scholar, Yaakov Lupu, shows how the practice of Mizrahi students joining Ashkenazic Yeshivot began long before the 1960s. He traces the exposure of Mizrahi communities to haredi influences back to the involvement of Lithuanian (mitnagdic) haredi organizations in schools in Morocco and their recruitment of Moroccan students, which began in the 1920s and continued throughout most of the 20th century.[59]

Still lacking, as previously noted, is an authoritative body of knowledge pinpointing the historical, social, and religious sources of Mizrahi haredism. Whereas Shlomo Deshen brings to light the significant role of senior Sephardic rabbis in Mandate Palestine[60] and Walter Zenner draws attention to the fact that the "militant conservatism of the Aleppian rabbinate prefigured the *haredi* orientation of the SHAS party,"[61] neither provides much detail about these "harbingers" of Mizrahi haredism as a socio-religious phenomenon.

In contrast with these only partially explored avenues, one topic has been studied intensively and in depth since the late 1990s—the halakhic writings of Ovadia Yosef, who, since the 1980s, has been the central religious figure within haredi Mizrahi Jewry. The first to provide an overview of the main elements of Yosef's writings was Binyamin Lau. In several articles followed by a doctoral thesis and a book, Lau analyzed Yosef's ambitious goal of "returning the crown to its ancient glory" (*lehaḥazir 'atarah leyoshenah*)—broadly, a call for the revival of classical Sephardic learning and halakhic decision-making. Other significant aspects of Yosef's halakhic worldview are his determination that the Shulhan Arukh of R. Yosef Caro be accepted as the ultimate authority (with a few exceptions) for halakhic rulings in the land of Israel, ideally by both Sephardim and Ashkenazim; his insistence that the observant Mizrahi community be united under that one halakhic umbrella, even if this means the diminution of the authority of local and ethnic-communal tradition; his critique of haredi Ashkenazic modes of halakhic learning and decision-making; and his attempt, in keeping with Karo's approach, to reduce the influence of Jewish mystical sources on both the halakhic discourse and the ritual practices of rank-and-file Mizrahim.[62]

Zvi Zohar's analysis of Yosef's halakhic writings is generally similar to that of Lau. He takes as his point of reference the history of halakhic decision-making among North African and Middle Eastern Jewry, which provides important comparative insights.[63] Both Lau and Zohar agree that the most significant key to understanding Yosef's halakhic writings is his aim of restoring Sephardic learning and halakhic ruling methods to their former place of honor.

Other scholars point to a number of additional themes appearing in Yosef's halakhic corpus. In an essay appearing in this volume, Nissim Leon discusses the concept of granting (religious) merit to the masses (*zikui harabim*), primarily by means of expanding their familiarity with sacred texts. Religious elevation of the masses can be achieved, according to Yosef, by the increased involvement of rabbis and yeshiva students in the day-to-day life of Mizrahi Jews.[64] This issue appears, at least implicitly, in several other studies dealing with specific aspects of Yosef's halakhic writings. Two examples are the doctoral thesis of Ariel Pikard on Yosef's rulings in light of changing historical circumstances[65] and Elimelech Westreich's chronological analysis of Yosef's rulings as a dayan in the rabbinical courts, which shows how he insisted on applying Sephardic legal traditions to the definition of various halakhic aspects of the marital status of women in Israel, especially in complex situations such as levirate marriages.[66]

Although these scholarly works provide us with a wealth of information concerning Yosef's writings and ideological and halakhic agendas, they contain little in the way of biography, though two recent books—each of them authored by a pair of journalists—help to fill in the gap.[67] Still to be written is an analysis of Yosef's homiletics. Beginning in the 1940s, Yosef became known as a popular preacher who was able to speak to audiences representing different levels of knowledge and sophistication. His reputation as a preacher grew in the 1950s, when he began to give weekly sermons in a number of institutions, including the Porat Yosef yeshiva and local synagogues in Petah Tikvah. Years later, while living in the Talbieh neighborhood of Jerusalem, Yosef delivered sermons every Friday evening to a small Sephardic minyan meeting at the Great Synagogue. In addition, Yosef has for decades preached a halakhic sermon at a Bukharian synagogue in Jerusalem every Saturday night, and he also speaks at numerous other public gatherings associated with the festivals, campaigns to strengthen religious observance, and election meetings. In recent years, many of these popular gatherings have been broadcast via satellite or cable television, as well as being taped or filmed.

The content of these sermons naturally varies in accordance with the audience in attendance. In many sermons, Yosef takes issue with Ashkenazic haredi approaches toward learning and halakhic decision-making, often in a broadly humorous and at times somewhat disdainful manner. Yet in the Friday-night sermons he delivered for years, Yosef made extensive use of Ashkenazic homiletical sources as well as recounting stories related to the European Jewish scene, and he in no way denigrated Ashkenazic Jews. In other words, whether consciously or unconsciously, this aspect of his ethno-religious agenda was excluded from these particular sermons.[68]

Yosef's preaching, then, is an important component of his public activity, accounting for much of his enormous popularity and influence. A comprehensive analysis of this aspect of Yosef's career is thus likely to shed light on his central role within Mizrahi haredism.[69]

Challenges in the Study of Haredi Mizrahim

The scholarly focus on Shas, on the one hand, and on the towering religious and political presence of Ovadia Yosef, on the other, tends to create the perception that "Mizrahim" are a united and perhaps even monolithic group. This is not the case. In the political arena, Shas' spiritual guides represent a variety of haredi Mizrahi subgroups and their relationships are complex and often tense. For instance, there is manifest antipathy between followers of the late kabbalist R. Yitzhak Kaduri (d. 2006) and those of Yosef, notwithstanding their political cooperation. Similarly, several of the initial members of the Moezet Hakhmei Hatorah, Shas' rabbinical council, did not see eye to eye with Yosef on a wide range of issues, but rather regarded themselves as part of the Ashkenazic haredi yeshiva world and adhered to the rulings of R. Schach. Because Yosef was of the opinion that these disagreements would prevent the council from reaching consensus and from giving Shas representatives clear and and unified policy guidelines, he refrained from convening it for several years during the 1990s; during this time, he provided the party with authoritative rabbinical guidance, usually his own.[70]

By and large, however, despite such internal dissension and differences, Shas managed to present a united front at election time and to retain the support of all its diverse components. While Shas' success in this regard is manifest, the extent of Yosef's contribution to that success is far from clear—in particular, what influence he may have had on the majority of Shas voters who are not hardcore haredi Mizrahim, and what role he played in mobilizing and retaining support for the party.

While political tensions within a party are to be expected, the situation in the case of Shas is complicated by a number of religious issues that have implications for the broader haredi Mizrahi community. Yosef, Kaduri, and other leading Mizrahi rabbinical figures, both within the haredi and Shas camps and outside them, represent differing schools of belief, thought, learning, and styles of halakhic decision-making. As noted, Yosef is committed to the supremacy and authority of purely legalistic talmudic sources and halakhic principles in his rulings, whereas others, both within Shas and in the wider haredi Mizrahi realm, tend to view mystical-kabbalistic sources as equally authoritative.[71] These are not purely abstract or theoretical differences, but rather have direct and practical implications for daily life: for example, they determine which prayer book is to be used, which texts are to be studied, and how ritual practices are to be observed. Another major source of disagreement derives from Yosef's determination that the Shulhan Arukh of "Maran" (R. Yosef Karo) is authoritative in halakhic matters. The effect of this determination is to override local, regional-geographic, ethnic, and communal halakhic traditions that were maintained over the centuries in various parts of the Sephardic world. As a result, Yosef's position has been challenged and rejected by a number of rabbis of Libyan, Moroccan, and Tunisian origin.[72]

In sum, the rhetoric and image of unity that Shas projects does not reflect reality. As yet, however, a more accurate systematic study of the competing elements within the party is not available. While necessary for an understanding of the workings of Shas as a political entity, such a study would have far wider and deeper implications, as the party's internal differences and contradictions go to the heart of haredi Mizrahi "lived religion."[73]

These conflicts are manifest in synagogue life and rituals, for example. As observed in a number of Mizrahi synagogues in Jerusalem, there is generational tension between elderly, non-haredi Mizrahim (who rely on oral traditions and customs) and younger haredi Mizrahim (who strictly follow the authoritative written halakhic texts and rulings).[74] Such tensions often find expression in selecting the prayer book that is to be used by the worshippers in services; while the synagogues in question possess prayer books with Ovadia Yosef's imprimatur as well as more mystically oriented prayer books, they tend to make more use of the latter.[75] To be sure, the differences between the various prayer books may often appear minor, more a matter of nuance and order of service than of text, but this is a sensitive and symbolic issue for worshippers. Interestingly, some of them consider themselves to be followers of Yosef, yet in this instance of public worship, it appears that deep-rooted local communal custom serves to limit Yosef's influence.

Similarly, Yosef's views regarding certain popular Mizrahi celebrations seem to have limited impact on the wider Mizrahi public. An example is the Lag Ba'omer "hilula" festivity at the tomb of R. Shimon bar-Yohai in Meiron. Yosef has long counseled the God-fearing not to attend this annual celebration, since many of the participants are not scrupulous in their religious observance, and halakhic rules relating to the strict separation of the sexes and modesty of dress are widely flouted. Notwithstanding Yosef's views, many of his followers go to the hilula at Meiron.

Here and elsewhere, Yosef and much of his public are far apart. The scope and substance of the gaps between them have yet to be mapped out and defined, but their presence certainly indicates that much of Shas' support comes from persons who do not necessarily agree with its leaders' religious (or political) agenda. Moreover, Yosef's response (or lack thereof) to this state of affairs remains uninvestigated.

The gap between elite and popular views among haredi Mizrahim also finds expression in the weeky "Torah portion" pamphlets distributed in synagogues throughout Israel.[76] An initial study of the most popular haredi Mizrahi pamphlet of this kind, *Ma'ayan hashavu'a*,[77] suggests that it expresses certain popular notions that contradict those of Yosef and his loyal followers. One example relates to R. Yosef Hayim (popularly known as the Ben-Ish Hai; 1834–1909) a Mizrahi halakhic authority whose rulings continue to be influential among haredi Mizrahim. Yosef's categorical rejection of Hayim's halakhic approach has been documented.[78] However, within the pages of *Ma'ayan hashavu'a*, we find attempts to reconcile their differences. In one pamphlet there is an imaginary discussion between them, during which Hayim (appearing to Yosef in a dream) praises one of the latter's books, even though in the introduction to it, Yosef had highlighted the differences between them.[79]

Although extensively studied with regard to the Ashkenazim, little research has been done on Mizrahi *hozrim bitshuvah* (newly religious).[80] In addition to the newly religious, the Mizrahi community also contains numerous individuals who were originally traditional in their religious outlook but who have gradually become stricter in their religious observance. These are known as the *mithazkim* (lit. "growing stronger"). The existing knowledge on hozrim bitshuvah and mithazkim indicates that certain Ashkenazic hasidic groups—notably Chabad (Lubavitch) and Bratslav, but also Gur, Belz, and Karlin—conduct activities aimed at encouraging *hazarah bitshuvah* as part of their ideological agenda. In other groups, especially among the mitnagdim and the Mizrahim, such activities are pursued by individual rabbis who generally are not part of the religious leadership. Thus, within the haredi Mizrahi religious and educational leadership, there is a perceptible ambivalence toward such activists as Reuven Elbaz,[81] Nissim Yagen (circa 1941–2000), and Amnon Yitzhak, in part because of their popularization of fundamental religious beliefs such as reward and punishment.[82] Nevertheless, among rank-and-file haredi Mizrahim, Elbaz, Yagen, and Yitzhak enjoy high status and popularity.

The Ashkenazic and Mizrahi approaches toward religious outreach differ greatly. Whereas Ashkenazic activists tend to view nonobservance among Ashkenazim as initially ideological—that is, as a continuation of secularism and principled rejection of religion—and later as a result of ignorance resulting from lack of "proper" education, Mizrahi activists regard this phenomenon among their brethren as religious laxity rather than outright denial.[83] Although this distinction may be based on inaccurate or outdated notions, it has nevertheless resulted in differing styles and methods of encouraging hazarah bitshuvah. For example, working on the assumption that their audience is likely to deny or reject basic beliefs, many mitnagdic activists emphasize rational arguments seeking to prove, say, the existence of God or the historical accuracy of the biblical account of the revelation of the Torah at Mount Sinai. In contrast, Mizrahi activists, who take it for granted that they are dealing with believers, focus on persuading them to put their beliefs into practice by observing the mitzvot in a more rigorous fashion—often, as noted, by resorting to concepts of reward and punishment.

Since Mizrahi haredism as a widespread phenomenon did not exist prior to the late 1970s (at the earliest), it seems safe to assume that many of its early proponents themselves underwent some process of religious return or strengthened commitment to religious observance. Indeed, it may well be the case that hozrim bitshuvah or mithazkim constitute the norm within the haredi Mizrahi population, which contrasts starkly with the situation among Ashkenazic haredim, where the newly religious are a small minority. In any event, more research is needed to clarify the varying types of Mizrahi religious returnees and the extent to which they are accepted by haredi Mizrahim from birth.[84] What is known is that approximately 25 percent of Shas voters may be regarded as haredi Mizrahim, as defined by several parameters including dress, religious lifestyle and observance, and the schools in which their children are educated. The large majority of Shas voters, however, fall short of these rigorous standards and manifest a wide range of expressions of what might be termed "soft," fluid, and traditional religiosity, which share in or accept some dimensions of hardcore Mizrahi haredism. Closer examination and analysis of these variations in Mizrahi religiosity are essential if we are to gain a deeper understanding of both the haredi Mizrahi and the Shas phenomena.

As noted, some of Shas' original support came from former National Religious Party voters and others associated with the religious Zionist (also known as the national religious) camp.[85] Furthermore, a number of leading figures in the haredi Mizrahi sector were formerly associated with state organs controlled by the NRP, most notably Ovadia Yosef, who served as chief rabbi.[86] However, whereas the phenomenon of Mizrahim leaving NRP circles and becoming haredim has not been studied, that of haredi inroads within the national religious sector—resulting in the rise of the Zionist-haredi subgroup popularly known as *hardal* (an abbreviation of *haredi-leumi*)—has received attention. Hardalim espouse the ideology of religious Zionism and attach religious value to the state of Israel, while at the same time accepting Ashkenazic haredi modes and standards of religious observance and education. A recent study has examined schools associated with the hardal ideology, but no similar research exists with regard to religious Zionists who turned to the haredi Mizrahi option, even though this process casts light on both religious Zionism and haredi society.[87] For example, keeping in mind the Ashkenazic haredi ideological and theological ambivalence toward Zionism and the state of Israel, what impact do hardalim, be they Ashkenazic or Mizrahi, have on these haredi views? What, if any, is their role in the noticeable haredi leaning toward the political Right in Israel over the last decade and a half in terms of attitudes toward the land of Israel, territorial withdrawals, and (albeit to a much smaller degree) army service?[88] Finally, are these religious Zionists who joined the haredi world at various levels—without completely disassociating themselves from the religious Zionist world—yet another source of influence promoting the growing involvement of haredim in Israel's economy and work force, as well as their increasing interest in higher education?[89]

A notable lacuna in the study of Shas, haredi Mizrahim, and Mizrahi haredism concerns the role of women in this phenomenon. Thus far, to the best of my knowledge, two studies have appeared: Anat Feldman's essay documenting the women's organization affiliated with Shas, "Margalit em beyisrael," which points to women's importance in both the political and social spheres of this movement,[90] and Tamar El-Or's anthropological study of Mizrahi women in a small town in the center of Israel and their gradual turn to religious belief and observance. El-Or offers a detailed ethnography based upon participation in various religious activities, such as learning groups and public sermons and events, and highlights the role of charismatic personalities, both male and female, in enhancing this process among Mizrahi women.[91]

Finally, Mizrahi haredism is not limited to Israel. Similar developments have occurred in Sephardic communities in North and South America and in France.[92] Apart from familial ties, the diaspora and Israeli haredi Mizrahi communities are also economically, socially, religiously, and institutionally interconnected. In addition, some diaspora Mizrahi communities and individuals have come under the influence of Ashkenazic haredim, particularly those of Chabad—for example, Syrian communities in the United States and Latin America and Mizrahi immigrants from Israel in New York.[93] Academic scholarship on haredi Mizrahi communities in the diaspora has scarcely begun.

Conclusion

To date, the two most studied aspects of Mizrahi haredism are Ovadia Yosef (in particular, his halakhic writings) and the Shas party. The focus on Yosef is understandable since he serves not only as the central religious figure among haredi Mizrahim but also as the spiritual leader of Shas. With the exception of Zvi Zohar's essay in this volume, there has been no systematic overview of other Mizrahi halakhic authorities of the 20th and 21st centuries, and thus no comparative perspective from which to view Yosef's halakhic accomplishments. Nor has there been a critical biography of Yosef or any content analysis of his popular sermons, though such a study, as noted, is likely to enrich our understanding of his halakhic writings. Finally, the impact of Yosef's writings on his "true believers" is yet to be researched.

Regarding Shas, we have a picture of this party's conduct; several possible explanations for its growth and staying power; important although not conclusive information about the circumstances leading to its establishment; and an analysis of its political behavior in the Knesset. However, we still know very little about Shas' political leaders and representatives in parliament, the nature of the relationships between the party's politicians and religious leaders (who decides what and how?) and between Shas and other religious parties, both Zionist and haredi, and the attitudes and characteristics of this party's voters.

In contrast to the growing scholarship focused on Ovadia Yosef and on Shas, there is far less material concerning Mizrahi haredism as a religious, cultural, and historical phenomenon. In other words, whereas several aspects of haredi Mizrahi leadership, whether religious or political, have been explored, we know little about rank-and-file haredi Mizrahim. In part, this situation reflects the belated academic awakening on the part of historians, sociologists, and anthropologists to the general phenomenon of haredi Mizrahim; it is also the case that critical primary sources for the study of Mizrahi haredism have yet to be analyzed. For example, I know of only one systematic study dealing with Shas' daily (later, weekly) newspaper, *Yom leyom*.[94] Similarly, as noted, there has been only sparse analysis of the various Torah-portion pamphlets that are specifically associated with haredi Mizrahi groups. The consequence of these lacunae is that the boundaries and substance of Mizrahi haredism have not been defined, either in their own terms or in relation to the cardinal question of how and to what extent it is similar to or differs from Ashkenazic haredism. In addition, Shas and the self-conscious Mizrahi identity that it is promoting has had a profound impact upon Mizrahim in Israel as well as on Israeli society, the details of which are yet to be explored.

Notwithstanding the gaps, the existing scholarship has revealed the complexity of this phenomenon. We are undoubtedly facing a multifaceted, heterogeneous subgroup that, while characterized as "haredi," does not quite fit the classic haredi framework. A more concentrated effort to uncover, document, and analyze the wider contexts of this socio-religious development is required if a broader understanding— not only of contemporary Israeli society, but of Jewish society as a whole since the last decades of the 20th century—is to be obtained.

Notes

I thank Richelle Budd Caplan, Nissim Leon, Nurit Stadler, and especially Peter Medding for their comments, constructive criticism, and suggestions on earlier versions of this article.

1. Chaim S. Karelitz, "Beoznei aḥeinu me'edot hamizraḥ," *Diglenu* 1–2 (336–337) (Tishrei 5745 [Sept. 1984]), 3. In addition, see G. Safran, "Haḥashash shehuva lifnei shmoneh shanim," *Yated neeman* (14 Shevat 5753 [5 Feb. 1993]), in weekend supplement, 11.
2. Martin A. Cohen, "The Sephardic Phenomenon: A Reappraisal," *American Jewish Archives* 44, no. 1 (1992), 3–5.
3. For a discussion of more general differences between the Ashkenazic and Sephardic experiences in the modern era, see Shlomo Deshen, "The Emergence of the Israeli Sephardi Ultra-Orthodox Movement," *Jewish Social Studies* 11, no. 2 (2005), 78–88.
4. See Jacob Katz, "Orthodoxy in Historical Perspective," in *Studies in Contemporary Jewry*, vol. 2, *The Challenge of Modernity and Jewish Orthodoxy*, ed. Peter Y. Medding (New York: 1986), 3–17; Moshe Samet, "The Beginnings of Orthodoxy," *Modern Judaism* 8, no. 3 (1988), 249–270.
5. See Michael K. Silber, "The Emergence of Ultra-Orthodoxy: The Invention of Tradition," in *The Uses of Tradition: Jewish Continuity in the Modern Era*, ed. Jack Wertheimer (Cambridge, Mass.: 1992), 23–85.
6. For a recent account, see Adam S. Ferziger, *Exclusion and Hierarchy: Orthodoxy, Nonobservance, and the Emergence of Modern Jewish Identity* (Philadelphia: 2005).
7. See Menachem Friedman and Yosef Shilhav, *Hitpashtut tokh histagrut: hakehilah haharedit birushalayim* (Jerusalem: 1985), 6.
8. See Menachem Friedman, *Haḥevrah haḥaredit: mekorot, megamot vetahalikhim* (Jerusalem: 1991), 6–26.
9. Ibid., 6–7.
10. See Menachem Friedman, "Life Tradition and Book Tradition in the Development of Ultraorthodox Judaism," in *Judaism Viewed from Within and from Without: Anthropological Studies*, ed. Harvey E. Goldberg (Albany: 1987), 235–256; idem, *Haḥevrah haḥaredit*, 70–88; idem, "The Lost 'Kiddush' Cup: Changes in Ashkenazic Haredi Culture: A Tradition in Crisis," in Wertheimer (ed.), *The Uses of Tradition*, 175–187. For a somewhat different analysis, see Haym Soloveitchik, "Rupture and Reconstruction: The Transformation of Contemporary Orthodoxy," *Tradition* 28, no. 4 (1994), 64–131.
11. Samuel Heilman and Menachem Friedman, "Religious Fundamentalism and Religious Jews: The Case of the Haredim," in *Fundamentalisms Observed*, ed. Martin E. Marty and R. Scott Appleby (Chicago: 1991), 198–219.
12. See Samuel C. Heilman, *Defenders of the Faith: Inside Ultra-Orthodox Jewry* (New York: 1992). On Heilman's failure to discuss Mizrahim, see Benny Kraut's review in *Central Conference of American Rabbis* 43, no. 1 (1996), 100–106.
13. See Roni Baum-Banai, "Shas - 'aliyatah vehitgabshutah: perek behistoriah ḥevratit-'adatit bimdinat yisrael" (Ph.D. diss., Tel Aviv University, 2004), 146; Binyamin Lau, *Mimaran 'ad maran: mishnato hahilkhatit shel harav 'Ovadyah Yosef* (Tel Aviv: 2005), 163–170.
14. For a detailed account, see Lau, *Mimaran 'ad maran*, 155–191. Yosef's ongoing association with the chief rabbinate is not exceptional among Mizrahi rabbis. For example, R. Ovadyah Hedaya was a member of the chief rabbinate in Petah Tikvah and also sat on the chief rabbinate's high court of appeals and on the council of the chief rabbinate. Several leading Ashkenazic haredi rabbis, among them Yosef Shalom Elyashiv, were also employed by the chief rabbinate at certain stages of their career, although none of them served as chief rabbi. However, whereas many of these Ashkenazic rabbis retrospectively developed a negative approach toward this institution, this is not the case with regard to Mizrahi rabbis (such as Yosef) who subsequently became leading figures among haredi Mizrahim.
15. For a discussion of *da'at torah*, see Yigal Mishol, "'Da'at torah': samkhut datit bayahadut haḥaredit - heibetim politiyim" (Master's thesis, The Hebrew University, 1998).

On the origin, development, practice, and implications of *da'at torah*, see Gershon Bacon, "Da'at torah vehevlei mashiah: lesheelat haidiyologiyah shel 'Agudat Yisrael' bepolin," *Tarbiz* 52, no. 3 (1983), 497–509; Lawrence J. Kaplan, "Daas Torah: A Modern Conception of Rabbinic Authority," in *Rabbinic Authority and Personal Autonomy*, ed. Moshe Sokol (Northvale: 1992), 1–61.

16. See Momi Dahan, *Haukhlosiyah haharedit vehareshut hamekomit* (Jerusalem: 1998), 7; Sergio DellaPergola, "Demography in Israel at the Dawn of the Twenty-First Century," in *Jews in Israel: Contemporary Social and Cultural Patterns*, ed. Uzi Rebhun and Chaim I. Waxman (Hanover: 2004), 40–41; Norma Gurovich and Eilat Cohen-Kastro, *Haharedim: tifroset geografit umeafyenim demografiyim, hevratiyim vekalkaliyim shel haukhlosiyah haharedit beyisrael 1996–2001* (Jerusalem: 2004), 73–83; Shlomit Levy, Hanna Levinsohn, and Elihu Katz, "The Many Faces of Jewishness in Israel," in Rebhun and Waxman (eds.), *Jews in Israel*, 267–271, 279; idem (Levy, Levinsohn and Katz), *Yehudim yisreelim: deyukan–emunot, shemirat masoret ve'arakhim shel yehudim beyisrael 2000* (Jerusalem: 2002), 10, 170.

17. S[hmuel] N. Eisenstadt, *The Absorption of Immigrants: A Comparative Study Based Mainly on the Jewish Community in Palestine and the State of Israel* (London: 1954). This book followed Eisenstadt's *Report on the Absorption of Immigrants in Israel with Special Reference to Oriental Jews* (Jerusalem: 1951), published by the Jewish Agency of Palestine and The Hebrew University of Jerusalem.

18. See, in chronological order, Alex Weingrod, *Reluctant Pioneers: Village Development in Israel* (Ithaca: 1966); Dov Weintraub, Moshe Lissak, and Yael Atzmon, *Moshava, Kibbutz and Moshav: Patterns of Jewish Rural Settlement and Development in Palestine* (Ithaca: 1969); Dorothy Willner, *Nation-Building and Community in Israel* (Princeton: 1969); Dov Weintraub, *Immigration and Social Change: Agricultural Settlements of New Immigrants in Israel* (Manchester: 1971).

19. Shlomo A. Deshen, *Immigrant Voters in Israel: Parties and Congregations in a Local Election Campaign* (Manchester: 1970); Harvey E. Goldberg, *Cave Dwellers and Citrus Growers: A Jewish Community in Libya and Israel* (Cambridge: 1972); Emmanuel Marx, *The Social Context of Violent Behaviour: A Social Anthropological Study in an Israeli Immigrant Town* (London: 1976); Moshe Shokeid, *The Dual Heritage: Immigrants from the Atlas Mountains in an Israeli Village* (Manchester: 1971).

20. See, chronologically, Shlomo Deshen and Moshe Shokeid, *The Predicament of Homecoming: Cultural and Social Life of North African Immigrants in Israel* (Ithaca: 1974); Shlomo Deshen and Moshe Shokeid, *Dor hatemurah: shinui vehemshekhiyut ba'olamam shel yoẓei ẓefon afrikah* (Jerusalem: 1977, 2nd ed. 1999); Shlomo Deshen and Moshe Shokeid (eds.), *Yehudei hamizrah: 'iyunim antropologiyim 'al he'avar vehahoveh* (Jerusalem: 1984); Shlomo Deshen (ed.), *Mahaẓit haumah: 'iyunim betarbut uvema'amad shel yoẓei hamizrah beyisrael* (Ramat Gan: 1986); Shlomo Deshen, "Hadatiyut shel hamizrahim: ẓibur, rabanim veemunah," *Alpayim* 9 (1994), 44–59; Moshe Shokeid, "The Religiosity of Middle Eastern Jews," in *Israeli Judaism: The Sociology of Religion in Israel*, ed. Shlomo Deshen, Charles S. Liebman, and Moshe Shokeid (London: 1995), 213–239.

21. Shlomo Deshen, "Haantropologim veheker hatarbuyot shel 'edot hamizrah," *Pe'amim* 1 (1979), 76–85, esp. 79–80 and the bibliography.

22. Examples include Yoram Bilu, "Psikhiatriyah masortit beyisrael: peniyot shel benei moshavim yoẓei maroko 'im be'ayot pesikhiatriyot ukshayei hayim lerabanim ulehakhamim" (Ph.D. diss., The Hebrew University, 1978); Walter Zenner, "Saints and Piecemeal Supernaturalism among Jerusalem Sephardim," *Anthropological Quarterly* 58 (1965), 201–218.

23. Haforum Lelimudei Hevrah Vetarbut, "Mangenonei kinun veyiẓur hayeda' hakanoni 'al mizrahim beyisrael," in *Mizrahim beyisrael: 'iyun bikorti mehudash*, ed. Hannan Hever, Yehuda Shenhav, and Pnina Motzafi-Haller (Tel Aviv: 2002), 290–293.

24. See, for example, Baruch Kimmerling, *Mehagrim, mityashvim, yelidim: hamedinah vehahevrah beyisrael—bein ribui tarbuyot lemilhamot tarbut* (Tel Aviv: 2004), 303; Shokeid, *Dor hatemurah*, 77–93.

25. One response to this struggle was a (nonviolent) protest movement known as the Black Panthers, which focused on improving the social and economic status of Israel's lower classes. On this movement, see Deborah Bernstein, "Hapanterim hasheḥorim; konflikt umeḥaah baḥevrah hayisreelit," *Megamot* 25, no. 1 (1979), 65–81; Yochanan Peres, *Yaḥasei 'edot beyisrael* (Tel Aviv: 1976), 160–176.

26. On the definition and characteristics of "strong religions," see Gabriel Almond, R. Scott Appleby, and Emmanuel Sivan, *Strong Religion: The Rise of Fundamentalisms around the World* (Chicago: 2003).

27. See Deshen, "The Emergence of the Israeli Sephardi Ultra-Orthodox Movement," 92–94; idem, "Hadatiyut shel hamizraḥim," 53–54; Heilman and Friedman, "Religious Fundamentalism and Religious Jews," 244–245; Friedman, *Haḥevrah haḥaredit*, 177–178. Although the phenomenon of Mizrahim studying at Ashkenazic institutions is well documented (see n. 60), no one has addressed the question of why these students did not choose to study at a Sephardic alternative such as the Porat Yosef yeshiva in Jerusalem. On the founding of this yeshiva, see Zvi Zohar, "The Sephardic Halakhic Tradition in the 20th Century," in this volume, 124.

28. Nissim Leon, "Hatenu'ah haḥaredit eẓel hamizraḥim beyisrael barei uveḥayei hapraktikah hadatit" (Ph.D. diss., Tel Aviv University 2005), 93–96.

29. Friedman, *Haḥevrah haḥaredit*, 184–185. See also idem, "Haḥevrah hadatit vehaḥaredit beyisrael leaḥar habeḥirot lakneset ha-12: megamot vetahalikhim," *Sekirah ḥodshit* 36, no. 5 (1989), 32–33. It should be noted that Friedman originally raised the economic issue with regard to Ashkenazi haredim; he later applied it to Mizrahi haredim. His point regarding the absence of a learning tradition applies only to Mizrahi haredim.

30. Friedman, *Haḥevrah haḥaredit*, 175.

31. The choice of the terms Sepharadim and Shomrei Torah, and not Mizrahim and haredim, is noteworthy, certainly with regard to the party's self-image. For details concerning Shas' municipal organization and initial electoral success, see Anat Feldman, "Gormim bizmiḥat miflagah ḥadashah: Hitaḥdut Hasefaradim Shomrei Torah (tenu'at Shas)" (Ph.D. diss., Bar-Ilan University, 2001), 32–42, 57–61.

32. See Heilman and Friedman, "Religious Fundamentalism and Religious Jews," 245–247; Friedman, *Haḥevrah haḥaredit*, 179–181; Binyamin Neuberger, *Hamiflagot beyisrael: hitpatḥutan, irgunan uma'amadan bama'arekhet hapolitit* (Tel Aviv: 1991), 137. For a more nuanced discussion of these forces and internal ties, see Feldman, "Gormim bizmiḥat miflagah ḥadashah," 26–32.

33. Friedman, *Haḥevrah haḥaredit*, 181–183.

34. Another ethnic party that lasted slightly longer during this period was Haihud Haarzi shel Hasepharadim Uvnei 'Edot Hamizrah, which won four Knesset seats in 1949 and two in 1951, but did not field a list in the 1955 elections; prior to the elections, its Knesset representatives joined the General Zionist parliamentary faction.

35. For more detailed discussion, see Baum-Banai, "Shas - 'aliyatah vehitgabshutah," 4–15, 31–34; Eliezer Don-Yehiya, "Datiyut ve'adatiyut bapolitikah hayisreelit: hamiflagot hadatiyot vehabeḥirot lakneset ha-12," *Medinah, mimshal veyaḥasim beinleumiyim* 32 (1990), 11–54; Hanna Herzog, "Ethnicity as a Product of Political Negotiation: The Case of Israel," *Ethnic and Racial Studies* 7, no. 4 (1984), 517–534; idem, "Political Factionalism: The Case of Ethnic Lists in Israel," *The Western Political Quarterly* 39, no. 2 (1986), 285–304; idem, "Midway between Political and Cultural Ethnicity: Analysis of the 'Ethnic Lists' in the 1984 Elections," in *Israel's Odd Couple: The 1984 Knesset Elections and the National Unity Government*, ed. Daniel J. Elazar and Shmuel Sandler (Detroit: 1990), 87–119; Neuberger, *Hamiflagot beyisrael*, 136–139, 150–153; Yoav Peled, "Towards a Redefinition of Jewish Nationalism in Israel: The Enigma of Shas," *Ethnic and Racial Studies* 21, no. 4 (1998), 703–728; Sammy Smooha, "Jewish Ethnicity in Israel: Symbolic or Real?" in Rebhun and Waxman (eds.), *Jews in Israel*, 63. Finally, compare this accepted view with Ephraim Yuchtman-Yaar and Tamar Hermann's "Shas: The Haredi-Dovish Image in a Changing Reality," *Israel Studies* 5, no. 2 (2000), 68–69; this article originally published as "Ha'yoniyut' shel Shas - dimui umeẓiut," in Peled (ed.), *Shas*, 343–390.

36. Samuel C. Heilman, "The Orthodox, the Ultra-Orthodox, and the Elections for the Twelfth Knesset," in *The Elections in Israel—1988*, ed. Asher Arian and Michal Shamir (Boulder: 1990), 135–155; cf. Friedman, "Hahevrah hadatit vehaharedit," 22–37.

37. Don-Yehiya, "Datiyut ve'adatiyut bapolitikah hayisreelit," 37–42. Although Shas today is identified mainly with Ovadia Yosef, his public involvement with Shas began only after he had completed his term of office as chief rabbi. Moreover, Yosef had some reservations regarding Shas, and he joined the party only after he found out that Schach and many Mizrahim were supporting it. See Feldman, "Gormim bizmihat miflagah hadashah," 50. Schach, meanwhile, withdrew his support from Shas prior to the 1992 elections (ibid., 46–49). On the recruitment of rabbis by the activists who founded Hitahdut Hasefaradim and Shas, see ibid., 42–54.

38. Aaron P. Willis, "Shas—The Sephardic Torah Guardians: Religious 'Movement' and Political Power," in Arian and Shamir (eds.), *The Elections in Israel 1992*, 121–141.

39. Hillel Frisch, "The Arab Vote in the 1992 Elections: The Triviality of Normality; the Significance of Electoral Power," in *Israel at the Polls, 1992*, ed. Daniel J. Elazar and Shmuel Sandler (Lanham: 1995), 103–110.

40. Gideon Doron and Rebecca Kook, "Religion and the Politics of Inclusion: The Success of the Ultra-Orthodox Parties," in *The Elections in Israel 1996*, ed. Asher Arian and Michal Shamir (Albany: 1999), 67–85.

41. Eliezer Don-Yehiya, "Religion, Ethnicity and Electoral Reform: The Religious Parties and the 1996 Elections," in *Israel at the Polls 1996*, ed. Daniel J. Elazar and Shmuel Sandler (London: 1998), 79.

42. Peled's initial analysis, from which the citations are taken, appeared in his article "Towards a Redefinition of Jewish Nationalism in Israel" (citations taken from pp. 705 and 720). A revised version containing data from the 1999 elections was published under the title "The Continuing Electoral Success of Shas: A Cultural Division of Labor Analysis" in *The Elections in Israel 1999*, ed. Asher Arian and Michal Shamir (Albany: 2002), 99–121.

43. Yisrael Ba'aliyah's election campaign focused on the need to wrest control of the Interior Ministry from Shas, since the latter's application of the laws of personal status in accordance with strict Orthodox criteria resulted, it was claimed, in the registration of thousands of recent Russian olim as non-Jews.

44. Etta Bick, "The Shas Phenomenon and Religious Parties in the 1999 Elections," in *Israel at the Polls 1999*, ed. Daniel J. Elazar and M. Ben Mollov (London: 2001), 55–101.

45. Michael Shalev and Gal Levy, "Hamenazehim vehamafsidim shel 2003: ideologiyah, mivneh hevrati veshinui politi," in *Habehirot beyisrael 2003*, ed. Asher Arian and Michal Shamir (Jerusalem: 2004), 257–266.

46. As head of the party, Deri served as minister of the interior. In 1999, he was convicted of corruption charges. He was sent to prison in September 2000; upon his release two years later, he did not resume political activity in Shas.

47. Etta Bick, "A Party in Decline: Shas in Israel's 2003 Elections," in *Israel at the Polls 2003*, ed. Shmuel Sandler, M. Ben Mollov and Jonathan Rynhold (London: 2005), 98–130.

48. For another example, see Asher Arian, "Miflagot besiman shinui muaz," in *Kez hamiflagot: hademokratiyah hayisreelit bimzukah*, ed. Dani Korn (Tel Aviv: 1998), 148.

49. Riki Tesler, *Beshem Hashem: Shas vehamahapekhah hadatit* (Jerusalem: 2002). This work is based upon her doctoral thesis, titled "Hamiflagah hatenu'atit keirgun kilayim: hamikreh shel tenu'at Shas" (The Hebrew University, 2000). In addition, see idem, "Mehirah shel mahapekhah," in *Shas - etgar hayisreeliyut*, ed. Yoav Peled (Tel Aviv: 2001), 210–279. On Shas' educational network, see Yamit Cohen-Shimony, "Zehutah hanashit shel habat hamizrahit hamithanekhet bemosdot hahinukh shel Shas" (Master's thesis, Bar-Ilan University, 2003); Varda Schiffer, *Ma'arekhet hahinukh haharedi beyisrael: tikzuv, pikuah uvakarah* (Jerusalem: 1998).

50. Feldman, "Gormim bizmihat miflagah hadashah," 26–57, 73–80; idem, "Hakamat tenu'at Shas: matarot vedarkhei pe'ulah," in *Shas: hebetim ra'yoniyim vetarbutiyim*, ed.

Aviezer Ravitzky (Tel Aviv: 2006), 405–443. In addition, see Baum-Banai, "Shas—'aliyatah vehitgabshutah"; Menachem Friedman, "The Ultra-Orthodox and Israeli Society," in *Whither Israel? The Domestic Challenges*, ed. Joel Peters and Keith Kyle (London and New York: 1993), 191–193.

51. Shlomo Fischer and Zvi Bekerman, " 'Kenesiyah' o 'kat'?," in Peled (ed.), *Shas— etgar hayisreeliyut*, 321–343. See also Shlomo Fischer, "Tenu'at Shas," *Teoriyah uvikoret* 12–13 (1999), 329–338.

52. Yuchtman-Yaar and Hermann, "Shas: The Haredi-Dovish Image in a Changing Reality," 68. In addition, see Gerald M. Steinberg, "A Nation that Dwells Alone? Foreign Policy in the 1992 Elections," in Elazar and Sandler (eds.), *Israel At the Polls, 1992*, 192–193.

53. Sara Helman and André Levy, "Shas ba'itonut hayisreelit," in Peled (ed.), *Shas— etgar hayisreeliyut*, 390–425.

54. Shlomo Fischer, "Kami'ot veliberalism politi: hairgun hamusagi shel hameẓiut vehalegitimaẓiyah shel hamedinah 'al pi tenu'at Shas," in *Ma'arbolet hazehuyot: diyun bikorti bedatiyut uveḥiloniyut beyisrael*, ed. Yehuda Goodman and Yossi Yonah (Tel Aviv: 2004), 249–277.

55. Aryeh Dayan, *Hama'ayan hamitgaber: sipurah shel tenu'at Shas* (Jerusalem: 1999); Yoel Nir, *Aryeh Deri: Ha'aliyah, hamashber, hakeev* (Tel Aviv: 1999); Menachem Rahat, *Shas - haruaḥ vehakoaḥ: eikh niẓeḥah Shas et hapolitikah hayisreelit* (Bnei Brak: 1998). Dayan's book is by far the best. For a critique of these books, see, for example, Yechiam Weitz, "Afui lemeḥeẓah," *Yedioth Aharonoth* (9 Oct. 1998), weekend supplement, 26.

56. Aaron P. Willis, "Sephardic Torah Guardians: Ritual and the Politics of Piety" (Ph.D. diss., Princeton University, 1993).

57. See the following works by Nissim Leon: "Separadim veharedim: ḥakirah etnografit 'al mashma'ut hashpa'at tenu'at Shas 'al tefisat hazehut hamizrahit vehaharedit veyaḥasah odoteihen" (Master's thesis, Tel Aviv University, 1999); "Kenes hateshuvah hahamoni baḥarediyut hamizraḥit," in *Ḥaredim yisreelim: hishtalvut belo temi'ah?*, ed. Kimmy Caplan and Emmanuel Sivan (Tel Aviv: 2003), 82–99; "Hatenu'ah haḥaredit eẓel hamizraḥim beyisrael"; "Hatesisah haḥaredit bekerev hayehudim hamizraḥim: temunot etnografiyot meeshnav beit hakeneset hadati," in Ravitzky (ed.), *Shas*, 165–194.

58. Neri Horowitz, "Shas vehaẓiyonut: nituaḥ histori," *Kivunim ḥadashim* 2 (2000), 30–61. On the tension between the religious and secular population regarding the education of immigrant children during the first years of the state, and Va'adat Frumkin, the commission appointed to investigate the matter, see Zvi Zameret, *'Alei gesher ẓar: haḥinukh beyisrael bishnot hamedinah harishonot* (Sdeh Boker: 1997), 141–160.

59. See the following works by Yaakov Lupu: " 'Haẓalat yahadut maroko letorah': hoẓaat talmidim mimaroko lishivot litaiyot aḥar hashoah," *Pe'amim* 80 (1999), 112–129; "Hahashpa'ah halitait 'al 'olam hatorah bemaroko mitḥilat hameah ha'esrim ve'ad 'aliyat Shas," *Kivunim ḥadashim* 2 (2000), 61–74; *Shas delita: hahishtaltut halitait 'al benei torah mimaroko* (Tel Aviv: 2004); "Shas: ha'omek hahistori," in Ravitzky (ed.), *Shas*, 123–152.

60. Deshen, "The Emergence of the Israeli Sephardi Ultra-Orthodox Movement," 94–95.

61. Walter P. Zenner, "Remembering the Sages of Aram Soba (Aleppo)," in *Critical Essays on Israeli Society, Religion, and Government*, ed. Kevin Avruch and Walter P. Zenner (Albany: 1997), 138, 144–145.

62. See the following works by Binyamin Lau: " ' 'Al mishmarti e'emodah lehaḥazir 'atarah leyoshenah': maavako shel harav 'Ovadyah Yosef lishmirat hahalakhah beereẓ yisrael," in *Etgar haribonut: yeẓirah vehagut be'asor harishon lamdinah*, ed. Mordechai Bar-On (Jerusalem: 1999), 214–228; "Shemirat minhagei 'edot mul aḥdut hahalakhah: 'iyun bemishnato hahilkhatit shel harav 'Ovadyah Yosef," *Akdamot* 10 (2001), 267–288; "Lehaḥazir 'atarah leyoshenah: 'iyunim bemishnato hahilkhatit shel harav 'Ovadyah Yosef " (Ph.D. diss., Bar-Ilan University, 2002); "Temurot ba'olam hahalakhah hasephardi: mimasoret lesifrut," in Caplan and Sivan (eds.), *Ḥaredim yisreelim*, 11–32; "Mekomah shel hakabalah bifsikato shel harav 'Ovadyah Yosef," *Da'at* 55 (2005), 131–152; *Mimaran 'ad maran*.

63. See Zvi Zohar, *Heiru penei hamizraḥ: halakhah vehagut eẓel ḥakhmei yisrael ba-mizraḥ hatikhon* (Tel Aviv: 2001), 312–353; idem, " 'Lehaḥazir 'atarah leyoshenah' - ḥazono shel harav 'Ovadyah," in Peled (ed.), *Shas—etgar hayisreeliyut,* 159–210.

64. See Nissim Leon, " 'Zikui Harabim' ": Ovadia Yosef's Approach toward Religious Activism and His Place in the Haredi Movement within Mizrahi Jewry," in this volume; idem, "Hatenu'ah haḥaredit eẓel hamizraḥim beyisrael," 86–90.

65. Ariel Pikard, "Pesikato shel harav 'Ovadyah Yosef lenohakh temurot hazeman" (Ph.D. diss., Bar-Ilan University, 2004); idem, "Harav 'Ovadyah Yosef behitmodeduto 'im 'dor haḥofesh vehaderor'," in Ravitzky (ed.), *Shas,* 228–284.

66. Elimelech Westreich, "Haganat ma'amad hanisuin shel haishah hayehudiyah be-yisrael: mifgash bein masorot mishpatiyot shel 'edot shonot," *Plilim* 7 (1998), 273–348, esp. 326–348.

67. See Lau, *Mimaran 'ad maran,* 25–133, as well as Neri Horowitz's discussion of Yosef's formative years, "Harav 'Ovadyah Yosef—hashanim heme'aẓvot," in Ravitzky (ed.), *Shas,* 194–228. Also see two full-length treatments: Nizan Chen and Anshil Pfeffer, *Maran: 'Ovadyah Yosef, habiyografiyah* (Jerusalem: 2004); Yossi Elituv and Zvi Alush, *Ben porat Yosef: ḥayav, mishnato umahalakhav hapolitiyim shel 'Ovadyah Yosef* (Or Yehuda: 2004). Chen and Pfeffer's book is the more informative.

68. For a detailed discussion, see Kimmy Caplan, "Haḥarediyut hamizraḥit vehadat ha'amamit: shnei mikrei mivḥan," in Ravitzky (ed.), *Shas,* 443–484.

69. See Leon, " 'Zikui Harabim.' "

70. Feldman, "Gormim bizmihat miflagah ḥadashah," 50–51; Friedman, "The Ultra-Orthodox and Israeli Society," 198.

71. See Kimmy Caplan, "Hael mitokh hakaletet—'al derashot udrashot muklatot ba-ḥevrah haḥaredit," *Yahadut zemanenu* 9 (1995), 194–195; Deshen, "The Emergence of the Israeli Sephardi Ultra-Orthodox Movement," 96–97.

72. Lau, " 'Al mishmarti e'emodah,' " 219–223; "Temurot ba'olam hahalakhah hase-pharadi," 12–30.

73. On the term "lived religion," see the introduction to *Lived Religion in America: Toward a History of Practice,* ed. David D. Hall (Princeton: 1997), vii-xiii.

74. See, for example, Deshen, "Hadatiyut shel hamizraḥim," 54. On the shift in focus among Ashkenazi haredim from mimetic and oral traditions to a text-based culture, see n. 10.

75. Yosef's prayer book was distributed to these synagogues free of charge by the Ministry of Religious Affairs at a time when this office was run by ministers representing Shas. I thank Moshe Samet for providing me with this information.

76. This widespread phenomenon has to date received limited attention. For three com-prehensive discussions, see Simeon D. Baumel, "Weekly Torah Portions, Languages, and Culture among Israeli Haredim," *Jewish Social Studies* 10, no. 2 (2004), 153–179; Kimmy Caplan, " 'Alonei parshat hashavu'a baḥevrah hayehudit haortodoksit beyisrael," in *Sifriyot veosafei sefarim,* ed. Moshe Sluhovsky and Yosef Kaplan (Jerusalem: 2006), 447–483; Jonathan Cohen, "Politics, Alienation, and the Consolidation of Group Identity: The Case of Synagogue Pamphlets," *Rhetoric and Public Affairs* 3, no. 2 (2000), 247–276.

77. Caplan, "Haḥarediyut hamizraḥit vehadat ha'amamit," 462–472.

78. See, for example, Lau, "Lehaḥazir 'atarah leyoshenah," 18–19; Zohar, *Heiru penei hamizraḥ,* 324–325.

79. *Ma'ayan hashavu'a* 74 ("Vayera") (25 Nov. 1991), 3; R. Ovadia Yosef, *Livyat ḥen: 'al hilkhot shabat lefi seder hamishnah berurah ubeur halakhah* (Jerusalem: 1986), 5–6.

80. The following are only a few examples: Janet Aviad, *Return to Judaism: Religious Renewal in Israel* (Chicago: 1983); M. Herbert Danzger, *Returning to Tradition: The Contemporary Revival of Orthodox Judaism* (New Haven: 1989); Lynn Davidman, *Tradition in a Rootless World: Women Turn to Orthodox Judaism* (Los Angeles: 1991); Debra R. Kaufman, *Rachel's Daughters: Newly Orthodox Jewish Women* (New Brunswick: 1993); William Shaffir, "The Recruitment of *Baalei Tshuvah* in a Jerusalem Yeshiva," *Jewish Journal of Sociology* 25, no. 1 (1983), 33–46. On the phenomenon in the Mizrahi sector, see Aviad, *Return to Judaism,* 22–23, 42–45; Michal Fechler-Rotenberg, "Signon rigshi/sikhli

shel ḥazarah bitshuvah bekerev nashim yisreeliyot" (Master's thesis, The Hebrew University, 1989); Yehuda Goodman, *Haḥzarah bitshuvah vezehuyot ḥadashot beyisrael bithilat shenot haalpayim* (Tel Aviv: 2002); Yehuda Mimran, "Defusei ḥazarah bitshuvah bekerev ḥozrim benei 'edot hamizraḥ uvnei 'edot ashkenaz haponim letipul nafshi" (Master's thesis, The Hebrew University, 1992); Leon, "Hatenu'ah haḥaredit eẓel hamizraḥim beyisrael," 170–175, 262–263.

81. On Elbaz's pioneering work with Mizrahi prisoners and youth, see Aviad, *Return to Judaism*, 30, 42.

82. For instance, Amnon Yitzhak has reportedly been criticized for not publicly supporting Shas. On Yitzhak, see Roni Giveon, " 'Yesh she'at raẓon gedolah 'akhshav bashamayim - tizkeru - she'at raẓon gedolah': kinsei haḥazarah bitshuvah shel harav Amnon Yiẓḥak - hebetim retoriyim vetiksiyim" (Master's thesis, The Hebrew University, 2003); Orli Waserzug-Ravid, "Retorikah shel omanut hamofa' bekenes haḥzarah bitshuvah," in *Yisrael bithilat hameah ha-21*, ed. Hillel Nosek (Tel Aviv: 2002), 123–158.

83. See the survey conducted by Shlomit Levy, Hanna Levinsohn, and Elihu Katz, *Emunot, shemirat miẓvot veyaḥasim ḥevratiyim bekerev hayehudim beyisrael* (Jerusalem: 1993), and their subsequent survey, *Emunot, Shmirat masoret ve'arakhim shel yehudim beyisrael 2000* (Jerusalem: 2002).

84. See Leon, "Hatenuah haḥaredit eẓel hamizraḥim beyisrael," 170–175, 262–263.

85. On the development and characteristics of this camp, its political arm, and the attitudes of its various subgroups toward the state and its institutions, see Gideon Aran, "From Religious Zionism to Zionist Religion: The Roots of Gush Emunim," in Medding (ed.), *Studies in Contemporary Jewry*, vol. 2, 116–144; idem, "Jewish Zionist Fundamentalism: The Bloc of the Faithful in Israel (Gush Emunim)," in *Fundamentalisms Observed*, ed. Martin E. Marty and R. Scott Appleby (Chicago: 1991), 265–345; Michael Feige, *Shtei mapot lagadah: Gush Emunim, Shalom 'Akhshav ve'iẓuv hamerḥav beyisrael* (Jerusalem: 2003); Charles S. Liebman and Eliezer Don-Yehiya, *Civil Religion in Israel: Traditional Judaism and Political Culture in the Jewish State* (Berkeley: 1983), 189–214; Charles S. Liebman and Eliezer Don-Yehiya, *Religion and Politics in Israel* (Bloomington: 1984), esp. 86–119.

86. For some preliminary comparisons between Shas and religious Zionism, see Dov Schwartz, "He'arot 'al haẓiyonut hadatit veShas: shnei modelim shel hitgabrut 'al mashber," in Ravitzky (ed.), *Shas*, 386–405.

87. For a summary of existing scholarship on the *hardal* phenomenon, see Mati Dombrowsky, "Miḥinukh mamlakhti dati letalmudei torah: tahalikhei hitbadlut baḥevrah haẓiyonit datit beyisrael" (Master's thesis, Bar-Ilan University, 2004).

88. See Yohai Hakak, *Meohalah shel torah lemaahal tironim: mifgash bein modelim tarbutiyim* (Jerusalem: 2003); Nurit Stadler and Eyal Ben-Ari, "Other-Worldly Soldiers? Ultra-Orthodox Views of Military Service in Contemporary Israel," *Israel Affairs* 9, no. 4 (2003), 17–49.

89. See, among others, Tamar El-Or, "Keshayim biftiḥat 'ḥalonot': haknayat mikẓo'a lenashim min hama'amad habeinoni/namukh," *Riv'on lekalkalah* 48, no. 4 (2001), 652–684; Yohai Hakak, *Bein kodesh letakhles: gevarim ḥarediyim lomdim mikẓo'a* (Jerusalem: 2004); Ya'akov Lupu, *Mifneh baḥevrah haḥaredit: hakhsharah mikẓo'it velimudim akademiyim* (Jerusalem: 2003).

90. See Anat Feldman, "Politikah, etniyut umigdar: irgun hanashim shel tenu'at Shas," in *Ishah bamizraḥ, ishah mimizraḥ: sipurah shel hayehudiyah bat hamizraḥ*, ed. Tova Cohen and Shaul Regev (Ramat Gan: 2005), 295–315.

91. See Tamar El-Or, *Mekomot shemurim: migdar veetniyut bimḥozot hadat vehateshuvah* (Tel Aviv: 2006). For an analysis of halakhic issues pertaining to women in Yosef's writings, see Lau, *Mimaran 'ad maran*, 202–220.

92. See, for example, Dominique Schnapper, "Israélites and Juifs: New Jewish Identities in France," in *Jewish Identities in the New Europe*, ed. Jonathan Webber (London: 1994), 173–174; Marta F. Topel, "Brazilian Ba'alot Teshuvah and the Paradoxes of their Religious Conversion," *Judaism* 51, no. 3 (2002), 329–347.

93. For example, a leading Syrian congregation in Brooklyn, Shaare Zion, was headed by Rabbi Abraham Hecht, a Chabad rabbi originally from Canada. See Moshe Shokeid, *Children of Circumstances: Israeli Emigrants in New York* (Ithaca: 1988), 139–161; Walter P. Zenner, "Syrian Jews in New York Twenty Years Ago," in *Fields of Offerings: Studies in Honor of Raphael Patai*, ed. Victor D. Sanua (Rutherford: 1983), 181–183; idem, "The Ethnography of Diaspora: Studying Syrian Jewry," *Contemporary Jewry* 19 (1998), 165–168; idem, *A Global Community: The Jews from Aleppo, Syria* (Detroit: 2000), 105–177.

94. Golan Guez, "Havnayat hazehut hahevratit be'iton tenu'at Shas 'Yom Leyom' " (Master's thesis, Bar-Ilan University, 2003).

Breaking Their Silence: Mizrahi Women and the Israeli Feminist Movement

Henriette Dahan Kalev
(BEN-GURION UNIVERSITY)

Political scientists tend to examine the impact of grass-roots activism in terms of visible output in the public sphere: for instance, how many laws were legislated, which desired policies came about, and whether decision-makers changed their minds as a result of grass-roots pressure. In this fashion, feminist movements are often evaluated on the basis of the impact they make, even though changes in women's status are the outcome of many factors—not all of them visible in the public sphere. Social changes most often begin with a shift in consciousness reinforced by economic and political factors, although the links between them are not always clear. Sometimes it appears as though every step forward is followed by two steps back; even irreversible processes are difficult to evaluate qualitatively, let alone quantitatively.[1] One example is an individual's acquisition of knowledge concerning the workings of political power via participation in social justice movements. Such experiences can be liberating and empowering, regardless of whether the movement's goals are actually attained.

In this essay, I examine first the relationship between Ashkenazic and Mizrahi women in the Israeli feminist movement, showing how Mizrahi feminism developed out of conflicts within the movement in a manner that reflected ethnic tensions present in the larger Israeli society. Following a discussion of the problems caused by economic policies promoting privatization and globalization, I present an account of three incidents in which Mizrahi women chose to "break their silence" in the face of economic oppression or exploitation. In conclusion, I point to an issue that has been inadequately discussed in the theoretical feminist literature—namely, the invisible link between the "social" and "psychic" aspects of women's oppression—and show its impact on both Mizrahi women and feminist movement activism.

The Feminist Movement in Israel

Early in the 1970s, in the aftermath of the Six-Day War, immigration to Israel from prosperous western countries increased markedly. Among the young migrants were women from Anglo-American countries who had been exposed to the feminist movement from the late 1960s onward. The ideas they brought with them, and the grass-roots activity that they initiated, marked the first significant steps in pursuit of women's rights in Israel.[2]

A local movement was founded, and slogans such as "liberation," "sisterhood," and "women's rights" were prominently aired. Annual conferences were attended by women from most sectors of Israeli society, including Israeli Palestinian women and American Jewish immigrants (the latter joined the movement in disproportionate numbers). Although Ashkenazic women were in the majority, there were also Mizrahim;[3] similarly, there were both religious and secular women in the movement. While few in numbers, Israeli feminists were enthusiastic and committed, confident that they were at the threshold of women's liberation.

Before long, however, tensions surfaced as some women came to the realization that they were not on an equal footing with others in the movement. Feelings of deprivation were especially salient among the ranks of the Mizrahi and Palestinian Israeli women, who discovered that they were not kept apprised of all the movement's meetings and events. They were also disturbed by the fact that they were routinely assigned menial tasks such as mailing flyers or preparing placards for demonstrations, and rarely if ever served as movement spokespersons either abroad or in the local media. They felt that they were slowly being marginalized, their voices gradually being silenced. As one Mizrahi woman put it:

> What do they [the Ashkenazic women] know about what it means to be a Mizrahi woman—a woman with many children, religious? They close their ears to us, they are patronizing.... They give you all the reasons in the world to feel like a stranger. No opportunity to open your mouth—nobody to talk to, anyway. A club...of feminist Neturei Karta—most of the time even the language is different. It's a club for immigrants where the domain and language is English.[4]

Whenever Mizrahi women tried to bring up the issue of being excluded for ethnic reasons, their claim was dismissed as irrelevant. Hence, many of them left the movement.[5]

By the early 1980s, it was clear that the Israeli feminist movement comprised almost exclusively Ashkenazic women activists who were mainly concerned with "upper-class" issues such as the struggle for greater representation of women on corporate boards, in political parties, and in higher education, as well as the celebration of sexual preference. At times, the class-based nature of an issue was not immediately apparent. For instance, the movement invested a good deal of its energy and almost all its resources in a highly publicized campaign to have women accepted to the pilots' training program of the Israel Defense Forces. Success, it was believed, would open doors for all women, although only those with high educational attainments (who more often than not came from the upper middle class) would be eligible. Thus, for Mizrahi women who came from the lower class, and for Palestinian Israeli women or religious women who did not even serve in the army, pilot training was not even a theoretical option. Meanwhile, socioeconomic issues that were of particular concern to poorer women—improving work conditions in factories, for instance, or encouraging more women to complete elementary school[6]—were largely ignored.

While almost everyone in this initial group of Mizrahi feminists belonged to the middle class and many had acquired higher education, most of them had grown up under deprived conditions and maintained their sensitivity to problems affecting the poorer population. Supporting the movement's agenda, they nonetheless had different priorities: for them, the equal opportunities sought (and sometimes already attained) by the Ashkenazic feminists were still in the realm of fantasy.

Although the patronizing attitude of the leadership and its elitist order of priorities caused growing resentment among the Mizrahi feminists, it was not until 1994 that these differences came out in the open. At the tenth annual feminist conference held that year in Givat Haviva, a small group of Mizrahi feminists disrupted the proceedings, claiming that the Ashkenazic women did not represent their special concerns and accusing them of betraying feminist ideals of sisterhood, solidarity, and equality. The movement's leadership rejected the charges. The debate between the two groups ended in a bitter deadlock, with many participants—both Ashkenazic and Mizrahi—walking out of the conference. Shortly thereafter, the movement split.[7]

The tumultuous conference at Givat Haviva is now regarded widely as a milestone in the development of feminist consciousness in Israel. Debate continued over the course of the following year not only within feminist circles but also among academics, in the media, and at the grass-roots level.[8] The conference left a legacy of soured relations among Israeli feminists, and the movement as a whole never recovered fully from being labeled upper-class, sectarian, and uncommitted to ideals of female solidarity and equality. Emergent ideological differences now came into the open, in this way demonstrating that the Israeli feminist agenda was not monolithic. Indeed, ethnic, class, religious, and national interests proved to be stronger than feminist sentiments of sisterhood.

The pattern of subordination to a hegemonic group that developed within the Israeli feminist movement has parallels in U.S. feminist movements since the 1980s, as has long been noted and extensively discussed.[9] Both the Israeli and American cases demonstrate that, although women may share common experiences of oppression because they are women, this does not preclude them from oppressing women who are not of their class or ethnic group.[10] Put generally, the conclusion is that the common fate of being oppressed as women is not a sufficient condition for generating solidarity; as is the case with subordination among men, better-off women tend to subordinate those women who are worse off. In other words, class ties may well be stronger than gender ties, and material interests lead upper-class women to identify with males of their own class, rather than with women from the lower classes or from different races or ethnic groups.

Following the split with the larger feminist movement, Mizrahi feminists began to meet separately and in the following year organized a conference of their own, which took place in May 1995 in Netanya. There they spoke for the first time about their complex experiences of ethnic and gender oppression. Some reported that discussing these issues freely was itself liberating and empowering.[11] In speaking of their past wounds, these women discovered that their personal experiences and perspectives had a collective dimension, connected as they were to the public sphere and to their socialization into the Zionist ethos. Their common individual experiences began to take the form of a Mizrahi women's collective narrative that fostered solidarity and helped define a Mizrahi feminist agenda.

The topics discussed at the first Mizrahi feminist conference reflected two major concerns. First was a deeply felt need to highlight the gap between official Zionist history as taught in school and Mizrahi women's own personal biographies, which included the history they had learned from their parents. Second was a need to expose and publicize the painful experiences of their parents' generation and their own experiences as children. Many of the women expressed a sense of urgency stemming from their belief that their own history was insufficiently recognized—and also misrepresented—by the rest of Israeli society.[12] At the conference, participants fulfilled the feminist ideal of translating "the personal into the political," in accordance with one of the main tenets of feminist thinking dating back to the 1970s.[13] Their avid desire to discuss questions relating to the politics of identity, the dominant view of Israeli history, and gender and race discrimination in Israel was incorporated into their agenda, moving it strongly in the direction of a history of marginalization, identity crisis, and economic deprivation.[14]

Within the broader context of the existing Israeli feminist discourse, Mizrahi feminism represented the interests of women who were at (or who identified with) the bottom layers of Israeli society, and who sought to expose the hidden mechanisms that made it more difficult for marginalized women to make their voices heard. This process of feminist social formation did not occur in a void. While the poverty and depressed circumstances of Mizrahi women were part of a social issue that had existed since Israel's establishment, the intersection between gendered and ethnicized experiences of disadvantage was not simply the coming together of two separate forms of deprivation. Rather, the compounding of these different yet inseparable social dimensions strengthened the walls of the societal enclave barring Mizrahi women from equal access to civil and social rights. Experiencing a more complex pattern of deprivation than Mizrahi men, they were thus in an even weaker position—and even more inclined to remain silenced.[15] Yet in order to escape that pattern, that silence needed to be broken. This was accomplished at the first Mizrahi feminist conference, where participants met with women very much like themselves.[16]

In spite of the emancipating experiences at their first conference, Mizrahi feminists soon discovered that speaking out did not lead to tangible gains. Years earlier, beginning in the 1980s, Israel had begun to pull back from its earlier welfare commitments. Now, worsening economic conditions worked to "re-silence" those among the Mizrahi women who only recently had begun to make their voices heard.

The Challenges Confronting Mizrahi Feminism

In the years following the conference, Mizrahi feminists such as Mira Eliezer and Netta Amar struggled on behalf of deprived women and children in the slums, especially in Israel's big cities. Most women prominent in the movement were lower middle-class, having become slightly better off economically and somewhat better educated than their sisters in the slums, and they were able to share their collective narratives with other women who, they believed, had undergone the same experiences of marginalization. Joining them were a number of younger Mizrahi women who were university students. Gradually, the Mizrahi feminist agenda began to shift from its initial orientation of seeking to uncover the causes of past deprivation to a focus on the present—namely, the conditions of poverty and unemployment within which the third and fourth generation of Mizrahi women were trapped, and which now also affected new immigrants from Russia and Ethiopia. Mizrahi women of the third and fourth generation in Israel worked hand in hand with new immigrants, thereby sharpening their own experience of deprivation. The agenda was promoted by a small group of activists mainly from the Tel Aviv and Jerusalem area, some two dozen in number, who held conferences and staged demonstrations. In 1999, they founded Ahoti (from *aḥoti*, lit. "my sister"), whose name reflected the founders' commitment to feminist sisterhood.[17]

At Ahoti's inaugural conference, organized mainly at the grass-roots level, participants included Mizrahi feminists as well as representatives of other marginalized groups of women such as Ethiopians, Palestinian Israelis, and lesbians. Most of the discussion focused on the actual rather than the theoretical or ideological: immediate problems such as economic recession and the rising unemployment in the outlying towns, exploitation of female labor, single motherhood, issues concerning elementary education, and deepening gaps between women in Israel's central region and those in development towns on the periphery. The term "globalization" often came up in discussion.

This shift of focus from historical deprivation and identity crisis to women's poverty in contemporary Israel was indicative of Mizrahi feminism's openness to issues confronting women at the grass roots, regardless of their country of origin. Moreover, it helped to remove the stigma of sectarianism that hitherto had been attached to Mizrahi feminists by other Israeli feminist organizations and by the media. The 1999 conference declared 2000 to be "the year of women workers." Shortly afterwards, Ahoti took up this project. The worsening situation of women workers as a result of Israeli leaders' globalization policies led to a focus on socioeconomic issues among Mizrahi activists. Their agenda included five main goals: 1) expanding the circle of feminists to include working women and those who lived in peripheral settlements; 2) integrating class politics with the varied and complex identity politics of many groups in Israeli society—Jews, Arabs, Ethiopians, Russians, Mizrahim, and women in general; 3) giving immediate assistance to low-income women, particularly in the area of legal counseling as to their rights; 4) bringing the current discourse between Jewish and Arab women factory workers into Israeli feminism; and 5) disseminating information on a variety of issues of particular importance to working women—for instance, the rights of pregnant women, sexual harassment in the workplace, how to read a pay slip, and how to join a labor union.[18]

Significantly, Mizrahi women activists were the first to address the corrosive and elitist influence of economic globalization on Israeli social policies, an issue hitherto neglected by the Israeli feminist movement. This new Mizrahi feminist agenda appealed especially to women located at the bottom rungs of Israeli society, a number of whom sought to bring their problems to the attention of the public and to raise women's consciousness regarding the need for action.

Four aspects of the influence of globalization in Israel were particularly relevant to the new Mizrahi feminist agenda: the privatization of industry; the opening up of the economic market (industrial and monetary systems) to the competition of the world market; the privatization of social services, and the shifting focus of economic enterprise from production to financial services. From the very first, Israeli society had been marked by gaps between poor and rich, with various economic growth policies running counter to the stated national political goal of attaining a more equal society.[19] These gaps, moreover, were highly correlated with ethnic, national, and religious cleavages, and as a result, society was divided economically into Mizrahim and Ashkenazim, religious and non-religious, Arabs and Jews, and immigrants and veterans.[20] Notwithstanding, Israel until the 1970s was widely considered to be a welfare state that provided its citizens with many basic social services, including education, health, housing, and pension and social security payments. The state was also the country's largest employer.[21] It was variously involved in the largest 100 companies (10 percent of which it owned), and more than 71 percent of the grants and subsidies given to Israeli industry came from the state.[22] Workers were protected by a single strong trade union movement (the Histadrut) and by labor laws thought to be comparable to those in European social-democratic countries. In addition, the state controlled the financial sector, closely regulating its activities and even owning many major institutions, including banks.[23] To round out the picture, women during this period were (as they mostly still are) the second breadwinner in heterosexual families.[24]

Israel began to move in the direction of globalization and to retreat from its welfare state commitments in 1979, when the coalition government led by Menachem Begin—the first non-Labor prime minister—adopted a policy of privatization and economic liberalization. Over the next 25 years, industry, the financial institutions, and social services slowly but steadily privatized, with the effects, however, being felt mainly (and negatively) by the lower-middle and lower classes. Whereas many lower-class women were formerly able to make ends meet by having more than one job, they now increasingly found themselves out of work, and in many cases had difficulty even feeding their children. During the 1980s and 1990s, economic reforms included the cutting of budgets for education, health, and the municipalities; reduced social service payments and decreased subsidization of basic commodities such as food; a cutback in aid to struggling industries; and increased competition and lessened protection in the employment sector, which led both to the weakening of the trade union movement and the introduction of private manpower firms and practices in hiring. The negative effects of these reforms were felt most acutely in the development towns in the Negev and in the north, where the population was (and is) largely Mizrahi.[25]

This is where Mizrahi feminism met globalization. The question facing women activists was: Did this situation carry the seeds of protest? Were the terms of extreme subordination of the women at the bottom of society—the first to be fired when textile and food factories were closed and workers were exploited—severe enough to generate change and motivate women to break their silence? And how might this be done? In the framework of the women workers project, Ahoti activists took up the challenge by traveling to Israel's outlying towns to meet with women factory workers, cashiers, and cleaners employed by private manpower companies, among others. They provided them with information about employee rights and encouraged them to unionize within the workplace. To their surprise, they discovered that the women were fully aware of their rights but had done nothing to realize them—and were unwilling, moreover, to attempt to unionize. At first the activists attributed this to the women's lack of experience in organizational activism. Only later did it become clear to them that the women workers, mostly new immigrants from Russia and Ethiopia, feared confronting their employers. Given the scarcity of employment opportunities in the development towns and the relatively high rate of unemployment, they were reluctant to speak out for fear of being branded "troublemakers." Such a label would not only jeopardize their present jobs but would hurt their chances of getting work elsewhere.

Exacerbating the situation was the fact that the power of unions in Israel generally, and in the development towns, in particular, had been seriously eroded as a consequence of privatization and globalization. Women workers were increasingly forced to deal with employer exploitation on their own and were afraid to fight for their just and legal rights. Although many of those exploited had cases that almost certainly would have stood up in court, they dared not take action.[26]

Ahoti activists tried in vain to encourage these women to break their silence. At a certain point, frustrated, some of the activists became disillusioned and disheartened and reverted to their previous identity politics agenda, emphasizing such issues as the distinctiveness of Mizrahi feminist art, literature, and media.[27] Meanwhile, the frustration and confusion regarding the realities faced by women workers, combined with internal disagreements over whether to focus on identity politics or on globalization, brought the "year of women workers" project to an end. Ironically, this occurred just as a number of women in southern development towns began to make their voices heard in protest.

Between 2000 and 2004, three significant cases of protest on the part of exploited Mizrahi women living in Negev development towns came to public attention. These protests were spontaneous and personal and were not connected to any organization, including Ahoti. For this reason, the claim may be made that social justice activism in this field did not lead to significant change. I would argue, however, that the work promoted by Ahoti, while not bearing immediate fruit, may have had an indirect influence on those women who spoke out.

Three Case Studies of Protest

Vicki Knafo's March to Jerusalem

The first, and perhaps best known, of these protests was initiated by Vicki Knafo, who in the summer of 2003 was a 43-year-old, twice-divorced mother of three children living in the town of Mitzpe Ramon. The sole breadwinner of her family, Knafo had worked over the years in various temporary jobs in which she earned less than the minimum wage. Like many others in her position, Knafo received an income supplement—in her case, equal to her monthly wages—from the National Insurance

Institute of Israel. As a result, while she lived below the poverty line, she "wasn't starving."[28] However, in June 2003, as part of the economic recovery plan, a cut in supplemental income payments went into effect. On the verge of starvation and "one step from suicide," Knafo decided to take action. Since she had no money for a bus ticket and no patience to wait for other single mothers to get a bus organized, she decided to march to Jerusalem—some 200 kilometers away—and to camp outside the Ministry of Finance, located in the row of government buildings close to the Knesset.

Knafo began her protest on July 1, 2003 and after five days reached her destination. By then, she was no longer on her own. Her roadside walk in the heat of an Israeli summer had quickly attracted widespread media coverage, and Knafo was soon accompanied on the way by other single mothers, unemployed workers, and social activists, including five members of Ahoti.[29] Upon their arrival, they were met by more individuals who sought to express their solidarity and encouragement. While Knafo did not manage to meet any senior government economic officials during the days that followed, thousands of people came to visit her and provided her with food, clothing, and a tent. Some of these people were mothers who joined her protest. Two weeks after Knafo's arrival in Jerusalem, some 300 single mothers (and a few fathers) and a large number of children were encamped in more than 40 tents opposite the Knesset.

Finance Minister Binyamin Netanyahu, a master of media communication, was deeply committed to privatization as the solution to Israel's economic ills. In his view, the key to economic reform and advancement lay in balancing the budget by means of cutting government outlays on social welfare programs such as old age pensions, child support, and unemployment benefits. He pursued such policies rigorously, even though this resulted in increased unemployment (which was further exacerbated by the influx of foreign workers, who were paid lower salaries than those required by law for Israelis). Eventually, Netanyahu invited Knafo for a meeting on condition that she come alone. Knafo, for her part, wished to be accompanied by social activists and economic experts who had offered her help. Negotiations for the meeting continued for weeks but generated only media hype, until eventually Knafo could no longer bear the public spotlight. This, together with the end of the summer school vacation, led her to pack up and return with her children to Mitzpe Ramon in September 2003. During her lengthy protest, Knafo had only the briefest of meetings with Netanyahu.

Ahoti activists were among those who spent time with Knafo in Jerusalem, discussing the steps she should take with regard to both the negotiations with Netanyahu and her contacts with the media and with representatives of other NGO's. At a certain point, Ahoti's voice was lost among all those willing to assist, since its only resources were time and solidarity (whereas other groups were in a position to provide financial support, food, tents, and professional advice and publicity). After returning to Mitzpe Ramon, Knafo ended her relations with Ahoti and most of the other groups.[30]

Throughout her stay in Jerusalem, Knafo was open to advice from those who came to offer sympathy and support. At the same time, fully aware of her inexperience in social activism, she refrained from making major decisions. Eventually, the powerful energy fueled by her protest dissipated as Knafo found herself pulled in different directions by groups and individuals who, in many cases, had their own agenda to promote.

Did Knafo's protest fail? In the course of three months spent by Knafo (and others who had joined her) in front of the Ministry of Finance, Netanyahu was forced to hear what she had come to tell him—via the media, if not necessarily firsthand. In this sense, given Knafo's initial resolve to do no more than tell the finance minister what she thought, her protest can be judged a success. For Knafo personally, the experience was certainly sobering. She learned much about the public sphere and about social activism against injustice. She learned about other, less immediately relevant matters, such as how the media handles scoops and how it feels to be a celebrity—both admired and criticized—and was also exposed to new terms and concepts in which her economic distress might be expressed. In all these respects, Knafo's protest was both important and successful on the personal level, even though it may have attained little in the way of political achievement or social change. No laws were passed, none of the desired policies were adopted, and decision-makers did not change their minds as a result of Knafo's protest. Likewise, Ahoti activists did not have any discernible impact as a result of their participation in this act of public protest. Nevertheless, it may not be going beyond the facts to suggest that Knafo's initial protest may well have led to a shift in consciousness that was then reinforced by the economic and political experiences associated with the event. However, because it is hard to quantify, it is very difficult to evaluate the extent of this shift.

From Workers to Bosses: The Mitzpe Atzmaut Textile Factory

Three years earlier, another Mizrahi woman from Mitzpe Ramon, Havatzelet Ingbar, had launched a different kind of protest against economic policies that had brought her family to the verge of starvation.

Ingbar, a married mother of four, had worked for 14 years as a seamstress in the Mitzpe Atzmaut textile factory. In July 2000, it became known that the factory was on the verge of bankruptcy. In the past, depending on the volume of its orders, the factory had periodically laid off workers; Ingbar and others were routinely fired and rehired about twice a year. Although the workers belonged to a union—Ingbar herself was a union representative—there had previously been no organized protests. As she explained: "We could do nothing, since there were so many other unemployed women waiting at the doors of the factory, and with even a hint of our fighting for our rights, we would have found ourselves immediately thrown into the streets."[31] Now, however, as word spread that all 57 employees at the factory were about to permanently lose their jobs, Ingbar and a few of her fellow workers walked off the floor, thus beginning a wildcat strike. Acting spontaneously, they gave little thought at first to the goals or the consequences of their action.

Their first step was to close the factory gates. Following this, their pressing priority was to attend to the needs of their children. Mothers with small children arranged with their husbands and relatives to have the children brought to the factory so that they could care for them at night. They also requested a supply of blankets and food sufficient for a protracted sit-in: "Because we are not going to let anybody in or out until we have a solution to our situation. We have nowhere to go, and we may die here. We are here until we hear what the Histadrut or the government have to offer us as a solution."[32]

The women's actions brought the media to Mitzpe Ramon—a rare occurrence. Dramatic images of women shouting and burning tires were broadcast, and there was a sense that the protest was likely to spread to other Israeli towns. After the first flush of excitement, however, the media lost interest and moved on. Neither did any representatives of the government show any interest. Nevertheless, the women carried on and permitted no one, including the owner, to enter the factory. After three weeks, a number of social justice organizations from Jerusalem and Beersheba became involved and sought to draw public attention to the situation. Some six weeks after the sit-in began, when the matter was almost forgotten, the head of the Histadrut, Amir Peretz, announced that he was going to visit the factory.

Upon his arrival, Peretz asked the strikers to open up the gates and hear what he had to say. He was allowed to enter and stayed inside for several hours. During the discussion, tension was high both inside the factory and among the crowd outside. At the end of the meeting, the Histadrut leader emerged together with Ingbar and another activist, Avigayil Yifrah, and issued a startling public statement: the workers, with Histadrut assistance in the form of a loan of NIS 1,000,000 (about $250,000), would purchase the failing factory. The women had agreed to end their strike as soon as the Histadrut made good on its promise and contracts for the purchase of the factory were signed. "We were shocked," Ingbar later recalled, "but we had nothing to lose."

The atmosphere was euphoric. The media celebrated a "victory for justice," focusing their attention on the leading personalities and on the reactions of the public at large, while ignoring the seeds of failure incipient in the initiative. The reality was that the Israeli textile industry was in crisis as a result of fierce competition from the Far East, Jordan, Egypt, and the Gulf states. More specifically, the factory in Mitzpe Ramon was deeply in debt. Only later did Ingbar and her fellow workers discover that its net worth was no more than about NIS 250,000. Beyond the additional NIS 750,000 in funding provided by the labor federation, all debts were to be assumed by the factory's new owners, namely, the women themselves. Moreover, the physical plant and equipment were old, and there were no capital reserves to enable the factory to survive unregulated competition emanating either from Israel or overseas. At the time of the sale, these realities—known not only to the owners but also to Histadrut leaders and to others involved in the textile sector (such as the Textile and Fashion Industries Association)—was not made clear to the women workers. They now proceeded to become factory owners by purchasing shares at NIS 5,000 each. Money for the shares came out of the NIS 1,000,000 loan provided by the Histradrut, since none of the women could afford NIS 5,000 out of their meager earnings as textile workers.

Ingbar recalls: "When the Histadrut offered to have us go for it, I was shocked. Me? How would I do both the sewing and the management? What do I know about business and commerce? But we were so excited, first, because he [Peretz] honored us with his visit, and second, who could afford to refuse such an offer when there was nothing else on the horizon? We had nothing to lose, so we decided to go for it."

Over the next few weeks, many individuals made their way from the center of the country to Mitzpe Ramon, a distant town on Israel's southern periphery, in order to offer moral support and professional advice. Among them were financial advisers, accountants, managers, and experts in marketing and human resources. The constant flow of visitors to the factory and their embrace of the women who had taken it over became a media festival in which anonymous female workers were transformed into national heroines, serving as a beacon of hope for others similarly disadvantaged. Two television producers came to document the process whereby women who had always been workers became businesswomen managing their own factory. Textile merchants also lent them moral and material support, placing larger orders than they required so as to give the women extra encouragement. A few weeks after the factory's purchase, it reopened in a colorful ceremony.

Ahoti activists were among those who offered help and support when the women's strike first hit the media. When asked what the women needed, Ingbar immediately requested scissors and chairs. It was at this point that the women's shockingly difficult working conditions were exposed. Under the previous owners, the women had sat for hours at a time on old and uncomfortable chairs and were not allowed to change their position; not surprisingly, many of them reported suffering from chronic backache. Yet the factory's needs went far beyond new chairs, scissors, or medical assistance. Ahoti, with no budget of its own, attempted to raise money by turning to a Jerusalem philanthropist, without success. As in the case of Knafo, the Ahoti activists found themselves unable to offer anything beyond moral support and solidarity. In addition, since most of them came from Tel Aviv or Jerusalem, it was not easy to travel to Mitzpe Ramon on a regular basis.

As noted, the seeds of failure were present from the outset, though these were either hidden from view or downplayed. The women in the factory did their best to become directors, managers, marketers, and accountants as well as factory workers, but they faced tremendous difficulties and obstacles. The worst was their lack of familiarity with Israeli political and bureaucratic institutions and processes. Moreover, most of those with whom they had to work were men, who, as Ingbar recalled, "could not bear the idea that a subordinated woman from yesterday would become their boss in the factory or an equal negotiator for resources today." In their interactions with the Histadrut, the ministries of finance, labor, and welfare, and local government authorities, the women were perceived as totally inexperienced; according to Ingbar, "they ate us alive." Management power games and manipulation were new to her and her friends. They did not know how the system worked, and more significantly, they were very minor players on the political scene, unable to pull strings, to apply pressure, or to persuade others to further the factory's interests. During the first year, Ingbar encountered both external and internal obstacles emanating from local officials, technicians, and some of her fellow workers. Men in managerial positions, she recalled, could not accept the dramatically transformed situation in which women "who knew nothing" were now speaking to them as equals. The initial expectation was that the women would quickly learn to function as managers, and in almost no time would be doing business as usual. These expectations were not fulfilled, however, and the task of overcoming the weighty external and internal obstacles and complications proved to be beyond them. The factory limped along, buyers gradually lost their patience, and after almost a year, Ingbar finally gave up and resigned; some time later, Yifrah resigned as well.

As with the case of Vicki Knafo, it is difficult to evaluate the success or failure of the Mitzpe Ramon women's act of protest. On an individual level, both Ingbar and

Yifrah found themselves unemployed once they had quit their managerial positions. Since the initial struggle was aimed at preserving jobs, they were clear losers. On a broader level, however, the revolt at Mitzpe Atzmaut was an unprecedented event in which a group of women workers, by virtue of their protest, eventually became managers of the factory in which they worked and had previously been exploited. To be sure, this turn of events led to no real change in the public arena and had no perceptible effect on other blue-collar women workers. At the same time, the women at Mitzpe Atzmaut experienced significant change. They gained a rare opportunity to look into the world of their employers, seeing from within how management and business is carried out. They had face to face contact with representatives of government ministries and business, with those who formerly determined how much they should earn or who bought the products they produced. They learned how it felt to be responsible for other people's salaries and to ensure that products were manufactured and delivered on time. The lasting effects of such experiences are difficult to evaluate and measure, but they have most likely led to shifts in consciousness or professional abilities among workers who were transformed overnight into managers.

The "Lionesses" of Beersheba

In January 2004, three women in their 40s—Yehudit Ben-David, Ahuva Mor-Yosef, and Michal Magen—entered a supermarket in Beersheba. They filled their shopping carts and then asked to speak to the manager, informing her that they intended to walk out without paying for what they had taken. Over the course of the following two months, this scenario was repeated in other supermarkets in the city. In a flyer signed by "The Three Lionesses," the women explained that they were acting out of desperation. "The economic depression and the recent removal of the subsidies on bread and basic food have brought us to starvation," they wrote. "We are left with no choice. We have to protect our children. We have decided to take direct action to fill our shopping carts with food and bring it to our children. It's time to stop being shy and silent. If you're a single mother, join us. Together we'll succeed."[33]

All three women were without regular employment. Mor-Yosef had worked as a supermarket cashier but five years previously had suffered a heart attack. "While I was recovering, they fired me," she told a foreign reporter. "Now they say I'm too old to hire." In a different interview, one of the women declared: "We are the silent victims of Bibi Netanyahu. . . . I clean stairways occasionally . . . but it's not enough for the rent and food and electricity . . . we have no electricity, so we are no longer ashamed [to steal]."[34] All three women were divorced, and their ex-husbands were not providing alimony.

Hearing of the women's protest, the Beersheba branch of the Shatil organization contacted the Lionesses and tried to encourage them to organize self-help—for instance, a project to bake and distribute bread among the city's poor population. But the women were too angry to conform by restricting themselves to socially acceptable activities, preferring instead to continue their challenge against the social order. They refused to act like "good girls" and instead resorted to criminal acts. In March, for instance, they were arrested (not for the first time) for attempting to invade the Knesset cafeteria.[35] Although they gained a certain amount of media exposure, their protest did not generate widespread public debate or support from other women. On the contrary, many people condemned the women for disturbing the public order and for providing a bad example to their children.[36] After April 2004, the Lionesses no longer received media coverage.

Conclusion

What can be learned from each of these three case studies? In each instance, women who had experienced years of economic deprivation and exploitation in silence suddenly broke out in protest. What motivated them? As indicated by the women themselves, what brought them to their moment of crisis was the fear that they would no longer be able to provide for their children. This was particularly so in the case of the Lionesses, who, forced to choose between being "good mothers" who would feed their children and "good citizens" who would maintain public order and obey the law, chose the former. In other words, the gender motivation, the commitment to motherhood in accordance with the values with which they had been raised, obliged them to take action. Until the moment of crisis, the point at which they could no longer "make do," the women in Beersheba—as with the factory workers in Mitzpe Ramon and with Vicki Knafo before June 2003—refrained from taking action. In all these cases, it seems, the women's spontaneous radical action was motivated not by social or feminist ideology but by their gendered consciousness of their traditional role and responsibility as mothers.

Does this mean that there is a gender difference in the motivation of the oppressed to rebel and to break the silence? Would fathers have done the same had they been in the same situation? Would they have used the same rhetoric in order to justify their protest? Although the question of why and when people rebel has preoccupied historians and philosophers of revolution (such as Hannah Arendt) and social scientists (such as Ted Gurr),[37] these scholars discuss the matter in terms of a class or civil rights struggle, without taking up aspects of gender—namely, biological, economic, psychological, and sexual differences between males and females. Similarly, while feminist literature has dealt extensively with the circumstances of inequality, it, too, has barely addressed the question of how, why, and when women, as opposed to men, choose to rebel instead of continuing to remain silent, thus carrying on in a framework of exploitation and humiliation. Moreover, in the case of the Israeli feminist movement, in which tension developed between Mizrahim and Ashkenazim, there is an additional ethnic factor to consider (similar to the racial factor underlying the tension between, for instance, African American and white American feminists). When the ethnic factor is intertwined with the gender factor, the "silencing forces" are compounded.

Whereas feminist scholars, despite different approaches, agree that sexual subordination is the common denominator at the root of women's oppression and silence,[38] they tend to ignore the public sphere—that is, such issues as how political practices, legislation, and economic consequences of globalization are connected to the formation of personal and gendered identity. Put somewhat differently, the feminist literature leaves a gap between the "psychic" (that is, forces operating on the individual level) and the "social" by ignoring the relations between the geopolitical or global context and the acting person, that is, the agent. An exception in this regard is Gayatri Chakravorty Spivak, who draws a distinction between the first world and the third world in her landmark work, "Can the Subaltern Speak?"[39] Yet in the era of globalization, there are situations in which *both* worlds exist: one can live in the "third world" even in a "first world" country, with the lives of women at the bottom of "first world" societies resembling those of women in the third world.

Hence, to be a Mizrahi woman and mother in an outlying town in Israel in the era of globalization raises issues of feminism different from those confronting an upper-class mother in Tel Aviv. Spivak criticizes the methods by which third world women's issues are formulated in contemporary western literature. She argues that, paradoxically, third world women are prevented from speaking when white men come to "save" them from brown men and thereby take over the representation of their interests. Similarly, when feminists take action in order to generate social change, the inner differences among them—for instance, whether they are white Americans or Indians—become transparent.[40] Ahoti and Shatil activists who tried to provide support and solidarity to the women in the cases discussed here also followed western patterns of action, which had the effect of silencing the "subaltern" women who took action.

In the case of Ahoti feminists, the dilemma was precisely this gap between the psyche and the social—between the women's need to discuss their ethnic and identity subordination, on the one hand, versus the imperative to "break the silence" with regard to economic oppression and deprivation, on the other. This was a dilemma that the activists faced both when attempting to support the struggling women and when trying to restructure their own agenda. In each of the three case studies, the protesting women had not previously heard of Ahoti, and their interactions with movement activists were no different from those with representatives of other non-governmental organizations. Thus, the gap that the activists were theoretically able to bridge between the psycho-ethnic and the socioeconomic remained unbridged.

As noted, it is very difficult to determine the success or failure of acts of spontaneous protest, and all the more so when issues of ethnicity and gender are factored in. In analyzing the three case studies through the lens of gender, it becomes apparent that the women acted first and foremost as mothers. They felt that they had the right to go public because socially structured norms expected them to function as good mothers. What they did, in effect, was to appeal to the public's sense of justice, delivering a message that went roughly as follows: "We were brought up and expected to be good mothers, but under the current economic conditions, it is impossible for us to fulfill our role." In this respect, the women took feminist action by politicizing the role of the mother, thrusting their issues, via the media, into the public arena (whether the state, the finance ministry, or the Histadrut labor federation). Instead of remaining silent or regarding their "incompetence" as mothers as a sign of personal failure, they placed responsibility for their economic distress back in the public sector, where they felt it belonged. In this respect, Ahoti had no influence on the women before, during, or after the events precisely because it failed to grasp the gendered aspect of the struggle and to work in the direction of politicizing the issue of motherhood.

Similarly, the issue of ethnicity needs more clarification. Whereas the women involved in two of the three acts of protest were Mizrahi, some of the workers at the Mitzpe Atzmaut textile factory were immigrants from southern parts of Russia (mainly Georgia).[41] The point was noted by the media, which thereby suggested that the Mizrahi women were economically disadvantaged in the same manner as new immigrants. This implicit comparison ignores the fact that many women of Mizrahi origin live in outlying towns, in a society where the gap between Mizrahim and Ashkenazim has always played a role in Israeli political dynamics. Moreover, the political consciousness of Mizrahi women is rooted in three decades of oppression and exclusion. This long-term oppression, according to Mizrahi feminist activists, resulted from their being made to feel inept, both as women and as Mizrahi—placed even lower on the socio-hierarchical ladder than were Mizrahi men. Consequently, these women comprise a category of their own, different from both Mizrahi men or non-Mizrahi women: a point worthy of notice in any further research regarding the Israeli feminist movement.

Notes

1. Dafna Izraeli, "Hamigdur ba'olam ha'avodah," in *Min, migdar, politikah*, ed. Dafna Izraeli, Ariella Friedman, Henriette Dahan Kalev, Sylvie Fogiel-Bijaoui, Hanna Herzog, Manar Hasen, and Hannah Naveh (Tel Aviv: 1999), 167–212.
2. Henriette Dahan Kalev, "Tensions in Israeli Feminism: The Mizrahi-Ashkenazi Rift," *Women's Studies International Forum* 24 (2001), 1–16.
3. On the number of women of Mizrahi origin in Israel, and the problems of obtaining precise figures, see Henriette Dahan Kalev, "Ma'arakhot hitargenut 'azmit: vadi salib ve-hapanterim hashehorim, hashlakhot 'al hama'arekhet beyisrael" (Ph.D diss., The Hebrew University, 1991).
4. Brachah Seri, quoted in the newsletter *Kol haishah* 19 (1983), 4.
5. Dahan Kalev, "Tensions in Israeli Feminism," 16.
6. Ibid., 11.
7. Ibid., 16.
8. Ibid.; idem, "Ma'arakhot hitargenut 'azmit"; Vicki Shiran, "Shlish, shlish, shlish, reva', reva', reva'," *Noga* 26 (1993), 26; Mira Eliezer, "'Avarnu kivrat derekh," *Miz'ad sheni* 4 (Jerusalem) (July–Aug. 1996), 25.
9. See, for example, Alison Jaggar, *Feminist Politics and Human Nature* (Totowa: 1988), 77–78; and Bell Hooks, *Feminist Theory from Margin to Center* (Boston: 1984), introduction.
10. Alice Walker, "Definition of a Womanist," in *Making Face, Making Soul*, ed. Gloria Anzaldúa (San Francisco: 1990), 342; Barbara Smith, *The Truth that Never Hurts* (New Brunswick: 1998); Henriette Dahan-Kalev, "On the Logic of Feminism and the Implications of African American Feminist Thought for Israeli Mizrahi Feminism," *The American Philosophical Association Newsletter on Feminism and Philosophy* (Spring 2003), 111–117.
11. Dahan Kalev, "Tensions in Israeli Feminism"; idem, "On the Logic of Feminism"; idem, "The Gender Blindness of Good Theorists: An Israeli Case Study," *Journal of International Women's Studies* 4 (2003), 126–147.
12. Dahan Kalev, "Tensions in Israeli Feminism."
13. Sara M. Evans, *Tidal Wave: How Women Changed America at Century's End* (New York: 2003).

14. Dahan Kalev, "Tensions in Israeli Feminism."

15. Lois McNay, "Subject, Psyche and Agency: The Work of Judith Butler," *Theory, Culture and Society* 16, no. 2 (1999), 175–193.

16. Catherine Krupnick, "Women and Men in the Classroom: Inequality and Its Remedies," *On Teaching and Learning, The Journal of the Harvard Danforth Center* (May 1985), 18–25.

17. Ahoti was founded by me and by Netta Amar, an attorney. We were soon joined by other Mizrahi feminists, among them the late Vicki Shiran, Vardit Damry Madar, Esther Eilam, and Ilanit Trabelsi.

18. These goals were formulated by me and by Netta Amar in April 2000. The extended agenda was sent as a funding application to the Hadassah Foundation in New York, in November 2001.

19. Henriette Dahan-Kalev, "Defusei dikui beyisrael: wadi salib," *Teoriyah uvikoret* 12–13 (1999), 31–44.

20. Ibid.

21. Yitzhak Katz, *Hafratah beyisrael uva'olam* (Tel Aviv: 1997).

22. Report by State of Israel, Government Companies Authority (1997), online (in Hebrew) at http://www.gca.gov.il/reshut/1997/heb/ikar/draft3_1.htm. In the course of privatization, the number of government employees was cut back. In 2004, the state employed some 500,000 workers, versus 1.6 million in the private sector; comparable figures for 2002 are 501,700 for the government sector and 1,040,000 (not counting foreign and Palestinian workers) in the private sector. See table in http://www1.cbs.gov.il/shnaton57/download/st10_12.xls; also Arieh Nahmias, "Yaḥasei 'avodah beyisrael 2004: ẓemiḥah ushevitah," online at http://openu.ac.il/Adcan/adcan40/adcan-6.html.

23. Shimshon Bichler and Nitzan Yehonatan, *Miriv̲ḥei milḥamah ledividendim shel shalom* (Jerusalem: 2001), 68–119.

24. Shlomo Swirski, Eti Connor-Atias, Vered Krouz, and Anat Harvest, *Mabat 'al hatakẓiv* (report published by the Adva Center for Social Research) (Tel Aviv: 2002).

25. The Manufacturers Association of Israel reports that, over the course of six years (1994–2000), the number of textile workers declined from 45,000 to 22,000. However, over the course of a decade including this period (1994–2004), the value of textile goods exported from Israel grew from $1,008,000,000 to $1,094,000,000. Two factors are responsible for the inverse relation between number of workers and the growth of exports: the reduction in wages, and improvements in technology. See http://www.industry.org.il/SubIndex.asp?Category ID=111.Following the signing of the Oslo accords in 1993, a number of Israeli textile factories moved their operations to Egypt, Jordan, or the United Arab Emirates, where manpower costs were cheaper. Today there are about 80,000 Israelis employed in some 800 small and medium-sized firms. In the course of one year—2003—some 12,000 textile workers lost their jobs when their factories shut down. See table 14 (employment in industry) in the yearbook of the Israel Central Bureau of Statistics, online at http://www.sbs.gov.il/publications/industry2003/tab14.xls.

26. In Kiryat Gat, for instance, a group of Ethiopian women hired by a cleaning agency declined to bring a suit against the company, despite conditions of exploitation. Similarly, two women in the town who were working a full, eight-hour day, but being paid for only five hours, refused to take action. This information was reported to me by Einav Himi Vaknin, an Ahoti activist who met with the women in Kiryat Gat in July 2001.

27. For instance, Shula Keshet, a Mizrahi artist, curated an exhibition titled "My Sister" in the Ami Steinitz art gallery in Tel Aviv in the spring of 2002.

28. Interview with Vicki Knafo, Jerusalem (21 July 2003).

29. I had met Knafo two days before the onset of her hike, when we were both interviewed on the Israeli educational television network (I was invited to appear because of a different issue involving the privatization of state lands in defiance of a high court decision). Hearing of Knafo's plan to hike to Jerusalem, I decided to inform fellow members of Ahoti and suggested that they organize a solidarity demonstration. Over the course of the following

month, I met with Knafo approximately twice a week. In August, I left for a sabbatical abroad.

30. The exception was an organization called Shatil, funded by the New Israel Fund (an American Jewish philanthropy), which provides managerial counseling to newly created activist organizations. Knafo's relationship with Shatil is worthy of more extensive analysis. In an interview conducted about a year after her protest, Knafo said that Shatil had "exploited me in order to promote [its] own interests." See Itzik Saporta, "Hama'avak hahevrati 'al pi Knafo" (3 Oct. 2004), online at www.haokets.org/article.asp?ArticleID=788.

31. I met with Havatzelet Ingbar several times between August 2002 and February 2003. All quotes are from interviews conducted with her during this period.

32. Ibid.

33. Flyer published in Beersheba, calling on single mothers to join the group.

34. Chris McGreal, "Trolley Dash: The Last Resort of Hungry Israelis," *Guardian International* (19 Feb. 2004), online at www.guardian.cou.uk/international/story/0,,1151077,00.html; Zvi Alush, "Robin Hood, hagirsah hanashit," *Yedioth Aharonoth* (1 Jan. 2004), 16.

35. *Kolbi* (Beersheba) (4 March 2004), 24.

36. Osnat Vazana, "Zot lo haderekh," *Sheva'* (Beersheba) (25 Dec. 2003), 14.

37. Hannah Arendt, *On Revolution* (New York: 1977); Tedd R. Gurr, *Why Men Rebel* (Princeton: 1970).

38. In an article on the work of the gender theorist Judith Butler, Lois McNay discusses the problem of an "autonomous subject instituted through constraint" and the relation between the "psyche" and the social. However, she keeps these two dimensions entirely separate, whereas I would argue that the cause for women's silence lies somewhere between the two. Social and materialistic issues are rarely analyzed within the same context as psychic and genderial issues. Hence the dichotomy between the social-materialistic and psychic-genderial persists, and the forces that keep women silenced remain hidden within the gap between the two sides. See McNay, "Subject, Psyche and Agency." In an attempt to untangle the complexity of this situation, feminist scholars look in many directions and attempt to provide some generalizing explanations. Luce Irigaray looks into the psyche (*Speculum of the Other Woman*, trans. Gillian C. Gill [Ithaca: 1985]); Judith Butler into subject formation (*Gender Trouble: Feminism and the Subversion of Identity* [New York: 1990]); and Julia Kristeva into semiotics (*Tales of Love*, trans. Leon S. Roudiez [New York: 1987]). They and many other scholars have produced fascinating theoretical explanations and suggestions regarding methods for "breaking-through" on the part of oppressed women.

39. Gayatri Chakravorty Spivak, "Can the Subaltern Speak?" in *Marxism and the Interpretation of Culture*, ed. Cary Nelson and Lawrence Grossberg (Chicago: 1988), 271–313.

40. Ibid.

41. See, for example, Yitzhak Elam, "Shimush bekoah ezel 'olei maroko ve'olei gruziyah," *Megamot* 24 (1978), 159–170.

Conditional Homelands and Diasporas: Moroccan Jewish Perspectives

André Levy

(BEN-GURION UNIVERSITY)

There are a number of popular notions regarding the relationship between "home-lands" and "diasporas" that are found as well in most of the scholarly literature on the subject. Taken together, these notions coalesce into what I have elsewhere termed the "solar system model," which posits a symbolic center (the homeland) surrounded by peripheral diasporic orbits.[1] Although ties exist between various components of the diaspora, the essential relationship of this model is between each diaspora and the homeland, and this relationship is mainly static and unidirectional. That is, the homeland serves as a symbolic center, a locus for longing and identification, and the relationship between the various diasporas is an outcome of their mutual identi-fication with the symbolic center.[2] The structure of the solar system model is thus essentially dichotomous, and it is reproduced in rhetoric that contrasts the "eternal" or "holy" homeland with the "temporal," "profane," or "alienating" diaspora.

Yet this model is both limiting and limited. It limits our understanding of the extremely complex relationship between the homeland and various diaspora com-munities. Furthermore, by depicting both homeland and diasporas in a fixed orbit, as it were, the model is indifferent to the varying perspectives of different diaspora communities—both to the homeland and with each other.

It is my claim that this model is constructed by means of mundane and ceremonial nation-state rhetoric.[3] By "nation-state rhetoric," I refer to all utterances that both confirm the state as a natural and everlasting entity and that envision it as the ulti-mate incarnation and embodiment of a people.[4] A clear indication of the linkage between nation-state rhetoric and the construction of a bipolar (center/diaspora) model is the common recourse to a religious or mythical terminology that associ-ates antiquity with sacredness and authenticity. As Eric Hobsbawm and Terence O. Ranger note: "Modern nations and all their impedimenta generally claim to be the opposite of novel, namely rooted in the remotest antiquity, and the opposite of con-structed, namely human communities so 'natural' as to require no definition other than self assertion."[5] The dichotomy between an other-worldly or holy place, on the one hand, and earthly or profane spaces, on the other, nurtures sociocultural and political constructions in which people are either "outside" or "inside" their own authentic, traditional, and natural place.[6] Such constructions, in turn, destabilize any notions of belonging to a significant "place" anywhere other than the homeland. In other words, according to the solar system model, symbolic power lies exclusively within the homeland, and there is an implicit demand that people in the diaspora be alienated from their "host" nation-states: there is no possibility of "belonging" simultaneously to more than one place.

Thus far I have emphasized the powerful, almost omnipotent status of nation-states. Yet nation-states are currently under political and theoretical attack as globalization and transnationalism gain in potency.[7] Both of these processes undermine notions of territorial fixity and exclusivity. As James Clifford has pointed out, there is a tension between "routes and roots": more and more individuals leave their place of birth and set down roots in other places as distinctive cultural groups, while challenging *as such* the image of rootedness in one place that is so often underscored in nation-state rhetoric.[8] No wonder, then, that the most flagrant critiques of nation-state rhetoric position themselves, whether concretely or metaphorically, in diasporas. Daniel and Jonathan Boyarin, for instance, criticize the political actualization of the Israeli nation-state on the grounds that Zionism, the ideology on which it rests, negates the diaspora, whereas diasporic existence is based on a higher moral life, since (unlike the Zionist state) it does not conflate genealogy and the possession of political power.[9] Yet even these critical voices do not challenge the underlying structural premises of the solar system model, namely, that "diasporas" exist in counterpoint to a mythical "homeland."

In contrast, this article seeks to demonstrate the inconsistencies in the underlying premises of the solar system model by examining the complex relationship of Moroccan Jews, whether still living in Morocco or relocated, with the "place" of the nation-state of Morocco as opposed to that of Israel. I do this not as another "diaspora voice" (though my personal perspective is clearly influenced by my being a Moroccan-born Israeli) but rather as an anthropologist who conducted extensive fieldwork in Morocco between 1990 and 1991 and who since has revisited it frequently for shorter periods of time. Following a brief introduction to the history of the relationship between Moroccan Jews and their Muslim surroundings, I offer a number of observations in the form of ethnographic "snapshots," which focus on the contrasting (and often ambiguous) image of Israel and Morocco as either "homeland" or "diaspora." At issue is a basic question: To what extent do nation-states such as Israel succeed in maintaining their position as a symbolic center vis-à-vis "their" diasporas? Specifically, how do Moroccan Jews now living in Israel perceive Morocco (and, by extension, Israel) when they return there for a visit? Conversely, how do Jews still living in Morocco regard Israel? Does Morocco now serve both as diaspora and as a symbolic center in its own right? If so, what does this mean for the solar system model that posits a fixed relationship between homelands and diasporas?

Jews in Morocco Today

Muslims and Jews lived together in Morocco for many centuries before European political forces, particularly French colonialism and Zionism, generated significant and deep social changes that eventually resulted in the mass emigration of Moroccan Jewry.[10] However, the split between Jews and Muslims predates French colonial rule and was not an outcome of the French divide-and-rule policy.[11] In precolonial Morocco (that is, prior to 1912), Jews were usually considered a "tolerated" minority that was allowed to maintain its religious autonomy within certain political, social, and symbolic constraints. These limitations were embodied in their status as *ahl al-dhimma* (people of the covenant), which, in daily experience, was translated into various forms of protection, on the one hand, and discrimination, on the other. As *dhimmis*, the non-Muslim subjects of the sultans or of local patrons, Jews suffered from several ritualistic humiliations and obligations.[12] For example, Jews were not allowed to ride horses (for these are noble beasts), to wear shoes in the vicinity of mosques, to dress colorfully, or to bear arms. Probably the most persistent obligation throughout history was the *jizya*, a personal tax levied on *dhimmis*.

Yet framing the relationships between Jews and Muslims in the formal status of *dhimma* is oversimplifying a highly complex political and sociocultural existence.[13] Moroccan Jews always had ambivalent relationships with Muslims. Although there was a high level of economic interaction, there was also a tendency to refrain from more intimate social contact. As was true of many other Jewish diasporas, Zion for Moroccan Jews was a far-off utopia, although the local community did have contact with Jews from there who were known as *shadarim* (an acronym for *sheluḥei derabanan*, rabbinical emissaries) who came to collect donations for their yeshivot. Journeys were made in the opposite direction as well: some Moroccan Jews went to Eretz Israel and settled there, never returning to their families.[14] Surely, such journeys symbolically accentuated the religious split between Jews and Muslims.

French colonialism strengthened this separatist inclination and historical developments in the following era accelerated the split.[15] The rapid changes in the post-independence "old-new" Moroccan state heightened the "Arabization" of Morocco and encouraged its identification with Islamic culture.[16] Hand in hand with this political and cultural process were the Zionist activities that grew more widespread in the postcolonial era.[17] Many Jews felt caught in the middle;[18] during the 1950s, almost all of them pondered the wisdom of emigrating and the vast majority actually did.[19] At its peak in the 1940s, the Jewish population of Morocco numbered more than 250,000, whereas the community today totals between 3,000 and 4,000 members.[20] Clearly, such a massive emigration would not be possible without the silent consent of the Moroccan authorities, and especially without King Hassan II's agreement. Indeed, the latter adopted a hands-off position, so to speak, regarding the emigration of "his Jewish subjects" from Morocco, and he maintained this position even when he was accused of being a "collaborator with the Zionists."[21] Moreover, throughout his reign, Hassan II aspired to the role of a mediating and moderating actor in the Middle East. This position resulted in the "special relationship" between Morocco and Israel, as highlighted by Prime Minister Shimon Peres' visit to Morocco in 1986.[22] It is important to stress that the unique bilateral relationship between the two states cannot be explained purely by realpolitik (that is, the Moroccan desire to gain U.S. political and financial support, via the Jewish lobby), although one should not discount this consideration. After all, throughout the centuries, Jews had attained positions of great influence in the Moroccan court.[23]

As the Jewish presence in Morocco diminished, its concentration in Casablanca increased. In 1951, for instance, 20 percent of the Jewish population lived in Casablanca. By the early 1990s, roughly 70 percent of the Jews (at the time, some 4,000 individuals) lived there. Meanwhile, Jewish institutions contracted or closed down entirely in the smaller towns and cities. Jewish schools, to give one example, have had to limit the number of their classes.

The impact of French colonialism and Zionism was not limited to those who emigrated but also had a decisive influence on the lives of the Jews who stayed. Moreover, both of these ideo-political movements further strained the already delicate relationship between Jews and Muslims. These political forces, as well as the strengthening of Morocco's Arab traits, increased the Jews' inclination to distance themselves from the Muslim community. Similarly, the massive Jewish emigration to France and Israel resulted in a smaller, more inward-oriented community. Today, it maintains institutions that provide an impressive variety, range, and level of Jewish services and thus reinforce the image of a small yet self-reliant Jewish enclave in the midst of the overwhelmingly Muslim population.

Keeping in mind these complex sociocultural, political, and historical contexts, I now turn to two sets of ethnographic vignettes: the first taken from a trip made by Moroccan-born Israelis back to the land of their birth, and the second demonstrating Jewish Moroccans' relationship with the Israeli "homeland."

Returning to Morocco

Spring of 1986. It is twilight as the three busloads of Israeli tourists enter Morocco, following a journey that began in Malaga, Spain. We are all returning to the country of our birth after a separation that has lasted three or four decades—when we left Morocco, none of us thought we would ever be able to return for a visit.[24] Enthusiasm is high, and when the buses finally stop, the people pour out hurriedly, each hoping to be the first to touch Moroccan soil. The gentle breeze carries with it a forgotten blend of smells: blossoming citrus flowers and sweet mint. Someone kneels, takes a clod of earth, and kisses it. There are silent tears, and a strong sense of bewilderment. David Hazzan mumbles in Hebrew (mainly to himself): "So many Arabs!" Realizing the absurdity of his comment, he immediately adds, "Well, what was I expecting to find here? Chinese?"

What lay behind our bewilderment? In part, it was the sense that we were participating in a paradoxical enactment of the "dream of return,"[25] in which Morocco was the desired and sacred place—momentarily, at least. Indeed, comparisons and associations with the migration to Israel had been made even before we reentered Morocco. In perhaps the most grandiose reference to past migration, made while we were traveling along the southeastern coast of Spain (heading toward Morocco), our Israeli escort had noted that we were traversing the same route taken by our forefathers when they were expelled from Spain in 1492.[26] Like them, he said, we were leaving Spain in the direction of Morocco. While this comparison between our trip and the expulsion from Spain (*gerush sefarad*) confirmed the neat dichotomy between exile (*golah*) and homeland, it was not clear what our escort might have had in mind in terms of a "homeland" versus a "diaspora." This ambiguity perhaps attested to a subtle challenge to the taken-for-granted assumption that Israel was the homeland and Morocco the diaspora.

A fairly prudent estimate suggests that, over the last two decades, about two thousand Israelis have visited Morocco each year in organized "tour" groups. In the spring of 1987, I joined one such group as part of my research, and after our return to Israel, I held about 40 interviews with most of the 28 tour participants, as well as with members of other groups. Although my main research regarding these travels was conducted some time ago, I still keep track of the phenomenon. To my amazement, the structure and basic premises of these trips have not changed in any meaningful way over the years.

As was common practice, we began our journey shortly before Lag Ba'Omer, which marks the *hilula* (anniversary of death) of R. Shimon bar-Yohai.[27] Our highly standardized three-week itinerary was structured as follows: after two days in Spain awaiting the proper documentation (as will be seen, we were not traveling on our Israeli passports), we proceeded to travel along the southeast coast of Spain toward Algeciras, then sailed to Ceuta and took a bus to Tangiers. Our first three days in Morocco were marked by extensive travel as we visited sites in 10 different cities and towns, including Tangiers, Ouezzane (tomb of R. Amram Ben-Diwan), Fes (tomb of Lala Soliqa), Meknès, Salé (tomb of R. Raphael Enkaoua), Rabat, and Casablanca. After spending the Sabbath in Casablanca, we left on Saturday night for the tomb of R. Yihya Lakhdar in Beni Hammed, to celebrate the great *hilula*. On the following days, we visited sites in Marrakech (including the tomb of R. Raphael Hacohen) and Ourika (tomb of R. Shlomo Belkhanes) before heading south to Agadir, on the Atlantic Ocean. From there we made our way up the coast to Essaouira (Mogador) (tomb of R. Hayim Pinto), Azemmour (tomb of R. Avraham Mul–Ness), and finally back to Casablanca, where we dispersed for 10 days of private touring. Before returning to Israel, some of the group went to France.

In tours of this sort, the initial decision to travel was usually made in family gatherings: one person would raise the suggestion and two to four people would decide to come along. Sometimes other friends or acquaintances joined the group. Few people traveled alone. The ages of the participants generally ranged between the late 30s and early 60s; in the group I linked up with, only four participants were over 70. In most cases, one of the members of the group (who had recruited other participants) served as a group escort and traveled for free. The Moroccan Tourist Bureau assigned a local guide, who served as a mediator between the travelers and the local population.

This was the first time most of the participants had left Israel, and for almost all of them, the tour represented their first encounter with the region where they had spent their childhood and adolescence. They were returning to Morocco after an absence of two to three decades, during which time they were certain that they would never see their native land again. No one, not even the very few who had been to Morocco once or twice before, claimed that the trip was for the purpose of relaxation. On the contrary, most of them expressed very profound reasons for their travel—for example, the desire to visit the tombs of parents or of other family members. One person claimed that he was traveling with a marble tombstone from Israel to place over his father's rapidly deteriorating grave, while others considered bringing their parents' bones back to Israel. Still others linked their visit to the desire to complete emotional business left unfinished as a result of their hasty departure from Morocco. One participant planned to return to Israel with an aged father who had not been allowed to make aliyah to Israel with his children when a selection policy (during the 1950s) was in force; another planned to bring back a sister who had become ensnared by the charms of a Muslim suitor and had married him.

During the trip itself, many of the travelers were looking for evidence to confirm their memories of past times and places. They were hoping to meet up with the same sites, smells, sounds, people, and feelings they remembered with longing. Reflecting later on the trip, Michel, the youngest on our bus, said: "I wanted to be back where I grew up . . . to take a walk around the neighborhood, to feel young again. I wanted to see if I could do the same things again." For all the travelers, finding "the same . . . " and even more so, "doing the same . . . " was a way of ascertaining their ability to attain an unmediated contact with their past. No wonder the voyage had aspects of a pilgrimage, as people constantly strove to "get there," to be in touch with a place laden with both sacred and mundane memories.

Yet the attempts to reconnect unreservedly with Moroccan soil did not go unchallenged. The challenges came from multiple directions: both from the prevailing Israeli and Moroccan reifying national rhetoric and from daily encounters with Jews and Muslims in Morocco. By "reifying national rhetoric," I refer to strategies of essentialism produced by invoking biogenetic or cultural resemblance. Put more simply, this rhetoric underlines ideas that "all citizens are, in some unarguable sense, all alike."[28] The consequence was a reaffirmation of the "natural order of things"—that is, Israel as being the homeland and Morocco the diaspora.

According to Erik Cohen, Israeli "ethnic festivities" (a term that can include tours of this sort) testify to the "symbolic diasporization" of Israel; they manifest longings for, and even invocations of particular traditions related to diasporic existence that were vigorously rejected by Zionism.[29] Not surprisingly, many social scientists who are deeply influenced by the classical Zionist agenda have criticized such ethnic manifestations, at times linking them to the (undesirable) strengthening of the right-wing Likud party.[30] Such criticism is not limited to the world of academia but appears as well in the public sphere. Back in the 1980s, for instance, the state-sponsored evening television news program (at the time, there were no others) featured an interview with King Hassan II. A number of Moroccan-born Israelis were invited to the studio to view the interview, which was taped in Morocco. Following the interview, in which the king issued a warm invitation to "Morocco's eternal sons" to return to the land of their birth, the (Ashkenazic) anchorman turned to his studio guests and asked for their reactions. When they responded enthusiastically, he reproached them. He could not understand, he told them candidly, why they, as Israelis, could still express such deep feelings toward Morocco, and he wondered aloud whether their love for Morocco was an expression of alienation from Israel. According to his reasoning, it was not plausible to regard both places as "home."[31]

A similar notion was communicated to the Israelis visiting Morocco. We all felt a certain anxiety when encountering the Moroccan bureaucracy, whether in the form of border policemen, bank tellers, or hotel desk personnel. Each time we had to show the *laissez passer*, the document issued by the Moroccan consulate, we felt our ambiguous status as returnees-cum-tourists. Our Israeli passports had been left at the consulate, and the unimpressive piece of paper we were given in exchange had a short paragraph of text in which it was requested that the holder be accorded "free passage into the country, and aid and protection as needed" ("de regagner librement ce pays et de lui accorder aids et protection en cas de besoin"). Most passports, it is true, make use of similar terminology, but this document seemed to be accentuating our total dependence on protection—a notion that resonated with remote memories of the Jews' status in Morocco as *dhimmis*. Our entry to Morocco was semi-clandestine: while the *laissez passer* identified each of us as former Moroccan citizens, our current citizenship was left blank. Thus it symbolically annulled our Israeli citizenship, indicating in this way its inability to deal with our "belonging" to both countries.

Obtaining this document was itself a complex and delicate procedure that underlined just how far removed we were from the way things were done in Morocco. In the first years following the opening of Morocco's borders to Israeli Jews, groups desiring to visit the country had to travel via Malaga, where the *laissez passer* would be issued. My group met with the Moroccan consul there, who congratulated each and every one of us in a little speech echoing King Hassan's invitation. He welcomed us, referring to us as "sons of Maghreb" and invoking the warm Muslim-Jewish relationships of the past. When he first began his speech, he spoke in French, whereupon a loud protest was made: "Speak in our language!" The consul smiled in satisfaction and switched to Maghrebi Arabic. "Anyone who wishes to stay in Morocco is welcome to do so," he said. "Those who are not interested in staying— may God lead them back safely to their homes."

This encounter was shot through with ambiguity. While some of the Israeli tourists were pleased by the face-to-face reception, seeing it as a sign of cultural intimacy (thus their demand to "speak in our language"), others were more ambivalent, noting the consul's deliberate omission of Israel in his remarks ("may God lead them back safely to their *homes*"). "We entered Morocco like thieves in the dark," a traveler named Joe remarked bitterly. His comment was indicative as well of things to come. We were instructed by our Israeli escort to keep our nationality under wraps—not to mention it at hotel registrations, for instance, or in any other encounter. He also instructed those men who ordinarily wore *kipot* to wear berets instead. His anxiety was so intense that, while still in Spain, we were asked to refrain from speaking Hebrew in public.

The tension surrounding our journey interfered with our desire to reconnect smoothly with the vistas of our past. At every stage of our journey we were forced to acknowledge our "inauthentic" status as Moroccans. Attempts to overcome this hindrance failed repeatedly. Our inability to convey our sense of being native Moroccans was noticeable even in small incidents, such as when we were invited by Moroccans to feel "at home" or were politely requested to act "as if you were in your own house." Such rhetoric underlined our alienation from Morocco, as it placed us in the category of "guests" rather than kin.[32]

Our failure was frustrating, hard to swallow, but above all disconcerting. While in Essaouira, a beautiful port city on the Atlantic, we visited the old Jewish cemetery.

There we met an old beggar who introduced himself as one of the last Jews of the city, appointed by the community officials to serve as a custodian of the dead. Members of the group were delighted to meet someone who could offer testimony about an authentic, remote, and cherished past, as well as informing us about the current situation. The beggar responded happily to our numerous questions, telling us many stories about people both living and dead. He reported about the handful of Jews who had remained with him in Essaouira, adding sadly that almost everyone had either migrated to France or Canada or else had gone to Dar-el-Beida (Casablanca). Others, he whispered fearfully, had gone "there"—meaning, to Israel. We were both moved by his stories and baffled by his reluctance to mention the Jewish state.

Before we got back on the bus, the beggar asked us for a donation. The people in the group responded generously. A minute before departing, one of them asked the beggar to say the customary kaddish prayer. He mumbled something and appeared to be confused. It was only then that the travelers realized that the beggar was not a Jew but rather a Muslim pretending to be a Jew in order to receive a donation. After their initial shock, they looked mainly embarrassed. They were bothered not so much by their being deceived as by their inability to distinguish a Muslim from a Jew. Their apparent lack of cultural savoir faire—a skill that had come to them so "naturally" in the past—was yet another indication of their being foreigners in Morocco.

These ethnographic vignettes reveal just how significant was the reality of the nation-state on this journey to Morocco. On the one hand were the manifestations of the travelers' bond with Morocco, such as when one of them kissed the soil upon his arrival. On the other were many mundane events in which the state was in some way invoked. For instance, local secret police, conspicuous in their dark suits, popped up every time the buses stopped in a large city. (They were probably assigned to protect us.) Then there was the presence of the king, the embodiment of the Moroccan state. Hassan's portrait hung on innumerable walls and was to be found even at Jewish cemeteries and at the shrines of revered Jewish ẓadikim. The king was also present in a more real sense when, as he did every year, he sent official emissaries to bless the pilgrims who came to the main Lag Ba'omer hilula in Ben Hammed. Armed soldiers and police (state symbols of protection and control) were positioned near the sites. Not only was Morocco's flag, with its red background and green star, raised high above the hilula compound, but the state colors were apparent as well in the red and green candles that were lit in honor of the ẓadikim.

On the broader political front, it was the involvement of state functionaries, beginning with the very highest level of leadership (Hassan II and Shimon Peres) that initially brought about the opening of borders to Moroccan-born Israeli Jews. Yet on a day-to-day basis, national rhetoric was implicated in our group's repeated failure to reconnect with the past.[33] The nationalistic rhetoric that was so interwoven with the trip came to dominate it, imposing an "in" or "out" view that deterred participants from embracing both countries. It played a key role in the construction of a partition between past and present, between here and there, and between homeland and diaspora. (Recall, for instance, the words of the Moroccan consul in Malaga.) Yet nationalist rhetoric was employed by the travelers as well. During dinner at the first hotel we stayed at, a waiter came and smilingly offered some oranges.

Wishing to reveal the fact that he was aware of our being Israelis, he added: "These are good like the ones you have," whereupon the person to whom he offered them responded ambiguously, "both are ours!"

Here as elsewhere in the context of modern travel, nationality serves as a key symbol defining identity. In the example I have just noted, the (ambiguous) expression of national identity underlined the semi-clandestine nature of the trip. Even more significant, however, is the way in which the "host" (the waiter) adopted an "us" versus "them" categorization, whereas the traveler, at this initial stage of the journey, attempted to counter it. As has been seen, further attempts on the part of the travelers to bypass the "us"/ "them" dichotomy met with repeated failure. In consequence, the travelers reverted to the national identity attributed to them by the Moroccans, and expressions on the order of "in Israel, things are better"—which indicated their growing anger and frustration—became stronger and more frequent as the journey progressed.

In this sense, the travelers to Morocco gradually employed a rhetoric that reinforced the solar system model by affirming and reaffirming the overpowering importance of the homeland. In contrast, as will be seen, Jews in Morocco constantly questioned the model.

"Homeland" from the Perspective of the Diaspora

Dining with me in June 2004 in a newly restored Jewish restaurant—bombed a year before by Al-Queida—Beber Kadosh offers a pessimistic forecast regarding the Jewish community in Morocco. "We are about to vanish," he says. Yet he doesn't seem to be saddened by the prospect. "We [the Jews] are a unique species in Morocco. We are like a rare flower. We should be protected like a rare flower. We should be marked with a special lapel pin so that we are recognized as a rare species that must be treated with care."

Beber Kadosh's half-joking, half-serious statement attests to the nuanced and ambivalent feelings of Moroccan Jews toward their country. Rooted in Morocco's soil, they are at the same time at risk of vanishing altogether. Thus the need to mark them as different and in need of care. Taking the imagery a step further, one can argue that Morocco is beautified by its Jews, who become all the more precious as their numbers dwindle. It should be kept in mind, however, that protected flowers usually become rare because of harsh circumstances. Indeed, Kadosh's call for protection struck a chord in my (perhaps oversensitive) ear. It invoked associations of distant times when Moroccan Jews were defined as *dhimmis*, tolerated and protected but also seen as pariahs.

Death and continuing emigration are further diminishing the rapidly aging Moroccan Jewish community. The main Jewish communal organization, the Comité de la communaute, has an employee who deals with the issuance of passports. According to him, a "passport is the Jew's modern walking stick." In other words, despite their feeling deeply rooted in Moroccan soil, Jews wish to keep their options open. Passports and visas are thus central emblems in their lives and the focus of much discussion, especially during moments of political tension. In addition, the smaller the community gets, the more its members feel estranged from the larger Moroccan society and long for a return to "the good old days."[34] What remains to been seen is whether such longings operate as a mechanism that enhances Jewish identification with Israel.

In fact, Moroccan Jews do not view Israel as an exclusive symbolic center, and their attitudes toward the Jewish state are ambivalent. Their reflections regarding emigration to Israel and the practical difficulties involved in going there are particularly telling. Above all, moving to Israel is seen as an indication of personal failure; in the popular view of things, it is only those who are not successful in Morocco and who lack the (desired) cultural capital to cope with life in France or in French Canada who make aliyah. Jews cannot avoid confronting the gap between the (sometimes simplified) ideological rhetoric of longing for Israel and the day-to-day struggle over collective and personal existence in Morocco.

It seems plausible to assume that emigration would drain Morocco of its symbolic Jewish resources, especially when Israel is the country of destination.[35] Consider, for instance, the symbolic meaning of "zadik migration" from Morocco to Israel that has been documented so thoroughly by Yoram Bilu and others.[36] These anthropologists describe a striking phenomenon: bringing to Israel the remains of sainted figures, often following a dream in which they appeared to various individuals to request their removal and reburial.[37] Interestingly, however, the massive emigration has worked in the opposite direction, enhancing Morocco's allure as a symbolic center—to the point of its competing with Israel. In an intriguing turn of events, Morocco has become a symbolic center that retains its own diaspora communities, mainly in France, Canada, and Israel. Thus, Jews in Morocco did not turn into a minority ethnic group in their own country but have rather established their own diaspora communities that encourage nostalgic feelings toward Morocco.

The Comité de la communaute, for instance, organizes and provides funding for hilula events held in various Moroccan Jewish "diasporas." In this manner, Jewish communities outside it cultivate a collective, as well as a mythical memory of the Maghreb. Charlotte Szlovak's film *Retour à Oujda* tells the story of tourists from France visiting the regions of their childhood in Morocco, as does Izza Genini's film *Retrouver Oulad Moumen*.[38] And there are, of course, tours such as the one I have described, which contribute to the perception of Morocco as a symbolic center. "Heritage tours" that mix hagiolatric features with tourism intensify the feeling that the Maghreb is a focus of admiration and longing. In many respects, Morocco becomes what Victor W. Turner describes as a "center out there."[39]

Paradoxically, what seems to underlie the transformation of Morocco from a typical diaspora to one that is also a center is the diminishing of its native Jewish population. That is, emigration from Morocco is what generates the establishment of diasporic communities outside it.[40] Clearly, however, demographic dwindling also poses a critical problem for the community vis-à-vis its "diasporas" in Israel, France, or Canada. After all, numbers matter: demographic inferiority goes against the notion of Morocco's having symbolic centrality for Moroccan Jews living abroad. It also weighs heavily on the dealings of Jews still living in Morocco with the "diaspora" communities. In 1990, for instance, the French journalist Gilles Perrault published *Notre Ami le Roi*, a highly critical account of Hassan II's often violent regime. Perrault described in detail the numerous arrests made without charge and the "disappearance" of political rivals. Following the book's publication, the atmosphere in Morocco became politically charged, with national television reporting on tension between Morocco and France. Overt and orchestrated support for Hassan worried Moroccan Jews, who viewed it as a sign that the throne was in danger. This, they feared, boded ill for them. "Any change . . . every political change hurts first and foremost Jews. . . . This is what our history teaches us," explained Jacques Levy, a member of the community. They were thus greatly relieved when letters of support for the king began to arrive from "their" diasporic communities and were especially pleased when a letter from Morocco's former chief rabbi, Shalom Mesas (then in Israel), was quoted at length on Moroccan television.[41] Their disappointment that no such support came from the Montreal-based Moroccan community highlighted Moroccan Jews' sense of marginality vis-à-vis their brethren in Canada. In the words of Dédé Haruse, a regular visitor at one of the popular Jewish social clubs, the Cercle de l'Alliance, "We are no longer important for Jews there."[42]

Such feelings of disappointment are highly revealing of Moroccan Jews' hopes that their country might serve as a symbolic center. Indeed, both their expectations and their disillusionment point to the existential paradox already noted: namely, the demographic weakening that marginalizes the Moroccan Jewish community also gave rise to the Moroccan Jewish diasporic communities and turned Morocco into a homeland. It is important to add, however, that this demographic dwindling within the Moroccan Jewish homeland has not prevented the development of various manifestations of self-esteem and expressions of a sense of historical uniqueness and symbolic centrality. A particularly fascinating example of the latter involves the attitude toward Hebrew—the ancient holy language later "revived" by the Zionists for use in everyday life.

As part of my goal to maintain contact with Moroccan Jewish youth, I decided upon my arrival to Morocco to teach Hebrew in one of the Jewish schools in Casablanca. To my surprise, I had to respond to a number of questions and reservations concerning my abilities. To my "Israelo-centric" eyes, it seemed as though the local school administrators had peculiar ideas on the matter. They believed that Hebrew was a sacred language that could not be separated from its cultural context and historical significance. From this it followed that in order to teach Hebrew, one had to know (among other things) Jewish law, midrash, biblical commentaries, the details of religious rituals, and the meanings of Jewish holidays. In short, they needed to be assured that I could teach more than the language in its "narrow sense." I, for my part, came to realize just how deep were my own "Zionist" assumptions about the language. For me, Hebrew was an Israeli symbolic asset, since it had been "revived" by Zionist activists (in particular, Eliezer Ben-Yehuda).

These conflicting attitudes toward the proper teaching of Hebrew were highlighted in a conversation conducted (in Hebrew) between Moïse Nahon, the chief supervisor of Hebrew instruction, and the Hebrew instructors at Casablanca's most prestigious Jewish school, the École normale hebräique. Here it should be noted that Nahon came from France: most Jewish high schools awarded a *diplome de bachelier* (the equivalent of an academic high school diploma) that, by arrangement with the

Moroccan government, was administered by France.[43] In any event, Nahon's views, like mine, were expressed from an "outside" perspective. In the course of the conversation, Morris Levy, one of the most prominent of the local Hebrew instructors, argued that it was best for Hebrew to be taught only by male instructors. As he explained:

> Our male instructors [*morim*] as opposed to female instructors [*morot*] possess a substantial knowledge of holy subjects [*limudei kodesh*]. Teaching Hebrew is not like instruction in any other common language . . . French, for example. Hebrew has extremely deep cultural layers that encompass a multitude of Jewish studies. Female teachers—at least in Morocco—do not have these qualifications. Thus, they cannot serve as Hebrew teachers. We cannot, for example, confine ourselves to the pure analysis of its syntax. Hebrew is not something external or foreign to us. We are deeply involved in it.

A second teacher, André Ovadia, voiced his total agreement, then turned to me. "Tell me, André," he said, "how do they teach Hebrew in your schools? Do they teach it as any other language?"

At this point, Nahon broke in. "Yes," he said, "that's the case in Israel. And I strongly believe that it should be so." He continued:

> We must teach its internal logic, its syntax, like any other language. It is, after all, a common language! In France, the Torah is also taught in this way. We treat it like any other text of fiction. We treat the historical facts with great caution and doubt. We certainly ignore belief . . . unlike what you are doing here. . . . It is true that we have instructors who believe in these holy texts, and then they tend to relate to them the way that you do. But they have to clarify to their students that they believe in the text and that they treat it as holy.

Apparently, Jewish teachers in Morocco are both aware of the cultural project in which they are involved and are deeply engaged in it. While showing awareness of alternative forms of Hebrew instruction, such awareness does not translate into acceptance or tolerance toward these competing modes of instruction.

In a different incident, an argument broke out between two Hebrew examiners (from France) and local teachers. The examiners had come to test the oral abilities of the students as part of a series of exams for their French *baccalaureat*. The local teachers claimed that the French examiners were heavily influenced by the Israeli attitude toward Hebrew, accepting uncritically its underlying assumptions (among them, that mastery of a language must be defined in part as an ability to converse freely in it with Israelis). In addition, the local teachers claimed, the French examiners—who had spent years in Israel—were prejudiced in favor of Israeli Hebrew and consequently took it for granted that the ultimate test for oral mastery of the language was the ability to communicate with Israelis. "Not only do I not have to accept such an assumption," Morris Levy asserted with passion, "but Israelis speak Hebrew incorrectly. They make many mistakes. Thus they certainly cannot stand as the standard against which one should measure verbal ability!"[44]

This attitude manifests a rejection of the symbolic imposition of the homeland (Israel), in this case, by refusing to accept its symbolic domination regarding the Hebrew language. Language turns out to be not only a key device for cultural distinction, but also a political device—that is, a powerful determinant of symbolic domination.[45] In the eyes of the local teachers, Morocco is a legitimate alternative and an even more genuine symbolic Jewish center, since Israel is "contaminated" by its secularity. Like anti-Zionist ultra-Orthodox Jews, they distinguish between the state of Israel and the land of Israel.[46] But unlike them, they do not negate Zionism.

Of course, one should not overestimate the implications of this local language battle. In this particular instance, the battle is as good as lost: the French examiners naturally get to have the last word, since they are the ones who are authorized by the French educational system to set the standard. More precisely, Morocco allows for "foreign" exams on its soil, and a French staff administers them, according to Israeli standards of correct Hebrew. Note, too, that the French examiners themselves embody a two-phase process: the standard is set by Israel and accepted by a powerful Jewish diaspora (in France). The latter then sends its officials to a minor diaspora country (Morocco) and there the examiners conclude that Moroccan oral Hebrew is "archaic." Perhaps the message is that French (cultural) colonialism has not entirely lost its grip? Yet the local teachers did not hesitate to voice their protest and dissatisfaction. And such protest is no empty, "symbolic" gesture; it is a political practice that threatens to undermine Jewish Israeli hegemony and to erode its legitimacy as a symbolic center. That is, the very awareness of Israel's symbolic hegemony as expressed by Moroccan Jews is what initiates a process of undermining its "natural" and transparent character.

Conclusion

As seen in the ethnographic snapshots presented here, migration to the homeland, as well as its political renewal, do not guarantee the homeland's becoming an uncontested symbolic center. Indeed, quite the opposite can happen. It is a hazardous enterprise; the political actualization of the utopian "dream of return" carries within it the seeds of its own rejection.[47] That is to say, as long as the "dream of return" remains in the realm of millenarian aspirations, it poses no threat. But when it becomes a tangible reality or is actualized through political and social processes, the "reality" it materializes is by definition far from the dream. Hence, the homeland is bound to be challenged as the symbolic center. This refusal to accept unconditionally the symbolic centrality of the homeland is particularly pronounced in the case of Morocco, specifically because of the demographic marginality of the local Jewish community.

It appears that both native Moroccan Jews and Moroccan-born Israelis live in a place that is perceived as being both homeland and diaspora (even though Israel is indisputably the "traditional" homeland). Most Moroccan Jews feel estranged from the Moroccan political regime at the same time as they are nostalgic about "ideational" Morocco, which—like a traditional homeland—is located mostly in the past. Yet they have more or less the same attitude toward Israel; they dream about the land of Israel but criticize its political manifestation in the state of Israel. Moroccan-born Israelis, for their part, are disappointed when they return to Morocco for a visit and discover that attempts to reconnect with their past are continually thwarted. In short, both Morocco and Israel pay the price of their political materialization. In both cases, Jews escape to nostalgia, the idealized past.

As we have seen, Moroccan Jews and Israeli Moroccans reject the demand of the nation-state for an ultimate and inflexible loyalty to one "place," aspiring instead for multidirectional links between the homeland and the diaspora. In this sense, the narrow vision of the nation-building project is rejected. Interestingly, even Jews living in Morocco have sentimental feelings toward the state; at the same time, they are nostalgic about Israel even though they do not intend to immigrate to it. Something similar could be said about Israeli Moroccans.

With all this, the position of both groups toward the solar system model does not dramatically undermine the rhetoric of homeland versus diaspora. (As has been seen, such rhetoric, of course, is also employed by the nation-state.) Nonetheless, this essay proposes an alternative positioning of Moroccan Jews at both ends of the dichotomy. And in so doing, I call into question, if only slightly, the underlying structure of this analytical model.

Notes

1. André Levy, "Center and Diaspora: Jews in Late-Twentieth-Century Morocco," *City and Society* 13, no. 2 (2001), 247–272; idem, "The Diaspora that Turned into a Center: Contemporary Jews in Morocco," in *Homelands and Diasporas: Holy Lands and Other Places*, ed. André Levy and Alex Weingrod (Stanford: 2005), 68–96.

2. Robin Cohen, *Global Diasporas: An Introduction* (Seattle: 1997); William Safran, "Diasporas in Modern Societies: Myths of Homeland and Return," *Diaspora* 1, no. 1 (1991), 83–99.

3. In other words, the state is not conceived here as an entity even though it appears as such, since people act "on its behalf." On the notion of a state as a "true entity," see James C. Scott, *Seeing Like a State: How Certain Schemes to Improve the Human Condition Have Failed* (New Haven: 1998); on the more mundane manifestations of a nation-state, see, for instance, Michael Billig, *Banal Nationalism* (London: 1995).

4. Michael Herzfeld, *Cultural Intimacy: Social Poetics in the Nation-State* (New York: 1997).

5. Eric Hobsbawm and Terence O. Ranger, *The Invention of Tradition* (Cambridge: 1983), 14.

6. See, for example, Arjun Appadurai, who aptly determines that "[n]atives are not only persons who are from certain places, and belong to those places, but they are also those who are somehow *incarnated*, or confined, in those places" ("Putting Hierarchy in Its Place," *Cultural Anthropology* 3 [1988], 36–49).

7. André Levy, "Diasporas through Anthropological Lenses: Contexts of Postmodernity," *Diaspora* 9, no. 1 (2000), 137–157; Khachig Tölölyan, "Rethinking Diaspora(s): Stateless Power in the Transnational Movement," *Diaspora* 5, no. 1 (1996), 3–36. By "globalization," I refer simply to a process that involves a (relatively) free traffic of capital, including human beings as a labor resource. Transnationalism, in this context, accentuates the fact that the free traffic of goods and people manages to overcome nation-state borders.

8. James Clifford, "Diasporas," *Cultural Anthropology* 9, no. 3 (1994), 302–338.

9. According to the Boyarins, the conflation of blood criteria of belonging and political strength gives rise to the danger that racist discrimination will be employed against minorities. See their article, "Diaspora: Generation and Ground of Jewish Identity," *Critical Inquiry* 19, nos. 3–4 (1993), 693–725; cf. Clifford, "Diasporas," who gently accuses the

Boyarins of being ethnically chauvinistic. On the premises of nation-state rhetoric, see also Sander L. Gilman and Milton Shain (eds.), *Jewries at the Frontier: Accommodation, Identity, Conflict* (Urbana: 1999).

10. On the earlier history of Muslims and Jews in Morocco, see, for example, André N. Chouraqui, *Between East and West: A History of the Jews of North Africa*, trans. Michael M. Bernet (Philadelphia: 1968); Hayim Zeev Hirschberg, *Toledot hayehudim beafrikah haze-fonit: hatefuẓah hayehudit bearẓot hamaghreb mimei kedem ve'ad zemanenu*, 2 vols. (Jerusalem: 1965); Mohammed Kenbib, *Juifs et musulmans au Maroc, 1859–1948: Contribution à l'histoire des relations inter-communautaires en terre d'Islam* (Rabat: 1994).

11. Charles-Robert Ageron, *La décolonisation française* (Paris: 1991).

12. Daniel Schroeter, "From Dhimmis to Colonized Subjects: Moroccan Jews and the Sharifian and French Colonial State," in *Studies in Contemporary Jewry*, vol. 20, *Jews and the State: Dangerous Alliances and the Perils of Privilege*, ed. Ezra Mendelsohn (New York: 2003), esp. 105–110.

13. Bat Ye'or's *The Dhimmi: Jews and Christians under Islam* (Rutherford: 1985) is an example of an overly simplistic approach.

14. See, for example: Hirschberg, *Toledot hayehudim beafrikah haẓefonit*.

15. On the rapid changes in Morocco during this time, see Mark I. Cohen and Lorna Hahn, *Morocco: Old Land, New Nation* (New York: 1966).

16. John P. Entelis, *Culture and Counterculture in Moroccan Politics* (Boulder: 1989); Rahma Bourqia, "States and Tribes in Morocco: Continuity and Change" (Ph.D. diss., University of Manchester, 1987); Michael W. Suleiman, "Morocco in the Arab and Muslim World: Attitudes of Moroccan Youth," *The Maghreb Review* 14, nos. 1–2 (1989), 16–27; Mark A. Tessler, "The Identity of Religious Minorities in Non-Secular States: Jews in Tunisia and Morocco and Arabs in Israel," *Comparative Studies in Society and History* 20, no. 3 (1978), 359–373.

17. Michael M. Laskier, "Developments in the Jewish Communities of Morocco: 1956–76," *Middle Eastern Studies* 26, no. 4 (1990), 465–505; Lawrence Rosen, "A Moroccan Jewish Community during a Middle Eastern Crisis," *The American Scholar* 37, no. 3 (1968), 435–451; Norman A. Stillman, *The Jews of Arab Lands in Modern Times* (Philadelphia: 1991); Agnès Bensimon, *Hassan II et les juifs: histoire d'une l'émigration secrète* (Paris: 1991); Shmuel Segev, *Mivẓa' 'yakhin': 'aliyatam haḥashait shel yehudei maroko leyisrael* (Tel Aviv: 1984); Yaron Tsur and Hagar Hillel, *Yehudei ẓefon afrikah bameot ha-19 veha-20* (Tel Aviv: 1995).

18. See, for instance, Albert Memmi, *Portriat du Colonisé* (Paris: 1973).

19. During this same period, almost all of Algerian Jewry went to France, along with about half of the Tunisian Jewish community. About 25 percent of the Moroccan Jewish community emigrated to France. See Michel Abitbol, *Yahadut ẓefon afrikah hayom* (Jerusalem: 1981).

20. *American Jewish Yearbook* (1950, 1960, 1970); AJDC Reports (1990, 1994).

21. During that period, walls in Casablanca (and elsewhere) were clandestinely decorated by Arabic rhyming grafitti saying (in free translation): "The bold king sold the Jews for wheat." This was a reference to Hassan's agreement to help the Zionist state in return for wheat he received from the United States.

22. On the long-term motivations of the monarch's policy toward Israel, see Mark A. Tessler, "Moroccan-Israeli Relations and the Reasons for Moroccan Receptivity to Contact with Israel," *The Jerusalem Journal of International Relations* 10, no. 2 (1988), 76–108. See also Mark A. Tessler and Universities Field Staff International, *Continuity and Change in Moroccan Politics* (Hanover: 1984).

23. To illustrate the complex and multi-layered Moroccan politics toward Jews, I would like to briefly recount an event that I witnessed while attending an evening sponsored by the Oeuvre de Secours à l'Enfance (OSE), an organization that nowadays supplies basic medical care for Jews. The evening's program consisted of a presentation of the organization's budget and some fund-raising, followed by refreshments. One of those present was the mayor of Casablanca. His participation had not been taken for granted; after all, he was responsible

for some four million citizens, and even the Jewish community did not consider this particular event to be of major import. Yet not only did the mayor attend, he also showed himself to be highly knowledgeable about the OSE's budget (remarking about some of the items funded by the organization) and even made a donation. Following the business portion of the evening, we were directed to a rich buffet on the second floor. One of the rabbis who attended the event offered a prayer on behalf of the king (*tefilah lishlom hamalkhut*). To my amazement, the mayor seemed to know the prayer—or was at least familiar with its general rhythm—since he said "amen" whenever required. Moreover, when the rabbi ended the prayer, the mayor asked him why he had skipped the customary prayer for the well-being of the congregation (*tefilah lishlom hakahal*). The rabbi proceeded to say this prayer as well, and when he finished, the mayor introduced his young son and asked the rabbi to bless him. The son stood in respectful silence as the rabbi put his hands on the boy's head and recited phrases from the Psalms.

24. Over a period of several decades, Israel did not have overt or formal diplomatic relations with Morocco. Israelis were not allowed to visit during this time.

25. See William Safran, "Diasporas in Modern Societies: Myths of Homeland and Return," *Diaspora* 1, no. 1 (1991), 83–99.

26. In fact, both Jews and Muslims were expelled from Spain; in 1492, the Moorish kingdom of Grenada surrendered to Ferdinand V and Isabella. However, the final expulsion of the Muslims did not take place until more than a century later, between 1609 and 1614.

27. *Hilula* is an Aramaic word that literally means marriage. In the context of hagiolatry, however, it refers to an annual celebration held on the anniversary of the death of a zadik, which in this context refers to a saintly figure.

28. Michael Herzfeld, *Cultural Intimacy: Social Poetics in the Nation-State* (New York: 1997), 27.

29. Erik Cohen, "Ethnicity and Legitimation in Contemporary Israel," *The Jerusalem Quarterly* 28 (1983), 111–124.

30. Uri Ram, *The Changing Agenda of Israeli Society: Theory, Ideology and Identity* (Albany: 1994). The linkage here is quite subtle; see, for instance, Yohanan Peres and Sara Shemer, "Hagorem ha'adati babehirot lakneset ha'asirit," *Megamot* 28 (1984), 316–331. In their concluding remarks, Peres and Shemer offer four explanations of Mizrahi voting patterns while ignoring Ashkenazic patterns of voting. Even Hanna Herzog's careful analysis, in her article "Haomnam 'adatiyut politit?," *Megamot* 28 (1984), 332–352, conceptualizes the "ethnic vote" as a "Mizrahi vote."

31. *Yoman hashavu'a*, 21 Oct. 1994.

32. Cf. Michael Herzfeld, *Anthropology through the Looking-Glass: Critical Ethnography in the Margins of Europe* (Cambridge: 1987). This failure to retrieve the past in Morocco's memory-laden landscape seems to correspond to Alfred Schutz's claim concerning the inability to reconnect with the past. See his article "The Homecomer," *American Journal of Sociology* 50, no. 5 (1945), 369–376. According to Schutz, it is the constant flux of social life that is responsible for the inability to recapture past realities; as the truism has it, one cannot go back in time by going through space. Schutz, however, focuses on individuals who seem to be liberated from sociocultural or political constraints or contexts. I would argue that such constraints and contexts—particularly the state context, and especially its bureaucratic institutions—are of great significance. Cf. Michael Herzfeld, *The Social Production of Indifference: Exploring the Symbolic Roots of Western Bureaucracy* (New York: 1992).

33. André Levy, "Homecoming to Diaspora: Nation and State in Visits of Israelis in Morocco," in *Homecomings: Unsettling Paths of Return*, ed. Fran Markowitz and Anders H. Stefansson (Lanham: 2004), 92–108.

34. André Levy, "Controlling Space, Essentializing Identities: Jews in Contemporary Casablanca," *City and Society* (1998), 175–199.

35. See, for instance, the discussion concerning the dramatic dwindling of sacred shrines in Morocco in André Levy, "The Structured Ambiguity of Minorities towards Decolonisation: The Case of the Moroccan Jews," *The Maghreb Review* 19, nos. 1–2 (1994),133–146.

36. See the following works by Yoram Bilu: "Saint Veneration among Moroccan Jews in Israel: Contents and Meanings," in *New Directions in the Study of Ethnic Problems*, vol. 8, ed. Naama Cohen and Ora Ahimeir (Jerusalem: 1984), 44–50; "Dreams and Wishes of the Saint," in *Judaism Viewed from Within and from Without: Anthropological Studies*, ed. Harvey E. Goldberg (Albany: 1987), 285–313; "Rabbi Yaacov Wazana: A Jewish Healer in the Atlas Mountains," *Culture, Medicine, and Psychiatry* 12, no. 1 (1988), 113–135; "The Role of Charismatic Dreams in the Creation of Sacred Sites in Present-Day Israel," in *Sacred Space: Shrine, City, Land*, ed. Benjamin Z. Kedar and R.J. Zwi Werblowsky (London: 1998), 295–315; "The Sanctification of Place in Israel's Civil and Traditional Religion," *Studies in Jewish Folklore*, 19–20 (special issue for Dan Ben-Amos) (1998), 65–84; *Without Bonds: The Life and Death of Rabbi Ya'akov Wazana* (Detroit: 2000). Also see André Levy "Hilula rabah ve'azeret teshuvah: nituaḥ mikreh," in *Meḥkarim betarbutam shel yehudei ẓefon afrikah*, ed. Yissakhar Ben-Ami (Jerusalem: 1991), 167–179.

37. In some cases, a replica of their shrine has even been erected, similar to the duplication of 770 Eastern Parkway—home of the late Lubavitch rebbe—in Kfar Habad, the main center of the Israeli Lubavitch movement. See Alex Weingrod, "Changing Israeli Landscapes: Buildings and Uses of the Past," *Cultural Anthropology* 8, no. 3 (1993), 370–387.

38. At one screening of the film in Jerusalem, most of those in the audience were former residents of Oujda, and they were far from passive—gesturing toward the screen whenever familiar sites from the town were shown and laughing whenever they recognized someone. A question and answer period featuring the film's director had been on the program, but instead of asking questions, members of the audience preferred to talk with one another, sharing their reminiscences and attempting to locate past acquaintances. As the director later commented: "It became a town meeting."

39. Victor W. Turner, "The Center Out-There: Pilgrim's Goal," *History of Religions* 11 (1973), 191–230.

40. For the Israeli perspective, see Yoram Bilu and André Levy, "Nostalgia and Ambivalence: The Reconstruction of Jewish-Muslim Relations in Oulad-Mansour," in *Modern Sephardi and Middle Eastern Jewries: History and Culture*, ed. Harvey E. Goldberg (Bloomington: 1996), 288–311. For the French perspective, see Joelle Bahloul, *The Architecture of Memory: A Jewish-Muslim Household in Colonial Algeria 1937–1962*, trans. Catherine Du Peloux Ménagé (Cambridge: 1996).

41. On the Moroccan monarchy's concern to underline its good relationship with the Jewish minority and its moderate attitude toward Israel, see Mark A. Tessler, "Moroccan-Israeli Relations and the Reasons for Moroccan Receptivity to Contact with Israel."

42. Interview with Dédé Haruse, October 1990.

43. Moroccan high schools that aspired to have their pupils pursue higher learning at prestigious French universities were obliged to have them undergo a number of matriculation exams that were supervised by French educational authorities.

44. Under different circumstances, I heard someone make an interesting distinction: "In Israel, one does not speak Hebrew. One speaks Israeli!"

45. Pierre Bourdieu, *Distinction: A Social Critique of the Judgment of Taste*, trans. R. Nice (Cambridge, Mass.: 1984).

46. Boyarin and Boyarin, "Diaspora."

47. Fran Markowitz, "Criss-Crossing Identities: The Russian Jewish Diaspora and the Jewish Diaspora in Russia," *Diaspora* 4, no. 2 (1995), 201–210.

Sephardic/Mizrahi/Arab-Jews: Reflections on Critical Sociology and the Study of Middle Eastern Jewries within the Context of Israeli Society

Harvey E. Goldberg
Chen Bram
(THE HEBREW UNIVERSITY)

Israeli society has undergone extensive changes since May 1948, and there have also been significant shifts and debates regarding the ways in which people understand these developments. Differing currents appear in public discourse, historical writings, and in the work of social scientists. This essay, undertaken by two anthropologists, assesses the contribution of "critical sociology" to the understanding of those aspects of Israeli Jewish society and culture that have their historical roots in Asia, Africa, and the Middle East. We focus on the interaction between the historical and cultural identities of specific immigrant groups and their descendants, on the one hand, and the negative stereotyping of these groups—in particular, their being lumped together in a single overarching category as a prelude to processes of social, political, and cultural exclusion—on the other. Our analysis offers an understanding of the experiences of Middle Eastern Jews in Israel that takes the varying research traditions into account.[1]

As is well known, the thinking of Shmuel Noah Eisenstadt dominated the sociological analysis of Israeli society for the first two decades after the establishment of the state.[2] He analyzed, for example, the far-reaching implications of creating a state (with its coercive and bureaucratic functions) for a Jewish population that hitherto had been voluntarily organized. In examining Israel's large immigration intake after 1948, Eisenstadt and others gave little weight to the significance of historical-cultural differences between the various groups.[3] Whereas an early paper of his had focused on "Oriental Jews,"[4] the subsequent predominant analysis involved the formulation of general variables that were then applied to all immigrant populations. Eisenstadt adopted mid-20th-century American sociology's dominant modernization paradigm that viewed whole societies as either "traditional" or "modern." Applying this dichotomous model to Israeli society, he introduced a third type of society, "transitional." While this category bridged the pasts of many Jews from Muslim countries and their expectations regarding the future Israeli society, it did not deal in depth with the particularities of culture or identity.[5] Underlying Eisenstadt's triadic classification was the desire to understand factors that encouraged or impeded "absorption" into the new society, which was envisioned as being built upon the values of modernity common to contemporary western nation-states, and led mainly by Jews of European origin.

Although greatly influenced by American sociology, early Israeli sociology did not take up the former's intense interest in issues of discrimination and prejudice. Thus it largely overlooked the manifestations in Israel of ethnic stereotyping and its impact on individuals, as well as outright discrimination and formal and informal discourse that devalued Middle Eastern culture.[6] Neither did it relate explicitly to the linkages between ethnic origins and access to power and resources. Instead, it offered a semantically flat and ostensibly neutral theoretical notion of "institutional dispersion"—the unskewed economic and political distribution of immigrants from different backgrounds—as the measure of successful integration.

By the 1970s, however, the validity of Eisenstadt's modernization model was widely questioned by social scientists. Challenges and alternative approaches that coalesced under the heading of "critical sociology" highlighted a number of themes. Functionalism (which Eisenstadt had adopted) was criticized for assuming consensus and ignoring conflict within society.[7] "Dependency theory" was invoked as a means of both better understanding Israel's ties with global economic and political forces, and of characterizing relations between stronger and weaker groups within the society.[8] Critical sociologists also argued that there was a tight fit between sociological perspectives and prevailing assumptions of the dominant agenda-setting forces within the society.

Active for more than a generation, critical sociologists have created a field that has entered the mainstream of sociological scholarship. Within it, over time, different theoretical strands—and disagreements—have emerged.[9] For example, Gershon Shafir and Yoav Peled welcome the contribution of Sammy Smooha, whose model of society takes account of conflict, but criticize him for not attempting to place his later work on Palestinians in Israel within the same analytic framework as Middle Eastern Jews.[10] Hannan Hever, Yehouda Shenhav, and Pnina Motzafi-Haller, the editors of *Mizraḥim beyisrael* (Mizrahim in Israel) point out that critical "post-Zionist" analysis has ignored questions of Mizrahi ethnicity.[11] In general, that book and Shenhav's *Hayehudim ha'aravim* (The Arab-Jews) emphasize links between culture, power, and identity, focusing on processes of inclusion and exclusion in Israeli society. These writers insist that Zionist ideology both created "Eastern ethnicity" and simultaneously devalued and limited it. They also highlight cultural matters and "alternative voices," both of which, in their view, received only limited attention in earlier critical writings.[12]

While we value these approaches, we would argue that they have not gone far enough. Thus, for example, the questions of precisely how much and to what extent power plays a role in everyday practice and discourse need to be determined by scientific investigation and empirical examination.

The burden of this essay, therefore, resides in the following interrelated themes:

1. Critical approaches to the study of Israeli society have emphasized the role of "the political" and the state in explaining issues of ethnic stratification and ethnic identity. While it is important to "bring the state back in"[13] to social research, this emphasis sometimes blurs the analytic distinction between state and society. It assumes that what happens at the highest political levels is reproduced automatically in local situations, without taking note of processes of interaction and variation that might be revealed by empirical examination.

2. One indication of the way in which assumptions about power continue to infuse social analysis is the persistence of binary modes of discourse, whether expressed in the categorization of groups or in analytic concepts that evoke bipolar images such as "hegemony" and "resistance." It is at least as important to be aware of what binary terminology and modes of analysis overlook as to understand what they help reveal. As Roland Calori notes, binary reasoning tends to "think about change as the replacement of one truth by a new truth, in terms of either . . . or," rather than seeking insight from difference, diversity, complexity, and tensions.[14]

3. Critical analysis has emphasized the significance of the factors of exclusion in shaping an inclusive "Mizrahi" ethnic category in Israeli society. It is now widely recognized that Mizrahim do not constitute a monolithic category and hence that the term is inadequate. Nevertheless, it continues to appear. As a result, the existence of more particular identities alongside or within a broader Mizrahi identity is obscured, and investigation of the often intricate relations between these identity levels is overlooked.

4. In addition to missing or ignoring segments of Israeli society and culture that do not fit neatly into the Mizrahi or Ashkenazic classification, the recourse to binary thinking irons out differences in the histories of the various Middle Eastern groups, both in their countries of origin and in their subsequent experiences in the Yishuv and Israel.

To concretize our points, our discussion is divided into three parts. We first explore the evolution of terms referring to ethnic groups in Israel—whether "Mizrahim" versus "Ashkenazim," particular identities such as "Kurdish" or "Bukharan" Jews, or broader terminology referring to "communities of origin" (*'edot*). Next we examine the maintenance of binary assumptions even by those who claim to critique them, bringing examples from the historical analysis of Zionism among Middle Eastern Jews (which often ignores the movement's variable forms and each Jewry's particular Zionist perspective). Third, we show how, in the analysis of Israeli society, the emphasis given to the mechanisms of hegemonic power results in a situation in which manifestations of pluralism are overlooked or discounted—in particular, the varying ways in which people from Middle Eastern backgrounds interact with, and influence, powerful institutions. In conclusion, we briefly discuss theoretical, methodological, and analytical issues relating to the further exploration of how ethnicity actually works—that is, how it is manifested "on the ground" in Israeli society.

Evolving Ethnic Categories

The various terms utilized to discuss "Sephardic" or "Mizrahi" groups, and their linkage to issues of power, have changed over time. Several points emerge from a historical purview. For one thing, the emphasis on power differentials, which underlies the binary distinction made between (powerless) Middle Eastern Jews and (powerful) European Jews, tends to overlook the historical origins of a plurality of Middle Eastern identities as well as the role played by even relatively "powerless" groups in shaping ethnic discourse. It is therefore useful to adopt a perspective in which popular ethnic categorizations, "official definitions" such as census categories, and social science concepts are all examined.

Historically, Sephardic traditions gained a foothold both outside and within the Middle East. While there emerged an overlap between the notions of "Sephardic" and Middle Eastern Jewry,[15] the two identities remained partially distinct. Thus, Jews residing in the Middle East who maintained Judeo-Spanish speech and held collective memories of an Iberian past distinguished themselves from local Jews who spoke Arabic and reflected the surrounding culture—even if the latter had also absorbed some Sephardic cultural influence. For instance, during the 17th-19th centuries in Aleppo, Jews originating in Europe referred to the local Jews as *musta'arabim* and adopted the term *francos* in reference to themselves.[16] Both in the 19th century and at the beginning of the 20th, when Jews from Europe came into contact with Jews from the Middle East in Ottoman and Mandate Palestine, "Sephardic" and "Ashkenazic" did not become, as might have been expected, blanket terms synonymous with "East" and "West." Instead, groups from Middle Eastern countries continued to identify themselves, and be identified by others, in specific communal terms (for instance, "Mugrabi" "Urfeli," "Halebi," "Yazdi," and the like).

Only with the large-scale immigration to Israel after 1948 did the binary division with an orientalist flavor begin to emerge. At the level of daily interaction, it became increasingly common to categorize persons on the basis of their country rather than their community of origin (as, for instance, "Moroccans" or "Iraqis"), a practice that lumped together individuals from very different backgrounds (for instance, Casablanca and the Atlas Mountains in Morocco; or Kurdistan and Baghdad in Iraq). As Dorothy Willner noted at the time, the Israeli tendency to assign identity by country of origin could be attributed to cognitive overload: the need to deal with extreme social complexity seemed to call for such shorthand labels.[17] Social scientists did not generally question this mode of classification, although Efrat Rosen-Lapidot's recent ethnographic work in France indicates that at least one group, Tunisian Jews, tend to adopt identities based upon their specific community of origin, rather than on their "Tunisian-ness."[18]

At the governmental level, immigration officials classified immigrants by country of origin, and the Central Bureau of Statistics subsequently broadened the term into "continent of origin." The latter classification soon became the basic element in demographic and sociological analysis that facilitated discussion of the differences between European and Middle Eastern Jews.[19] Obviously, such categories were at best rough approximations of social realities. For example, the "Africa" category often covered individuals both from North and South Africa, with the latter being English-speaking immigrants mainly of East European origin (in popular ethnic terminology, they were known as *Anglosaksim*, along with Jews from England and America). Similarly, countries that bridge Europe and Asia, such as Turkey and the former Soviet Union, also generated problems of classification.

Dvora Yanow provides a useful perspective on census-taking and public policy issues when she notes that scholars "argue that 'race' and 'ethnicity' and their associated categories are created by states and societies to establish and reinforce a hierarchy of population groups with attendant power and status."[20] However, her assumption that "states" and "societies" are always in tandem may be too simplistic. For one thing, ethnic labeling does not always begin at the state level; for another, several ethnic labels for the same group may coexist or overlap. Finally, the question of how the spread of ethnic labels and images within society affects the way in which such labels are used within state bureaucracies requires empirical investigation.[21] For example, Jewish immigrants from the former Soviet Union were at first categorized by the Israel Central Bureau of Statistics as coming from Europe. Later, as different governmental bodies confronted the diversity among ex-Soviet immigrants, they distinguished between the Asiatic and European parts of the former empire—which in itself was more a reflection of popular images than of careful ethnographic-historical research.[22] In sum, ethnic categorizations, which have profound policy implications, are often the outcome of a complex interaction between popular labels and official classifications.

More generally, the terms used in discussing ethnic phenomena have varied and have been subject to debate. Whereas romantic reference was once made to the in-gathering of the "tribes" of Israel, the term that eventually became common was *'edot* ("communities"). Typically, this was a shorthand for *'edot hamizrah* (the Eastern communities), for in the post-state period there was almost no reference to European *'edot*.[23] This terminological imbalance has been variously interpreted.

Smooha argues that this usage refers to an "ethnoclass" rather than to a place of origin. As such, he maintains, the term *'edot* allows unexamined assumptions about differences in class and status to remain in place.[24] Both he and Shlomo Swirski, who emphasizes power differentials, prefer the term *Mizrahim* (Easterners) because it highlights the issue of social power and emphasizes that these differences are anchored in the disadvantaged situation of Mizrahim within Israeli society rather than in their immigrant past.[25] From this perspective, the term *'edot hamizrah* also serves to mask (and thus perpetuate) power differentials between ethnic groups. Furthermore, it assumes or implies that Middle Eastern immigrants are "traditional" as compared with Europeans, who are "modern," as well as drawing (negative) attention to the linkages between them and "Arabs."[26]

It is beyond doubt that this ethnic classification involved stereotypes that affected the immigrants' economic status, social prestige, and access to power, as did educators' expectations and social workers' assumptions about the norms of family life. Nevertheless, discarding the term *'edot* and replacing it with another global category such as "Mizrahim" also highlights certain social processes while obscuring others. Thus, according to Yehouda Shenhav, the term *'edot hamizrah* represented the (once) hegemonic discourse imposed from above, whereas "Mizrahim" reflected the politics of identity emanating from below.[27] In our view, however, both terms suppress a pluralist view of Mizrahi/Middle Eastern communities.

It is not necessary to defend the usage of the term 'edot hamizraḥ to recognize that, historically, it offered a plural view of these groups that represented a commonsense response to reality. For at least one generation after statehood, immigrants to Israel from Europe consisted mainly of the remnants of families and communities that had survived the Second World War, while those from Middle Eastern countries came as families, whole communities, or total populations. In the latter case, preexisting ties were maintained or re-constituted after arrival, often reinforced by processes of geographic concentration and segregation in peripheral regions and depressed urban neighborhoods (which reflected a combination of policy decisions, resource differentials, immigrant choice, and unintended consequences). This situation enhanced the possibility of maintaining cultural continuity via the organization of local community synagogues, festival celebrations, and the conduct of religious life adapted to the new and changed surroundings. In the area of religious terminology, 'edot hamizraḥ became an accepted way of defining the liturgical tradition and order of synagogue services and rituals, as set down in prayer books printed in accordance with "Nusaḥ sefarad ve'edot hamizraḥ." Equally important, such expressions of ethnocultural continuity and variation were considered legitimate within a setting that otherwise stressed nation-building and homogeneity. These factors, along with the preexisting historical diversity among groups generally thought of as "Sephardic" or "Oriental," justified the language of plurality with reference to Jews from Middle Eastern countries, despite the invidious meanings often attributed to terms like 'edot.[28] It is important therefore to distinguish between the mobilization of terminology to reinforce social stratification and the terms accepted as meaningful or legitimate by the groups in question.

The same warning may be applied to the succeeding common label—Mizrahim. In contrast with 'edot hamizraḥ, it connotes ethnic differences that overlap with class, political protest, and socialization in Israel, involving varying degrees and forms of social and cultural exclusion. A few critical researchers have examined empirically the socioeconomic differences between various groups within the broad Asia-Africa category.[29] Similarly, some groups maintain that grouping all "Easterners" in a single category is not consistent with their sense of self-identity and devalues their particular heritage and social standing; hence, they continue to distinguish, both publicly and in academic research, between Sephardim and Orientals.[30] So, too, Jews from Turkey insist that they are Sephardic but not Mizrahi, and Jews from Iran prefer to be viewed separately as the 'edah iranit rather than be placed under the general rubric of "Oriental Jews."[31] Conversely, Jews from Bulgaria report that Israelis of European origin tend not to regard them as Sephardim because they seem to be "Europeans like themselves."[32] In sum, all these examples suggest that the category of "Mizrahim" requires further clarification, and its relationship with other classification practices needs to be examined in a situational context.

As noted, the use of the term Mizrahim was advocated by Shlomo Swirski as early as 1981, leading Shafir and Peled to credit him with having "pioneered the study of the Mizrachim from their own point of view, rather than that of the Ashkenazi elite."[33] Baruch Kimmerling, however, views Swirsky's book very differently, suggesting that it was a "political manifesto" that first influenced young Mizrahi intellectuals and later percolated more widely.[34] Kimmerling points out that Swirski criticized "the plural form of the term *Mizrahiyim* and made a claim for the unity among emigrants from different Eastern countries." This, he argues, is far from the study of "the Mizrahim from their own point of view," being rather the imposition of an external interpretation upon a social category that might be accepted by some within it but rejected by others.

There is something to be said for both these readings of the significance of Swirski's book. Clearly it represented a new analytic approach that also resonated with political perceptions and feelings increasingly common among many younger Mizrahim.[35] Neither is it an either/or issue whether "Eastern" Jews should be characterized globally as opposed to having their diversity emphasized (consider the differences between Jews from Yemen, Iraq, and "Bukhara"—all in Asia, for example). That is to say, accepting insights linked to the term "Mizrahim" does not require the abandonment of a research approach highlighting ethnic specificity. In our view, overarching categories that highlight the Mizrahi/Ashkenazic divide, may exist simultaneously with approaches that accord significance to the plurality of groups and the differences within them.[36]

It should also be noted that the "power to define" lies partly with the weaker social groups. Thus, "Ashkenazim" is largely an artifact created by the term's being paired with (or juxtaposed against) the Mizrahim.[37] Israelis of European background who grew up around the time of statehood have often claimed that, as children, they did not realize that they were Ashkenazim, nor were they aware of a Sephardic/ Ashkenazic dichotomy even when they lived in manifestly mixed neighborhoods. In conversations with us, they insisted that they saw themselves as *Israelis*.

There are various ways in which the emergence of *Ashkenaziyut* is reflected in the quotidian use of terminology. Those who did recognize the Ashkenazic category as relevant in the generation after statehood associated it with the traditional religious life of their European parents or grandparents. This may be echoed in everyday Arabic speech in Jerusalem, which refers to ultra-Orthodox Jews dressed in "typical" garb as *siknaj*.[38] Another indication that "Ashkenazic" takes on meaning according to historical context is the way it is used by recent immigrants from the region of the Caucasus. To them, the term refers specifically to Russian or Ukrainian Jews (who often look down upon them), rather than to Israelis of European background. Thus, the current contrast between Ashkenazim and Mizrahim is a (re)invention reflecting emerging ethnic stratification in Israel.

The reemergence of the Ashkenazic category in the ethnic lexicon, which probably took root sometime in the 1970s, may be read as attesting to the success of Middle Eastern Jews in converting what once was simply assumed to be the (Jewish) Israeli standard into only one of a number of normative ways of being Israeli. If "hyphenation" is required to distinguish between different "kinds of" Israelis, clearly the Ashkenazic option is not the only, and hence not necessarily the normative, one. Gil Eyal (citing Tom Segev's documentation of an early statement by Zalman Aranne) interprets Aranne as being aware that the use of these global classifications would eventually highlight the fact that the state is no more than the rule of one group over the other.[39] An insistence on the term "Ashkenazic," then, underlines how, in the course of two to three decades, Middle Eastern Jews "Ashkenazified" the Ashkenazim, and in so doing called their hegemony into question.[40] It is not only the creation of a new distinct category of "Ashkenazic Israelis," parallel to the ethnicization of the term "WASP" in the United States, that is noteworthy, but the success in making "Ashkenazic" a commonsense way of attributing identity to a large sector of Israeli society.

In recent years, the complexity of the discourse of ethnic classification has been brought to the fore by the (re)introduction into social science discussion of the term "Arab-Jews," as exemplified in Shenhav's book of that name (*Hayehudim ha'aravim*). A study of Mizrahi experiences in Zionist and Israeli contexts, *The Arab-Jews* utilizes the terms both descriptively, to refer to Jews from Middle Eastern countries, and as a means of accentuating dilemmas they encountered in the intertwined spheres of nationalism, religion, and ethnicity.

An analysis of the Arab linguistic and cultural background of many of its members is indeed necessary for an understanding of Israeli society. However, the global characterization of Mizrahim as *Arab* excludes Jews from non-Arab Middle Eastern countries such as Turkey and Iran,[41] marginalizes Jews living in areas in which Greek, Turkish, or Arabic was the lingua franca, yet whose primary language was Judeo-Spanish, and ignores those living in territories of the former Soviet Union, variously labeled "Bukharan Jews," "Jews of the Caucasus," "Georgian Jews," and "Krymchaks."[42] But beyond the questions of the extent to which a chosen label fits the targeted population, and whether it is economical, is the issue of its biases and attendant connotations. Many uses of the term "Arab Jews" (with or without a hyphen), both by critical sociologists and others, are intended for rhetorical purposes. The idea that "being Jewish" and "being Arab" can overlap is not surprising to anyone familiar with the Jewish Middle Ages, nor is the adoption of Arabic speech by a large segment of the Jewish world, which led to the creation of various versions of Judeo-Arabic language and culture, both oral and written. This notion was succinctly put in the oft-cited statement of S.D. Goitein that Jews in Yemen were "the most Jewish and most Arab of all Jews."[43] Only when the clashing nationalisms of the modern world serve as the primary point of reference does the idea of someone being both Arab and Jewish become an "impossibility" that must be dislodged.

It is more than a little ironic that two very different scholarly works feature "Arab Jews" in their titles. *The Last Arab Jews*, by Abraham Udovitch and Lucette Valensi, focuses on the Jews of Djerba, who were (and are) known for their tenacious observance of Judaism and its local customs.[44] Shenhav, however, chooses this term, among other reasons, because it highlights the "secular" aspects of Jewish life in Iraq that, for ideological reasons, were not recognized by the Zionist emissaries (*shelihim*) sent by the Yishuv.[45] This difference correlates with these books' varying goals. Whereas *The Last Arab Jews* provides a detailed account of the history, social structure, and daily life in Djerba, the analysis in *The Arab-Jews* is aimed primarily at exposing the biases and obfuscations of regnant *discourse about* Jewish life in Arab lands, particularly Iraq. This comes through clearly in an extensive footnote critiquing a comment made by Albert Memmi.[46]

We do not take issue with the legitimacy of the term "Arab-Jews" or its perspective on Jewish life in Arabic lands. Indeed, we agree that the question of how Jews in the Middle East integrated into (and/or were in friction with) local society, culture, and sense of nationhood needs greater attention and understanding.[47] However, we do have serious reservations about the employment of such terms and labels when they override or discount the complexity and diversity of Jewish life in Middle Eastern settings—placing all Middle Eastern Jews into a single homogenizing category that precludes appreciation of their historic variability and potential for plural identities in the contemporary world.

Consider, for instance, the Jews of Iraq, who once constituted one of the largest Jewish communities in the Middle East. One outstanding feature of life in Iraq in the first half of the 20th century was the Jews' active participation in modern Arabic literature. A recent study by Reuven Snir examines this development and explores how it has been used in ideological debates. Snir shows that Arabic literary activity among Jews was not a common phenomenon.[48] While this fact does not detract from the historical and theoretical importance of Iraqi Jewish writing in Arabic, it does underscore the need to uncover a variety of socio-historical contexts before moving toward generalizations.

The homogenization of a multiplicity of "non-Ashkenazic" categories in the single term "Arab-Jews" is also surprising, given recent efforts by critical analysts to unpack or disaggregate the simple Mizrahim/Ashkenazim dichotomy.[49] The latter would pave the way to recognizing notions like "mizrahiyut" or "Arab Jews" as part of the current vocabulary of Israeli culture, while at the same time permitting an empirical examination of the behavior of those who, to some degree and in various contexts, both identify themselves in these terms while also giving expression to other, more particular identifications.[50] In our view, although critical analysis recognizes the weakness of simple binary contrasts, it continues to perpetuate some of the very notions it seeks to deconstruct, as is evident in its persistent recourse to binary models. This has profound implications for the analysis of Israeli society and for the understanding of Middle Eastern Jewish communities in the pre-state period.

Mechanisms of Binarism and Its Expression in History

To some degree or another, all social scientists employ (and thus reinforce) concepts that are established by officials, that appeal to common sense, and/or are popularized by the media. Thus, Israeli social discourse has internalized the "given-ness" of a society divided into two separate homogenous rubrics of "Easterners" and "Europeans," despite considerable empirical evidence to the contrary. Critical sociology does not constitute an exception to the rule, and theories emanating from it have not succeeded in escaping the inherent blinders of existing categories.

At times, to be sure, it may be necessary to use binary categorizations because these represent the observed phenomena and capture the trends in areas such as economics, education, residence, and political participation.[51] But the documentation and analysis of the ongoing (and widening) social gaps that determine individuals' location in the social structure are insufficient in the realms of identity and culture. The latter are not independent of the processes of stratification, but neither are they merely a reflection of them. Of equal significance are the various categories that the *actors themselves apply* in ordering and interpreting their situation and experiences. In not admitting these considerations, critical sociologists remain over-reliant on binary categories.

We begin by illustrating how binarism is reproduced through language. Some biases built into language are found on the opening pages of *Mizraḥim beyisrael*, which seeks explicitly to break out of the straightjacket of prior discussions of ethnic divisions in Israel. On the one hand, the collection is titled "Mizrahim in Israel," not "The Mizrahim . . . ," which reflects its claim that "there is no single clearly distinguished Mizrahi identity, but rather many identities taking shape simultaneously, growing out of complex relationships of inclusion and exclusion."[52] On the other hand, from the beginning of the first substantive chapter, the focus is on rescuing *"the* Mizrahi subject from the framework of hegemonic discourse in Israel,"[53] and phrases with a definite article (*ha* in Hebrew) appear frequently (albeit not consistently) throughout the succeeding pages.[54] The use of the Hebrew definite article conveys a sense that there exist given social categories that are self-explanatory.[55]

Nor is the sense of a fixed Mizrahi category confined to *Mizraḥim beyisrael*. Shafir and Peled's book includes a chapter titled "Mizrachim and Women," which employs a Mizrahi-Ashkenazic opposition to describe the ethnic divide. Although well aware of this binary term's history and of the fact that there is variation within each category, Shafir and Peled still fall victim to a kind of "double-think." While claiming at one point that "[t]he widely used Ashkenazi-Mizrachi distinction is an Israeli social construct that reflects ambivalent attitudes and disguises important differences between the Mizrachim themselves," Shafir and Peled go on to generalize about "the two Jewish ethnic groups."[56] Moreover, part of the variation between Mizrahim is attributed to economics: "About one-third of Mizrachim can now be classified as belonging to the middle class."[57] In this way, the authors acknowledge that their generalizations selectively ignore one third of a social category; this is especially surprising, given the importance of social class in their analysis.

The chapter titled "Mizrachim and Women" may encode a message at other levels, suggesting the unchanging nature of an East-West dichotomy, notwithstanding current insights regarding the ways in which gender roles are constructed categories.[58] Social science has not always easily drawn parallels between gender and other forms of inequality and domination (such as class and race); the tendency became widespread after the social protests of the 1960s. These parallels carry a certain historic irony with regard to Jews from Middle Eastern backgrounds, where in some instances Muslim discourse compared Jews to women, implying an "essential" but limited place for them in society.[59]

Beyond the ways in which binary categories shape perceptions of Israeli society today, they also bias the attempts of critical sociology to examine the past, as is exemplified by studies of Middle Eastern Jews in the Yishuv and of the history of Jews in Middle Eastern countries in the modern era. Consider, for example, the Jews from Yemen, who began immigrating in significant numbers after 1881, and who attained symbolic significance during the period of the Yishuv. Recent research has revealed the problematic nature of their treatment by the European Zionist leadership, as well as the complex relationships between them and other groups, particularly Sephardim and Mughrabim.[60] Critical sociologists view the history of Yemenite Jews in Palestine as emblematic of Mizrahi-Ashkenazic relationships in general. Shafir and Peled, for instance, assert that the experience of Yemenite Jews is "the most revealing case" of Mizrahi-Ashkenazic relationships.[61] *Mizraḥim beyisrael* explicitly adopts the strategy of taking one episode to represent the whole, namely, Yehudah Nini's historical study of ten Yemenite families who, after having lived for almost 20 years in Kinneret, a collective settlement (*moshava*), were expelled to make room for newcomers from Europe and resettled elsewhere.[62] Thus, in its conclusion, Nini is criticized for presenting his study as a "historical miniature" and as a marginal episode from which it was not possible to generalize.[63] What is striking in both Shafir and Peled's book and in *Mizraḥim beyisrael* is the resort to the synechdoche: making one group—Yemenites—stand for "the whole" Mizrahi experience, rather than addressing a diversity of historical circumstances and developments in which varying forms of Eastern-ness are also evident.

It is noteworthy that critical sociologists have not studied the Sephardic entrepreneurial families that formed an economic elite in Palestine early in the 19th century.[64] Although their prominence declined somewhat as European migration increased and the labor movement's influence grew, they continued to play an important economic role—for instance, in banking—throughout the Mandate period. Also ignored is the role played by Bukharan Jewish merchants and traders in the development of Jerusalem (their activities came to an end when the new Soviet regime confiscated their wealth). Clearly, a part-for-whole argument focusing only on these established "Mizrahim" would produce a very different analysis from that derived from the Yemenite case. The latter, to be sure, is of historical importance for any discussion of the emergence of hegemonic patterns and orientalist attitudes in the Zionist project, but discussions of Zionism and Jews in the Middle East cannot rest solely on it. Rather, they must examine the issue at all levels and in all its complexity, cover all cases, and take into account contrary examples, instead of using synechdochic logic that ignores or discounts them to arrive at global assessments.

In *The Arab-Jews*, Yehouda Shenhav rethinks some basic issues connected with the encounter of European Zionism with Middle Eastern Jews.[65] While the book as a whole is intended to portray *mizrahiyut* as a diverse phenomenon with "broad margins," its first chapter offers a method for using one case as a paradigmatic historical episode enabling generalization. This chapter focuses on a series of events and developments in Iraq and Iran during the Second World War, using these as the "methodological" and "theoretical" baseline for studying the attitudes and the relationships of Zionism and the incipient Israeli state both to Eastern Jews and to the "Arab-ness" of their history, culture, and identities. Shenhav claims that here, for the first time, there was an organized attempt by Zionist emissaries to recruit Jews in an Arab region for Zionist immigration, following the Yishuv leadership's adoption of a policy aimed at bringing about large-scale Jewish migration to Palestine from Middle Eastern lands. Shenhav takes this as his "zero-point" because it relates to a specific Eastern group before global categories such as " 'edot hamizrah" were established by the homogenizing discourse and practices of state bureaucracies. The emissaries' activities in educating and recruiting Jews (mostly

Iraqi) for Zionist emigration were facilitated by the involvement of Solel Boneh, a Histadrut company, in the erection and running of oil refineries in Abadan, Iran, as part of the Yishuv's support for the British war effort.

Shenhav's discussion situates the emissaries on a shifting boundary between colonialism and nationalism. Their capacity to act was dependent on British rule, and they enjoyed primacy vis-à-vis local Jews because of their link to the imperial power. From the perspective of Zionist ideology, they sought to fulfill its elevated goal of incorporating Iraqi Jews into a new collectivity that gave expression to their shared Jewish identity. An analysis of the emissaries' reports and letters reveals the conceptual and value struggles that the presumed hegemonic *shelihim* encountered in seeking the re-creation, in the Zionist image, of local Jews who were deeply engaged in an Arab milieu.

Significantly, Shenhav's analysis of the Abadan endeavor treats Jews in Iran and in Iraq as a single entity. Not only does this approach incorporate from the outset a concept that it seeks to interrogate—namely, the creation of a broad category of "Easterners"—it also ignores the very different histories and cultures of these two Jewish populations. In fact, although the events under discussion are centered in Abadan, Shenhav gives very little specific information about the Jews of Iran. We will return to the question of how his analysis tends to merge groups and categories. First, however, we indicate a reservation about assigning prototypical status to this particular historical episode.

While the Abadan-emissary project was the first instance of a new Zionist policy, it was soon followed, as will be seen, by meetings between Libyan Jews and Palestinian Jewish soldiers participating in the British conquest of Libya from Axis forces. First broached in the summer of 1942, the idea of recruiting Solel Boneh workers for the oil refineries in Abadan took shape over the ensuing months. In addition to the British concern over the shortage of oil from Asia that led to increased production in Abadan, there was the fact that German and Italian forces led by Fieldmarshal Erwin Rommel were advancing from Libya into Egypt, coming within 100 kilometers of Cairo. Only in late October 1942 did the British forces succeed in breaking through the Axis lines, thus finally reversing the direction of the war in North Africa. Meanwhile, the leadership of the Yishuv, increasingly aware of the multidimensional uncertainties facing it, strongly encouraged Jews to enlist in the British armed forces: among its concerns was the possibility that Britain would retreat from Palestine, regroup elsewhere, and leave the Yishuv to its fate. This seeming convergence of Jewish, Zionist, and British colonialist interests could not have been taken fully for granted when the Abadan project was first envisioned. Furthermore, the perceptible divergences in these interests may well have been significant both in the substance of the Yishuv's decisions and in their timing. The assumed link between British imperial and Zionist interests, and the assumption that the latter was an arm of the colonialist enterprise (which permeates Shenhav's data) is far from being proven.

In his analysis, Shenhav brings to light the complexity and paradoxes of the situation, emphasizing the diverse backgrounds of the *shelihim* and the fluidity of their discourse and practice, which varied "according to interests, partners, and the circumstances in which they operated."[66] Yet in contrast with this sensitivity toward context, the "European-ness" of the Zionist project is taken as a given, and the ethnic backgrounds and experiences of the emissaries are left unexplored.[67] While in principle one may analyze texts in isolation from individual biographies, an examination of individual emissaries and *their* ethnic trajectories, in our view, is capable of adding both color and additional levels of meaning to the story.

In the case of the emissaries to Abadan, at least three were neither European nor Ashkenazic. Hai Yissakharov (mentioned in *The Arab Jews*) probably was of Bukharan origin, whereas Rashi Yissakharov and another emissary, Yerahmiel Asa (also mentioned in the book), came from families originating in the Caucasus that, in the 1920s, settled in an area of Tel Aviv near the site of the old central bus station.[68] From his early teenage years, Asa belonged to Hanoar Ha'oved, a Zionist socialist youth movement. Together with two other youngsters of Caucasian background, he was part of a collective (*gar'in*) that settled in the Galilee, where it first reconstructed the site of Tel Hai and then founded Kibbutz Hulata. This part of his biography— together with the astonishment shown by members of a Baghdadi synagogue at his secular appearance and mien[69]—would seem to attest to his "assimilation" into European *halutzic* culture. However, judging by the experience of Rashi Yissakharov, who grew up in the same Tel Aviv neighborhood, the reality may have been more complex. Rashi, unlike Asa, continued to live in Tel Aviv, where he eventually became a manager in Solel Boneh. He was a central figure in the local Caucasian synagogue and was active in Caucasian communal organizations. Then, as now, "Caucasian Jew" was an ambiguous category—as reported in interviews with Rashi, many East European Jews expressed surprise when learning of his origin ("But you're not a *frenk*; you're one of us, aren't you?"). At his funeral in 2003, his son noted that Rashi frequently referred to his Caucasian roots, even though he had never visited the Caucasus.

Thus, while Yerahmiel Asa and some like him moved firmly into the Zionist establishment, other Caucasian Jews took different routes. In general, relationships between Caucasian Jews and the Zionist movement were shot through with ambivalence, as became evident, for example, with regard to the individuals who sought to emigrate to Palestine after 1918 and to those who, a decade later, wished to be accepted in agricultural settlements, but were told to wait for settlements meant especially for "*'edot mizrahiyot*."[70] Given their later voluntary activities among Caucasian newcomers in the 1970s and 1990s that firmly "reconnected" them to their particular past, it is highly unlikely that such ambivalence was foreign to Asa and Rashi Yissakharov. The latter maintained close ties with the new immigrants who, in the 1990s, became members of the Caucasian synagogue in south Tel Aviv that he headed, and with whom he communicated in Juhuri (Judeo-Tat), their spoken language.

Moreover, the hypothesis that, decades earlier, these individuals were conscious of their non-European past cannot be gainsaid. Indeed, during his term as a member of Knesset representing the Ahdut Ha'avodah party (1958–1959),[71] Asa proposed a policy of *shizur tarbuyot* (the interweaving of cultures, as in a carpet) in place of the dominant "melting pot" model.[72] Finally, with regard to Hai Yissakharov, Shenhav describes an incident where the ethnic/national characteristics of the Palestinian Jews were compared to other groups in Abadan and reports Yissakharov's response:

"He as a Jew demands the same conditions as the English do as Englishmen."
One can only wonder whether Hai Yissakharov's sensitivity to ethnic issues in the
Yishuv prompted this remark.[73] In any event, close examination of the orientations
and activities of these non-Ashkenazic emissaries in Abadan and elsewhere not
only brings to light data that challenge the binary conception of ethnic difference,
but also uncovers the roots of alternative conceptions of group diversity in the
Zionist/Israeli context.

Shenhav's analysis of the situation at Abadan also focuses attention on an emissary of far different origins—Enzo Sereni, who came from a very established
Italian Jewish family.[74] Like his fellow *shelihim*, Sereni found himself in a conceptual bind. On the one hand was the recognition that, linguistically and culturally,
the Jews of Baghdad were part of the local Arab(ic) culture and language. On the
other hand, the emissaries were committed to values that emphasized the community's Jewishness and Zionist potential. Citing Homi K. Bhaba, Shenhav insists that
such ambivalence and internal contradictions are characteristic of colonialist discourse, and he uses this theoretical focus to portray Sereni's difficulties in seeking to
isolate definitive elements of Jewish identity and "difference" in the local Arab
Jewish world. Unable to distinguish physically between Jews, Muslims, and Christians, Sereni found more subtle evidence of difference, such as the local Jews'
ability to identify members of the three religious communities on the basis of
speech. Left unexplored by Shenhav is an analysis of Baghdadi Jews' sociolinguistic
practices and what implications these had for their identities. For this, other sources
of information and methods of study are required.[75]

To analyze such situations solely via the prism of colonialist theory's tortured
conceptualizations of ambivalences, contradictions, and "boundaries" (both repressed and vacillating) is to fail adequately to take note of and account for their
intricacy. Relating to the speech of Jews in Baghdad only as revealed in documents
in Zionist archives, and seeking to understand it in terms of theory anchored in other
climes, comes at the cost of ignoring available evidence provided by Iraqi Jews
themselves. Put generally, critical analysis, representing theoretical emphases that
privilege certain issues, does not necessarily open the door to understanding past or
present "Mizrahi" experiences at the level of actual individuals. Paradoxically, the
attempt to reveal the meanings imposed on others by hegemonic discourse has
resulted in a resort to the same kinds of generalization that the critical analyst sought
to discredit and discard.

More broadly, in the case of Zionism, critical theory's eagerness to uncover the
hidden assumptions of dominant social groups results in their terms of reference
being taken as the starting point. This, in turn, may amount to a certain complicity in
the suppression of alternative points of view. A significant example is assigning
Zionism wholly to European Jewry. Thus, Shafir and Peled begin their discussion
with the simple assertion that "[t]he Zionist movement was a European movement,"
and Shenhav offers an analysis of what he calls "the first practical encounter between the Zionist movement and the Jews of Arab lands."[76] There can be no doubt
that Zionism developed primarily in Europe and that for many years its most significant political activities (outside of Palestine) were conducted in the European

arena. So, too, there are useful insights to be had by teasing out, as does Shenhav, both the colonialist and nationalist drives among the emissaries in Abadan, and by examining the ideas that emerged among Zionist activists in that setting.[77] What we do call into question, however, is this discourse's wholesale dismissal of Zionism as a meaningful development in Jewish life in Middle Eastern and Asian countries, about which there is now a considerable literature.[78]

It is a truism that Zionism appeared first in Europe and only later in the Middle East (and that it was not a major factor there). However, this does not justify *excluding* this part of the world from Zionist history. In fact, when Zionism did develop in Middle Eastern countries, it had a real social base, such as the aspirations of Jews for fuller societal participation (often stimulated by education in Alliance Israélite Universelle schools), which largely were blocked because neither local Muslims nor colonizing Europeans easily accepted upward Jewish social (and political) mobility. It also manifested a degree of cultural creativity, most prominently with regard to the Hebrew language; so, too, Zionist-sponsored sports flourished, in part because it was exempt from the legal restrictions on political activity that were commonly found in colonial situations. Those Zionist-inspired developments are not uniform, but rather exhibit interesting variations that reflect the different challenges facing Jews in each country. Although such phenomena may appear to be relatively minor elements in the "big picture," to remove them from scholarly purview is to adopt the Eurocentric lenses that critical theory seeks to replace. In our view, a historical examination of Zionism among the Jews of Libya, to take but one example, is sufficient to undermine the claim made in *The Arab-Jews* that its analysis of the experiences of the Zionist emissaries in Iraq and Iran offers a general model applicable to all other settings, irrespective of their particular conditions and contexts.

As noted, the success of the Eighth Army in pushing back the Axis forces in Libya brought about direct contact between Jewish soldiers from Palestine and Jewish communities in both Cyrenaica and Tripolitania in late 1942 and early 1943. These events have been partially described and analyzed, and we have no doubt that a "critical" study would enrich an understanding of them. But one comparative point needs emphasizing. Zionism had already begun to have a significant impact among Libyan Jews in the period just before the Second World War, and perhaps even earlier.[79] To be sure, the extent of that impact has often been exaggerated, partly due to a popular tendency to overestimate the strength and contribution of Zionism, following the immigration of whole Jewish communities, or large portions of them, to Israel. An example of such exaggeration is the now oft-repeated statement that the soldiers arriving in Tripoli from Palestine met a "community that spoke Hebrew."[80] This claim is not entirely baseless, however, as systematic efforts to teach modern Hebrew began in the 1930s in Tripolitania (a study of the revival of Hebrew in Israel in the 1950s ranked Libyan Jews as one of the immigrant groups among whom the use of the language was most widespread).[81] Moreover, in contrast with the situation in Baghdad, Zionism was the only nationalist option available to Libyan Jews, who were caught between a Fascism turned antisemitic and a Muslim environment in which nationalism was both weak and severely repressed by Italian colonial rule.

Furthermore, in Libya, unlike Iraq, Arabic was not part of the educational curriculum of Jewish youth. In brief, soldiers from the Yishuv who interacted with Libyan Jewry faced practical and conceptual challenges that were very different from those encountered by the Zionist emissaries in Iraq and Iran. To be sure, individual elements of these situations were similar, but their overall constellations varied significantly.

Curiously, the notion that Zionism is an entirely European phenomenon and movement resonates with another view that most critical sociologists reject strongly, namely, the classic distinction in Zionist historiography between those who, over the centuries, came to live in the land of Israel for religious reasons and those who were inspired by Zionism. As noted, Eisenstadt had used this notion to differentiate between "Oriental Jews," whose immigration "into Palestine did not imply a break with their traditional social and cultural structures," and the pre-state, ideologically motivated halutzim, or pioneers, from Europe.[82] The distinction between "Old" and "New" Yishuv that most likely inspired this subsequent sociological contrast along ethnic lines has been scrutinized and questioned from several quarters.[83] It is therefore surprising that a "critical" perspective easily continues a differential view of Zionism along a simple East/West line.

What seems to us not only more appropriate but also necessary is an open-ended examination of how the idea of Zionism was interpreted and became significant in different sectors of Jewry. As a corollary, one must go beyond the simple division between West and East. The claim that coming to Palestine was envisioned as an ordinary move "within the region" that demanded little cultural adjustment may be relevant with regard to immigrants from Arabic-speaking Aleppo or Baghdad. However, there is no prima facie reason for assuming that Palestine was more "natural" a setting for Jews from Kurdistan or Afghanistan than for those from Galicia or Volhynia. In sum, we must be wary of the simplified and often orientalist images affecting all theoretical schools that have characterized the discourse on Zionism. Similarly, it must be recognized that all-encompassing schemes have a tendency to prejudge (and misinterpret) the histories of a number of specific Middle Eastern communities, and in doing so have failed to take into account significant particular and plural "Mizrahi" experiences.

The Search for Plurality

The previous section illustrated how analysis based on explicit and implicit binary models skews the understanding of some historical developments. Several biases are thereby perpetuated. Theory is privileged over the complexity and plurality of ethnic identifications. State power is placed center stage, while society is relegated to the background. Even the growing trend of revealing "resistance" to hegemony retains the centrality of issues regarding power and the state. While some critical sociologists have been surprised by their unexpectedly "discovering" social life "on-the-ground," or "from below," one is tempted to suggest that attention to plurality, and an interest in phenomena far removed from the arenas of power, would have uncovered and dealt with its presence from the outset. This is not to call for abandoning one approach and replacing it with the other, but rather to propose the undertaking of additional ethnographic research capable of revealing the complex interplay among the various factors, which critical approaches have undervalued.

Some of these points are taken up in Adrianna Kemp's study of "resistance" on the part of immigrants in *moshavei 'olim* in the early 1950s, which appears in *Mizraḥim beyisrael*.[84] Kemp applies the notion of resistance to settlers who tried (often successfully) to leave a moshav, as well as to those who opposed signing formal contracts outlining their obligations to the cooperative settlement institutions that had set them up in the new villages. She argues that resistance to "control" is often a subtle matter manifested in mundane, everyday activities and in itself is worthy of attention above and beyond the now familiar tale of Mizrahi public protest. The data that she interprets in the light of this theoretical approach are taken from Knesset records, Zionist archives, and the daily press.

In her analysis, Kemp takes for granted what has become "canonized" knowledge—namely, that immigrants from Middle Eastern countries were forced into peripheral areas. While not disputing this view as an overall first assessment, we would suggest that Kemp's "discovery" of acts of resistance presumes a monolithic settlement process. It is noteworthy that she does not refer to the extensive anthropological literature on these very issues, such as the moshav studies of Dorothy Willner or Alex Weingrod.[85] This omission is puzzling, given the use (in quotation marks) of the phrase "ḥaluẓim ba'al korham," which is virtually a translation of Weingrod's title, *Reluctant Pioneers*.[86]

Willner's book, in particular, deals with these matters at length, providing historical background and analysis of the relevant ideological and institutional factors.[87] Willner distinguishes a phase in the process, termed the "rationalization" of settlement procedures, which follows an improvisation phase. Rationalization is concerned with "the land settlement agencies' legal authority to effect settler compliance in the absence of consensus." Willner also points to the contextual variation of this process, noting that the new policy of "ship to village" settlement (which depended, at least formally, on immigrants agreeing to be sent to the designated village), was instituted in response to the social and economic difficulties of the transit camps (*ma'abarot*).[88] She claims that this policy, which resulted in the scattering of the immigrants in many small and distant villages, weakened their restricted (but still real) bargaining power by cutting them off from the flow of information that reached the vast mass of diverse immigrants in the larger and more centrally located transit camps. Her ethnography explains the administrators' motivations and intentions but also records the cajoling, at times deception, and even coercion that manifested themselves in relations between bureaucrats and moshav settlers. Based on contemporary field observations, Willner's account is consistent with the picture drawn by Kemp, except for Kemp's portrayal of a uni-directional and monochromic "control" (*shelitah*). Although Willner's account takes note of power differentials, it also provides a nuanced sense of interactions between those in power and those subject to it, demonstrating that negotiation, as well as "control" or "resistance," is a significant factor worthy of study.

Esther Meir-Glitzenstein's subsequent historical study of immigrants from Iraq after their arrival in 1950–1951 supports Willner's analysis.[89] Originally sent to peripheral areas, many of these Iraqi immigrants forced their way into ma'abarot in the center of the country—although, as she also points out, the "ship to village" policy made it relatively difficult for immigrants to circumvent the planning authorities. Another field study from the 1960s shows that immigrants from Iraq and Libya in three ma'abarot (which eventually became the town of Or Yehudah) overcame attempts to "scatter" them in outlying rural settlements.[90] These points fit in with Gil Eyal's recent observation that some groups of early immigrants remained in "no-man's-land" in rundown and often abandoned housing, alongside Arab populations on the seams of the poorest urban areas, simply because they lacked the resources to move out.[91] In Eyal's account, the interaction between authorities and settlers forms part of what is shown to be a highly complex situation.

Ethnographic accounts of moshav settlement also reveal the presence of both consensual and coercive processes. Immigrants from rural Tripolitania who established a village in the Sharon plain in 1950, and who were interviewed in 1964, gave several reasons why they had found the moshav option attractive.[92] These included the opportunity to get out of the ma'abarah, their desire to remain with people they knew, the ease with which they could maintain a religious lifestyle, and their lack of urban employment skills. More recent work by Esther Schely-Newman has shown the power of moshav women from Tunisia to fashion and refashion the significance of their settlement experiences by means of storytelling, a perspective on moshav life ignored by all previous accounts.[93] While these accounts do not undermine the general framework of limited choice that such settlers faced, they do suggest that recognizing from the outset the possibility of interaction between immigrants and authorities, and of plural situations and paths, is a more useful starting point for research than a governing theoretical notion that initially obscures settler initiatives and varied responses—only later to "discover" them.[94]

Significantly, these former Tripolitanian villagers did not see themselves in broad ethnic terms as either Sephardim or Mizrahim.[95] For them, as for others, the consolidation of these terms as widely meaningful and applicable took place over time. Similarly, the meaning of these terms in the Israeli ethnic lexicon—their social connotations and applications—continued to evolve without necessarily erasing the significance of more particular identifications. This may be seen especially in the political sphere, where the emergence of Shas looms large, but it is also manifest in other realms.

The Shas party offers an instructive example. While it claims to raise a single "Sephardic" banner, it is based culturally on a far from seamless integration of various ethnic identities and religious modes. Although it has structured itself around salient figures who highlight the constituencies of Jews from Iraq and Morocco, it also makes provision for representation of a number of different particular ethnic communities on its Knesset list (for instance, from the Bukharan community).[96] At a cultural level, the movement sought to link the rationalist halakhic worldview of Ovadia Yosef and the ecstatic devotion to *zadikim* that continues to be an important element among Jews from Moroccan backgrounds.[97]

Moreover, the electoral rise of the party has not led to religious unification. The relationship between the overall and particular identities is shifting and dynamic. Notwithstanding the boost they have enjoyed from Shas' success, rabbis representing different communities have expressed their objections to Ovadia Yosef's attempts to institute a single Sephardic halakhic standard.[98] This is well illustrated in the case of Levi Nahum, born in Tripoli but educated in yeshivot in Israel, who has undertaken the initial publication and reissue of books written by rabbis in Tripoli.[99] One of these, published in 1987, included a *haskamah* (statement of approval) from Ovadia Yosef. More recently, he published a siddur that followed the liturgical tradition (*nusaḥ*) of Tripoli. Based upon the well-known tradition of Leghorn (a community in Italy that influenced many North African communities), it includes liturgical commentary and rulings by R. Yaakov Raqah, a 19th-century Tripolitan scholar, as well as the contemporary prayer for the state of Israel. Significantly, in its preface, Nahum cites a passage by the renowned kabbalist Isaac Luria to the effect that each "tribe" in Israel should remain loyal to its own *nusaḥ*. While not explicit, his disagreement with Yosef's position is manifest. More broadly, Nahum's story is that of an ongoing search for an ethno-religious "home" that adequately conveys his particular identity and commitments. Similar developments appear in other communities; for example, a new set of *maḥzorim* (High Holiday prayer books) called *Nusaḥ Kavkaz*[100] was published in 2003 and distributed at the opening of a magnificent synagogue in the town of Tirat Hacarmel. What these cases indicate is that the matrix within which these searches have proceeded is "Mizrahi," but that they involve shifts between broad and local ethnic categories and reflect both European and Eastern religious traditions.

The plurality and negotiation of ethnic categories is not confined to relatively unknown figures like Levi Nahum or other barely visible phenomena. It also takes place in the Israeli public sphere, even if not always recognized as such. A good case in point is the popular singer Sarit Haddad. Interviews reveal that many Israelis assume she is "Moroccan," but in fact her background is more complex. Haddad was born into a family from the Caucasus named Hoddedatov that moved to Hadera in the 1970s. Given binary assumptions of hegemony, one might have assumed that the logical move would have been to "Ashkenazify" in order to become more "fully Israeli." Nevertheless, Haddad chose a "Mizrahi" option; the name Haddad, Arabic for blacksmith, was found among Jews (and Christians, but usually not Muslims) in many Middle Eastern settings. The choice is not surprising if one views Mizrahi music as having become one of Israel's mainstream traditions. Moreover, such a choice can signify the downplaying of the traditions of a specific group.[101] In general, then, it demonstrates not only that individuals can move between and seek to change categories, but also that historical developments may shift the center of gravity of such categories, even while an illusion that they are "given" is maintained.

What such processes reveal, we suspect, is the gradual acceptance of "Middle Eastern-ness" as part of Israeli life, accompanied by "resistance" to such acceptance, on the one hand, by those who see it as threatening and, on the other hand, by those who have a political stake in retaining *mizraḥiyut* as a distinct category.[102] Both because of the manipulation of binary categories and the presence of plural identifications, the study of ethnic perceptions and actions is a fluid field full of paradoxes. For example, binarism, and the "success" of the Mizrahi category, may result in the marginalizing of groups that do not easily fit into it. Thus, in small towns in Israel, one can observe how Caucasian Jews are subject to exclusionary practices by those of North African origins.[103] At a more formal level, certain developments and phenomena are characterized precisely by their undefinedness, their fluidity, and their openness to choices made by individuals and families. Consequently, the meeting of "East and West" in Israel has given rise to many social and cultural manifestations that have not received adequate scholarly attention.

The term "hybridity" (an outgrowth of post-colonial theory) is now used commonly to refer to processes whereby elements from diverse traditions are combined, often in novel ways. That term deserves to be treated with caution, however, because of its connotation of being able to identify the original cultural elements from which hybrid forms emerge, which in many cases is a difficult if not impossible task. It is also necessary to take into account more labile structures, experimentation, and creativity. At a social level, for example, there now may be residential areas that reflect so much marriage across categories that it is meaningless to place them in any accepted grouping. In the realm of culture, the variety of forms of folk dancing currently exhibit "mixtures upon mixtures," including the mobilization of global trends into local trends (or vice versa). These phenomena often defy easy labeling and call for more descriptive or ethnographic work to begin to grasp their social and cultural significance.

Given that ethnicity is clearly linked to stratification in Israeli society, there has been surprisingly little research on patterns of interethnic marriage and their implications.[104] A recent study by Barbara Okun that examines education as a major influence on marriage choices partly fills the gap.[105] She points to the decreasing significance of social hierarchy as a factor determining the scope of interethnic marriages, but notes as well the continuing relevance of a European/Mizrahi dichotomy. Focusing on marriage patterns among Israeli offspring of "mixed" Mizrahi-European marriages (who, in the 1995 census, were relatively few in number), Okun found that when such individuals chose spouses who were born to "non-mixed" parents, the choice was related to education—that is, the more educated were more likely to find partners with solely European ancestry, whereas the less educated tended to choose a spouse of wholly Mizrahi origin.[106] In short, marriage alone does not entirely overcome the stratificational consequences of the ethnic divide.

These findings lend weight to the argument that the disappearance of ethnic differences via interethnic marriage, as epitomized by the "happy ending" of Ephraim Kishon's film, *Salah Shabati*, reflects a hegemonic worldview.[107] Beyond such a critique, however, it is necessary to explore the significant empirical questions regarding "mixed" marriages, which over time have become increasingly common. For instance, to what extent do mixed couples explicitly identify with one group rather than another? Do they seek either to integrate their different traditions; to cut themselves off completely from the past by stressing their "Israeli-ness"; or to create a "multicultural" mode of being Israeli that allows for expression both of their different backgrounds and the other cultural influences to which they have been exposed? And how do such phenomena mesh with (or strain against) other social processes and choices, such as the move to new neighborhoods with greater ethnic mixing;[108] the selection of schools; the maintenance of ties with members of extended families who are to various degrees "religious," "traditional," or "secular";[109] and individuals' needs to express their identity in the course of life-cycle developments?

So, too, an examination of such aspects of everyday life may reveal self-perceptions that not only reflect different levels and sources of ethnic identification, but also illuminate the links between ethnicity and other social forces such as class or religion. This does not imply abandoning one conceptual paradigm (ethnicity) and replacing it with another, but rather the adoption of a research orientation capable of dealing with the variety of social and ideational factors at work "on the ground." In our view, considerable progress in understanding ethnicity in Israeli society can be made by determining which elements and categories of ethnicity are meaningful to which "sorts" of people, and by delineating the conditions in which they become salient or, alternatively, attenuated.

Conclusion

This essay has assessed aspects of the ways in which critical sociology has shaped the understanding of the experiences of Jews from Middle Eastern lands in Israeli society. Our arguments should not be taken as a challenge to the whole edifice. Rather, in criticizing some features of critical sociology's methods and conclusions, our main intent has been to characterize both its strengths and weaknesses. These can be summed up in two related claims. Critical approaches have provided useful insights into how hegemonic structures have excluded Jews defined as "Eastern," but have been less successful in documenting and grasping developments reflecting the distinctiveness and creative adaptations of those groups themselves. As a corollary, analysis based on binary categories and assumptions, which has been a major feature of this approach, has greatly hindered comprehension of both the histories and the empirical experiences of "Eastern" groups in Israel. Unfortunately, critical sociology did not follow its success in revealing how binary thinking was constructed by showing how to disentangle from its undesirable consequences.

Indeed, we would argue that critical sociology has maintained some of the assumptions of the earlier canonical approach. Not unlike the title of Joseph Ben-David's article in the early 1950s, which implied that one had to choose between "ethnic differences *or* social change,"[110] some of the works discussed here imply that a focus on Mizrahim or Arab-Jews necessarily *replaces* research that highlights individual ethnic identities. Our claim is that an emphasis on particular identities, as viewed by participants, should be *added to* the paradigm of critical research, because broad and specific identifications may both exist simultaneously and interact in varied ways.

Closely related to our urging greater attention to the plurality of ethnic expressions is a call for research to take a step back from issues of politics and the state, and from other matters that involve striving toward "the center." No one can deny the pervasiveness of the political and the dominant role of the center within Israeli life. This does not preclude considerable variation in the manner in which politics is conducted—at the center and at the local level, and in relations between them. Particularly important from our present perspective is the need for a detailed empirical examination of the variety of forms that politics assumes at diverse local levels. We therefore urge investigating the various situations in which state-hege-monic and broad political forces interact with a plurality of local institutions, actors, and identities (including cases in which the last appear to be neutralized or sub-merged in the background) in order to bring to light the whole range of Mizrahi ethnic and religious expressions.

These substantive claims lead to two more points that situate critical sociology vis-à-vis other research thrusts. One by-product of the critical approach has been to downplay ethnography and dismiss its contribution to the recording and interpre-tation of the variety of experiences of Middle Eastern Jews. This, in our view, is based on a very partial reading of the discipline of anthropology, in general, and Israeli research literature, in particular.[111] While ethnographic research often has overlooked power when making explicit formulations, the implicit assumption in both anthropology and folklore is that "significant human contact and creativity flowed from the margins to the centers more often than the reverse."[112] Applying this to our present concerns, and given the diversity that exists within Israeli society, we believe that one simply cannot know in advance which "peripheral" feature of society or culture might be found to be central. The social sciences cannot afford to abandon its methodological commitment to explore social life without theoretical dictates, since such dictates often work to exclude various fields or aspects of social life as "irrelevant."

Moreover, while theory is crucial, its drawbacks as well as its power must be kept in mind. Critical theory has furthered the understanding of Israeli society but—like other theories—has led to a situation in which areas close to those it has illuminated have been made invisible by its glare.[113] Shenhav, for instance, characterizes the story of the emissaries in Abadan as a "laboratory for [the study of] the hybrid-ization of ethnic identities"[114]—using a scientific image that was also popular among first-generation Israeli social scientists. Not surprisingly, the insights derived from Shenhav's analysis represent a continuation of a tendency to "sociologize history" that characterized the pre-critical approach.[115] A complementary approach, stemming from the natural history background of anthropology, emphasizes gath-ering data in the field. When Franz Boas, at the turn of the 20th century, formulated his ideas about culture and conducted fieldwork in accordance with them, he insisted that the more varied and analytically complex a phenomenon (like culture), the more it had to be studied as a product of history. In our view, to the extent that researchers prove capable of integrating varied theoretical insights and of taking complexity and plurality into account, both empirically and theoretically, we will learn that much more about Israeli—or indeed any—society.

Notes

This article is a joint effort to which the authors contributed equally. It is partially based on research supported by the Israel Science Foundation (grant no. 907/02); a grant from the Memorial Foundation of Jewish Culture (to Harvey Goldberg and Hagar Salamon); support from the Shaine Center for Research in the Social Sciences (to Harvey Goldberg); a grant by the Maurice Amado Foundation Research Fund in Sephardic Studies, UCLA (to Chen Bram); and a research grant from the Ben-Zvi Institute (to Chen Bram). Field data relating to the Caucasus Jews were gathered by Bram, and those concerning Jews from Libya by Goldberg. We both thank Hagar Salamon for comments on an earlier draft of the article.

1. The term "Middle Eastern" is used here inclusively to refer to Southwest Asia and North Africa. It does not help to insist on strict geographic definitions. Jews from Turkey may not see themselves as "Middle Easterners" even though they come from the region, whereas the activities of Jews from Iraq who moved, say, to India continued to be relevant to those still residing in Baghdad. Not all Jews of the Persian cultural sphere (for instance, those in Central Asia or the Jews in the Caucasus) reside in the Middle East in a narrow sense. Interestingly, western specialists in Middle Eastern studies have only recently expanded their purview to include those areas, in contrast to scholars of Jewry in the Middle East, who have always viewed "Bukharan" Jews as an example of "Eastern" Jewry. Our discussions of terminology should make clear that each term or phrase delineating cultural or ethnic phenomena has its advantages and drawbacks.

2. For the most comprehensive source, see Shmuel N. Eisenstadt, *The Absorption of Immigrants: A Comparative Study Based Mainly on the Jewish Community in Palestine and the State of Israel* (London: 1954).

3. Joseph Ben-David, "Ethnic Differences or Social Change?," in *Integration and Development in Israel*, ed. Shmuel N. Eisenstadt, Rivkah Bar-Yosef, and Chaim Adler (Jerusalem: 1970), 368–387 (originally published in Hebrew in *Megamot* 3 [1952], 171–183); Harvey Goldberg, "Historical and Cultural Dimensions of Ethnic Phenomena in Israel," in *Studies in Israeli Ethnicity: After the Ingathering*, ed. Alex Weingrod (New York: 1985), 179–200; Harvey E. Goldberg and Hagar Salamon, "From Laboratory to Field: Notes on Studying Diversity in Israeli Society," *Hagar: International Social Science Review* 3 (2002), 123–137.

4. Shmuel N. Eisenstadt, "The Oriental Jews in Palestine (A Report on a Preliminary Study in Culture-Contacts)," *Jewish Social Studies* 12 (1950), 199–222.

5. Daniel Lerner's *The Passing of Traditional Society: Modernizing the Middle East* (Glencoe: 1958) was one of the first social science works to deal with the notion of a "traditional" society. At the time, much of the emphasis was on the rural sector of "developing" societies, despite the fact that most Jewish immigrants to Israel did not come directly from rural settings. Their classification into "traditional" and "transitional" sectors appears in Eisenstadt, *The Absorption of Immigrants*, 118–124; the link with modernization theory appeared somewhat later. See also Henriette Dahan-Kalev, " 'Adatiyut beyisrael— nekudat mabat post-modernit," in *Moderniyut, post-moderniyut vehinukh*, ed. Ilan Gur Zeev (Tel Aviv: 1999), 197–231, and the discussion below.

6. See, for instance, Theodor Adorno, Else Frenkel-Brunswik, Daniel J. Levinson, and Nevitt R. Sanford, *The Authoritarian Personality* (New York: 1950); and Gordon Alport, *The Nature of Prejudice* (Cambridge, Mass.: 1954). Some researchers from the United States did attend to these issues, for instance, Judith T. Shuval, "Patterns of Inter-group Tension and Affinity," *International Social Science Bulletin* 8 (1956), 75–123, and Walter P. Zenner, "Ambivalence and Self-Image among Oriental Jews in Israel," *Jewish Journal of Sociology* 5 (1963), 214–223.

7. Sammy Smooha, *Israel: Pluralism and Conflict* (London: 1978).

8. Shlomo Swirski and Deborah Bernstein, "Mi 'avad bemah, 'avur mi utemurat mah? Hapituah hakalkali shel yisrael vehithavut halukat ha'avodah ha'adatit," *Mahbarot lemehkar ulevikoret* 4 (1980), 5–66.

9. Overviews of, and specific perspectives within, critical analysis appear in recent publications that address questions relating to Jews from the Middle East. See Hannan Hever, Yehouda Shenhav, and Pnina Motzafi-Haller, (eds.), *Mizrahim beyisrael: 'iyun bikorti mehudash* (Jerusalem: 2002); Gershon Shafir and Yoav Peled, *Being Israeli: The Dynamics of Multiple Citizenship* (Cambridge: 2002); Yehouda Shenhav, *Hayehudim ha'aravim: leumiyut, dat veetniyut* (Tel Aviv: 2003); Baruch Kimmerling, *Mehagrim, mityashvim, yelidim: hamedinah vehahevrah beyisrael bein ribui tarbuyot lemilhamot tarbut* (Tel Aviv: 2004);

Yossi Yonah and Yehuda Goodman (eds.), *Ma'arbolet hazehuyot: diyun bikorti bedatiyut uvehiloniyut beyisrael* (Jerusalem: 2004); Amnon Raz-Krakotzkin, "The Zionist Return to the West and the Mizrahi Jewish Perspective," in *Orientalism and the Jews*, ed. Ivan Davidson Kalmar and Derek J. Penslar (Waltham: 2005), 162–181; Gil Eyal, *Hasarat hakesem min hamizrah: toledot hamizrahanut be'idan hamizrahiyut* (Jerusalem: 1995), 108. (An English version has recently been published as *The Disenchantment of the Orient: Expertise in Arab Affairs and the Israeli State* [Stanford: 2006], but page citations refer here to the Hebrew version.) The current spate of books presenting overall political and cultural perspectives on Israeli society was noted by Alex Weingrod ("Habrerah haantropologit," paper delivered at the annual meeting of the Israel Anthropological Association, Sederot, May 2005).

10. Shafir and Peled, *Being Israeli*, 32–33. We agree that a major challenge in the study of Israeli society is not to "ghettoize" the topic of Arab groups within it (see Goldberg and Salamon, "From Laboratory to Field").

11. Hever, Shenhav, and Motzafi-Haller (eds.), *Mizrahim beyisrael*, 24–25.

12. See also Ella Shohat, *Zikhronot asurim: likrat mahshavah ravtarbutit* (Tel Aviv: 2001); idem, "The Invention of the Mizrahim," *Journal of Palestine Studies* 29 (1999), 5–20; Dahan-Kalev, " 'Adatiyut beyisrael."

13. Theda Skocpol, "Bringing the State Back In," *Items* 36 (1982), 1–8. An overview of the complexity of state-society relations in Israel is found in Baruch Kimmerling, "State Building, State Autonomy, and the Identity of Society: The Case of the Israeli State," *Journal of Historical Sociology* 6 (1993), 397–429.

14. Roland Calori, "Learning from Diversity: Philosophical Perspectives," *International Review of Sociology* 13 (2003), 591–605, esp. 597–598.

15. Harvey Goldberg, "Introduction: Culture and Ethnicity in the Study of Israeli Society," *Ethnic Groups* 1 (1978), 163–186.

16. In a historical development that is not clear, the term was transmuted in (Palestinian) Yiddish into *frenk*, and it became a pejorative way of referring to all "Sephardim." See Zenner, "Ambivalence and Self-Image among Oriental Jews in Israel."

17. Dorothy Willner, *Nation-Building and Community in Israel* (Princeton: 1969), 200.

18. Efrat Rosen-Lapidot, "Défrancophonisme in Israel: Bizertine Jews, Tunisian Jews," in *Homelands and Diasporas: Holy Lands and Other Places*, ed. André Levy and Alex Weingrod (Stanford: 2005), 270–295.

19. Anat Liebler, "Hastatistikah kearkhitekturah hevratit—'al kinunah shel halishkah hamerkazit lestatistikah kemosad apoliti" (Master's thesis, Tel Aviv University, 1998); Calvin Goldscheider, "Ethnic Categorization in Censuses: Comparing Observations from Israel, Canada and the United States," in *Census and Identity: The Politics of Race, Ethnicity, and Language in National Censuses*, ed. David I. Kertzer and Dominique Arel (Cambridge: 2001), 76–77.

20. Dvora Yanow, "From what *Edah* are You?" Israeli and American Meanings of 'Race-Ethnicity' in Social Policy Practices," *Israel Affairs* 5 (1999), 184. Terminological development is also discussed in Hanna Herzog, *'Adatiyut politit: dimui mul meziut* (Tel Aviv: 1986) and Zvi Ben-Dor, "Hahistoriyah hamuflaah shel hamizrahiyim," in *Hamahapekha hamizrahit: shalosh masot 'al haziyonut vehamizrahim*, ed. Inbal Perlson (Jerusalem: 1999), 87–106.

21. Michael Herzfeld, *Cultural Intimacy: Social Poetics in the Nation-state* (New York: 1997).

22. Chen Bram, "Visibility in Immigration: The Case of Caucasus Jews," paper presented at the Van Leer Workshop on Immigration, Jerusalem, February 2005.

23. This is a simplification, as evidenced by those ultra-Orthodox Ashkenazim who were known as the *'edah haredit* or by the title *Edot* that was given to the folklore and ethnology journal published in the late 1940s by Raphael Patai, which featured articles on European and Middle Eastern groups. Virginia Dominguez's *People as Subject, People as Object: Selfhood and Peoplehood in Contemporary Israel* (Madison: 1989), discusses more recent usages of the term.

24. Sammy Smooha, "Bikoret 'al girsah mimsadit 'adkanit shel hagishah hatarbutit besoziologiyah shel yahasei 'edot beyisrael," *Megamot* 29 (1985), 73–92, which relates to

Eliezer Ben-Rafael's *The Emergence of Ethnicity: Cultural Groups and Social Conflict in Israel* (Westport: 1982); see Ben-Rafael's reply, " 'Adatiyut: teoriyah umitos," *Megamot* 29 (1985), 190–205. See also Smooha's *Social Research on Jewish Ethnicity in Israel, 1948–1986* (Haifa: 1987).

25. Shlomo Swirski, *Israel: The Oriental Majority* (London: 1989), Eng. version of *Lo nehshalim ela menuhshalim* (Haifa: 1981), 1, 60–61.

26. Joëlle Bahloul, "The Sephardic Jew as Mediterranean: A View from Kinship and Gender," *Journal of Mediterranean Studies* 4 (1994), 197–207; Goldberg, "Historical and Cultural Dimensions of Ethnic Phenomena in Israel."

27. Shenhav, *Hayehudim ha'aravim*, 26.

28. The situation was variable: Jews from Iraq distanced themselves from the term *'edot hamizrah* even as Baghdadi Jews drew a distinction between themselves and the northern Kurdish Jews. See Esther Meir-Glitzenstein, " 'Olei 'irak beyisrael: hamaavak veha-hishtalvut," in *'Edot—'edut leyisrael: galut, 'aliyot, kelitah, terumah, umizug*, ed. Avshalom Mizrahi and Aharon Ben-David (Netanya: 2001), 509, 519; see also n. 31.

29. On differences between Jews from Africa and Asia during the early years of immigration, see Shafir and Peled, *Being Israeli*, 78; a more extended discussion is found in Karin Amit, "Mizrahim le'umat ashkenazim: hahalukah haetnit hadikhotomit vehazlahatam shel benei hador harishon vehasheni beshuk ha'avodah hayisreeli" (Ph.D. diss., Tel Aviv University, 2001).

30. See, for example, Issachar Ben-Ami (ed.), *The Sepharadi and Oriental Jewish Heritage: Studies* (Jerusalem: 1982).

31. Walter Weiker, *The Unseen Israelis: The Jews from Turkey in Israel* (Lanham: 1988), 1–2; Judith Goldstein, "Iranian Ethnicity in Israel: The Performance of Identity," in Weingrod (ed.), *Studies in Israeli Ethnicity*, 237–258. See also Haggai Ram, "Lo mizrah velo ma'arav, lo hurban velo geulah: haziyonut vihudei iran," *Teoriyah uvikoret* 26 (2005), 149–75. Ram argues that the case of the Jews of Iran challenges conventional dichotomies.

32. Guy Haskell, *From Sofia to Jaffa: The Jews of Bulgaria and Israel* (Detroit: 1994), 140–141.

33. Shafir and Peled, *Being Israeli*, 32.

34. Kimmerling, *Mehagrim, mityashvim, yelidim*, 323, n 2.

35. See, for example, Yigal Nizri (ed.), *Hazut mizrahit: hoveh han'a bisvakh 'avaro ha'aravi* (Tel Aviv: 2004).

36. An example is the way in which people from three different regions in Tunisia—Djerba; the town of Sfax in central Tunisia; and Bizerte in the north, have preserved and reworked their traditions in Israel. See Shlomo Deshen, "Ritualization of Literacy: The Works of Tunisian Scholars in Israel," *American Ethnologist* 2 (1975), 251–259; Esther Schely-Newman, *Our Lives Are But Stories: Narratives of Tunisian-Israeli Women* (Detroit: 2002); Rosen-Lapidot, "Défrancophonisme."

37. See, for example, Shafir and Peled, *Being Israeli*, 74; cf. Hever, Shenhav, and Mot-zafi-Haller (eds.), *Mizrahim beyisrael*, 17, where there is an explicit attempt to avoid highlighting this contrast.

38. There may or may not be a connection between *siknaj* and Nathan Alterman's term *shiknozi*, which he placed in the mouth of Yemenite domestic helpers in Tel Aviv ("the rag is Yemenite and the boss is *shiknozi*") in his "Shir Hateimaniyot" (Song of the Yemenites [female domestic helpers]), in his *Pizmonim veshirei zemer*, part 1 (Tel Aviv: 1977), 31. Another example of how European Jews and their cultural patterns were coded by Middle Easterners is the emergence (and passing?) of the term *vusvus* (from the Yiddish "what? what?") as an appellation for Ashkenazim.

39. Eyal, *Hasarat hakesem min hamizrah*, 105. Aranne is cited by Tom Segev in his *1949: The First Israelis* (New York: 1986), 174.

40. Cf. Edward Said, *Orientalism* (New York: 1978), ch. 2, on the theme of "orientalizing the oriental." The input of Mizrahi speech to the emergence of a new meaning of "Ashkenazic" was only one factor at work. See Dahan-Kalev, " 'Adatiyut beyisrael," 211, 224–225, which also stresses the emergent nature of the term.

252 Harvey E. Goldberg and Chen Bram

41. *Hayehudim ha'aravim*, which discusses an important episode in Iran (see below), cites many references to Jews in Iraq, but few on Jews in the former country.

42. Michael Zand, "Notes on the Culture of the Non-Ashkenazi Jewish Communities under Soviet Rule," *Soviet Jewish Affairs* 16 (1986), 379–442; Chen Bram, "Hakarah, he'ader hakarah vehakarah sheguyah bikvuẓot bekerev 'olei ḥever ha'amim," in *Rav tarbutiyut barei hayisreeli*, ed. Ohad Nahtomi (Jerusalem: 2003), 163–191; Anatoly Khazanov, *The Krymchaks: A Vanishing Group in the Soviet Union* (Jerusalem: 1989).

43. See the autobiographical sketch of Goitein in Robert Attal, *A Bibliography of the Writings of Shelomo Dov Goitein* (Jerusalem: 1975), xxiii.

44. Abraham L. Udovitch and Lucette Valensi, *The Last Arab Jews: The Communities of Jerba, Tunisia* (Chur: 1984).

45. A review by Yitzhak Dahan ("Waters of Babylon," *Azure* 19 [2005], 164–171) characterizes this picture as a generalization. Another review suggests that the book generalizes from its view of Iraqi Jewish experience to all Middle Eastern groups. See Galit Hasan-Rokem, "Haim mitaḥat lekhol ḥasifah mistateret hakhḥashah ḥadashah?" *Haaretz* literary supplement (4 April 2004). Cf. Shohat, "Invention of the Mizrahim," which offers a different assessment of Jewishness among Jews in Iraq.

46. Shenhav, *Hayehudim ha'aravim*, 267, nn. 62–63. Responding to Muammar Ghaddafi's call to Jews to return to their Arab homeland, Memmi had written an essay, which appeared in *Haaretz* on September 27, 1974, in which he outlined five factors that contributed to an inaccurate, idealized view of Jewish life in Arab lands. According to Shenhav, "Memmi forgets to place his position in the setting of current politics." Shenhav's point is questionable not only because Memmi himself indicates that he is no stranger to the idea that thought is shaped by politics (see his *Dominated Man* [Boston: 1969]), but perhaps even more so on epistemological grounds—attributing political motives to the historian's analysis and assessments is no substitute for evaluating them scientifically in terms of methods, evidence, and coherence.

47. Ammiel Alcalay, *After Jews and Arabs: Remaking Levantine Culture* (Minneapolis: 1993). On Iraq, in particular, see Nissim Qazzaz, *Hayehudim be'irak bemeah ha'esrim* (Jerusalem: 1991); Bram, "Hakarah, he'ader hakarah vehakarah sheguyah bikvuẓot bekerev 'olei ḥever ha'amim"; and Nancy Berg, *Exile from Exile: Israeli Writers from Iraq* (Albany: 1996). For a critical view of how Zionism and Egyptian nationalism alike read the history of Jews in Egypt through ideological lenses, see Joel Beinin, *The Dispersion of Egyptian Jewry: Culture, Politics, and the Formation of a Modern Diaspora* (Berkeley: 1998).

48. Reuven Snir, *'Araviyut, yahadut, ẓiyonut: maavak zehuyot biẓiratam shel yehudei 'irak* (Jerusalem: 2005).

49. Hever, Shenhav, and Motzafi-Haller (eds.), *Mizraḥim beyisrael*, 17.

50. Dahan-Kalev, "'Adatiyut beyisrael," stresses the importance of a contextual approach in studying ethnicity in Israel.

51. Hever, Shenhav, and Motzafi-Haller (eds.), *Mizraḥim beyisrael*, 17.

52. Ibid., 9–10.

53. It is possible to read "the *Mizrahi* subject" as referring to a topic of discourse, in which case use of a definite article is reasonable. The sentence, however, is followed by a quote from W.E.B. DuBois discussing "How does it feel to be a problem?," and the next paragraph refers to Gayatri Spivak's "Can the Subaltern Speak?," which makes it appear that the text is emphasizing actors, not "topics."

54. See ibid., 16, where the definite article appears three times: on lines 4 ("lisheelat hazehut hamizraḥit"), 14 ("hagdarat hazehut hamizraḥit"), and 18 ("hamizraḥiyut"), even as the discussion depicts how the category is socially constructed ("mizrahiyut" without a definite article also appears on the page). The inconstancy also appears on the next page (17), which opens with the claim that Mizrahi identity is fluid, insists toward the end of the page that the plural form is appropriate to the topic, but at the end of the second paragraph emphasizes the intention of the volume to "examine anew *the* Mizrahi topic" in Israel— expressed as "hasugiyah hamizraḥit," though it would have been possible to write "sugiyot hakeshurot lemizraḥiyut" (topics concerning Eastern-ness, or other related formulations).

We invite the Hebrew reader to peruse that chapter, along with the final one in the volume, and to judge to what extent the definite article *ha* might have been dropped from other phrases containing the term Mizrahi without affecting the meaning of the sentence.

55. The use of the Hebrew definite article in reinforcing unquestioned homogeneity appears in other central spheres of Israeli life, notably religion. Thus, "Judaism" becomes "hayahadut" and Jewish law is presented as "hahalakhah." On the importance of studying religion and ethnicity in Israel together, see Harvey E. Goldberg, "Ethnic and Religious Dilemmas of a Jewish State: A Cultural and Historical Perspective," in *State Formation and Ethnic Relations in the Middle East*, ed. Akira Usuki (Osaka: 2001), 47–64. This is also a theme in Shenhav, *Hayehudim ha'aravim* and in his "Haglimah, hakluv ve'arafel hakedushah: hashelihut haziyonit bamizrah kepraktikah gevulit bein 'leumiyut hilonit' le'teshukah datit'," in Yonah and Goodman (eds.), *Ma'arbolet hazehuyot*, 46–73. Penina Motzafi-Haller, "Datiyut, migdar uma'amad be'ayara midbarit," in ibid., 316–345, also examines the topics together. Other examples appear in this paper, but without extended discussion of the point.

56. Shafir and Peled, *Being Israeli*, 74 (n. 1), 78, 82. The phrase "the two groups" appears a second time on page 82, as does "the two ethnic groups" in material that they quote. Binary categorization is a conscious choice, because after pointing to different statistics concerning people from "Asia" as compared to "Africa," Shafir and Peled state that "the significant social reality is that both groups have been viewed as a uniform Mizrachi population" (ibid., 79). Our question is: viewed by whom, in which contexts, and based on what evidence?

57. Ibid., 78.

58. Ibid., ch. 3; Judith Butler, *Gender Trouble: Feminism and the Subversion of Identity* (New York: 1999).

59. See Harvey E. Goldberg, *Jewish Life in Muslim Libya* (Chicago: 1990), ch. 5.

60. Nitza Druyan, *Beain marvad-kesamim: 'olei teiman beerez yisrael,1881–1914* (Jerusalem: 1981); Yehudah Nini, *Teiman veziyon: hareka' hamedini, hahevrati, veharuhani la'aliyot harishonot meteiman, 1800–1914* (Jerusalem: 1982). See also notes 64 and 78.

61. Shafir and Peled, *Being Israeli*, 75–76.

62. Yehudah Nini, *Hehayit o halamti halom: teimanei kineret—parashat hityashvutam ve'akiratam, 1912–1930* (Tel Aviv: 1996).

63. This critique is misplaced, as it ignores both Nini's aim of elucidating the Kinneret affair's historical complexity as well as his reference to it as a "metaphor" (*mashal*) that has wider implications for the understanding of Israeli society. See Hever, Shenhav, and Motzafi-Haller (eds.), *Mizrahim beyisrael*, 299; cf. Nini, *Hehayit o halamti halom*, 15–17.

64. Joseph Glass and Ruth Kark, *Sephardi Entrepreneurs in Eretz Israel: The Amzalek Family, 1816–1918* (Jerusalem: 1991).

65. Shenhav, *Hayehudim ha'aravim*.

66. Ibid., 48.

67. Ibid., 43.

68. On Hai Yissakharov, see ibid., 42, 58, and 61; on Yerahmiel Asa (formerly Isaiylov), see ibid., 100. Data on Rashi Yissakharov are from interviews by Chen Bram. See his " 'Mitnagdim anu lehityashvut meyuhedet shel 'edot mizrahiyot,' yehudei hahar mekavkaz: 'al hakarah, hishtalvut vezehut," in Mizrahi and Ben-David (eds.), *'Edot—'edut leyisrael*, 547–571. Various terms have been applied to Caucasus Jews. They are at times referred to as "Caucasian Jews," sometimes as "Mountain Jews" (*heharariyim* or *yehudei hahar*), and now are often called *Kavkazim*.

69. Shenhav, *Hayehudim ha'aravim*, 100.

70. Mordechai Altshuler, *Yehudei mizrah kavkaz: toledot hayehudim heharariyim mereishit hameah hatesha' 'esrei* (Jerusalem: 1990), 506–509, 512; Bram, "Mitnagdim anu lehityashvut meyuhedet shel 'edot mizrahiyot."

71. Asa replaced another member of Knesset, Avraham Abas, and for this reason served for only two years. As Esther Meir has shown, relations between Mapai and leaders of "Mizrahi" origin were not merely a matter of the former co-opting the latter. See her article "Mehuyavuyot mitnagshot: hamanhigut hamizrahit beMapa"i bishnotehah harishonot shel hamedinah," *Yisrael* 5 (2004), 63–97. Meir does not include Asa in her discussion. The fact

that Asa was considered by members of his party to represent "Sephardim" (and replaced another MK representing this sector) can also be inferred from his position on the board of the Federation of Sephardic Communities. In addition to being an emissary in Abadan, Asa was sent on state missions to Iran, Iraq, and Turkey in 1954 and 1955.

72. Bram, "Mitnagdim anu lehityashvut meyuḥedet shel 'edot mizraḥiyot," 555.

73. Shenhav, *Hayehudim ha'aravim*, 58; we offer this as a *possible* interpretation.

74. We are grateful to Sergio DellaPergola for pointing this out to us. Sereni's father was a noted physician, and he himself earned a doctoral degree.

75. In this regard, see Haim Blanc, *Communal Dialects in Baghdad* (Cambridge, Mass.: 1964), which is based on field research among immigrants in Israel in the 1950s and on the speech of Muslims and Christians whom Blanc interviewed elsewhere. This monograph is a pioneer effort in conceptualizing the realm of "communal dialects," a sociolinguistic phenomenon that is by no means peripheral (cf. David M. Bunis, Joseph Chetrit, and Haideh Sahim, "Jewish Languages Enter the Modern Era," in *The Jews of the Middle East and North Africa in Modern Times*, ed. Reeva Spector Simon, Michael M. Laskier, and Sara Reguer [New York: 2003], 113–141). While the Jews spoke a Judeo-Arabic dialect, to what extent and in which ways it differed from the speech of Muslim (or Christian) groups was everywhere an empirical question. The hyphenated term Judeo-Arabic has long been used to describe an empirical linguistic phenomenon that is one aspect of an ongoing social involvement, along with the maintenance of difference, that characterized Jewish life in Muslim settings for centuries (Goldberg, *Jewish Life in Muslim Libya*).

76. Shafir and Peled, *Being Israeli*, 74; Shenhav, *Hayehudim ha'aravim*, 26–27. Shohat ("Sephardim in Israel") was influential in arguing that there was no resonance between Zionism and the experience of Jews in the Middle East.

77. See Amnon Netzer, "Persian Jewry and Literature: A Sociocultural View," in *Sephardi and Middle Eastern Jewries: History and Culture in the Modern Era*, ed. Harvey E. Goldberg (Bloomington: 1996), 240–255. The experiences of the Zionist emissaries in Iraq might also be fruitfully compared with the encounter of Jewish Palestinian soldiers in the British Eighth Army with Libyan Jews. See Yoav Gelber, *Toledot hahitnadvut*, vol. 3 (Jerusalem: 1983), 95–131. See also Maurice Roumani, "Zionism and Social Change in Libya at the Turn of the Century," *Studies in Zionism* 8 (1987), 1–24. The Libyan case is discussed below.

78. For a brief but cogent statement, see Zvi Yehudah, "Diyun" in Yehudah Nini, *Yahasan shel Ḥibat Ẕiyon vehatenu'ah haẕiyonit le'aliyah meteiman* (Jerusalem: 1977), 42–45. Specific studies are cited in Goldberg (ed.), *Sephardi and Middle Eastern Jewries*, 25–26. Regarding Jews in the Caucasus, see Yisrael Kloizner, "Hatenu'ah haẕiyonit bekavkaz bereishitah," *Shvut* 8 (1981), 86–98; Bram, " 'Mitnagdim anu lehityashvut meyuḥedet shel 'edot mizraḥiyot."

79. Early developments are described in Roumani, "Zionism and Social Change in Libya at the Turn of the Century." For overviews, see Renzo De Felice, *Jews in an Arab Land: Libya, 1835–1870*, trans. Judith Roumani (Austin: 1985), and Yaakov Hajjaj-Liluf, *Toledot yehudei luv* (n. p.: 2000). For the perspectives of two Zionist emissaries and one local leader, see Ben-Zion Rubin (ed.) *Luv—hedim min hayoman* (Netanya: 1988).

80. Amishadai Guweta, "Irgun 'Ben-Yehudah' uveit hasefer 'Hatikvah,' " in *Sefer yahadut luv*, ed. Frija Zuarets, Amishadai Guweta, Zuriel Shaked, Gavriel Arviv, and Frija Tayar (Tel Aviv: 1960), 144.

81. Roberto Bachi, "A Statistical Analysis of the Revival of Hebrew in Israel," *Scripta Hieroslymitana* 3 (1956), 229.

82. Eisenstadt, "The Oriental Jews in Palestine," 202.

83. Gur Alroey, *Imigrantim: hahagirah hayehudit leerez yisrael bereishit hamaeh ha'esrim* (Jerusalem: 2004), 32–33; Hanna Herzog, "Hamusagim 'yishuv yashan' ve 'yishuv ḥadash' behe'arah soẕiologit," *Cathedra* 32 (1984), 99–109; Shenhav, *Hayehudim ha'aravim*, 78–84.

84. Adriana Kemp, " 'Nedidat 'amim' o 'habe'erah hagedolah': shelitat medinatit vehitnagdut bisfar hayisreeli," in Hever, Shenhav, and Motzafi-Haller (eds.), *Mizraḥim beyisrael*, 36–67.

85. Willner, *Nation-building and Community in Israel*; Alex Weingrod, *Reluctant Pioneers: Village Development in Israel* (Ithaca: 1966).

86. Kemp, " 'Nedidat 'amim' o 'habe'erah hagedolah'," 39.

87. Willner, *Nation-building and Community in Israel*, 169–199.

88. Ibid., 190.

89. Meir-Glitzenstein, " 'Olei 'irak beyisrael."

90. Erik Cohen and Yosef Katan, *Kehilah ketanah bemerḥav metropolitani: meḥkar kehilati 'al or yehudah beezor tel aviv* (Jerusalem: 1966).

91. Eyal, *Hasarat hakesem min hamizraḥ*, 108.

92. Harvey E. Goldberg, *Cave Dwellers and Citrus Growers: A Jewish Community in Libya and Israel* (Cambridge: 1972), 54–56.

93. Schely-Newman, *Our Lives Are But Stories*.

94. Such a research orientation also was formulated early on in anthropological research. See Alex Weingrod, "Reciprocal Change: A Case Study of a Moroccan Immigrant Village in Israel," *American Anthropologist* 64 (1962), 115–131.

95. Goldberg, *Cave Dwellers and Citrus Growers*, 86. This statement refers to people considered adults upon settling on the moshav in the early 1950s. Younger people were sensitive to ethnic categories in contexts outside of the moshav.

96. For example, Knesset members Raphael Pinhasi from the veteran Bukharan community, or Amnon Cohen from the Bukharan immigrant community of the 1970s. By contrast, no subgroup affiliated with the party is from a family originating in the Caucasus. Perhaps because the "ethnic" aspect of Shas seems so obvious, it has prompted little research. One of the few studies to date is that of Anat Feldman, "Hakamat tenu'at Sha' 's: matarot vedarkhei pe'ulah," in *Sha' 's: hebetim tarbutiyim vera'yoniyim*, ed. Aviezer Ravitzky (Tel Aviv: 2006), 428.

97. Yoram Bilu, "Personal Motivation and Social Meaning in the Revival of Hagiolatric Traditions among Moroccan Jews in Israel," in *Tradition, Innovation, Conflict—Jewishness and Judaism in Israel*, ed. Zvi Sobel and Benjamin Beit-Hallahmi (Albany: 1991), 47–69. Field research by André Levy, while not directly concerned with Shas but reflecting the period during which that movement grew, shows the intricate and creative processes involved in such an incremental confluence of different religious cultures. See André Levy, "Hilula rabah ve'azeret teshuvah: nituaḥ mikreh," in *Meḥkarim betarbutam shel yehudei zefon afrikah*, ed. Issahar Ben-Ami (Jerusalem: 1991), 167–179. See also the essays by Kimmy Caplan and Nissim Leon in this volume.

98. Zvi Zohar, " 'Lehaḥazir 'atarah leyoshenah'—ḥazono shel harav 'Ovadyah," in *Sha' 's: etgar hayisreeliyut*, ed. Yoav Peled (Tel Aviv: 2001), 159–209. See also Nissim Leon's essay in this volume.

99. Cf. Shlomo Deshen, "Ritualization of Literacy."

100. *Nusaḥ yehudei kavkaz* appeared on the cover, but the first page also carried a subtitle: *Keminhag hasefaradim uvnei 'edot hamizraḥ yozei kavkaz* [According to the custom of the Sephardim and *'edot hamizraḥ* from the Caucasus].

101. Motti Regev and Edwin Seroussi, *Popular Music and National Culture in Israel* (Berkeley: 2004), 191–247. A discussion of Haddad's music (pp. 233–235) contains no reference to her background, but Chen Bram has witnessed Caucasus Jews commenting on her omission of their music in a performance. A discussion of social messages in Haddad's songs would also be interesting; some lyrics challenge patriarchal power. Whereas one might label this as especially "Mizrahi" or else as equally relevant to Israeli society generally, some young women from the Caucasus express the view that it relates specifically to their situation.

102. See, for example, Hagar Salamon, "The Ambivalence over the Levantinization of Israel: 'David Levi' Jokes," *Humor: International Journal of Humor Research* (forthcoming).

103. Bram, "Visibility in Immigration."

104. Yochanan Peres, *Yaḥasei 'edot beyisrael* (Tel Aviv: 1976), provided a view of the situation until the early 1970s. For a generation after statehood there was a slow but steady increase in the rate of marriages crossing the European-Middle Eastern divide, reaching the

level of about one-fourth of all marriages. In social class terms, rates were low in the extremes of the socioeconomic scale but higher in the middling ranges where cross-*'edah* marriages did not entail major shifts of status for either partner. The broad estimation of one-fourth of all marriages crossing the Asia-Africa/Europe-America rubrics was still in place in the 1980s. See Uziel ,O. Schmelz, Sergio DellaPergola, and Uri Avner, *Ethnic Differences among Israeli Jews: A New Look* (Jewish Population Studies, No. 22) (Jerusalem: 1990), 37–50. Neither of these studies examined possible interesting patterns of endogamy within and "marriage exchange" among specific country-of-origin groups. See, however, Sergio Della-Pergola essay in this volume, esp. 24–25.

105. Barbara S. Okun, "The Effects of Ethnicity and Educational Attainment on Jewish Marriage Patterns: Changes in Israel, 1957–1995," *Population Studies* 55 (2001), 49–64; idem, "Insight into Ethnic Flux: Marriage Patterns among Jews of Mixed Ancestry in Israel," *Demography* 41 (2004), 173–187; Binyamin Gshur and Barbara S. Okun, "Generational Effects on Marriage Patterns: Jewish Immigrants and Their Descendants in Israel," *Journal of Marriage and the Family* 65 (2003), 287–310.

106. Okun, "Insight into Ethnic Flux." On the general importance of generational differences when studying ethnic-related trends, see Amit, *Mizrahiyim le'umat ashkenazim*, 100–111.

107. Hever, Shenhav, and Motzafi-Haller (eds.), *Mizrahim beyisrael*, 300–301. On cultural analysis of *Salah Shabati* and its reception in different audiences, see Goldberg and Salamon, "From Laboratory to Field," 127.

108. Schmelz, DellaPergola, and Avner (eds.), *Ethnic Differences among Israeli Jews*, 34–37.

109. One could obviously expand the list of categories here. On "traditionality," see Yaakov Yadgar and Yishayahu [Charles] Liebman, "Me'ever ledikhotomiyah 'dati-hiloni': hamasoratim beyisrael," in *Yisrael vehamoderniyut: leMoshe Lissak beyovlo*, ed. Uri Cohen, Eliezer Ben-Rafael, Avi Bareli, and Efraim Ya'ar (Jerusalem: 2007), 337–366.

110. Ben-David, "Ethnic Differences or Social Change?" (emphasis added). See also Harvey Goldberg, "The Changing Meaning of Ethnic Affiliation," *Jerusalem Quarterly* 44 (1987), 39–50.

111. Hever, Shenhav, and Motzafi-Haller (eds.), *Mizrahim beyisrael*, 292–294 (emphasis added). Space does not permit further discussion here.

112. Renato Resaldo, Smadar Lavie, and Kirin Narayan, "Introduction," in Smadar Lavie, Kirin Narayan, and Renato Rosaldo, *Creativity / Anthropology* (Ithaca: 1993), 2. This statement reflects upon the work of anthropologist Victor Turner, and it would also hold true for one of the people who influenced him, French ethnographer Arnold Van Gennep.

113. The image is taken from Talcott Parsons, *The Structure of Social Action* (Glencoe, Ill.: 1949), 17.

114. Shenhav, *Hayehudim ha'aravim*, 48.

115. Goldberg and Salamon, "From Laboratory to Field"; Goldberg, "Introduction: Culture and Ethnicity in the Study of Israeli Society," 166.

Review Essays

The Shaping of Israeli Historiography of the Holocaust

Orna Kenan, *Between Memory and History: The Evolution of Israeli Historiography of the Holocaust, 1945–1961.* New York: Peter Lang, 2003. xxviii + 139 pp.

Holocaust historiography, whose origins go back to the event itself, has expanded immensely in recent decades. The initial lack of historical distance highlighted the inherent problematics of the field, which has been marked throughout by recurrent controversy and the emergence of different schools of thought. In recent years, a number of scholars have examined the factors and circumstances that shape the landscape of Holocaust research—in particular, its national, social, and geographical settings. For example, in a most interesting Ph.D. thesis, Conny Kristel analyzed the work of three Dutch Jewish historians who wrote comprehensive histories of the Holocaust of Dutch Jewry.[1] Nicolas Berg generated intense debate among German historians with his lengthy (776 pages) critical study of West German historians.[2] In November 2004, Yad Vashem organized a conference titled "Holocaust Historiography in Context: The Emergence of Approaches and Research Centers." And Israeli historiography has come under scrutiny in two Ph.D. theses, one of which, authored by Orna Kenan, has now been published as *Between Memory and History*.[3]

Kenan's volume covers the period from the establishment of the state of Israel in 1948 through the Eichmann trial of 1961 (viewed by the author as the turning point in Israeli Holocaust historiography) before concluding with a 15-page overview of Israeli Holocaust historiography from 1961 until the present. Kenan focuses primarily on the 1950s, seeking to explain the historiography of this period against the background of the Yishuv's approach to the Holocaust in the 1940s, on the one hand, and the beginnings of research conducted among survivors and resistance fighters in D.P. camps between 1945 and 1948, on the other. Kenan's approach, which is both analytical and descriptive, is based on archival material, newspapers, and scholarly studies on Israeli society in the 1950s.

Kenan's basic thesis is that there was a deep "interaction between memory and historical writing in shaping Israel's historiography of the Holocaust period." As she elaborates:

The destruction of a major part of European Jewry, followed shortly thereafter by the establishment of the state of Israel, started an ongoing process of engagement between a past that continues to influence the life and identity of the nation and a present in which the nation's changing sense of self leads to successive transformations in the perception of that past. In this process, historical narration and collective memory often seem interwoven. Indeed...for each changing phase in the memory of the Holocaust, a related move in its historiography also took place (pp. xiv–xv).

Specifically during the 1950s, as a result of Israel's establishment and the need to strengthen national identity, one witnesses the "imposition of a Zionist paradigm of explanation of the Holocaust," which included the negation of exile (*shelilat ha-galut*) (p. 73), on the one hand, and the creation of a pantheon "occupied by the partisans and ghetto fighters" (p. 75), on the other.

A basic issue that must be dealt with in any work of this type is the matter of definitions. What is historiography, what should be included under the rubric of Israeli historiography of the Holocaust, who are the professionals, and who are the Israeli historians of the Holocaust? Kenan does not deal systematically with these issues. She does briefly allude to the relationship between history and memory and clearly opts for an approach that, following Eric Hobsbawm and Amos Funkenstein, emphasizes the interwovenness of the two. However, she fails to define what kind of studies are to be included in the category of (academic) historiography as opposed to various forms of popular writing such as journalism and memoir. Throughout the book, it becomes apparent that Kenan considers school books, memorial services, and *yizkor bikher* (memorial volumes) to be "historiography." However, the manifestly professional products of academic historiography such as *Yad Vashem Studies*—which began publication in 1957—are omitted. As a result, the concept of historiography is blurry, and what Kenan presents us with are only some of the popular historical images in the collective memory of Israeli society.

This is a troublesome matter, given that the main thrust of public "memory" of the Holocaust in Israel during the 1950s differed greatly from the academic subjects being researched at the time. Whereas the Israeli public was obsessed with the issues of Jewish resistance and heroism, and debates about their meaning for the nation (with collaboration as their negative polar opposite), scholarly writing from the mid-1950s focused on a broad array of issues. Most prominent, of course, was research on two subjects: antisemitism in all its variations, and resistance. But in addition, as evidenced by the titles of some of the articles appearing in the first three volumes of *Yad Vashem Studies*, published in the years 1957 to 1959, there was considerable interest in research methodologies; Jewish organizations in Germany during the first years of the Nazi regime; the year 1938 as a crucial point in the development of anti-Jewish policies; the Jews of France; the German foreign office and the Palestine question, 1933–1939; the role of the Gestapo in obstructing and promoting Jewish emigration; Jewish refugees in the U.S.S.R. during the Second World War; and the anti-Nazi boycott movement in the United States. Clearly, the foci and concerns of public memory of the Holocaust are far narrower in scope than those of scholarly research on that subject.

Regarding the "professional historians," Kenan, in a sweeping statement, declares that

[i]n *Eretz Yisrael* as well as throughout the West, during the two decades following the war, professional historians—whether they were Jewish historians or not—did not address the history of the Jewish catastrophe in Europe. If we take the most illustrious Jewish historians of the 1940s . . . (in the Anglo-Saxon world), and in Jerusalem . . . , none of them turned to the history of the Shoah (p. xv).

I firmly disagree with this observation. Numerous "professional" historians throughout the West dealt with the Holocaust during the two decades in question, among them Jacques Presser and Lou de Jong in the Netherlands; Wolfgang Scheffler, Martin Broszat, and Helmut Krausnick in West Germany; and Raul Hilberg in the United States. Some of them—there were, of course, others—were engaged at the time in writing doctoral dissertations on Holocaust-related topics. Yet even if Kenan's statement is taken to refer only to *established* professional historians, it is inaccurate. (Presser, for instance, was at the time a professor of modern history who had previously written about the French and American revolutions.)

To be sure, most established university-based historians did not deal with the Holocaust during the first two postwar decades. The reason for this is quite obvious: it is one of the basic assumptions of historiography that only with the passing of time—perhaps several decades—can the distance and perspective required for historical analysis be attained. The writing of "instant history" was thus quite novel, and in the case of the Holocaust it was undertaken mainly by survivors with some historical training, for whom it was a tool for coming to terms with their own past.[4] Especially in the D.P. camps following the war, these "professionals" were assisted by others who wanted to record what had happened while their memories were still fresh.

In addition, as Kenan herself shows, as a result of the Holocaust, many old-guard members of the "Jerusalem school" who dealt with other historical periods began to look into antisemitism in earlier periods.[5] In that sense, they too were involved in an aspect of Holocaust research. This phenomenon was not confined to Israeli historiographers; throughout the world, whether in the United States (Hannah Arendt, Theodor Adorno), Great Britain (James Parkes), France (Jules Isaac, Leon Poliakov) or, of course, Germany, historians—along with political scientists, psychologists, and philosophers—turned their attention to the study of the origins and development of antisemitism *in light of* the Holocaust.

As noted, historiography—the writing of history in accordance with certain disciplinary rules and principles—is traditionally associated with university history departments and research institutions. In this regard, Kenan focuses on Yad Vashem, the Holocaust Martyrs' and Heroes' Remembrance Authority. She describes the heated polemics between two "camps" of historians at the institution during the second half of the 1950s. The first consisted of younger historians, students, and protégés of Prof. Ben-Zion Dinur, one of the world's leading Jewish historians, whom he brought together in the Institute for the Study of the Destruction of European Jewry and Its History in Recent Generations, under the joint auspices of Yad Vashem and the Hebrew University. The second included some of those historians previously referred to—namely, survivor historians of Polish origin, who did not have any formal university affiliation but who had begun to engage in Holocaust research while still in the D.P. camps. After coming to Israel, some of them had worked at Beit Lohamei Hagetaot (Ghetto Fighters' House)—which, established at Kibbutz Lohamei Hagetaot in 1950, was Israel's first Holocaust museum.

Kenan regards the conflict between these two camps as a battle over the primacy of the Zionist paradigm. Yet she misses some major points relating to the context of the debate and its implications. For instance, why should there be any discussion of the views of historians at Yad Vashem? Wasn't its institutional purpose commemorational and monumental in nature? Indeed, in the initial discussions regarding the basic concept of Yad Vashem (some of which took place as early as 1942), the commemorative and monumental aspects were uppermost. But when this memorial institution was officially established in 1953, it embarked on a different path. Dinur, who at the time was minister of education, was appointed chairman of Yad Vashem; for him, commemoration was equated with historical research, not monuments. Thus, for the first years of its existence, Yad Vashem centered its activities on the gathering of archival materials, on research, and on publication.

Although this cannot be documented, it appears that Dinur conceived of Yad Vashem somewhat along the lines of the Institut für Zeitgeschichte in Munich, which had been established by the West German government in order to research Nazism and the Third Reich (it later became a leading institution in this field). He may also have had in mind the YIVO Institute (in New York), the Jewish Historical Institute (ŻIH) in Warsaw, or the State Institute for War Documentation in Amsterdam. Yet despite these models, the decision to steer Yad Vashem in the direction of historical research was not the most obvious course to take, and it thus calls for analysis and explanation. Unfortunately, Kenan does not address the issue.

Neither does Kenan examine the state of university-based historical research in Israel in the 1950s (or, for that matter, in the years following 1961). Was Israeli historiography at all comparable to German or American historiography? I doubt this. For one thing, the academic base was much smaller. Until 1955, Israel's only university was the Hebrew University in Jerusalem, which had two separate history departments for general and Jewish history. Apart from the handful of historians teaching there, a number of others, some of them employed as high school teachers, published their research findings in *Zion*—at the time, Israel's sole historical journal. Kenan mentions the fact that a number of survivor historians were taken on at Yad Vashem despite some reservations about their professional level. What she fails to note, however, is that Dinur, via the Institute for the Study of the Destruction of European Jewry and Its History in Recent Generations, succeeded in getting some Hebrew University doctoral students, such as Nathaniel Katzburg, Uriel Tal, Daniel Carpi, and Bela Vago, and others, including Leni Yahil and Shaul (Eschwege) Esh (who hitherto had specialized in linguistics and ancient Jewish history) to focus their research on topics relating to the Holocaust. He thus began training a cadre of professional Holocaust historians. Moreover, in 1958, with the establishment of the Institute of Contemporary Jewry, Holocaust studies began to be offered at the Hebrew University (Esh taught the first course). In the following year, a Holocaust chair, the first in the world, was established at the recently founded Bar-Ilan University.

In a chapter titled "Israel's 'Pantheon' and the 'Silence' of the Survivors during the 1950s," Kenan claims that Israeli public discourse in the 1950s emphasized the negation of the exile to the extent that only fighters and resisters could be integrated into the national pantheon of heroes. Other survivors had no place in this pantheon and were reduced to "silence." According to Kenan, "the imposition of a Zionist paradigm of explanation on the Holocaust . . . hindered the survivors' natural desire . . . to publicly acknowledge, experience and mourn their loss" (p. 73).

This thesis is not new. It was formulated by several post-Zionist authors in the 1980s and 1990s,[6] and it has also been expressed in certain literary works, especially those of Aharon Appelfeld. Yet in the last decade, research by Dalia Ofer, Hanna Yablonka, and Judith Baumel has demonstrated that, at the time, survivors were intensely involved in a number of Holocaust-related issues such as restitution, the establishment of an official Holocaust commemoration day, and the bringing to trial of collaborators.[7] Kenan herself discusses the media coverage of the debate within Yad Vashem at the end of the 1950s and indicates that the general public—undoubtedly "Zionist"—supported the survivor historians as against Dinur and his entourage (the "Zionist establishment"). In other words, within a Zionist society and even among Zionist elites, there could be different "Zionist" approaches.

Dinur saw the Holocaust as the culmination of antisemitism that was an inherent feature of the Jews' abnormal national existence in exile. As a historian, he was interested in the ways in which antisemitism—especially its "modern" variant—had developed into the Nazis' murderous campaign. For this reason, Yad Vashem's initial research program focused on periods well before the actual Holocaust. Kenan characterizes this approach as "Zionist." But were the survivor historians who chose another path of research any less Zionist? Their stated approach was to view the Jewish people in *organic* terms. The Holocaust, in their interpretation, had proved that this organism was "ill," and it was the historian's task, as it would be with a physician, to analyze the sources of illness, offer a prognosis, and point to ways in which the diseased body might be cured. Accordingly, the survivor historians urged an emphasis on Jewish society between 1933 and 1945 and not so much on the Germans and antisemites who had initiated and carried out the destruction and murder before and during the Nazi period. In their view, the focus should be on such issues as the failure of Jewish leadership and the lack of solidarity by Jews elsewhere (including those of the Yishuv), in addition to more "uplifting" aspects of Holocaust history, in particular the physical and spiritual resistance demonstrated by Jews.[8] They, too, prescribed the establishment of a strong Jewish state in Israel as the cure for the nation's endemic ills. In sum, the Yad Vashem debate should be seen as revolving around the proper "meaning" of the Holocaust (and Holocaust research), and its proper analysis and interpretation, from *different Zionist viewpoints*—a point that Kenan overlooks entirely.

Similarly, Kenan attempts to explain the phenomenon of *yizkor bikher* as resulting from the "imposition of a Zionist paradigm of explanation" of the Holocaust. In her view, in order to "give vent to [their] repressed impulse" to publicly acknowledge, experience, and mourn their loss, surviving members of *landsmanshaftn* were encouraged to write about their wartime experiences (p. 73). While this is an interesting explanation, Kenan brings no proof to sustain her claim. In addition, the hypothesis itself is open to question: what about *yizkor bikher* that were conceived or published outside of Israel? Why is it that such commemorative books were almost entirely limited to East European communities (Poland, Czechoslovakia, the eastern parts of Hungary)—did West European survivors have no need to "give vent to this repressed impulse"? And finally, why were the historical chapters in many of these books written by historians? A more plausible explanation, I believe, is that the *yizkor bikher* were a kind of monument for vanished Jewish communities in Eastern Europe, generally behind the Iron Curtain and inaccessible to tourists, and a collective tombstone for the many individual lives whose traces had been destroyed there. Thus, *yizkor bikher* should be seen as a complex mixture of commemoration, mourning, working-through, and historiography that emerged in the context of the Cold War and that represented a typically East European Jewish concept of communality.

As noted, Kenan regards the Eichmann trial as the turning point in Israeli Holocaust historiography. This is the case, she explains, because of

> the emotional reaction of Israelis to the trial of Adolf Eichmann.... The amount and intensity of survivors' testimonies provoked countless questions and uncertainties which shuddered [sic] the simplified image of the passive victims, which had prevailed until then vis-à-vis the dominant image of the "heroic" Israeli or, its mirror image, the heroic fighter (p. 77).

Fully half of the chapter dealing with the Eichmann trial focuses on public discourse rather than historiography, and when Kenan finally arrives at the historiography, she claims that "the fundamental change that occurred as a result of the Eichmann trial became evident in the fact that antisemitism became the subject of serious historical research" (p. 84). To support this contention, Kenan quotes from the writings of Shmuel Ettinger, Jacob Talmon, and Jacob Katz. Talmon, however, had done "serious" research on antisemitism back in the early 1950s, whereas Katz dealt explictly with the topic from the end of the 1950s and was clearly aware of its significance well before then.[9] Moreover, some of the young historians brought by Dinur to Yad Vashem during the second half of the 1950s researched antisemitism in various countries, with Katzburg focusing on Hungary, Vago on Romania, and Tal on Germany. Yahil's doctoral thesis on the rescue of Danish Jewry (completed in 1964) had earlier arisen out of her work at Yad Vashem, not because of the Eichmann trial.

In all, scholarly research on antisemitism was well-advanced in Israel before the Eichmann trial. But the most important factor in the development of Holocaust research in Israel was the change in direction at Yad Vashem following the resolution of its internal debate and the ouster of Dinur. Under Arye Kubovy (who replaced him), Yad Vashem channeled its resources into monumental commemoration. The Institute for the Study of the Destruction of European Jewry was disbanded, and support for the work of the survivor historians at Yad Vashem was virtually withdrawn. Many of them moved to the Hebrew University's Institute of Contemporary Jewry, which soon replaced Yad Vashem as Israel's main center of Holocaust research. Within its walls a new generation of scholars blossomed; among them were to be found Yehuda Bauer, Dov Levin, Shaul Esh, and later, Yisrael (Israel) Gutman. Thus, contrary to Kenan's claim, the first turning point in Israeli Holocaust historiography dates back to the end of the 1950s. A second turning point occurred during the first half of the 1970s, as a result both of the growth in Holocaust awareness in the 1960s (due, among other things, to the Eichmann trial, to the impact of Rolf Hochhut's play *The Deputy* [1962], Arthur Morse's critical study of U.S. behavior during the Holocaust, *While Six Million Died* [1967], and, probably most of all, to the apprehensions and memories stirred up by the Six-Day War) and of the growth of the university system and the increasing popularity of Holocaust studies among both scholars and students. In the long run, then, Dinur and his emphasis on historical research proved victorious. Israeli historiography increasingly focused on internal Jewish issues of the Holocaust era, leaving "perpetrator history" to German (and a handful of other) historians.

Kenan's failure to explore certain contextual issues seems partly the result of her ignoring a number of important archival sources, among them Meir (Mark) Dworzecki's papers at Yad Vashem[10] and the archives found at the Hebrew University and at YIVO. In addition, Kenan has not systematically checked bibliographic sources—periodicals, conference proceedings, and articles found on RAMBI (an online index of articles on Jewish studies, produced by the Jewish National and University Library at the Hebrew University). Similarly, the topics of Holocaust courses taught at Israeli universities from 1958 onwards are overlooked.

More regrettable is Kenan's neglect of an invaluable resource for contemporary historians: interviews. Many of the Holocaust historians mentioned (and unmentioned) in *Between Memory and History* were still alive when Kenan began her research in the late 1990s, among them Joseph Kermisz, Jozeph (Melkman) Michman, Yehuda Bauer, Israel Gutman, Daniel Carpi, Leni Yahil, Otto Dov Kulka, Nathaniel Katzburg, Zwi Bacharach, Livia Rothkirchen, Mendel Piekarcz, Aharon Weiss, Shmuel Krakowski, Joseph Walk, and Saul Friedlander; some of them are still active in the field. By foregoing interviews, Kenan missed an opportunity to gain first-hand insight into the motivations and worldviews of many of the major figures in Israeli Holocaust historioigraphy.

Between Memory and History also contains a number of regrettable mistakes. For instance, Kenan states: "Already in 1940 Jabotinsky called for the speedy evacuation of a million Polish Jews and their resettlement in Palestine within one year" (p. 8). In fact, Jabotinsky's plan was proposed in 1936; over time, it underwent an interesting evolution.[11] She writes that "Rabbi Abraham Hacohen Kook helped the authors of textbooks geared for the national-orthodox schools to formulate this [Zionist] interpretation [of Jewish history] in religious terms." Kenan is here speaking of the 1950s—but since R. Kook died in 1935, it would be more accurate to say that his religious justification of Zionism served as the basis for these textbooks. The historian H.G. Adler is identified as an East European survivor, one of the "factographers" who "made extensive use of full texts, replicating documents with brief explanations that did not distort the records in their original form" (p. 52). In fact, Adler was not from Eastern Europe and his work was interpretive in nature; I suspect that Kenan has mixed him up with Joseph Wulf. Similarly, the career of Isaiah Trunk is ascribed to Philip Friedman (pp. 110–111, n. 47). Even more troubling is Kenan's disregard of a whole series of scholars who played important roles in the history of Holocaust research both before and after 1961. To mention only one particularly egregious example: Shaul Esh, who taught the first Holocaust course at an Israeli university; wrote path-breaking works; established important contacts with German researchers and integrated the research on Jews with work done on "perpetrators," is mentioned only once, in a single sentence, as "one of the leading Israeli scholars of the Shoah and Nazism, as well as chief Editor of Yad Vashem's publications" (p. 53).

As a Holocaust historian who has dedicated much of his work to historiography, I had high expectations upon starting Kenan's volume. Some of her findings are indeed valuable, especially those concerning the emergence of research in the D.P. camps. Overall, however, *Between Memory and History* is both distorted in its analysis and lacking in insight. We remain in need of an Israeli counterpart to Nicolas Berg's fine work on German Holocaust historiography.

DAN MICHMAN
Bar-Ilan University
Yad Vashem

Notes

1. Conny Kristel, *Geschiedenis als opdracht: Abel Herzberg, Jacques Presser en Loe de Jong* (Amsterdam: 1998).
2. Nicolas Berg, *Der Holocaust und die westdeutschen Historiker: Erforschung und Erinnerung* (Göttingen: 2003).
3. The other work is Boaz Cohen's doctoral dissertation, "Hameḥkar hahistori hayisreeli 'al hashoa, bashanim 1945–1980: meafeyanim, megamot vekivunim" (Bar-Ilan University, 2004), which I supervised.
4. For a formulation of this idea, see Hans G. Adler, *Der verwaltete Mensch* (Tübingen: 1974), foreword.
5. On the "Jerusalem school," see David N. Myers, "Was There a 'Jerusalem School'? An Inquiry into the First Generation of Historical Researchers at The Hebrew University," in *Studies in Contemporary Jewry*, vol. 10, *Reshaping the Past: Jewish History and the Historians*, ed. Jonathan Frankel (New York: 1994), 66–92.
6. See, in particular, Tom Segev, *The Seventh Million: The Israelis and the Holocaust* (New York: 1993).
7. Among other works, see Dalia Ofer, "Israel," in *The World Reacts to the Holocaust*, ed. David S. Wyman (Baltimore: 1996), 836–923; Hanna Yablonka, *He'asor harishon, 1948–1958* (Jerusalem: 1997), 41–56; Judith Tydor Baumel, " 'In Everlasting Memory': Individual and Communal Holocaust Commemoration in Israel," *Israel Affairs* 1 (1995), 146–170.
8. See several articles by Joseph Kermisz and Nathan Eck in *Yedi'ot Yad Vashem* 1 (1954); ibid., 2 (1954); ibid., 4–5 (1955); also see Nathan Eck, *Hato'im bedarkhei hamavet* (Jerusalem: 1960); Nachman Blumental's remarks at the First International Conference on the Research of the Holocaust and Heroism, Jerusalem, July 1947, Yad Vashem Archives, AM 1/237.
9. Richard I. Cohen, "How Central was Anti-Semitism to the Historical Writing of Jacob Katz?" in *The Pride of Jacob: Essays on Jacob Katz and His Work*, ed. Jay M. Harris (Cambridge, Mass.: 2002), 125–140.
10. From the end of the 1940s, Dworzecki had lobbied for the establishment of a Holocaust studies chair at the Hebrew University. As noted, such a chair was eventually established at Bar-Ilan University in 1959, and Dworzecki became its first incumbent.
11. See Dan Michman, *Hashoah veḥikrah: hamsagah, minuaḥ vesugiyot yesod* (Tel Aviv: 1998), 147–153; English version, *Holocaust Historiography: A Jewish Perspective: Conceptualizations, Terminology, Approaches, and Fundamental Issues* (London: 2003), 205–214.

The Rabin Assassination: Looking Back at a National Trauma

Dana Arieli-Horowitz, *Yoẓerim be'omes yeter: reẓaḥ Rabin, omanut upolitikah* (Creators in overburden: Rabin's assassination, art and politics). Jerusalem: Magnes Press, 2005. 407 pp.

Lev Greenberg (ed.), *Zikaron bemaḥloket: mitos, leumiyut, vedemokratiyah* (Contested memory: myth, nation, and democracy). Beersheba: Humphrey Institute for Social Research, 2000. 169 pp.

Charles S. Liebman (ed.), *Reẓaḥ politi: reẓaḥ Rabin ureẓiḥot politiyot bamizraḥ hatikhon* (Political assassination: the murder of Rabin and political assassinations in the Middle East). Tel Aviv: Am Oved, 1998. 160 pp.

Yoram Peri: *Yad ish beaḥiv: reẓaḥ Rabin umilḥemet hatarbut beyisrael* (Brothers at war: Rabin's assassination and the cultural war in Israel). Tel Aviv: Babel, 2005. 405 pp.

Yoram Peri (ed.), *The Assassination of Yitzhak Rabin*. Stanford: Stanford University Press, 2000. 386 pp.

Writing in the wake of the assassination of President John F. Kennedy and on the basis of a comparison between the United States and Italy, Sidney Verba once argued that, whereas major crises can have an integrative or disintegrative effect on a given society, they usually reinforce whatever tendency happens to be stronger.[1] Thus, in fragmented political cultures, national trauma invariably leads to a deepening of internal rifts rather than to their healing. Israel is a classic example of this second kind of body politic, so it is not surprising that the assassination of Yitzhak Rabin on November 4, 1995 led to an intensification of existing conflicts. Immediately after the tragedy, politicians of all persuasions expressed the hope that it would prove to be a transforming event that would bring Israelis together. However, this was not to be the case. After a very brief respite, politicians became engaged in a fierce debate regarding the causes of the assassination. This, in turn, led to a wide variety of accusations and counter-accusations and to a general escalation of tension in an already highly volatile political arena.

All the books reviewed in this essay reflect this situation in one way or another. Yoram Peri, a former aide of Rabin's, is at pains to point out that his work on the assassination does not derive from scholarly curiosity alone; it has also provided a form of solace or therapy in the wake of a highly traumatic event. The essays in the volume edited by Charles S. Liebman are described by him as a blend between scientific analysis and personal reflections—a description that can be applied as well to Lev Greenberg's edited collection—whereas Dana Arieli-Horowitz's more recent collection of interviews with a number of prominent Israeli artists was specifically designed to examine their response to what was, for many of them, "a point of no return" (p. 11).

How did conflicts within Israeli society lead, perhaps inexorably, to Rabin's assassination, and how were they intensified by it? Some of the authors and contributors in these volumes put forward their own causal explanations of the assassination; others analyze the public discourse in order to delineate the various explanations offered by opposing sectors of the Israeli body politic.

In both *The Assassination of Yitzhak Rabin*, an edited collection, and in his book *Brothers at War* (*Yad ish beaḥiv*), Peri points out that a reading of ancient and modern history draws attention to the ubiquity of assassinations and to the fact that they are particularly common in regimes characterized by a high level of violence and a low level of political legitimacy. In his view, the presence of these conditions in Israel made it more likely that an assassination would occur. Agreeing with Peri are a number of contributors to *The Assassination of Yitzhak Rabin*. In an article titled "One More Political Murder by Jews," Nachman Ben-Yehuda analyzes a total of some 90 planned, attempted, and successful assassinations since 1882, the vast majority of which took place prior to the establishment of the state of Israel. Rabin's assassination, he contends, is the latest killing in a longstanding struggle for legitimacy between competing symbolic universes within Zionism. In contrast, while Ehud Sprinzak's essay, "Israel's Radical Right and the Countdown to the Rabin Assassination," focuses on recent political trends, he, too, argues that the assassination was the culmination of a process of delegitimization of the Labor government and of the prime minister at its helm.

Other contributors to Peri's volume arrive at a similar point from a more psychological perspective. In " 'Let Us Search Our Path': Religious Zionism after the Assassination," Aviezer Ravitsky shows how the personal identity of religious Zionists, which had been greatly enhanced by the settlement activity of Gush Emunim, suffered a blow with the rise to power of the Labor government and the ensuing peace negotiations with the Palestinians. This, combined with the widespread fear regarding the possibility of territorial concessions in the event of an agreement, made the resort to violence more likely. In a similar vein, Israel Urbach applies a number of concepts from his work on the suicidal behavior of individuals to help understand the phenomenon on a national level. In "Self-Destructive Processes in Israeli Politics," he contends that right-wing extremists found their messianic dream of a Greater Israel threatened by the Oslo accords; in consequence, both their own lives and those of others became completely meaningless.

Most of the contributors to *The Assassination of Yitzhak Rabin* agree (with, of course, the benefit of hindsight) that the assassination was bound to happen. Why, then, did Israel's political leaders chose to ignore the "red lights and warning signals," the writing on the wall? According to Peri in *Brothers at War*, their failure was the outcome of a "false collective consciousness"—that is, a traditional and deeply felt sense of Jewish victimhood, enhanced in the period following the Holocaust, which gave rise to a widespread belief that evil was an external phenomenon. Such a perception prevented both politicians and the general Israeli public from identifying internal sources of iniquity in general and violence in particular. Together with an unbounded confidence in the resilience of Israeli democracy and the prowess of the country's defense forces, this deceptive self-image led to a misplaced complacency before the assassination and to total shock in its wake.

The existence of a "false collective consciousness" is, I believe, highly doubtful. For one thing, the first war in Lebanon and the first intifada had already raised serious doubts about the efficacy of the Israel Defense Forces. Still more significant is the fact that for many years, particularly during the period of Likud rule from 1977 to 1984, the Labor party and its allies expressed concern about the level of political violence, some even predicting the outbreak of civil war.[2] There was, it seems, a tendency to exaggerate rather than to underestimate the internal sources of evil—which, according to the Israeli Left, were all to be found on the right of the political spectrum.

This argument reappeared in the wake of the assassination. As Peri and many of the contributors to his work and the other edited volumes point out, Labor leaders drew attention to the steady escalation of right-wing political violence in the years prior to the assassination. Time and again, they recalled the increasingly severe attacks against both Palestinians (from sporadic vigilante attacks to the "Jewish underground" of 1984, to Baruch Goldstein's massacre of Muslim worshippers in the Cave of the Patriarchs ten years later) and left-wing Jews (from the violence against the Labor party in the 1981 elections to the killing of Emil Greenzweig in February 1983). Significantly, however, their criticism was directed almost exclusively at the political and spiritual leaders of the secular and religious right-wing parties, or what is widely referred to as "the national camp" (*hamaḥaneh haleumi*), whose verbal violence (rather than the physical violence of their more extreme followers) was singled out as the root of the problem and the real danger to the stability of Israeli society.

Although the leaders of both the secular and the religious parties in the Likud-led coalition rejected the charges of verbal violence, they could not avoid dealing with them. In some instances, as Ravitsky points out, there were political and spiritual leaders who accepted these strictures, calling on their colleagues and followers to engage in soul-searching and mend their ways. But as Peri and others demonstrate, most of those accused of verbal violence and incitement rejected these allegations. At times, they charged that the Israeli Left was exploiting the action of a lone actor—"a wild weed" (*'esev shoteh*), as Rabin's assassin, Yigal Amir, was most often characterized—in order to stigmatize the nationalist religious camp to which he allegedly belonged. On other occasions, the blame was transferred to those on the Left. Thus, right-wing parliamentary and extra-parliamentary leaders, both secular and religious, contended that "the war of words" in the early 1980s had actually been sparked by the incessant incitement against Menachem Begin and Ariel Sharon during the Lebanon War that emanated from its opponents on the Left. They also made frequent reference to certain deprecatory remarks, attributed to Rabin, putting down the Jewish settlers and their opposition to the Oslo accords—arguing, in effect, that the assassination was a victim-precipitated crime.

In this way, the debate following the assassination did not revolve around the perpetrator, but rather around those who allegedly incited him. In sum, both sides sought to divest themselves of responsibility by placing the blame firmly on their political opponents. However, as is usually the case, their arguments tended to reinforce rather than change peoples' attitudes and, in so doing, exacerbated the already deep divisions in Israeli society.

Not surprisingly, with the passage of time, the debate over responsibility for Rabin's assassination has become less pervasive. It now tends to take place primarily during the period leading up to the annual remembrance day and has become part of the broader issue of how best to commemorate both the event and Rabin's memory. But the major protagonists and underlying issues remain the same: the "peace camp" and the "national camp" are still pitted against each other, with each seeking to promote its own reading of the event while simultaneously rebutting the views of its political rivals.

Writing about "the struggle to forget" in *Brothers at War*, Peri notes that there was a great deal of opposition to establishing an official remembrance day. It took almost two years for the Knesset to enact the required legislation; since then, Peri claims, representatives of the nationalist camp have used their positions and influence to play down the importance of the Rabin assassination in schools and other state institutions (pp. 196–197). The Left, for its part, has continually criticized Likud-led governments for failing to give due recognition to Rabin's "peace legacy" in official commemoration ceremonies held at the Knesset and at Rabin's grave on Mount Herzl. In consequence of this perceived effort to blur the message of Rabin's life and legacy, leaders of the "peace camp" hold their own annual rally in Rabin Square, the site of the assassination. In this way, they ensure that their message gets across, albeit mainly to their own followers.[3]

In general, the apparent impossibility of reaching consensus over the Rabin legacy and the lessons to be learned from his assassination have led to a depoliticization of official commemoration activities. Peri notes that, in the mass media, the focus is increasingly on individuals' private recollections of Yitzhak Rabin, particularly during the period before he entered politics. At the same time, Ministry of Education commemorative programs are now likely to emphasize very general issues such as violence in the schools and in the society at large, rather than the assassination itself (pp. 217–221). Unable to agree on the political significance of Rabin's life and death, both the governmental agents of memory and the mass media choose in the main simply to avoid it.

Lev Greenberg's edited collection, *Contested Memory* (*Zikaron bemaḥloket*), also takes up this question. In an essay titled "Commemorating Yitzhak Rabin and Commemorating His Commemoration," Michael Feige describes the widespread tendency to evade the substance of the issue by relating more to the act of commemoration than to what is actually being commemorated—with car stickers declaring that "we will not forgive and we will not forget" or enjoining others "to remember and not to forget" capturing the essence of this trend. In her article in this collection, "Between Jerusalem and Tel Aviv," written only three years after the assassination, Vered Vinetsky-Seroussi points out that there are many who feel no need to remember Rabin, as is made manifest by the different approaches of Israel's two largest cities to Rabin's commemoration. Although the prime minister, in accordance with official protocol, was buried on Mount Herzl and made an honorary citizen of the nation's capital, the municipality deemed it sufficient to name only one road after him (albeit the one leading to the new complex of government buildings), and even this was done with very little fanfare long after Rabin's death. In contrast, the Tel Aviv municipality immediately altered the name of the place where the assassination occurred, from Kings of Israel Square to Rabin Square. The different responses of the country's two major cities, in Vinetsky-Seroussi's view, both reflect and reinforce the rift between the secular Left and the religious Right. In the eyes of many, Tel Aviv and Jerusalem have come to represent rival worldviews within Israeli society.

The contrasting images of Israel's two metropolises—"the eternal capital of the Jewish people" versus "the city that never stops"—provide an ideal backdrop for an examination of Dana Arieli-Horowitz's *Creators in Overburden (Yozerim be'omes yeter)*,[4] a collection of interviews with Israeli artists who, according to Arieli-Horowitz, view themselves as "the hub of Israeli secularism" and who, in contrast to the country's political elite, continue to grapple seriously with the Rabin assassination.

Not all artists, of course, react in the same way. There are those who decided not to respond to the assassination (and other political events) in order to avoid sinking into depression. David Gerstein, for instance, feels that doing art for art's sake is "an existential need" and is "a way of saving one's soul" in an overpoliticized society such as Israel (pp. 15–16).[5] According to Arieli-Horowitz, however, other artists who previously felt this way changed their mind in the wake of the assassination, seeing it as an attack on their most cherished values. Moreover, almost all the artists interviewed in this volume understand their political role as being very different from that of the rival political and ideological camps in the debate over the legacy of Yitzhak Rabin—each with its own leaders and followers. They are derisive of works that take the form of propaganda for a particular cause and instead advocate the use of art as a way of making people think. Moshe Gershuni, for instance, argues that this is an inherent feature of painting: as the only non-linear art form, it cannot provide solutions but is rather like "a system of question marks" serving to open the minds of the audience (p. 73).

The ways in which the artists have gone about this task have varied in accordance with their understanding of the significance of Rabin's assassination. Those who see it as an infringement of universalistic values tend to relate to Yitzhak Rabin as a private citizen rather than as the person who symbolized the body politic. A number of artists chose to focus on an impersonal feature of the event—the bloodstains rather than the victim—in order to emphasize the tragedy of any loss of human life. This stance is best exemplified in a painting by Deganit Brest, in which words spoken by the doctor on duty that night at Ichilov hospital are placed in the center of the canvas: unaware of the identity of the injured person before him, the doctor had described Rabin as "an old man in a suit" and as "a very old man with a face as white as snow." In contrast, those artists who saw the assassination in more particularistic terms—as a threat to the solidarity of Israeli society or as a serious breach of Jewish tradition—resorted to completely different themes. Most often, they incorporated biblical motifs and other Jewish iconography into their work, with many direct references (or more subtle allusions) to the sacrifice of Isaac, the Sixth Commandment prohibiting murder, or traditional mourning customs. Artists in this group attempted to show how Yigal Amir had committed a heinous crime even in terms of the tradition he claimed to represent.

A number of the interviewees make mention of the fact that the nationalist camp has not produced any significant artistic response to the assassination. Some of them attribute this to the Israeli Right's lack of need or desire to relate to the murder of a political leader who was prepared to give up parts of the holy land to the Palestinians. Others adopt a much more radical stance. The sculptor Buki Schwartz, for instance, contends: "Art is on the Left. Art is done by people who are concerned about human rights and about man as man rather than relating to people as creatures that you can destroy and kill because they are expendable at that particular time" (p. 47). In his opinion, and in that of many other artists interviewed here, those in favor of a Greater Israel have not simply failed to produce an artistic response to the assassination; their lack of humanitarian values makes them totally incapable of doing so.

The controversy surrounding the Oslo accords, which formed the backdrop for events leading to Rabin's assassination, is seen by all the authors and contributors in these volumes as part of a much broader struggle over the shaping of the collective Israeli identity. In an address given on the third anniversary of the Rabin assassination, the historian and former Labor foreign minister Shlomo Ben-Ami used a term that has become increasingly popular in the United States—"culture war"—in describing the split between the "Jewish" and the "Israeli" side of the body politic. According to Ben-Ami, the common demominator of the nationalist camp is not its stance on the territorial issue but rather its "revolt against the state of Israel" (*Contested Memory*, p. 154).

Taking this idea a step further, Peri bases much of his analysis in *Brothers at War* on the dichotomy between "retro" (conservative) and "metro" (cosmopolitan) culture that was articulated by John Sperling following the 2004 presidential elections.[6] Summarizing the significance of the Israeli "great divide," Peri writes:

> We are talking about two worldviews that are based on conflicting visions of man and the world. The differences of opinion relate to issues such as religion and the church, the environment, human rights ... and many other matters from the right to hold firearms to the right of the United States to determine by force the nature of the regime in states around the world (p. 74).

Of course, the areas of controversy in Israel are, in certain cases at least, very different from those in the United States. However, after analyzing conflicts regarding Israeli collective identity—among them, the clash between those who see themselves primarily as Jews and those who regard themselves first and foremost as Israelis; between citizens whose principal allegiance is to the state of Israel and others who are committed above all to the land of Israel—Peri concludes that in Israel, as in the United States, there is a great divide between "retro" and "metro," and that the debate concerning the assassination and legacy of Yitzhak Rabin must be looked at within the context of this culture war.

It should be noted that Peri, Vinitsky-Seroussi, and other authors who point to a dichotomy between conflicting cultures, ideologies, or symbolic universes within Israeli society describe "ideal types" rather than providing a complete and accurate representation of the competing worldviews. In particular, they draw attention to the widespread acceptance of ethno-nationalism rather than political nationalism as the basis for membership in the Israeli collective, even among adherents of the supposedly cosmopolitan and universalistic "metro" culture. Thus, as Amnon Raz-Krokotzkin points out in his contribution to *Contested Memory*, titled "The Rabin Legacy: On Secularism, Nationalism and Orientalism," the propensity to adopt a particularistic stance is evidenced not only by the longstanding discrimination against Israeli Arabs, but also by the nature of the public discourse about the Rabin assassination and, more broadly, about the secular-religious divide in Israel, which is always conceived as being solely of an intra-Jewish nature. Paradoxically, therefore, public discourse on this matter emphasizes the common denominator between Jews on both sides of the divide, while excluding the country's Arab citizens from discussion.

Moreover, with regard to Rabin's assassination, Raz-Krokotzkin argues that the secular Left camp was able to "decontaminate" itself by placing causal responsibility on the national religious camp, and thereby retain its enlightened self-image.[7] Yet the truth of the matter, Raz-Krokotzkin maintains, is that Yigal Amir's heinous crime is attributable to Zionism as a whole, not just its religious-messianic interpretation. In other words, this crime is best understood in relation to the nationalistic elements of Jewish identity, common to both camps, rather than the religious elements that are primarily the province of only one camp.

This stance has garnered very little support beyond the small but vocal group of post-Zionist scholars. A more common tendency, as noted, has been to reconstruct Rabin's biography and to create a new version of him as an Israeli culture hero. As Haim Hazan points out in his contribution to *The Assassination of Yitzhak Rabin*, titled "Rabin's Burial Ground: Revisiting the Zionist Myth," the official "agents of memory" have sought to emphasize the universally human elements of the Zionist ethos at the expense of its more specifically nationalistic features. By including only those elements of Rabin's life story that were incommensurate with the assassin's ideological stance, those who eulogized the prime minister created a distance not only between the perpetrator and his victim, but also between their own symbolic universe and that of Yigal Amir's ideological collaborators.

More than a decade has elapsed since the Rabin assassination. Over time, there have been manifold changes in the alignment of forces in the Middle East, some of which are noted in these volumes. In *Brothers at War,* for instance, Peri examines the responses both to the assassination of Rehavam ("Gandhi") Zeevi, the leader of the right-wing Moledet party, by Palestinian terrorists in October 2001, and to the Israeli disengagement from Gaza and northern Samaria in August 2005. In fact, the debate surrounding these two events proceeded on essentially the same lines as did that regarding the assassination of Yitzhak Rabin. These, too, were part of the ongoing culture war in Israeli society. Unfortunately, however, Peri's analyses are tainted by a certain lack of objectivity and seem to be unduly swayed by his concern to honor Yitzhak Rabin's memory and legacy.

Peri, of course, is well aware of the extent to which biographies are a social construct. He himself draws attention to the different ways in which Rabin's colleagues and followers have reconstructed his life history and even iconized him in the wake of the assassination. Nevertheless, he finds it difficult to adopt this neutral stance toward those who created a less flattering portrait of the prime minister. Instead of analyzing the logic of their retrospective interpretations, he admonishes them for undermining Rabin's legacy and minimizing the significance of his assassination.

This problem is particularly acute in Peri's treatment of the aftermath of Zeevi's assassination. He points to the favorable reconstruction of Zeevi's life history and to the ways in which the reaction to his death mirrored that engendered by Rabin's assassination. Everything was the same, he notes, from the granddaughter's eulogy at the funeral to the establishment of an institute in the victim's memory. However, rather than accepting these responses as a legitimate expression on the part of a rival ideological camp, Peri castigates what he calls "the Rabinization of Gandhi" and bemoans the negative effect this has allegedly had on the commemoration of Rabin's life and death (pp. 225–227).

Brothers at War was written during the protracted and often bitter struggle over the disengagement plan. In his opening chapter, Peri lists the different means by which the leaders of the "orange campaign"[8] questioned the legitimacy of the government's decision to withdraw from settlements in Gaza and northern Samaria, in particular, the claim made by Ariel Sharon that "the fate of Netzarim is the same as that of Tel Aviv." Thus, according to its opponents, the disengagement plan was a violation of a campaign promise that had moved many voters to choose the Likud rather than one of the smaller and more extreme right-wing parties. While accepting the veracity of this claim, Peri dismisses it on the grounds that many foreign leaders (as well as previous Israeli prime ministers) had behaved in exactly the same manner. Ehud Barak, Benyamin Netanyahu, and—most importantly for him—Yitzhak Rabin had all taken a rigid stance on the occupied territories during election campaigns but had adopted more flexible policies after gaining office. Breaking promises is nothing out of the ordinary; everyone does it because, as leading Israeli politicians have been wont to say (in the words of a popular Hebrew song), "what you see from here, you don't see from there." At the same time, Peri is highly critical of the leaders of the nationalist religious camp who used the issue of broken promises against Sharon, castigating them for appealing to democratic principles that they themselves do not believe in. Rather than viewing this kind of discourse as a legitimate means of gaining political support against the disengagement, Peri portrays it as "a tactic designed to please the ear of innocent Israelis" (pp. 67–68).

As noted, Peri's book went to press at the height of the controversy about the disengagement plan and before it was actually implemented. It therefore makes no mention of the restraint shown by the vast majority of settlers and their supporters and, even more importantly, the moderating influence of their spiritual mentors at the time of the withdrawal. This rather unfortunate timing was most probably due to the desire to bring out the book in time for the tenth anniversary of Rabin's assassination. Had it been released a little later, Peri would have had the opportunity to relate to the gap between the rhetoric and actions of the nationalist religious camp on this occasion, and this in turn may have led him to a more nuanced reading of "retro" culture.

Authors differ regarding the depths of disagreement between the rival camps in Israeli society and the extent of support within the nationalist religious camp for the use of illegal and even violent means to further its cause. Many of them, however, are of the opinion that there is a severe crisis of legitimacy. In his essay in *The Assassination of Yitzhak Rabin* titled "At the Last Moment," Gadi Yatziv points out that this crisis does not stem from a feeling that the state is unable to meet the demands and expectations of its citizens, as is the case in many western countries. Rather, in certain sectors of the nationalist religious camp, there is a basic questioning of the government's right to rule.

It is this kind of stance that prompts Michael Walzer's call for a "politics without God." In "Democracy and the Politics of Assassination," which appears in the Liebman collection, Walzer argues that the increasing influence of religion in the public realm leads to an understanding of political issues in absolute terms and consequently leaves no room for any kind of give and take. For this reason, Walzer insists, Israel should follow the example of many other western democracies and separate religion and state. Politics should be limited to more mundane issues, whereas the search for truth and the work of redemption should go on elsewhere.

The present state of mind of the religious Right suggests that bringing it around to this point of view is a tall order. In this regard, however, two points must be borne in mind. First, the nationalist religious camp is much more heterogeneous than Peri and many of the authors in his and the other edited volumes would have us believe.[9] Second, and even more important, religious Zionism before the Six-Day War was of a very different ilk. It stood for "Torah va'avodah," the integration of Torah with worldly pursuits, a balance between tradition and modernity. Albeit today very much in the minority, there are still those within religious Zionism who believe in an alternative to what Walzer aptly refers to as the politics of ultimacy. All those in favor of recreating such a synthesis—including, ironically enough, adherents of the future-orientated "metro" culture—should hope for the realization of the traditional Jewish plea that our days be renewed as of old.

GERALD CROMER
Bar-Ilan University

Notes

1. Sidney Verba, "The Kennedy Assassination and the Nature of Political Commitment," in *The Kennedy Assassination and the American Public: Social Communication in Crisis*, ed. Bradley S. Greenberg and Edwin B. Parker (Stanford: 1965), 357.

2. For a detailed analysis of this stance, see Gerald Cromer, "The Voice of Jacob and the Hands of Esau: Verbal and Physical Violence in Israeli Politics, 1977–1984," in *Studies in Contemporary Jewry*, vol. 18, *Jews and Violence: Images, Ideologies, Realities*, ed. Peter Y. Medding (New York: 2002), 149–167.

3. Significantly, this annual rally is held on the Saturday night closest to November 4. Official ceremonies, in contrast, take place on the 11th of Heshvan—the Hebrew anniversary of Rabin's death.

4. "Yoẓerim be'omes yeter" is better translated as "overburdened creators."

5. Although Arieli-Horowitz quotes Gerstein in her introductory chapter, the interview itself does not appear. This is unfortunate, given the fact that his stated views seem to differ greatly from those of the other artists.

6. John Sperling, Suzanne Helburn, Samuel George, John Morris, and Carl Hunt, *The Great Divide: Retro vs. Metro America* (Sausalito: 2004).

7. This term is borrowed from an intriguing analysis of the response to the assassination of former Italian prime minister Aldo Moro in 1978. See Robin Erica Wagner-Pacifici, *The Moro Morality Play: Terrorism as Social Drama* (Chicago: 1986).

8. The color orange was adopted as an identifying feature of the campaign against the disengagement plan; over time, opponents of the plan became known as "the oranges" (*haketumim*).

9. This point is made very forcefully in an article written by Asher Cohen and Stuart Cohen, "Mah atem roẓim mehaẓiyonut hadatit," *Haaretz* (29 Nov. 2005).

Book Reviews

Antisemitism, Holocaust, and Genocide

Jack R. Fischel and Susan Ortmann, *The Holocaust and Its Religious Impact: A Critical Assessment* (Bibliographies and Indexes in Religious Studies, no. 54). Westport: Praeger, 2004. 335 pp.

Whoever thinks that this book deals mainly with the theology of the Holocaust (a subject of particular interest to this reviewer) is likely to be disappointed. Its basic theme is actually Christianity and the Holocaust, such that a better title would have been *The Holocaust and Its Religious Roots*. The annotated books and articles—including several from web sites—are quite varied, ranging from medieval Jewish history to the memoirs of Holocaust survivors. Yet these categories are covered very selectively. Much more numerous are discussions of the extent to which Christianity or Christians were responsible for what happened. Coverage is limited to the English language. The annotations are sometimes quite lengthy, depending, it seems, on the importance the compilers assign to the item.

An irritating feature of this otherwise useful bibliography is the large number of typos and even more the Germanic influence, which is especially noticeable in the punctuation: a comma, for example, before each use of the word "that" as a conjunction. One cannot help but wonder about the level of editing that allowed such an obvious error, repeated in annotation after annotation, to pass.

The bibliography is divided into four parts: "Christian Anti-Judentum," "From Anti-Judentum to Anti-Semitism," "The Moral and Religious Response to the Genocide of the Jews," and "Post WW II Responses to the Holocaust." A useful feature for those unfamiliar with the topic is the book's glossary, which features terms associated with the Holocaust and with Jewish and Christian theology. A closer classification of the articles would have been useful—within each section, listings are organized by author—but this deficiency is rectified, to some extent, by the index, where one can find books and articles organized according to frequently discussed topics such as the behavior of Pope Pius XII during the Holocaust.

AVRAHAM GREENBAUM
University of Haifa

Yosef Gorny, *Between Auschwitz and Jerusalem*. London: Valentine Mitchell, 2003. 250 pp.

Between Auschwitz and Jerusalem is the English translation of a book published in Hebrew in 1998, five years after the opening of the Holocaust Museum in Washington, D.C. Yosef Gorny begins with a comparison between this museum and Yad Vashem. The architectural differences between the two buildings reflect a significant change in the way in which the Jewish collective identifies with its two modern components—the Holocaust and the state of Israel. Until fairly recently, the Holocaust and Israel could be seen as inseparable partners in the same historical destiny. The Holocaust justified the striving for a state and empowered the nation in its existential struggle, whereas the state ensured the vitality and continuity of the collective that had endured the Holocaust.

Yet from the beginning, immediately after the Second World War, the connection between the Holocaust and revival was complex and fraught with tension. The historical and psychological explanation for this tension was to be found in the attempt to transform the helplessness of the Jews in the Holocaust into a positive political and intellectual tool in the struggle to establish a state. At first, the dialectical tension between these two elements worked in the direction of unity between Jews in Israel and in the American diaspora. By the late 1980s, however, the contradiction between these two elements was no longer dialectical but had rather become an expression of estrangement between the center of Jewish experience— the state of Israel—and the large Jewish community in the United States.

Gorny's book centers on the transition from dialectical to post-dialectical tension; it is a historical piece of research that does not deal with Holocaust history. It examines streams of thought that touch on the Holocaust, but not on the moral, theological, or psychological questions that arise from it. Gorny focuses on consciousness, but in the collective, national, and social sense rather than in the individual, psychological sense. What interests him is not so much the form of collective memory as its underlying political and ideological motivations, though he also points to the ways in which public memory in its various forms becomes itself a factor in the crystallization of the collective consciousness.

Attitudes regarding the Holocaust as an element of collective identity evolved differently in the United States and in the state of Israel. It took much longer for American Jewry to move from the stage of "suppressed knowledge" to that of consciousness and recognition of the Holocaust as a component of Jewish collective identity. Holocaust consciousness, as an emotional phenomenon, began to develop in the 1970s and reached its culmination in 1993 with the opening of the Holocaust Museum, which became a pilgrimage site for millions. This move from one extreme to the other was influenced by the special character of American Jewry, in particular its gradual transformation from an immigrant community (benefiting from the liberal-democratic regime and economic opportunity of the host country) to a community equal in status to that of any other. The best evidence of American Jewry's initial public detachment from the Holocaust is provided by the Eichmann affair. Eichmann's capture in 1960 prompted widespread discussion and disagreement, and his trial received extensive coverage in both the general and the Jewish media. Hannah Arendt's coverage of the trial and the book that emerged from it, *Eichmann in Jerusalem: The Banality of Evil*, generated even greater controversy, which swept through intellectual circles that had hitherto been remote from all Jewish affairs. However, the excitement did not serve as the basis for systematic, in-depth discussion of the Holocaust as either a historical phenomenon or in terms of its significance for Jews.

In Israel, in contrast, in the first decade of statehood, the Holocaust was a public and national issue, whether with regard to criticism of the Yishuv leadership's policies and behavior during the war, which surfaced during the Kasztner affair, or to discussions concerning reparations and relations with Germany. The Eichmann trial itself and its reverberations served both directly and indirectly to heighten Holocaust consciousness in the newly established Jewish state.

Thus, in Israel, as opposed to the American Jewish diaspora, the inculcation of knowledge of the Holocaust as part of the collective identity served the ideological purposes of crystallizing the unity of the new society, and to that extent preceded efforts to create a Holocaust consciousness. Consequently, the stage of suppressed knowledge was comparatively shorter in Israel than it was in the United States. Moreover, the lines between the stages of knowledge and of consciousness were more blurred in Israel, owing to the early public emphasis on instilling the lesson of the Holocaust. Nonetheless, more concerted efforts to develop Holocaust consciousness began with the changes in government and accession to power of Menachem Begin in 1977.

The book concentrates mainly on the stage of Holocaust consciousness when it, together with religious belief and Israel's place in the world, became an increasingly important component of the Jewish collective identity. Gorny systematically tracks the development of "public thinking" in this sphere, stressing the ideological positions of those seeking to influence Jewish and general public opinion, while at the same time drawing comparisons in this regard between Israel and the diaspora.

Between Auschwitz and Jerusalem presents various forms of intellectual discourse on the nature of the connection between the Holocaust and the state. The first chapter, titled "The Statist Discourse, or The Eichmann Syndrome," opens the discussion in terms of both time and content. Gorny focuses not on the conduct or outcome of the trial but rather on the uproar concerning the right of the state of Israel, as representative of the Jewish people, to put Eichmann on trial, as well as on Hannah Arendt's stand on this question in particular and her general attitude toward the Jewish state. Chapter 2, "The Theological Discourse, or Faith and Politics," discusses the three-sided connection between (religious) faith, the Holocaust and the state, as Gorny considers the question of God's place in history; the metaphysical and mysterious connection between the Holocaust and the state; and the relationship between policy and morality from a religious perspective. This chapter is followed by "The Academic Discourse, or History and Ideology," which deals with attempts by scholars (mainly historians, sociologists, and philosophers) to give the Holocaust an objective explanation, especially with regard to its particular versus universal character. Showing how the various stands taken by participants in this discourse related to their a priori ideological outlook, Gorny endeavors to reveal the connection between methodology and ideology. In the following chapter, "The Ideological Discourse, or Ideology and Politics," he moves Holocaust discourse from the halls of academe to the public plane, where its political-ideological nature is more explicitly revealed. Closing the cycle on the relationship between the state and the Holocaust, "The Pundits' Discourse, or Ethnicity and Politics," revolves around the establishment of the Holocaust Museum. In this chapter, Gorny addresses the status of Jews as an ethnic group in the United States and poses the question of whether their historic experience there expresses their Jewish destiny, or whether it first and foremost has a universal message. The political dimension of the chapter refers to the relationship of American Jews with other ethnic groups that bear historic memories of persecution and discrimination. The book concludes with "The Mythical Ethos of the Holocaust and the State," which sums up the issue in light of developments in Jewish history over the last century.

I will conclude this overview on a personal note. I read Gorny's book in its original Hebrew version as soon as it was published, since at the time I was engaged in research on the relationship between the state of Israel and American Jewry. Influenced by what Gorny had written, I decided to visit the Holocaust Museum on my next trip to the United States. During my visit, I, too, was struck by the differences between it and Yad Vashem. In the intervening years, Yad Vashem has undergone extensive renovations and has recently inaugurated what is essentially a new and entirely different museum. Now scholars are faced with the challenge of adding another chapter to Gorny's research.

ARIEL FELDESTEIN
Sapir College

Gábor Kádár and Zoltán Vági, *Self-Financing Genocide: The Gold Train, the Becher Case and the Wealth of Hungarian Jews.* Budapest: Central European University Press, 2004. 413 pp.

During the first four and a half years of the Second World War, the Jews of Hungary lived under the illusion that they would escape the tragic fate that had befallen the other Jewish communities in Nazi-dominated Europe. Identifying themselves as Magyars of the Jewish faith—loyal and patriotic citizens whose destiny had been intertwined with that of the Magyars since the Revolution of 1848–1849—they firmly believed that Hungary would never betray or abandon them. Their illusions were shattered immediately after the German occupation of Hungary on March 19, 1944, when they found themselves subjected to the swiftest and most barbaric campaign of destruction in the Nazis' war against the Jews.

The SS, who were relatively few in number, were able to complete their murderous mission in Hungary only because of the wholehearted cooperation of the newly established quisling government of Döme Sztójay. Almost immediately after the occupation, the Germans and their Hungarian accomplices launched a systematic campaign to bring about the isolation, expropriation, and ghettoization of the Jews as a prelude to their subsequent deportation. As part of its criminal campaign against the Jews, the Sztójay government transformed thievery and plunder into a state industry, instituting a spoliation and confiscation program that the rapacious elements of Hungarian society both applauded and took full advantage of.

Self-Financing Genocide is a thoroughly revised, updated, and enlarged English version of *Aranyvonat* (The gold train), which the authors published in 2001. It is a comprehensive and fully documented account of the Hungarian chapter of the Final Solution, with an emphasis on the expropriation of Hungarian Jewry—one of the richest communities in prewar Europe. It also provides a fascinating account of the fate of the Jewish wealth that Hungarian Nazis smuggled out of the country just before its liberation by the Red Army, an odyssey that came to be known as the "Hungarian Gold Train." The authors of this remarkable work, Gábor Kádár and Zoltán Vági, are among the best of the young historians in post-Communist Hungary focusing on the Holocaust and the postwar era. The English edition of *Aranyvonat* is enriched by the incorporation of new documentary materials they unearthed in various Hungarian and foreign archives and via their work for the United States Presidential Advisory Commission on Holocaust Assets in 2000–2001.

The volume is divided into three parts. The first part provides a succinct overview of the special characteristics of the Holocaust in Hungary. The authors enable the reader to gauge the magnitude of the tragedy by providing a thoroughly documented account of the demographic and economic status of Hungarian Jewry before the German occupation. They then critically review the avalanche of increasingly draconic measures taken by the SS and its Hungarian accomplices to bring about the speedy implementation of the Final Solution. While the radical elements of the Sztójay government outdid the SS in their eagerness to "solve" the Jewish problem as quickly as possible, they were clearly less enthusiastic about sharing the confiscated Jewish wealth. As Kádár and Vági demonstrate convincingly, the Germans and the Hungarians competed fiercely to obtain possession of the Jews' plundered wealth.

It is this competition that constitutes the thrust of the second part of the book, along with its fascinating account of the Hungarians' attempt to salvage their share of the loot on the eve of the *Götterdämmerung*. Fearing the rapidly approaching Red Army, the Hungarian authorities managed to acquire a train that took much of this stolen treasure to Austria. The crates were clearly labeled by their contents—jewelry, gold and silver, precious stones, valuable paintings, furs, rugs, and so forth.

In a narrative that is both spellbinding and persuasive, the authors identify the many Hungarian officials involved in the roundup of the loot and the acquisition and guarding of the "Gold Train." Particularly gripping is the account of the train's vicissitudes in Austria following that country's liberation by the Allies. As the authors recount, some of the freight on the Gold Train fell into the hands of American and French authorities. Many of those entrusted with safeguarding its valuable contents, including both Hungarian and Allied personnel, lined their own pockets. In the late 1940s, part of the loot was returned to Hungary only to be sequestrated by the pro-Soviet Communist regime in the name of socialism.

A considerable part of the Jewish wealth ended up in the pockets of SS *Obersturmbannführer* Kurt A. Becher, Heinrich Himmler's personal representative in Hungary during the German occupation. His role in Hungary, including his dealings with Rezsö (Rudolph) Kasztner, a leader of the Zionist-controlled Relief and Rescue Committee of Budapest, is the subject of the third part of this remarkable book. In contrast to Adolf Eichmann, who was an ideologically driven "idealist" dedicated to the implementation of the Final Solution, Becher was a calculating realist. A member of a Waffen-SS unit that reportedly committed many atrocities in the occupied territories of the Soviet Union in 1942 and 1943, Becher, presumably realizing the approaching inevitable defeat of the Axis, decided during his subsequent assignment in Hungary to pursue two basic goals: personal enrichment and the acquisition of foolproof alibis. The authors provide convincing evidence about how Becher managed to achieve both objectives, emerging—following his clearance by both the Allies and the German authorities—as one of the richest persons in postwar Germany. According to Kádár and Vági, the self-serving accounts of Becher and Kasztner with regard to the rescue of Jews (both in Budapest and in several Nazi concentration camps) were basically unfounded and calculated to serve as alibis after the collapse of the Third Reich.

Self-Financing Genocide is bound to become the standard work on the spoliation of Hungarian Jewry during the Nazi era. It is—and will continue to be—of great value not only to those interested in the practical issues of restitution and reparation, but also to everyone interested in unraveling the details of the Final Solution in Hungary.

RANDOLPH L. BRAHAM
Graduate Center/City University of New York

Renée Poznanski, *Jews in France during World War II*, trans. Nathan Bracher. Hanover, N.H.: Brandeis University Press, in association with the United States Holocaust Memorial Museum, 2001. xxv + 601 pp.

Over the years, there have been three distinctive approaches to research on the fate of the Jews in France during the Second World War. The first, launched in 1981 by Robert Paxton and Michael Marrus, focused on French Jews as victims of the Vichy authorities. By the 1990s, however, there appeared two additional approaches that shared the common starting point of Jews as actors in their own destiny. Thus, in the second approach, a group of scholars connected with Yad Vashem (notably Lucien Lazare) emphasized how Jews fought back; resistance, whether armed or social, was presented as symbolic of the Jews' determination to live or die as free men. The third approach, in contrast, looked at the political aspects of the struggle. Adam Rayski advanced a political analysis of the Jewish organizations' programs and activities; Richard Cohen and I (in separate works) emphasized the differences between the organizations and how these were overcome; and Maurice Rajfus condemned the native French Jewish leaders, claiming that they had to all intents and purposes abandoned foreign-born Jews in France in order to ensure their own survival.

With this as background, we can better appreciate Renée Poznanski's decision to deal with what has been omitted from these earlier studies. As important as it is to understand how organized Jewry ultimately overcame its political differences, we still need to get a sense of how the overwhelming majority of French Jews reacted to their increasingly desperate situation. Making use of a wide range of sources, Poznanski describes the conditions under which three quarters of the Jews in France survived the Second World War. Rather than retrace earlier debates about the causes and consequences of communal divisions, she chooses to ignore them—which is not to say that political divisions did not have a bearing on the ways in which French Jewry reacted to the Nazi threat, but rather to recognize that the overwhelming majority was probably unaware of these disputes.

Divided into twelve chapters that are chronologically and thematically organized, *Jews in France during World War II* outlines the difficulties confronting the Jewish population across the demarcation line that divided the country. Poznanski's study consists of two parts. The first seven chapters move from a discussion of the composition of the Jewish community, to the shock arising from the introduction of the race laws, to the introduction of the "yellow star" in the summer of 1942. Until that point, the Jewish population generally chose to abide by restrictions placed upon them while simultaneously seeking means to ensure their material existence. Poznanski refers to this period as an "inward movement." One may or may not agree with this characterization, which implies that legal persecution contributed to the unification of the various Jewish communities. This, however, is questionable, especially given the fact that foreign-born Jews were treated measurably worse than the native French Jewish population until 1943, even though both groups suffered from the same repressive regulations. Unification between the two groups ultimately occurred, but only when they realized they were facing a common fate.

In the next five chapters, which are the most important part of this study, Poznanski first presents a graphic depiction of daily life in various camps. Two of the Jewish camps in the occupied zone were established in May 1941, following the arrest of immigrant Jews. A third, Drancy, was created following the mass arrest of men, women, and children in July 1942. Many other camps were in the Vichy zone, some established at the outbreak of the war in order to intern the "enemy aliens," mainly Jewish refugees who had fled Germany, Austria, and Czechoslovakia. After presenting this material, Poznanski offers an account of the selections and subsequent mass deportations from the camps in July and August 1942. The chronological presentation of the book allows us to understand what was to follow: the dispersal of the Jewish population, accompanied by the authorities' relentless hunt for those who remained. The continuous threat of arrest and deportation led many to flee the cities and seek refuge in hamlets or small country towns. Indeed, this major shift of habitat helps explain why many more Jews survived the Holocaust in France than in other countries.

Here Poznanski omits discussion of at least one issue worthy of attention—the function of rumors in the decision-making process of each family. If my own family's experience lends itself to generalization, this form of unofficial information played an important role in deciding what needed to be done or considered. Admittedly, the history of rumors and their influence might be difficult to trace, but there can be no doubt that they played an important role, especially in places where

Jews lived in relatively large numbers. How else can we explain the fact that, once word got around that there was safety in the Italian zone of occupation, thousands acted accordingly?

This point aside, it must be said that Poznanski's extremely well researched, sensitively written, and generally well-translated volume has essentially filled in the remaining gap in the wartime historiography of the Jews in France, and signifies the end of all-encompassing studies. Future research in this field is likely to be limited to the examination of Jewish life in particular areas or camps, or of the lives of leading French Jewish personalities—and all future studies will be greatly indebted to Poznanski's work.

JACQUES ADLER
University of Melbourne

Rochelle G. Saidel, *The Jewish Women of Ravensbrück Concentration Camp.* Madison: University of Wisconsin Press, 2004. 279 pp.

In May 1939, a concentration camp for female political prisoners was established in the tiny community of Ravensbrück, located north of Fuerstenberg in what would later become East Germany. Although small women's camps had existed in Nazi Germany from 1933 onward, the majority of women taken into custody for anti-Nazi activity had been incarcerated until then in prisons rather than in camps. All of the 974 inmates of Ravensbrück in May 1939 were characterized as German anti-fascists (including Social Democrats and Communists); 137 of them were also Jewish. At the time, however, their Jewishness was considered incidental.

The camp's original purpose was to incarcerate and punish female political prisoners and to make use of them as slave labor. Following the outbreak of the war, the number of inmates in Ravensbrück increased, with transports from Nazi-occupied countries arriving almost daily. All of the prisoners were sent out to work, mainly outdoors and under inhuman conditions. Torture and solitary confinement were routine. There was also a network of satellite camps near Ravensbrück, many of which contracted with private companies to produce goods for the war effort.

Apart from being a concentration camp, Ravensbrück also served as a central training camp for newly hired female SS auxiliary guards who were later transferred to other camps throughout the Third Reich. Although the camp was designed to hold 5,000 women at any given time, it often contained more than 30,000 prisoners. In all, between 1939 and 1945, some 132,000 women from 23 countries were imprisoned in Ravensbrück, including political prisoners, Jehovah's Witnesses, Gypsies, prostitutes, lesbians, and criminals. Jews comprised about 20 percent of the camp population. Of the total number of prisoners, only about 15,000 survived.

In a well-researched and moving study, Rochelle Saidel has chronicled the history of the camp at Ravensbrück and the story of the Jewish women who survived it. On her first visit to the Ravensbrück memorial site some 25 years ago, Saidel was intrigued by the official (Communist) commemoration at the camp, which made no reference to Jews. As the Jewish women imprisoned during its early years had all perished, and those who arrived later usually stayed for only a short time, almost nothing had been written about them.[1]

Saidel focuses on three basic topics. The first I refer to as "Shoah"—the history of the camp and its Jewish inmates' fate—with chapters dealing with forced labor, the transfer to satellite camps, the death march from the camp, the rescue of some inmates to Sweden, and liberation. Earlier chapters provide a detailed and in-depth account of the history of Ravensbrück, its workings, and the overall fate of its Jewish inmates. Later chapters describe these events through the eyes of survivors who were interviewed by Saidel. Here it should be noted that, rather than relying on the traditional form of historical narrative and its plethora of written documentation, Saidel has chosen to adopt a new historical methodology that places oral documentation on the same level as written. The question is whether such a methodology reflects some version of relativism and "new historicism" that consider any given individual narrative to be as factually correct as any other. Although I assume that Saidel, a veteran researcher, does not go along with these trends, a fuller discussion of her attempts to verify the oral testimonies through cross-referencing would have served to resolve any doubts as to her awareness of the pitfalls of relying solely on oral documentation. In addition, she has wisely chosen to concentrate upon descriptions of individual experiences, thus lessening the necessity to corroborate personal testimonies when describing major events in the history of the camp. The result, however, is at times slightly disjointed; it is left to the reader to make the connections between the various testimonies in order to mold them into a smooth and seamless narrative.

The second topic, which is integral to the nature of the book, is that of "biography." Here, too, Saidel focuses upon the individual nature of testimony and, making skillful use of her material, presents the history of a number of notable Jewish inmates whose stories either exemplify a category or are the exception that proves the rule. Among those profiled is Gemma LaGuardia Gluck, the sister of New York mayor Fiorello LaGuardia, to whom an entire chapter is devoted. (Imprisoned because she had a Jewish mother, LaGuardia Gluck survived the war and came to the United States after liberation.) Accounts of other individuals are interspersed at various points in the book, comprising the innovative research on which this study is based.

Although this is a book about Jewish women during the Holocaust, the third topic, "gender," appears by itself only in brief, mainly in a chapter toward the end of the book titled "Gender and Women's Bodies." Feminist theory is unfortunately missing in this section, and there is little mention of the extensive and varied research in the field of gender and women's studies over the past two decades. Several years ago, Gabriel Schonfeld, the editor of *Commentary*, published a vehement attack on gender study of the Holocaust. Claiming that the lives of women during the Holocaust may or may not have been different from those of men, he lashed out against "scholars" who manipulated the Holocaust in order to further a feminist agenda and ridiculed what he portrayed as the false scientific methodology of some of their works. Schoenfeld (and several other scholars) argued that, even if the experiences of Jewish men and women may have differed somewhat during the Holocaust, the ultimate picture should be shaped by knowledge of their similar fate.[2]

As a scholar well-versed in Holocaust studies, Saidel was no doubt aware of this criticism and of the debate that it engendered, and it is disappointing that she chose not to address this topic in depth, instead limiting her discussion to one very narrowly circumscribed chapter. Yet perhaps this decision was shaped by the nature of her material. This volume, after all, places its emphasis on Jewish (as opposed to non-Jewish) inmates of the camp, and on the workings of Ravensbrück as a concentration camp. The inmates' experiences are described and analyzed as those of persecuted Jews who—since this was a women's camp—also happened to be women. Overall, Saidel views them as belonging to the larger corpus of "Jews under Hitler" rather than "persecuted women under the Nazis."

This conclusion is, of course, debatable and there may be other reasons why Saidel chose to locate her study far from the cutting edge of gender discourse and deep in the heart of more traditional Holocaust historiography. Be that as it may, *The Jewish Women of Ravensbrück Concentration Camp* is an important contribution to our understanding of the Holocaust, the world of the concentration camps, and the lives of Jewish women under Nazi rule.

JUDITH BAUMEL-SCHWARTZ
Bar-Ilan University

Notes

1. The following sources are noted in Saidel's bibliography: Denise Dunfurnier, *Ravensbruek: The Women's Camp of Death* (London: 1948); Christian Bernadac, *Camp for Women: Ravensbrueck* (Geneva: 1978); Marie-Jo Chombart de Lauwe, et al. *Les Français à Ravensbrueck* (Paris: 1965).
2. Gabriel Schoenfeld, "Auschwitz and the Professors," *Commentary* 105 (June 1998), 42–46; idem, "Controversy—Holocaust Studies: Gabriel Schoenfeld and Critics," ibid. 107 (1998), 14–25.

Biography, History, and the Social Sciences

Judith Deutsch-Kornblatt, *Doubly Chosen: Jewish Identity, the Soviet Intelligentsia, and the Russian Orthodox Church*. Madison: University of Wisconsin Press, 2004. 200 pp.

This pioneering study examines the conversion of members of the Russian Jewish intelligentsia to Russian Orthodoxy during the post-Stalin era. Though popularly discussed, this phenomenon has generally been overlooked in academic research, perhaps in part because it was never very widespread, but also because of what Judith Deutsch-Kornblatt terms a "general squeamishness toward the topic of conversion" (p. x).

Why, indeed, did some Russian Jews become "Russian Jewish Orthodox Christians," especially given traditional antisemitism in the Russian Orthodox Church and the fact that in Soviet Russia, unlike Russia of an earlier period, such conversions were entirely voluntary in nature, uninfluenced by considerations such as career advancement or educational opportunity? In *Doubly Chosen: Jewish Identity, the Soviet Intelligentsia, and the Russian Orthodox Church,* Deutsch-Kornblatt seeks to understand "a larger narrative about the meaning of Jewish identity in Russia" (p. 22). She looks at two groups of Russian Jewish Christians, those who were baptized in the mid-1960s to early 1970s, and those who entered the Church in the late 1980s and the 1990s. For both "the 1960s generation" and the "1980s generation," she concludes, conversion was not simply a religious decision but also a political or cultural statement.

Deutsch-Kornblatt points to a thirst for belief that developed in the post-Stalin era, which was a time of profound ideological vacuum and gradually diminishing faith in Communism. Soviet Jewish intellectuals who converted during the 1960s considered their baptism to be not only a religious step but also a "political statement of dissent" and an expression of "the individual personality" suppressed by the Soviet collectivist ideology (p. 132). Generally corroborating Gauri Viswanathan's findings that a willful change of religion may be viewed as an act of opposition,[1] Deutsch-Kornblatt shows that, for these Jews, conversion most often signified opposition to Soviet ideology rather than to Judaism (whose precepts were unknown to most of them). Among other incentives for conversion, she cites the "strong acculturation of Russian Jews and their sense of belonging to the great tradition of Russian literature, music, and art" (p. 8), and the intelligentsia's rediscovery of Nikolai Berdyaev, Pavel Florensky, Vladimir Soloviev, and other Russian religious philosophers. Soloviev, who emphasized the spiritual chosenness of the

Jewish people, was particularly influential, as were certain charismatic figures of the time, notably Father Alexander Men.

In "a central paradox of this study," Deutsch-Kornblatt reports that most of the converts, both in the 1960s and later, felt "*more*, not less Jewish after their baptism than before" (p. 96). This was particularly true of the later converts, whose conversion took place in a context of far greater freedom. In this, the "Russian Jewish Christians" differed from the non-Russian Jewish converts from Judaism, who tended to discard their Jewishness in an attempt to attain full integration into the larger society.

On this point, however, it is quite possible that the findings may have been different had the sample of respondents been more systematically selected. Deutsch-Kornblatt's qualitative study is based primarily on in-depth interviews with 35 converts from Judaism who were chosen "largely by word of mouth" (p. 29). Although this method (known as "snowball sampling" or "chain referrals") is an efficient way to gain access to marginal groups or to collect information on confidential topics, it does not generally result in a good cross-section of the population being examined. In this instance, emigrants are heavily overrepresented, with almost all of the respondents from the 1980s generation currently living in Israel or in the United States. The sense of an enhanced Jewish identity and "double chosenness" (p. 15) may not be shared by those former Jews who remained in the former Soviet Union.

Surprisingly, Deutsch-Kornblatt virtually omits any discussion of the late 1970s to early 1980s. This was a time when Russian Orthodoxy came increasingly into vogue—but so did Judaism, to the extent that a number of previous converts abandoned Christianity. At this point, the Soviet context of oppression no longer serves as an adequate explanation regarding those who sought to combine Jewish identity and Christian faith. Although Deutsch-Kornblatt discusses at length the "double identity" of Oswald Rufeisen (Brother Daniel), a Polish-born Jew who converted during the Holocaust, whose case is irrelevant to the Soviet context of this book,[2] she barely overcomes the limitations of her proposed explanatory model.

As it happens, almost all of Deutsch-Kornblatt's respondents were connected in some manner to a group of intellectuals allied with Father Men. Defined by Russian scholar S. Lezov as the "bearers and customers of liberal subculture in Russian Christianity,"[3] the overwhelmingly majority of this group consisted of ethnic Russians (Men, murdered in 1990, was himself born to Jewish parents and baptized, together with his mother, into the banned Catacomb church). Yet apart from a number of references to traditional antisemitism in the Russian Orthodox Church, *Doubly Chosen* makes virtually no mention of the interactions of Jewish Christians with their non-Jewish counterparts. Consequently, it may seem that the rejection of Russian Orthodox antisemitism is exclusively a Jewish Christian concern—particularly considering that the respondents' commitment to struggle against this "genetic disease" is regularly emphasized. Yet in the absence of any mention of support for this stance within the Russian Orthodox community, the adherence of Jewish Christians to Russian Orthodoxy seems puzzling, to say the least.

Further, while the cultural and sociopolitical context of the 1960s is depicted systemically, that of the 1980s is given in a haphazard and sometimes confusing manner. Deutsch-Kornblatt quotes without comment the wife of one convert of the late 1980s who thus explained her husband's act: "At the time, it was dangerous to practice Judaism. So he went through Buddhism before he came to Orthodoxy" (p. 85). What is this supposed to mean? The Soviet Union at this point was in the era of *perestroika*, which was characterized, among other things, by far greater openness toward religion, including Judaism. This tendency became evident toward the celebration of the 1000th anniversary of Russia's baptism in 1988, and found its legal expression in the 1990 Law on Freedom of Conscience and Religious Organizations. It is thus hardly appropriate to speak, as the author does, of "apocalyptic times" (p. 92) or "the shattering effects of the glasnost and perestoika" (p. 31) with regard to young Jewish intellectuals who, for the most part, were both enthusiastic supporters and beneficiaries of reforms.

Doubly Chosen also contains a number of inaccuracies that could easily have been avoided. For instance, the peak year for Jewish emigration from the Soviet Union/ Commonwealth of Independent States in the period 1968–1990 was 1990, not 1979; and the playwright and songwriter Alexander Galich did not emigrate to Israel but rather arrived in Norway in 1974 (he later lived in Munich and Paris). More serious is Deutsch-Kornblatt's misinterpretation of a key term in Russian: "When I would ask my subjects about their conversions (*perekreshchenie*), almost all would explain that they did not 'convert'. . . . Instead, they consistently used the term *obrashchenie*, meaning a turning toward or entrance into something new" (pp. 56–57). In fact, the word *perekreshchenie* means transbaptism, that is, baptism to another Christian confession, and therefore cannot be used to denote conversion from a non-Christian denomination. *Obrashchenie* is the correct term for "out" conversion.

Notwithstanding these reservations, this subtly and perceptively written book is a valuable study that will be of interest to a broad range of scholars and university students.

DINA ZISSERMAN-BRODSKY
The Hebrew University

Notes

1. See Gauri Viswanathan, *Outside the Fold: Conversion, Modernity and Belief* (Princeton: 1998), who notes that "conversion is a subversion of secular power," which "can best be grasped as an outcome of particular historical conjuncture" (p. 3)
2. The "double identity" of Cardinal Jean-Marie Lustiger, who described himself as a "fulfilled Jew," is also noteworthy.
3. S. Lezov, "Yest' li u russkogo pravoslaviia budushcheie?" *Znamia* 3 (March 1994), 173.

Zvi Gitelman (ed.), *The Emergence of Modern Jewish Politics: Bundism and Zionism in Eastern Europe*. Pittsburgh: University of Pittsburgh Press, 2003. 288 pp.

In 1897, two great political movements that would fundamentally change the lives of East European Jewish communities were established: Bundism and Zionism. A century later, the authors of this collection of essays inquire into the diverse facets of modernization brought about by these opposing political movements, while also dealing with cultural issues that stress the interaction between politics and the arts.

In his introductory essay, Zvi Gitelman credits the Bund, in particular, with being an agent of democratization that opened up new spheres of activity for previously marginalized groups in the Jewish community—namely, women and the under-privileged classes. Zionism, in contrast, appealed mainly to a middle-class clien-tele. The fact that the Bund nevertheless ended up being one of the "great losers" of history is attributed largely to the murderous violence of the Nazis, although Gitelman also cites the movement's location in Eastern (as opposed to Central or Western) Europe and its use of Yiddish as a lingua franca.

In late tsarist Russia, it was specifically the middle-class Jewish milieu that was characterized by western notions of emancipation and integration. As Benjamin Nathans shows, Jewish lawyers were prominent in promoting the notion that only the abolition of legal discrimination could combat Jewish isolation and victimi-zation. Nathans also explores the reciprocal influences between the two movements and concludes that both the Bundists and Zionists pursued the goal of civic equality at a time when the liberal Jewish elite increasingly "flirted" with Jewish nation-alism and collectivism. (Which ideas these Jewish liberals developed in the face of glaring social evils remains unanswered.)

Antony Polonsky treats the different Gentile contexts of Jewish political models in Eastern Europe. He describes the position of the Bund and that of Zionist groups in the semi-authoritarian Poland of the interwar period, along with the divergent processes of political fractionalization, on the one hand, and nation-building, on the other. In Lithuania, in contrast, the concept of Jewish national autonomy was actually realized for a brief time after the First World War; Polonsky asks about the reasons for its failure and calls into question the option of a secure diaspora ex-istence in Eastern Europe, though he touches only in passing on the parallel nation-building of other East European ethnic groups.[1]

Gershon Bacon focuses on the political strategy pursued by the conservative re-ligious Agudas Yisroel party in Poland. Despite ideological differences with the Zionists, the two groups often worked together, since they needed to collaborate both in the parliament and in the *kehilot*. It can be argued, of course, that the Zionists were by no means the "inventors" of the modern political party, and that Agudas Yisroel might just as easily have taken the Gentile conservative parties as a role model.

In separate essays, Daniel Blatman and Samuel Kassow examine the two Jewish labor parties, the Bund and Poale Zion Left, during the time of the Second Polish Republic. Kassow's contribution recalls that the political concept of Poale Zion Left was inadequately rooted in the East European context. To be sure, its repre-sentatives, like the Bundists, were supporters of Yiddishism. At the same time, they also operated in a conceptual triangle oriented toward Moscow, Palestine, and the diaspora. The inherent difficulties of satisfying all three fronts eventually led to Poale Zion Left's growing focus upon Palestine and a rapprochement with the Zionist mainstream by the latter half of the 1930s. The Bund, in contrast, was able to establish its roots in diaspora Jewish life by means of a network of auxiliary organizations. Daniel Blatman illustrates this both for the Bund's women's organization, the Yidishe arbeter froy (YAF), and for the Bund-dominated Jewish trade unions. As he shows, the Bund also succeeded in becoming fully integrated into the Polish trade union council while continuing to maintain its own separate organizational structure, not least through the Jewish craftsmen's union. Blatman also addresses the question (discussed at the time among Bundists) of the extent to which Jewish women served as "agents" of polonization and acculturation to a higher degree than did men. Further research is urgently needed in this area.

Michael Steinlauf explores the importance of politics for Jewish youth in interwar Poland. Making use of autobiographies found in the YIVO archives, his work underscores the fact that new institutions such as lending libraries, youth clubs, and summer camps (which were mostly run by political organizations) became increasingly important anchors of Jewish identity outside the family, replacing religious ties. Steinlauf also notes the relationship between linguistic orientation and class membership, but his remarks remain fragmentary. Further research in this area is also desirable. David Fishman, for his part, has little new to say about the Bund and Yiddish culture. His attempt to play down the importance of the Bund for the development of the Yiddish linguistic and cultural movement is sketchy and unconvincing.

The close relationship between art and politics in East European Jewish communities is the focus of three contributions. In an impressive essay, Ruth Wisse examines the political visions of Y.L. Peretz, describing their essence as a "will to powerlessness," which also found expression in Peretz's literary work and in his understanding of the "Diaspora politics of culture" (p. 131). Seth L. Wolitz explores two competing schools in the visual arts: that of Marc Chagall and the Vitebsk school, and that of the Bezalel group. While Bezalel can be seen as an artistic translation of Zionist ideology, the more successful Vitebsk group was dedicated to the concept of *doikeyt*, which promoted the Jews' symbiotic relationship with an East European homeland. Accordingly, the Vitebsk artists took up numerous Gentile motifs, and Wolitz quite rightly speaks of the hybrid nature of this artistic tendency. David Aberbach's contribution on Hebrew literature in late tsarist Russia takes a similar approach: he describes the reciprocal influences between Russian and Hebrew literature as a cross-cultural encounter.

The essays by Jonathan Frankel on Bundists in the United States and by Maud Mendel on relations between French Jews and immigrants from Eastern Europe before, during, and after the Second World War point to Bundism's failure—in contrast with Zionism—to gain a foothold outside of Eastern Europe. Ronald Grigor Suny, a specialist on Armenia, ends the volume with an outsider's look at the Jewish political movements. His essay emphasizes their significance for a new comparative historiography across nations, one that gives greater emphasis to the interrelationships between minority and majority populations, thereby deconstructing the master narratives of national history. One might add that this volume provides still more evidence that history's "beautiful losers" such as the Bund deserve far more academic attention than the self-righteous victors.

GERTRUD PICKHAN
Free University (Berlin)

Note

1. In his recent study of Polish and Jewish socialists before 1918, Joshua Zimmerman has demonstrated the many correlations with Jewish models of identity. See his *Poles, Jews, and the Politics of Nationality: The Bund and the Polish Socialist Party in Late Tsarist Russia, 1892–1914* (Madison: 2004).

Jeffrey S. Gurock, *Judaism's Encounter with American Sports* (The Modern Jewish Experience). Bloomington: Indiana University Press, 2005. x + 234 pp.

One might expect a man who has been successively a high school basketball player, a college lacrosse team member, a college and high school basketball coach and, past his 50th birthday, still a marathon runner, sooner to be a jock than an Orthodox Jew and a productive, respected American Jewish historian. But all these constitute parts of Jeffrey Gurock's life. In the present work, he notes, he has achieved his enduring desire to combine in written form the athletic and the academic. Hence, the reader of *Judaism's Encounter with American Sports* will find its focus shifting back and forth between Professor Gurock, Yeshiva University historian, and Jeff, coach and advocate for religiously observant Jewish athletes. Throughout, Gurock arouses interest and, among older readers, nostalgia, with the aid of a style that is often redolent of newspaper sports pages.

The reader should note Gurock's title. It implies that he does not deal with the accomplishments of such Jewish professional athletic champions as Hank Greenberg or Sandy Koufax but rather with sports within a specifically Jewish, mainly Orthodox, communal or academic framework. Thus the likes of Sid Luckman at Columbia or Marshall Goldberg at Pittsburgh, both of them collegiate Jewish football heroes, are omitted in favor of Jewish youths who formed the basketball teams of schools like Rabbi Jacob Joseph High School or Yeshiva College. Gurock dwells at some length on such institutions, unwavering in their Orthodoxy, that wrestled with questions involving sports competitions and especially the settings in which they took place. The rabbis who headed strictly Orthodox yeshivot, which in postwar America were increasing both in number and in religious rigor, would have liked to discontinue the inter-yeshiva games beloved of their pupils but felt unable to do so. Yet if they had to accept games, they would not tolerate boys and girls enjoying one another's company as spectators, nor would they allow cheering squads composed of girls who were, in their conception, skimpily dressed. Reluctantly accepting the games, they regretted that yeshiva youth lavished more admiration on their schools' players than on outstanding Talmud students.

The principals of the Orthodox schools at the center of Gurock's interest also debated whether they should admit Conservative schools to the yeshiva high school athletic leagues. They usually refused to accept them, over the dissent of moderates in their midst. This issue points to a significant weakness in Gurock's work: he gives little attention to sports' relation to Judaism in non-Orthodox, not to mention Reform or secular, Jewish institutions, perhaps because only the Conservative schools among them even took notice of the questions that exercised the Orthodox. It goes unmentioned that, by approximately 1910, Hebrew Union College possessed a well-equipped gymnasium, whose adjacent walls displayed photographs of teams composed of future Reform rabbis. The Jewish Theological Seminary's gymnasium of 1930 was merely a large room that is now used for other student purposes. No Orthodox institution possessed a gymnasium worthy of the name until Yeshiva University's fine facility was erected in the 1970s.

Gurock also devotes much less space to Jewish centers, synagogue centers, and YMHAs, compared with the Orthodox schools. At the Jewish centers, sports and dances were the main (and, in many places, practically the only) activities. The centers sometimes issued statements expressing concern for their members' development as Jews, but these were mostly perfunctory in tone. Despite their ties to synagogues, synagogue centers did not differ much. During the suburban building boom of the 1950s and 1960, there was sharp rivalry between the two types of center. Gurock quotes extensively from rival spokesmen, especially rabbis, yet says little about what actually went on in the respective centers. He does refer to Cleveland's wealthy Reform congregation, Tifereth Israel—known as The Temple—which abolished its long-established center in the 1920s. However, he misstates the reason it closed. It was not snobbish exclusiveness, an attempt to keep away the mass of East European Jews who lived nearby. Rather, its powerful rabbi, Abba Hillel Silver, insisted that The Temple's members should participate with other Jews in a community center serving Cleveland Jewry as a whole. The Temple thereafter confined itself to worship and religious education.

Gurock's heart is in sports at Yeshiva University, essentially its basketball team, whose occasional victories in major competition thrilled yeshiva youngsters. During a few years of glory in the early 1950s, Yeshiva gained fame in the metropolitan newspapers' sports pages. Alone of the Orthodox institutions, it was a degree-granting college, and it began to attract public high school graduates as students. The stars of the basketball team came mainly from this source and, within Yeshiva, opinions were divided regarding the propriety of the new Jewish studies program designed to accommodate them and others. Teams at the only other Jewish university of that time, Brandeis, are not mentioned.

When Jeff takes charge, *Judaism's Encounter with American Sports* is not a carefully balanced book, owing to the author's infectious enthusiasm for Orthodox young sportsmen. The early chapters, however, are the work of Professor Gurock, and these are well balanced indeed. Gurock presents the little that is known about ancient and medieval Jewish sports before moving on to his central theme, the mass arrival of East European Jewish immigrants in America. He finds a lack of physicality among the immigrants; his very doubtful claim is that many of the more robust Jews were Bundist revolutionaries who preferred to remain in Russia to fight the regime. Actually, all sorts of Jews left Russia, and it appears impossible to classify them ideologically. Yet it is true that, by and large, the immigrants knew little and cared less about sports. They had to work long and hard just to earn a living, and their children's fervor for the professional sports that so excited the American people puzzled and sometimes antagonized them.

Years before radio, youngsters from the Lower East Side would trek to Park
Row, the newspaper street facing City Hall, to learn the latest baseball scores before
they appeared in print. My father, the son of immigrant workers and no athlete,
would walk to Park Row and was proud that he had seen in action the great Giants
pitcher Christy Matthewson. I, his son, also no athlete, am proud that I saw the
nonpareil Carl Hubbell, also of the Giants, put down the St. Louis Cardinals. I
merely suggest that the enthusiasm of young Jewish spectators for professional
sports might also belong in *Judaism's Encounter with American Sports*. As it is, its
precision and documentation demonstrate Professor Gurock's known scholarship,
while its fervor shows Jeff playing hard alongside the professor.

LLOYD P. GARTNER
Tel Aviv University

Uzi Rebhun, *Hagirah, kehilah, hizdahut: yehudei arzot habrit beshilhei hameah
ha'esrim* (Migration, community, and identification: Jews in late 20th-cen-
tury America). Jerusalem: Magnes Press, 2001. xi + 281 pp.

For many years, the social sciences did not fare well as a branch of Jewish scholarship. Although *Statistik der Juden* was included among the disciplines constituting
Jewish studies in the programmatic statement issued in 1819 by the Verein für
Kultur und Wissenschaft der Juden, a survey of the curricula of American colleges
and universities during the period of 1923 to 1968 indicated the almost total absence
of courses on the social scientific study of the Jews.[1] In the late 1960s, there was only
one tenured professor in the United States whose primary field of interest was the
sociology of the Jews (Marshall Sklare), and not a single scholarly organization
served as a marketplace of ideas for the field. It is only in the last three decades or so
that the situation changed, the Jewish community first becoming aware of its need
for independent research and later funding the gathering and distribution of statistical data. Fortunately, we now have a younger generation of bright and well-trained
people who specialize in Jewish social research. Though their number is small, they
are rapidly transforming the field from a proprietary marginal enterprise into a
"normal" science. The book under scrutiny is a fine example of the coming of age of
Jewish social science.

Uzi Rebhun's work is valuable from several perspectives. First, while the vast
majority of scholars who work on American Jewry are themselves American Jews,
Rebhun was born and trained in Israel. Consequently, his work views American
Jewry from an external perspective. Second, Rebhun gears his book not only to
experts in the field but also to scholars who are not trained in statistics or social
science methodology. In his first chapter, for instance, he explains the logic of
survey research (the method most frequently employed by sociologists and de-
mographers) and offers statistical models showing how various patterns of correlations are consistent with the assumptions of some models and inconsistent with

those of others. His discussion—the best of its kind that I have ever read—enables non-experts to follow the arguments and findings presented in the remainder of the book.

As indicated by its title, a main theme of this work is migration. Over the course of the late 19th and early 20th centuries, the geographic distribution of Jews changed radically as they were faced with the collapse of their historic social order. During the period of the great trans-Atlantic migration (ca. 1880–1924), proportionally more Jews migrated to the United States than did members of any other ethnic or religious group. Even within their new homeland, Jews continued to be highly mobile— both socially and geographically. Rebhun offers a comprehensive report detailing the "what" and "why" of Jewish American geographic mobility and then focuses his inquiry on the relationship between Jewish identification and geographic mobility, seeking to show its direction, sources, and consequences. In other words, assuming that there is, in fact, a relationship between geographic mobility and level of Jewish identification, with Jews who migrate more frequently (or farther) tending to have "weaker" Jewish identities, what is the direction of the causal flow? Is it the moving that weakens Jewish identification, or is it rather that those with a weaker sense of Jewish identification are the ones most likely to be mobile?

Rebhun's first two chapters discuss geographical mobility on the abstract level. In succeeding chapters, he shifts to an empirical mode, that is, from concepts to indicators. Measuring mobility in terms of the frequency and distance of moves both over the course of a lifetime and over the course of the most recent five-year period, Rebhun demonstrates the way in which micro-level phenomena lead to macro-level consequences. For instance, he shows how, as certain neighborhoods undergo decline, those who have less of an investment in local institutions are among the first to move, whereas those who are more attached to local institutions are among the last. This simple, micro-level phenomenon accounts for the macro-level regularity in which local Reform temples follow their constituencies to more desirable locations while hasidic *shtieblakh* remain in place, often until the bitter end.

The Jews, of course, were not the only ethnic group to immigrate en masse to the United States. Upon their arrival, different groups chose different areas in which to live, their choice being determined both by the skills and human contacts that they brought with them from the "old country" and by the opportunities available at the time. Yet another valuable feature of this book is Rebhun's presentation of the geographical distribution of various ethnic groups over the course of time and his comparison of the mobility of whites in general with that of Jews. Among the similarities in "mobility history" is the Northeast region's gradual loss of population, both of Jews and of whites in general, between 1900 and 1990—though this region, as he shows, continues to be the geographic center of gravity for American Jewry.

Rebhun also focuses on the components of Jewish identification, consisting of both religious and ethnic (or "tribal") elements, showing that, between 1970 and 1990, American Jews underwent structural assimilation rather than secularization. In 1970, the average American Jew was tied to a Jewish community consisting of family, friends, and Jewish communal organizations. While secularization had already made major inroads in the Jewish community, as late as 1990 it had not eroded the loyalty of most American Jews to certain non-demanding religious behaviors such as attending a Passover seder (as compared with, say, maintaining a kosher household), although other aspects of Jewish peoplehood—such as religious endogamy and maintaining an all-Jewish friendship circle—had declined further during the same period. Here and in the succeeding chapters, Rebhun offers a remarkably clear analysis of some very complex social processes that link the elements of Jewish life in a modern society that rewards ability and hard work but sets a very high price for "making it."

PAUL RITTERBAND
University of Haifa

Note

1. Paul Ritterband and Harold S. Wechsler, *Jewish Learning in American Universities: The First Century* (Bloomington: 1994), 174.

Yuri Slezkine, *The Jewish Century.* Princeton: Princeton University Press, 2004. 438 pp.

It is hard to recall another work focused on modern Jewish history that has attracted as much attention in recent times as this book by Yuri Slezkine. In part, the extraordinary reception accorded *The Jewish Century* is to be explained by the sheer esprit and verve of the writing. It is truly astonishing that somebody raised in Russia and arriving in the United States only as a young adult should be able to produce such a sparkling English text, replete with a seemingly inexhaustible string of aphorisms and paradoxes, the one more polished than the next.

Beyond the style, though, and more important, is the substance—or rather, perhaps, the methodology. In analyzing the role played by the Jewish people in the 20th-century world, Slezkine advances bold generalizations with a breathtaking recklessness. Such an approach is refreshing. Originating as it does largely in the scholarly traditions of continental Europe (Hegelianism, Marxism, and, it would seem, phenomenology), this approach cannot but attract startled attention when lined up next to the cautiously empirical historiography predominant in the English-speaking world generally and in the field of Jewish studies particularly. (In this context, it is perhaps worth recalling the lasting impact made by Hannah Arendt's *Origins of Totalitarianism*, another work untrammeled by merely empirical inhibitions and likewise rooted in modes of thought ultimately traceable to German philosophical idealism.)

For all the great variety of detail that enriches *The Jewish Century*, its key line of argument can be briefly summarized, hopefully without undue distortion. As his starting point, Slezkine recalls that the Jewish people had developed over many centuries as a primary example of a trading and relatively urbanized minority, forced to survive on its wits in the midst of predominantly agrarian, militarized, largely feudal ("Apollonian") societies. In this context, he coins the term "Mercurian" to describe not only the Jews but all the groups that have fulfilled a similar middleman role in modern times—among them, the Parsees in India, the overseas Chinese in southeast Asia, the Indians in East Africa, the Lebanese Christians in South America, and the Armenians in Eastern Europe and the Middle East. (These are the "mobilized diasporas," to use John Armstrong's terminology from his well-known article of 1976.)[1]

Slezkine grants that for all its unusually high levels of literacy, numeracy, and economic adaptability, the Jewish people contributed almost nothing to the early stages of modernization as advanced by the scientific and industrial revolutions. It was only the interlocking process of emancipation and integration that brought about a truly dramatic transformation, as Jews seized on the opportunities inherent in the dynamics of modernization with unexampled enthusiasm and innovative drive. In the approximately 50 years before the First World War, in the German, the Habsburg, and even the Russian empires, they attained astonishing rates of upward mobility in whatever channels were opened up to them: specifically in the free professions; industrial and mercantile entrepreneurship; finance; newspaper publishing and journalism; the arts and sciences.

All this was as nothing, though, when compared to the leading positions that Jews had won for themselves in the Soviet Union by the 1930s in every sphere of responsibility, whether in government and the armed forces, industrial enterprise, scientific and academic research, or literature and music. And a remarkably similar development unfolded in the United States a generation or so later, when access to the inner sancta of society and the economy was first attained by those Jews who were the grandchildren and great-grandchildren of the exodus from Eastern Europe.

While the Apollonians were being forced inexorably by the modernizing juggernaut to transform themselves into Mercurians, the Jews, for their part, had a head start. Or, as Slezkine puts it: "Modernization . . . is about everyone becoming Jewish. Some peasants and princes have done better than others, but no one is better at being Jewish than the Jews themselves" (p. 1).

But while emancipation and economic opportunity were bringing Jews in from the cold, a parallel development—nationalism—was emerging to keep them out. In contrast to Eric Hobsbawm, for example, and in line with both Ernest Gellner and Anthony D. Smith, Slezkine treats nationalism not as a transient but as an integral and cardinal factor in the process of modernization. "The [mechanized] Weberian world," he writes, "could be sustained—indeed conceived—only within states that posed as tribes." Taking a familiar example, he adds (*pace* Eugen Weber) that peasants could become Frenchmen only "if France stood for Patrie as well as Progress" (p. 61).

Unavoidably, so the argument runs, the Jewish people was uniquely involved in the nationalist turn: in its origins and, still more, in its consequences. The Old Testament, with its foundational tale of national heroes, nation-building, and a Chosen People, had provided the archetypal model for the emergent European nation-states. But if the modern nation, like the ancient, increasingly defined itself as "ascriptive and blood-bound," it could hardly open itself up to those primordial aliens in its midst, the Jews. No sooner had the Jews expressed themselves eager to become, for example, Germans—"for who needed chosenness . . . if everyone was becoming Jewish anyway?"—than "the Germans themselves became 'chosen' " (pp. 61–62).

With the neutral society thus exposed as a dream doomed to failure, the search for alternatives, "the Jewish revolution," was set in motion, manifesting itself quintessentially in three major and competing ideologies or, in Slezkine's words, the three "great modern prophecies": nationalism (expressed, in its specifically Jewish form, as Zionism); Marxism; and Freudianism. In their Jewish context, as he describes it, they were all three the product of "patricidal" rebellion on the part of the generation of the sons against their upwardly mobile fathers who had escaped the ghetto only to suffer exclusion and insult.

And these same three ideologies largely shaped not only Jewish but also world history in the 20th century: Marxism, through the rise and fall of Communism in Europe; Freudianism as a "salvation religion" exerting enormous influence on American society; and nationalism as ultimately the most potent force in the competition to mobilize mass society.

The fissionable power encapsulated in the nationalist idea revealed itself in its most devastating form, of course, in the genocidal onslaught of the Nazi regime against the Jewish people—an onslaught justified by a theodicy which envisaged "all the corruption of the modern world . . . as caused by one race, the Jews" (p. 103). However, it was also nationalism, whether that of the Russians or of the many other territorially rooted ethnic nationalities in the Soviet bloc, that underpinned the eventual expulsion of the Jews, starting in 1940, from virtually all positions of authority in the Communist states.

It is into this same framework that the author slots the creation of Israel, the product of Zionist ideology, which argued that "it was not for everyone else to become like the Jews, but for the Jews to become like everyone else" (p. 2)—one more radical ideology that failed, if only in part, because Israel has so conspicuously been unable to gain recognition from world opinion as a normal country. In the last resort, it is only in the United Sates, concludes Slezkine, that the Jewish people has found a setting that is "the least revolutionary," the most Mercurian, based neither on "tribal descent" nor on "the cult of the national soul" (p. 67), and therefore most compatible with its character.

What, then, are we to make of this book? It will surely continue to be widely read, and understandably so. The author is not afraid to tackle the big questions, and to hazard answers of exceptional clarity and wit (indeed, one cannot help wondering how much may be written tongue-in-cheek). His chapter on the Soviet Jewish experience, over a quarter of the book and one hundred pages in length, is impressively perceptive and informative, gaining in interest because, as he tells us, it is partially inspired by the life story of his Jewish grandmother.

Nevertheless, it seems to me that the highly schematic and architectonic character of *The Jewish Century* has been bought at a very high price—too high. It brings with it significant sins of omission. No attention at all, for instance, is paid to the remarkable resurgence of ultra-Orthodox Judaism over the last few decades (after all, it is quite possible that one of Tevye's descendants, who are followed in imagination by Yuri Slezkine throughout the book, would today be living in Bnei Brak, Borough Park, or Stamford Hill).

More important, though, are the sins of commission. The idea of placing Freudianism on a par with Marxism and nationalism as one of the three great ideologies shaping the 20th century fits neatly into the tripartite conception of the book, but is surely a gross exaggeration. The preference for tidy formulations that gloss over complex realities similarly produces such hyperbolic characterizations of Zionism as "the most eccentric of all nationalisms" (p. 2) and of Israel as "a state of exemplary Apollonians among universal (Western) Mercurians" (p. 367).

Underlying all such issues is the fundamental problem that the facts which Slezkine marshals do not give substance to the claim that the last century was the Jewish century. The Jews were significantly, sometimes greatly, overrepresented for brief periods (no more than a few decades, at most) in a number of select spheres in a few states; but even then—because in comparative terms the Jewish people is miniscule—they were nearly always in a minority at whatever they were doing. Of course, the belief that despite all this, the Jews were somehow of vast importance, imposing radical change on their host societies, has always been an obsession of the paranoid Judeophobic mind. And it is the consequent genocide, the Holocaust, which alone might, perhaps, justify the idea of the Jewish century. However, that issue is by no means central to the book under review; the entries for the Holocaust in the index take up less space than those for Gypsies.

Yuri Slezkine is philosemitic, and his book can be read as a celebration of Jewish vitality, enterprise, courage, and imagination. But to employ the Jews as a symbol, as a metaphor, for modernization in all its major manifestations is intellectually irresponsible and cannot be justified. Karl Marx famously turned Hegelianism on its head, substituting a materialist for an idealist explanation of history, while retaining the same dialectical framework. It is hard to escape the uncomfortable conclusion that *The Jewish Century* has similarly tipped the antisemitic paradigm upside down while leaving its structure intact.

JONATHAN FRANKEL
The Hebrew University

Note

1. John A. Armstrong, "Mobilized and Proletarian Diasporas," *American Political Science Review* 70, no. 2 (June 1976), 393–408.

Aaron Surasky, *Melekh beyofyo: toledot ḥayav po'alo vedarko bakodesh shel maran hagaon R. Yeḥezkel Abramsky* (The life and holy path of R. Yehezkel Abramsky), 2 vols. Jerusalem: n.p., 2004. 902 pp.

R. Yehezkel Abramsky's long life was spent in three centers of Judaism, each with its distinctive character. He began in Russia, steeped in religious tradition but modernizing; then in England, with its freedom and assimilation; and finally in the new, sovereign Israel, where the most venerable and the newest in Judaism existed in uneasy embrace. Throughout, Abramsky was unswervingly Orthodox, an outstanding representative of talmudic learning and of community leadership in that spirit.

Born in 1886 to pious parents in a White Russian village that lacked enough Jews to constitute a steady minyan, Abramsky studied Talmud at home until he left at the age of 17 to learn at the yeshivot of Slobodka, Telz, and Mir. Native talent and diligent study made him a recognized traditional scholar as a young man, and his reputation steadily increased with the years. His foremost master, he said, was R. Hayim Soloveichik of Volozhin and then of Brest-Litovsk, whose innovative, analytic method of Talmud study powerfully influenced Abramsky and the realm of yeshivot in general.

After 1918, Abramsky, now married and serving as the rabbi of several small communities, had to contend with religious persecution on the part of Russia's Communist regime. Persecution continued when, in 1923, he removed from Smulyan to become rabbi of the prominent community of Slutsk, where Talmud learning still flourished even among humble Jews. It is interesting to note that, at this date, Jewish notables of Slutsk were able to follow the traditional practice of sending a delegation to Smulyan in order to lure Abramsky away. Some time later, however, fearing especially for the religious future of his growing sons, Abramsky became anxious to quit Communist Russia. He was elected rabbi of Petah Tikvah while he and his family were still waiting to receive the necessary exit permits; someone else was appointed in his place. This fiasco, together with Abramsky's determined adherence to traditional Judaism, set in motion a chain of events that led to his arrest and hunger and misery in a labor camp in Siberia. Liberated after "only" one year of his five-year sentence thanks to continuous pressure from abroad, he was allowed to leave Russia, though not with all of his family.

Abramsky came to England in 1931 to take up the post of rabbi of the largest immigrant congregation in the East End of London, and several years after his arrival, his older sons were permitted to quit Russia and join him there. In his new country, Abramsky became familiar with an assimilated Jewish community that enjoyed freedom, was respectful of Judaism, but was fervent neither in Jewish learning nor in religious observance.

Upon his retirement in 1952, Abramsky settled in Jerusalem, where he found that the realized dream of a Jewish state brought a new set of dilemmas. He was quickly accepted into Israel's rabbinic leadership, a rare occurrence among newly arrived diaspora rabbis. He took an active role in seeking to resolve some of Israel's dilemmas, such as women's military service and kashruth in public institutions, in the spirit of Agudath Israel, with which he became affiliated. However, teaching and writing, rather than politics, were his main preoccupations. He commuted for years to the Slobodka yeshiva in Bnei Brak, where he delivered regular discourses (shi'urim) in Talmud, probably in a mixture of Hebrew and Yiddish. The singular erudition and clarity of his shi'urim, given in synagogues and in yeshivot both in England and in Israel, were a major source of Abramsky's renown.

This long, eventful life has been chronicled by Aaron Surasky, whose work, however, is less a biography than a hagiography. R. Abramsky is portrayed in glowing terms of reverence—wise, learned, and benevolent to the point of infallibility. While no one questions his deep learning and distinction as a Talmud lecturer, there is such a thing as too much. Moreover, the reader who desires a full account is likely to be disappointed. There is almost nothing about Abramsky's personal life and family apart from a description of his imprisonment in Russia, nor about the social and communal environments in which he lived and labored, and to which he reacted. There is, however, a long chapter about the family and ancestors of his first wife, whom he married in 1909, which a contemporary reader will find superfluous. With his long, broad beard, Abramsky cut quite a handsome figure, and he was also well known for his quick wit and sharp tongue, but few examples are provided. Finally, readers oriented to history will have to struggle to distill historical information from the pages of Surasky's book.

Recognized by Chief Rabbi Joseph H. Hertz as England's foremost East European rabbi, Abramsky was appointed *av beit din*, or head of the rabbinical court, in 1935. This move on Hertz's part suggests a strategy of bringing the gradually Anglicizing immigrant Jewry into the orbit of official Anglo-Jewry. Initially, the objection was raised that a rabbinical judge (*dayan*) who did not yet know English could not hear cases involving individuals who spoke only in that language. Sir Robert Waley Cohen, the managing director of Shell Oil and the lay ruler of the United Synagogue, provided him with a teacher of English. Even before he undertook the potent position of *av beit din*, Abramsky demanded that the kosher meat trade, which operated under beit din supervision, cease selling animal hindquarters, since these had not been porged of "the sciatic muscle that is on the socket of the hip" (see Gen. 32:33). Negotiations over this costly concession lasted almost a year, until Abramsky had his way—a singular demonstration not only of his personal stature but also of the established Jewish community's larger concern to draw its immigrant majority into the official community. Such vigorous independence, which Abramsky manifested with regard to other issues as well, had been unthinkable or very risky in Communist Russia, and later in Israel it was subordinated to party politics. His years in England were thus the high point of Abramsky's service to the Jewish community.

On the rabbinical court, *Dayan* Abramsky seems to have exerted a dominating influence over his colleagues. He got along well with the two potentates of the community, Chief Rabbi Hertz and Waley Cohen, although the men quarreled sharply with one another. His Saturday afternoon shi'urim, delivered in Yiddish to sizable audiences at an Anglo-Jewish synagogue, are remembered with admiration to the present day. A different undertaking, presumably conducted in English, was the weekly discussion group that met in *Dayan* Abramsky's home, which began when a young man whose religious observance was wavering was invited to visit one Friday night following the Sabbath meal. Within a few weeks, the one young visitor had become a group of 20, and these individuals continued to gather until the Second World War intervened. Abramsky was thus fully engaged in Jewish communal affairs, while evidently taking no part in the issues of British life. With the outbreak of war, he became active in the efforts to rescue Holocaust survivors and to assist those who made it to Britain. It is characteristic of the present book that little mention is made of these efforts.

In the realm of scholarship, Abramsky's permanent achievement is his *Hazon Yehezkel*, a voluminous commentary on the Tosefta, the "supplement" to the Mishnah, which he began around 1912 and later reached 12 large volumes, many of them published after Abramsky's death in 1976. Written in fine Hebrew, *Hazon Yehezkel* is traditional in scope and conception, and does not deal either with philological or historical issues. There are two divisions to the commentary, an explanation of the text practically word by word, and novellae (*hidushim*). *Hazon Yehezkel* is paralleled (or perhaps, as some maintain, rivaled or surpassed) by Saul Liberman's *Tosefta kifshutah*. It is remarkable that two contemporary rabbinic scholars of the highest stature independently undertook a massive edition and commentary on the long-neglected Tosefta. Sadly, neither author lived to complete his work. A comparison of these two monumental works illustrates the contrast between the old and the new in rabbinic scholarship.

Abramsky lived in an age of Orthodox decline, whether under the circumstances of oppression in Russia, ready assimilation in Britain, or marginalization in Israel. The present work takes little account of these circumstances. With its shortcomings— but with a welcome abundance of photographs and reproductions of letters—it is a testament of reverent admiration for a notable figure who lived in deep religious faith before the current resurgence of Orthodoxy.

LLOYD P. GARTNER
Tel Aviv University

Language, Literature, and the Arts

Samantha Baskind, *Raphael Soyer and the Search for Modern Jewish Art*. Chapel Hill: The University of North Carolina Press, 2004. 260 pp.

As its title suggests, *Raphael Soyer and the Search for Modern Jewish Art* focuses on two different issues: Jewish elements in the art of Raphael Soyer, and what is involved in the term "modern Jewish art." However, it is not Soyer's search for such an art that is discussed, but rather the author's search for it, using Soyer as an examplar. The attempt to merge these two elements into a single unit is the greatest failing of this otherwise informative and well-researched book. To do justice to each part, we must view each one individually.

The best feature of this book is its detailed description of the life and work of Raphael Soyer, in particular its discussion of specific problems confronted by the artist. Baskind's analysis of the works and their meaning is perceptive and exacting, and on the whole very convincing. She brings out clearly the artist's dilemma as an immigrant to America and his need to integrate into mainstream American art, even if this meant eschewing any overt expressions of his Jewishness for most of his life. Nevertheless, she finds various hidden levels of Jewish identity in his work, from his view of himself as a "New York painter," to his identification with the homeless and his expression of alienation from his surroundings. Toward the end of his life, Soyer finally became confident enough to openly express his Jewish identity in his illustrations for Isaac Bashevis Singer's books. In each case, Baskind provides a good deal of welcome detail on the artistic, sociological, and psychological background for the choices Soyer made. She carefully dissects the experience of immigrants in the American melting pot and the different attitudes to it in the 1920s, when Soyer began his work as an artist, and in the 1960s and 1970s, when ethnic identity became popular and Soyer could revert to his Jewish roots. The book thus becomes in part the odyssey of a Jewish immigrant who wants to become an American and his final realization that he can also be a Jew.

There are, however, a few problems here, primarily because Baskind makes it sound as if she has rediscovered Soyer. She makes the odd assertion that Soyer has been left out of all but general books on American art and that he is mostly mentioned in books on Jewish art (pp. 5, 7). Moreover, although much of what she writes is in fact new, she only rarely credits ideas she has taken from others, most notably Milly Heyd and Ezra Mendelsohn.[1] Ten years before the publication of Baskind's book, Heyd and Mendelsohn had discussed the process of acculturation that led Soyer to reject his Jewish identity, albeit without the richness of source material that

Baskind brings. They, too, stressed Soyer's universalism and leftist politics, as well as the notion that Soyer's call for social justice had Jewish roots, ideas that Baskind develops further.[2] In some cases, as in her discussion of *City Faces* (1958), Baskind blends in their analysis of the work with comparisons and conclusions of her own, without properly crediting their research.[3] In another instance, she misinterprets their argument that Soyer identified with the homeless Walter Broe because he was "a persona through which the artist's views on society and the human condition were expressed" as referring only to the physical resemblance between them, where in fact her own analysis actually develops their idea and gives it substance.[4] Since Baskind's own writing is full of insights, and goes very far beyond the range of the Heyd and Mendelsohn article, it is unclear why she did not properly acknowledge their work.

At times, Baskind twists the facts to suit her interpretations. For instance, in trying to prove that Soyer was interested in the Jewish notion of repairing the world (*tikun 'olam*), she subverts the meaning of the inscription from Isaiah 57:20 that appears in Soyer's painting *How Long Since You Wrote to Mother?* (Pl. 4, pp. 96, 98–100). Rather than concentrate on the actual inscription, "The wicked are like the troubled sea," she stresses Isaiah 58:6–7:

> No, this is the fast I desire: to unlock fetters of wickedness, and untie the cords of the yoke to let the oppressed go free; to break off every yoke. It is to share your bread with the hungry, and to take the wretched poor into your home; when you see the naked, to clothe him; and not to ignore your own kin.

This, she argues, depicts the ideal world after a return to Jerusalem, thus suggesting a Zionist context. In reality, these verses immediately follow Isaiah's harangue against the Jews for their attention to ritual while disregarding the poor, and they are meant to point out the proper way for a Jew to act. The correct interpretation would actually have bolstered Baskind's hypothesis on the "Jewishness" of the social justice that Soyer is promoting, whereas the Zionist context seems utterly misplaced.

Misinterpretation and insufficient acknowledgement of the work of others also mar Baskind's discussion of Jewish art per se. She explores a wide range of writings on modern Jewish art in order to try to determine what it is. Although a new and serious approach to this problem is always welcome, this is not what the reader is given here. Baskind merely repeats ideas that are part of the consensus among serious researchers on Jewish art: namely, that there is no truly "Jewish" style, and that what we usually find in modern art are hidden references to the artist's experience as a Jew. Yet, although Baskind refers both to Avram Kampf's groundbreaking exhibition of 1975, *Jewish Experience in the Art of the Twentieth Century* and to the books he wrote on this subject, she concludes that his definitions are confused (pp. 57–58, 76), even though she herself makes use of them.[5] To show that her approach is "new" and "up-to-date," she quotes Nicholas Mirzoeff: "The diasporic visual image is necessarily intertextual, in that the spectator needs to bring extratextual information to bear on what is seen within the frame in order to make full sense of it" (p. 219, n. 57). This is a postmodern description of any study of iconography and iconology, and it has long been established practice by serious researchers of Jewish art, including Kampf. In the future, Baskind should beware of belittling the contributions of others in order to stress her own role as a pioneer. For instance, she downplays the contribution of the journal *Jewish Art*: "Occasionally a modern Jewish artist, most notably Marc Chagall, is discussed, but typically in connection with openly Jewish subject matter" (p. 6). Actually, since its inception in 1974, *Jewish Art* (formerly called the *Journal of Jewish Art*) has published no fewer than 38 articles on 24 different modern Jewish painters and sculptors[6] as well as 17 articles on schools of modern Jewish art and on general issues such as Jewish artists' use of Christological and mythological imagery and their own highly personal symbolism. For her part, Baskind makes no more headway than anyone else in developing a theoretical framework for modern Jewish art.

On the whole, I sympathize with her attempt to combat misunderstandings about modern Jewish art and the tendency to disregard the importance of an artist's Jewish background. However, the way to fight this is not through theorizing but rather through the kind of in-depth work she presents here with regard to Soyer. Had she concentrated only on this portion of her book, it would have gained in stature. Yet despite its flaws, and despite occasional errors,[7] *Raphael Soyer and the Search for Modern Jewish Art* is a highly commendable book that should be appreciated by anyone interested in American Jews, or the problems of expressing Jewish (or, for that matter, any other minority) identity in art.

ZIVA AMISHAI-MAISELS
The Hebrew University

Notes

1. Milly Heyd and Ezra Mendelsohn, " 'Jewish' Art? The Case of the Soyer Brothers," *Jewish Art* 19 (1993), 195–211.

2. Ibid., 201–203.

3. Heyd and Mendelsohn, " 'Jewish' Art?," 199; cf. Baskind, *Raphael Soyer and the Search for Modern Art*, 119–123.

4. Ibid., 206; cf. Baskind, 79–109, and esp. p. 218, n. 37.

5. Strangely, Baskind leaves Kampf out of her overview of writings on the problem of modern Jewish art. It is only on p. 57 that she mentions him, noting only his treatment of works by Soyer. Compare her comments on the importance of the Jewish experience, esp. pp. 64 and 195, with Kampf's introduction to his exhibition, esp. pp. 7–8. Baskind later credits Heyd and Matthew Baigell with Kampf's original ideas (p. 212, n. 21).

6. Of these articles, ten are admittedly on Chagall, whom even Baskind acknowledges to be the major modern Jewish artist (p. 162).

7. For instance, a Russian shtetl is not a ghetto, as she suggests it is on p. 66.

Bryan Cheyette and Nadia Valman (eds.), *The Image of the Jew in European Liberal Culture 1789–1914*. London: Vallentine Mitchell, 2004. 247 pp.

With Jewish writers of the caliber of Saul Bellow, Henry Roth, and Philip Roth, to name only a few in modern American literature, and with characters such as Shylock in a continuing line in English literature, there has been a plethora of studies of attitudes toward Jews and Jewishness in both America and England. *The Image of the Jew in European Liberal Culture* breaks new ground in dealing with Jews in the 19th century in Europe, concentrating on attitudes toward Jews in four countries— Britain, Germany, France, and Italy. The texts discussed are considered against a background of general European liberalism and in contexts not only of instances of antisemitism but of philosemitism and of the relation between the two. The book opens with a short but incisive introduction by the editors. They first delineate the general background of previous relevant work, and then place the contributions that follow in illuminating contexts. The book, comprising 11 essays, is divided into three sections, "After Enlightenment," "Fin de Siècle Jews," and "After Dreyfus." Unfortunately, while all the contributions are professionally competent, solidly written, and well researched, with a wide range of citations, most tend to lack sparkle. However, three essays—one in each section, as it happens— stand out both in the quality of their writing and in the scintillating nature of their analyses.

In the first section, Florian Krobb offers a lively account of the depiction of Jews in the second half of the 19th century in Germany, particularly in the work of Theodor Fontane, an author who "paradoxically, was labelled a 'Philo-semitic Antisemite' " (p. 79). But it is Michael Galchinsky whose work is most notable in this section, despite the ponderous title of his essay: "Africans, Indians, Arabs, and Scots: Jewish and Other Questions in the Age of Empire." In contradistinction to the implicit assumption of several contributors to the volume, he insists that "the Jewish Question" was not the central concern of European discussions of marginality, being merely a "subset" of such discourse. Focusing on attitudes in 19th-century England, he conclusively demonstrates, with reference to some particularly prominent writers, that the marginal groups named in his title were as much a focus of interest as were Jews.

Galchinsky is most illuminating in his analyses of the attitudes of Edmund Burke and Thomas Macaulay, contrasting what he calls Burke's "thick description" of the African slave trade in his "Sketch of a Negro Code" with his "thin depiction" of Jewishness in his famous book on the French Revolution. No Jews actually appear in the latter text, although they figure as a metonymy for Jacobinism. Burke regards the Revolution as an attack on Christianity, and therefore views it, figuratively, as "Jewish." In contrast, his discussion of African slaves deals with concrete details of their behavior and their treatment. Macaulay, for his part, in two parliamentary speeches in the 1830s, elaborated on what should be the proper treatment of all British subjects, including the Jewish religious and racial minority in England and the correspondingly other but huge group of Indians in India. He advocated the same sort of tolerant attitude toward Jews as that which had made Catholics good Englishmen, declaring there was nothing in the Jewish character that made them unfit for "the highest duties of civilisation." But this was implicitly English civilization, as became clear in his insistence that the Indian school curriculum be based on English texts, since Macaulay believed that Indians, like Jews, could only benefit from exposure to English culture. Galchinsky concludes that Macaulay "tried to ameliorate" the suffering of both marginalized groups "while ensuring the maintenance of English Christian power" (p. 55).

An outstanding essay in the section on fin de siècle Jews is Marilyn Reizbaum's "Max Nordau and the Generation of Jewish Muscle." She links and contrasts Nordau's famous work *Degeneration* (1892) with his Zionist tracts, particularly the short piece "Muscle-Jews" (1903). Nordau encapsulates his sense of the degeneracy of the 1890s in his image of the "impotent despair of a sick man." His views were colored by those of his teacher, Cesare Lombroso (on whom there is an article in this section by David Forgacs). Reizbaum shows how this image of the sick man is strikingly countered by Nordau's later evocation of the physically strong and healthy Zionist. It is these two views of the Jew that Nordau bequeathed to the 20th century.

Reizbaum brilliantly links Nordau with three 20th-century works. The most fascinating link is made with Pat Barker's *Regeneration* (1991), the first volume of a trilogy that is perhaps one of the finest achievements of the century (Reizbaum does not discuss the other two volumes). *Regeneration*—implicitly held against Nordau's *Degeneration*—is set in a mental hospital during the First World War and has two historical figures among its main characters, the shell-shocked poet Siegfried Sassoon and the psychologist W.H.R. Rivers. The drama posits mental collapse (degeneracy) against physical fitness, both epitomized by the Jew, Sassoon. Reizbaum next turns to the film *Chariots of Fire*, which features an exceptional Jewish athlete. Finally, she discusses James Joyce's *Ulysses*, although she disappointingly fails to do justice to the depiction of Bloom, this being the more surprising since she has recently published a book on Joyce.

The most illuminating, and also most skillful essay in the last section of the volume is Edward J. Hughes' "Textual and Tribal Assimilation: Representing Jewishness in *À la Recherche du Temps Perdu*." Marcel Proust would seem to have been destined to be ambivalent about Jews since, as Hughes points out, his mother was Jewish, though he omits to mention that she converted to Christianity on her marriage. The result was that, in his major work, Proust projected "contrasting perspectives on Jewishness" (p. 155). Marcel's mother is the focus of Proust's favorable attitude toward Jews. She is linked suggestively with the Esther and Ahasuerus tapestries in the church at Combray, with the Esther figure projecting "the beauty of the mother's Jewish features" (p. 159). But then the "unreliable" Albertine is also associated with Esther, as is the prostitute Rachel, whom Marcel meets in the brothel to which his Jewish friend Bloch takes him. Thus the novel establishes what Hughes calls a "dialectic of opprobrium and adulation" (p. 160). The opprobrium is particularly heaped on Bloch, who is shown to be the kind of Jew who makes a point of expressing anti-Jewish sentiments, and who is said by the narrator to be "ill-bred, neurotic and snobbish." There is a devastating description of the mature Bloch in the final assembly at the end of the narrative. Hughes is excellent in his account of the deft use Proust makes of the device of intertextuality in his portrayals of various characters. Although one cannot expect a comprehensive treatment of so vast a work as *À la recherche* in a single essay, one would nevertheless have welcomed an attempt to deal with the presentation of Swann (the most

interesting Jew in the text), with Marcel's beloved Jewish grandmother, and also
with the reverberations in the narrative of the Dreyfus affair.

H.M. DALESKI
The Hebrew University

Yaron Peleg, *Orientalism and the Hebrew Imagination*. Ithaca: Cornell University
    Press, 2005. 153 pp.

Unlikely as it may now seem, Jews and Arabs were once routinely imagined together, as "cousins" belonging to the same Oriental, Semitic family. The year 2005
was particularly fruitful in recalling this fact. Along with Yaron Peleg's book, it saw
the appearance of an anthology, *Orientalism and the Jews,* edited by me and Derek
J. Penslar, as well as Gil Anidjar's *The Arab, the Jew: A History of the Enemy,* which
expanded on some important work from the final years of Jacques Derrida. The idea
of the Jews as an "Oriental" (that is, Middle Eastern) people was sometimes used
against them by Jew-haters, as evidenced by the term "antisemite." Yet despite
what a superficial reading of Edward Said might suggest, orientalism was not always
intended as a condemnation of the Orient. In fact, for most of the 19th century, the
prevailing attitude toward the East was one of romantic fascination. It is true that the
Orient was in many ways constructed as Europe's feminized, impassioned, and
premodern Other, but to romantics this was more of a compliment than an insult.

Peleg's excellent work shows that in the so-called "Hebrew revival" period (ca.
1900–1930) there was a tendency to adapt such romanticism to the vision of a new
kind of Jew, and in particular a new kind of Jewish man. Peleg deals with a number
of writers but focuses essentially on three: David Frishman (1859–1922), Moshe
Smilanski (1874–1953), and L.A. Arielli (Levy Arieh Orloff, 1886–1943). The first
two adopted romantic orientalism (although in Frishman's case with some reservations), while the last rejected its assumptions with wizened scorn.

David Frishman was a diaspora Jewish nationalist who fostered modern Hebrew
literature, yet was not a Zionist. Notwithstanding his doubts concerning the viability
of the Yishuv, he was quite impressed with the Zionist settlement when he visited
Palestine in 1911. According to Peleg, Frishman's inspiration, like that of other
Hebrew orientalists, was primarily Russian in origin. That is, some of the Zionists in
Palestine regarded Arabs in much the same way as Russians regarded Cossacks:
namely, as wildly primitive yet familiar blood relatives, possessed of a violent
sexualized energy that could revitalize a nation in decline—whether Russian or, in
this case, Jewish. (Indeed, watchmen in the early Yishuv often wore Cossack hats.)
Frishman, however, did not write about Arabs; his orientalized Cossacks appeared
rather as biblical Israelites. Peleg suggests that the sensuous vitality of these characters was meant to counter the pallid, bookish un-masculinity of the East European
Jew, though one may well wonder about Frishman's own hang-ups. In his "Be-
headed Heifer," for example, the Israelites follow up their military victory by raping
the enemy's women throughout the night before killing them in the morning—

except for the virgins, whom they display for sale in the market, their nakedness covered only by a flimsy cloth.

In describing the same characteristics of virile bellicosity that Frishman sees in the biblical Israelites, Moshe Smilansky refers instead to contemporary Palestinian Arabs. Although Smilansky is patronizingly dismissive in some of his fiction, a number of stories collected under the title *The Sons of Arabia* feature blue-eyed, blond Arabs (de-Semitized macho males in the mold of the ideal *sabra*), who serve as a model for the "New Jew" of the Yishuv. Peleg notes that such stories transfer Max Nordau's notion of " 'muscular Judaism' from the Slavic peasants of Eastern Europe [admired by Nordau] to the society of fighting Bedouins in the eastern Mediterranean" (p. 78). At times a Bedouin noble savage becomes the Kipling-like bosom buddy of a handsome Jewish warrior. At other times, we are reminded of the disturbing sexuality seen in Frishman's work, as when a sheik's son kidnaps the wife of another Bedouin sheik and, after two days of ecstatic sexual happiness, kills her before falling on the swords of the soldiers coming to arrest him.

The pessimist of the three writers, L.A. Arielli, left for America after 14 years in Palestine and did not share his colleagues' romantic dreams. Arielli's major theme is not the exuberant future but what he saw as the decaying present. Peleg pays particular attention to Arielli's play, *Allah Karim!* which ends with the killing of an Arab intruder by a Jewish watchman. The killing transforms the main Arab character (who at first naively trusts the mock love of a patronizing Jewish woman) into an avenging murderer—we would now surely call him a terrorist. In the final scene, the woman, Naomi, exclaims, "A land that nurtured strong and vigorous men like our ancient heroes, and even like this savage Arab, is worth living in—living and fighting" (p. 118). Troubled masculinity surfaces once again: Naomi has no kind words for her Jewish male contemporaries, only for "our ancient heroes" (à la Frishman) and the "savage Arab" (à la Smilansky). Arielli's similarity to the other two writers, despite his jaded pessimism, is perhaps even greater than Peleg recognizes.

According to Peleg, the fact that all three writers had some positive attitudes toward Arabs complicates what he calls the post-Zionist view. One does wish, though, that he had engaged these post-Zionists more specifically, since it is likely that not all of them view early Hebrew literature as manifestly, rather than surreptitiously, dismissive of Arabs. (That it was *subtly* colonialist is generally admitted by Peleg.) Should he continue along the lines of this outstanding work, Peleg might wish to situate each writer in a broader context, not merely within Hebrew literature and early Zionist history. For instance, Frishman's construction of the biblical Jew as an oriental relative of the Arab has long and strong Christian roots, as seen in such writers as Robert Lowth or Johann Gottfried Herder. Smilansky's noble Arab character probably has its origins not only in the author's experience in Eretz Israel but also in the romance novel and popular cinema of the time: the author could not have failed to notice the phenomenal success his contemporary, Rudolf Valentino, was having with *The Sheik*, Hollywood's first blockbuster. And the gender anxieties of all three writers recall the general male malaise among Jews familiar to most of us from the contemporary Viennese milieu of Sigmund Freud and Otto Weininger (who is in fact briefly mentioned by Peleg). But no one can be asked to do everything; and, as a significant contribution to our understanding of the complexities of

Jewish attitudes to Arabs in the early 20th century, *Orientalism and the Hebrew Imagination* does far more than enough.

IVAN DAVIDSON KALMAR
University of Toronto

David M. Schiller, *Bloch, Schoenberg, and Bernstein: Assimilating Jewish Music.* Oxford: Oxford University Press, 2003. vii + 199 pp.

A concert held in November 2004 in the Berliner Philharmonie, conducted by Daniel Barenboim, included two choral works: Arnold Schoenberg's *A Survivor from Warsaw* (1949), followed by Brahms' *German Requiem* (1869). While this is a well-established order—first the short modern piece, then the longer classical one—the program was obviously a reversal of the historical narrative. Yet the dissonant world of *A Survivor from Warsaw*, with its male chorus singing the Hebrew "Shma yisrael" in unison within an English narrated frame, served to render the *German Requiem*, with its verses from the Old Testament, into a grand lamentation for European Jewry. Such is the power of musical performance: to contextualize its objects of experience in a certain time, for a certain audience, and in relation to other currently heard works and sounds. This is particularly true regarding the music composed by Jews since they first ventured onto the frontiers of Western classical music in the 19th century. Composed on the brink of modernism, their works often assimilate foreign elements while in turn being assimilated within larger and therefore different musical contexts. It is mainly when contextualized that their complex structure of meaning comes to the fore.

"Assimilating Jewish Music" is the subject of David Schiller's fine book, which he has chosen to locate within the rich and intricate American Jewish cultural milieu. Skillfully framing his research and argument, Schiller concentrates on Schoenberg's *A Survivor from Warsaw* and two other works—Ernest Bloch's *Sacred Service* (1933) and Leonard Bernstein's *Symphony no. 3: Kaddish* (1963)—that are related to three crucial moments in the history of modern American Jewry. The main chapters are organized via a threefold methodology: biographical or psychological criticism related to the composers' intentions and reflections, the works' reception history, and an analysis of their musical structure and style.

Following Zygmunt Bauman, Hannah Arendt, and other eminent thinkers, Schiller is well aware of the paradoxes and aporias of assimilating music and of its intricate relations with such concepts as modernism and postmodernism, racism and universalism, unity and eclecticism, and nationalist versus gender identity. He is also conscious of the European context, in particular, Wagner's long-lasting impact on the musical "Jewish question," as well as the "crisis of the Holocaust" that directly impinges on the cultural specimens he studies. It is this complexity that guided him in choosing these specific works as representative of their times and sensibilities. Though Bloch and Schoenberg are European immigrants whereas Bernstein is American-born, all of the composers maintain, to varying degrees, a precarious "situatedness" in Gentile culture, and all of them, as it were, are entangled in a triangle that seems to emerge from the book: that of survival, memory, and vision, as manifested through narrative, dialogue, and prayer—primarily the kaddish.

Schiller's methodological and conceptual frame enables him to provide a thick description of each of the works. He shows how the (somewhat naive) post-romanticism of *Sacred Service* embodies the paradox of the intentionally universal that was received as local and communal; how the classical modernism of *A Survivor from Warsaw* provides a means of coping with the aporia of Holocaust representation; and how the post-modernism of *Kaddish* expresses Bernstein's grappling with a complex identity—religious, sexual, familial—through ancestral legacies both communal and musical. This, I find, is the most compelling section of the book.

Although Schiller's analysis is well informed and thought out, a more profound examination of the phenomenon under scrutiny—choral works inspired by, if not intended for, a religious experience—seems to be missing. Whereas his interpretation of the musical métier of the *Kaddish* in terms of Bernstein's declared musical models is richly convincing; his reliance on Schoenberg's compositional aesthetics and theory is likewise pertinent; and his anchorage in Bloch's essays and letters is illuminating, Schiller fails to penetrate the musical works as historical, anthropological, and psychological objects. Apart from a discussion of each work's basic set of tones or motific combination, their musical unfolding is in the main discussed formally, with little reference made to phenomenology or semiotics. This is true as well with regard to the reception history: in adhering to the responses of a handful of critics, primarily those who lived close to the time of the first premieres, Schiller misses the possibility of viewing the works in relation to the cultural practices of concert- and synagogue-goers, although this matter is slightly touched upon in the case of *Sacred Service*. One has the feeling, sometimes, that the authorities cited in this book function as crutches for the author (he often repeats the same quotations), though he no doubt could have managed on his own.

Semiotics and phenomenological awareness, I would like to stress, should not be seen as mere academic decoration, but as the very tools of the enterprise undertaken by this kind of book, namely, bringing to the fore the cultural import of a relatively neglected chapter in modern Jewish art—that which is embodied in sonic configurations. This relates first and foremost to the experiential world of the oratorio—so central in the general history of assimilatory Jewish music, starting with Mendelssohn—whose encoded forms of participation and expression function as a tacit legacy with which these works maintain a vital dialogue (though only one of them is officially categorized as "oratorio"). More particularly, when Bloch conflates his previously composed melodies of "dream" and "consolation" for the sake of his culminating kaddish, one is curious to know how this semiotic correlation determines the listener's musical perception in relation to the apotheosis it is supposed to fashion. In addition, some kind of phenomenological-aesthetic framework might have aided Schiller in dealing with the "unanswered question" of the representation of the Holocaust, beyond Adorno's contradictory assessment of *A Survivor from Warsaw*.

As is true of most of the artists and critics appearing in this book, Schiller's knowledge of the relevant Jewish customs and Hebrew texts and contexts is somewhat lacking (for instance, he mainly knows the kaddish as a memorial prayer, whereas it also functions, as in Bloch's work, as a repeating unit of prayer that stands by itself). Yet this very flaw points to the book's great strength—its insider perspective on American Jewish music. *Assimilating Jewish Music* may indeed be read as a labor of love that adds an important layer to our growing understanding of the auditorial worlds of modern Jewry, embedded as they have been in the turbulent dramas of their time.

RUTH HACOHEN
The Hebrew University

Donald Weber, *Haunted in the New World: Jewish American Culture from Cahan to The Goldbergs*. Bloomington: Indiana University Press, 2005. xiii + 250 pp.

"Never never never be ashamed you're Jewish," the abrasive stand-up comedian Jules Farber yells to a group of matrons in Wallace Markfield's novel *You Could Live If They Let You* (1974). "Because it's enough if I'm ashamed you're Jewish." That emotion, according to literary scholar Donald Weber, is characterized by psychologists as a yearning for invisibility, and it throbs throughout American Jewish cultural expression. Shame is what overcomes Morris Cominsky, Esq., at an elegant uptown dinner party in the silent film *His People* (1925), when his father unexpectedly shows up from Delancey Street and seeks recognition. The father is repudiated, but nevertheless reassures his son: "Remember, Morris, we always have on Friday night gefulte fish" (pp. 53–54). Shame runs throughout the recollections of Ira Stigman (hint: drop that "n"), who records in Henry Roth's *Mercy of a Rude Stream* (1994–1998) his own youthful and "deplorable table manners...his jerky, ravenous, noisy, chomp-chomp, despite efforts to deport himself with restraint, with a little decorum" (p. 77).

But shame can also mean Fanya's calculation of the price of assimilation in Anzia Yezierska's *All I Could Never Be* (1932)—the futility of trying "to acquire from the Gentiles their low voices, their calm, their poise.... I lost what I had—what I was" (p. 46). Seeking to disavow an Old World style that was off-key in the 20th century, both "greenhorns" and the native-born progeny of immigrants were so eager to shed the humiliating status associated with their religious and ethnic origins that psychologically illuminating art (both high and popular) could result. *Haunted in the New World* is a smart, attentive study of the cultural consequences of *oysgrinung*— the "greening-out" process that required of such upwardly mobile Jews an incessant vigilance and "self-monitoring" (p. 107).

As the above examples suggest, the biggest emotional charge is gastronomic. At the table, the conflict of the generations can be transformed into class differences as well, just as the consumption of forbidden food can also signify for the arrivistes the abandonment of an entire way of life. In Yezierska's *Salome of the Tenements* (1922), Sonya Vronsky is suddenly lifted through the caprice of romance into genteel society, and is so dazzled in one dining room that she proclaims: "I'm so starved I could eat up the shells of the oysters and all!" (She is reminded of her lowly origins only when a butler has to place the correct fork in front of her, leaving her "shamed and confused" [p. 35].) But Weber is less interested in what happens to the division between kosher and *treyf;* less interested in *what* Jews eat, than in *how* they eat. In *The Jazz Singer* (1927), audiences are introduced to Al Jolson when he is on the road, pursuing a career as an entertainer rather than a cantor. He doesn't just eat a plateful of ham and eggs; he wolfs them down. Jack Robin (né Jakie Rabinowitz) is a *freser* who has not adopted the genteel habits of the larger community. Such compulsive eating habits show the durability of his ethnicity, even after his piety has lapsed.

This *oysgrinung* is what Weber tends to call Americanization. But this kind of assimilation could be discerned wherever and whenever the Jews of the modern era entered civil society, and it is hardly peculiar to the United States. There was a joke told by Berlin Jews that mocks such impulses for inclusiveness, as one restaurant patron tells another: "You don't have to order pork so loudly. We already know you are Jewish." In the United States, Weber implies, the self-consciousness of this struggle was spent by the mid-20th century, for his book ends in the 1950s, with Gertrude Berg's "Molly Goldberg," the "Yinglish" records of Mickey Katz, and Saul Bellow's *Seize the Day* (1956). Jewish culture was about to become both more blatantly ethnic and more pervasive, but readers of *Haunted in the New World* can infer that the conflict between generations is over. What was once embarrassing, the author argues, was becoming sentimentalized, the stuff of nostalgia.

Weber looks closely at about two dozen works—novels, films, and television programs, in particular—and does so with much astuteness. The limitation of his book is not its lack of comprehensiveness; his right to select the evidence worthy of analysis should not be impugned. What is missing is a certain historicity. Postwar novels of antisemitism such as Arthur Miller's *Focus* (1945) and Bellow's *The Victim* (1947) are explored without serious consideration of the concurrent decline of such bigotry after the Second World War. The defense of feeling that Weber detects in *Seize the Day* was not sustained once Bellow realized that, by the 1960s, the case for emotional emancipation was being overstated.

And what happened at the dining tables once Jews were allowed to sit above the salt, having learned which fork to use? More sedate standards of propriety got punctured, though not only by Jews. At least in popular culture, blacks and Southern whites were also responsible, in their own ways, for refusing to abide by what seemed to be rather arbitrary rules of decorum. Democratization thus continued to wreak havoc on the very idea of privilege founded in class-based distinctions. The inclusion of once marginal groups has meant that authenticity has often trumped artifice and candor can become more admirable than civility. But social control still needs to be achieved, and at least some ideals therefore have to be projected in order to avoid giving offense or inflicting hurt. The arbiters of etiquette—of good breeding—need not, however, come from "good stock." They can be Jews, like "Miss Manners," the *nom de plume* of Judith Perlman Martin, who speaks with unsurpassed authority in contemporary America on the subject of courteous conduct.

Nor were any advice columnists ever more influential than the Friedman twins, known to their readers as Ann Landers and "Dear Abby" Van Buren, who offered common sense and tart wisdom in an era of anxiety and uncertainty, when even a status such as "insider" or "outsider" was so easily subverted.

STEPHEN J. WHITFIELD
Brandeis University

Religion, Thought, and Education

David Ellenson, *After Emancipation: Jewish Religious Responses to Modernity.*
Cincinnati: Hebrew Union College Press, 2005. 547 pp.

Students of modern Judaism will find invaluable information and deep insights into
contemporary Judaism in this welcome collection of essays taken from the writings
of one of the outstanding historians of our time, David Ellenson. Twenty-three essays that appeared in a variety of publications have been gathered in this book, and
although they vary in length, style, and subject matter, they are certainly deserving of
appearing together in a permanent format. Furthermore, even though they were not
originally connected to one another, these essays form a logical and coherent whole.

With its concern for Jewish life and the continuation of Jewish existence, Ellenson's work transcends dry historical research in which history is examined for its
own sake. In these essays, the past is rigorously examined in order to illuminate
the present and to give guidance for the future. Although deeply identified with
the Reform movement (presently serving as president of Hebrew Union College—
Jewish Institute of Religion), Ellenson neither indulges in polemics nor adopts a
narrow partisan view. His aim, rather, is to understand all forms of modern religious Judaism, how they emerged, and what they stand for, without passing judgment.
Thus he examines Orthodox responsa, Orthodox-Reform and Orthodox-Conservative
disputes, the curriculum of the Jewish Theological Seminary in comparison with its
Orthodox and Reform counterparts, and the new Conservative siddur (for which he
has nothing but praise). In each case, we understand the issue at hand better than
before because he is not content to accept the conventional approaches to his subject
matter.

Ellenson's personal concerns are never far from the surface: one can sense his own
point of view through his comments concerning others and their work. In his preface,
he offers a brief account of the formulation of his own religious sensibilities. Born
into an Orthodox family in Newport News, Virginia, he lived in an environment that
was steeped in traditional Judaism yet tolerant of other movements—a community
that aspired to be part of the general Southern society under circumstances in which
this was not always possible. His break with Orthodoxy does not seem to have been a
revolt and a rejection, but rather an intellectual exploration of other ways of thinking
during his university years that led him eventually to rabbinical studies at the institution he now heads.

In his first essay, "Judaism Resurgent?" (originally published in vol. 17 of this
journal),[1] Ellenson attempts to chart the evolution of American Jewry. At first

insular yet at the same time striving to adopt universal American values and ways of life, it developed into a community that proudly affirms its peculiarity at a time when its continued existence is threatened by assimilation and intermarriage. The question, then, is whether the Jewish community will be able to sustain itself in America's open environment.

Subsequent discussions of 19th-century European Jewish life, which to my mind constitute the heart of this volume, explore the ways in which various groups dealt with emancipation and modernity. Ellenson's forte is the examination of specific, limited historical events with the aim of demonstrating how these events reflect an entire worldview. Through the particular he sheds light on the general, using each carefully constructed case to illuminate a major problem of its time. Thus in "Samuel Holdheim and Zacharias Frankel on the Legal Character of Jewish Marriage," he explains the major thrust of Liberal Judaism as being an attempt to find acceptance in German society at that time, and he shows the different way in which the Historical-Positive school approached the issue.

In similar fashion, Ellenson devotes an entire essay to the different approach taken toward the prayers for rain in the prayer books of Abraham Geiger and Isaac Mayer Wise, and in this fashion analyzes two different approaches to Reform Judaism. As he states in conclusion: "The treatment they accorded *Gevurot Geshamim* and *Tal u-Matar* in their *siddurim* is a single detail that reflects the nature of their larger Jewish project. Their model of how to calibrate the demands of the past against the present provides a rich legacy for the people Israel even today" (p. 236).

Particularly informative is Ellenson's essay on "Emancipation and the Directions of Modern Judaism: The Lessons of Melitz Yosher." This was a book that was written to justify the practices of Adat Yeshurun, an Amsterdam congregation that modified many common Ashkenazic practices in the community while still claiming to adhere to traditional Judaism and Jewish law. Ellenson demonstrates that these modifications were indeed all within the scope of Jewish law and were intended to create a synagogue service that would be more acceptable in the modern community. Thus aesthetics and decorum were emphasized, and many practices were established that later became common in Reform congregations. The kaddish prayer was recited in unison rather than by individual mourners, the priestly blessing was curtailed, certain prayers were eliminated so that those that remained could be said with greater meaning and devotion, and a weekly homiletical Shabbat sermon was instituted. Ellenson's conclusion is telling. "*Melitz Yosher* shows that religious change need not be radical. It can be rooted in tradition.... For these Jews, a complete compatibility between Jewish and western values and aesthetics is perceived as attainable" (pp. 117, 120). One feels that this conclusion represents Ellenson's own view, as well as being the goal toward which he aspires as a leader of the American Reform movement.

This is an important volume for anyone concerned with the future of religious Judaism in today's world. It demonstrates that a true historian is one whose insights into the past can also be used as a guide to the present.

REUVEN HAMMER
Jerusalem

Note

1. David Ellenson, "Judaism Resurgent? American Jews and the Evolving Expression of Jewish Values and Jewish Identity in Modern American Life," in *Studies in Contemporary Jewry*, vol. 17, *Who Owns Judaism? Public Religion and Private Faith in America and Israel*, ed. Eli Lederhendler (New York: 2001), 156–171.

Peter Eli Gordon, *Rosenzweig and Heidegger: Between Judaism and German Philosophy*. Berkeley: University of California Press, 2003.

Once acclaimed as an inspired guide for the perplexed of our times, the meaning and consequence of Franz Rosenzweig's writings have since come into question. Peter Eli Gordon, having criticized recent efforts to read Rosenzweig as an existentialist, an ethicist, a proto-postmodern, or a hermeneutical or quasi-psychoanalytic thinker, ventures a novel interpretation. His bold, even audacious revaluation examines Rosenzweig's stance on a variety of topics related to German philosophy and Judaism in comparison with that of Martin Heidegger, whose own relations with these subjects remain controversial, to say the least. In Gordon's view, Rosenzweig and Heidegger's strikingly similar and yet intransigently opposed positions on several key issues emerge against a common background: "Restored to its German philosophical context," Rosenzweig's famous (or infamous) appeal for "a peculiarly Jewish way of being in the world" expresses a quest for " 'primordial' " sources marking a critical break from the metaphysics of identity, totality, and eternity. Gordon elucidates this "characteristic tension within Weimar culture between archaism and modernism" with a generous reading of contemporaneous sources (pp. 4–5). How this tension marks "the waning of idealist epistemology and the ascent of existential ontology" (p. 276) is the more trenchant problem, however, toward which the book gestures inconclusively.

The content of Gordon's argument unfolds in a richly detailed account of the intellectual background to the similarities and differences between Rosenzweig and Heidegger. The first chapter effectively introduces Hermann Cohen's neo-Kantian promotion of a causal logic—the " 'principle of origins' "—in his defense of a hypercritical epistemology relying on pure, a priori ideas for its claims to scientific (essentially, mathematical) knowledge. Cohen's key insight was that being originates in the thought of "the nothing" or in the negation of a privation, the overcoming of a lack. This principle would come to frustrate both Rosenzweig, who considered the multiplicity of being prior to the unity of thought, and Heidegger, who pleads for " 'a more original questioning' " than any strictly logical method for causally or conditionally relating one thing to another (such as that adopted by Leibniz's principle of sufficient reason or Cohen's principle of origins) (p. 50). In their eyes, Cohen had failed to resolve the tension between the particularity of experience and the universality of value. By contrast, Rosenzweig and Heidegger followed a "resurrection of metaphysics," which led them to elevate the idiosyncratic features of a unique life above a universalizable system of laws.

The second chapter makes a signal contribution to Rosenzweig scholarship with its generous reading of his important 1913 dissertation, *Hegel und der Staat* (published in 1920), which remains sadly understudied since it is only available in the original *Fraktur* (an archaic German font) edition or in a sole French translation. Gordon reconstructs Rosenzweig's youthful argument that "Hegel's mature idea of the state first appeared as a 'reconciliation' to the theological and metaphysical problem of fate," (p. 104), which involves Judaism and Christianity in the quest for an ever more meaningful life. On Rosenzweig's reading, the figure of Jesus in early Hegel and the state in late Hegel would each putatively reconcile the fate of the finite individual to the infinite whole from which its individuality had fatefully broken. This reading, Gordon surmises, could have led Rosenzweig into the trap of assuming that he could replace the totalizing state or the reconciling Jesus with the doctrine of Israel's election.

The long "experimental" Chapters 3 and 4 bring the insight of what Rosenzweig took from Hegel to illuminate the "sheer strangeness" of his work of 1921, *Star of Redemption* (p. 121). These two chapters neatly divide Gordon's treatment along the *Star*'s implicit division between the critique of totality, or move "beyond metaphysics," and the resolution of fate in the people Israel, a "redemption-in-the-world" (p. 112). The question is what makes the transition, if not Hegelian dialectics.

On the one hand, Gordon argues, Rosenzweig's refusal "to find in death a higher and salvific purpose" (p. 113) leads him to critique all totalities in a search for an irreducible, primordial feature of life. Unlike Idealism's "knowledge of the all" or the failure of the philosophical tradition to uncover its "original 'sources,' " as Heidegger put it (p. 139), Rosenzweig treats human finitude and mortality not as the limit of experience but, rather, as its condition. Like Heidegger, and inverting Cohen, Rosenzweig fits a philosophical trend that finds in "the derivation of being from existence" a "resistance to our concepts"—that is, our mathematical certainties (pp. 160–161 and n. 68). He proposes that a confrontation with the nothingness of experience that is something in experience (namely, death) would uncover the disunity of beings that precedes the ontological reduction to *a* being. As an alternative to Robert Gibbs' reading of Rosenzweig as a postmodern for whom there are no definitive interpretations, and Leora Batnitzksy's reading of him as a Gadamerian for whom there are strong interpretations, Gordon suggests that Heidegger and Rosenzweig find "a way of being" available "through our purposeful and directed way of living" (p. 183). Moreover, this way "implies that life holds a salvific meaning" because love, in Rosenzweig's terminology, stands "victorious" over death (pp. 189, 175).

On the other hand, the notion that finitude limits any experience to this world contradicts Rosenzweig's famous claim about the people Israel's "eternal life," which inhabits a real dimension " 'outside of time agitated by wars' " (p. 208). Perhaps, as Gordon insists, Rosenzweig would never reduce a particular existence to a universal principle, even one as non-conceptual as Emmanuel Levinas' "ethics." Nevertheless, Rosenzweig implies that "community is ontologically prior" and presents a "holism" that conjoins time and eternity (pp. 202–205). On Gordon's reading, therefore, Rosenzweig's "community" takes the place of Hegel's "fate." Although his claims about Jewish "blood" could amount to an "argument in favor of Jewish uniqueness," Rosenzweig admits that eternal life is "purchased . . . at the cost of the unredeemed world." Thus Rosenzweig grants Judaism "permanence" by replacing its organic political history with a crude political "decisionism" and its "rules of kinship affiliation" (pp. 207, 214–219). Like Hegel's Jesus and state, then, redeemed "Jews" are *in* the world but not *of* it. Such redemption, like Heidegger's concept of "authenticity," betrays a "self-sufficient constitution" without reference to worldly horizons of meaning. In addition, Heidegger's authenticity and Rosenzweig's redemption share the features of temporal unity, future-directedness, and a "heritage" (pp. 222–224). In this context, Gordon goes on to suggest what distinguishes Rosenzweig's redemption from Heidegger's authenticity.

Gordon makes a controversial distinction. Undoubtedly it is ironic to associate the Nazi philosopher Carl Schmitt and even Hitler more closely to Rosenzweig than to Heidegger. Some might even argue that it is inappropriate (though this criterion is validly eschewed in Gordon's preface). More to the point, however: is it accurate? I think Gordon hangs his claim about Rosenzweig's (as opposed to Heidegger's) unhappy "chauvinism" on a weak thread, namely, that to Rosenzweig the "community of blood" enjoyed by Jews "holds for our [people] in a *wholly particular way*" (pp. 214, 211 n. 26). Granted that the ambiguous German word *besonderer* marks Israel as "distinguished," would it make Rosenzweig's redemption unambiguously more "collectivist" and "exclusive" than Heidegger's "individualist" and "inclusive" authenticity (cf. pp. 228–229 n. 56)? Such a global claim will reasonably come into question, given the fact of Rosenzweig's subsequent refining of his views about Jewish identity as well as Heidegger's commitment to German identity, an issue on which one may now consult James Phillips' book *Heidegger's Volk: Between National Socialism and Poetry* (2005). And should we not suspect the distinction's resemblance to Saint Paul's critique of Judaism, which Gordon rightly credits as inspiring Heidegger (p. 227, n. 53)? Moreover, if their "nonparticipation" and "dissociation" could provide, as Batnitzky and Richard A. Cohen have mistakenly argued, the basis for a "universal hope" presented in Rosenzweig's Jews, then why not also read Heidegger's devotion to the Greeks and the poets in a similar fashion (p. 230)? And why must Jews' or Greeks' "indifferent" immersion *in* the world not, in its way, affect the "transfiguration" *of* it? Is "refusing transcendence" a straightforward gesture for either thinker to make (pp. 231, 227, and passim; cf. Heidegger's complex view of "grounding" in his 1955–1956 lecture series *The Principle of Reason*)? It is, finally, all the more surprising that Gordon later cites approvingly "Rosenzweig's ecumenical portrait of the new thinking," which "readily admits paganisms' legitimacy alongside Judaism and Christianity" (pp. 302–304).

Chapter 4 lands on this basic paradox: Heidegger's authenticity takes its cue for a "locus of value" and "normativity" from theism, and Rosenzweig's redemption anticipates "secularism." Both reconfigure time and eternity. And though Rosenzweig has the "probity to register this metaphysical collapse" in religious terms, Heidegger insists that the abolishment of metaphysics makes the translations of "philosophy and theology exceedingly difficult." Both get stuck at the impasse of a putative holism that tries to encompass within itself (for instance, life) what remains outside its limits (for instance, death or fate). Unsurprisingly, both thinkers abandon philosophy and theology for "a poetic and narrative form" of translation (pp. 232–236).

Fittingly, Chapter 5 explores the contemporary reception of Rosenzweig and Martin Buber's joint translation of the Hebrew Bible into German (beginning in 1924), suggesting how the translation's characteristic archaisms and neologisms seek "to restore an original [saying] even if it must endure the exile of being in another language" (p. 249). The Buber-Rosenzweig translation would largely emphasize the "difference" between the German and Hebrew over the "identity" of them, as in Luther's (and Mendelssohn's) translation. But Gordon pinpoints the intriguing ambiguity in Rosenzweig's and arguably also Heidegger's "difference" theories of translation. Since they each assert the priority of the original language to impress its distinctive features on a translation, Rosenzweig and Heidegger undermine the present authority of the target language; but this assertion further leads each thinker to affirm the "present" authority of single "past" tradition—biblical for Rosenzweig, and Greek for Heidegger.

The central paradox noted above is more broadly discussed in Chapter 6's tantalizing account of Rosenzweig's "Exchanged Fronts," his written response to the momentous 1929 "Davos Disputation" between Heidegger and Ernst Cassirer. In it, Rosenzweig makes the surprisingly insightful claim that Heidegger radically pursues Cohen's mature interest in the finitude of human being that resists the transcendence of eternal truths (cf. Heidegger's 1928 lectures, *The Metaphysical Foundations of Logic*). Though mostly a reflection of his own reading of Cohen's late writings, Rosenzweig's essay provides insight into the dilemma he and Heidegger faced. As a human being "first discovers its existence within horizons it had no share in creating," its recognition of this situation forces it into "a this-worldly recoil," "an 'opposition' " that simultaneously admits its dependence on the temporality of being and satisfies a "longing for ultimacy," the original essence of truthfulness (pp. 302, 288). Rosenzweig and Heidegger paradoxically seek a metaphysic that is not tricked by its own transcendence.

The book reaches an unlikely conclusion in its insistence that the real issue that relates and separates Rosenzweig and Heidegger is how differently each thinker replaced idealist epistemology with existential ontology, dualisms of all kinds with putative variations on "holism" such as redemption and authenticity. But how coherent are their supposed holisms? Rosenzweig was, on this reading, inconsistently attracted to God's transcendence and Jewish exceptionality, whereas Heidegger "thankfully abandoned" such pretensions (despite a "stubborn" attachment to the pre-Socratics' and German poets' "immediacy" or direct access to a "heritage"). Hence the notion that Rosenzweig embraces a "brave and unlikely fusion" of philosophy and theology and that Heidegger "stakes a covert appeal to what he openly denies" raises more questions than it answers (p. 302). It remains an open question whether the fate of enduring, even enjoying life "despite" its finitude turns one's " 'being aware' of groundlessness" into "a new dispensation" for either thinker (pp. 312, 309). And yet the lively manner in which the book proceeds and the detailed information it supplies merit a close reading by anyone with a general interest in modern Jewish thought or German Jewish intellectual history.

GREGORY KAPLAN

Rice University

Tamar Ross, *Expanding the Palace of Torah: Orthodoxy and Feminism.* Waltham: Brandeis University Press, 2004. xxiv + 324 pp.

Tamar Ross' *Expanding the Palace of Torah: Orthodoxy and Feminism* is both timely and of vital concern. Most of the book surveys in depth the dilemmas of Jewish Orthodoxy vis-à-vis feminism, in particular, the attempts being made to accommodate feminism within the Orthodox community and especially within accepted halakhic and philosophic parameters. It seems, however, that within the normative framework of Orthodoxy, such efforts cannot resolve the dichotomy between Orthodoxy and feminism. Despite some successful attempts to bridge the gap on a number of specific issues, it appears that even the most liberal and open-minded of Orthodox *poskim* (decisors of Jewish law) and philosophers either cannot or will not solve the basic problems.

Ross' thoughtful, intelligent, learned, and even loving discussion of the matter, which comprises about two thirds of the volume, is without doubt a major contribution. But in spite of her formidable knowledge of halakhah, she is first and foremost a philosopher, both by training and by inclination. Since she finds within contemporary philosophic and halakhic discourse no satisfactory solution either to practical questions or to ethical and philosophical quandaries, Ross proposes a philosophical theory, which she calls "cumulative revelation."

For Ross, revelation is a cumulative and dynamic process that reveals over time its ultimate significance. Throughout the ages, there have been successive hearings of God's voice, the revelation at Sinai being but the first of these. In order to keep within the realm of Orthodoxy, Ross takes an all-inclusive approach, maintaining that integral elements of halakhic Judaism handed down from the past, which appear today to be immoral and untenable, are not to be rejected outright. They, too, remain part of God's message:

> God's voice does not express itself through the reverberation of vocal chords (at Sinai). His word is heard through the rabbinical interpretation of the texts. History, and particularly what happens to the Jewish people—the ideas and forms they accept as well as the process of determining those they reject—is essentially another form of ongoing revelation, a surrogate prophecy (p. 198).

Ross' approach is thought-provoking and perhaps convincing, but is not as radical as it may first appear. Ross herself shows how it is rooted in certain classical Judaic texts, including halakhic ones. She clearly has no wish to break with tradition, as is evident, for instance, in her ambivalent response to Blu Greenberg's seminal work, *On Women and Judaism: A View from Tradition* (1981). While she embraces

Greenberg's courage in openly setting out the difficulties in halakhic positions, she distances herself from Greenberg's more radical approach toward change within Orthodoxy.

Despite its undoubted achievements, *Expanding the Palace of Torah* left me somewhat dissatisfied. Although I tend to agree with Ross' depiction of the larger picture, the application of her philosophy to specifics is at times vague and wanting. On the practical plane, Ross does not really solve very much: we are still left with the same down-to-earth difficulties and problems that first prompted a feminist critique of Orthodoxy. The specific meaning of each new revelation is difficult to fathom. Despite a few classical Jewish literary sources that may hint at such an approach, her theory of "cumulative revelation" appears to lie outside Orthodox consensus.

Throughout the book, the reader is accosted by the substantial problems that confront Orthodoxy on matters involving accepted standards of morality, with the challenge of feminism responsible for only one of a number of such moral impasses. Orthodox Judaism, which is wont to deny the validity of many accepted contemporary outlooks and positions, has a real problem if it wishes to avoid both rigid fundamentalism and the rejection of generally accepted morality and modernity. Historically, Judaism has found place within its orbit for slavery, animal sacrifice, insularism, biblical anthropomorphism, and polytheism—and, of course, if not partial misogyny, then at least inequality between the sexes and a system of patriarchy—to name but a few concepts and practices that are completely at odds with contemporary intellectual and moral standards.

Tamar Ross, with great intellectual integrity, is aware of these moral deviations, sees them as integral parts of historic Judaism, and cannot accept them today philosophically or morally. It seems to me, however, that the most pressing problems today (as even Ross would probably admit) are the ongoing normative problems not solved by accepted halakhic authorities, which are the products of the traditional halakhic way of thinking.

Before arriving at her novel philosophical theory, Ross dissects in detail the sundry attempts to improve the lot of women within the halakhic framework. Her sad conclusion is that even the most far-reaching attempts to accommodate feminism and halakhic Judaism are found wanting. If so, one may ask, why the tenacious clinging to Orthodoxy? Why doesn't Ross go the way of, say, Alice Shalvi, a formerly Orthodox feminist who moved into the fold of Conservative Judaism? Ross' answer (given in a somewhat different context) is that "I *am* ideologically committed to the tradition as it stands as the basic grammar that governs the way I relate to the world and my religious experience" (p. xxi). It seems to me that the answer to this question is more complex: having been born into and raised in a loving, intellectual, and warm Orthodox home and environment, Ross cherishes her religion and its normative practice. Knowing full well that Judaism, for all its thought and philosophy, is above all a normative religion, she cannot bring herself to view its norms lightly—not to take them seriously would be fatal both to her philosophy and to her psychology. As she herself writes, "the ultimate message of Judaism, over and above the notion of monotheism, is the centrality of *halakhah* to the religious way of life" (p. 136).

I tend to agree with Ross that changes within Orthodoxy with respect to women's issues will come about as a result of the women's learning revolution now underway. In the future, as women increasingly become scholars of the law, they will gain clout in the Orthodox Jewish community. But even here, Ross hedges her assertions. "Even in cases not directly relating to sex and gender," she writes,

> the likelihood is that women entering halakhic discussions will have their own unique input regarding the implications of any given issue. Bringing different considerations to bear may lead to different judgments.... To the extent that there is a typically feminine way of looking at the overall balance, these different criteria too could lead at times to modified conclusions (p. 240).

Six pages earlier, she takes a more limited view: "I do not suggest that any given *halakhah* would be decided differently by a woman" (p. 234).

Ross' worldview is essentially that of a lengthy process, with no substantial new "revelation" just around the corner. She offers no concrete solutions for today's women who long to take part in Judaism's normative and religious life, or for those chained to recalcitrant husbands who refuse to give them a *get*, all of whom have experienced halakhic intransigence, conservatism, and anti-feminism. What can "cumulative revelation" offer to the modern-day *'agunah*? What moral force do Ross' philosophy and halakhic approach have, if they merely tell women that things may change in another 20 or 30 years? Ross would probably reply that it is not the purpose of her book to supply solutions to pressing problems. I suppose that I am one of the people she is referring to when she writes that "a segment of my readership may find my own suggestions characteristically theoretical and vague" (p. xx).

I hope that the reader of this review will not be left with the wrong impression. *Expanding the Palace of Torah* is one of the most intellectually stimulating books I have read in the past few years. Ross writes with clarity, intellectual honesty, erudition, empathy, humanity, and great wisdom. Her outstanding grasp of Jewish thought, philosophy, and Jewish law are all eminently displayed in this volume, which is destined to become a classic in Jewish studies.

SHMUEL SHILO
The Hebrew University

Hava Tirosh-Samuelson (ed.), *Women and Gender in Jewish Philosophy*. Bloomington: Indiana University Press, 2004. vii + 356 pp.

Edited by Hava Tirosh-Samuelson, *Women and Gender in Jewish Philosophy* fills a critical void in Jewish philosophy and should be of intense interest to students of that field as well as those of gender and Judaic studies, and feminist theory. The book lends itself to two levels of reading. Readers will first of all find discussion of epistemology, politics, and philosophical anthropology. Tirosh-Samuelson has gathered some of the best and the brightest scholars of medieval and modern Jewish philosophy in the United States. (The contributors are: Sara Pessin, Idit Dobbs-Weinstein, Heidi Ravven, Jean Axelrod Cahan, Tamar Rudavsky, Leora Batnitzky,

Laurie Zoloth, Claire Katz, Nancy Levene, Suzanne Stone, Sandra Lubarsky, and Randi Rashkover.) At a second level, the book raises serious methodological questions. Scholars interested in gender, feminism, and Jewish studies are usually unversed in philosophy, whereas for most students of Jewish philosophy—including many of the contributors to this volume—feminism and gender do not represent primary areas of interest. At issue then is the character of a collection of scholarly essays about a field that as yet does not exist. The point is underscored by Tirosh-Samuelson in her introduction: "*the volume does not constitute a feminist Jewish philosophy*" (p. 3).

Instead, *Women and Gender in Jewish Philosophy* is billed, perhaps somewhat casually, as a collection of essays by "Jewish women philosophers who think about Jewish philosophy in light of feminist philosophy" (p. 3). As also noted by Tirosh-Samuelson, the collection displays no consensus about the nature and practice of either Jewish or feminist philosophy. This lack of consensus contributes to the appeal of the volume, leaving it fundamentally open-ended, exploratory, and non-dogmatic. The essays nevertheless revolve around contested and intersecting theoretical topoi: epistemology and the tension between human embodiment and abstract reason; community, relationship and alterity; and political power and disempowerment. As argued by Dobbs-Weinstein, Jewish and feminist philosophy invite the reader to consider the *continuities*, not the discontinuities, between sensibility and intelligibility, passion and action, and necessity and freedom (p. 56). To these we might add the continuities between mind and body, individual and society, and pure and practical reason. These are the varied topoi at the basis of the (alleged) affinities identified by the authors between Jewish and feminist philosophy.

Depending on their own intellectual disposition, feminist and nonfeminist readers of Jewish and western philosophy will either welcome or resist the analysis of familiar thinkers in the new light cast by feminist theory. Ibn Gabirol, Maimonides, Gersonides, Spinoza, Buber, Rosenzweig, Levinas, Gilian Rose, and David Novak alongside Aristotle, neo-Platonism, and Marx are variously marshaled to lend support for an emergent, contemporary discourse about women, gender, and Jewish philosophy. At the same time, the association requires constant disclaimers that threaten to scuttle the project at its very root. These caveats follow an identical logic throughout the text, which can be paraphrased as follows: "despite the obvious fact that Ibn Gabirol was not a proto-feminist"; "despite Maimonides' explicit use of negative stereotypes"; "despite the fact that Marx rejected Jewish religious community"; "despite the fact that Buber, Rosenzweig, and Levinas uncritically reified 'the feminine' "; "despite the fact that at first glance Rose and Novak have little to say to Jewish feminists such as Miriam Peskowitz and Rachel Adler"—despite all this, they are all brought into a complimentary conversation with modern feminist theory and Jewish philosophy. Like any act of disavowal, the limits of these discursive couplings are simultaneously marked and overshot.

This rhetorical strategy underlines the almost thoroughgoing plasticity of philosophy and hermeneutical revision. At its best, this look at women and gender in Jewish philosophy forces willing and unwilling readers (both feminist and Jewish) to weigh how male authors invested in androcentric patterns of thought and culture require more careful readings that probe the surfaces of their own work and look past philosophical clichés and stereotypes (about reason, about women). Key players in the history of Jewish philosophy provide philosophical frameworks that are now grafted onto new theoretical contexts that enrich its study. Instead of reading the history of Jewish philosophy through Kantian or Straussian prisms that exaggerate the collisions between strict purity of reason over against an "other" (not just revelation, the more familiar rubric in Jewish studies, but also sensation and imagination), the contributors bring a more vivid life and a new coherence to medieval and early modern Jewish philosophy, as well as to the larger practice of reason. The effect brings philosophy down from the heights of pure reason, away from mysticism toward the thick texture of lived human experience. As Dobbs-Weinstein notes, a certain type of feminist reading contributes not just to the liberation of contemporary women and men, but also to the liberation of philosophy from its own most obvious historical limits.

That said, *Women and Gender in Jewish Philosophy* is over-invested in a history that cannot meet more contemporary requirements. Judged in the light of feminist theory, the Jewish philosophical tradition will always fall short—but of this, the reader will get no firm sense. While each essay is excellent, the sum is not quite equal to the parts. A collection of scholarly essays is supposed to represent a second-order discourse that builds upon established bodies of work. In this case, we have a second-order discourse without a first-order discourse upon which to reflect. The book fails to find what Pessin calls "a feminist ground" (p. 28) because no such ground exists in the history of medieval, modern, or even contemporary Jewish philosophy. The volume cries out for foundational work in feminist, Jewish philosophy; as it is, the contributors are left in a lurch. Overconfident and self-assured in their own readings, they exhibit no "anxiety of influence," no agon between contemporary women philosophers and their male precursors, no "madwomen in the attic"—that tortured sense at the creation of new discourse as its practitioners struggle to assert themselves in relation to the old.

Zachary Braiterman
Syracuse University

Zionism, Israel, and the Middle East

Yoram S. Carmeli and Kalman Applbaum (eds.), *Consumerism and Market Society in Israel*. Oxford: Berg, 2004. 208 pp.

Yoram Carmeli and Kalman Applbaum's edited collection is based on several assumptions. First, "consumerism" has become a constitutive element of the Israeli economy, polity, and state—as significant as production had been in the past. Second, the rise of consumerism is connected with the privatization of businesses and the decline of state involvement in welfare programs, which in turn has resulted in growing socioeconomic differentiation. And finally, we are witnessing the pluralization of Israeli society and the crystallization of group diversity, which blur the image of the "average" or "mainstream" Israeli.

Working with these assumptions, *Consumption and Market Society in Israel* aspires to offer a kind of composite portrait of Israel as a consumerist society. Beyond the insights to be found in any given essay, the volume's novel approach is itself a contribution to the abundant literature dealing with Israeli society. Nonetheless, this is a somewhat problematic collection, containing as it does two distinct strands, one of them more useful than the other. On the one hand are various essays that describe and analyze data and processes that have largely gone uninvestigated in the Israeli context. On the other hand, many contributions display an unfortunate tendency to discuss consumerism in postmodernist terms—that is, through radical relativistic criticism—and to apply this quite hazardous, loose, and verbose approach to the Israeli reality. The result is a number of chapters that are virtually unreadable, in contrast to others that are both innovative and interesting.

Thus, Carmeli and Applbaum's introduction offers a conceptual, and quite pointless, discussion of various consumerist behaviors (described only vaguely) that are interpreted as reflecting deep and complex psychological processes involving attitudes toward the state, immigration, and collective identity. A similarly sterile approach is to be found in Fran Markowitz and Natan Uriely's discussion of what goes on in a Beersheba shopping center frequented mainly by a lower-middle- and lower-class clientele. Markowitz and Uriely are convinced that the way in which individuals buy clothes, television sets, or fruit in this particular mall "reveal some of the complexities involved in the interrelationship between people and goods, people's identities and the Zionist nation-state, and the possible alternative that merchandising and merchandise pose to them" (p. 32). The ensuing argument, which relies heavily on clichés such as the "hegemony of the State," tends more toward ideological elaboration than scholarship. Julia Bernstein and Carmeli's essay about immigrants from the former Soviet Union is similarly flawed. Here, too, the subjects of the research become objects of abstract and ideological generalizations—many of which, it should be noted, sharply contradict empirical findings concerning this group's linguistic and political behavior, their collective identities, attitudes toward Israel, and perceptions of their own diaspora.[1]

Amalia Sa'ar and Tania Forte's essay about consumerism across national and gender divides and Tania Forte's piece about "the power and production of homes in Galilee" resort to the same kind of conceptualization, although here the authors refer as well to more precise data and offer some interesting analysis. Some contributions focus on the presentation of empirical data and add to scholarly knowledge. For instance, Daphna Birenbaum-Carmeli's essay about a residential Tel Aviv neighborhood sheds light on the development of Israel's middle class as manifested in the construction of residential areas alongside exclusive and expensive shops and boutiques, which serve as symbols of a high social status. In addition, Birenbaum-Carmeli points to the development of a secular, "consumption-class" culture in which intra-Jewish ethnic cleavages are of little significance: in the neighborhood in question, Jews of European origin comprise 60 percent of the population, compared with 40 percent of Middle Eastern or North African origin. Her conclusion, which is corroborated by other works,[2] is that there is a lack of symmetry in Israeli society between the middle and upper "non-ethnic" classes and the lower socioeconomic classes in which ethnocultural origins are more salient.

Equally interesting is Ronit Grossman's study of a kibbutz guest house that was originally conceived as a kind of "bubble"—that is, tourists could see what collective life in the kibbutz was like without disturbing its members' daily routines. Over time, however, the kibbutz itself underwent a transformation, becoming much more similar to the "outside world" represented by the tourists. Another essay focusing on a non-mainstream Israeli group is Tamar El-Or and Eran Neria's fine study of haredi walkers. El-Or and Neria follow up several recent studies showing that many of the common secular Israeli stereotypes regarding the ultra-Orthodox "ghetto" are based on superficial observation and are completely unfounded. According to El-Or and Neria, the boundaries of this community are in reality looser than they seem and are crossed continually. All in all, "more secular practice is seen in the city—done by ultra-orthodox people . . . contemporary Jerusalem is less 'holy' . . . because that population [has adopted] new practices, many secular in character" (p. 92).

Finally, Rebecca Rajman and Adriana Kempit tackle an intriguing topic that has rarely, if ever, been addressed: namely, migrant workers' affiliation with Evangelical churches. The authors contend that, for these workers, especially those who are staying in the country illegally, the churches constitute a space in which they can acquire a public presence, at least in the context and limits of the migrant population, and thus forge a new social and cultural identity. In so doing, they take advantage of the special status accorded religious institutions by state authorities, which gives them autonomy and statutory protection from state interference in their affairs. Paradoxically, within the church, they may also become part of Israeli society, since many of the Evangelical churches evince strong support for Zionism and the state of Israel.

In sum, *Consumption and Market Society in Israel* can be recommended for those essays that offer original analysis based on solid data. The volume as a whole, however, would have made an even weightier contribution to our knowledge of the subject if only its editors (and several of the authors) had opted for a less confusing and obtrusively ideological line of argument.

ELIEZER BEN-RAFAEL
Tel Aviv University

Notes

1. Among many other works, see, for instance, Eliezer Ben-Rafael, Mikhail Lyubansky, Olaf Glöckner, Paul Harris, Yael Israel, Willi Jasper, and Julius Schoeps (eds.), *Building a Diaspora: Russian Jews in Germany, Israel, and the USA* (Leiden: 2006).
2. See, for instance, Ephraim Ya'ar, "Change and Continuity in Israeli Society: The Test of the Melting Pot," *Israel Studies* 10, no. 2 (2005), 91–128.

Michael Dumper, *The Politics of Sacred Space: The Old City of Jerusalem in the Middle East Conflict.* Boulder: Lynne Rienner, 2002. xi + 185 pp.

Whatever your views regarding the sanctity of Jerusalem for Jews, it is foolish to deny that Jerusalem is holy to Muslims and, in a spiritual sense, to Christians as well.[1] Michael Dumper's recent study, *The Politics of Sacred Space: The Old City of Jerusalem in the Middle East Conflict,* is premised on this notion of multiple "holiness," and that perspective makes his book a useful addition to any library on Jerusalem.

Dumper, a British academic, has written previously on issues regarding Jerusalem from a largely Palestinian perspective,[2] and there can be little doubt where his sympathies lie. This study focuses on the Old City, that is to say, the area of Jerusalem "within the walls." It therefore excludes not only Israel's West Jerusalem but also the Palestinian and (in Dumper's nomenclature) "settler" areas of East Jerusalem (pp. 13–15).

One of the most promising aspects of Dumper's book is his attention to "the relationship between holy cities and the modern state in general" (p. 9). Thus he calls our attention to parallels between Jerusalem, on the one hand, and Rome, Mecca, and Najaf, on the other.[3] While he promises far more than he delivers in terms of constructing a general theory or taxonomy, bringing our attention to this "underdeveloped and under researched area" (ibid.) is a real plus. In particular, Dumper provides useful distinctions between what was designated a "holy place" under the Sublime Porte (linked, as it were, exclusively to Christian sacred sites) and its expansion by the Mandatory authorities as well as the U.N. to include a variety of Jewish and Muslim sites. He notes quite correctly the recent proliferation of such sites, pointing out that "once a site is elevated to a list, certain rights and obligations will flow to that site and eventually lead to nationalistic claims" (p. 21).

Dumper's working assumption is that there will be no peace without some accommodation of Palestinian interests in Jerusalem. At the same time, he veers from the traditional Palestinian proposals of internationalization, extraterritorialization, or shared administration. Such "regimes," as he terms them, "are no longer feasible." In addition, it would take "enormous political will on the part of an Israeli government to reverse the gains made by the settlers in taking over properties throughout the Old City" (pp. 7–8).

Dumper traces with varying degrees of success the developments in each of the three religious communities in the Old City in the years following the 1967 war. His discussion of Muslim and Christian activities covers ground that is generally neglected. His analysis of developments in the Jewish quarter, however, is far less useful.

In dealing with the Muslim quarter, Dumper focuses on the activities of the Waqf, providing a detailed picture of both its assets and responsibilities. He discusses the work of restoration programs, including the restoration of suq al-Qattamin (an architecturally significant market area in the Old City) and the development work of the Jerusalem Development and Investment Company and the Old City of Jerusalem Revitalization Program. He also discusses changes in *sharia* (Islamic) law that allow for innovation and flexibility in the Waqf's style of management.

Dumper's review of Jewish expansion efforts in the Old City largely describes the efforts of such groups as Ateret Cohanim to project a Jewish presence in areas often adjacent to the Jewish quarter. For some reason he lumps together Christian support groups such as the International Christian Embassy (not even located in the Old City) with settler groups and messianic movements such as the "Temple Mount faithful" (*neemanei har habayit*), and he treats as one the efforts to increase Jewish settlement in the Muslim quarter and those to advance the rebuilding of the Temple. I found this particular section of the book to be dated—focused on the 1980s—and less developed than I had hoped. Missing, for example, is a detailed account of the activities of Irving Moskowitz, the benefactor of the Har Homah neighborhood and of Jewish groups seeking to purchase residential units in Jabel Mukaber, and a clearer appraisal of former mayor Ehud Olmert's relations with the settler community. Whereas Dumper asks the relevant questions—for instance, "Were the settler groups proxies of the state in a covert policy to acquire property and extend Israeli influence in the Old City?" (p. 61)—his analysis is far thinner and far less useful than one would expect.

Dumper's discussion of the Christian community revolves around the increasing cooperation between the various Christian groups (excluding the pro-Israeli Protestant evangelicals, whom the established groups both fear and disdain) in opposing various Israeli policies. Pointing out that the Christian community is undergoing a demographic decline, he does not really analyze the extent to which Christian emigration reflects a fear of Muslim domination (as those on the Israeli Right suggest), or else is more the outcome of a higher social and educational status and the resultant desire to take advantage of opportunities abroad or escape what Israelis refer to as "the [current] situation" (*hamaẓav*).

For Dumper, the turning point in relations with the Christian community occurred in 1990, with a partially successful effort by settler groups to take over part of the

St. John's hospice in the Christian quarter, an act that led to riots and the tear-gassing of the Greek Patriarch. Since that time, Dumper tells us, the Christian denominations have become more united in their approach to the Israeli authorities, and the previous Israeli approach of making special deals so as to "pick" off denominations no longer seems to work. According to Dumper, the Christian leadership no longer believes Israel's promises to protect access to holy sites. While not discussed in his book, the events surrounding the siege of the Church of the Nativity in Bethlehem in 2002 have only (from the Christian perspective) added to this fear.

As an aside, it is worth noting the dramatic distance between Israeli judgments (largely self-congratulatory) regarding its protection of the holy places since 1967 and Dumper's report of the emphatically held Christian (let alone Muslim) view that Israel fails in this responsibility. From Dumper's perspective, the problem lies with security needs that often result in closure. Thus, while foreigners have fairly untrammeled access to the holy places, Christians who live in the West Bank normally do not. As the Christian churches do not define their ministry along the geographical lines of the 1967 border, this creates obvious problems.

The concluding chapter of Dumper's book proposes solutions for some of the practical problems connected with management of the holy places after any negotiated settlement. This "technocratic" discussion seems strangely disconnected from his earlier political analysis. Here his focus is on issues such as "questions of shared administration of certain holy sites, of pilgrim quotas, property ownership and use, rights of access and reparation" (p. 7). He draws parallels from the management of pilgrim flows in Mecca during the *hajj,* which does not seem particularly apposite. He dwells on the recent history of Muslim-Jewish interaction at the Cave of the Patriarchs—the history of which cannot be viewed as an interreligious success story—while referring only in passing to the experience of Nebi Samuel, which might provide more instructive lessons for the future "sharing" of holy sites.

Dumper's most pointed contribution is his suggestion that an interreligious commission be created to "manage" issues related to the holy places and the Old City. As he himself points out, this idea is not new. It was envisioned in Article 14 of the Mandate for Palestine (although the British never succeeded in securing agreement on how each religious group would be represented). Dumper returns to the concept and makes a useful contribution in unpacking the kinds of activities it might undertake in aid of a permanent settlement. He assumes that a permanent settlement will lead to an explosion of pilgrimage (largely, he suggests, from Islamic countries of Southeast Asia, West Africa, and Central Asia [p. 150]), and he believes that a management body can come to some agreement on such issues as quotas for pilgrims of the various faiths; the assignment of access times to different religious communities; the staging and timing of religious events; and the creation of alternate pilgrimage routes. In Dumper's view, "an interreligious council of some kind that can have input into the negotiating process may be the sina qua non for peace in Jerusalem" (p. 168).

Dumper's study predates efforts to build the Jerusalem wall (or fence) and therefore does not account for the effects that separating eastern Jerusalem from the Palestinian "hinterlands" in the West Bank may have on "sacred space" issues. In particular, he does not discuss the concerns of the Christian churches, the various representations of Roman Catholic congressmen (including Congressman Henry Hyde) to Israeli officials on their behalf, and the Israeli response. That surely is "the politics of sacred space."

MARSHALL J. BREGER
Columbus School of Law, Catholic University of America

Notes

1. Nonetheless, some Jewish figures continue to make this denial. See, for instance, Daniel Pipes in *New Republic*, 28 April 1997 (pp. 16–18); a useful corrective is Zvi Werblowsky, *The Meaning of Jerusalem to Jews, Christians and Muslims* (Jerusalem: 1983).
2. See Michael Dumper, *The Politics of Jerusalem since 1967* (New York: 1997); idem, *Islam and Israel: Muslim Religious Endowments and the Jewish State* (Washington, D.C.: 1994); idem, "Israeli Settlement in the Old City of Jerusalem," *Journal of Palestine Studies* 21, no. 4 (Summer 1992), 32–53.
3. The Jerusalem-Mecca parallels were earlier developed in an excellent book by F.E. Peters, *Jerusalem and Mecca: The Typology of the Holy City in the Near East* (New York: 1986).

Dvora Hacohen, *Immigrants in Turmoil: Mass Immigration to Israel and Its Repercussions in the 1950s and After.* Syracuse: Syracuse University Press, 2003. 325 pp.

This book, an English translation of Dvora Hacohen's 1994 monograph on the "great immigration" of 1948 to 1953,[1] provides a highly useful narrative of Israeli immigration policy during the tumultuous first years of the state's existence.

The book begins with the post-independence stream of immigration from Eastern Europe. The number of immigrants who had survived the Holocaust became so great that, by the summer of 1948, they accounted for one third of all new recruits to the Israeli army. Mass immigration from Eastern Europe unleashed power struggles involving the World Zionist Organization, the Jewish Agency, Mosad le'aliyah bet (originally an underground immigration movement), and the newly formed Israeli government. Hacohen does a fine job navigating the reader through these internecine quarrels concerning immigration and settlement, but provides insufficient analysis regarding how this bureaucratic maze developed in the first place. Greater sensitivity to the array of polarized ideologies and centers of power—diaspora versus Israel, Zionist versus non-Zionist, socialist versus bourgeois, and secular versus religious— would have made for a richer and more illuminating account.

The author could also have made more of the relationship between immigration policy in the wake of the U.N. partition resolution of November 1947 and the question of the future of Palestine's Arab population. She quotes from David Ben-Gurion's speech of December 3, 1947 in which he voiced the assumption that the new Jewish state would have a sizable Arab minority. This threat, Hacohen argues, motivated Ben-Gurion's call for the immigration of two million Jews as soon as possible after independence. Such an analysis challenges the argument, often made by Israel's critics, that the Zionist mission of "ingathering the exiles" precluded the establishment of a Palestinian state and foreordained massive expulsions of Palestinians and expropriation of their land. Unfortunately, Hacohen does not expand upon her point, and the succeeding chapters, which deal with mass immigration of Jews from the Middle East and North Africa, do not consider the extent to which immigrant absorption was dependent upon an available supply of abandoned Arab lands, and to what extent immigration and military policies influenced each other.

In her second chapter, Hacohen notes the similar basis of Israeli immigration policy toward Jews from Eastern Europe and the Middle East. Whenever—and wherever—windows of opportunity for mass Jewish emigration appeared, Israeli officials felt compelled to act quickly, and they also hoped that the temporary permission to emigrate in one land might lead other states to act similarly. In an interesting corrective to the view that Israeli officials colluded with Middle Eastern rulers to force their Jews to leave for Israel, Hacohen cites the cases of Libya, whose Jewish exodus was entirely voluntary, and Turkey, whose Jewish community organized its own exodus at a time when neither the Jewish Agency nor the Joint Distribution Committee believed them to be in mortal danger. One wonders, though, about the impartiality of Hacohen's judgments concerning Arab Jewish communities' states of mind. For example, she claims that the Iraqi government's bill of 1950 that allowed Jews to immigrate was a source of unmitigated joy: "The Jews could hardly contain their excitement" (p. 78). Another recent book, Esther Meir-Glitzenstein's *Zionism in an Arab Country: Jews in Iraq in the 1940s* (2004) offers a much more nuanced analysis of Iraqi Jewish public opinion.

Hacohen is more convincing when she demonstrates the intensely practical approaches taken by immigration officials to the most audacious of schemes. The tension between the pragmatic and the romantic that lies at the root of the Zionist project was nowhere more visible than in the story of the mass immigration of Yemenite Jewry. Packed into a refugee camp in Aden that was maintained by the Joint Distribution Committee and eventually airlifted to Israel in Operation Magic Carpet, these were the Jews whom Ben-Gurion visited at Tel Hashomer hospital, where he was moved to proclaim: "I understood at that moment what it means to 'rejoice with trembling.' I shuddered with excitement at this great and terrible sight. Yes—these are the birth pangs of the Messiah" (p. 69).

The ensuing chapters focus on the herculean challenges facing the immigration officials and their inability to formulate an effective policy in the face of constant infighting and a woeful lack of resources. Levi Eshkol, treasurer of the Jewish Agency and director of its settlement department, strove to restrict the immigration, fearing that it was leading the young state to economic ruin, but he was undermined by the Mosad le'aliyah bet, which fostered unrestricted immigration both on principle and (given the Mosad's strong base in the left-wing Mapam party) as a means of embarrassing the Mapai-led government. At first, immigrants were dumped into camps with few employment opportunities. In order to get the immigrants off the dole, another solution was proffered in 1949: the transit camp, or *ma'abarah*, which was to be attached to an existing town, so as to enable immigrants to be integrated directly into the local economy and give them access to social services provided by local councils. The transit camps, however, hardly fulfilled the hopes invested in them. They were shoddily constructed, often on unsuitable land; they were over-crowded; and the inhabitants' social, educational, and medical needs overwhelmed the local authorities.

Hacohen's institutional-historical narrative is useful but often lacks color. More-over, apart from one tantalizingly brief reference to competition within the transit camp in Hadera between representatives of Iraqi and Syrian Jews, the reader gets little sense of the interethnic conflicts that raged in the closed and impoverished atmosphere of the *ma'abarot*. Hacohen does, however, offer some eye-opening material in the book's penultimate chapter on civil unrest in 1951. She writes of mass black marketing of consumer goods, uprisings, and looting by immigrants in Petah Tikvah, Kfar Ono, and Holon. The mass, unauthorized flight of immigrants from the ma'abarot led the government to attempt a draconian form of population control: the denial of social services to those who abandoned their designated transit camp. The legislation, however, was filled with loopholes and all but impossible to enforce. Late in 1951, some restrictions on immigration were finally applied: this factor, combined with a decline in the number of Jews seeking entry into Israel, finally gave the battered Israeli economy a bit of relief. No sooner had the immi-gration problem begun to subside, Hacohen notes, that a new problem emerged: emigration. In 1952, there were 13,500 departures as against 24,000 arrivals, and in the following year, 3,000 more Jews left the country than immigrated to it. The problem lay not only in the numbers of Jews leaving but also in their socioeconomic and demographic profile: younger, healthier, and better educated than the average Israeli.

The book's analytical and methodological frameworks are a bit out of date. Only in a brief final chapter does the author engage with recent critical sociological literature, which claims that a colonial relationship existed between the Israeli Ashkenazic elite and the new immigrants, and that "Mizrahi" Jewry was invented out of a welter of Middle Eastern and North African Jewish communities. Hacohen writes very much within a Zionist discursive framework, freely employing terms such as "ingathering of the exiles" or referring to the mass immigration as "one of the most miraculous events in the history of the state and the Jewish people" (p. 11). Nevertheless, this is a well-crafted historical monograph, based on solid archival research and a commitment to accuracy.

DEREK J. PENSLAR
University of Toronto

Note

1. Dvora Hacohen, *'Olim base'arah: ha'aliyah hagedolah uklitatah beyisrael, 1948–1953* (Jerusalem: 1994).

Don Handelman, *Nationalism and the Israeli State: Bureaucratic Logic in Public Events*. Oxford: Berg, 2004. 272 pp.

This book sets out to identify the bureaucratic logic underlying public events in Israel. Don Handelman, an anthropologist, defines public events as "sites of performance whose designs are intended in relatively coherent ways to convey participants into versions of social order" (p. 4). His confidence that an observer of such events may identify the practices by which they are turned into social and political ordering devices, stems from a long tradition within the social sciences that dates back to the development of the modern bureaucratic state, especially in Europe.

The side-by-side development of the centralized European state and the social sciences led to a close association between them. Social scientists were expected to provide the taxonomies, classifications, structures, and statistical data necessary for the functioning of the bureaucratic state, and in this way became major advocates of its "legal-rational" nature. The association reached its peak in Max Weber's sociology, which was rooted both in the structure of science and in that of the Prussian state of the late 19th century.

Ironically, however, Weber's promise to apply scientific logic to politics came when the bureaucratic state was beginning to adopt different forms. His idealized Prussia could hardly serve as a useful model for a century marked by ultranational movements, messianic ideologies, and global political and economic forces. This, however, did not deter sociologists, anthropologists, and political scientists from advancing the notion that contemporary political life moved in accordance with a rational bureaucratic logic.

Many continued to model the state, despite its structural and normative instability, in arboreal terms. Consider Handelman's depiction of the state: "the shaping is tree-like, deeply rooted, in place, a fundamental of origins and ancestry and reaching unbroken from the distant past into the far future, centered stably around an axis mundi that opens in all directions and planes, unmoving, vertical, tall, hierarchical . . . " (p. 33). With this model in mind, no wonder the feeble, self-doubting, insecure Zionist presence in Palestine at the beginning of the 20th century turns into "a highly centralized, bureaucratic proto-state, the precursor of the present state" (p. 22); or that a ceremony in 2001, marking the end of search-and-rescue operations at the "Versailles Halls" in Jerusalem (whose upper floor had collapsed during a wedding, killing 23 guests), becomes associated with 18th-century French absolutism. "The State made order at Versailles," Handelman declares.

Nationalism and the Israeli State provides a variety of cases in which the state "creates, reproduces, legitimates, changes, and sanctifies itself through everyday practice" (p. 7). In addition to the Versailles case, the author analyzes the ways in which the state delineates categories of citizenship and nationality; disseminates national symbols through the celebration of holidays and birthdays in kindergartens; and encourages the presence of uniformed military personnel at Holocaust memorial gatherings in order to advance the formula that "the State saves the Israeli Jews from the fate of the Holocaust dead" (p. 117). He concludes by arguing that the conspicuous military presence and role in Israeli public events amplifies the national while dampening and subduing free will, and that Zionism is triumphant mainly "as a bureaucratic state whose infrastructures are organized through mono-thetic classification torqued through with emotions of the national" (p. 206).

I would like to follow the author's analysis of one of these cases—the Versailles memorial ceremony—as a means of highlighting, and casting doubt upon, his at-tempt to apply Foucault's belief in the power of the state to impose social order in contemporary Israel. My argument is that the ceremony, like other public events discussed here, represents not a bureaucratic logic "deeply embedded in the rou-tine grounds of daily life in modernity" (p. 5), but rather its absence. If anything, it represents a failed attempt by a state bureaucracy to assert a role within a vibrant civil society—which Handelman, like many observers of Israeli politics, mostly ignores.

Israelis, like people everywhere, are very concerned with the price and quality of their housing. The availability, reliability, and behavior of the contractors who build and renovate their homes are among the most common topics of discourse in the country. The dramatic collapse of the Versailles floor, caught on video, naturally sparked great concern on a personal level. For months, the public and the press were preoccupied with the nature of the material (invented by an Israeli engineering firm) from which the dance floor/ceiling was made, the licensing process that allowed its use in a public facility, and the tolerance for improvisation in Israeli culture. It is safe to assume that Israeli families watching the wedding video, which showed dozens of frightened people falling through the floor, were mainly concerned with the quality of the ceilings and roofs of their own homes, schools, and workplaces.

It is thus quite an exaggeration to turn the event into a metaphor "too close to the greatest of ongoing, pervasive fears among Israeli Jews—the terror that the State could cave in upon itself" (p. 7). Although a disaster of this kind sparks at first the thought that an act of terror may be involved, it immediately became clear that this was a case of flawed construction—which then led to a whole set of concerns, none of which had much to do with the state.

True, Israelis often view the state as responsible for their security and well-being, yet very few of them consider it the sole protector of their individual safety. This could clearly be seen during the Lebanon war of 2006, when civic organizations did not wait for the slow-to-react state to take care of the tens of thousands of citizens who found themselves under rocket attacks in northern Israel. Handelman is correct in his assertion that the Versailles collapse touched deep chords within civic society, but he misses the point when he assumes that "the ruined remnants of Versailles had to be mended, domesticated, controlled. And this had to be seen to be done, and could be done only by official organs of the state" (p. 7). The state played a role later when an official committee of inquiry was set up, as a result of which several of those responsible were sent to jail, but the initiative of some officials who hastily organized a memorial ceremony cannot be described simply as a response to citi-zens' expectations or as functional in any other way. It was, at best, an expression of these officials' frustration over their incapacity to mend, domesticate, or control anything.

Although the author takes note of the ceremony's idiosyncrasies—for instance, the fact that soldiers of the Home Front Command (which conducted most of the search and rescue operations) could be seen standing, talking, joking, and milling about in front of the stage, he does not hesitate to frame the scene as an "embodiment of the nation-in-arms" (p. 8). The "nation-in arms" image, which ignores the rich network of civil relations in Israel, is supported by such facts as the use of the Hebrew term *hityaḥadut* in Israeli ceremonies, which, according to the author, connotes "the coming together, the joining together of people, of people and memory, of the living and the dead, so that all are closed off together, enwrapped (and at times enrapt) in communion among themselves" (p. 9). The term, however, has the opposite meaning (*hityaḥadut* connotes a turning inward in moments of grief and prayer, *away* from the crowd). And although the Jewish mourner's kaddish prayer, said in the ceremony, does denote communal support for individual mourners, this hardly justifies its consideration as a pillar in a process of turning Israel into "a military family, the family-in-arms, given birth by crisis, cradling the state with its arms" (p. 9).

Handelman analyzes various activities taking place within Israel's civil society, such as birthday celebrations or Mother's Day, as building blocs of a collective national entity inspired by bureaucratic logic. One wonders, however, what the kindergarten children observed by Handelman during a Hanukah celebration would have said had they found out that inviting their families to celebrate the holiday with them was tantamount to a state effort to encompass the individual within the national and to appropriate the family as the basis of "the nation-in-arms and the family-in-arms" (p. 61). One also wonders what they would have said had they been told that their candle-lighting ceremony in the early evening (when, incidentally, Jewish holidays begin) was designed by a bureaucratic logic to evoke the uplifting illumination of the holiday from the depths of despair, and that their participation in a circle dance with their mothers "blurs the distinctiveness of particular families, their parents and children, their adults and youngsters. Distinct family units disappear" (p. 66).

Nationalism and the Israeli State makes an important contribution in highlighting political functions that can be attributed to public ceremonies and in providing good anthropological tools to observe them. That contribution would have been enhanced, in my opinion, had the civil dimension in Israeli life been given the weight it deserves.

MICHAEL KEREN
The University of Calgary

Shulamit Reinharz and Mark Raider (eds.), *American Jewish Women and the Zionist Enterprise*. Waltham: Brandeis University Press, 2005. 393 pp.

Without aiming to provide the final word on any gender-related area of American Jewish history or Israel studies, *American Jewish Women and the Zionist Enterprise* offers a most comprehensive and stimulating single-volume account of the interplay between the lives of American Jewish women and the creation of the state of Israel.

Edited by Shulamit Reinharz and Mark Raider and originating in a symposium held at Brandeis University in 1999, this collection also draws richly from new archival research and interpretation, reprinted scholarly works, and memoir literature. Without exception, the essays offer new methodological approaches to ostensibly familiar topics such as Hadassah, or else break ground in uncharted scholarly territory.

The book is divided into four parts. The first, "Three Generations of American Jewish Women and the Zionist Idea," deals with Emma Lazarus, Henrietta Szold, and Marie Syrkin. This is followed by "American Jewish Women's Organizations and the Zionist Enterprise" (focusing on Hadassah but also featuring less-researched organizations such as the Mizrachi Women of America) and "Aliyah, Social Identities and Political Change." Concluding the book is a section titled "Women Report and Remember"—several short, oral history accounts by American Jewish women who came to settle, at least temporarily, in Mandatory Palestine.

As noted, Hadassah receives a good deal of attention. Of particular note are Mira Katzburg-Yungman's "Women and Zionist Activity in Erez Israel: The Case of Hadassah, 1913–1958" and Mary McCune's "Formulating the 'Women's Interpretation of Zionism': Hadassah Recruitment of Non-Zionist American Women, 1914–1930," both of which incisively probe the secrets of this organization's success and staying power. Katzburg-Yungman surveys the way in which traditional Jewish concepts and practices, among them *pidyon shevuyim* (ransoming of captives), found expression in distinctive Hadassah projects such as Youth Aliyah, and she provides what is surely the most succinct and accurate extant scholarly description of the subtle ways in which these projects, utilizing a mix of American and Yishuv resources, evolved over time. Her deceptively simple, yet powerful conclusion is that Hadassah's impact lasted in Israel after 1948 because its "non-political" projects focused on the welfare of the Yishuv generally, rather than exclusively on women's concerns. McCune offers a persuasive account of how Henrietta Szold and her Hadassah followers selected family and social welfare issues that appealed broadly to American Jewish women, which they then used to increase membership at the expense of non-Zionist organizations, especially the National Council for Jewish Women.

A number of other essays examine Hadassah (and, more broadly, American women's Zionism) comparatively, either by contrasting it with other Jewish organizations or by locating it in the context of Jewish history. Allon Gal opens his piece by declaring that "Henrietta Szold's Zionist views were basically a product of the democratic qualities of American culture" (p. 25) and then goes on to argue that she conceptualized Zionism as an extension of Judaism rather than as a revolt against its two-thousand-year link with *galut* (exile). In fact, as Gal movingly shows, Szold retained a nostalgia for the Baltimore landscape of her youth. His unstated thesis is that Szold's insistence on *continuity* alongside change in the development of the Yishuv essentially grafted the outlook of Conservative Judaism onto Zionism.

In her groundbreaking essay on Bessie Gotsfeld and the Mizrachi Women of America, Baila Round Shargel looks at Hadassah from the vantage point of religious Zionism in America and shows that the former did not enjoy a monopoly on educational and social welfare projects in the Yishuv. Mark Raider's contribution on the Pioneer Women's Organization (today Naamat USA) deftly points out that the "non-political" Hadassah women were often drawn emotionally toward the pioneering halutz models of Labor Zionism. He also argues that Hadassah was not quite as inclusive an organization as was seemingly indicated by its burgeoning membership lists in the 1920s and 1930s—thousands of less acculturated Jewish immigrants preferred the socialist-communalist messages of Pioneer Women. Esther Carmel-Hakim investigates how the different social conditions of Canadian Jewry might have influenced the approach of Hadassah-WIZO Canada, in particular with regard to its decision to support an agricultural training school for women at Nahalal.

What is less well developed in these and other essays is the question of how American Zionist women viewed the American, as opposed to Jewish, component of their identity, and to what extent being American could both enhance and complicate their Zionist efforts. For instance, as viewed through the prism of the increasingly dominant Labor Zionist ideology, American Jewish women were doubly handicapped—considered unfit for pioneering communalism because they were both women and "soft" Americans. Some American women Zionists (Golda Meir being the best known) fought the stereotype by deliberately modeling their behavior on that of the halutzim. Others, including Sara Bodek Paltiel, the first American-born graduate of the Hadassah Nursing School and a founding member of Kibbutz Kfar Blum—the subject of a moving essay authored by her niece—seem to have accepted the stereotype but defined themselves as "not typical Americans" (p. 223).

An interesting methodological issue is raised by the editors' decision to feature Marie Syrkin as the representative of "third generation" American Zionist women (following Emma Lazarus and Henrietta Szold, who represent the first and second generations, respectively). Rather than personifying "third generation" Zionism, Syrkin would seem to represent an alternative *political* view—that is, pragmatism rather than the political idealism espoused by Szold. In choosing Syrkin (rather than her own political idol, Golda Meir), the editors may well have taken the view that the ultimate measure of these women's value as historical subjects was not their actual impact but rather the extent to which charismatic figures such as Syrkin, Meir, or Irma Lindheim (a former Hadassah president from an affluent New York background, who later joined Kibbutz Mishmar Haemek) represented the existential dilemmas and struggles of American Jewish women both of their own generation and of subsequent ones. This focus on the politics of identity leads to extremely creative scholarly contributions, such as Shulamit Reinharz's discussion of Lindheim's colorful life. At the same time, it demands a conscious rethinking of the scholars' goals when, in such a highly politicized field as Zionist affairs, they focus on individuals who did not, in the conventional sense, "make history."

This focus on the politics of identity necessitates a recognition that Hadassah's historical singularity need not be considered solely, or even primarily, in terms of its impact on the state of Israel, even though Katzburg-Yungman is surely correct when she concludes that Hadassah "play[ed] a pivotal role in the development of the state" (p. 172). Perhaps just as important, Hadassah derived its unique power from the balm it offered both to the ambitious (and often troubled) women in its leadership stratum, and to its rank and file membership. Reinharz hints at the need to revise images of altruistic mission, and to view the Hadassah experience more realistically in American terms of pragmatic self-interest, when she cites the example of Jane Addams: "Irma [Lindheim] belonged to a generation influenced by American Christian middle-class women reformers like Jane Addams (1860–1935), who declared that she created Hull House in Chicago not to save poor immigrants, but to save herself" (p. 258).

American Jewish Women and the Zionist Enterprise contains a few technical errors, including the reference to influence "radiating from Kiryat Shemonah to the northernmost corners of the country" (p. 217); Ruth Halprin Kaslove's assertion that her mother "was the only woman to serve on the Agency until long after the state of Israel was established" (p. 328); the publication date listed in footnote 13 (p. 141); the exclusion of Judah Magnes from the list of Ihud founders (p. 68, footnote 10); and, apparently, the substitution of the word "compatible" for "incompatible" in Lawrence Oliphant's reflection on the impact of American life on Jewish identity (p. 10). These are incidental and do not detract from the masterful impression left by the superbly edited text. Nor, of course, do the irresoluble methodological issues broached above minimize the collection's status as one of a handful of books that should long serve as required reading for anyone seriously interested in the history of American Zionism.

MATTHEW SILVER
Max Stern College of Emek Yezreel

Stephen Spector, *Operation Solomon: The Daring Rescue of the Ethiopian Jews.* New York: Oxford University Press, 2005. 279 pp.

In 2005, I reviewed a book in this journal on Operation Solomon authored by Israel's former ambassador to Ethiopia,[1] in which I noted that Stephen Spector had prepared an as yet unpublished manuscript on the same theme. Spector's book has now come out, and very readable it is, too! Spector, a professor of English at the State University of New York, Stony Brook, is clearly a master raconteur. Although he is not an expert on Ethiopian Jewry (and to his credit does not claim to be), he clearly knows how to tell a good story. Operation Solomon, in which 14,310 Ethiopian Jews were airlifted to Israel within a day and a half, as the future both of Jews in Ethiopia and of the Ethiopian government headed by Mengistu Haile Mariam was hanging in the balance, contains all the elements of a drama. Spector recounts the events leading up to the operation and its aftermath with excitement and aplomb, and in exquisite detail.

Beyond Spector's narrative gift, the most impressive feature of this book is the list of public archives and unpublished documents that he perused in order to construct a well-nigh definitive story. The public documents include reports from the U.S. Department of State, the Jewish Agency, and the Hebrew Immigrant Aid Society (HIAS). The unpublished documents, which are of far greater interest, include unclassified and limited official-use documents from the U.S. Department of State, a wealth of handwritten records of meetings and telephone memos from the Joint Distribution Committee (JDC), and miscellaneous private memoirs and correspondence of key figures including Senator Rudy Boschwitz and Uri Lubrani, the former Israeli ambassador to Ethiopia who was called in to head the negotiations with the Ethiopian government. All of this is complemented by more than 200 oral history interviews conducted with experts on Ethiopian Jewry, Ethiopian Jewish activists and religious leaders, Israelis involved in Operation Solomon, and U.S. Representatives of Congress.

Spector surveys the history of the Jews in Ethiopia and swiftly brings the reader to 1988 and to the events culminating in Operation Solomon. He recounts the extraordinary role in bringing Jews from the villages to the capital by "an obscure American woman" (p. 27) named Susan Pollack, the resident director in Addis Abeba of the American Association for Ethiopian Jews (AAEJ), an advocacy organization whose raison d'être was "rescue." The question of accountability is treated indirectly: was Pollack right to instigate such an "ingathering" in Israel? Did she have a right to intervene? Spector describes in breathtaking manner the conditions in Addis Abeba as the Jews streamed to the capital at a time when rebel forces were knocking at the gates, waiting to take over. He tells of the negotiations at the governmental level to release the Jews and airlift them to Israel, and the race against time to fly them out before the Marxist government collapsed. The tale is told in dramatic narrative style, unfolding chapter by chapter and supplying shifting perspectives of the various people involved.

Nevertheless, truth is intangible and there remain some conundrums that appear insoluble. Most prominent among them is the mystery regarding $35 million that was transferred from the Israeli side to the Ethiopian side in exchange for the release of Ethiopian Jewry. At first, the representative of the Ethiopian government, Kassa Kebede, provided the Israelis with an erroneous bank account number in New York; it was a bonds rather than a cash account. More troublesome, the number was that of a private account and not an official Ethiopian government account. Zvi Barak, the Jewish Agency treasurer representing the Israelis, pointed out to Spector that neither the name of Ethiopia's ruler, Mengistu Haile Mariam, nor that of Kassa Kebede was on the account, but that it may have been a front. According to Spector, the correct bank account number may finally have been given to the Jewish Agency by Bob Houdek, chief of mission in the American Embassy in Ethiopia from 1988 to 1991, who then transferred the information to Israeli ambassador Asher Naim, who in turn passed it on to Zvi Barak. Spector also claims that Operation Solomon was already in movement before the monies were actually transferred.

Operation Solomon has a double and at times competing agenda: a detailed and accurate description of events that led up to the rescue operation, and a case study of the difficulty of compiling oral evidence and the quest for "truth." Spector explains that he tried to recover the reality of events fairly and honestly. However, narratives based on memory and self-presentation are inescapably influenced by the need to reconstruct experience in ways that make sense, both personally and historically. In the book, he presents conflicting accounts of the same events, different interpretations of the same acts, dreams and miracles, and various understandings of historical "facts" and conventional wisdom. Overlaying this is Spector's own sense of drama, conveyed in sentences such as: "In Washington D.C., watching the airlift on T.V., Susan Pollack wept" (p. 175), or descriptive phrases such as "[Kassa's] sullen face" (p. 153), or "the Israeli's gut instinct" (p. 120). More problematic are the two chapters about a young woman named Chomanesh and her family, who are composite characters. Unfortunately, the interview transcripts are not provided and the one interview with Kassa Kebede that appears in Appendix 3 is not given verbatim, but is instead subject to Spector's interpretation. All of this contributes to the impression that this book is more in the nature of a novel, an unreal series of events dramatized by a gifted author, as opposed to a serious academic book published by Oxford University Press. This is a pity, given the author's meticulous and wide-ranging research.

SHALVA WEIL
The Hebrew University

Note

1. Asher Naim, *Saving the Lost Tribe: The Rescue and Redemption of the Ethiopian Jews* (New York: 2003).

STUDIES IN CONTEMPORARY JEWRY

XXIII

Edited by Ezra Mendelsohn

Symposium–Jews and Sports

Michael Alexander, *The Jewish Bookmaker: Gambling, Legitimacy, and the American Political Economy*

Diethelm Blecking, *Jewish Sports in Poland, 1918–1939*

Sergio DellaPergola, *Dream and Disenchantment: Massimo Della Pergola and the Invention of the Italian Toto*

Gabriel Finder, *"Boxing for Everyone": Jewish DPs, Sports, and Boxing*

Sander Gilman, *Thoughts on the Jewish Body, Baseball, and the Problem of Integration*

Jeffrey Gurock, *Hakoah Vienna's U.S. Tour in 1926 and American Jewish Pride and Priorities*

Anat Helman, *Sports in the Young State of Israel*

André Levy, *Playing for Control: Sports and Jewish-Muslim Relations in Morocco*

Stephen Norwood, *American Jewish Muscle: Forging a New Masculinity in the Streets and in the Ring, 1890–1940*

Edward Shapiro, *From Participant to Owner: The Role of Jews in Contemporary American Sports*

Tamir Sorek, *Ethnic Why Did Beit-Shean Let Betar Win? Latent Ethnic Solidarity and the Sports Ethic in Israel*

... plus essays, review essays, and book reviews

Note on Editorial Policy

Studies in Contemporary Jewry is pleased to accept manuscripts for possible publication. Authors of essays on subjects generally within the contemporary Jewish sphere (from the turn of the 20th century to the present) should send two copies to:

> The Editor, *Studies in Contemporary Jewry*
> The Avraham Harman Institute of Contemporary Jewry
> The Hebrew University
> Mt. Scopus, Jerusalem, Israel 91905

Essays should not exceed 35 pages in length and must be double-spaced throughout (including intended quotations and endnotes).

E-mail inquiries may be sent to the following address: Studiescj@savion. .huji.ac.il.

Abstracts of articles from previous issues may be found via our website: http:// icj.huji.ac.il/StudiesCJ/studiescj.html.